THE BLACKWELL COMPANION TO CRIMINOLOGY

BLACKWELL COMPANIONS TO SOCIOLOGY

The *Blackwell Companions to Sociology* provide introductions to emerging topics and theoretical orientations in sociology as well as presenting the scope and quality of the discipline as it is currently configured. Essays in the Companions tackle broad themes or central puzzles within the field and are authored by key scholars who have spent considerable time in research and reflection on the questions and controversies that have activated interest in their area. This authoritative series will interest those studying sociology at advanced undergraduate or graduate level as well as scholars in the social sciences and informed readers in applied disciplines.

The Blackwell Companion to Criminology

Edited by

Colin Sumner

Advisory Editor
William J. Chambliss

Blackwell Publishing

BLACKWELL PUBLISHING
350 Main Street, Malden, MA 02148-5020, USA
9600 Garsington Road, Oxford OX4 2DQ, UK
550 Swanston Street, Carlton, Victoria 3053, Australia

First published 2004 by Blackwell Publishing Ltd
First published in paperback 2007 by Blackwell Publishing Ltd

2   2008

Library of Congress Cataloging-in-Publication Data

The Blackwell companion to criminology / edited by Colin Sumner.
       p. cm.—(Blackwell companions to sociology)
    Includes bibliographical references and index.
    ISBN 978-0-631-22092-3 (alk. paper)
    ISBN 978-1-4051-7562-3 (paperback: alk. paper)
    1. Criminology. I. Sumner, Colin. II. Series.
HV6025.B544 2003
364—dc21   2002155267

A catalogue record for this title is available from the British Library.

Set in 10.5/12.5pt Sabon
by Kolam Information Services Pvt. Ltd, Pondicherry, India
Printed in Singapore
by Utopia Press Pte Ltd

For further information on
Blackwell Publishing, visit our website:
www.blackwellpublishing.com

Contents

Preface

This has been a mammoth enterprise and I am grateful to the contributors for making it feasible with their support, good spirit, and responsiveness to my editing. Considering they are a distinguished bunch, and therefore very busy, their commitment and patience reflect the altruism for which academics rarely get credit. Of course, some were not able to join us, in fact a whole contingent who were to write on ethnicity, but this *Companion* intends to be around for a while so there will be future opportunities for growth. Sadly, Rosa del Olmo and Sue Lees died during the early stages of the book and we miss their respective contributions on Latin America and the delinquency of girls. A project like this is a labor of love, so I am grateful to Susan Rabinowitz at Blackwell USA for inviting me to pull the collection together, my old friend Bill Chambliss for assistance with US matters, my wife, Pat, for her constant encouragement, and, especially, Ken Provencher, Blackwell's manager for this project, for his unfailing understanding and good cheer.

The shape of this collection of essays reflects some choices. Criminology is far too vast to be compressed, however selectively, into one volume. From the outset, I have aimed primarily at high quality and a cutting edge with a global standpoint. The most fundamental feature of the volume is an international range of expert contributors, around a base of essays from North America, who tackle their subject matter from a global perspective, either in the sense of reviewing their fields or locating crime issues within international debates and historical parameters. My intention was not to be comprehensive but to deliver a volume that would stimulate development within criminology across the globe. The book therefore contains predominantly sociological criminology, to reflect contemporary thinking and current key issues. For the same reasons, it also combines established authorities in the field with some outstanding younger scholars. I have attempted to edit the volume actively to provide a collection that would, for several years to come, serve undergraduates everywhere in their appreciation of both fundamental issues and areas of growth within criminology.

With these aims in mind, the volume had to combine theoretical or general insights with explorations of specific empirical areas. A broad theoretical overview section is a must for any international volume, apart from its inherent value as a binding thread for the book and for criminology as a whole; hence Part I. I then decided to select two standard areas within criminology which had a global significance and two areas which were at the forefront of recent criminological thinking. The first criterion produced Part II, "Juvenile Delinquency and Justice for Youth," and Part III, "Punishment and its Alternatives"; the second accounts for Part IV, "Gender and the Masculinity of Crime" and Part V, "Capital, Power and Crime." I sought essays for Parts II and III which were innovative and fresh; for Parts IV and V which were summative yet moved things further forward. Finally, for the last section, I wanted a topic which might capture a global criminological imagination and mark this volume as international and contemporary. This led to Part VI, "Globalization, Crime, and Information," which looks at topics specifically reflecting the globalization of crime issues and the huge role of information in today's criminal justice systems.

The first part of the volume focuses on a key theoretical issue within the international study of crime and society: the relation between the nation-state, criminal justice, and social control. My own essay explores the historical and current meanings of the criminological axiom that crime and deviance are social constructions, with a view to sharpening our use of the word "social" in an age of globalization and sustained divisions within and between populations. The following essay by Dario Melossi traces the history and meaning of the concept of social control, comparing its American origins to its current European forms. Both these essays provide readers with a critical background in sociological theories of crime, law, and deviance, while pointing to the importance today of issues relating to communications, culture, and globalization for understanding the possibility of social control. They also evidence the displacement of jurisprudence and law by sociology and social control, a theme that is taken further in Markus Dubber's essay. Dubber uses offenses of possession to illustrate the extent to which the legal or due-process model for dealing with crime has been suffused with the politically defined "war on crime." He poses the question of justice within a war setting. The blurred and neglected relation between war and crime underlies Wayne Morrison's essay on genocide. Outlining the significance of criminology's neglect of genocide, Morrison argues that any criminology which remains bound to the nation-state is unsustainable as an intellectual enterprise in postmodernity. All four essays in this section pose fundamental questions for criminology in the twenty-first century and open up themes which are explored in the rest of the volume.

Part II, on juvenile delinquency, begins with another challenge to a fundamental notion within criminology. Jack Katz and Curtis Jackson-Jacobs present a sustained interrogation of the meaning and value of "the gang" in US criminological research on juvenile delinquency. Through a close analysis of the methodology and analysis of gang research, the authors show that the causal claims for the role of gangs in promoting criminal violence are simply not sustained by the evidence or the methodology. In the next essay, Mark Fenwick examines the traditional idea in criminology that Japan's low official rates of crime are an exceptional case warranting a special explanation based on culture. He questions the success of "reintegrative shaming" (Braithwaite) in Japan, pointing to high recidivism rates, the prevalence of punitive crime-talk in civil society, low public confidence in policing, poor treatment regimes, and low investment in the criminal justice system. Both Katz and Fenwick would support the idea in Hayward's essay that criminology needs to pay more detailed attention to the relationships between consumer culture and crime. Drawing on advances in cultural theory, Hayward shows how the relationships between commoditization and crime can be understood in more depth. His essay draws attention to the youthful accomplishment of identity through material means, the need to emphasize the new subjectivities of the consumer age in revising Mertonian cultural strain theory, and the value of more sophisticated ideas about the impulsivity and sensation-seeking involved in juvenile crime. The final essay in this section, by Elrena Van der Spuy, Wilfried Schärf, and Jeffrey Lever looks at successive legal attempts to "tame" South Africa's youth in the context of the moves away from apartheid. Youth crime and violence remain high in South Africa: this fact and the lack of success in establishing a youth justice system are placed within the context of the structural imperatives of underdevelopment and the need to advance a "criminology of the South." All the essays in this part testify to the importance of placing juvenile crime and its definition within more precisely defined and researched historical and sociological contexts.

Part III deals with punishment and looks closely at its less discussed and less fashionable alternatives. Pat O'Malley opens it up with an enquiry into the erosion of modernist penal reform and the reversion to expressive violence in punishment, placing this development within the contexts of postmodernity and globalization. O'Malley reviews contemporary penal theory and argues for a more exact explanation of the connections between social transformations and changes in penal policy, rejecting epochal theories of structural crisis in favor of accounts which fully encompass the details of the prevailing political ideologies, such as neo-liberalism, that produce policy change. The current "punitive turn" warrants our attention to the state of non-custodial sentences, and in the next essay, Barry Holman and Robert Brown trace the historical roots of alternatives to prison and provide a summary of the wide range of community-based sanctions available today in the USA. They argue that the evidence does not justify a "nothing works" philosophy but that too many non-custodial measures produce increased surveillance or net-widening rather than offender-specific treatment. This essay is followed by that of Mark Lipsey, Nana Landenburger and Gabrielle Lynn Chapman which provides a detailed assessment of the research evaluating the effectiveness of rehabilitation schemes. The authors identify the themes in a variety of approaches that produce greater effectiveness, rather than prizing any one approach, and emphasize the socially valuable outcomes of multi-modal schemes with certain types of offender. The final essay in Part III, by Laureen Snider, examines the roots of one particular and current wave of punitiveness, that aimed at female offenders. Documenting the increased incarceration of women internationally and the history of female incarceration, she explains why reformist movements within criminology, including feminisms, have not stemmed this tide of punitiveness. Her detailed review locates the latter within contemporary changes in political economy.

Moving on from Snider's essay, Meda Chesney-Lind's opener to Part IV, which focuses on gender and crime, looks closely at criminological ideas about the female offender and locates her within broader social and historical contexts. She questions the apparently rising level of girls' violence, arguing that there is an undergoing relabeling of girls' offenses as criminal which produces this statistical effect. She also looks closely at the link between increased female incarceration and the mandatory sentences involved in "the war on drugs" as a war on "communities of color," emphasizing that the mass incarceration of African American women in the USA has been a function of the failure to address issues of racial inequality. The second essay in this section, by Adrian Howe, calls for the maleness of violence to be unequivocally addressed by criminology. The essay critically reviews the "denial" within criminology of the issue of male violence, and argues that there is an effective discursive erasure of the maleness of violence. Criticizing work on masculinities for assisting this process, Howe demands that men's violence be addressed head on as a "massive social problem." Richard Collier's essay follows by providing an extensive assessment of the masculinity literature within contemporary criminology and the way masculinity has been problematized. Focusing on the ideas of hegemonic masculinity and diverse masculinities, the issue of specific male subjectivities is addressed through critiques of both socialist work on the dominant masculinity and psychoanalysis-inspired portraits of the male psyche. Collier emphasizes that there remain some very important questions about exactly what it is about masculinity that produces criminal behavior and about why "men arguably remain the unexplored, desexed norm of criminology." In the next contribution to this contemporary debate, Mary Bernstein examines the roots of homophobia and the criminalization of same-sex erotic relations through the sodomy statutes in the USA. Stressing both the cultural and social-structural reasons for homophobia, she draws attention to the "homosocial" nature of societies at different points in history which works to oppose lesbian and gay rights. The final essay in Part IV is Elizabeth Comack's study of the interplay between gender and race in the criminalization of the rejected Other. She uses the notion of law as an ideological gendering and racializing practice to interpret the legal processing of a sample of defendants, a high proportion of whom were Aboriginals charged with violent crime in Manitoba. Her research demonstrates the extent to which legal discourse and practice are infused with both gendered and racialized stereotypes.

Part V deals with crimes related to capital and the state, both global and national. Amedeo Cottino leads off with an assessment of criminological work on "white-collar" and corporate crime. He argues that criminology needs to transcend disciplinary boundaries if it is to make an effective job of studying white-collar crime and spelling out its huge implications. Observing how often the serious crimes in this area are excused by elites with no little interest in the matter, Cottino calls for a more structural analysis of violence and of the content of the penal law. The following contribution by Pearce and Tombs examines the links between multinational corporations (MNCs) and crime and the reasons why the routine criminal activities of the MNCs are unlikely to receive the

attention of the law. Their study draws upon the oil industry to illustrate the
ways in which MNCs can ensure their wishes and rights transcend the social and
legal considerations of either nations or the international community. Like
Cottino, they too doubt that criminology is at present equipped or ready to
deal with international crimes whilst it remains tied to nation-state-based
notions of crime and crime control. In the next essay, Karen Joe Laidler documents the contemporary drug scene in Hong Kong, in both its global and local
dimensions. Long positioned internationally as a colony with a thriving drug
trade, Hong Kong's illegal entrepreneurs have adapted to independence by
furthering their local drugs trade. That trade has taken on the patterns evidenced
elsewhere on the planet and has seen a big shift from heroin and opiate use
toward psychotropic drug use, notably amphetamines such as ecstasy, marking a
strong connection with the growth of a vibrant leisure industry geared to the
youth culture. Laidler's study illustrates the location of crime within a global
market culture. The last essay of Part V, by Alexis Aronowitz and Monika
Peruffo, shows that transnational market forces need not be politically legitimate
yet can still evade the sanctions of international law. The authors look closely at
human trafficking in West and Central Africa, documenting how it is now
censured by the UN as "transnational organized crime" yet thriving as part of
a clutch of serious criminal activities involving the economic and sexual exploitation of some of the poorest people on the planet. Aronowitz and Peruffo
indicate the links between the old and new forms of slavery and how this illicit
market thrives upon the internationally sustained if not condoned underdevelopment and poverty of Africa.

Last and certainly not least, Part VI contains a range of studies illustrating the
importance of globalization and "the information society" to contemporary
forms and patterns of crime. Maureen Cain's opening essay shows how globalization can lead to the localization of acute economic problems related to
policing and crime, through a case study of private security officers in the
Caribbean. She demonstrates how taking an IMF loan influenced the economy
and private policing of Trinidad and Tobago in recent years. It markedly affected
both the range and amount of illegalities and the structure of private policing by
opening the territory to the full blast of international market forces. Globalization is not necessarily the penetration of capital into "the periphery" but can be
its export to "the center," causing a "glocalization" of crime conditions in the
periphery. The following essay by Thomas Mathiesen, in contrast, illustrates
how the formation of a supranational economic and political bloc such as the EU
can produce the growth of a massive level of surveillance activity, officially for
the purpose of detecting and preventing serious cross-border organized
crime. The concept of "Fortress Europe," embodied most notably in the Schengen agreement, convention, and information system, has generated a high-
technology super-state organization of information, yet organized cross-border
crime, argues Mathiesen, is less under threat as a result than political freedoms,
and we face a "new McCarthy era" with global dimensions.

The manipulability and misuse of information pertaining to crime has no
better illustration than the interpretations of the official US crime statistics
acutely observed in the essay by Bill Chambliss. He demonstrates in detail
ways in which misleading numbers and misinterpretations of numbers can be

produced by both official agencies and independent criminologists. Chambliss argues that this massaging of information can create and sustain major myths within both criminology and society, such as the supposed magnitude of the US murder rate compared to that of other nations and the alleged recent rise in violent youth crime, and deplores the increasing politicization of crime statistics. The following contribution from Aaron Doyle and Richard Ericson turns our attention to the information networks and the role of the police within them. Its main purpose is to observe the ways in which the police are these days, first and foremost, knowledge producers who are increasingly driven by the knowledge needs of other institutions. As in the UK, the possibility of the Canadian police actually catching an offender is severely limited by the sheer volume of form-filling and data collection, meeting either the needs of accountability or the demand for information from other institutions such as insurance companies. Policing in the information age is very much knowledge production and net-working within knowledge management systems. This "virtuality" of crime illustrated in the three preceding essays, and the inevitability of resistance to it, is developed in the final essay of the volume, by Paul Taylor. He points to the growth of internet hacking as a form of political resistance to the globalized information society. Taylor documents the growth of electronic civil dis-obedience and argues that it is an "imaginative and defensible attempt to re-appropriate new information technologies for society's benefit." Observing the immateriality of contemporary capitalism, Taylor sees the new crime of com-puter hacking as a major challenge to and within globalization.

As I write, the growing possibility of war against Iraq and of more incidents of international "terrorism" highlight more than ever not only the political rele-vance of a global analysis of crime and justice but also the sheer necessity of international approaches within any criminology committed to both scientific and useful knowledge, using interdisciplinary methods and thinking, rising beyond conventional theory and the limiting parameters of nation-state-based criminology, and confronting the realities of the information age in a globalized market. Our *Companion* may be discomforting at times but it is a companion for a discomforting new century which requires us to see "the big picture" and its implications for smaller, more local, scenes of crime and injustice. We have tried to capture some key criminological snapshots of both big and small, and their interrelationship, which will help the contemporary student of criminology make sense of the world.

Colin Sumner
February 2003

Contributors

Editor: Colin Sumner is an investment manager and writer. He was Professor and Head of the Law School at the University of East London and for many years a Lecturer in Criminology and Fellow of Wolfson College, University of Cambridge. He has been a Visiting Professor at the Universities of Barcelona, Hamburg, Berkeley, Simon Fraser, Queen's (Kingston), St. Mary's, and Dar es Salaam. His books include *Reading Ideologies* (1979), *The Sociology of Deviance* (1994), *Social Control and Political Order* (ed. with Roberto Bergalli, 1997), *Violence, Culture and Censure* (ed., 1997), *Censure, Politics and Criminal Justice* (ed., 1990), and *Crime, Justice and Underdevelopment* (ed., 1982). He edited a book series with the Open University Press entitled *New Directions in Criminology* and, with Piers Beirne, founded and edited the journal *Theoretical Criminology*.

Advisory Editor: William J. Chambliss is Professor of Sociology and Co-Director of the Institute on Crime, Justice and Corrections at the George Washington University. He is the author and editor of over twenty books, including *Power, Politics and Crime*; *Making Law* (with Marjorie Zatz, 1999), *Law, Order and Power* (with Robert Seidman, 1971), *On the Take* (1988), and *Organizing Crime* (with Alan A. Block, 1981).

Alexis A. Aronowitz worked for the United Nations Interregional Crime and Justice Institute and the UN Office on Drugs and Crime where she coordinated research activities within the framework of the Global Programme against Trafficking in Human Beings. Alexis received her PhD in Criminal Justice from SUNY at Albany. She currently teaches criminology courses at the University College of Utrecht, is writing a book on human trafficking, and is conducting research into hate crimes in Western Europe. She has held research positions at the Dutch Ministry of Justice and the International Police Institute at the University of Twente and has published in the fields of human trafficking, hate crimes, tax fraud, and police priorities.

Mary Bernstein is Associate Professor of Sociology at the University of Connecticut. Her research, which has appeared in the *American Journal of Sociology* and the *American Sociological Review,* focuses on sexuality, social movements, and the law. She recently published *Queer Families, Queer Politics: Challenging Culture and the State* (ed. with Renate Reimann, 2001). Currently, she is completing a book on lesbian, gay, bisexual, and transgender political strategies and legal change.

Robert A. Brown is a Visiting Professor of Criminal Justice in the School of Public and Environmental Affairs at Indiana University Purdue University Indianapolis (IUPUI). He received his doctorate in Criminal Justice from the University of Cincinnati. He is a former senior case developer for the National Center on Institution and Alternatives' Client Specific Planning (CSP) program. His research interests include intermediate sanctions, drug courts, and policing.

Maureen Cain was the Chair of Sociology at the University of the West Indies, Trinidad, before returning to become Reader in the School of Law at the University of Birmingham. She was the recipient in 1988 of the American Society of Criminology's Sellin-Glueck Award and is the current President of the British Society of Criminology. Maureen has held various appointments at Brunel, the London School of Economics, the Institute of Criminology in Cambridge, the European University Institute, and La Trobe University. She has published six books including *Society and the Policeman's Role* (1973), *Growing Up Good: Policing the Behaviour of Girls in Europe* (1989), and *For A Caribbean Criminology* (forthcoming, 2004), and was for many years the Editor of the *International Journal of the Sociology of Law.*

Gabrielle L. Chapman is the Director of Planning and Research at the Tennessee Department of Corrections and a doctoral candidate in sociology at Vanderbilt University.

Meda Chesney-Lind is Professor of Women's Studies at the University of Hawaii at Manoa. Her books include *Girls, Delinquency and Juvenile Justice* (with Randall G. Shelden, 1998), which received the American Society of Criminology's Michael J. Hindelang Award; *The Female Offender: Girls, Women and Crime* (1997); and *Female Gangs in America* (ed. with John M. Hagedorn, 1999). Her most recent book is *Invisible Punishment: The Collateral Consequences of Mass Imprisonment* (co-edited with Marc Mauer, 2002). In 2001 she received the Bruce Smith Sr. Award from the Academy of Criminal Justice Sciences for "outstanding contributions" to criminal justice.

Richard Collier is Professor of Law at the University of Newcastle upon Tyne. He has published widely in the area of gender and law and his publications include *Masculinity, Law and the Family* (1995) and *Masculinities, Crime and Criminology* (1998). He is presently writing a book on law and fatherhood. Other current research interests include studies of men, law and "work–life" balance, and gender, law, and the corporatization of universities.

Elizabeth Comack is a Professor of Sociology in the Department of Sociology, University of Manitoba. Her recent publications include: *Locating Law: Race/*

Class/Gender/Sexuality Connections (ed., 2006), *Criminalizing Women: Gender and (In)justice in Neo-liberal Times* (co-ed., 2006), and *The Power to Criminalize: Violence, Inequality and the Law* (with Gillian Balfour, 2004). She is presently writing a book entitled *In Here/Out There: Men, Masculinity, Violence, and Prison* which is based on interviews conducted with men at a provincial prison in Manitoba.

Amedeo Cottino is Professor of Sociology of Law at the University of Turin. He has studied and taught for many years in Sweden where he received his Ph.D. His books and articles include *Equality before the Penal Law* (ed. with Claudio Sarzotti, 1995), *Organized Crime* (1998), *Disonesto ma non criminale: La Giustizia e i Privilegi dei Potenti* (2005), and *European Legal Systems* (ed., with P. Robert, 2000) and have also dealt with issues of labor laws: *Il Mercato delle Braccia* (ed., 1973) and *Il Problema dell'Efficacia della Legge* (1973); Swedish social democracy: *La Social Democrazia Svedese* (1981); and alcohol politics: *L'Ingannevole Sponda* (1991).

Aaron Doyle is Associate Professor of Sociology at Carleton University, Ottawa. His books include: *Arresting Images: Crime and Policing in Front of the Television Camera* (2003), *Insurance as Governance* (with Richard Ericson and Dean Barry, 2003), *Uncertain Business: Risk, Insurance and the Limits of Knowledge* (with Richard Ericson, 2004) and *Risk and Morality* (co-edited with Richard Ericson, 2003).

Markus Dirk Dubber is Professor of Law and Director of the Buffalo Criminal Law Center at the State University of New York, Buffalo. He is editor of the *Buffalo Criminal Law Review* and has recently published *Victims in the War on Crime* (2002).

Richard Ericson is Professor and Director, Centre of Criminology, University of Toronto. His most recent visiting appointments include positions at All Souls College, Oxford and Université Paris X-Nanterre. His most recent books are *Policing the Risk Society* (with Kevin Haggerty, 1997) and *Governing Modern Societies* (ed. with Nico Stehr, 2000). His forthcoming work includes: *Insurance as Governance* (with Aaron Doyle and Dean Barry), and *Uncertain Business: Insurance and the Limits of Knowledge* and *Risk and Morality* (both with Aaron Doyle).

Mark Fenwick is Associate Professor in the Faculty of Law, Kyushu University, Japan. He studied for his Master's and doctorate at the Institute of Criminology, University of Cambridge. He has written various articles in the field of criminology, and his research interests include legal theory and the sociology of law.

Keith J. Hayward is Senior Lecturer in Criminology at the School of Social Policy, Sociology and Social Research, University of Kent. He has a Master's from the Cambridge Institute of Criminology and a doctorate from the University of East London. His research interests include criminological theory, social theory, youth crime, popular culture, and terrorism and fanaticism. He is the author of the forthcoming book *City Limits: Crime, Consumerism and the Urban Experience*.

Barry R. Holman works with statutory agencies, foundations and non-profit organizations, researching and developing community-based alternatives to incarceration for adults and youth. He taught sociology and criminology at the George Washington University and Northern Michigan University. His degrees are from the University of Wisconsin-Superior and the George Washington University. He works from his home in Bend, Oregon.

Adrian Howe is Professor of Criminology at the University of Central Lancashire. She has written *Punish and Critique* (1994) and edited *Sexed Crime in the News* (1998). Her most recent contribution to the field of sexed violence is "Provoking polemic: Provoked killings and the ethical paradoxes of the postmodern feminist condition" (*Feminist Studies*, 2002).

Curtis Jackson-Jacobs is a graduate student in the department of Sociology at the University of California, Los Angeles. Work based on his Master's research with college-student crack-cocaine users has appeared in the journal, *Contemporary Drug Problems*. His current ethnographic research examines violent fights among young Americans.

Jack Katz is Professor of Sociology at the University of California, Los Angeles. He is the author of *Seductions of Crime* (1988) and *How Emotions Work* (1999).

K. Joe Laidler is Associate Dean of the Faculty of Social Sciences and Associate Professor in Sociology at the University of Hong Kong. At present, her research in the United States includes studies on the use patterns and problems associated with club drugs in California; the relationship between alcohol and drug use and violence among female gang members, and alcohol and drug cessation during adolescent pregnancy. She is also working on a number of drug-related studies in Hong Kong.

Nana A. Landenberger is a Research Associate at the Vanderbilt Institute for Public Policy and a clinical psychologist with several years' experience in providing cognitive-behavioral treatment to adult offenders.

Jeffrey Lever has worked in the Departments of Sociology at the Universities of Stellenbosch, Cape Town and the Western Cape for 25 years. He is a former President of the South African Sociological Association and edited the *South African Sociological Review* from 1992 to 1996. He is currently joint managing editor of the *African Sociological Review* published by the Council for the Development of Social Research in Africa, Dakar, Senegal. He is a Visiting Fellow of the Department of Sociology at Rhodes University, Grahamstown.

Mark W. Lipsey is a Senior Research Associate at the Vanderbilt Institute for Public Policy Studies and Director of the Center for Evaluation Research and Methodology at Vanderbilt University.

Thomas Mathiesen has been Professor of Sociology of Law at the University of Oslo since 1972. He is the author of a number of books in English and other languages on the sociology of law, criminology, the sociology of power and counter-power, and media sociology. He is a co-founder of the Norwegian prisoners' movement.

Dario Melossi taught at the University of California, Davis, for several years, and is now a Professor of Criminology in the University of Bologna. His books include *The Prison and the Factory* (with Massimo Pavarini, 1981), *The State of Social Control* (1990), and *The Sociology of Punishment* (ed., 1998). He has a new book (in Italian) on the development of criminological theories in connection with theories of the state and social control. Since his return to Italy, he has been researching migrants' criminalization in the context of the construction of a European Union.

Wayne Morrison is Director of the External Programme for Laws, University of London, and an academic member of the School of Law, Queen Mary College, University of London. He has published *Theoretical Criminology* (1995), *Jurisprudence: from the Greeks to Post-Modernism* (1997), and a contemporary edition of *Blackstone's Commentaries on the Laws of England* (2001). He is currently working on a history of the criminological imagination and its silences.

Pat O'Malley is University Professorial Research Fellow, Faculty of Law, in the University of Sydney. He is an author and editor of many publications in the field of risk, and a member of various Australian government bodies concerning crime and justice. Editor of the Cambridge University Press *Law and Society* series, he serves on the editorial boards of many journals in the field, including the *British Journal of Criminology, Economy and Society, Theoretical Criminology*, and *Law and Society Review*. In 2000 he received the Sellin-Glueck Award from the American Society of Criminology. His recent work has focused on risk-based models in the government of social problems, including two edited collections: *Crime and the Risk Society* (1988) and *Crime Prevention in Australia* (1997).

Frank Pearce is a Professor of Sociology at Queen's University, Kingston, Ontario. His first book on corporate crime was *Crimes of the Powerful* (1976) and his most recent is *Toxic Capitalism* (with Steve Tombs, 1998). He also recently published the second edition of *The Radical Durkheim* (2001). He is currently working on the implications for social theory of the work of the Collège de Sociologie, founded and organized by Georges Bataille and colleagues in Paris in the late 1930s.

Monika Peruffo is currently Trafficking Focal Point for the International Organization for Migrations Mission in Colombia, South America. She received her Ph.D. in Sociology of Law from the State University of Milan. She has been working in international cooperation projects for the EU and the UN Interregional Crime and Justice Research Institute (UNICRI). In her work with UNICRI, she specialized on trafficking in women and children, particularly from the Balkans and from Nigeria, and on the worst forms of child labor, such as commercial sexual exploitation and bonded labor. She now works for the Global Alliance Against Traffic in Women (GAATW) in Thailand, where she coordinates international advocacy activities.

Wilfried Schärf is Associate Professor at the Institute of Criminology at the University of Cape Town, South Africa. He is the principal editor of *The Other Law: Non-state Ordering in South Africa* (2001) and is currently working on a monograph on African justice systems. He has contributed to the post-apartheid transformation of the justice system through the National Crime Prevention Strategy, the White Paper on Safety and Security, and the Law Commission working group on Community Dispute Resolution Structures.

Laureen Snider is a Professor of Sociology at Queen's University in Kingston, Ontario, Canada. She has written extensively on the punishment of women and on corporate crime. Her books include *Bad Business: Corporate Crime in Canada* (1993) and *Corporate Crime: Contemporary Debates* (coedited with Frank Pearce, 1995).

Elrena van der Spuy is a Senior Lecturer attached to the Department of Criminal Justice, Faculty of Law, at the University of Cape Town. She is a former Director of the Institute of Criminology at UCT. Her primary research interests revolve around issues of policing. She has published on aspects of South African policing reform, transnationalism in policing, and the impact of donor assistance to criminal justice reform in post-conflict societies.

Paul A. Taylor is Senior Lecturer in Communications Theory, Institute of Communications Studies, at the University of Leeds. His previous work includes *Hackers: Crime in the Digital Sublime* (1999) and his recent publications focus upon the phenomenon of hacktivism and digital culture in general. He was recently appointed as the evaluator of the Economic and Social Research Council's *Virtual Society?* programme.

Steve Tombs is a Professor of Sociology at Liverpool John Moores University and Chair of the human rights charity The Centre for Corporate Accountability. Recent publications include: *Beyond Criminology? Taking Harm Seriously* (2004), co-edited with Dave Gordon, Paddy Hillyard, and Christina Pantazis; *Unmasking the Crimes of the Powerful: Scrutinising States and Corporations*, with Dave Whyte (2003); and *Safety Crimes*, also co-authored with Dave Whyte (2007). He is co-author of *Corporate Crime* (1999) with Gary Slapper, and *Toxic Capitalism* (1998) with Frank Pearce. He also co-authored *People in Organisations* (1996) and co-edited *Risk, Management and Society* (2000).

Part I
Crime, Justice, and Societies

1

The Social Nature of Crime and Deviance

COLIN SUMNER

No *Companion to Criminology* in the twenty-first century would be a truly sociable companion unless it explored the meaning and value of "the social" in an age of suspicion and distrust. Most of the contributions to this volume are sociological in nature, reflecting the predominance of sociology within global criminology. They deal with phenomena often described by sociologists as socially constructed but usually seen, conversely, by the public as the antisocial activities of antisocial individuals. This difference of standpoint suggests a problem.

Criminologists are concerned with the ways that social conditions and institutions produce or construct crime and deviance. Many argue that psychological, psychiatric, legal, medical, and other perspectives based upon the individual as the root cause of social phenomena are not the best ones for understanding or explaining crime and deviance, while accepting that they may have more to offer in the practical day-to-day handling of individual offenders. Criminologists concerned with explanation rather than detection or treatment tend to take the view that collective or aggregate phenomena are the result of collective or aggregate conditions, just as Durkheim saw consistent suicide rates over time as a direct index of persistent social realities (1970 [1897]), or as Marx saw forms of law as a reflection of predominant social relationships (see Marx and Engels 1968). For most criminologists, social facts require social explanations.

Therefore, it might be useful for criminology students to explore what this means: to know, or to think critically about, what is social about crime and deviance. Too often the meaning of the social nature of crime and deviance is taken for granted and the professional usage of the term "social" has become sloppy, with the result that it is too often unclear that anything specific is being gained by describing crime and deviance as "social" problems. This essay seeks to outline and clarify what we have understood as the social construction of crime and deviance and to bring out what has become problematic about this understanding.

The Growth of the "Social"

If crime and deviance are social constructions, what does that mean at the beginning of the twenty-first century? Does it have the same value or meaning as an idea as it did in 1946 when Mannheim published *Criminal Justice and Social Reconstruction*? In that book, Mannheim talked of "the crisis in values" which "confronts the criminal law" and described criminal law as "a petrified body, unable to cope with the endless variety of problems created by an ever-changing world and kept alive mainly by tradition, habit and inertia" (1946: 3). He argued that, after the devastation of World War II, the public, democratic, and "scientific" elements in the penal system needed extension in order to achieve greater representativeness and efficiency, at the expense of the private, the vested interests of elites, and the inconsistent, amateurish prejudice too often displayed.

Criminal law, for Mannheim, had to represent society, as a collection of diverse classes of people with divergent interests, and the construction of a democratic social order required the scientifically informed criminalization of "antisocial behavior." If the behavior was not antisocial it should not be criminalized, Mannheim maintained, warning, however, that not all antisocial behavior should be criminalized and that many such behaviors were better regulated outside of the penal system. For Mannheim, the social dimension of criminal law was the extent to which it democratically expressed the interests and needs of a broadly defined public. In short, social objectives were paramount and were to be achieved at the expense of the private, the sectional, and the purely procedural.

The key objective in 1946 was the (re-)construction of a social order which had public legitimacy, not an open playground for the vested interests of either the free market or the closed shop of establishment technocrats. The cost to the public purse was not the key issue. Society, Frank claimed in his *Society as the Patient* (1948), was the problem not the individual, and society had to be reconstructed as a healthy, efficient entity for the benefit of the majority, or even, ideally, all. Within the dominant ideologies of that time, the "social," however variously understood in the UK, Germany, the USA, or the USSR, was synonymous with social democracy, collective interests, scientific planning, welfare-statism or at least the good of the people, and the prevention of any reoccurrence of mass gangsterism, free-market selfishness, widespread poverty, and national degeneration. Social construction demanded that social policy and social issues be uppermost in a scientifically informed program of legislation.

During the period from 1946 to 1965, when quantitative analysis of factors correlated with "delinquent behavior," or delinquency prediction based on official statistics dominated criminological methods, even some psychiatrists inclined to see the main causes of criminal or delinquent behavior as "sociological" (e.g., West 1967). By the heyday of the labeling perspective in sociology, from around 1965 to 1975, which analyzed criminal or deviant acts as the products of authoritative social groups and institutions labeling it as such, it was becoming axiomatic that crime and deviance were statuses constituted by social definitions, pressures, milieux, institutions, interactions, factors and choices; by basic collective features of human association which make up what we think of as society. The rise of socialist, feminist and postmodern criminologies, from 1968 to the present day, anchored this standpoint firmly, while developing the caveat that societies were very much ruled by dominant classes, men, and powerful discourses. Today, even biological or constitutional criminologies, dating back to the 1880–1940 era, have become "sociobiological" in their approach.

The ideal of "the social," or a planned collective development of communities, had emerged much earlier than the twentieth century. Writers like Hobbes, in the seventeenth century, had understood that without some kind of "social contract," or collective compromise of interests for the common good, the greedy world of business and commerce would lead to poverty and powerlessness for the economically marginal or dispossessed, and thus to extensive urban crime and political disorder (see Taylor, Walton, and Young 1973). Foucault (1967, 1977) observed that this early phase of commercialization and urbanization had generated the elements needed for the later birth of criminology in the nineteenth century – as part of the scientific armory of the "social administration," or state management, of large populations by tiny but powerful economic, political, and military elites. These elements included the fear of urban crime and disease, political instability, the rise of a Protestant work ethic, a militaristic approach to public order, the ascendancy of the new rationalist or "natural" sciences in both technology and the study of human behavior, and a growing awareness of the close relationship between moral health, political order and a prosperous economy (see Sumner 1990b). For Foucault, the field of "the social" was the territory governed by "biopolitics," or the "scientific" administration of populations for the health of the economy and the nation.

The emergence of mass-manufacturing capitalism and mass society by the early twentieth century accelerated social, social-administrative, social-ist, social-scientific and social-welfare tendencies as movements for the reform or mitigation of the worst effects of capitalism. A "social" world or "society" was increasingly not just a vision of a healthy collective order but also a fact of modern capitalism, institutionalized within new political parties and legislation aimed at the diminution of mass poverty and political chaos. Concomitantly, we witness the long decline of the old idea that crime and deviance were behaviors expressing the power of an extraterrestrial Evil through weak and deficient, ultimately godless, individuals who had to be constantly suppressed by the godly and truly good institutions of law enforcement.

In this modernist view, crime was a "social fact" (Durkheim 1938 [1897]), not an individual aberration; a fact resulting from the condition of our society. It was a normal feature of social life, reflecting the forms and levels of our social development. It was not something mysterious which spewed strangely from hearts of darkness, but rather something more prosaic and earthly which directly reflected the extent, form, and success of our attempts at social integration. Some convicted criminals, Durkheim observed, may well be disturbed individuals but the typical rates, patterns, and forms of crime were demonstrably related to the level of social integration; the degree to which particular social groups were integrated into the norms of society via organized and interconnected social institutions. This was the vital factor: too little integration caused crimes underpinned by normlessness, moral disarray, or social isolation, too much caused the crimes brought about by dictatorship, excessive suppression, and overregulation (see Sumner 1994: ch. 1). For example, the official statistics, he argued, clearly showed that a Protestant, unmarried male in an urban area was far more likely to commit suicide than a married Catholic female in the countryside; similarly, but conversely, a prisoner trapped without hope or prospects was more likely to commit suicide than someone with aspirations and possibilities. For Durkheim, it was ultimately a question of a systemic balance between the needs of the social and the needs of the individual. In this perspective, the behaviors we define as crime are not already "out there" but are those which outrage the collective sentiment today and in that way are relative to contemporary social norms and the social mood to enforce them. The "social" world, the realm of society, does not just produce offensive behaviors but also perceptions of offensiveness, and thus crime and deviance are always doubly socially constructed.

Both of these aspects of the social production of crime and deviance were, for Durkheim, facts of life in any society, and in a new or modern world with new scientific methods and philosophies they were to be studied within sociology and planned out in social administration, with the same degree of unemotional, scientific logic as we would expect in the field of particle physics. Indeed, during the time Durkheim was writing, Einstein published his theory of relativity, a theory which added to our understanding that even the physical world only appeared to us in forms relative to our standpoint (for more on this, see Sumner 1994). From a modernist position, crime was primarily a social problem and could best be tackled through the new sciences of society. It contained no secret about "criminal minds," but was the outcome of mundane social circumstances and systems.

The age of moral absolutes, of the Manichaean vision of clear differences between right and wrong, was rapidly being eclipsed by an age of moral relativism. It was becoming clearer, as Nietzsche (1969 [1887]) observed, that good intentions could produce very bad results and vice versa, and that one man's nobility is another's cynical exploitation of inherited power. Earlier, Marx's *Capital* (1970 [1867]) had asked who was the criminal and who was the victim in a world driven increasingly by the search for vast profits and transnational powers. Who was the vandal (see Stone 1982): the working-class youth who damaged public monuments or the industrialist who destroyed the environment to make money and then erected monuments to himself in public? What was moral and healthy, or immoral and sick, was becoming deeply ambiguous in a fast-changing commercial world which, to paraphrase Marx and Engels (1968: 38), was revolutionizing all existing social relations and vaporizing the rural traditions of pre-capitalist economies. Not only was crime a social fact but it was a rapidly changing one; moving with the changes in our emotions, circumstances, and customs.

The mass slaughter of the Great War of 1914–18 led to the discovery of "shell shock" or post-traumatic stress disorder, and the rise of a sociologically aware psychiatry of social disorganization. The gap between individual human weakness and unnatural social disaster was narrowing; the former seemed understandable in the circumstances and the latter became the bigger problem. Radical developments in post-impressionist art after 1900, such as the cubist work of Picasso or the visceral screams of Grosz's expressionism, reflected not just our shock at the new (see Hughes 1981), but also our realization that reality was not simply out there to be painted, that the view was relative to the viewer, and that what we saw was coming from within our increasingly tormented souls (see Sumner 1994: ch. 3). The savage within began to accompany the savage without. Our nascent utopias of a social world were threatened by historical psychological baggage. Jung feared that all our grand ideals, whether they be "the solidarity of economic interests" or "international social democracy," had "failed to stand the baptism of fire – the test of reality" and the "gnawing doubt" of "modern man" had left him (and maybe her) in search of a soul, in a state of "almost fatal shock" at the sight of the "catastrophe" of modernity (Jung 1933; see Sumner 1994: 74).

With the rise of fascism in the 1930s, in both its national (Germany) and social (the USSR) forms, and of social democracy in America and Britain, social blockages in the old world were swept aside by undammed waves of long-suppressed popular aspirations. The search for social ideals and the drive for their realization was conducted in distressingly uncertain as well as depressingly difficult economic and political conditions: who was to say any more that the crimes that mattered sprung from individual hearts of darkness or from social states of disorganization? Individuals seemed mere pawns in social history and the latter lay in the hands of individual rulers, powerful states, and huge corporations more powerful than mere kings, queens, bishops, and knights ever were. The social and the individual were becoming intertwined and blurred in the madness of the age. How else could the later atrocities of the 1939–45 war be explained?

Relativism and relational thinking grew apace in many fields of work and thought. It was increasingly clear that what we expressed, whether in the sublime work of art or the sublimations of criminal activity, was a reflection of our relation to the social world or society, what we wanted from it and what it was doing to us. In this vision of the interactivity between individual and social circumstances, the field of criminology in the 1930s, through the work of the School of Sociology in the multicultural "melting pot" of Chicago, absorbed the notion of the social and converted it fully into a cause of crime, viewing the patterns and rates of crime as expressions of social disorganization. The definition of action as criminal was increasingly seen as related or relative to the standpoint of both the offending subject and the community, the legislator or the police officer, with their specific economic, political, or cultural interests, needs, and perceptions. Crime and deviance were now understood as products of "social intercourse." The social was becoming not just the external societal but the interactive field of all human relations. The value and meaning of the criminal law was increasingly understood as relative to the social problems it addressed and its ability to ameliorate them. The crime or deviance of an individual was now grasped as a clear reflection of the individual's experiences of society and social circumstances.

Several major historical events and processes in the rest of the twentieth century finally fixed this interactive sociological standpoint as the fundamental assumption, or *Grundnorm*, for any rational or scientific study of crime and deviance. In brief summary, these events and processes included:

- the further growth of great cities and more urban migration bringing new waves of widespread petty delinquency and organized crime;
- the growth of huge multinational corporations able to bend, create, or flout the law at will and thus to make a mockery of the claim of equality under the law;
- the Depression of the 1930s and widespread poverty in the Third World ever since, forcing many to scavenge unlawfully, but understandably, for survival;
- World War II, with its mass killing by both sides in the name of a free society under the rule of law and the Holocaust, with its bureaucratic annihilation of millions of alleged deviants, scapegoated mainly on a racist basis; the later criminalization of genocide;
- the post-1945 construction of corporatist welfare states dedicated to "planning out" the roots of deviance, degeneracy, and dissent in relative deprivation and institutional disorganization;
- the growth in affluent societies in the West of deviant or delinquent subcultures between 1955 and 1975, evidencing apparently incontrovertibly the power of the link between "bad company" and "bad behavior";
- the violent suppression, externally and internally, of decolonization and other nationalist or "terrorist" movements by old and new imperial powers, posing complex new questions about the social value of violence;
- mass social deviance, or individualistic and hedonistic self-expression, via the "revolution in manners and morals" (Allen's phrase, referring to the USA of the "roaring" 1920s: Allen 1969) and the "cultural revolution" of Europe in the late 1960s, challenging the necessity or value of many conservative aspects of existing capitalist culture;
- the rise of feminism(s) after 1970 confronting the idea of a "natural" order of things with the notion of a violent male order derived from a centuries-old patriarchal culture of domination;
- the massive rise in official "volume crime" rates, during the whole post-1945 era in most Western societies, sitting grinning in apparent contradiction to growing affluence and burgeoning law-enforcement industries;
- the rise of political "dissidence" in both East and West on such a grand scale as to result in a questioning of both capitalist and communist societies and, indeed, of the very nature and purpose of state societies at all;
- the rise of huge regional economic blocs, treaties, and organizations, such as the EU, the NAFTA, and the OAU, which, alongside the multinational corporations, began to undercut the power of the nation-state and forced many to question "who rules" and whose norms actually defined crime and deviance;
- the colossal labor migrations, globalization of labor markets, and expansion of travel generally, raising sharp issues about the validity or applicability of the national or moral basis of laws and blurring the distinctions between crime and rights, deviance, and cultural diversity;

- the massive environmental destruction following the increasingly global penetration of the economic order, confirming our worst fears about the lack of social regulation of capitalist economies.

All of these huge changes conspired and converged to confirm that crime and deviance are doubly socially constructed, as practical or behavioral responses to social conditions and as social censures reflecting the emotions, ideologies, and values of powerful social groups.

Today, in a new century, we still understand the world as an interactive field of human relations and impersonal forces within which individuals and groups do make choices, but only within the great swirl of social change and within the contexts, constraints, and pressures of huge institutions, structures, and processes operating on a global scale. The "dead hand of the past," as Marx called history, remains ever-present around and within us alongside visions of the future. As always, the social combines past, present, and future in a series of dialectics between the individual and the collective. In that sense, it is still a social world. To paraphrase Durkheim (1970 [1897]) from a hundred or so years before, even when, in our individualistic world of "alternative lifestyles," we think we have escaped the social bond, we remain inextricably within its clutches. However antisocial the criminals or deviants, or even the lawmakers, they too are social beings, "hot-wired" into society's circuits and networks.

Nevertheless, what the rest of this essay will bring out is that within this very broad understanding of the "social" there are actually several competing meanings with significant differences of emphasis. Already, aware readers may have inferred that the social can be used to mean the general, the aggregate, the public, the collective, the shared, the democratic, the cultural, the societal, or the official and state-sanctioned. These terms carry very different connotations and can import sharply different meanings to the idea that crime and deviance are social phenomena. For example, it is very different to suppose that crime is a collective problem needing collective solutions than to take it as a cultural issue needing cultural answers or as a state problem requiring state attention. My main objective is to elucidate the historic meanings of the social within criminology, and, secondarily, to begin to indicate a problem in the meaning and valuation of the social which criminology in the twenty-first century will have to confront. As such, the essay will raise far more questions than it answers and may well be uncomfortable for those who want a one-line dictionary-style definition. A good companion is one who asks questions, not one who constantly reiterates well-worn answers.

THE SOCIAL IN EARLY CRIMINOLOGY AND SOCIOLOGY

Before 1914, most commentators did not see crime as a social form, although we should not forget the number of writers who saw social conditions causing crime in the nineteenth century, such as Quetelet, Dickens, Marx, Mayhew, and Booth (see Mannheim 1965: chs. 19–21). Early criminologists, such as Goring and Lombroso, tended to examine convicted criminals as if engaged in a "a zoology of social sub-species" (Foucault 1977: 253; see Beirne and Messerschmidt 1991).

They, and their followers within a positivist criminology based on the natural science methods of that time, analytically dissected the moral constitution of captive criminals in prison as degenerate forms of the human species, claiming to find that they possessed constitutional abnormality, mental deficiency, weak moral conscience, and emotional deficits. Anatomical criminology was moving on: two centuries before, surgeons had physically dissected the actual corpses of executed criminals in medical science's search for the symptoms of evil. Even as late as 1919, Giddings, an early American sociologist, was claiming that there were "seven devils": the depraved, deficient, deranged, deformed, disorderly, dirty, and devitalized (Sumner 1994: 40). Criminology was born out of social change, yet with a belief in the pre-social nature of the criminal: the "man–beast" in famous novels about Count Dracula, Frankenstein, and Dr. Jekyll, raging carnally in popular urban demonology in the same rogues' gallery as the "unciv-ilized savage" of the overseas territories colonized during that period (see Pick 1989; Gilman 1985). Anthropology, popular literature, and medical science combined with a bastardized Darwinism to produce the idea of the "other," the strange, foreign, criminal, and alien as a degenerate subhuman form not worthy of humane treatment: a precondition of the series of savage, inhuman, strange, criminal, and "animal" massacres, incarcerations, tortures, executions, and genocides from 1880 onward as Europe colonized the world. America had already completed the genocide and bantustanization of its "first nations."

A new age of imperialism and internal colonialism was underway. Accom-panying the formation of an industrial capitalist mass society, was a view of all those who did not or would not fit in with its relentless expansion as in some way "not human" and therefore as expendable as animals or insects. In line with its times, early criminology tried very hard to prove that criminals were consti-tutionally defective. At this stage, they were portrayed as pre-social. Describing them as antisocial came later, in the mid-twentieth century; once a sense of society had been forged in the ruling imagination.

At the same time, there was the jurisprudential argument that the declining traditional forms of regulation were natural or pre-social. Ross, the American sociologist, in 1901 described them as automatic, spontaneous, and instinctive (Ross 1969). This supposedly "natural control" was founded on tight family, interpersonal, and communal bonds and a moral consensus. It was the regula-tion of the community by the community, of like-minded people by like-minded people, and as such it treated conforming or even deviant people as its own, as fellow humans struggling to keep in tune with the great spirits, and seriously nonconforming people as nonhumans divested of spiritual communion, or as aliens lacking the qualities of the community. "Social control," that key concept of twentieth-century sociology, was, on the other hand, for Ross, a form of regulation which was planned, conscious, and scientifically informed (see Sumner 1997a). It combined natural control with a machine-like, mass legal system. It centered on the principle that true rule or effective order could only really occur through the consent, participation, and commitment of most sections of society. Social control, with its very American insight into the "melting pot" of fast-changing multicultural societies, recognized everyone, conformist or criminal, in principle as an ontological, legal, and political part of the social whole and capable of either supporting or destroying the social fabric of goodwill and loyalty. Deviants, criminals, or dissenters were to be seen as human but at odds with the project of the society and its desired social norms, and the term "anti-social" gradually emerged to describe the status of their offenses.

Ross understood that the processes of industrialization were creating a new form of society, a highly diversified and differentiated form, which could sweep away valuable bonds and norms of traditional human interaction unless the forms of regulation were also modernized to become forms of social control unifying the disparate sections of the territory with "equal rights" and "due process." The binding of living tissue, in Ross's terms, was being replaced by "rivets and screws," in other words what we call today the machinery of criminal justice. This new system had to be imbued with social values appealing to and protecting all or most sections of society, or else it would be merely an impersonal machine helpless to prevent the excesses of economic individualism or to promote the welfare of the many.

The savagery of the colonialists' violence, whether in the USA itself or in Africa and elsewhere, had, Ross observed, destroyed the indigenous natural community-based controls of the colonized (and, it is arguable, of the dispossessed everywhere, namely the working class and women) with the result that not only had the colonizers lost their innocence as self-proclaimed disseminators of an egalitarian rule of law representing a collective will, but they had also created a demoralized and deregulated mass of potential resistance fighters. Social control was essential for the new society to hold together domestically and internationally – both to rein in the excesses of the powerful *and* to incorporate the new dispossessed within the new wealth of nations. This of course remains very poignantly true today, although resurgent free-marketeers frequently forget its wisdom and social policy experts have to remind them equally frequently of the value of "social capital" (see Putnam 1995, 2001). Social control was and is a modern form of rule which had to be integrative, representative, and fair, while also involving an impersonal machinery of justice which could mass-process large numbers of people at a low cost. Today, we still try to maintain this difficult balancing act, but what Ross's great insight shows is that the idea of the criminal or deviant as an evil demon beyond the pale of humanity is not at all a required ideological tool of modern social control but actually a throwback to an age of pre-social control. We can expect it to disappear one fine day when we have finally absorbed Ross's lessons about the requirements of social control such as community participation and integration. It seems that we are still learning them.

One of the first, and still, powerful components of the modern field of population management, and therefore practical social control, was immigration regulation, a subsystem which suggests that modern societies prefer the cheaper option of exclusion rather than a costly inclusion. In 1921, Harry Laughlin, working for the US Eugenics Record Office – an auspicious location, like today's equivalents, vitally involved in official classifications of "all types of individuals who require social care or attention of one sort or another" – defined the "socially inadequate" as including:

(1) Feeble-minded, (2) Insane, (3) Criminalistic (including the delinquent and wayward), (4) Epileptic, (5) Inebriate (including drug habitués), (6) Diseased

(including the tuberculous, the syphilitic, the leprous, and others with chronic infectious segregated diseases), (7) Blind (including those with greatly impaired vision), (8) Deaf (including those with greatly impaired hearing), (9) Deformed (including the crippled), and (10) Dependent (including children and old folks in "homes," ne'er-do-wells, tramps, and paupers). (Laughlin 1921: 56)

This list reveals the perceived extent of the "antisocial": Laughlin quotes sociology professors of the time as defining the list as "public charges" and "social debtors." It reminds us that, as Foucault (1967, 1977, 1980a) and others have argued, "social" administration was set up to manage the unproductive sectors of society, those fragments of population who do not produce wealth. The "antisocial" was in 1921 in practice still those population sectors costly to the state. Social control was expensive: the way of free-market society – "free trade, liberty, and gunboats" – where the rich get richer and the poor die early or in prison, was increasingly deplored in the liberal conscience, but it was at least cheap for the state.

The desire for "social welfare," or better state care of public charges, grew fast after 1900, but it was in constant conflict with a desire to remove the costly "public charges" from sight, one of whose most portentous expressions was the pseudo-science of eugenics, an early sort of "ethnic cleansing" theory. In the New World, the costly, dangerous, and diseased elements were frequently screened out by immigration policy, although we should not forget the internal ethnic and class cleansing achieved through such legislation as the sexual sterilization laws (see McLaren 1990). In the old world, as we saw from 1939 to 1945, some of the perceived enemies of the "pure" society, desirous of purity in body and mind, were forcibly eliminated in large numbers. McLaren argued, in relation to early Canadian social policies, that:

> the rise of eugenics symptomized a shift from an individualist to a collectivist biologism by those who sought to turn to their own purposes the fears raised by the threat of "degeneration". Individualism, materialism, feminism, and socialism were said to be rampant. The purported surges in venereal disease, tuberculosis, alcoholism, divorce, and labor unrest were pointed to by the nervous as evidence of the erosion of traditional values. Early Victorian science had reassured the middle class of the harmony of religious and scientific truths and the possibility of social peace and industrial harmony. This vision had been momentarily lost. (1990: 27)

This insight helps us understand why Hitler's hit list of "costly" elements included not just Jews but communists, intellectuals, homosexuals, and avant-garde artists, as well as no small number of foreigners in general. Like Stalin, he saw the "big issue" of the "social" as the problem of cleansing out the various threats to the order of the diseased national-social state. Biologism, the belief in the biological or ethnic basis of crime and other individual weakness, had, indeed, been collectivized.

This is a reminder of how words can mean many different things. The "social," even in the hands of socialists, feminists, or nationalists, did not yet mean much more than a collectivized and mythical ethnic purity of body and mind or an obsessively patriotic elevation of core indigenous characteristics to an almost sacred status (McLaren 1990; Amatrudo 1997; Sumner 1994: ch. 2).

As such, its progressive features were all too often contained within an ethnicized totalitarianism of vested national interests and the new religion of moral purity. Today's excesses of both "political correctness" and its opposite, England-for-the-English-style racism, thus had their forerunners, and they were forged in the violent vortex of authoritarian nationalism, nation-state formation, and the ethnic persecution of foreign elements. We are instructed in a very important lesson: what the social means at any point in time is very much an expression of its historical milieu. It may well be that the social has no transhistorical meaning; maybe nothing but our jaundiced attempts to make things better for ourselves.

THE STATE CONSTRUCTION OF SOCIAL DEVIANCE: THE SOCIAL NATION OF NEW-DEAL SOCIOLOGY

It makes less sense historically to talk of the social construction of crime and deviance between 1900 and 1945 than to speak of the state deployment of categories and administrative systems to construct crime and deviance as "social" problems confronting the "nation" or "the free world." As in the post-decolonization Third World after 1960, crime control was a primary means for defending the nation-state against its supposed enemies and social control a means of keeping a constant eye on deviants, dissenters, and other potential threats to the state. Nation-building using crime control and public administration is not new, nor particularly social. In fact, given the nature of the capitalist state, especially in its imperial forms in colonial and "puppet" societies, such practice was and is usually autocratic, partisan, and bigoted along class, ethnic and gender lines – anything but social or collective. Nation-state building or rebuilding has frequently been a form of antisocial exclusion; a form which ideologically inspired the Holocaust, many genocides, much ethnic cleansing, and, in its less violent forms, a whole range of class-based, gendered, and racist institutional practices and visions which supposed that the ethnic ghettoes of social deviance, like Vietcong villages, continuously reproduced themselves. These images may seem florid but they also reappear in the dry prose of today's positivist criminology: see, for example, Farrington's recent statement that "[I]t is clear that problem children tend to grow up into problem adults, and that problem adults tend to produce more problem children" (1997: 400). Such positions express no more than the archetypal fear of the ever-procreating devil present in unwanted, resistant, or expensive sections of the population: the eternity of evil and therefore the eternal enemy of the state.

Nation-building, with its mythical or ideological legend of the nation as an ethnically pure singularity, has involved a process of naming, shaming, and excluding its costly, offending, and threatening elements as foreign impurities, degenerations, or instruments of the devil – rather more than a process of recognizing them as the unwanted offspring of their parent body politic who needed care, integration, rights, and recognition, not only to preserve the moral integrity of that parent as a spiritually viable and sustainable whole but also to give them their due as their parents' progeny. The gain of the twentieth century in this respect seems to be the dubious one that exclusion is more internal than external: frontier borders have disappeared and internal "exclusion camps" of all kinds have multiplied. The social in twentieth-century practice was distorted by and often turned into the sectional.

Durkheim (1938 [1897]) was a forerunner in trying to teach us that deviant elements in the body politic were there to teach us something, namely, as Frank (1948) was later to articulate, that society itself was imperfect, dis-eased or full of tensions. By the mid-twentieth century, we were describing labeled criminals and deviants as "social problems" and "social issues"; we had begun to take some responsibility for our offspring. This new, if fragile and distorted, sensibility was becoming a central feature of what we still today call social democracy.

The new society of the 1930s' US New Deal still understood itself to a certain extent within the language of a medical model, but the core of its thinking was the new managerial–administrative planning essential to social democracy and the new social control. Wirth (1931) had called for a "clinical sociology" linked to child guidance work; some US sociologists had observed Hitler's social planning within Germany with no little respect; frontier culture was criticized in favor of an intellectual urban liberalism which would match the gangsters with strong state management, social security, and incorporated trade unionism. A federal welfare state began to emerge in the USA to match Hitler's national socialism and Stalin's union of soviet republics. The concept of social deviance was born in 1937, combining psychoanalysis, social policy, and sociology in a potent union (see Sumner 1994: ch. 4), conveying the idea that one could study scientifically the manifest behavioral symptoms of social disorganization and neutrally classify them generically as deviations from social norms.

The new US scholarship of the 1930s, influenced by the systemic failures of Prohibition, sleaze scandals, and the Depression, recognized that if *so many* were forced to work for the Mob or hustle for survival the root of their "sin" could not be their individual personalities but the collective failure to provide jobs or social security and to regulate society with honesty and sensitivity. Bad boys were no longer failures evidencing personal deficiency, and bad girls still had not been scientifically discovered, but in the writings of labor historians such as Tannenbaum (1938) they became products of over-zealous moralism, punitive thinking, and over-heavy policing, scapegoats for collective anxieties about the future, vehicles through which social frustration articulated itself aggressively, and even victims of a gun-ridden "frontier culture" which the parent community did nothing to regulate and everything to support. Bad boys became social products and social responsibilities. It was not a matter of liberal tolerance. Society, said Tannenbaum, through its parents, communities, legislators, and authorities, really was more to blame in the detailed causation of juvenile delinquency than the youthful perpetrators themselves. The social construction of crime and deviance could therefore only be studied logically and accurately by examining the everyday interactions between rulemakers and rulebreakers producing criminalization, namely the conflicts between elders and their offspring, authorities and their citizens, communities and their rebels.

This was no small change. It broke sharply from earlier criminology with its unilateral natural science gaze at supposedly inanimate objects. The emerging socially conscious interactionism neither saw the offender as the sole cause of his actions nor his offending act as externally driven by objective forces: it saw offenses as products of social interaction between lawbreakers and lawmakers. Crime was no longer an individual disease but a social dis-ease, tension, conflict, or dysfunction. Tannenbaum claimed that society overdramatized crime as evil, at the expense of self-critical reflection (see Sumner 1994: ch. 5), and society gradually came to terms with the idea that crime was a social outcome which could only logically be treated with "social" work, "social" welfare, "social" planning, and sociology (the study of "the social").

Despite the profound issues facing many societies of the 1930s, the social interactionist perspective completely downplayed or even ignored the huge role of structural conflicts, for example, between capital and labor, city and country-side, public office and individual enterprise, or between countries heading toward war, in producing the patterns of everyday interaction. The emerging concept of the social was very much a parochial one, tending to take for granted the increasingly international, master structures of economy and politics driving modern societies; a weakness which *ab initio* reduced the meaning of the social to the remaining main sector of human intercourse – the cultural. Culture was much discussed and researched in the 1930s and what was understood as "the social" was very much reduced in reality to "the cultural" or patterns of behavior involving systems of norms (see also Mannheim 1965: 422, where he observes that the concept of culture "remains so vague and ill-defined").

Nevertheless, Roosevelt's New Deal recognized that society produced its own problems and could therefore begin to cure them itself through social measures based upon a national–cultural consensus. "Inadequates" and "public charges" now became "deviants," and since they were seen as socially produced, they were called "social deviants." As Goffman later sardonically put it in his *Asylums*: "A crime must be uncovered that fits the punishment" and "the character of the inmate must be reconstituted to fit the crime" (1968a: 334; see also Sumner 1994: 206–31). The punishment by the time we reached the 1950s was to be less physical and more mental or cultural. After a long world war witnessing the practical value of loyalty, and in a period of full employment demanding labor, motivated compliance to the cultural norms of the nation-state or welfare society was prized as a vital force. Deviant motivations had to be rechanneled through "treatment," "social work," "education and training," "operant conditioning," "community development," and of course "participation."

"Social deviation," as the generic category for the individual expression of society's cultural failures and weaknesses, was studied by the "social sciences" of social administration and sociology. These were the names of the fields demanded by the logic of the thinking. In contrast, it should be noted, conventional criminology from the 1950s to the 1970s derided and dismissed much of these new sciences of the social, absorbing only those elements consistent with its acceptance of external causation driving weak individuals to crime: that is, accepting only those forms of sociology and social administration which did not introduce choice, subjectivity, symbolism, cultural meaning, reflexivity, and interaction. It could absorb those types of sociological analysis which did not take heed of the interactionist–culturalist advances of the 1930s and persisted in portraying delinquency as an effect of supposedly "objective" and "external" factors. Social science in general, from 1940 to the mid-1960s, also mostly did just that, mainly focusing on class–status differentials, "sink" housing estates, low-income divorced parents, poor housing, maternal deprivation, and the improvement of systems of social administration.

Goffman's later definition of deviance in *Stigma* (1968b) reminds us that by the 1960s social deviants were clearly more cultural deviants than public charges or societal products, although they were still viewed as costly, and that not much else had changed apart from the generic name of those blamed internally by the capitalist collective for its problems:

> If there is to be a field of enquiry called "deviance", it is social deviants as here defined that would presumably constitute its core. Prostitutes, drug addicts, delinquents, criminals, jazz musicians, bohemians, gypsies, carnival workers, hobos, winos, show people, full-time gamblers, beach dwellers, homosexuals, and the urban unrepentant poor – these would be included. These are the folk who are considered to be engaged in some kind of collective denial of the social order. They are perceived as failing to use available opportunity for advancement in the various approved runways of society; they show open disrespect for their betters; they lack piety; they represent failures in the motivational schemes of society. (1968b: 170–1)

Sociology in the United States had grown rapidly after the war and we saw a partial cashing-in of the logic of the new sciences of the social within mainstream, functionalist, sociology. Social deviants were now fully cast as cultural rejects in need of counseling, probation, a haircut, or national service to revive their lapsed motivational compliance to society's norms and to emphasize the nonviability or dysfunction of any alternative lifestyle. The products of faulty socialization, not social inequality or discrimination, they simply needed resocialization and the "social problem" would be resolved. Not all sociologists fell in with this new postwar conservatism. Interactionism retained a critical edge. Edwin Lemert (see Sumner 1994: ch. 8; Lemert and Winter 2000), for example, noted the fact that cultural definitions of deviance rarely seemed to apply to bankers, politicians, generals or industrialists and remained the expressions of elite values, and Goffman (1968a) acutely observed the detail of society's cynicism in searching for (what Cohen [1973] later called) "folk devils" to quench its thirst for an enemy and action. Goffman argued, for example, that certified madness is more a matter of contingency or bad luck than anything else, pointing out that most mad people live outside of the mental institutions and that there are many who are not mad when they enter mental institutions but are when they leave. Many regimes in mental hospitals over the last two centuries today look insane in their methods, if they were meant to be curative of madness rather than productive of it, and some very disturbed people, with official records of psychiatric treatment, became leaders of nations in the twentieth century.

What Goffman grasped was that, in a highly differentiated, culturally diverse society, we could all always anytime be labeled as deviant in some way or other if we were unlucky, and that it is therefore a case of "there but for the grace of God go I." The question whether there is something common to, and individually different about, those labeled as socially deviant, on his analysis, really misses the point, just as it would be silly to research what it was that lottery winners had in common that produced their success in buying a winning ticket, other than the fact that they bought the ticket. What social deviants had in common was that they had been selected for labeling as such; they were awarded losing tickets. The power of the social to produce crime was thus, in Goffman's writings, forcefully delivered – through the idea of symbolic power exchanges within social interaction or a highly culturally loaded allocation. Individual peculiarity, Goffman understood, was real, but in a culture that praised and fostered it as a birthright it could hardly be the cause of official censure or certification as deviant or criminal. The "social question" for such, later very influential, American sociologists of crime and deviance of the 1960s concerned the social features which culturally labeled deviants had in common as people who had been through the same labeling process; in the same way that we can sensibly study what happens to lottery winners during and after their success but not whether their idiosyncrasies made them buy a winning ticket. You cannot knowingly buy a winning lottery ticket, unless the game is "fixed." It was now a question of what society did to people in labeling them as criminal or deviant.

The even more radical ideas that you could unconsciously or consciously buy what was very likely a losing ticket and that the whole game is completely corrupt and fixed from the outset were only to be fully resurrected by the critical criminology of the 1970s.

The "social" in Goffman's work, and that of other leading symbolic interactionists such as Becker (1963) and Matza (1969), had become the cause of scapegoating and discrimination. It had become a batch of institutions set up to "manage" all those categories of people censured and symbolized as deviants or as threats to "civilized society," and thus it dutifully produced them through its bureaucratic processes. In that sense, society had become a villain, and the only villain we could rationally apprehend and interrogate. Most scientists of "the social," whether orthodox or liberal, overlooked the fact that so-called social deviants usually did not reject but actually expressed conventional capitalistic values – norms of property acquisition, aggressive upward mobility, competitive selfishness, and geographical mobility – and all too frequently acted in league with authoritative institutions. This "oversight" was the root of many analytic problems later. It rather betrayed the fact that "the social" was now, in truth, officially at odds with unrestrained capitalism, or, put another way, that capitalism itself generated huge internal conflicts between its individualistic core logic and the collective aspirations it encouraged.

Tending to assume an eternal welfare state and an immutable normative-political consensus marking "the end of ideology" (Bell 1960), sociology as a whole developed an amnesia toward what had just happened on a collective global scale, namely the Holocaust and mass slaughter (Sumner 1994: ch. 7; Bauman 1989: 3). Communism and fascism were now allegedly history, and mainstream sociology, in what became known as social theory, proceeded to forget that history and to develop a theoretical language which declared that everything was now social, including biology, science, and history itself. Talking of social relations, social norms, social roles, social interaction, social forms, and social systems, "social" theory often took the form of an elaborate abstraction which encoded the social in a massive blandness (Mills 1970), turning a mere pipe dream, the hope for a truly social world, into a universal fact of life – everything had now become social and not a little vacuous. The social was everywhere but was largely vacant – of history, economics, jurisprudence and the blood and thunder of the harsh realities of social inequality. Little was said in postwar social theory up to 1968 about what Gouldner (1975: ch. 2) called "the master institutions" of political economy, the state, and imperialism, and their deeply antisocial logics and effects. The core drivers and destroyers of the social world (or culture) had been evacuated: sociology's discourse became correspondingly empty and the social had lost its political edge and economic roots, becoming merely cultural.

If everything was covered by "welfare," there could be no reason for delinquency – so social deviants, in both social administrative and interactionist sociologies, became "rebels without a cause" (Bell 1960; see Sumner 1994: ch. 7) or mere (sub-)cultural stylists. The antisocial official violence of the twentieth century, with its wars, colonialisms, barbaric cruelty, economic disasters, autocratic states, and numbing bureaucracies were for a while forgotten. Hope overcame realism. Instead, we were given a long sentence in the punitive pedagogy of social science: social deviations were said to be the result of the breakdown of social norms in social interaction, brought about by faulty socialization into social roles and institutions by weak parents and by a lack of social integration into well-defined communities. Everything had become social or cultural, but capitalism and the state still got off scot-free, and students could be forgiven for producing statements like "crime is a product of social, cultural and political contexts," which blurred the meaning of the social and undermined its distinctiveness. For what is economics or politics if everything is social? Indeed, the disciplines of economic and political science receded as the tide of sociological supremacism tended to turn everything into a branch of sociology. Economies became social relations of production and distribution; political institutions became the social organization of power; and culture the artifacts of social consciousness. Neither economics nor politics could apparently teach sociology anything, since its captive scientific specialty was the social and that was all there was. The world had suddenly, and quite mysteriously unless we take into account Bretton Woods, the World Bank, the United Nations, and the Marshall Plan, become a society and its contents were all social: animalism or ethology, biological needs and drives, human nature, economic laws, political realism, and the historically impossible had all been banished by the mid-1960s. Everything had become merely social, in the sense of cultural; every entity reduced to a semantic point in a consensual sea of cultural differences.

In the late 1960s and throughout the 1970s, the non-cultural returned with a vengeance. Deviant sociologists like Mills pointed out the very antisocial behavior of economic and political elites; ethologists like Lorenz observed the ways in which we behaved like unconscious animals; radical psychoanalysts, such as Fromm and the Jungians, claimed the persistence of primeval patterns of being; Marxists contended that a truly social world could only be created on the basis of the socialization of the means of economic production; and philosophers attempted to articulate the eternal and absolutely meaninglessness of existence, social or otherwise. The social, however, in becoming everything, had lost its specific historical significance.

The Resurrection and Later Devaluation of the Social Ideal in Critical Criminology

With the rise of a more structural–historical or "critical" criminology by 1970, and the subsequent flourishing of a range of critical criminologies right up to the present day, we registered a remembrance of class struggle, imperialism, the Holocaust, propaganda, and what it felt like to rebel. We remembered Tannenbaum's insistence that society was very much a hope, a dream, inchoate, ill-formed, often hijacked by private or selfish interests, and altogether at odds with the sustained drive to wealth, power and domination. We remembered his insight that those labeled deviant, delinquent, and criminal were often rebels – and rebels with good cause. "All along the watchtower" the rebels came into view: workers, the colonized, women, homosexuals, avant-garde artists, communists, nationalists, ethnic minorities and, of course, youth. The deviants rediscovered their political history and resisted their medico-psychiatric treatment by the clinicians of the welfare states (see Pearson 1975). Their deviance was now, in their eyes, mere difference and pathology a mere social attribution by unsympathetic observers. Critical criminologists put new topics onto the map: most notably domestic violence, corporate crime, crimes of the state, rape, "social crime," and political crime. A critical sociology of law emerged exposing the links between social divisions, power and law. Much of this critical work examined the inequities of social structure, some explored the positive aspects of deviant consciousness and subcultures, and much was historical.

History was back on the agenda, along with Marx, politics and political economy (see Thompson 1975). Fights, strikes, wars, divorces, unilateral declarations of independence, reclaim the night marches, and scuffles all broke out. Poverty and genocide were rediscovered all over the planet, there all the time in our midst. Inevitably, this return of history and materialism meant a revision of the social.

Some critical criminologists embraced revolutionary socialism and a complete overhaul of the state. *The New Criminology* (Taylor et al. 1973) criticized sociological criminology, both orthodox and interactionist, and called for a fully "social theory of deviance"; crime became part of the political struggle, a response to unacceptable social norms and conditions. The social world was turned upside down. Social deviants became heroes in exhibiting antisocial attitudes; they became the healthy ones faced by an unhealthy society. Simultaneously, the state acquired the attribute of being antisocial, as the sponsor of evil and as the maker and defender of boundaries on maps which divided people against each other. Welfare was declared a "con," a sham incorporating and pacifying the lower classes. Rights were dismissed as ephemeral masks concealing recalcitrant "structural inequalities" and the fact that "might is right." Later, the state was further denounced as the defender of the twin faiths of patriarchy and racism, and the central agency of the unintelligence involved in the destruction of the environment.

The social had returned to being an aspiration rather than a vacuous fact; the hard fact was the US military-industrial complex relentlessly bombing Vietnam, and just as hard were the discovery of Stalin's labor camps, the genocide in

Cambodia, and the dissolution of the socialist soviet republics. The achievement of the social and the true nature of the social itself were no longer identified with social administration, social welfarism, or socialism; all these were now discredited as antisocial state strategies for the maintenance of the powerful. Indeed, the general political drift was that we could somehow magically become social in a world without a state. The social had now for many become "the good life," where "all you need is love" and "authentic" human action for there to be peace and harmony. Getting in touch with the true self, and real feelings, was a recipe for a "new age," providing one ignored the anger, frustration, fear, and envy.

Other critical criminologists, probably the majority, from 1970 to the present, produced a stream of research and analysis amounting to a materialist deconstruction of the social state, exposing and describing the many ways in which it had failed to deliver and in which it concealed massive social divisions and inequities (see Chambliss and Seidman 1971; Beirne and Messerschmidt 1991; Garland 1990; Taylor 1999). The term "social" in these writings became a neutral reference to aggregate conditions brought about by history. It lost much of its positive normative weighting. Its rhetorical force as signifier of desired change was fragmented into manifestos for specific causes, such as those of the working class, women, anti-racism, anti-imperialism and local communities. All of this produced a devaluation of the present social. Critical criminology, inevitably with its exposés and critiques, reduced the "social" dimension of social relations to its specific economic, political, or cultural elements as lodged within specific historical and geographical settings, and thereby devalued the inherited meaning of the word. The meaning of the social, for many, was in abeyance but nobody, to my knowledge, actually rejected its use in principle. Whether the social world was portrayed in terms of class divisions, or divisions of gender, ethnicity, nationality, region, or age, the point was that it was being deconstructed into its fragments. The fragmented picture produced was the fragmented world we critical criminologists saw. It was a world where crime, realistically, was a sign of problems and conflicts and a destructive and unhelpful, individualistic, antisocial blight on our hopes for progress; and where deviance was as much a sign of difficulty as of creativity. We remembered that Marx and Engels described petty crime as the parasitic acts of a demoralized lower working class, and critical historians of the 1970s even developed the idea of "social crime" to mark off that small sector of volume crime which actually benefits the community. The world we saw was not one of moral consensus based upon a universal morality, but one of division ordered by amoral force and the moralistic censure of the crimes and deviations of the lower classes. Crime in this way became more of a censure authorized by the powerful than a behavior peculiar to the poor (see Sumner 1990a: ch. 2) – in an antisocial world no behavior has uncontested meanings and disapproval is more a sign of powerful interest than moral purity.

This devaluation and fragmentation of the concept of the social has been accelerated by the celebration of political economy, the cultural, the specific, the local, the historical, and the subjective in the analysis of crime and deviance. The grand abstractions of modernist sociology were, like "The Wall," being taken down brick by brick. Feminist work also challenged the erection of inflexible, ahistorical, broad abstractions as a masculinist form of thought and thus openly devalued the general in favor of the particular. The various feminist criminologies since the 1970s have shared much with critical criminology in general, but there have been some key disagreements over the social nature of crime and deviance. The big area of convergence is that many feminist criminologies regard patriarchy as a *social* form of domination, not a biological or natural one; their view of the social world has been that it is so dominated by a self-interested patriarchy that law did not represent the interests of women and was therefore sectional not universal (see Smart 1989; Gelsthorpe and Morris 1990; Howe 1994; Dobash et al. 1995; Daly and Maher 1998). In this way, for feminist criminology generally, the "social" as a field of consensus, positivity, and constraint on established power was still to be constructed. The existing "social" left too many female victims unprotected. Feminism brought the victim back into criminology in a big way, especially the victims of domestic violence and rape. Forms of crime and criminal justice were consistently portrayed as expressions of male power and as discriminatory. The key concept in this picture has been the sociological one of gender: the idea that the roles, capacities, and rights of each sex, and the norms governing relations between the sexes, are historical and cultural in origin and have been passed on through socialization processes. Gender and gender relations are thus themselves social or cultural constructions and amenable to political change.

The significant area of disagreement lies with the more anarchic tendencies within criminology and concerns the utopian view of the social world resurrected in the late 1960s. Feminists overall have rejected the anarchistic view of the future social because it said little about the reconstruction of gender relations and roles needed to give women equity with men. While there is much ambiguity within feminist criminology, as in socialist criminology, about the value of using the state or legal reform to achieve greater equality and of using the concept of equality as a justification or goal for women's causes, feminist work in recent years has implicitly been geared to change in the present rather than in some distant future. Indeed, its position has been that the utopian vision of the social needs considerable reworking before it can ever happen; a position shared with most socialist criminology. In addition, an important part of feminist criminology has moved away from critical criminology on the issue of the roots of existing social forms: these writings suppose a transhistorical sociobiological propensity of males toward aggressive domination and of females toward a passive nurturance (e.g., Brownmiller 1975; Daly 1984). This tendency demands a revolution in the power balance between men and women before a truly social world can be constructed; no "socialist" revolution could take place before this. When we add in the anti-racist view, expressed in more recent times, that the class and gender revolutions cannot be truly social advances without the removal of divisions of ethnicity, it is clear that the critical criminologies were calling for a thoroughgoing reconstruction of the existing social world.

Critical criminologies over recent years have in effect devalued the supposed social dimension of human relations, deconstructing it as a concealment of sharp divisions of class, race, and gender. In so doing, they sometimes forget the role played by socialists and feminists in constructing the social in the first place, notably within social democracy, socialism, social work, and social policy.

History rarely goes backward or forgets for long, and it may be that all we are seeing now is not so much a demolition of the social as its reworking; a deconstruction and a rebuild. Certainly, no critical criminologist is advocating the progressiveness of the free market or a return to "a natural order."

The tendency of critical criminology to denigrate the existing "social" was given a boost during the 1980s by postmodernism, following or interpreting the work of Foucault, whose work on crime in many respects mirrored that of the late 1960s' "new" criminology with its celebration of deviation from the social. At home with things being upside down, inside out, or even nonexistent, postmodernists were soon announcing, with all-too-ready enthusiasm, that socialism was dead and that "the social" was merely talk, a discourse amongst other discourses, simply a means to domesticate the healthily wild lower orders (cf. Henry and Milovanovic 1996; Stanley 1996). They were also generally quick to decry forms of thought and talk in general as mere strategies of domination. The "social" became simply a dominant-class discursive tactic for the defleaing of the "dangerous classes" so that they did not spread any more contagious diseases (Foucault 1977, 1980a, 1980b). Crime and deviance in postmodernist thought became discursive categories of control within a panoply of dominant scientific, medical, and legal discourses which, when invested in powerful campaigns and maneuvers, served in the regulation of the populace and to deliver healthy workers every Monday morning; key terms in the rationalization of rule.

The socialization of the population into "civilized" habits, in the eyes of Foucauldian sociology, was simply rendering it into captivity. "Civil" society was denied its status as a field of fierce debate and was portrayed as a system of normative institutions which attempted a humane containment of that many-headed hydra, the people. Prisons were no more an instrument of humane containment than the university, the hospital, or the family; the police no more a means of policing the masses than the television set. The difference between a radio, a baton and a marriage disappeared – they were now all part of the wallpaper of domination. The difference between humane and inhumane systems of power vanished in Foucault's work: both the moderate monitoring of "disciplinary" systems to induce motivated compliance, such as the new managerialism or surveillance systems, and the terroristic penality of spectacular executions, such as the public stoning or hanging, were portrayed as mechanisms of population management. Somewhat inconsistently, at the same time as postmodernists dismissed differences of this sort, they celebrated the "differences" of socially deviant groups. Power was seen as ubiquitous and eternally negative; difference as ubiquitous but eternally positive.

"Difference" in fact became a hallmark of postmodern "cool" after about 1985. Postmodernists hailed society as a vast sea of differences, all of which should be respected, except of course those they themselves disapproved of. The distinguishing qualities of women, blacks, and other previously suppressed groups were positively valued; whereas it is hard to remember any essays on "the difference" of neo-Nazi skinheads. Nevertheless, the postmodernists were in line with popular thinking, at least among the young. Deviance was now being revalued generally and the merits of the social were devalued in one further respect. The social world became identified with prison. It was a straitjacket, somebody else's tired old moral clothes, an excuse for discipline through monitoring, audit, review, examination, surveillance and retraining, and therefore control or suppression.

Foucauldian criminologists talked of "the social" as a discourse translated into power, as a rhetorical and tactical figure which put people in yet more chains and thus extended the historical reign of the will to dominate. They celebrated the subversion of dominance generally, in public or in private. Following Foucault and Nietzsche, they cheered on anything that achieved a sublime moment out of the eternity of postwar blandness and rejected the new modality of "disciplinary power" (Foucault 1977) as yet more domination. In fact, for Foucauldians, it seems, disciplinary power was worse than power expressed through spectacular public terror in that it required our consent and self-subjugation to the rhythms of modernist industrial warehousing and management in all its forms. Those of us, even during the late 1960s, who never developed any excitement for being publicly mutilated, even though it had the great merit of not requiring our consent, may see disciplinary power as an historic improvement over "the penality of terror," since at least we could say "no" – which is a little difficult after being beheaded or pulled apart by four horses à la Damiens (Foucault 1977: 3). Some might even argue that the fate of the early seventeenth-century poor prior to the advent of, say, foundlings' hospitals was far worse than modern systems of surveillant social security. The gains of social reform were forgotten. For Foucauldian criminology reform or progress was a discursive illusion: we are all so incorporated into the networks of social discipline that we do not say "no" and have therefore lost our souls and not just our heads. It also overlooked the extent to which resistance was a profound part of the very constitution of the modern "social." Without resistance it would not exist, however limited and flawed.

To downplay resistance in the formation of societies is to ignore the crucial role played by the rejection of excess in the formation of any system of discipline or form of social regulation. This refusal to draw a line against excess left Foucauldian postmodernism unable to generate a new basis for a "social" world; a position which tended toward the anarchic, the amoral, and the indiscriminate. It was also a position which, with the benefit of hindsight, amounted to a mirror opposition to the over-controlling, moralistic, often authoritarian and discriminatory managerialist systems embedded deep in the heart of modernist forms of organization (see Clarke and Newman, 1997, on the managerialist state). Foucauldianism replaced disciplinary power with a celebration of excess. It amounted to an indiscriminate support for political and cultural amorality, overlooking Nietzsche's cynicism (1969 [1887]) about the *ressentiment* of rebel groups and their capability of replacing one policing system with another of equal abhorrence.

THE SOCIAL AS CULTURE

As the preceding argument has explained, the "social" in post-1945 sociology has lost its economic and political meanings. It has become a neutral term devoid of its normative reforming message. It is now "off-message" in an age of spin. It connotes a bygone age of integrated communities, welfare states, militant trade unions, and class politics. In the UK, politicians avoid it for electoral success and the public associates it with a bleeding-heart liberalism exempting offenders from individual responsibility. If it has any residual active and positive meaning in a contemporary sociology which has largely rendered it an anodyne abstraction, it refers to the *cultural* dimension of human life, standing in opposition to the economic and political. In a multicultural globalized world that means mere differences of style; no longer differences in essence. Diversity is now the anti-norm, or norm, depending on how you look at it. The social as the fabric of society, the state-backed political consensus of welfarism, has been replaced by the idea of the universality of difference or the normality of deviation. With the globalization of mass commodity exchange, the "fall of The Wall," and the discrediting of politics in general, there is no universal political principle which commands more assent than that of respect for the specificity or identity of others. The "other," that alien figure that gave rise to the concept of culture in the 1930s, has not only been pardoned through an historic political amnesty but hailed as a hero of progressive change: the image of Mandela is perhaps the exemplar of this trend. "Others" are now respected and it is supposed that even our economic and political relationships are mere expressions of cultural attitudes. Conversely, there is a disrespect for or suspicion of the familiar, the traditional, the fixed, and the established.

Specifics are now pivotal because they give identity in an age of postmodernity when the global expansion of capitalist social structures actually de-differentiates people and places. Commoditization on a global scale reduces people and things to commodities and therefore their value in a global market. The globally marketable is synonymous with "cool" and national–cultural artifacts or styles only survive well if they are marketable. When so many things are hybrid, multicultural, mobile, or mixed in character, sociologists downplay the pure or essential in order to be accurate. As travel, exchange, movement, and globality destroy, blur, or mix real differences, our cultures celebrate difference. Nothing is essential or pure any more because nothing and nobody are just one thing: we are all a mixed bag, a hybridity that defies fixing in official or general words; these words seem to restrict, fix, and control, whereas subcultural argot or the vernacular give control and identity. The social, in a globalized and depoliticized age of commoditized mass information, has become merely culture: a diverse, accumulated, and anonymous mix of meaning-giving attributions and talk which uses the meanings of the past and present along with allusions to a desired future. Culture can thus be anything.

When any object can be an art form, or any feeling just, or any act moral, as in postmodern culture, there is no obstacle to reversing or subverting the meaning we give to things. Anything can become anything; ironically, the perfection of the free-marketeer's fantasy. In this context, crime can be seen by some as seductive, as a sublime moment or "buzz" in an otherwise bland, powerless, and pointless existence; a signifier of "action," or even power, in a disenfranchised cultural desert; victims' pain unimagined in a world that is losing its social imagination (see Katz 1988). Empathy and foresight can be difficult, or just too painful, for generations trapped in the hyperreality of a media network which frequently portrays violence as glamorous and lionizes serious crimes. Crime, alongside war, for many postmodernists and sociologists of postmodernity, has become very much a media event. No longer social but cultural, crime can also be a fashion, a style accoutrement, giving identity where none exists (to rephrase A. K. Cohen's 1955 view of subcultures) and a form celebrated in the new gangster movies, simultaneously dispensing and parodying the hard masculinity of white or black working-class entrepreneurs in a materialistic culture. Philosophical materialists might say that little has changed: Chicago gangs were also models of fascination in the 1930s (and in film ever since) when organized crime was rife, stimulated profitably by the criminalization of disapproved substances which anaesthetized the pain of "the vale of tears" (Engels's phrase) with its rapid change, downright misery, and much insecurity.

Cultural studies has taken over so much of sociology and we even now have "cultural criminology" (e.g., Ferrell and Sanders 1995) which proclaims the culturalness of much to do with crime. But what of economics and politics, and "the social"? It has become common within contemporary criminology to say that crime and deviance are "cultural" phenomena. Sadly, this escape route avoids the question. The obsession with the "cultural" does little more than redesignate some things we once called "social," because they were common or collective in character, at the same time as not addressing things we really wished would be more collective in character, such as capitalism and the state, and their relation to the cultural. Too much cultural studies or sociology today is a description of popular current meanings with no discernible methodology for establishing or defending their veracity or value as facts-in-existence or their effects in general or in particular. To talk of capitalism, state, and class is on the other hand, especially if it involves statistics, distinctly unfashionable.

Nevertheless, culturalist thinking does reflect something important about our times. In the twenty-first century, it would be cretinous to suppose that the world's ills are a result of the genetic or psychological weaknesses of a few rotten apples in an otherwise healthy barrel, if only for the reason that there would be little agreement on the application and meaning of terms like ills, genetic, psychological, weakness, rotten, and healthy. Things now have different and multiple meanings, far removed from the monolithic and absolute moral syntax of any mythical "Golden Age" of monocultural, slow-moving communities, bound to the land, and tightly bonded in an incestuous parochialism. Crime and deviance are contested moral judgments, censures (see Sumner 1990a: ch. 2) that mean different things to people in practice. Breaking someone's rules or norms in a multicultural world is no longer a simple fact with no argument followed by the punishment of the offender; more likely it is the basis for a conference hosted by a university to discuss who is the victim of whose oppression. Moral norms are contested, as are their forms of enforcement. The historic lineages of moral judgment have been fragmented and challenged through exposure to political, academic, and media examination. The information age has passed through secularization and moved on to a virtual de-moralization. The effect of this is to dissolve moral certainty and moral positions themselves, the very cement of "the social," without which "the social" can have no binding material foundations.

By illustration, many members of the public would today claim that censure and policing have disappeared for all practical community purposes, and that any attempt to protect oneself from crime is as likely to lead to arrest as the original criminal act. In many of today's Western societies, crime matters *are* often upside down: no convicted criminal is executed but many kill themselves (e.g., young offenders in secure institutions); more people are killed on the roads or at the workplace than in interpersonal conflicts; many murder convictions are made despite the absence of a corpse and there are hundreds of thousands of "missing persons" annually with no crime recorded; witnesses and victims often seem to be punished more than offenders; television and newspapers feed in frenzy on the dramas of crime and trial by media often overtakes the legal process; and social deviance is so often expressed virtually yet internationally on the Net. In today's world, realistically, crime and justice *have to be* constructed or interpreted using cultural devices or knowledge – because they have acquired an immateriality and lack of obviousness, or they are just plain absent.

It is little wonder that people from non-Western societies see the West as corrupt, decadent and lacking "faith," as "Babylon," as an Augean stables in need of cleansing. The tides of history are reversed: it is "others" who now see themselves as civilized and the West as in need of moral restoration. It is not surprising in this context that armed militants should arise from the mass of "others" who feel victimized by the Western powers to begin a jihad against them. As long as the West continues to support one kind of terrorism, such as that in Israel, it will generate another, opposed, kind, such as that of al-Qa'eda.

What is censured as crime or deviance is now so obviously a political issue (see Bergalli and Sumner 1997; Sumner 1997b). Adherence to legal principle is seen by politicians as lawyers' blocking efficient justice, and politicians make decisions about the length of individual sentences. Most crime is not the subject of trials with contested arguments and evidence but is summarily processed through the expedient guilty pleas of the vast majority of charged but unrepresented persons; a process frequently not even requiring the presence of the offender, or witnesses, or lawyers, or a victim or even (who knows how often?) an offense. The bulk of real punishment is not in the form of the prison sentence or even a fine but in the loss of work, status, finance, and family, and, as such, is imposed on the offender's relatives as much as upon the offender. Perhaps in a completely postmodern control system, as Scheerer once sarcastically suggested to me (see also Scheerer and Hess 1997), the authorities would simply allocate crime convictions monthly to the whole population randomly using the electoral register – this way, a more efficient, less expensive and more democratic system could be produced without recourse to time-consuming legal issues at all. The fact is that what we now have by way of a national regulatory system, for most offenses, has by and large moved away from social control involving shared meanings, participation, representation, and assent toward a fully computerized cyber-control programmed to meet police performance targets, combined with regular media spectacles to put flesh-and-blood conviction into what would otherwise be an anonymous grind with a very low percentage of actual detections. We have, in the round, a vast amount of crime, deviance, and rule-infraction with very low actual detection rates, but we also have spectacular and vast amounts of fictional or factional crime drama on television where the police always "get their man." We have added a new, entirely virtual, penality of terror onto modern disciplinary power. In this new all-purpose control system, the postmodern culturalist perspective makes a lot of sense of something which appears to have little – and certainly bears little resemblance to a system of *social* control.

Culturalism points to the fact that there are often many definitions or views of "the crime or deviance situation" involving complex questions about chains of victimization and the length of lineages of oppression. It sees us now enmeshed in a network of conflicting meanings and perceptions; a fact which tempts many to think that the best view, even if profoundly uncomfortable and ultimately impractical, is a relativist one denying relevance or validity to any moral code. Morality, like the social, has become immaterial in a world that prizes the absence of moral–evaluative judgment and celebrates the removal of any kind of discrimination or discretion. Even rights, rules, and evidence seem increasingly immaterial. Justice now too often means mechanical rubber-stamping or sheer emotional pressure conforming to politically correct but ephemeral "spin," irrespective of morality, rights, rules, or evidence. These latter terms, and the philosophies and practices they refer to, have been ditched by contemporary sociology and cultural studies into the categorical dustbin of modernist epistemology – as terms of an old discourse (see also Bauman 1989: 174–5). Discourse is all: "all that is solid melts into air" (Shakespeare) – even crime and justice. It is, however, rarely so to the general public whose common sense not only distances it from the bland talk of politicians but also the mystifications of social science. That public, as in Mannheim's day, still needs democratic representation to enable the freedom to be different but also protection from crime, and the provision of a criminal justice system which produces social justice.

Ultimately, despite its contemporary relevance, to say that crime and deviance are cultural forms tells us little in the long run when culture can mean anything and everything; and no more than the social did when it meant anything and everything. Crime, either as a behavior or as a censure, undoubtedly has an important cultural dimension, but we need to move beyond the infinity of specifics toward some new universals which might act as guides and restraints; otherwise anything could be censured or approved, depending on the political and cultural standpoint of the decision-maker. Observing the cultural dimension of crime and deviance cannot blind us to its potential for complete anarchy – a condition which must be at the mercy of the rich and powerful rather than under the control of the poor and meek, and therefore one of potentially massive injustice. Nor can it be allowed to render us open to just any form of collective regulation, whether arbitrary, partisan, or cybernetic. To be progressive, criminology has to be reconstructive and contribute to this process of moving beyond the cultural.

This new century requires us to recognize that we do censure others and that the big issues surround the question of exactly how "social" is a censure of something or somebody as criminal or deviant. These issues are (a) whether our censures are democratically supported censures or mere partisan instruments of self-interest, (b) whether even our democratic censures will benefit anyone and produce a healthy society, (c) what social and individual health mean and how is their meaning to be constructed, (d) how censures are to be fairly applied in a mass multicultural society, and (e) to what purpose we censure. The social is now a question, not an answer.

A Happy Ending?

Whether we use the word "social" in any meaningful way or even at all, today most of us believe that society as we knew it has gone. The privatization of public services is its key indicator. As one ex-health-service worker said to me, explaining why she had quit: "the feeling has gone." No academic has summarized it more succinctly. In the UK, Margaret Thatcher once declared that society did not exist and waged a war against sociology, trade unions, and the welfare state. The return to free-market economics, the "rolling-back" of welfare, and the politics of neo-liberalism from 1979 onwards meant that we are back to a new type of Hobbesian war of all against all, with the power of commercial interests winning most battles. The "social" institutions, practices, or values which mean anything are those we have re-created or protected in our own pockets of resistance. They are the gains or conservations of a recalcitrant human desire to remain human and therefore part of a collective. The idea of a society has become a mere dream again, not a reality. The reality is a continuous struggle to maintain associations, and the values and norms of association, in an increasingly materialistic but immaterial world. Many of us understand those values, both as principles and as things of great worth, whether as forms of social capital, spiritual sustenance, or pleasure, but the world of globalized capitalism constantly pulls us in other directions toward that all-consuming black hole that is the dominance of things, individualist greed, and impersonal organization.

But we have to dream to achieve. A reconstructed "social" has to become a strong utopia again. Optimists would see it in process of reconstruction through social democracy, or perhaps the anti-globalization movement; pessimists view the reformers as stricken with the same old Nietzschean will to dominate, destroying much more social value than they create. The social cannot be sensibly used as a descriptor of societal reality today other than meaning that it has been collectively produced: but then do "we" really feel guilt for the crimes of the powerful? Were their historic sins really "our" crimes?

Crime and deviance are much better understood not as social constructions but as the dominant censures of the day, reflecting dominant economic, political, and cultural interests and preferences and targeting the groups, individuals, and acts offending those interests and preferences. A particular censure of crime or deviance, *and* the level of its enforcement, may approximate to some democratically shared "social" value to some degree, and may even contribute to some poorly defined social health, but as a whole censures and their enforcement tend to reflect the antisocial interests of capital, patriarchy, and ethnicities. In that way, the major "crimes" often remain uncensured and unpunished. The body of dominant censures in the capitalist world is barely more "social" than it ever was. Humanity in all its interdependent forms has, for example, a profound social or collective interest in the preservation of the environment and indeed the planet itself, but international authorities do little to censure or regulate environmental destruction or to support a healthy diversified survival. Disease, dis-ease, and crime also remain interlinked, at considerable expense to the wealthy nations: the cost to the USA of the crime of September 11, 2001 far exceeds the cost needed to reduce disease in Africa to bearable levels, to compensate the scarred people of Bhopal (see Pearce and Tombs 1993), or to produce a solution in the Middle East – and this suggests that the international social policies of the United States should address causes before dealing with expensive symptoms. This fact takes us back to the early eighteenth century in Europe, just before the last rise of a biopolitics to produce a more social order, or even to Germany in 1945 just before the Marshall Plan. Faced with the potential damage of violent resistance, epidemics of disease, global deflation, and environmental tragedy, today's rulers must face the fact of interdependence in a global economy and recognize their own self-interest, let alone ours, and begin a new wave of social reconstruction. As always, crime and deviance cannot be disentangled from the social facts of collective life.

It is misleading to say that crime and deviance are social constructions when there is so much doubt, confusion, and fear about what "the social" actually is or when they are so often a response to social destruction. The twenty-first century may well demand answers to all the questions that the twentieth century left very unresolved: questions about the limits to the legal rights of the individual or the corporation over the good of the collective, the life-giving priority of our social obligations, the ethical means whereby social justice is to be achieved either locally or internationally, the nature and limit of political representation, the possibility of survival without the reconstruction of some kind of social order, and the possibility of reconstructing a social order at all. These answers will, we can only hope, produce a radical re-drawing of the map of social censures and our way of, and purpose in, enforcing them.

References

Allen, F. L. (1969) The revolution in manners and morals. In M. Plesur (ed.), *The 1920s: Problems and Paradoxes*. Boston: Allyn & Bacon.

Amatrudo, A. (1997) The Nazi censure of art: Aesthetics and the process of annihilation. In C. S. Sumner (ed.), *Violence, Culture and Censure*. London: Taylor & Francis, 63–84.

Bauman, Z. (1989) *Modernity and the Holocaust*. Cambridge: Polity.

Becker, H. (1963) *Outsiders*. New York: The Free Press.

Beirne, P., and Messerschmidt, J. (1991) *Criminology*. San Diego: Harcourt Brace Jovanovich.

Bell, D. (1960) *The End of Ideology*. New York: The Free Press.

Bergalli, R., and Sumner, C. S. (eds.) (1997) *Social Control and Political Order: European Perspectives at the End of the Century*. London: Sage.

Brownmiller, S. (1975) *Against our Will*. London: Secker & Warburg.

Chambliss, W. J., and Seidman, R. B. (1971) *Law, Order, and Power*. Reading, MA: Addison-Wesley.

Clarke, J., and Newman, J. (1997) *The Managerial State*. London: Sage.

Cohen, A. K. (1955) *Delinquent Boys*. New York: The Free Press.

Cohen, S. (1973) *Folk Devils and Moral Panics*. St. Albans: Paladin.

Daly, K., and Maher, L. (eds.) (1998) *Criminology at the Crossroads: Feminist Readings in Crime and Justice*. New York: Oxford University Press.

Daly, M. (1984) *Pure Lust*. London: The Women's Press.

Dobash, R. E., Dobash, R. P., and Noaks, L. (eds.) (1995) *Gender and Crime*. Cardiff: University of Wales Press.

Durkheim, E. (1938) [1897] *The Rules of Sociological Method*. New York: The Free Press.

Durkheim, E. (1970) [1897] *Suicide*. London: Routledge & Kegan Paul.

Farrington, D. P. (1997) Human development and criminal careers. In M. Maguire, R. Morgan, and R. Reiner (eds.), *The Oxford Handbook of Criminology*. Oxford: Clarendon Press, 361–408.

Ferrell, J., and Sanders, C. S. (eds.) (1995) *Cultural Criminology*. Boston: Northeastern University Press.

Foucault, M. (1967) *Madness and Civilization: A History of Insanity in the Age of Reason*. London: Tavistock.

Foucault, M. (1977) *Discipline and Punish: The Birth of the Prison*. London: Allen Lane.

Foucault, M. (1980a) *Power/Knowledge*. New York: Pantheon Books.

Foucault, M. (1980b) *The History of Sexuality. Vol. 1*. New York: Vintage.

Frank, L. K. (1948) *Society as the Patient: Essays on Culture and Personality*. New Brunswick, NJ: Rutgers University Press.

Garland, D. (1990) *Punishment and Modern Society*. Oxford: Clarendon Press.

Gelsthorpe, L., and Morris, A. (eds.) (1990) *Feminist Perspectives in Criminology*. Milton Keynes: Open University Press.

Gilman, S. L. (1985) *Difference and Pathology: Stereotypes of Sexuality, Race, and Madness*. Ithaca: Cornell University Press.

Goffman, E. (1968a) *Asylums*. Harmondsworth: Penguin.

Goffman, E. (1968b) *Stigma*. Harmondsworth: Penguin.

Gouldner, A. W. (1975) *For Sociology*. Harmondsworth: Pelican.

Henry, S., and Milovanovic, D. (1996) *Constitutive Criminology*. London: Sage.

Howe, A. (1994) *Punish and Critique: Towards a Feminist Theory of Penality*. London: Routledge.

Hughes, R. (1981) *The Shock of the New: Art and the Century of Change*. London: BBC Publications.

Jung, C. (1933) *Modern Man in Search of a Soul*. London: Kegan Paul, Trench, Trubner.

Katz, J. (1988) *Seductions of Crime: Moral and Sensual Attractions in doing Evil*. New York: Basic Books.

Laughlin, H. H. (1921) The socially inadequate: How shall we designate and sort them? *American Journal of Sociology*, 27(1), 54–70.

Lemert, C. C., and Winter, M. F. (eds.) (2000) *Crime and Deviance: Essays and Innovations of Edwin M. Lemert*. Lanham, MD: Rowan & Littlefield.

Mannheim, H. (1946) *Criminal Justice and Social Reconstruction*. London: Kegan Paul, Trench, Trubner.

Mannheim, H. (1965) *Comparative Criminology: Vol. 2*. London: Routledge & Kegan Paul.

Marx, K. (1970) [1867] *Capital. Vol. 1*. London: Lawrence & Wishart.

Marx, K., and Engels, F. (1968) *Selected Works*. London: Lawrence & Wishart.

Matza, D. (1969) *Becoming Deviant*. Englewood Cliffs, NJ: Prentice-Hall.

McLaren, A. (1990) *Our Own Master Race: Eugenics in Canada, 1885–1945*. Toronto: McClelland & Stewart.

Mills, C. W. (1970) *The Sociological Imagination*. Harmondsworth: Penguin.

Nietzsche, F. (1969) [1887] *On the Genealogy of Morals/Ecce Homo*. New York: Vintage.

Pearce, F., and Tombs, S. (1993) US capital versus the Third World. In F. Pearce and M. Woodiwiss (eds.), *Global Crime Connections*. London: Macmillan, 187–211.

Pearson, G. (1975) *The Deviant Imagination*. London: Macmillan.

Pick, D. (1989) *Faces of Degeneration*. Cambridge: Cambridge University Press.

Putnam, R. D. (1995) Bowling alone: America's declining social capital. *Journal of Democracy*, 6, January.

Putnam, R. D. (2001) *Bowling Alone: The Collapse and Revival of American Community*. New York: Simon & Schuster.

Ross, E. A. (1969) *Social Control: A Survey of the Foundations of Order*. Cleveland, OH and London: Press of Case Western Reserve University.

Scheerer, S., and Hess, H. (1997) Social control: A defence and reformulation. In R. Bergalli and C. S. Sumner (eds.), *Social Control and Political Order*. London: Sage, 96–130.

Smart, C. (1989) *Feminism and the Power of Law*. London: Routledge.

Stanley, C. (1996) *Urban Excess and the Law*. London: Cavendish.

Stone, C. (1982) Vandalism: Property, gentility and the rhetoric of crime in New York City 1890–1920. *Radical History Review*, 26, 13–34.

Sumner, C. S. (ed.) (1990a) *Censure, Politics and Criminal Justice*. Milton Keynes: Open University Press.

Sumner, C. S. (1990b) Foucault, gender and the censure of deviance. In L. Gelsthorpe and A. Morris (eds.), *Feminist Perspectives in Criminology*. Milton Keynes: Open University Press, 26–40.

Sumner, C. S. (1994) *The Sociology of Deviance: An Obituary*. Buckingham: Open University Press.

Sumner, C. S. (1997a) Social control: The history and politics of a central concept in Anglo-American sociology. In R. Bergalli and C. S. Sumner (eds.), *Social Control and Political Order*. London: Sage, 1–33.

Sumner, C. S. (ed.) (1997b) *Violence, Culture and Censure*. London: Taylor & Francis.

Tannenbaum, F. (1938) *Crime and the Community*. New York: Columbia University Press.

Taylor, I. R. (1999) *Crime in Context*. Cambridge: Polity.

Taylor, I. R., Walton, P., and Young, J. (1973) *The New Criminology*. London: Routledge & Kegan Paul.

Thompson, E. P. (1975) *Whigs and Hunters: The Origin of the Black Act*. London: Allen Lane.

West, D. J. (1967) *The Young Offender*. Harmondsworth: Penguin.

Wirth, L. (1931) Clinical sociology. *American Journal of Sociology*, 37, 49–66.

2

Theories of Social Control and the State between American and European Shores

Dario Melossi

The question of social control – defined as such – first emerged within North American society at the beginning of the twentieth century. It accompanied the further development of that society, and was "exported" to Europe and continents where sociology flourished, especially after World War II. It is an idea closely related to a type of society defined as "democratic," with a very special understanding of democracy: a society where social order is largely based on the participation of a large number of its members and the construction of a consensus therein. From this perspective, the first kind of democratic mass society was in fact the United States (together with a few Northern European societies) in the first half of the twentieth century. After World War II, and then again after the end of the so-called "Cold War" in 1989, this model was slowly and tentatively extended from these pioneering areas into the furthest reaches of the world, from continental Europe to Japan, from Asia to Latin America.

Whereas up to the second half of the nineteenth century, political theory dominated the rhetoric of social order and its construction, basing it in such concepts of political and legal philosophy, as the state, the social contract, and individual rights, at the turn of the century this conceptual equipment did not seem to be able any longer to capture the peculiar circumstances of the construction of consensus in a mass democratic society (Melossi 1990). Tocqueville, in his profoundly visionary and far-seeing *Democracy in America* (1961 [1835–40]), had already noted the peculiarities of a society where power rests on social interaction and the construction of a consensus internal to such interaction. It was, however, with the making of the first radically "modern" society, the United States after the conclusion of the Civil War, with the accompanying phenomena of accelerated industrialization, urbanization, and mass immigration, that the traditional tools of political science appeared for the first time wholly obsolete. These new developments particularly concerned ideas of the state and sovereignty that were both contemptuously rejected by the founder of modern political science in the United States, Arthur Bentley:

> The "state" itself is...no factor in our investigation. It is like the "social whole": we are not interested in it as such, but exclusively in the processes within it. The "idea of the state" has been very prominent, no doubt, among the intellectual amusements of the past, and at particular times and places it has served to give coherent and pretentious expression to some particular group's activity...I may add here that "sovereignty" is of no more interest to us than the state. Sovereignty has its very important place in arguments in defence of an existing government, or in verbal assaults on a government in the name of the populace or of some other pretender, or in fine-spun legal expositions of what is about to be done. But as soon as it gets out of the pages of the lawbook or the political pamphlet, it is a piteous, threadbare joke. So long as there is plenty of firm earth under foot there is no advantage in trying to sail the clouds in a cartoonist's airship. (Bentley 1908: 263–4).

Alessandro Passerin d'Entrèves noted, about statements such as this one by Bentley, that "[t]he disruption of the notion of the State in modern political science is such a challenging and portentous event that it is surprising no detailed study should yet have been made to account for it and to explain it" (1967: 60).[1]

This was the social and political environment within which the concept of social control was instead created. Contrary to the traditional conceptualizations of political theory, social control belonged in the realm of the social – and was part of the theoretical toolbox of a rising corporation of social scientists. It also had, however, another interesting particularity: it was not intended for a philosophical description of the world. It was rather linked with an idea of social intervention and reform, "social engineering," as it was revealingly called at the time. It was not an instrument to describe the ideal and impose it on civil society through the might of the political and legal weaponry, as had traditionally happened in continental Europe. It was instead an instrument for building social order from within the very core of civil society.

As soon as "social control" took its very first steps, however, it became evident that many were the ways in which it could be conceived. First of all, social control could be one or many, or conceptions of social control could refer to a "monist" or a "plural" view of the world and the type of social order therein. In a related way, social control could be connected to either a conflictual or a consensual view of that same world, so that on the one hand we may schematically think of monist-and-consensual theories of social control and on the other of plural-and-conflictual theories of social control. Finally, another crucial distinction soon became clear. Social control could be seen either as a "reaction" to something undesirable happening within the social context (a rupture of balance, a deviance, an event to be censured (Sumner 1994)), or as a force or power that "constituted" social order in an active, suggestive, affirmative manner (Foucault 1978 [1976]). Whereas in the former case social control expressed the power to say "no," in the latter case it expressed the power to suggest behavior. It is often the case, finally, that monist and consensual theories of social control tend to be reactive (in this case it is the rupture of the original balance, "deviance," that the social scientist has to explain) and that plural and conflictual theories tend to be affirmative and suggestive (and in this case the burden of proof is rather placed on the strategies and mechanisms of social control).

FROM THE ORIGINS TO THE CHICAGO SCHOOL

Edward A. Ross was the first, in 1901, to introduce the term "social control" as a major organizing theme of sociology. Framed in the dominant social Darwinian scheme of the time, the term itself was derived from a rather casual usage in Herbert Spencer's *Principles of Sociology* within the treatment of what the British philosopher called "ceremonial institutions" (1904 [1879]: 3–35). However, already in Ross's work, one can find some of the main themes that relate the birth of sociology in Europe in the nineteenth century to its future development in North America in the next century. Ross connects a critique of capitalism (McMahon 1999: 9) and of the traditional reliance on "the state" by ruling elites on both sides of the Atlantic, to a critique of economics and political science, the two prestigious and age-honored disciplines with which the newborn discipline of sociology had to contend. As Engels had stated some time earlier, when he referred to a "state" that is on its way out "into the museum of antiquities, next to the spinning wheel and the bronze axe" (1972 [1884]: 232), so for Ross the antics of "Government" are "archaic" and belong in "the museum of history" (1959 [1901]: 80; see also McMahon 1999: 37, 47, 51). This kind of observation would have become a *leitmotiv* of early twentieth-century North American social sciences, from the innovative Arthur Bentley, as we have seen above, to the main representatives of the Chicago school of sociology. At the same time, Ross established a connection between the shifting reliance of the social system on either "political" means, "operating through prejudice of fear," or "ethical" means, "mild, enlightening and suasive," and the basic nature of such a system, whether it is constituted through heterogeneity or homogeneity (1959 [1901]: 124–5). The greater the degree of heterogeneity, the greater the reliance on "political" means (a line of thought that can also be traced from Tocqueville to Durkheim to Gramsci [Melossi 1990: 100–3]).

Ross's idea of democracy typified a Midwestern, agrarian, nativist democracy (McMahon 1999: 107–35), as C. Wright Mills was famously to point out in one of his early essays (1963a [1943]). Accordingly, the problem of assimilation of new immigrants was paramount in Ross's interests, from the standpoint of a superior moral attitude typical of the American, white, and Protestant Commonwealth and contemptuous of the poor manners of the newcomers, often non-Protestant, non-urbanized and of "suspicious" "race" (Southern Europeans, Jews, etc.). Ross's position represented therefore the American counterpart to an elitist position that had developed for a few decades already in European social sciences, expressing fear and resentment for the unwelcome entrance of "the crowd" or "the masses" into the social and political life of European societies. This attitude had found voice in works such as Gustave Le Bon's *The Crowd* (1960 [1892]) or Scipio Sighele's *La folla delinquente* (1985 [1891]) (*The Delinquent Crowd*). In so doing, European *class* elitism was transformed into a class *and ethnic* elitism in America. The migrant "surplus" masses that crowded the European countryside and that moved to European cities, either to embark on the adventure of migration or to remain as a "reserve army of labor" for domestic capitalism, were then doubly labeled "uncivilized" and "dangerous," first by their own elites, then by the elites of the host countries, such as Argentina or the United States (Teti 1993; Salvatore and Aguirre 1996).

However, such a backward-looking attitude, if it was perhaps appropriate to the old-fashioned socioeconomic and class structure of Continental Europe (rapidly evolving toward their disastrous Fascist outcomes), became quickly unacceptable within the context of the fast-paced development of the United States in the Progressive Age. The elitist attitude was certainly not to disappear. Rather, its intentions and goals were to be transformed into a project of inclusion and incorporation of these emerging crowds within the main social covenant. The concept of social control, the "great social secret" Ross had discovered (McMahon 1999: 31–56), became central to this new enlightened elitist project, at that crucial juncture in the development of American social science encapsulated within the Chicago School of Sociology and Pragmatism – the only genuinely "American" philosophical orientation. It was a concept of social control that was all-pervasive because it responded to the need of the new society to incorporate large masses of newcomers in its midst, on grounds of a factual cooperation rather than through the traditional authoritarian instruments of politics and the law.

Many of the themes announced in Ross's pioneering contributions were to be developed in that budding school of sociology, at Chicago, particularly by Robert E. Park, the man who would personify, intellectually and administratively, Chicago sociology. In his German dissertation, *Masse und Publikum* (*The Crowd and the Public*, 1972 [1904]), Park tried to give an answer to the fervent debate that had been central to European social sciences. Park had formerly been a journalist, and he was not afraid of the crowd. On the contrary, in a typical "American" manner, he conceived of the crowd not as a dangerous, dark, subversive force, but as something that could be domesticated, tamed, enlightened, by turning it into a "public opinion." This had already been Durkheim's position in *Professional Ethics and Civic Morals* (1958 [1898–1900]) but Durkheim, in a characteristically French way, had seen this project as the task of the state, "the organ of the social thought" (Durkheim 1958 [1898–1900]: 49–51). For Park instead it is the free intellectual enterprise of the elites that could fulfill that civilizing function. It is no surprise then that, in Robert E. Park and Ernest W. Burgess's extremely influential *Introduction to the Science of Sociology*, social control is proclaimed "the central problem of society" (1969 [1921]: 42). At about the same time, Park studied the issue of "the immigrant press" and "its control" (1970 [1922]). This was a very charged political issue in those years, following the International Workers of the World (IWW) famous "free-speech fights," World War I and the debate about the loyalty of the enemy immigrants, and especially the "red scare" after the Bolshevik revolution in Russia. In this essay, characteristically, Park concluded that the only way to break down ethnic or political barriers was to favor the development of immigrant discourse toward a shared and more universalistic conceptual and linguistic horizon, a position that was very much like the one being advanced at the same time in the dissenting opinions on matters of free speech submitted by the most enlightened and innovative members of the Supreme Court, such as Justices Louis Brandeis and Oliver Wendell Holmes (Kairys 1982).

The author, however, who would give theoretical dignity to such views and who would develop and make them available for theorizations of a later period, was George Herbert Mead, a philosopher in strict contact with the tradition of American pragmatism and especially with John Dewey. The point of view of pragmatism was deeply connected with the construction of a mass democracy in "progressive" America. Democratic political life – as well as a dynamic industrial capitalist society – both required a convinced, consensual acceptance by society's members. The problem of the construction of consensus – the way in which the members of a common enterprise come to see "eye to eye" on matters of common concern – set the stage for Mead's theory of social control. For Mead, in a move that was intendedly antagonistic to a Cartesian type of philosophy, the constitution of "society" and "self" are one and the same thing. The process that links these two aspects is indeed social interaction, because the development of a self – and eventually of a strong "I" – and of social control, are predicated on the specifically human ability of assuming the attitude of the other, an other which, in its most developed form, is a "generalized other" (Mead 1964 [1925], 1934). The development of the self is possible only insofar as the self is subjected to social control, the process by which our very impulse toward developing our personality and individuality pushes us to assuming the standpoint of others – the very premise of individualism.

Only in so doing will we eventually become able to assume the position of the "I" and strive therefore for freedom and "authenticity." However, to place at the center of the social process the issue of interaction means to place at the center of the social process the question of communication, and therefore also of the mass *media* of communication. Especially at the level of the generalized other, in fact, communication becomes paramount, and face-to-face interaction gives way to more generalized, universalistic, and standardized forms of communication. This is the juncture at which the more specifically political struggles in the arena of social control open up, and the tensions and conflicts between democracy and social control become sharpest. It follows in fact from Mead's ideas that those agencies that have the highest power to constitute a universe of shared meanings in society are those which are able to exercise the deepest form of social control. It also follows from this (not only from Mead's ideas but from the whole *oeuvre* of the Chicago School), that the whole superimposition of legal and political structures basically rests on social control and the only chance of such structures being somehow effective lies in trying to influence the general constitution of meaning, entering in competition, so to speak, with other agencies and other conceptual structures. The distribution of the chances of influencing the constitution of meanings is not at all reflective, however, of the distribution of political rights, which are of course individualized. On the contrary, such distribution has become more and more concentrated in society, following and accompanying the concentration of economic and political power – an overall line of thought that was expressed in terms of political philosophy by John Dewey in *The Public and Its Problems* (1927).

The New Deal and Social Control

Some of the themes that had been developing at a micro-sociological or theoretical level within American sociology between the Progressive Age and the 1920s were to become common parlance in the dramatic period that followed the aftermath of the "Black Friday" of October 29, 1929 when the most serious economic crisis in the history of the United States was set in motion by a spectacular crash of the stock exchange. During the next three years, prices and production plunged, whereas bankruptcies and the number of the unemployed skyrocketed to previously unseen heights. In 1932 Franklin Delano Roosevelt was elected President in a landslide on the basis of a program where he announced a progressive "New Deal" to the American people.

Many contemporaries interpreted this succession of dramatic events as the definite demise of capitalism or, at the very least, of a phase in its history, unbridled "laissez-faire" capitalism. Whereas the role and function of the federal government started to be greatly strengthened in all areas of economic, political, and cultural life, Americans were obliged to give much more attention to the events that were taking place at the same time in Europe. There, the co-mingling of the political and the economic had taken two different paths, on the one hand with Communism, in the land of the Bolshevik revolution, and on the other with Fascism, or, as it was later called in Germany, with a "nationalist" variety of "socialism." With the New Deal Roosevelt chose to follow a third way, so to speak, in which massive "social" powers of intervention and "control" of the economy would not be accompanied by policies of publicization and nationalization of property. In so doing, Roosevelt helped to create the complex political and economic model of capitalism that was to triumph first over Nazi-Fascism in 1945 and then over Communism in 1989.

The ideas and conceptualizations of a "social" type of "control" that had been developing in the country for almost thirty years – Ross's influential and pioneering book having been published in 1901 – came at that point to full fruition. The idea of social control moved from the areas of urban sociology, sociology of deviance, social philosophy, and the philosophy of education, to the center stage in social organization, the fields of economics, and the law. John M. Clark's *Social Control of Business* (1926), Adolf A. Berle, Jr. and Gardiner C. Means's *The Modern Corporation and Private Property* (1932), Roscoe Pound's *Social Control Through Law* (1942) (whose concept of social control had been explicitly influenced by Ross (Geis 1964)), as well as the production of a "realist" strain of legal philosophy by authors who were often also involved in the politics and administration of the New Deal, were the intellectually remarkable consequences of this redefinition of the main themes and motifs of society.

At the same time, the coming to maturity of an American strain of welfare and regulated capitalism within the framework of mass-democratic society – most dramatically emphasized in the recognition of unions' rights after a bitter struggle between the federal government and a backward-looking Supreme Court – was to profoundly change the contours of American society. The mobilization of all the energies and forces of society during the economic recovery and the war economy was to give the nation a sense of cohesion and compactness, and also of a worldwide role that went far beyond the Monroe Doctrine. Together with the stop to the massive immigration that had character-ized the country between the second half of the nineteenth century and 1924 (when Congress established strict quotas based on national origin), this situation helped to reformulate the focus of sociology from the fragmented, conflictual, and open-ended outlook of pragmatism and the Chicago School to a more unified, consensual, and structured vision of the world that would accompany the move of the core of American sociology from Chicago and the Midwest to the East Coast and especially the great Eastern universities. In fact, the social theory that a young professor at Harvard, Talcott Parsons, was to develop between *The Structure of Social Action* (1937) and *The Social System* (1951) probably constituted the clearest expression of this conceptual change. Through an original incorporation and revisitation of the great European sociological authors of the previous period, from Durkheim to Weber, from Pareto to Freud, Parsons redefined the central problem of sociology as "Hobbes' problem of order" (Parsons 1937: 89–94), strengthening and powerfully structuring sociol-ogy's traditionally competitive stance toward economics and political science. There was continuity and at the same time rupture in Parsons's proposal. Sociology's traditional aversion toward the radical methodological individual-ism of economists, lawyers, and political scientists was strongly reaffirmed but this was done within a masterful reconstruction of a concept of a social system in which normative, "moral" and "non-rational" elements were decisively emphasized.

Within such a complex program also the role and function of "social control" were greatly reformed. The process of "socialization" of the young within the social system was now paramount, and Parsons redefined social control essen-tially as the reaction against a "deviance" that has its origins in the failed socialization of individuals or groups. Chicago's often empiricist and atheoreti-cal but stimulating and suggestive concept of plural and conflictual social worlds – that well mirrored the life of the city in the age of great migrations – gave way to a society which conceived itself as having to accomplish a process of social-ization (and, in the background, "Americanization") into a unified and cohesive social system, a system that had defeated the economic crisis, and that was readying itself for the defeat of the twentieth-century (Fascist and Communist) competitors on the global scene. Within its national laboratory, this social system was already experimenting with the project of exporting the specific and novel type of social organization it had discovered and developed, eventu-ally setting the stage for its worldwide hegemony.

Parsons's intellectual solution to the Hobbesian problem, somehow resulting out of an integration of Durkheim with Freud, was the idea of an "internal-ization" of the sovereign that mirrored closely some of Freud's "meta-psychological" works, such as *Totem and Taboo* (1955 [1913]). While at the same time developing Chicago's main motifs but also "normalizing" them, Parsons incorporated Hobbes's voluntary, rationalist, social-contractual solution within each individual, a non-rational product of his or her successful socializa-tion. Accordingly, the concept of "deviance" was demoted from an effect of a wanting social organization, à la Shaw and McKay (1942), or even of an alternative social organization, à la Sutherland (1973 [1942]), to that of a wanting process of socialization, ultimately rooted in the individual. Accordingly, mental illness became the paradigm of deviance, in the same way in which psychotherapy became the paradigm of social control (Parsons 1977 [1970]). It is significant that in the theory of deviance closest to Parsons's, the "theory of anomie" of his student and colleague at Harvard, Robert K. Merton (1938), the lack of internalization of norms concerning either the prescribed goals of society or, and especially, the means to be used in order to reach such goals, is conceived to be the source of deviance. Deviants became therefore either opportunists or misfits, with lip-service being paid to a residual category of "rebelliousness."

Neo-Chicagoans

While triumphant Parsonianism, as the appropriate *Weltanschaung* of the age, was progressively conquering center-stage, another more subterranean line of thought was developing post-Chicagoan motifs, especially in their more interesting Meadian variations. In the 1940s Edwin Sutherland, C. Wright Mills and Edwin Lemert further worked on an interactionist, plural, and conflictual concept of social control and pointed in the direction of what would later bloom as "labeling theory" under different social conditions.

Almost straight from one of the most loved German philosophers in Chicago, Georg Simmel (1955 [1908]), Edwin Sutherland developed his central notion of how "normative conflict" from the standpoint of society appears as "differential social organization" and from the point of the individual appears as "differential association"; a theory of "criminal behavior" that rested on a concept of general human behavior and social organization (1973 [1942]).

Even closer to Mead was, however, the early work of C.Wright Mills, first in his dissertation, later published as *Sociology and Pragmatism* (1966 [1942]), then in essays such as "Situated action and vocabularies of motive" (1963b [1940]), where Mills developed Mead's concept of social control in a linguistic and historical-comparative direction that, through his collaboration with Hans Gerth (Gerth and Mills 1946), put him in contact with Weberian sociology. In Mills's view – a linguistic view fostered in those years also by other Pragmatist-inspired theorists, as Kenneth Burke (1969 [1950]) – social control is exercised through the establishment of "typical" or "normal" "vocabularies of motive." In these contributions by Mills transpired the increasing disillusionment of the Pragmatists, especially John Dewey (1927), with the "corruption" of democracy brought about by the crystallization and stiffening of its essential lymph, public debate, within a field of mass media of communication more and more occupied by large corporations, and dominant economic, cultural, and political centers. This argument would be eventually spelled out at length in what appears today to be C. Wright Mills's most "visionary" contribution, *The Power Elite*, a book published almost half a century ago, in 1956, but whose message appears (unfortunately) to have become more and more topical!

A clear overturn of Parsons's "homeostatic" concept of social control could then be found in a strikingly innovative piece by young sociologist Edwin Lemert in one of his early articles (1942), where he opposed a concept of "active" social control, "a process for the implementation of goals and values," to Parsons's "passive" concept, as he later explained (1967a [1964]: 21). He was also to present an idea of social control as *producing* deviance, the process that, a few years later, Lemert was to term a "secondary" concept of deviation (Lemert 1951, 1967b). The legacy of Sutherland, C. Wright Mills (who would die prematurely in 1962 at the age of only 45!) and Ed Lemert, who would be among the protagonists of the successive movement, would loom very large in the renewal of sociology, and especially of a critical "sociology of deviance" inspired to labeling theory, during the 1960s and early 1970s.

SOCIAL CONTROL BETWEEN LABELING THEORY AND A RESURRECTED LEVIATHAN

Howard Becker's famously sharp statement, in his introduction to *Outsiders* (1963: 9), that "deviant behavior is behavior that people so label," authoritatively opened the season of a "labeling theory" according to which official social controls, created by "moral entrepreneurs," perform a crucial role in *constituting* deviance, at the same time as deviants, so defined, reproduce themselves and their activities through the coming into being of more secluded and smaller circles of social control. Becker remained true to the Pragmatist and Chicagoan roots of his thinking in eschewing any reference to "the state" and referring instead to "moral entrepreneurs," such agencies, for instance, as the Federal Bureau of Narcotics of the Treasury Department that in the 1930s had created "the marijuana menace." However, this "stateless" quality of social control was not to last during times increasingly characterized by a sharpened sense of social and political conflict.

"The state" in fact was to re-enter the scene prominently with the contributions by David Matza. Matza, first together with Gresham Sykes (1957) and then in *Delinquency and Drift* (1964), maintained that "techniques of neutralization" of moral censorship open up the possibility for a mood, or condition, of "drift," within which the neoclassical element of "will" (1964: 181) leads the would-be deviant toward his or her path of deviance. Together with individual will, in the politically hot late 1960s, the other pole of the classical contractualist coupling, the state, was to re-emerge. So it did in fact in the following, crucial work by Matza, *Becoming Deviant* (1969), where the steps of Howard Becker's marijuana-smoking deviant subject are retraced anew under the constellation of "the ban" imposed by a sinister-looming "Leviathan," in a view that was heavily and unavoidably marked by the conflicts of the time, from the Vietnam War to the civil rights struggle, from the student movement to antiwar demonstrations.

Matza's work clearly marked a milestone in the development of future discussions of deviance and social control. Matza's neo-anarchist indictment of the indecent travesties of power – which was at the same time committing the most egregious crimes and labeling as such what seemed to be, in comparison, rather minor occurrences (1969: 157) – connected with the contemporary reappearance, within European social and political theory, of a neo-Marxist critique of the state, most famously represented by the almost contemporary essay by French philosopher Louis Althusser, "Ideology and Ideological State Apparatuses" (1971 [1970]).

In this connection, labeling eventually went to feed a "critical" or "radical" criminology movement that bloomed vividly in the mid-1970s in the United States (especially around the Berkeley School of Criminology, closed by an act of authority in 1976), the United Kingdom (with the National Deviancy Conference), Europe (with the European Group for the Study of Deviance and Social Control and many journals), and various organizations and journals in Latin America (Bergalli 1997). However, especially in the United States, the call by David Matza and others for a renewed respect of the individuality, dignity, and free will of the deviant soon became hegemonized by a rapidly escalating reactionary counter-tendency that I have dubbed a "revanche criminology" (Melossi 2000). This literally "reactionary" counter-tendency changed the value-sign of Matza's coupling of the individual and Leviathan, and tried to restore the good rights of Leviathan vis-à-vis what was described as a mounting wave of illegality and crime committed by the most downtrodden elements of the working class and especially by ethnic minorities. These theoretical developments accompanied the age of the US "great internment" in the last quarter of the twentieth century (Beckett 1997; Chambliss 1999; Garland 2001).

One of the (indeed very minor) victims of all this turmoil in the 1970s was a sense of the (separate) history of concepts of state and social control, concepts that became instead almost inextricably joined in an Orwellian "1984" dystopian view (Cohen 1985) to which many other intellectual strains contributed, such as the latest results of the apocalyptic view of the Frankfurt School (Marcuse 1964), and the rising star of Michel Foucault's ambiguous concept of Panopticism (1977 [1975]: 195–228). The confusion was not diminished by the fact that these were all conceptual weapons used in violent political critique of *both* rapidly decaying socialistic totalitarian societies in the East, *and* socialism *and* welfarism in the West, from the perspective of a rising neo-liberal critique. It is no surprise then that in a much repeated statement, Stanley Cohen could dub social control a sort of "Mickey Mouse concept" (1985: 2) even if, one should note, Cohen's own contributions (Cohen 1985, Cohen and Scull 1983), however rich in empirical detail, did not do much to make the concept any less so, especially in theoretical terms, by failing to problematize the relationships of the state to social control.

THE CURRENT PREDICAMENTS OF SOCIAL CONTROL

It is quite true, however, that theories of social control have found it difficult to resist the onslaughts of the last quarter of the twentieth century, an onslaught coming from two opposing and apparently polarized fields, one from Europe and the other from their own American backyard. The European onslaught followed in the steps of Foucauldian developments, in which themes and suggestions that had been familiar to American social and political science for almost a century were reshaped, transformed, and translated into a language unrecognizable to social scientists. The American onslaught consisted instead in a progressive obsolescence of the "social" aspect of social control within sociology and especially criminology, in the context of a type of culture David Garland has recently defined as a "culture of control" *tout court* (2001).[2]

In the hot, hot, late 1960s, when napalm bombs were falling on the very, very, faraway jungles, villages, and cities of Indochina, when students were clashing with police in numerous American campuses, when Black Panthers were patrolling the streets of West Oakland, and when "crime" and a "drug market" had been surging for many years of the decade, sociologists raised and trained in the Parsonian paradigm reacted to what was happening in very different ways. On the one hand, as we have seen, theories of social control were bent toward an increasingly critical guise, becoming intertwined with politics and "the state," in a converging mode with the hegemony of a Marxist/anarchist paradigm within equally riotous Europe. On the other hand, a right-wing, revanchist response was taking shape, which went to join the more general transformation of the American mind that tentatively emerged under the Nixon years and then affirmed itself more and more under the Reagan and Bush Sr. presidencies. This was a response that essentially identified the crucial problem of American society in a coming-apart of the social fabric, a relaxation of all the principal agencies in the production and reproduction of morality, a re-emergence of an animalistic anarchistic uninhibited "monster" lurking within each one of us but especially in those who – as Marx would have said – had less to lose and more to gain, those at the bottom of social stratification, who also happened to be those belonging to certain ethnic minorities.

Parsons had identified "the central problem of society," as we have seen, in the "Hobbesian problem of order," but his answer, along Durkheimian and Freudian lines of reasoning, had been different from that of Hobbes. For him, the solution was no longer the (legitimate) might of Leviathan but was the incorporation, the internalization, of Leviathan within each one of us. The deviants were those for whom, for whatever reason, such internalization had gone somehow wrong. These were the deviants to whom was to be applied a remedial, homeostatic, reactive type of social control. In *Causes of Delinquency* (1969), Travis Hirschi was to give a slightly different twist to this familiar story. "The question", he wrote, is not "Why do they do it?" It is rather, "Why don't we do it?," to which a somewhat cynical comment ensued: "[t]here is much evidence that we would if we dared" (1969: 34). The tables were therefore turned, in a sense, in a direction that became increasingly popular in the years to come, a concept of criminality and deviance as a mundane, almost trivial, occurrence. The next step was to be the utmost lack of interest in the makeup, morality, and destiny of the "doers" and an increasing interest instead in ways of protecting "us," the potential victims, a "criminology" of "everyday life" (Felson 1998). Hirschi's answer to "Why don't we do it?" turned out to be not very dissimilar from the traditional answers. We do not do it because we have "bonds" to society of various sorts, we have an emotional investment in relations with others, both significant and anonymous, and therefore we restrain ourselves from our most luciferous impulses. Is this very different from saying that deviants do it because they are not restrained?[3] Apparently not, but the point is, in my view, that this whole orientation of deviance studies contributed to a sense of taken-for-grantedness of criminal behavior and "criminals." Such taken-for-grantedness meant also a fundamental lack of interest, sympathy, and compassion for the destiny of "the other." From here the path was certainly not too long to the next stage, when the image of a deviant "predator" "lurking in the dark," a street-fighting animal, a "monster" rich in specific historical connotations, became central to the American economy of representation (Melossi 2000). This imagery climaxed around the time of the presidential contest between George Bush and Michael Dukakis in 1988, when Republicans unabashedly played the card of "Willie" Horton, "a wonderful mix of liberalism and big black rapist,"[4] going in and out of the American court and prison systems.

The other path along which theories of social control traveled most productively in the last quarter of the twentieth century was one where the term "social control" was seldom used, the "European" path indicated in the work by Michel Foucault, especially in *Discipline and Punish* (1977 [1975]). Whereas, on the one hand, Foucault's stress in *Discipline and Punish* on the "dialectic" – as Horkheimer and Adorno would have called it (1972 [1944]) – between a rhetoric of Enlightenment and liberalism centered in individual rights and safeguards, and a "penitentiary project" substantiating a very strong vision of man and society, was undoubtedly post-if not neo-Marxian, on the other hand his rejection of any type of teleological epistemology or writing of history locates him resolutely beyond Marx and Marxism. More particularly, Foucault was among the authors who, in a 1970s Europe that was at the same time exiting a period of intense hegemony of Marxist theory and experiencing a deep disillusionment with the hopes of what was then called "realized socialism," brought about a very healthy, even if somewhat puzzling, "disenchantment" with any preconstituted reading of the destiny of the social world. His damning critique, in the following "Introduction" to *The History of Sexuality* (1978, entitled in its French original *La volonté de savoir* [1976]), of some of the shibboleths of the immediately previous years, such as "repression," "liberation," and "the state" (picked up again thereafter in an essay called "Governmentality" (2000)[1978]) simultaneously touched a raw nerve and helped prepare a free slate on which new ideas, concepts, and visions could start afresh. Foucault's indication of the connections between the world of production and the apparatuses of cultural reproduction in the centrality of the imagery of the Panopticon in *Discipline and Punish*, his stress on what he called "Panopticism" in the welfare stage of industrialism and capitalism, and finally his decisive reclaiming of power relations from the state concept in *La volonté de savoir* and "Governmentalité," worked to constitute the signposts of a new manner of thinking social control even if, as already mentioned, "social control" is nowhere to be found within Foucault's conceptual toolbox. This very fact is, however, something that should give us pause, in light of the century-long development of the concept as we have reconstructed it, especially in relation to the tradition of American sociology.

As we have already mentioned, Foucault's conceptualizations and contributions belong inherently in European thought, and more specifically in that particular conjuncture of European thought in the 1970s when the disillusionment of Europeans with socialism and Marxist theory ushered in the realization – which was then celebrated under the label of "postmodernism" – that political thinking and acting could not be supported by any "grand narrative" somehow reassuringly "external" to our acting. The latter especially, however, had been the very starting point of American Pragmatism. As Richard Rorty wrote in 1983, "James and Dewey... are waiting at the end of the road which... Foucault and

Deleuze are currently travelling" (xviii). One has the impression, in other words, that Foucault allowed for the introduction within European social thought, through the elaboration of an apposite new vocabulary, of themes and motifs that had already been belabored at length within American political and social science, exactly at the point when the social model produced in the North American context was readying itself to become hegemonic over Europe and tendentially over the entire globe, with the impending fall of realized socialism. First in *La volonté de savoir*, when he wrote that "[i]n political thought and analysis, we still have not cut off the head of the king" (1978 [1976]: 88), and then in "Governmentalité," Foucault dismissed the concept of the state:

> the excessive value attributed to the problem of the state is expressed, basically, in two ways: the one form, immediate, affective, and tragic, is the lyricism of the cold monster we see confronting us. But there is a second way of overvaluing the problem of the state, one that is paradoxical because it is apparently reductionist: it is the form of analysis that consists in reducing the state to a certain number of functions, such as the development of productive forces and the reproduction of relations of production, and yet this reductionist vision of the relative importance of the state's role nevertheless invariably renders it absolutely essential as a target needing to be attacked and a privileged position needing to be occupied. But the state, no more probably today than at any other time in its history, does not have this unity, this individuality, this rigorous functionality, nor, to speak frankly, this importance. Maybe, after all, the state is no more than a composite reality and a mythicized abstraction, whose importance is a lot more limited than many of us think. Maybe what is really important for our modernity – that is, for our present – is not so much the statization of society, as the "governmentalization" of the state. (Foucault 2000 [1978]: 220)

If the reader thinks she might have read something of the kind recently, it may have been a few pages above, when we quoted the words penned by Arthur Bentley about eighty years earlier. At the same time, this "governmentalization," of the state but especially of society, had been discussed by American social scientists under the label of "social control." To make a long story short, Foucault explained to Europeans, in a language they could understand, a few essential things that Americans already knew. Such "things" would have soon concerned Europeans too, and had something to do with living under the new conditions characteristic of a globalized society. All of this is particularly relevant for the issue of social control. Foucault's emphasis on the intimate connections between "truth," "discourse," and "power," as well as his barely sketched critique of a state-centered model, unfolded within a type of society where social control – as Dewey, Mead, Mills, and many other North American sociologists had cogently predicted – was more and more the matter of constructing a common mind and language than that of manipulating laws and guns. In a mass democratic system – that only in the 1970s was coming to maturation in Europe – it could not be otherwise. The realization that the construction of this common mind and language was taking place within the arena of the mass media of communication was the inevitable corollary of such overall development.

In Conclusion: Law and Social Control

The broader concept of social control that one can reconstruct in the history of sociological thinking from Ross to Mead and Mills, to the labeling theorists to Foucault, carries remarkable consequences also for the usual criminological tendency to reduce social control to what Donald Black (1976) has termed "governmental social control," that is, the law. At this juncture, we find the increasing relevance of Emile Durkheim's sharp insight, that "punishment is above all intended to have its effect upon honest people" (1964 [1893]: 63). In other words, what we think as social control proper is subsumed under a much broader concept of social control that concerns the world of our representations. Within it, the legal definitions of good and evil certainly play a very important role but we should be aware of not taking them too seriously. On the contrary, "crime" can be seen as an instrument of social control, whereas this is framed through the concept of crime as "non-governmental social control" as in Black (1984), in the sense of "governing through crime" as in Simon (1997), or in the more literal and ominous version of Matza (1969) and the critical criminological tradition, i.e., as indeed a possible form of governmental social control. In a way opposite to the hubris of the law, which sees social control and deviance as something ordered by its will and command, these sociological perspectives portray the law (and indeed the state) as resting upon the social foundations of processes of control and deviance-definition. Within contemporary mass-democratic societies (and even more so in their "globalized" stage) the disenchantment with concepts of law, state, and sovereignty places the study of "social control" squarely at the center of our attention, in even closer connection with what Mead called "the process of communication," and in even sharper relief than when E. A. Ross pioneeringly claimed to have discovered the "great social secret."

Notes

1   The overall argument presented in this essay is belabored at much greater length in my *The State of Social Control: A Sociological Study of Concepts of State and Social Control in the Making of Democracy* (Melossi 1990). See also Melossi 1997, and in general the essays collected in Bergalli and Sumner 1997.
2   Unfortunately, Garland's promising reference to the "limits of the sovereign State" (1996) is not then followed through in its theoretical implications.
3   Later on, in a book co-authored with Michael Gottfredson (1990), Hirschi's theory switched to the concept of a lack of self-control, a want substantially invariant along the life of the (criminal) individual.
4   In the words of one of the producers of the political advertisement about Horton in the Bush campaign (Karst 1993: 73–4). Horton was the black Massachusetts convict who raped a white woman while on a furlough program when Michael Dukakis was Governor of the State, an episode that became a favourite card of George Bush's 1988 presidential campaign against the same Dukakis.

References

Althusser, L. (1971) [1970] Ideology and ideological state apparatuses. In L. Althusser, *Lenin and Philosophy*. New York: Monthly Review Press, 127–86.

Becker, H. S. (1963) *Outsiders: Studies in the Sociology of Deviance*. New York: The Free Press.

Beckett, K. (1997) *Making Crime Pay: Law and Order in Contemporary American Politics*. New York: Oxford University Press.

Bentley, A. F. (1908) *The Process of Government*. Cambridge, MA: Harvard University Press.

Bergalli, R. (1997) The new order in Spain and an Hispanic perspective on the history and meaning of social control. In R. Bergalli and C. Sumner (eds.), *Social Control and Political Order: European Perspectives at the End of the Century*. London: Sage, 34–51.

Bergalli, R., and Sumner, C. (eds.) (1997) *Social Control and Political Order: European Perspectives at the End of the Century*. London: Sage.

Berle, A. A., and Means, G. C. (1932) *The Modern Corporation and Private Property*. New York: Macmillan.

Black, D.(1976) *The Behaviour of Law*. New York: Academic Press.

Black, D. (1984) Crime as social control. In D. Black (ed.), *Toward a General Theory of Social Control*, Vol. 2, Orlando, FL: Academic Press, 1–27.

Burke, K. (1969) [1950] *A Rhetoric of Motives*. Berkeley: University of California Press.

Chambliss, W. J. (1999) *Power, Politics, and Crime*. Boulder, CO: Westview Press.

Clark, J. M. (1926) *Social Control of Business*. NewYork:Whittlesey House.

Cohen, S. (1985) *Visions of Social Control*. Cambridge: Polity Press.

Cohen, S., and Scull, A. (1983) *Social Control and the State*. Oxford: Martin Robertson.

Dewey, J. (1927) *The Public and Its Problems*. Denver:Alan Swallow.

Durkheim, E. (1958) [1898–1900] *Professional Ethics and Civic Morals*. Glencoe: The Free Press.

Durkheim, E. (1964) [1893] *The Division of Labor in Society*. New York: The Free Press.

Engels, F. (1972) [1884] *The Origin of the Family, Private Property and the State*. New York: International Publishers.

Felson, M. (1998) *Crime and Everyday Life*. Thousand Oaks: Pine Forge Press.

Foucault, M. (1977) [1975] *Discipline and Punish*. New York: Pantheon.

Foucault, M. (1978) [1976] *The History of Sexuality. Volume 1. An Introduction*. New York: Random House.

Foucault, M. (2000) [1978] Governmentality. In M. Foucault, *Essential Works of Foucault 1954–1984, Volume 3 (Power)*. New York: The New Press, 201–22.

Freud, S. (1955) [1913] *Totem and Taboo*. In S. Freud, *The Standard Edition*, Vol. 13. London: Hogarth, 1–161.

Garland, D. (1996) The limits of the sovereign state. *British Journal of Criminology*, 36, 445–71.

Garland, D. (2001) *The Culture of Control. Crime and Social Order in Contemporary Society*. Oxford: Oxford University Press.

Geis, G. (1964) Sociology and sociological jurisprudence: Admixture of lore and law. *Kentucky Law Journal*, 52, 267–93.

Gerth, H. H., and Mills, C. W. (1946) Introduction: The man and his work. In H. H. Gerth and C. Wright Mills (eds.), *From Max Weber: Essays in Sociology*. New York: Oxford University Press, 3–74.

Gottfredson, M. R., and Hirschi, T. (1990) *A General Theory of Crime*. Stanford: Stanford University Press.

Hirschi, T. (1969) *Causes of Delinquency.* Berkeley: University of California Press.

Horkheimer, M., and Adorno, T. W. (1972) [1944] *Dialectic of Enlightenment.* New York: Herder & Herder.

Kairys, D. (1982) Freedom of speech. In D. Kairys (ed.), *The Politics of Law. A Progressive Critique.* New York: Pantheon, 140–71.

Karst, K. L. (1993) *Law's Promise, Law's Expression: Visions of Power in the Politics of Race, Gender and Religion.* New Haven, CT: Yale University Press.

Le Bon, G. (1960) [1892] *The Crowd.* New York: Viking.

Lemert, E. (1942) The folkways and social control. *American Sociological Review,* 7, 394–9.

Lemert, E. (1951) *Social Pathology. A Systematic Approach to the Theory of Sociopathic Behavior.* New York: McGraw-Hill.

Lemert, E. (1967a) [1964] Social structure, social control, and deviation. In E. Lemert, *Human Deviance, Social Problems, and Social Control.* Englewood Cliffs, NJ: Prentice-Hall, 3–30.

Lemert, E. (1967b) *Human Deviance, Social Problems, and Social Control.* Englewood Cliffs, NJ: Prentice-Hall.

Marcuse, H. (1964) *One-Dimensional Man.* Boston: Beacon Press.

Matza, D. (1964) *Delinquency and Drift.* New York: John Wiley.

Matza, D. (1969) *Becoming Deviant.* Englewood Cliffs, NJ: Prentice-Hall.

McMahon, S. H. (1999) *Social Control and Public Intellect: The Legacy of Edward A. Ross.* New Brunswick, NJ: Transaction Publishers.

Mead, G. H. (1934) *Mind, Self, and Society.* Chicago: University of Chicago Press.

Mead, G. H. (1964) [1925] The genesis of the self and social control. In G. H. Mead, *Selected Writings.* Indianapolis: Bobbs-Merrill, 267–93.

Melossi, D. (1990) *The State of Social Control:A Sociological Study of Concepts of State and Social Control in the Making of Democracy.* Cambridge: Polity.

Melossi, D. (1997) State and social control *à la fin de siècle*: from the New World to the constitution of the new Europe, in R. Bergalli and C. Sumner (eds.), *Social Control and Political Order: European Perspectives at the End of the Century.* London: Sage, 52–74.

Melossi, D. (2000) Changing representations of the criminal. *British Journal of Criminology,* 40, 296–320.

Merton, R. K. (1938) Social structure and anomie. *American Sociological Review,* 3, 672–82.

Mills, C. W. (1956) *The Power Elite.* New York: Oxford University Press.

Mills, C. W. (1963a) [1943] The professional ideology of social pathologists. In C. W. Mills, *Power Politics and People.* New York: Oxford University Press, 525–52.

Mills, C. W. (1963b) [1940] Situated actions and vocabularies of motive. In C. W. Mills, *Power Politics and People.* New York: Oxford University Press, 439–52.

Mills, C. W. (1966) [1942]) *Sociology and Pragmatism.* New York: Oxford University Press.

Park, R. E. (1970) [1922] *The Immigrant Press and Its Control.* Westport, CT: Greenwood.

Park, R. E. (1972) [1904] *The Crowd and the Public.* Chicago: University of Chicago Press.

Park, R. E., and Burgess, E. W. (1969) [1921] *Introduction to the Science of Sociology.* Chicago: University of Chicago Press.

Parsons, T. (1937) *The Structure of Social Action.* New York: McGraw-Hill.

Parsons, T. (1951) *The Social System.* New York: The Free Press.

Parsons, T. (1977) [1970] On building social system theory: A personal history. In T. Parsons, *Social Systems and the Evolution of Action Theory.* New York: The Free Press, 22–76.

Passerin D'Entrèves, A. (1967) *The Notion of the State*. Oxford: Clarendon Press.

Pound, R. (1942) *Social Control Through Law*. New Haven: Yale University Press.

Rorty, R. (1983) *Consequences of Pragmatism*. Minneapolis: University of Minnesota Press.

Ross, E. A. (1959) [1901] Social control. In E. A. Ross, *Social Control and the Foundations of Sociology*. Boston: Beacon Press, 1–127.

Salvatore, R. D. and Aguirre, C. (eds.) (1996) *The Birth of the Penitentiary in Latin America: Essays on Criminology, Prison Reform, and Social Control, 1830–1940*. Austin: University of Texas Press.

Shaw, C., and McKay, H. D. (1942) *Juvenile Delinquency and Urban Areas*. Chicago: University of Chicago Press.

Sighele, S. (1985) [1891] *La folla delinquente*. Venice: Marsilio.

Simmel, G. (1955) [1908] The web of group-affliations. In G. Simmel, *Conflict and the Web of Group-Affiliations*. New York: The Free Press, 125–95.

Simon, J. (1997) Governing through crime. In L. M. Friedman and G. Fisher (eds.), *The Crime Conundrum*. Boulder, CO: Westview Press, 171–89.

Spencer, H. (1904) [1879] *The Principles of Sociology*, Vol. 2. New York: Appleton.

Sumner, C. (1994) *The Sociology of Deviance: An Obituary*. Buckingham: Open University Press.

Sutherland, E. H. (1973) [1942] Development of the theory. In E. H. Sutherland, *On Analyzing Crime*. Chicago: University of Chicago Press, 13–29.

Sykes, G., and Matza, D. (1957) Techniques of neutralization: A theory of delinquency. *American Sociological Review*, 22: 664–70.

Teti, V. (1993) *La razza maledetta: origini del pregiudizio antimeridionale*. Rome: Manifestolibri.

Tocqueville, A. de (1961) [1835–40] *Democracy in America*. New York: Schocken.

3

Criminal Justice Process and War on Crime

Markus Dirk Dubber

The year 1968 was a watershed year in the evolution of the modern American criminal justice process. This was the year Herbert Packer published his magisterial overview of American criminal law and procedure, *The Limits of the Criminal Sanction* (Packer 1968). There Packer famously distinguished between two competing models at work in the criminal justice process, the "due process model" and the "crime control model." In Packer's scheme, the due process model operates from a presumption of innocence and places a premium on accuracy. The crime control model, by contrast, proceeds from a presumption of guilt and focuses on efficiency. The goal of the first is to do justice, that of the latter to provide security. Although Packer was careful not to express too strong a preference for one or the other, his sympathies for the due process model were plain enough.

Also in 1968, presidential candidate Richard Nixon published a position paper on criminal justice, entitled "Toward freedom from fear." There he laid out his vision of the American criminal justice process as a war on crime, fought by "the peace forces" against "the criminal forces," "the enemy within" (Nixon 1968: 129–37). While Nixon was not the first to conceive of a war on crime, he was the first to have the vision and the power to put a program for the systematic and comprehensive eradication of criminal threats into action (Vorenberg 1972; Clear 1997). Three decades later, two million people were incarcerated, and another four and a half million under non-carceral state control, adding up to over three percent of American adults (Bureau of Justice Statistics 2001a; Bureau of Justice Statistics 2001b).

That same year, the United States Supreme Court decided *Terry v. Ohio* (United States Supreme Court 1968). In this case, the Court recognized a new type of police search and seizure without probable cause – with only "reasonable suspicion" – to suspect criminal activity. The Court thereby gave its constitutional imprimatur to the comprehensive enforcement regime of the war on crime; *Terry* "stops" and "frisks" proved supremely useful in the identification and incapacitation of criminal threats.

The final third of the twentieth century was the age of the war on crime, or rather – as we will see – the police action against criminals. At the outset of the twenty-first century, Packer's gentlemanly balanced analysis, matching due process against crime control, reads like a quaint missive from a sunken world of fair play and rationality in punishment.

In one sense, the crime war model is an extreme version of Packer's crime control model. The crime war model controls crime by controlling criminals. It eliminates threats not through deterrence or rehabilitation, but through incapacitation. It bends, and if necessary breaks, the rules of traditional criminal law to get and keep human hazards off the street, by employing new sweep offenses, like possession, to eliminate the enemy within.

In another sense, however, the crime war model goes far beyond Packer's crime control model. The crime war model proceeds not from the presumption that every defendant is guilty, but that *everyone* is guilty. The crime war is fought on behalf of the community of actual and potential victims against a community of actual and potential offenders, where the boundaries between the two communities track familiar, and politically potent, American socioeconomic friend–foe distinctions of race and class.[1] By 1995, over 800,000, or almost one-third, of African American males in their twenties were under carceral or non-carceral state penal control (Mauer and Huling 1995). In some urban centers, that proportion topped one-half (Tonry 1995: 4). At the end of 2000, black inmates accounted for 46 percent of state and federal prisoners, and 10 percent of black males between the ages of 25 and 29 were in prison, compared to one percent of white males in the same age group (Bureau of Justice Statistics 2001a: 1, 11).

The concept of "victims' rights" plays a central role in the political ideology of the war on crime. In the final analysis, however, the conflict between offenders and victims at the core of the crime war is regulated by the state. The essential division in the crime war model is not between offenders and victims, but between the state and everyone else. The primary function of the victims' war against offenders is to detract attention from the state's control of the entire population, victims and offenders alike, as a faceless mass of threats to its authority (Dubber 2002a).

This state-based model of the criminal process goes back far beyond Packer, or Nixon for that matter. It is rooted in the criminal administration model of the early twentieth century, developed by a new breed of continental criminologists – including Lombroso and Ferri in Italy and von Liszt in Germany – and championed by such American progressives as Roscoe Pound and Francis Sayre (Lombroso 1911; Ferri 1897; von Liszt 1883). The criminal administration model is a model of criminal, rather than crime, control. Treatmentism, as a theory of *control*, rather than of *punishment*, and of *social* control, rather than of *personal* punishment, is simply the criminological version of the crime control model. For treatmentism, from the outset, had two sides: progressive rehabilitation and repressive incapacitation. As Packer himself put it, without fully appreciating its significance, incapacitation is but "the other side of the rehabilitative coin" (Packer 1968: 55).

The criminal administration model itself can be seen as a modern, highly formalized, and vastly expanded version of the patriarchal model of criminal justice whose roots lie in the authority of the householder over his household. In modern criminal law the state is the true victim of crime; in premodern law it was the householder, and eventually the king as *parens patriae*, the householder of the realm whose peace extended over his kingdom as the householder's *mund* once covered his household and everyone, and everything, it encompassed. The king's peace of English common law is the state's (or "public") peace of today.

Rather than two models, due process and crime control, as Packer had proposed, there is thus only one: criminal control (cf. Griffiths 1970).[2] And the war on crime is its purest manifestation, stripped of naïve progressive assumptions about the curability of criminal pathology.

Taking Packer's analysis as its point of departure, this essay gives an overview of the crime war model in every aspect of the American criminal justice process.

THE WAR ON CRIME

When Nixon called for an all-out war on crime in 1968, the idea of an American war on crime was nothing new. In the midst of World War I, George Herbert Mead wrote a brilliant essay on the "psychology of punitive justice" that analogized American penal practice to a war on criminals, and the punitive emotions unleashed by crime to the emotions of battle (Mead 1918). In his account of the crime war, Mead could draw on the work of Durkheim, who had some twenty years earlier exposed the societal significance of the punitive urge directed at outside threats. The "unanimous aversion that the crime does not fail to evoke" helped "maintain inviolate the cohesion of society by sustaining the common consciousness in all its vigour" (Durkheim 1984: 69). Punishment helped modern society stave off anomie by providing its members with a shared characteristic, hatred for criminals perceived as external threats to the survival of society. Crime thus was "a factor in public health, an integrative element in any healthy society" (Durkheim 1984: 71).

Like Durkheim, Mead concluded that punitive emotions played an important role in the process of group identification through mutual identification and role-taking.[3] According to Mead, punishment "provides the most favorable condition for the sense of group solidarity because in the common attack upon the common enemy the individual differences are obliterated" (Mead 1918: 580–1).

Unlike Durkheim, Mead did not stop at analyzing this phenomenon of cohesion through punitive differentiation. He critiqued it, from the perspective of an early twentieth-century American progressive. Mead worried that the denial of differences on the basis of shared punitive emotions stood in the way of the public resolution of intracommunal, and very real, conflicts based on these differences.

Once criminal law turned into a war on criminal enemies, crime stopped being an internal societal problem reflecting intracommunal conflict. There was no room for the notion that society bore any responsibility for crime, and for the idea that the criminal justice system should seek to reintegrate offenders, rather than eradicate them as external threats to the very existence of society. To the crime warrior, progressive thinking of this type was not only wrongheaded, but positively dangerous: nothing less than the survival of the community was at stake.

But this was precisely Mead's thinking. Mead, a professor at the University of Chicago, was a proponent of the juvenile court experiment launched in Chicago at that time, which became a blueprint for the reform of American juvenile justice in the twentieth century. But Mead had bigger plans. To him, the juvenile courts were not just about juveniles. They illustrated an inclusive, and in his opinion more productive, approach to the problem of crime in general.

Here Mead reflected the progressive criminological wisdom of the day. There was no more significant distinction between (adult) crime and (juvenile) delinquency than there was between adults and juveniles. Crime was the symptom of a particular defect, an illness that could be treated, one way or another. If it was curable, it was incumbent upon the state to provide rehabilitative treatment. If it was not, incapacitative treatment was indicated. Crime was not a matter of justice, but a concern of public health. Criminal justice had nothing to do with punishment, a notion at once atavistic, barbaric, and most important unscientific, and everything to do with peno-correctional treatment.

Mead saw the progressive account of criminal justice as treatment as an alternative to the crime war model. Where the crime war presupposed differentiation, treatmentism presupposed identification. And where the crime war destroyed, treatmentism reintegrated.

This was not so, however. Mead here committed an error common among progressive thinkers about criminal justice at the time: he confused treatment with rehabilitation, conveniently ignoring the less savory side of treatmentist ideology, incapacitation. The main difference between the crime war model and the criminal administration model advocated by Mead and others at the time was that the latter did quietly what the former did openly. Both models proceeded from the assumption that offenders were different. The crime war model portrayed them as enemies, outsiders, and – quite literally – outlaws (see Radin 1936). The criminal administration model regarded them as deviant, abnormal, and morally defective.

The less benign underbelly of treatmentism, and its kinship to the crime war model, is obscured by Mead's focus on juvenile delinquents. That focus itself is of course telling – for the juvenile justice process is based on the fundamental differentiation between process participants – state officials – and the object of their attention – the juvenile. At any rate, once we leave the deceptively friendly confines of family court and enter the undeniably harsh world of the ordinary criminal process, the benevolent pretensions of the criminal administration model quickly give way to a more sinister reality.

In the United States, the vision of the criminal justice process as crime administration was worked out by, among others, Roscoe Pound, the father of the American branch of the sociological school of law and, as Dean of Harvard Law School, one of the most influential, and prolific, American legal scholars of the first half of the twentieth century. As with much of his work, Pound's views on criminal administration could build on the work of continental predecessors, including that of Franz von Liszt, whose famous "Marburg Program" of 1883 had laid out the treatmentist agenda forcefully and succinctly (von Liszt 1883).

Writing in 1927, Pound argued that modern penal thought regarded "penal treatment" as "interference to prevent disobedience," rather than as punishment (Pound 1927: xxxv). Criminal law was distinctive in that it did not concern itself with the rights, or interests, of individuals but with "social interests regarded directly as such, that is, disassociated from any immediate individual interests with which they may be identified" (Pound 1927: xxxii.) Criminal law did not mete out justice, but subjected to penal treatment persons who fit "well recognized types of anti-social individuals and of anti-social conduct" (Pound 1927: xxxiv).

The criminal justice process was designed to put this progressive vision into action. It was not a criminal justice process properly speaking, for its function after all was not to do justice, but to prevent disobedience. As a criminal administrative process it was instead dedicated to identifying and then treating those persons who displayed the relevant antisocial traits.

Pound's colleague on the Harvard Law School faculty, Francis Sayre, a few years later further spelled out what such a system of criminal administration might look like. In a 1933 article that continues to be frequently cited to this day, Sayre coined an entire new category of crimes, the aptly named "public welfare offenses." These were offenses, not crimes, against the public, not an individual, and its welfare, rather than a specific right or interest.

Sayre took notice of a general development "away from nineteenth century individualism toward a new sense of the importance of collective interests." This trend manifested itself in the criminal law in a "shift of emphasis from the protection of individual interests" toward "the protection of public and social interests" (Sayre 1933: 67). Since the modern criminal law was about safeguarding communal interests, or rather the "public welfare," the criminal *process* too had to be modernized. In the old days of punishment, "the criminal law machinery [!] was overburdened with innumerable checks to prevent possible injustice to individual defendants." Now the time of criminal administration had come: "We are thinking today more of the protection of social and public interest; and coincident with the swinging of the pendulum in the field of legal administration in this direction modern criminologists are teaching the objective underlying correctional treatment should change from the barren aim of punishing human beings to the fruitful one of protecting social interests" (Sayre 1933: 68). In Pound's words, the criminal process no longer could afford "extreme tenderness toward accused persons" (Pound 1927: xxxiv).

The point here is not whether Sayre and Pound were right to portray traditional criminal law as obsessed with the protection of defendants' rights. That assessment is unlikely to be shared by many students of Anglo-American criminal justice through the nineteenth century. What matters is that they *thought* the criminal process oversolicitous of defendants' rights. This perception, and critique, of course is all the more noteworthy when it is in fact mistaken. Whatever (few) rights the defendant enjoyed in American criminal law at the time, they needed to be curtailed.

In modern criminal administration, notions of guilt were out of place. As the modern criminologists – from Italy and Germany – reconceptualized criminality as "social danger," rather than as a form of wrongful conduct, so the criminal process had to follow suit. Since guilt no longer mattered, "defenses based upon lack of a blameworthy mind, such as insanity, infancy, compulsion and the like" became obsolete and needed no longer be inquired into (Sayre 1933: 78). The task of the criminal process was no longer to separate the guilty from the innocent – or at least the not guilty – but to identify "those with dangerous and peculiar idiosyncrasies" (Sayre 1932: 1018).

At the end of the first third of the twentieth century we thus find the main ingredients for the revision of criminal justice as a state regulatory scheme designed to eliminate threats to the community, and eventually the state itself, that culminated in the war on crime of the last third of the century. In a system of criminal administration, flexibility is key. State officials charged with protecting the community from harm must enjoy wide discretion to make expert judgments about which communal interests must be protected, how they ought to be protected, who may threaten them, and how these threats are best disposed of.

To ensure the necessary room for discretionary calls of this type, offenses should be defined broadly. Specific offenses merely specify a universal offense, *the* public welfare offense, i.e., anything that interferes with the public welfare. Just what offends, or might offend, the public welfare is left to the discretion of state officials. Here is Sayre's own non-exhaustive list of offenses against the public welfare (Sayre 1933: 78), which adds up to a mini-modern criminal code:

1 Illegal sales of intoxicating liquor;
2 Sales of impure or adulterated food or drugs;
3 Sales of misbranded articles;
4 Violations of anti-narcotic acts;
5 Criminal nuisances;
6 Violations of traffic regulations;
7 Violations of motor-vehicle laws;
8 Violations of general police regulations, passed for the safety, health or well-being of the community.

Note that offenses in these categories today make up the bulk of criminal law on the books and in action. Drug offenses and, of course, traffic and motor-vehicle offenses alone account for the vast majority of the business of the criminal administration system.

Once the state has determined which communal interests deserve its attention, it puts into place the most efficient means for their protection. Convenience is everything. Offenses must be easily detected and easily proved, with minimal constraints. Convenience in investigatory work requires abandoning, or at least reducing, constitutional, and statutory, protections against searches and seizures, curtailing the exclusionary rule in cases where these protections remain in place (so that evidence obtained in their violation will not be excluded from the trial). In substantive criminal law, offenses are to be defined with as few elements as possible – the fewer elements there are, the fewer elements the prosecutor has to prove. *Mens rea*, for example, is to be dispensed with. (In fact, that is how Sayre ended up marking the otherwise conveniently indefinable scope of public welfare offenses: they do not require proof of *mens rea*.) Defenses, we have already seen, are no longer necessary, either because the claims they were meant to defend against – like *mens rea* – need no longer be made by the state or because the general prerequisites for liability – like guilt – no longer exists. Claims of mistake, ignorance, insanity, infancy, duress, or entrapment are no longer relevant. Where defenses cannot be eliminated altogether, the burden of proving them ought to be placed on the defendant. Defenses become "affirmative" defenses.

Whatever elements cannot be eliminated must be conveniently proved. Here too the law of criminal evidence can shift the burden of proving – or rather disproving – them onto the defendant. Presumptions, some rebuttable, some not, come to the prosecutor's aid, allowing her or him to presume the proof of offense elements from otherwise innocuous facts (e.g., from presence to possession), and from other offense elements (e.g., from possession to possession with intent).

So much for the substantive requirements for liability. Now the process for diagnosing them must be rendered more convenient as well. Jury trials are replaced with bench trials, and bench trials with plea agreements – or trial by prosecutor. In Sayre's words, the goal is to transform the criminal process into "some form of administrative control which will prove quick, objective and comprehensive" (Sayre 1933: 69).

Note that Pound's and Sayre's vision of criminal law bears a striking resemblance to the crime war decried by their fellow progressive Mead. Offenders differ from the rest of us. In fact, they are defined in terms of their deviance from the social norm. And not only are offenders different from us, their deviance manifests itself in their anti-social behavior, their assaults on social interests. They are offenders against all of us, directly, rather than against individuals first. We, the community, are offended by crime as a community, rather than as individuals.

But criminal administration also differed from the war on criminals. The Pound–Sayre vision of the criminal process begins and ends with the state. By contrast, the state plays virtually no role in the crime war model, as described and critiqued by Mead. The traditional crime war is a war by the community against its enemies. Modern criminal administration, however, is only indirectly concerned with communal interests. Recall that its modus operandi is "interference to prevent disobedience." Criminal law is the mechanism by which the state enforces obedience to its commands. The paradigmatic offense of modern criminal administration ultimately is not an offense against public welfare, but disobedience to the state. It is the authority and eventually the survival of the state that is at stake, not the survival of the community. In the final analysis, the paradigmatic offense of modern criminal administration thus is the state authority offense, rather than the public welfare offense.

So crucial is the maintenance of the state and its superior status that criminal law is not used merely to punish disobedience. Instead criminal law "interferes" (for it can hardly punish prospectively) to *prevent* disobedience. Criminal administration seeks to identify and eliminate *threats* to the state's authority long before that authority in fact has been compromised.

In a word, criminal administration proceeds from the supposition that offenders are not just different, but also inferior. In this sense, it is not a war on crime in the true sense of the word. It is instead a police action against the threat of offense. Its model is not war, as an intercommunal conflict among equals, but the disciplinary authority of the householder. Wars are governed by the laws of war.

Police actions are not. Wars are declared with the consent of the governed. Police actions are prosecuted by the chief executive without that consent (Weiner and Ni Aolain 1996; Corn 1999).

To recognize another as an enemy in war is to recognize him, in certain respects, as an equal, as the fellow member of a community governed by common rules, the rules (and laws) of war. Consider, for instance, the radically different treatment of regular enemy soldiers and partisans or guerrillas in the case of capture. Much of the law of war on this issue is dedicated to determining who is entitled to the benefit of treatment as a prisoner of war. The distinction between prisoners of war and others essentially turns on that between members of organized military units and other combatants. According to the US Army's field manual on the law of warfare, the former "must at all times be humanely treated" and "are entitled in all circumstances to respect for their persons and their honor" (Department of the Army 1956: §§ 89–90). The latter may be shot on the spot (ibid.: §§ 80–2).

A war on crime in the true sense of the word treats the foe as equal to the friend, not inferior to him. Take, once again, the treatment of prisoners of war. Although failed escape attempts may give rise to disciplinary measures, *successful* attempts may not; recaptured prisoners of war "shall not be liable to any punishment in respect of their previous escape." (ibid.: § 167). Life in a prisoner-of-war camp must preserve the dignity of its inmates as full-fledged persons. So "the Detaining Power shall encourage the practice of intellectual, educational, and recreational pursuits, sports and games amongst prisoners," and a prisoners' representative is to have a voice in the administration of the camp (ibid.: §§ 114, 155–7).

In general, the law of war makes every effort to stress the equal status of prisoners of war and their captors. For instance, prisoners of war "shall be quartered under conditions as favorable as those for the forces of the Detaining Power who are billeted in the same area" (ibid.: § 101). They also are "subject to the laws, regulations, and order in force in the armed forces of the Detaining Power" (ibid.: § 158). And they may keep their uniforms, including indications of rank and medals (Department of the Army 1956: § 94).

Contrast the treatment of war enemies with that of offenders marked for penal treatment. Penal treatment in American correctional institutions begins with a ritual of differentiation and degradation. The object of correction is stripped of his connection to normal society. He is assigned a number, his possessions are confiscated, he is subjected to a full body "cavity" search, dressed in prison garb, and thoroughly cleansed. As a confirmed human threat, the convict–inmate is prohibited from possessing anything, except as specifically permitted by the warden (Conover 2000: 104–5). From the moment he enters the prison, the object of penal correction is subject to the virtually unlimited disciplinary authority of the warden and his subordinates. He is infantilized in both senses of the word – he will depend on the warden for sustenance as well as for discipline. He is not only Other, but inferior as well.

Given the marked inferiority of the objects of penal treatment, the law of war takes great pains to distinguish prisoners of war from convict prisoners. The internment of prisoners of war in "penitentiaries" is expressly prohibited (Department of the Army 1956: § 98). Not even for "disciplinary punishment" may prisoners of war be "transferred to penitentiary establishments (prisons, penitentiaries, convict prisons, etc.)" (ibid.: § 173).

As one might expect in a system designed to "prevent disobedience," the sanctions for disobedience in penal treatment are varied and strict. After all, prisoners are in prisons because they have already been diagnosed with abnormal obstreperousness – that is why they were convicted in the first place. Acts of disobedience, or other manifestations of a disobedient disposition, thus are subject to prison discipline, including the further differentiation and degradation implied in the use of solitary confinement and transfer to so-called "special housing units" in general. Prison discipline deprives inmates of "privileges," which are granted, and denied, at the discretion of the warden. These privileges, to possess certain items – such as a television set – or to wear certain clothes, or to don a particular hairstyle, or to earn money, or to leave one's cell, and so on, represent markers of normalcy and equality. To deny them to the prisoner, or to deprive her of them once given, is to reconfirm her status as Other and inferior.

In the realm of war, the object of penal treatment resembles the partisan more than he does the enemy. Unlike the partisan, he cannot be shot on sight. That is not the point, however. For even the partisan is not without rights. Constitutional protections available even to suspected criminals fulfill a function analogous to the provision in the law of war that partisans "be treated with humanity, and in case of trial, shall not be deprived of the rights of fair and regular trial" (ibid.: § 248). Note that these general protections spring from the offender's or partisan's "humanity" (insofar as constitutional rights are considered to be human rights). An inferior outsider is not without protection, but he enjoys rights only at the most abstract level, as a human. And common humanity all too often has proved all too thin to function as a reliable base for respectful treatment. There is another, more specific, parallel between criminals and partisans. They are entitled to a "fair and regular trial," but only "in case of trial." In the American criminal justice process, however, full-fledged trials are no more frequent than are trials of partisans in the heat of war. The vast majority (over 90 percent) of criminal cases are disposed of by plea agreement.

Disobedience and treatment

Another way of seeing the difference between criminal administration and a true crime war model is to take the treatmentist concern with *disobedience* seriously. The roots of the criminal administration model lie in the householder's inherent power to discipline the members of his household and to extinguish external threats to its welfare. Pound himself pointed out this connection. In his view, "the authority of the State to punish is derived historically from the authority of the head of a patriarchal household," among other things, including "magisterial discipline": "the Roman magistrate had *imperium*, i.e., power to command the citizen to the end of preserving order in time of peace and discipline in time of war" (Pound 1927: xxxiii). Pound was not alone in this belief. It was shared by Gustav Radbruch, a student of von Liszt's and a leading German progressive criminal law scholar and justice minister in the Weimar Republic, as well as by Theodor Mommsen, the great historian of Roman law (Mommsen 1899: 16–17, but note Strachan-Davidson 1912: 28–9). Radbruch contrasted the origin of the criminal law in household discipline, and more particularly in the householder's correction of his slaves, with that of international law in the resolution of disputes among heads of households (Radbruch 1950).

The state in the criminal administration model of Pound and Sayre occupies much the same position as the householder did in medieval law, or the *pater familias* in Roman law. Its authority is virtually unlimited, except by its notoriously ill-defined end, the welfare of the community. The paradigmatic offense of patriarchal and treatmentist discipline is what might be termed the communal welfare offense. Every act – or threat – of disobedience against the householder or the state is an affront against the communal welfare, and every sanction that enforces the authority of the householder or the state is justified in the name of safeguarding that welfare.

To this day, the state's power to punish is said to derive from its power to police (see LaFave and Scott 1986: 148). The police power, however, is nothing but the householder's disciplinary authority. According to Blackstone, the king, as the "father" of his people (Blackstone 1769: 176) and "*pater-familias* of the nation" (1769: 127), was charged with

> the public police and oeconomy [, i.e.,] the due regulation and domestic order of the kingdom: whereby the individuals of the state, like members of a well-governed family, are bound to conform their general behavior to the rules of propriety, good neighbourhood, and good manners: and to be decent, industrious, and inoffensive in their respective stations. (1769: 162)

This definition of the police power was quoted in every major nineteenth-century American treatise on the subject (Tiedeman 1886: 2; Cooley 1890: 704 n.1; Freund 1904: 2). The only adjustment American criminal law made to Blackstone's vision of police was to substitute the state, or the public, for the king. So criminal law no longer enforced the king's peace but the public peace instead.

State and patriarchal discipline are inherently differentiating and hierarchical. Both are grounded in the categorical distinction between the subject and the object of discipline, or treatment. Not only is the object of discipline (the slave or the criminal deviant) categorically different from the subject (the householder or the state); it is also fundamentally inferior. In these circumstances, punishment affirms difference and inferiority. It differentiates and degrades, provided that one keeps in mind that the differentiation and degradation are viewed as merely reaffirming a preexisting relationship. Through discipline, the slave-offender is revealed as, not made, Other and lower (see Garfinkel 1956: 421).

There's one final distinction between a crime war and penal treatmentism that deserves mention. The war on crime, as described by Mead, is open about its objectives and its methods. Penal treatmentism is not. Penal treatmentism goes about its differentiation and degradation in a roundabout way. What is more, it differentiates and degrades its objects for their own sake. Once punishment is reconceived as treatment of an ailment, the punished become beneficiaries of medical treatment. As patients they have neither reason, nor right, to require justification of their treatment. On the contrary, it's the *failure* to prescribe peno-correctional treatment that would require legitimation. Penal treatmentism, in other words, is essentially hypocritical (Morris 1968; Allen 1981).

The Model Penal Code (MPC)

After Pound's general outline and Sayre's invention of public welfare offenses, penal treatmentism found its final, and most important, manifestation in the American Law Institute's Model Penal Code (MPC), completed in 1962, six years before Packer's *Limits of the Criminal Sanction* and Nixon's manifesto for the modern police action on crime appeared (Dubber 2002b). The Model Code exerted enormous influence on all aspects of American criminal law. Most states recodified their criminal law on its basis, including New York, Texas, Illinois, Pennsylvania, and New Jersey (Singer 1988: 519). Even in jurisdictions that did not, courts frequently draw on the Code's analysis to elucidate unsettled issues. Aside from its considerable impact on American criminal law doctrine, the MPC also became the foundation for contemporary criminal law scholarship and teaching (Kadish 1988: 521).

Although it was not completed until the early 1960s, the origins of the MPC are roughly contemporaneous with Pound's and Sayre's work on criminal administration. Its conceptual backbone was in place by 1937, when its drafter, the great Herbert Wechsler, published a monumental article, "A rationale of the law of homicide," with his Columbia colleague Jerome Michael (Michael and Wechsler 1937). This article represented a sustained attempt to apply the idea of criminal administration to the entirety of criminal law. The criminal law was to become a system of peno-correctional treatment. Wechsler and Michael studiously avoided the term "punishment," as did virtually every other progressive writer on criminal justice. Punishment had become taboo (Hart 1958: 425). Every sanction is treatment, rehabilitative (if possible) or incapacitative (if appropriate). In his 1952 blueprint for the Model Penal Code, which streamlined the results of his 1937 article, Wechsler classified even capital punishment as an "extreme affliction sanction," rather than punishment (Wechsler 1952: 1123).

The Model Penal Code reflected penal treatmentism in various ways (Dubber 2002b). To begin with, fundamental principles of criminal law were reinterpreted in the light of treatmentism. So Wechsler called for the retention of the act requirement not as a prerequisite for liability, but as a "behavior symptom" for purposes of "diagnosis and prognosis" (Wechsler 1952: 1123). Offenders' conduct mattered insofar as it "indicates that they are disposed to commit crimes" (American Law Institute 1962: § 1.02(1)(b)). Those who displayed that disposition were not punished, but "subject[ed] to public control."

The "objective" of the criminal law was "to describe the character deficiencies of those subjected to it in accord with the propensities that they...manifest" (American Law Institute 1980: 157 n.99). The Code's treatment "diagnosis and prognosis" considered such things as whether the offender posed a "significant threat to the property system" or "manifested" particular "character traits" (American Law Institute 1980: 157).

The Code actually consisted of two codes, a "penal code" (contained in parts I and II) and a "correctional code" (in parts III and IV). The penal code in turn consisted of two parts, a general part (codifying general prerequisites of criminal liability) and a special part (defining specific offenses). The correctional code, now largely forgotten, amounted to a two-part code of penal treatment: part III, "treatment and correction," dealt with the conditions of penal treatment and part IV, "organization of correction," with the structure and operation of a department of corrections.

The penal code and the correctional code must be read together. In fact, they should be read backwards. For the point of the penal code is to provide the diagnostic tools for assigning the treatment that is applied according to the correctional code. In fact, one might read the penal code as a kind of crude, legalized nosology of criminal pathology – the criminal law's equivalent of the Diagnostic and Statistical Manual of Mental Disorders (better known as the DSM), the first edition of which was published by the American Psychiatric Association in 1952, the year Wechsler's blueprint for the Model Code appeared (Kirk and Kutchins 1992: 27).

The law of attempt provides a particularly stark illustration of the Code's treatmentist approach. As the Code drafters explained, "[t]he primary purpose of punishing attempts is to neutralize dangerous individuals" (American Law Institute 1985: 323). This focus on incapacitative treatment had several consequences. To begin with, the concept of attempt was expanded to reach any conduct "strongly corroborative of the actor's criminal purpose" (American Law Institute 1962: § 5.01(2)). In the drafters' view, the line between (non-criminal) preparation and (criminal) attempt had been crossed at that point where the offender manifested a sufficient level of dangerousness, or abnormal criminal disposition, that called for penal treatment in the form of public control.

The MPC drafters also did away with the so-called impossibility defense. What mattered was the offender's abnormal dangerousness, not the possibility – or rather the impossibility – of criminal harm. The offender's criminal disposition – the threat he poses as a criminal deviant – requires state intervention even if the particular conduct posed no threat to anyone or anything.

Finally, the MPC abandoned the distinction between the punishment for attempted and consummated crimes. Traditionally, attempts had been punished considerably less severely than consummated crimes. The distinction between attempt and consummation, however, appeared irrational to the MPC drafters. An offender who attempts a crime is just as dangerous, and suffers from the same general disposition to commit crimes, as one who happens to succeed in putting his plan into action. From the standpoint of penal treatment, there is no difference between the offender who lifts a wallet from another's pocket and one who tries to do the same but finds the pocket empty.

The MPC's treatmentist approach resulted in exceptionally harsh provisions on so-called inchoate, or incomplete, offenses in general. Attempt here is but one example of the Code's effort to heed Pound's motto for modern criminal law: not to punish but to "*prevent* disobedience." So, to take another example, the MPC endorsed the unilateral theory of conspiracy. This means that one person can be a conspirator even if the person he thinks he is conspiring with is not, say, because he is a police officer posing as a conspirator. In general, this view of conspiracy is not much favored, perhaps because it is hard to punish someone for entering into an agreement when that agreement was never in fact entered into. But, from the perspective of incapacitative treatment, it is irrelevant whether the person was right or wrong about his partner in crime. What mattered, once again, was that by at least *thinking* he had conspired to commit some crime he had manifested that all-decisive criminal disposition.

Then there is the inchoate crime of solicitation. For conviction of solicitation it is enough to have tried to encourage someone to commit a crime. It matters not whether the letter asking your friend to kill your next-door neighbor gets lost in the mail. Once again, having written it and put it in the mailbox is enough evidence of your criminal character to indicate the need for peno-correctional treatment.

The most inchoate MPC offense of all, however, tends not to be recognized as such. It is the offense of *possession*. Possession is the ultimate dangerousness offense. If attempt is an inchoate offense, possession is an inchoate inchoate offense. Possession occupies a central place in the Model Penal Code. For that reason alone it deserves a closer look. More important, however, possession also evolved into the favorite weapon in the modern war on crime as a police action against criminals, as envisaged by Nixon and as prosecuted over the past thirty years.

At the outset it is crucial to see that possession is not just an offense. It is a theory of criminal liability, or rather a method for the diagnosis of criminal character. It forms an integral part of a type of criminal process designed to incapacitate threats, rather than to do justice, or even to "control crime." Possession is the paradigmatic offense of the criminal administration model stripped of its progressive pretensions, of treatmentism without rehabilitation.

To see the doubly inchoate nature of possession, it helps to place it along a spectrum of dangerousness, or inchoacy. Possession comes in two basic varieties, simple and compound. Simple possession punishes possession, without more. Compound possession punishes possession with the intent to use the item possessed in some way (perhaps to sell it). At the end of pure dangerousness, or extreme inchoacy, is simple possession. Here we are farthest removed from the harm that the use of the object may cause. Then comes compound possession. Compound possession still does not inflict harm, but at least presupposes the intent to use the item possessed in a way that *may* be harmful.

Next is the *preparation* to use the item possessed. Unlike possession, however, "mere" preparation is not criminalized. That's so because traditional criminal law distinguished between preparation and *attempt*. A preparation that blossomed into an attempt becomes criminal. An attempt to use the object possessed is a preparation that has almost, but not quite, borne fruit. And eventually, on the other end of the inchoacy spectrum, we find the actual use of the possessed item. Beyond the spectrum of inchoacy altogether lies the actual use of a possessed item to inflict harm – say, by stabbing someone with a knife.

Possession, on the other end of the dangerousness continuum, thus amounts to an inchoate attempt. In fact, some courts have recognized an offense of attempted possession, or a conspiracy to possess, thus creating a triple inchoacy, an inchoate inchoate inchoate offense.

In addition to providing for various specific possession offenses (such as possessing false weights or measures, abortifacients, prison-escape implements, or obscene materials), the Model Penal Code defines two sweeping possession offenses in its general part, the part that contains the general principles of criminal liability that apply to all offenses: possession of instruments of crime, including firearms and other weapons, and possession of offensive weapons (American Law Institute 1962: §§ 5.06, 5.07). The first makes it a crime for anyone to "possess . . . any instrument of crime with purpose to employ it criminally," where "instrument of crime" includes "anything specially made or specially adapted for criminal use" or "anything commonly used for criminal purposes and possessed by the actor under circumstances which do not negative unlawful purpose."

This section encapsulates a mode of dangerousness diagnosis, rather than defining a particular crime. It prescribes incapacitative treatment for someone whose criminal disposition has manifested itself in the possession of some instrument "*commonly* used for criminal purposes" with the intent to commit some crime. It punishes criminal possession as possession by a criminal.

The inference from possession to criminal possession occurs with particular ease when the item possessed is a weapon. And a weapon, under the MPC, is broadly defined to include not only firearms but "anything readily capable of lethal use and possessed under circumstances not manifestly appropriate for lawful uses which it may have" (American Law Institute 1962: § 5.06(2)).

In addition to providing for rather generous definitions of possession and the items possessed, the Code also puts in place various presumptions designed to simplify the task of proving that these definitions have been met. So weapons are presumed to be possessed "with purpose to employ [them] criminally." That way the simple possession of a weapon transforms itself into a compound one.

And the simple possession itself may be presumed as well. If you are in a car with a weapon, you are presumed to possess it (American Law Institute 1962: § 5.06(3)). Mere presence thus turns into possession, which turns into possession, with intent to use "criminally."

In the end, the Model Code thus criminalizes being in the presence of "anything readily capable of lethal use." Presence alone constitutes a sufficiently reliable symptom of that all-decisive criminal disposition to warrant incapacitative treatment in the absence of proof to the contrary. Possession thus is an offense, a theory of criminal liability, and a mode of penological diagnosis all wrapped into one. It was the perfect doctrinal tool for a criminal process bent on the elimination of threats through incapacitative treatment.

Possession's considerable incapacitative potential, however, came at the price of flaunting virtually every rule of traditional Anglo-American criminal law. As English courts had recognized since the eighteenth century, possession had no *actus reus* because it was a state, or a relation, rather than a form of conduct. At best it was an omission (*not* not possessing) without a corresponding duty to act, another violation of established doctrine. In its strict liability version, it even lacked a *mens rea*.

But none of this mattered since, as Pound and Sayre had explained, the days of solicitude for criminal defendants, and of strict adherence to outdated constraints on state penal treatment were over. To the extent the violation of a legal principle posed a problem, it was resolved simply, and expeditiously: in its *actus reus* provision, the Model Code drafters simply *declared* possession to be a type of conduct (ibid.: § 2.01(4)).

Given its usefulness as a tool for the identification and elimination of human threats, it's no surprise that possession assumed a crucial role in the war on crime as a concerted campaign of mass incapacitation. The war on crime of the past thirty years seized the incapacitative tools laid out in the Model Code, and proceeded to sharpen them for greater effect.

Possession offenses today pervade American criminal law. In New York State, for example, there were at the last count 153 possession offenses, 115 of which were felonies. Eleven of the possession felonies were punishable by a maximum sentence of life imprisonment. In 1998, possession offenses made up 106,565, or a little less than one-fifth, of arrests in that state (Division of Criminal Justice Services 1999, 2000). A total of 33,219 (31.2 percent) of those originally arrested for possession went to prison or jail. In fact, one in every five prison or jail sentences handed out by New York courts in 1998 was imposed for a possession offense (Division of Criminal Justice Services 2000).

The most significant expansion of the scope of possession offense vis-à-vis the Model Penal Code occurred in the area of drug criminal law, a category of offenses not covered in the Model Code (American Law Institute 1962: 241). In 1998, there were 1.2 million arrests for drug possession offenses alone (Bureau of Justice Statistics 1999). Simple possession of large quantities of cocaine was punishable by a maximum sentence of life imprisonment in New York, and by a mandatory sentence of life imprisonment without the possibility of parole in Michigan (see United States Supreme Court 1991).

The process of possession police is highly efficient. Virtually all of the New York possession cases in 1998 were disposed of through a plea agreement of some sort, and virtually none resulted in an acquittal. There were well over 100,000 possession arrests, and 129 acquittals.

Possession offenses were easy to detect, and easy to prove. Every *Terry* stop-and-frisk amounted to a search for possession; and so did every arrest (with the requisite "search incident"). Any traffic stop could blossom into a possession investigation. The United States Supreme Court's criminal procedure jurisprudence is littered with cases in which the police stop a suspect for one reason or another, and end up finding possession evidence, intentionally or not. *Terry* itself involved a stop-and-frisk of burglary suspects, but resulted in convictions for gun possession (cf. Dubber 2002a).

Once possession evidence has been found, a possession case is quickly made, leaving the defendant no reasonable alternative to a plea agreement. Simple statutes with few offense elements, with modest *mens rea* requirements if any, easily circumvented with a host of presumptions, and the suspension of justification defenses like self-defense, all translate into open-and-shut cases. And unlike zero-tolerance offenses, such as jaywalking, or its predecessor as the sweep offense of choice, vagrancy, possession carries a big stick, with penalties up to and including life imprisonment without the possibility of parole.

Possession in the war on crime is a concerted campaign that involves all levels of American law enforcement. Take "Project Exile," for example. The idea behind this incapacitation program is strikingly simple: use the harsh federal gun-possession laws directed against convicted felons to take exceptional human threats off the street, and back to prison. Project Exile literally exiles offenders in two ways. Thanks to Draconian federal gun-possession statutes, it incapacitates them far longer than a state court sentence could. Moreover, by sending convicted possessors to remote federal prisons, rather than local institutions, the already considerable exiling effect of ordinary imprisonment is further enhanced. In the words of a Philadelphia police officer: "[t]hey're sent anywhere in the country, so they're separated from their families and there's no probation or parole under the federal guidelines, so they're doing their complete sentence" (Westervelt 2000).

Neither Sayre nor even the drafters of the Model Penal Code foresaw the transmogrification of their model of criminal administration into a massive incapacitation campaign, that would leave over six and a half million people, two million of them in prisons and jails, under the state's penal control by the end of the twentieth century. And neither did Herbert Packer.

Writing just six years after the publication of the MPC, he was still convinced that the due process model would continue what he regarded as its inevitable march of triumph over the dreaded crime control model. *Terry* had not happened yet – though it is hard to say if that would have managed to dampen his belief in progress. He saw the MPC as a monument of American criminal law reform, which it clearly was in the sense that it systematized a hopelessly haphazard body of doctrine. But he did not fully appreciate the nature of that systematization. While he was uneasy with the hypocritical replacement of punishment with treatment, he did not acknowledge the MPC's essentially treatmentist foundation, nor the deep affinity between treatmentism in substantive criminal law and crime control in the criminal process.

In 1968, Packer's analysis thus was out of date almost as soon as it appeared. The future of the American criminal process belonged to the crime war model of the criminal process. At least up until now.

THE FUTURE

The end of the war on crime may be in sight. Crime rates have been dropping recently, and the incarceration expansion has shown signs of slowing down. For the first time in almost three decades, the state prison population declined, albeit very modestly, during the last six months of 2000 (Bureau of Justice Statistics 2001a). Some states have begun to reduce some criminal sanctions, after decades of continuous increases (Butterfield 2001). As crime is losing political salience, it may transform itself from a crisis into a challenge once again, and from an emergency into a problem. How American society will respond to what in 1967, immediately prior to the imitation of the national police action against criminal threats, appeared as "the challenge of crime in a free society," remains to be seen (President's Commission on Law Enforcement and Administration of Justice 1967). It is doubtful whether the challenge of reconciling punishment with liberty will be met with a return to treatmentism, no matter in what guise.

Perhaps the beginning of a response can be found in 1968 as well, the very year that produced Packer's analysis of the criminal process, Nixon's crime war manifesto, and *Terry v. Ohio*. That year, Herbert Morris published the article that exerted considerable influence on the critique of rehabilitative ideology in subsequent years (Morris 1968). Though targeted specifically at rehabilitationism, the still reigning penal ideology of the time, "Persons and punishment" challenged treatmentism in general, as a system of social control. Morris called not merely for a reevaluation of comfortable rehabilitative attitudes toward punishment as cure. He instead suggested a model of a criminal *justice* process worthy of its name, one that gives offenders, and victims, their due as persons, rather than subjecting them to diagnosis and disposition. Thanks to the war on crime, this model of the criminal process has never been worked out. Perhaps the time of the justice model will come after the demise of its utter opposite, the criminal process as crime war.

Notes

1   On the political significance of the friend–foe distinction, see Schmitt 1996. For a treatment of (much of) modern criminal law as "foe criminal law," see Jakobs 1985.
2   Packer (and Griffiths) were unusual in their attempt to conceive of questions of the American criminal process not primarily as questions of constitutional criminal procedure or – what often amounts to the same thing – as questions of the jurisprudential ideologies of particular Justices on the United States Supreme Court, taken individually or aggregated onto "Courts" named after their respective Chief Justice, as in "Warren Court" (after Earl Warren, 1953–69), "Burger Court" (Warren Burger, 1969–86), or most recently "Rehnquist Court" (William Rehnquist, since 1986). Subsequent treatments of Packer's models of the criminal process generally approached the tension between the two in terms of the ideological differences between "the Warren Court" and "the Burger Court" in particular, with the former representing due process and the latter crime control, often concluding that they had more in common than some had feared (Arenella 1983; Dripps 1990).
3   Freud and the French sociologists Tarde and Salleiles arrived at similar conclusions, though not necessarily by the same route. (Freud 1922, 1963; Tarde 1912; Salleiles 1913).

References

Allen, F. A. (1981) *The Decline of the Rehabilitative Ideal: Penal Policy and Social Purpose*. New Haven, CT: Yale University Press.

American Law Institute (1962) *Model Penal Code (Proposed Official Draft)*. Philadelphia: American Law Institute.

American Law Institute (1980) *Model Penal Code and Commentaries (Official Draft and Revised Comments): Part II (Definition of Specific Crimes) §§ 220.1 to 230.5*. Philadelphia: American Law Institute.

American Law Institute (1985) *Model Penal Code and Commentaries (Official Draft and Revised Comments): Part I (General Provisions) §§ 3.01 to 5.07*. Philadelphia: American Law Institute.

Arenella, P. (1983) Rethinking the functions of criminal procedure: The Warren and Burger Courts' competing ideologies. *Georgetown Law Journal*, 72, 185–248.

Blackstone, W. (1769) *Commentaries on the Laws of England, vol. 4*. Oxford: Oxford University Press.

Bureau of Justice Statistics (1999) *Number of Arrests, by Type of Drug Law Violations, 1982–98*. Washington, DC: US Department of Justice.

Bureau of Justice Statistics (2001a) *Prisoners in 2000*. Washington, DC: US Department of Justice.

Bureau of Justice Statistics (2001b) *Probation and Parole in the United States, 2000.* Washington, DC: US Department of Justice.

Butterfield, F. (2001) States easing stringent laws on prison time. *New York Times,* September 2, 1.

Clear, T. R. (1997) Societal responses to the President's Crime Commission: A thirty-year retrospective. In US Department of Justice, Office of Justice Programs, *Research Forum, The Challenge of Crime in a Free Society: Looking Back, Looking Forward.* Washington, DC: United States Department of Justice, 131–58.

Conover, T. (2000) *Newjack: Guarding Sing Sing.* New York: Random House.

Cooley, T. M. (1890) *A Treatise on the Constitutional Limitations Which Rest Upon the Legislative Power of the States of the American Union (6th ed.).* Boston: Little, Brown.

Corn, G. S. (1999) "To be or not to be, that is the question": Contemporary military operations and the status of captured personnel. *Army Lawyer,* June, 1–18.

Department of the Army (1956) *Field Manual, The Law of Land Warfare.* Washington, DC: Headquarters, Department of the Army.

Division of Criminal Justice Services (1999) *Criminal Justice Indicators New York State: 1994–1998* (Dec. 13). Albany: State of New York, Division of Criminal Justice Services.

Division of Criminal Justice Services (2000) *Possession Related Offenses New York State* (Feb. 4). Albany, NY: State of New York, Division of Criminal Justice Services.

Dripps, D. A. (1990) Beyond the Warren Court and its conservative critics: Toward a unified theory of constitutional criminal procedure. *University of Michigan Journal of Law Reform,* 23, 591–640.

Dubber, M. (2002a) *Victims in the War on Crime: The Use and Abuse of Victims' Rights.* New York: New York University Press.

Dubber, M. (2002b) *Model Penal Code.* New York: Foundation Press.

Durkheim, E. (1984) Crime and punishment. In Steven Lukes and Andrew Scull (eds.), *Durkheim and the Law.* Oxford: Blackwell, 59–101.

Ferri, E. (1897) *Criminal Sociology.* New York: Appleton.

Freud, S. (1922) *Group Psychology and the Analysis of the Ego* (trans. James Strachey). New York: Norton.

Freud, S. (1963) *Civilization and Its Discontents* (trans. Joan Riviere and James Strachey). London: Hogarth.

Freund, E. (1904) *The Police Power: Public Policy and Constitutional Rights.* Chicago: Callaghan.

Garfinkel, H. (1956) Conditions of successful degradation ceremonies, *American Journal of Sociology,* 61, 420–4.

Griffiths, J. (1970) Ideology in criminal procedure or a third "model" of the criminal process. *Yale Law Journal,* 79, 359–417.

Hart, H. M., Jr. (1958) The aims of the criminal law. *Law and Contemporary Problems,* 23, 401–41.

Jakobs, G. (1985) Kriminalisierung im Vorfeld einer Rechtsgutsverletzung. *Zeitschrift für die gesamte Strafrechtswissenschaft,* 97, 751–85.

Kadish, S. H. (1988) The Model Penal Code's historical antecedents. *Rutgers Law Journal* 19, 521–38.

Kirk, S. A., and Kutchins, H. (1992) *The Selling of DSM: The Rhetoric of Science in Psychiatry.* New York: de Gruyter.

LaFave, W. R., and Scott, A. W., Jr. (1986) *Substantive Criminal Law* (2nd ed.). St. Paul: West.

Lombroso, C. (1911) *Criminal Man, According to the Classification of Cesare Lombroso.* New York: Putnam.

Mauer, M., and Huling, T. (1995) *Young Black Americans and the Criminal Justice System: Five Years Later*. Washington, DC: The Sentencing Project.

Mead, G. H. (1918) The psychology of punitive justice. *American Journal of Sociology*, 23, 577.

Michael, J., and Wechsler, H. (1937) A rationale of the law of homicide I & II. *Columbia Law Review*, 37, 701–61, 1261–325.

Mommsen, T. (1899) *Römisches Strafrecht*. Leipzig: Duncker & Humblot.

Morris, H. (1968) Persons and punishment. *The Monist*, 53(4), 475–501.

Nixon, R. (1968) Toward freedom from fear. *Congressional Record*, 114, 12936–7 (May 13).

Packer, H. L. (1968) *The Limits of the Criminal Sanction*. Stanford: Stanford University Press.

Pound, R. (1927) Introduction. In Francis Bowes Sayre, *A Selection of Cases on Criminal Law*. Rochester, NY: Lawyers Co-operative Publishing Co., xxix–xxxvii.

President's Commission on Law Enforcement and Administration of Justice (1967) *The Challenge of Crime in a Free Society*. Washington, DC: United States Government Printing Office.

Radbruch, G. (1950) Der Ursprung des Strafrechts aus dem Stande der Unfreien. In *Elegantiae Juris Criminalis: Vierzehn Studien zur Geschichte des Strafrechts* (2nd ed.). Basel: Verlag für Recht und Gesellschaft.

Radin, M. (1936) Enemies of society. *Journal of Criminal Law and Criminology*, 27, 328–56.

Salleiles, R. (1913) *The Individualization of Punishment* (trans. Rachel Szold Jastrow). Boston: Little, Brown.

Sayre, F. B. (1932) Mens rea. *Harvard Law Review*, 45, 974–1026.

Sayre, F. B. (1933) Public welfare offenses. *Columbia Law Review*, 33, 55–88.

Schmitt, C. (1996) *The Concept of the Political* (trans. George Schwab). Chicago: University of Chicago Press.

Singer, R. (1988) The 25th anniversary of the Model Penal Code: Foreword. *Rutgers Law Journal*, 19, 519–20.

Strachan-Davidson, J. L. (1912) *Problems of the Roman Criminal Law, vol. 1*. Oxford: Clarendon Press.

Tarde, G. (1912) *Penal Philosophy* (trans. Rapelje Howell). Boston: Little, Brown.

Tiedeman, C. G. (1886) *A Treatise on the Limitations of Police Power in the United States Considered From Both a Civil and Criminal Standpoint*. St. Louis: F. H. Thomas Law Book Co.

Tonry, M. (1995) *Malign Neglect: Race, Crime, and Punishment in America*. Oxford: Oxford University Press.

United States Supreme Court (1968) *Terry v. Ohio*, 392 US 1.

United States Supreme Court (1991) *Harmelin v. Michigan*, 501 US 957.

von Liszt, F. (1883) Der Zweckgedanke im Strafrecht. *Zeitschrift für die gesamte Strafrechtswissenschaft*, 3, 1–47.

Vorenberg, J. (1972) The war on crime: The first five years. *Atlantic Monthly*, May, 63–69.

Wechsler, H. (1952) The challenge of a Model Penal Code. *Harvard Law Review*, 65, 1097–133.

Weiner, R. O., and Ni Aolain, F. (1996) Beyond the laws of war: Peacekeeping in search of a legal framework. *Columbia Human Rights Law Review*, 27, 293–354.

Westervelt, E. (2000) Philadelphia's crackdown on criminals who possess illegal guns. *Morning Edition*, National Public Radio, March 23.

4

Criminology, Genocide, and Modernity: Remarks on the Companion that Criminology Ignored

Wayne Morrison

Almost all the survivors, [of Auschwitz] orally or in their written memoirs remember a dream which frequently recurred during the nights of imprisonment, varied in its detail but uniform in its substance: they had returned home and with passion and relief were describing their past sufferings, addressing themselves to a loved one, and were not believed, indeed were not even listened to. In the most typical and cruelest form the interlocutor turned and left in silence. (Levi 1986: 12)

companion 1 one who keeps company or frequently associates with another: a partner (*obs.*): spouse (*obs.*): higher rank of servant, who, though receiving pay, stands rather in the relation of a friend: fellow, rascal (*Shak.*): a member of an order, esp. in a lower grade: one of a pair or set of things: an often pocket-sized book on a particular subject (as in *angler's companion*). – *v.t.* to accompany. – *adj.* Of the nature of a companion: accompanying...

companion 2 (*naut.*) *n*. the skylight or window-frame through which light passes to a lower deck or cabin.... (*Chambers 20th Century Dictionary*)

CRIMINOLOGY AND GENOCIDE: AN UNACKNOWLEDGED COMPANIONSHIP?

This is an essay about being and companionship. It is a contribution to a book entitled *The Blackwell Companion to Criminology*. It is a collection of words, sentences, and paragraphs. Words, by their nature, oppose silence: words invoke presence(s). Through writing we institutionalize memory into history, we acknowledge different features of being human, and we identify those institutional forms and behavioral practices by which we establish our historical identities.

There is an inherent instability and irony in including genocide in a *Companion to Criminology*: criminology has not acknowledged genocide as any sort of companion.

What is criminology? Criminology is an academic discipline. Criminology is discourse; it is an heir to the *logos* tradition where language is regarded as both reflective and constitutive of, but also a tool of, humanity's inherent rationality. Criminology is a contribution to the project of subjecting the world, the place wherein humanity resides, to rational knowledge and control; but criminology must also "humanize" the edifices of those projects. Its subject is crime, but its universe is human nature and social life. Thus criminology has a metaphysical dimension, it serves to invoke images and realities of pain, loss, domination, transgression, censure, and extinction. Crime may be presented as banal or existentially exciting to its perpetuators, but the term covers a variety of events that both attack victims in a physical sense (sometimes even killing them) and undercut that most fundamental quality necessary for social existence, namely *trust in the world*. Criminology is in part an attempt to restore trust by explaining crime, by rendering it understandable, predictable and controllable. Yet that is a stabilizing role, a matter of reassurance; metaphysics is more than that. Beyond reassurance, humans need narratives of birth, identity, and belonging; and narratives that provide hope for the future. We desire transcendence, we need to hear the discourses of eschatology, we want to understand that the demeaning and humiliating aspects of our societies are not timeless features but edifices to be overcome. Thus criminology – as with social sciences in general – must be critical, else it is in danger of providing a fundamentalist metaphysic telling us to accommodate to the world, for it is the natural state of affairs.

But criminology is also ideology. Criminology is a canon of accepted texts and topics for research and teaching. Criminology is a set of activities – reading, writing, researching, talking, going to conferences, connecting data and theories, thinking . . . and obeying the "limits" of the "discipline."

Criminology is a modern academic discipline devoted to the study of crime and its surrounding influences that has largely ignored that range of mass murders, rapes and associated atrocities, that destruction of people and their culture, which have been loosely placed under the rubric of the term "genocide."[1] While there have been some recent attempts to incorporate the study of genocide, or at least to comment upon its absence, criminology, as a mainstream discipline, operates oblivious to genocide.

The statement that criminology has largely ignored genocide (and the "Holocaust" in particular) is easily sustained. One explanation proposed is that "it was rather too hurriedly placed in the category of 'political crime' and seen as too fuzzy for 'scientific' work" (Eryl Hall Williams, personal communication). A small group of writings exist on "political crime," defined loosely as "crime committed by a government for ideological purposes," but the concept of crime utilized is usually that of the existing state regulations which have been breached in the pursuit of political goals. Post-World War II criminology was expressly "positivist." While it is true that in the immediate post-World War II context the need for a more "humane" criminology was felt, particularly in Holland and in the Scandinavian countries, clearly influenced by the Nazi atrocities, there were virtually no direct writings. The Nazi experience appears to have been seen as a matter for social psychology and history rather than germane to criminology. The criminology of the time was marked by a lack of reflexivity and a rather unquestioning acceptance of its basic assumptions: there was no attempt to analyze to what extent criminological knowledges had contributed to the ease with which the Jews and others were able to be labeled as criminals and degenerates. The subject matter may have also been too personal for a discipline struggling to claim "scientific" status. British criminology came to be largely influenced by three Jewish refugees, Max Grunhut, Leon Radzinowicz, and Hermann Mannheim, who established criminology as an academic discipline in the universities of Oxford, Cambridge, and at the London School of Economics and Political Science (LSE), respectively. Eryl Hall Williams, for some time the sole criminologist in the LSE Law Department, had actually been an administrator at Belsen concentration camp after its liberation. None incorporated the Holocaust into their "criminology," although Mannheim included some writings on war crimes. Perhaps another reason is that if the "crimes" had not been justiciable (i.e., had been the actual subject of legal judgments resulting in punishments), then they were seen as not "solid" enough to be accepted as fit subjects for a serious "scientific" discipline. The development of a specific intellectual discipline devoted to the rational analyzing of crime, viz., criminology, has paralleled the development of criminal justice systems. In the absence of a supra-state institutional framework for judgment and punishment, no subject matter existed. Thereby Nuremberg, having provided a charter for possible future use and several new categories of "crime" (for example, waging aggressive war, crimes against humanity), was of such limited institutional impact that it provoked no associated "criminology" and the UN genocide convention has not produced any stream of legal cases. The Holocaust has made an occasional entry in texts in the general area of victimology. It is undoubtedly the role of spokespersons for the oppressed that motivates a small "critical" criminological interest in identifying the victims and situations of "state crimes." This, however, is mostly limited to highlighting the "abuses" of power of state governments in a descriptive way, with little sustained theoretical analysis of the meaning of "state crime."[2] Obedience research was the theme of Kelman and Hamilton's (1989) *Crimes of Obedience*, which was written in the shadow of the Holocaust's legacy, although the authors stated that they deliberately did not discuss the Holocaust or genocide, partly for personal reasons. That text focused on the My Lai Massacre in the Vietnam War and represents the only sustained attempt in criminology to develop an awareness of the role of obedience and authority as criminogenic forces.

Is this criminological silence surprising? Consider the basic facts.

1   The twentieth century was the century of high *modernity*; the time where the globe became "civilized" and "rationalized," wherein industrial techniques were constantly refashioned, a time where administrative bureaucracy became increasingly efficient. It was a period when time itself seemed to speed continually faster and it denoted a world where knowledge, wealth, and experiences of diverse ethnicities became universalized (albeit in partial and distorted ways).

2   In the twentieth century criminology became institutionalized as a scholarly discipline devoted to the "scientific study of crime and its surrounding influences." By the close of the century criminology was a major scholarly discipline with large conferences and networks of funding sources and publishing outlets.

3   The twentieth century was the "age of genocide"[3] (the intentional killing of others because they belong to a particular ethnic, religious, or cultural group). It was a century in which tens of millions (possibly hundreds of millions[4]) of human beings were exterminated as a deliberate consequence of state policy or operations. Moreover, it was the century which saw the establishment of a truly international body – the UN – a body which passed in mid-century a Genocide Convention giving positive recognition (in the jurisprudential sense) to the "crime."

4   Criminology ignored genocide – it did not consider it as part of its area of investigation, and the vast majority of criminological texts were written and discussed without any reference to it.[5]

If the logic of the above sequence should result in genocide being fundamental to criminology, what can be learnt from this absence?[6]

TALKING ABOUT CRIME AND CRIMINALS; NOT TALKING ABOUT GENOCIDE: CONSTITUTING THE LATE MODERN SUBJECT OF CRIMINOLOGY

Anyone who goes to the camps and hospitals along India's border with Pakistan comes away believing the Punjabi army capable of any atrocity. I have seen babies who have been shot, men who have had their backs whipped raw. I've seen people literally struck dumb by the horror of seeing their children murdered in front of them or their daughters dragged off into sexual slavery. I have no doubt at all that there have been a hundred "My Lays" [sic] and "Lidices" in East Pakistan – and I think, there will be more.

My personal reaction is one of wonder more than anything else. I've seen too many bodies to be horrified by anything much any more. But I find myself standing still again and again, wondering how any man can work himself into such a murderous frenzy." (Tony Clifton, Newsweek, June 28, 1971)

Such were the words of a journalist covering the plight of the millions of refugees who had fled from the actions of the Pakistani army in what was then East Pakistan, now Bangladesh (the total was to reach ten million). In the nine months between March and December 1971 nearly three million Bengalis died as a result of army action or cholera. The accounts written by journalists and scholars from India and Bangladesh freely use the term "genocide," however, the events occurred in the midst of the Cold War, and the major powers, the United States, the Soviet Union, China, and India, backed either Pakistan or supported the independence movement. As a result the UN never debated fully whether the events constituted genocide, nor were there war-crimes trials. The "truth" of the events and their legacy is contested. What is not contested is that, along with the other events of the twentieth century that can be labeled genocide, criminology takes no interest in accounting for these actions, nor does it see fit to include explanations for group and individual actions as part of its array of theoretical resources.

Social theory begins with observing something that arouses the sense of wonder…why? The above journalist experienced an acute sense of wonder, wrote his reactions, and moved on to another assignment, another scene. But the theorist is meant to reflect, to engage systematically with the material and attempt to transcend it. Social theory constantly moves between what is clearly observable, the empirical scene, the "agency" of the actors, the "micro," and the overreaching context, which is unobserved, but which is believed to "structure" the events, the "macro."

What are the consequences for criminology of ignoring genocide? Or, to put it another way, what is normal criminology? Take a representative text, *Talking about Crime and Criminals*, a 1994 book by Don Gibbons, a well-established American professional with around forty years' involvement as a criminologist. Its subtitle is *Problems and Issues in Theory Development in Criminology*, and Gibbons clearly argued for general theories of crime and an inclusive criminology. However, Gibbons did not include the millions of people killed in twentieth-century genocide, nor the hundreds of thousands of woman raped in his "talking." Nor was Kelman and Hamilton's *Crimes of Obedience* (1989), a book written to account for the type of military behavior displayed in the My Lai massacre, a discussed text. As a consequence, Gibbons could argue "that the accumulated evidence on biological and sociological factors in lawbreaking must be taken seriously," and that we must "give considerably more attention to the part played by individual differences in psychological characteristics between those who violate the law and those who do not" (1994: 204). Thus we find those favorite tropes of individualism, differentiation and normalcy; the stability of modern life is taken for granted and crime is something committed by the "other." He did, however, find considerable space for Gottfredson and Hirschi's *A General Theory of Crime* (1990).

Gottfredson and Hirschi's *A General Theory of Crime* put forward what has proved to be the most influential American theory in criminology in the 1990s. Their text was a sophisticated attempt to create a general theory which overcame the unstable dualism between the legacies of classical criminology (legalist definitions) and positivism by controlling its own dependent variable. The authors were clear that criminological theory must be faithful to the data on crime; it must "organize the facts about crime, whether demographic, social or institutional (1990: 274). What constituted that data? It is no surprise that again there is no inclusion of the millions murdered, the hundreds of thousands raped, the vast amounts of property confiscated, the houses occupied, in the cause of genocide. Instead they find that "the vast majority of criminal acts are trivial and mundane affairs that result in little loss and less gain" (1990: 16). From that basis they argue that criminality has much in common with accidents and other forms of "deviant" behaviors (i.e., illicit drug-taking), and is a function of low rates of "self-control." This self, however, is an abstracted self. Nowhere do they face up to the European traditions of social theory that asserts that all "selves" (and their psychologies) need to be understood in terms of social, historical, and economic processes; nor the narratives of taking control of the situation, or "another" and "yourself" that hold out to "individuals" a way of asserting their identity and self-worth in conditions where they are anything but in "control" (see Morrison, 1995 for a sustained, if rather diffuse, critique along these lines); nor is the normalcy of the (mainly) American statistics ever questioned.

Criminology thus produces a discourse on crime that reduces the existential power and attractions of crime and treats crime as mundane by ignoring the great "crime." Perhaps this is not surprising, as many genocides have been partially airbrushed from history. Consider that committed on the Armenian people by the New Turks between 1915 and 1917.

Surprisingly, the actual events are well documented (the following account draws upon Libaridian 2000). The Turkish Ottoman Empire had contained many minorities, often suffering persecutions, but never faced threats of extermination. However, as the Empire declined, in 1913 the Turkish government fell into the hands of a militarist wing of the Young Turks movement, which took the Empire into World War I on the side of Germany. Sometime around 1915 the same group developed a plan for exterminating the Armenian population of around 2–3 million living in the mostly rural area of Western Armenia, part of the Ottoman Empire since the sixteenth century.

There were several phases to the genocide. First, in April 1915, core elements of the religious, political, educational and intellectual leadership of the Armenian people – around 1,000 persons – were taken into custody and killed in a few days. Second, the Armenian draftees of the Ottoman army, numbering over 200,000, were eliminated through mass burials, burnings, executions, and exhaustion in labor battalions.[7] Then the remainder of the population, now without those males most likely to have resisted, were given orders of deportation.

> The fate of the deportees was usually death. Caravans of women and children, ostensibly being led to southern parts of the Empire, became death marches. Within six months of the deportations half of the deportees were killed, buried alive, or thrown into the sea or the rivers. Few reached relatively safe cities....Most survivors ended up in the deserts of Northern Mesopotamia, where starvation, dehydration, and outright murder awaited them. Subsequent sweeps of cities ensured the elimination of the Armenian people from the western and largest portion of their historic homeland. (Libaridian 2000: 204)

The process was supervised by a secretive organization that functioned as part of the government. The methods involved the torture of thousands, gleeful killings, burning and looting, rape, and the abduction of children, all of which were recorded in the letters and diaries of Western missionaries, journalists, travelers, diplomats, and later, the narratives of survivors. These activities required the acquiescence of large numbers of Turkish and Kurdish civilians. But while the government passed laws making it a crime to offer assistance to the Armenians (punishable with death by hanging in front of one's house and the burning of the house), several governors and sub-governors refused to follow orders. In addition, "many Turks and Kurds, especially in the Dersim region, risked their lives to save straggling Armenians, and Arabs throughout the Empire's southern provinces accepted and helped the survivors." The overall result, however, was devastating.

> Of the 2 to 3 million Western Armenians, 1.5 million perished during the Holocaust. Up to 150,000 of those who had accepted Islam or had been kept, stolen, or protected by Turks and Kurds survived in Western Armenia without, however, any possibility of preserving a sense of religious or national identity. Close to 400,000 survived by reaching the southern or Arab provinces of the Ottoman Empire.
>
> In addition to the death of some 50 to 70 percent of Armenians living under Ottoman Turkish rule, Armenians lost the right to live as a community in the lands of their ancestors; they lost their personal property and belongings. They left behind the schools, churches, community centers, ancient fortresses, and medieval cathedrals, witnesses to a long history. Survivors were forced to begin a new life truncated, deprived of a link with their past, subject to upheavals in the new lands where they suddenly found themselves as foreigners. The remnants of the largely peasant and rural population were now a wretched group of squatters on the outskirts of cities poorly equipped to handle an increase in population. (Libaridian 2000: 206)

This successful genocide influenced Hitler, who once asked, "Who today remembers the Armenians?" We could repeat his words, for "the denial of the Armenian genocide is an official policy of the Turkish government, supported by considerable financial resources and the connivance of intellectuals and academics who cherish the attention of those in power" (Chalk and Jonassohn, 1990: 250). The denial continues. In October 2000, the US House of Representatives agreed to a request from President Clinton to withdraw a draft resolution that labeled the actions as genocide. President Clinton had said that passing the resolution could put American lives at risk and inflame tensions in the Middle East. The Turkish government, a NATO military ally of the US, had fiercely resisted the proposal warning that US military planes might be barred from Turkish airspace and that Turkey might pull out of a possible $4.5 billion defense deal with an American contractor (BBC News Online, 20 October 2000). Conversely, in November 2000 the upper house of the French parliament approved a bill recognizing that Ottoman Turkey carried out a "genocide" against Armenians in 1915. This vote succeeded, in spite of opposition from the French government, and Turkey called it a "merciless distortion of historical fact," while the Armenian Foreign Ministry called it a "triumph of morals and justice in politics" (ibid., 8 November 2000). Also in that month, the European parliament approved a resolution calling on Turkey to recognize publicly that the killings were genocide (ibid., 16 November 2000).

Does criminological silence in the face of genocide denote that criminology is a mere servant of state power? Perhaps this charge is too extreme. The question remains, however: "How in these times can the logos of criminology be constituted without acknowledgment of these phenomena?" First let us consider the structure of criminology and its relationship to the state.

Criminology has seen itself as an applied science of modernization, perhaps more precisely, of *rational* modernity. Bauman argues that there is a particular link between modernity and genocide. He defines modernity "as of a time when order – of the world, of the human habitat, of the human self, and of the connection between all three – is *reflected upon*; a matter of thought, of concern, of a practice that is aware of itself, conscious of being a conscious practice and wary of the void it would leave were it to halt or merely relent" (1991: 5.) Moreover, "existence is modern in as far as it is effected and sustained by design, manipulation, management, engineering. The existence is modern in as far as it is administered by resourceful (that is, possessing knowledge, skill and technology) sovereign agencies. Agencies are sovereign in as far as they claim and successfully defend the right to manage and administer existence: the right to define order and, by implication, lay aside chaos, as that left-over that escapes the definition." In seeking the "macro" foundations of the Holocaust, Bauman systematically traces the gardening ambitions of the early part of the twentieth century. He argues that particular ideas of breeding combined with medical and social engineering notions into a program of the taming of nature, of the systematic designing of the future. Bauman draws upon the range of work dealing with the practices and opinions of doctors, scientists and bureaucrats. He summarizes that they were guided by a "proper and uncontested understanding of the role and mission of science – and by the feeling of duty towards the vision of good society, a healthy society, and orderly society. In particular, they were guided by the hardly idiosyncratic, typically modern conviction that the road to such a society leads through the ultimate taming of the inherently chaotic natural forces and by systematic, and ruthless if need be, execution of a scientifically conceived, rational plan." The criminology of the Nazi era is explored by Wetzell (2000), who argues against any simple ideological correlation between the state of criminological ideas and the ideological needs of Nazi Germany. The aim of criminology has been to find knowledge(s) concerning crime, and hence of social control, to enable the state to regulate the conditions of its society in such a way that crime is minimized. In its clearest modernist form, i.e., positivist criminology, the assumption was that there were real, identifiable forces at work that created crime and constituted "criminality" (defined as a relatively stable propensity of individuals to engage in crime). By implication, knowledge of those real forces, constitutive factors, and pathologies helped create and legitimate a power to alleviate or eliminate crime. Either the criminogenic social conditions that caused crime could be controlled, or criminals were to be identified and neutralized by elimination (either through death or incarceration) or reformation.

Perhaps thankfully, reality has proved more difficult to grasp; criminology has not turned out to be a successful "applied science." Criminology was and is a hybrid discourse. Criminological histories are written in the tension between the epistemologies of legalism and the social sciences (in particular, sociology), between the competing ontologies of crime and deviance. Legality defines the crime; sociology offers the relativism of anthropology's understanding of deviance. If legality offered certainty, clarity, and logic, sociology opposed this with reflexivity, relativism and continual questioning. Criminology offered two, somewhat competing, species of trust. Trust in the tablets of law to demarcate the good and the evil, the allowed and the prohibited, the safe and the dangerous; or trust in the facts of the scientists to give us an understandable and practicable mirror of the natural state of things. If, in modernity, we no longer knelt before the altars of the theologians' practices, we secured ourselves to the realities of the world through (social) contracts and the logic of legal inferences or the interlocking texts of expert (scientific) knowledge. Only we never quite were at home. Neither law nor science offered that mixture of community and eschatological finality characterizing religious belief. Not being at home, we never totally knew our own being.

Criminology should have been seen as especially compromised, for what else was its basic subject matter – crime, criminals, and criminality, and its seemingly logical consequence, punishment (and/or treatment) – if not "moral phenomena"? And how can one agree on the description of such moral facts in modernity in the face of contingency (relativism) and existentialism?

Instead of such reflexivity, however, came the discipline of the criminological canon, and the assumption of criminology's status as an applied science; an applied science whose objects mirrored the functional contours of a developing modernity. If modernity was constituted upon the grounding of secularization, a critique of caste and a drive towards functionalism and technological development, criminology's critique of class came late and its assumption of functionalism early. Within modernity's overall logic, functionalism contributed to a rearranging and modernizing of traditional political patterns and programs; within criminology, functionalism offered the solace of proper arrangement, and it allowed one to deny that the "normal" was a product of the political, the arbitrary, and the contingent.

Epistemologically, the main tactic was to downplay any awareness that the "normal" world was shaped by power and contingency, which might have forced criminologists into existentialism, in favor of claims to map the world, to issue a logos which reflected the functionalism of an ordering now made social, but still "natural." Criminologists sought to map the social–natural world: the replication of those Lombrosian diagrams of the face, Sheldon's photographs of the body, the Chicago School's concentric maps of social ecology in text after text attest to this only too well. To what extent did all this activity amount to the deducing of a few "moral" "facts" (such as postulates of societal norms, obligations, solidarity, images of the normal, right, and the good) from suppositions and superimposing or refracting images not unsettling to "common sense" nor disturbing the rights of the nation-state?

The symbolic space criminology worked within was the constitution of a social order within the boundaries of the *nation-state*. Assuming the reality and legitimacy of that entity – the province of classical legalism – adherents of the tradition of positivist criminology sought to constitute that space "peacefully" through identifying fit companions and those to be contained, to be treated or neutralized (Roshier 1989). And this was to be achieved through the "objectivity" of scientific activity. But reflexively, we now understand that the ordering was political, not natural. To give an example: "The purpose of Italian criminal anthropology [lay]...in the attempt to construct an ordered language for the containment of disorder and, through that language, to formulate the definition of a political subject by elaborating ever more closely the criteria for political exclusion" (Pick 1989: 138–9). The center of that politics was usually assumed rather than held as a part of the material to be analyzed. Criminology worked within the parameters of an imaginative domain focused around the nation-state (even when being "critical"). And for all its "knowledge," its currently most popular manifestation appears as state-sponsored criminologies of control (Garland, 2001). Mainstream criminology has not taken on board the lessons of genocide: and those like Nils Christie (1993, 1994, 2000) or Stan Cohen (2001), who have tried to, sound strange with their message. A message which might be paraphrased as *"do not trust the state and be careful of narratives of control. You may end up defined as the problem and controlled out of existence."*

CONFRONTING GENOCIDE: ISSUES OF UNIQUENESS, GENERALITY, AND RELATIVISM

It should not be necessary to recount in great detail the genocidal horrors of the twentieth century. The names and realities – for example, those of Turkish Armenia; the ghettos, the death squads, and the concentration camps of the Jewish Holocaust; the massacres, the rapes, and the rivers with their bobbing corpses that saw the birth of Bangladesh; the auto-genocide by which the Pol Pot regime sought to return Cambodia to year zero; the rapes and ethnic cleansing of Serbs in Bosnia; the intensity of the killing in Rwanda – constitute that other reality of the modern era.

What is important to grasp is the breath and depth of the questions "Why?" and "What are the implications for our understanding of humanity?"[8] And also our reluctance to face them.

Even academically, to confront genocide is unsettling. Silence becomes understandable since language appears unable to do "justice" to the horror and terror of it (Steiner 1977). Consider the Jewish Holocaust; the best-known instance of a consciously planned total genocide.[9] Faced with the array of sanctioned massacres, industrial killing, mobile death squads, the widespread torture, the obvious enjoyment that many perpetrators take from it, the individual and collective despair of the victims, one is tempted to think of hell and believe these are evidence of a collective madness. Yet the rational coordination, the conferences dedicated to minimizing the psychological impact upon the perpetrators, and the involvement of bureaucracy deny us the relief of anthologizing and differentiating the perpetrators as something constituted other than our own normalcy. All attempts to provide interpretative grids of sense seem compromised. As Bartov expressed it:

> our main difficulty in confronting the Holocaust is due not only to the immense scale of the killing, nor even to the manner in which it was carried out, but also to the way in which it combined the most primitive human brutality, hatred and prejudice, with the most modern achievements in science, technology, organization, and administration. It is not the brutal SS man with his truncheon whom we cannot comprehend; we have seen his likes throughout history. It is the commander of a killing squad with a Ph.D. in law from a distinguished university in charge of organizing mass shootings of naked women and children whose figure frightens us. It is not the disease and famine in the ghettos, reminiscent perhaps of ancient sieges, but the systematic transportation, selection, dispossession, killing, and distribution

of requisitioned personal effects that leaves us uncomprehending, not for the facts but their implications for our own society and for human psychology. Not only the "scientific" killing and its bureaucratic administration; not only the sadism; but rather the incredible mixture of detachment and brutality, distance and cruelty, pleasure and indifference." (1996: 67)

For Steiner, the Holocaust shows the contingency of civilization:

The cry of the murdered sounded in the earshot of the universities; the sadism went on a street away from the theatres and museums...the high places of literacy, of philosophy, of artistic expression, became the setting for Belsen....We know now that a man can read Goethe or Rilke in the evening, that he can play Bach and Schubert, and go to his day's work at Auschwitz in the morning. (1977: preface)

Does Auschwitz offer the extreme relativism? It seemed so to one survivor.

Concentration camp existence...taught us that the whole world is really like a concentration camp. The weak work for the strong, and if they have no strength or will to work – then let them steal, or let them die .... There is no crime that a man will not commit in order to save himself. And, having saved himself, he will commit crimes for increasingly trivial reasons; he will commit them first out of duty, then from habit, and finally – for pleasure .... The world is ruled by neither justice nor morality; crime is not punished nor virtue rewarded, one is forgotten as quickly as the other. The world is ruled by power. (T. Borowski, quoted in Friedrich 1994: 29)

Yet another was not so sure:

The evidence of Auschwitz has demonstrated many things about humanity. It has demonstrated that men (and women too) are capable of committing every evil the mind can conceive, that there is no natural or unwritten law that says of any atrocity whatever: This shall not be done. It has demonstrated that men can also bear and accept every evil, and that they will do so in order to survive. To survive, even just from one day to the next, they will kill and let kill, they will rob and betray their friends, steal food rations from the dying, inform on neighbors, do anything at all, just for one more day. The evidence of Auschwitz has demonstrated just as conclusively that men will sacrifice themselves for others, sometimes quite selflessly...The evidence has demonstrated, moreover, that those who share a commitment to some political or spiritual purpose, are at least as likely to survive as those who make survival their only goal. The evidence, in other words, is as contradictory as human nature itself. (Friedrich 1994: 101–2)

And yet many feel that it must be brought under rational comprehension, for example:

To understand genocides as a class of calculated crimes, such crimes must be appreciated as goal-directed acts from the point of view of the perpetrators: genocide is rationally instrumental to their ends, although psychopathic in terms of any universalistic ethic .... Modern premeditated genocide is a rational function of the choice by a ruling elite of a myth or "political formula" (as Mosca put it) legitimizing the existence of the state as the vehicle for the destiny of the dominant group whose members share an underlying likeness from which the victim is excluded by definition. (Fein 1979: 8)

But bringing genocide into a coherent modern disciplinary logos problematizes the notion of modernity itself. For if genocide is evil,[10] does the prevalence of genocide in modernity denote that aspects of modernity create the conditions for even greater evil then the pre-modern, or is it an aberration, is genocide the survival of the pre-modern in modernity?

GENOCIDE, THE (IN)COMPREHENSIBILITY OF EVIL, AND ITS REPETITION IN MODERNITY

In the twentieth century, we find genocide to be horrifying, morally unjust, and criminal, yet we go on committing it. For us the formula goes something like this: It never happened, and besides, *they* deserved it. Prior to the sixteenth century, when the Spanish in America began to have doubts about killing men whose souls they claimed they wanted to save, the formula would have read: *We* did it, and *they* deserved it. Even so responsibility would still be assigned to a god or, better yet, the victim. But with us, as genocide has become more repugnant, as it has come to seem unthinkable, it has actually become commonplace. Contemporary man deals in bad faith as well as death. (Smith 2000: 29)

The horror of the Holocaust is not that it deviated from human norms; the horror is that it didn't. (Bauer 2001: 42)

There are two master narratives for confronting modern genocide. Both agree that genocide is an embodiment of evil. The first asserts that modernity is a progressive unfolding of liberty, reason, and progress, in which examples of genocide, such as the Holocaust, are isolated outbreaks, perversions of modernity with little wider lessons. Each genocidal activity is thus considered a product of its own particularity, owned by the group who suffered and the perpetrators. The second asserts that modernity is a radically fractured and unbalanced program in which genocide is an inherent possibility; thus genocidal activities represent forms and features of the modernizing process, albeit at odds with others. Consider explanations of the Holocaust. The first narrative is actually comforting, it enables us to think of the Holocaust as not only a unique historical horror but as something truly other to our modern existence, something of which we need not concern ourselves. It was common after World War II to thus label the Holocaust as the work of a select few, inspired by Hitler's personal charisma and carried out by the social deviants of the SS. The research task was then to identify the characteristics and functioning of the perpetrators, assuming that their norms and personalities were somehow pathological. But the second narrative points out the vast role of those "ordinary" people, the doctors, the scientists, and the bureaucrats, who could kill in the name of a sane and rational employment, albeit speaking a language that disguised the nature of the task. Could the perpetrators be just like us? Were they ordinary men, or ordinary Germans (trapped in a particular historical circumstance)?

ORDINARY MEN OR ORDINARY GERMANS? SHOULD THIS BE A CENTRAL QUESTION FOR CRIMINOLOGY?

Genocide involves killing on an industrial scale. But it is achieved by aggregates of individual behavior. Consider the Holocaust.

> In mid-March 1942 some 75 to 80 percent of all victims of the Holocaust were still alive, while 20 to 25 percent had perished. A mere eleven months later, in mid-February 1943, the percentages were exactly the reverse. At the core of the Holocaust was a short, intense wave of mass murder. The center of gravity of this mass murder was Poland.... In short, the German attack on the Jews of Poland was not a gradual or incremental program stretched over a long period of time, but a veritable blitzkrieg, a massive offensive requiring the mobilization of large number of shock troops.... If the German offensive of 1942 [against the Soviet Union] was ultimately a failure, the blitzkrieg against the Jews, especially in Poland, was not.... How had the Germans organized and carried out the destruction of this widespread Jewish population? And where had they found the manpower during this pivotal year of the war for such an astounding logistical achievement in mass murder? (Browning 1998: xv–xvi)

In seeking answers Browning researched the conduct of Reserve Police Battalion 101, a group of "middle-aged reserve policemen" who became immersed in the very non-industrial killing involving physically rounding up thousands of Jewish men, women, and children and shooting them or herding them into transports to the death camps. In the period July 1942 to November 1943 the men of this Battalion, numbering at the most 500, rounded up and shot at least 38,000 defenseless Jewish men, women and children and deported at least 45,200 to death camps. Browning gives us a narrative of contingency and existential choice. In the early hours of July 13, 1942 the men were roused from their bunks and assembled before their commanding officer, Major Trapp, a 53-year-old career policeman.

> Pale and nervous, with choking voice and tears in his eyes, Trapp visibly fought to control himself as he spoke. The battalion he said plaintively, had to perform a frightfully unpleasant task. The assignment was not to his liking, indeed it was highly regrettable, but the orders came from the highest authorities. If it would make their task any easier, the men should remember that in Germany the bombs were falling on women and children.
>   He then turned to the matter at hand. The Jews had instigated the American boycott that had damaged Germany, one Policeman remembered Trapp saying. There were Jews in the village of Jozefow who were involved with the partisans, he explained according to two others. The battalion had now been ordered to round up those Jews. The male Jews of working age were to be separated and taken to a work camp. The remaining Jews – the women, children, and elderly – were to be shot on the spot by the battalion. Having explained what awaited his men, Trapp then made an extraordinary offer: if any of the older men among them did not feel up to the task that lay before him, he could step out." (Browning 1998: 2)

Significantly, a few men stepped out. Although there was adverse peer-group pressure, it was possible to avoid the action. But the majority did not choose to avoid the task. And among the majority who participated some clearly grew to enjoy the job, for this was only to be the first of many similar actions. And, once engaged in genocide the individuals found themselves existentially immersed in the physical task of killing, a task that splattered blood and sometimes human brains on uniforms that had to be cleaned, hands that had to be washed, minds that had to accept the scenes as necessary. But some came to find their calling in killing. Browning also tells us of the "Jew hunt," the search and seeking-out operations to locate small pockets of Jews or individual Jews who had somehow escaped from the sweeping operations. This was a previously neglected part of understanding the operation of the "Final Solution." "The Jew hunt was not a brief episode. It was a tenacious, ongoing campaign in which the "hunters" tracked down and killed their "prey" in direct and personal confrontation. It was not a passing phase but an existential condition of constant readiness and intention to kill every last Jew who could be found."(Browning 1998: 132)

Browning gives us a picture of the devastating potential of humanity. Using later work such as the psychologist Stanley Milgram's behavioral experiments – the famous Stanford experiments conducted in the 1970s – Browning suggests that under similar circumstances everybody has the potential to be a mass murderer. While Browning's text was read primarily by a narrow range of scholars, the same material was addressed by Daniel Goldhagen in a bestselling text entitled *Hitler's Willing Executioners* (1996). While savaged by most scholarly critics, Goldhagen's text was a huge public and commercial success and created a substantial debate both as to the nature of his claims and the politics of Holocaust scholarship. Goldhagen traced the main motivation for the Holocaust to German antisemitism and the unique force of German hatred of Jews, the cultural roots of which he claimed stretched back to Martin Luther. Goldhagen's text was also accompanied by quite explicit details of killings and many photographs – photographs which demonstrated the lack of distance between victim and killer as well as appearing to some critics to almost present a pornography of genocide. Conversely, Goldhagen's thesis is the less threatening; for there the genocide is a *German* problem, a matter of a specific historical situation and has few lessons for the rest of us; whereas for Browning *humanity* as such contains the potential.[11] If the Reserve Police Battalion was staffed by ordinary men, men who operated within a "murderous consensus" (a term borrowed from Bauer 2001: 83) as to the position of Jews created within a discourse of crime and control (both the Jews and the gypsies were portrayed by the Nazis as hereditary asocial criminals), then the criminological impact is clear. Do not trust the state or state-sponsored "science" to give you images of the dangerous "other," of crime and criminality and the global threat. Do not be ready to allow the state to readily mobilize its police to control the dangerous other: instead subject any and all such claims to critical analysis.

Addressing the Contemporary Problem of Criminology, Widening the Scope of the Terrain and Understanding "a New Experience of Crime"

In a text published in 2001 and which appeared to capture the mood of the times, *The Culture of Control: Crime and Social Order in Contemporary Society*, David Garland, a Scottish criminologist resident in New York, presented a picture of criminology – at least officially recognized criminology – as increasingly dominated by a "new iron cage" of coercive penal rationality. "Instead of addressing the difficult problem of social solidarity in a diverse, individuated world, our political leaders have preferred to rely upon the certainties of a simpler, more coercive, Hobbesian solution" (2001: 202). Garland's wide-ranging analysis was in large part constructed on his interpretation of the literature on everyday life in the USA and Britain and the "new experience of crime" therein. Garland's text was strangely both situated and unsituated. For although he was clear he referred to the "culture of crime control and criminal justice in Britain and America," his analysis was also of an unspecific "modern society," "contemporary society," "modernity," and "high crime societies." Thus this "history of the present" slipped into universality, whilst apparently making no claims to compare or speak about any locations other than the USA and Britain, nor to offer any analysis as to the global underpinnings of the everyday of those locations.

Throughout the 1990s New York assumed a highly symbolic position in debates within criminology and crime prevention. The city became a symbol of the fight against crime, the battle to prevent those visions of urban life inherent in the 1980s film *Blade Runner*, from becoming a reality of everyday life. New York, it was said, was the place where the almost-accepted-as-inevitable increase in crime was reversed as a result of zero tolerance and changes in policing strategies. New York had taken seriously the twin (and often contradictory) messages of the criminology of everyday life – rational calculation and opportunity theory *plus* targeting antisocial elements and not tolerating underclass behavior. The crime-control message of New York was transported around the Western world: it was a one-way process.

On September 11, 2001 two hijacked commercial airliners were deliberately flown into the twin towers of the World Trade Center, New York's highest buildings and symbol of its central role in the globalized economy, which collapsed with over 3,000 deaths. It was no longer possible to deny that everyday life had become global.

The events of September 11 profoundly shocked the American people and others worldwide. In a very postmodern fashion the events were shown live on TV and the Internet, throughout the world. They showed, all too clearly, that the routines of everyday life, the assumptions as to what normal security and trust were dependent upon, were only partial. Similarly, Garland's highly sophisticated "history of the present" was only a narrative of partial experiences of crime. His account of the path that criminology has taken to reach a state-sponsored *culture of control* downplayed the existence of a (admittedly less influential) critical tradition and concentrated upon that criminological discourse which found its data in the decisions made "within the institutions of the criminal justice state" (to transfer part of a sentence from Garland and Sparks, 2000: 19).

Toward a More Integrated Criminology for the Twenty-First Century?

The Norwegian Criminologist Nils Christie once wrote that criminology should offer a mirror to society. This essay has argued that it has clearly failed in that task, or at least offered only a phantom mirror. A mirror which neglected the genocidal reality of the twentieth century. Criminology has denied its companion. We have thus only a partial heritage and all theories presented to us need to be interpreted and understood in that light. Including genocide within the data to be analyzed changes our understanding of the "progress" of modernity, of the normality of crime and policing. It is perhaps to look in on the lower deck.

Yet those who have spent their adult life in trying to come to grips with genocide tell us there is both a depressing and an uplifting message in actually confronting genocide. The depressing message lies in the seemingly endless varieties of inhuman barbarisms that humans are willing to inflict upon other human beings; the uplifting message is for all the genocide, all the death, humanity, as such and as a moral project has not been destroyed by genocide (Bauer 2001).

What would a criminology look like that placed genocide within its arena of study? *How would talking about crime and criminals change?* There is not space here to attempt such a project. However, confronting genocide as part of the criminological enterprise would broaden the continuum of data and problems that would need to be analyzed. It would also mean that much of what is currently accepted as accounts of crime would be seen as extremely limited and localized discourse. How would *The General Theory of Crime* fare? Low rates of self-control, established by specific forms of childrearing practices, cannot explain the behavior of the perpetuators in the variety of situations where genocide has occurred.[12] But criminology would also be enriched and its problematics better positioned. For example, many of the themes in Jock Young's *The Exclusive Society* (1999) have a direct parallel in the literature on trying to understand genocidal situations; an altered text would have different boundaries, more complex layers of exclusion and injustice. Conversely genocide studies may have things to gain. To the criminological eye, the diversity of definitions of genocide within the sociological literature in genocide studies appears a reversion to the classical debates as to the nature of crime. A theory of genocide that incorporated the perpetuator's perspective might also be attempted; at least some strands in criminology have attempted to flesh out a more appreciative tradition.[13] Genocide studies may need to do likewise to get more rounded accounts.

If this were attempted, criminology would have to rewrite its history: it has existed in a truncated institutional imagination, a continual state of denial of subject. Because modernity meant to so many in the West, a grand transformation in terms of progress, wealth and technological power, of "civilization," it seemed as if genocide had to be kept away from the mainstream disciplines, such as philosophy, sociology, and criminology. Located in particular sections of history or German, or Cambodian, or Armenian studies, or more recently small centers of genocide studies, genocide becomes a series of individual plots, in which specific and locatable factors led to the specific configurations and where identifiable individuals can be identified and related as perpetrators. This partook in the myth of modernity's justice wherein modernity was seen as an increasingly coherent place of social order and where crime induced punishment and doing justice. To paraphrase Bartov, the myth allows us to believe that balance is possible: that the perpetrators can be located and destroyed in the justice of the "happy" ending. Thus the world is rendered safe, predictable, unthreatening. But genocide is far more complicated and complicating; its stories often have no clear beginnings, no casual personages, little clarity, and no resolution. But with genocide the story continues; the plot seems never resolved. "The world we inhabit is the same world that produced (and keeps producing) genocide" (Bartov 1996: 53). And the suspicion remains: perhaps criminology, that largely faithful servant of modernity's power, clothed its companion – genocide – with silence so that the state need not lose its hegemony. Criminology's knowledge truly was formed in the dialectic between those who accepted the subject/data produced by the state's criminal justice processes and those who wish to critique that. The dance, however, was constrained by the location of its beginnings: the terrain of the nation-state. That terrain is now intellectually wholly unsustainable, even if that Leviathan has not yet lost his dazzling clothes – nor should we forget that its power may be most dangerous as it retreats from its zenith. But then, perhaps amidst an often gloomy postmodernity, putting the task of understanding genocide into the mainstream might provide some ways into a proper understanding of criminology and the challenges of our times.

Notes

1   I will not in this essay recount the arguments and history concerning the term "genocide." It must be noted that there is considerable debate as to the benefits, scholarly or practical, in adopting any particular definition: a situation that closely parallels the debates as to the nature of "crime" in criminology. The legal definition was adopted by a United Nations Convention on Genocide approved on December 9, 1948: "In the present Convention, genocide means any of the following acts committed with intent to destroy, in whole or in part, a national, ethnical or religious group, as such: (a) Killing members of the group; (b) Causing serious bodily or mental harm to members of the group; (c) Deliberately inflicting on the group conditions of life calculated to bring about its physical destruction in whole or in part; (d) Imposing measures intended to prevent births within the group." That definition loosely followed the formulation offered by Raphael Lemkin (1944), when working in the US State Department during World War II to cope with what he saw as a new form of war, a war waged not on a nation but on "peoples." There are significant differences, however: in particular, while Lemkin understood genocide as a "crime" that destroyed the cultural potential of groups, the UN definition does not incorporate this more complex notion of the destruction of the contribution to the world of groups.

2 Some writing on the Holocaust and modernity, in particular Bauman's (*Modernity and the Holocaust*, 1989) thesis, has been picked up by the Norwegian Nils Christie (1993; 2nd ed. 1994; 3rd ed. 2000) in his *Crime Control as Industry: Towards Gulags, Western Style?*, which specifically, and rather uncritically, adopts the Bauman thesis and draws parallels with the development of a late modern industrial complex of prisons or "correctional facilities." Christie's readiness to use Holocaust references is unusual and dates from his Master's thesis for which he interviewed Norwegian concentration-camp guards. Colin Sumner, editor of the present volume, having outlined a criminological agenda to transcend the confines of the nation-state (Sumner 1982), published *Violence, Culture and Censure* in 1997, explicitly in commemoration of the Holocaust, with two essays on the subject by David Craig and Tony Amatrudo. The November 1997 and 1998 American Society of Criminology (ASC) meetings saw a budding interest in genocide. George Yacoubian presented a subject search of criminological journals and ASC papers to illustrate the virtual absence of any work on genocide. The University of Memphis has established a Genocide Studies center jointly between the Departments of Political Science and Criminal Justice, with the idea of applying criminological perspective to the subject. At the time of writing they have established an information resource on the Internet and have begun some projects, but the center is in its infancy. Alex Alvarez has recently completed the first book-length study self-consciously written from the standpoint of a criminologist: *Governments, Citizens, and Genocide* (2001). The Holocaust has been a clear determinant of the work of Stanley Cohen, in particular *States of Denial* (2001). But at the American Criminological Conference in November 2000, a conference with over 1,800 delegates, a round-table discussion on progressing the acknowledgment of genocide in criminology drew an audience of three (myself included). The 2001 conference had an audience of six to the session on genocide, which I take it would draw the response from a "positivist" analysis of a 100 percent increase in appeal!

3 Smith (2000: 21) describes the twentieth century as "an age of politically sanctioned mass murder, of collective, premeditated death intended to serve the ends of the state. It is an age of genocide in which . . . men, women and children . . . have had their lives taken because the state thought this desirable."

4 Rudolph Runnel, in *Democide* (1992) and *Death by Government* (1995), estimates that between 1900 and 1987 close to 170 million civilians (and disarmed prisoners of war) were killed by governments and quasi-governmental organizations (political parties, paramilitary groups); the vast majority were killed by non-democratic regimes. He defines this as "democide" (the killing of peoples), while he places 38 million of them as victims of "genocide" (using the definition within the UN Convention) of whom nearly 6 million were the Jewish victims of the Holocaust.

5 One can take virtually all texts and ask how general claims can be made as to the nature of crime in them if genocidal massacres are excluded as material for analysis. Many well-known works in criminology, such as Wilson and Herrnstein's *Crime and Human Nature* (1985), actually present a relatively narrow image of criminal activity.

6 This is not to say that this is not a novel question. "In the light of this record [of genocide in the twentieth century], one is prompted to wonder as to why the historical recurrence of a social phenomenon failed to register as a critical social problem, particularly among social thinkers and social scientists" (Vahakn 1995: 201). Bauman wrote *Modernity and the Holocaust* (1989) in the hope that it would move into the mainstream of sociology. But it remains an outside question, not part of the canon.

7 Vahakn describes how the military mobilization of Armenian males in 1915 meant
   that the most "threatening" portion of the Armenian population was concentrated
   and culled before the wider genocide was implemented.

> Though [the] mobilization had many other objectives, it served a major purpose for the swift
> execution of the plan of genocide. By removing all able-bodied Armenian males from their
> cities, villages, hamlets, and by isolating them in conditions in which they virtually became
> trapped, the Armenian community was reduced to a condition of near-total helplessness,
> thus an easy prey for destruction. It was a masterful stroke as it attained with one blow the
> three objectives of the operation of trapping the victim population: a) dislocation through
> forcible removal; b) isolation; c) concentration for easy targeting. (1995: 226)

8 As Smith puts it:

> If one starts from the present, one asks what weakens and erodes the moral constraints
> against genocide. If, on the other hand, one starts with the ancients, one has to ask how
> these restraints came about in the first place and when, and subsequently consider why
> they have not been more effective. If we just assume that such moral inhibitions have
> always existed, we distort the history of both genocide and society. (2000: 39)

Emmanuel Lévinas asks a related question:

> It is extremely important to know if society in the current sense of the term is the result of a
> limitation of the principle that men are predators of one another, or if to the contrary it
> results from the limitation of the principle that men are *for* one another. Does the social,
> with its institutions, universal forms and laws, result from limiting the consequences of the
> war between men, or from limiting the infinity which opens in the ethical relationship of
> man to man? (1985: 80)

9 I would accept Yehuda Bauer's argument (2001) that the Nazi plans for the Jews
   constituted the only known instance of a consciously planned annihilation of a race
   and therefore can be placed at the extreme – Holocaust – of the genocidal continuum.
10 As is widely accepted, e.g., Staub (1989).
11 Browning may somewhat underestimate the role of racial ideology which was
   central to the Holocaust. Racial ideology, however, has played a crucial role in
   most of the genocides of the twentieth century, an ideology that saw racial and
   ethnic plurality as a threat to state building.
12 Goldhagen (1996) begins his account of Reserve Police Battalion 101 with an
   occasion where one of the officers wrote a letter to higher authority refusing to
   carry out an order to get every man to sign a declaration that they would not loot or
   destroy Polish property. Such an order, he stated, was an affront and insult to the
   discipline and honor of the men, who could be trusted not to do such things.
13 Pace Matza (1969); as examples see Katz (1988); Morrison (1995); Hayward
   (2002); Presdee (2000); and the emerging field of "cultural criminology" generally.

References

Alvarez, A. (2001) *Governments, Citizens, and Genocide: A Comparative and Interdis-
ciplinary Approach*. Bloomington: Indiana University Press.
Bartov, O. (1996) *Murder in Our Midst: The Holocaust, Industrial Killing, and Repre-
sentation*. Oxford: Oxford University Press.
Bauer, Y. (2001) *Rethinking the Holocaust*. New Haven, CT: Yale University Press.
Bauman, Z. (1989) *Modernity and the Holocaust*. Cambridge: Polity.

Bauman, Z. (1991) *Modernity and Ambivalence*. Cambridge: Polity.

BBC News Online (2000) www.bbc.news.com

Browning, C. (1998 [1992]) *Ordinary Men: Reserve Police Battalion and the Final Solution in Poland*. New York: Harper Perennial.

Chalk, F., and Jonassohn, K. 1990 *The History and Sociology of Genocide: Analysis and Case Studies*. New Haven, CT: Yale University Press.

Christie, N. (1993, 2nd ed. 1994, 3rd ed. 2000) *Crime Control as Industry: Towards Gulags, Western Style?* London: Routledge.

Cohen, S. (2001) *States of Denial: Knowing About Atrocities and Suffering*. Cambridge: Polity.

Fein, H. (1979) *Accounting for Genocide*. New York: The Free Press.

Friedrich, O. (1994) *The Kingdom of Auschwitz*. Harmondsworth: Penguin.

Garland, D. (2001) *The Culture of Control: Crime and Social Order in Contemporary Society*. Oxford: Oxford University Press.

Garland, D., and Sparks, R. (2000) Criminology, social theory and the challenge of our times. In D. Garland and R. Sparks (eds.), *Criminology and Social Theory*. Oxford: Oxford University Press, 1–22.

Gibbons, D. (1994) *Talking About Crime and Criminals: Problems and Issues in Theory Development in Criminology*. Englewood Cliffs, NJ: Prentice Hall.

Goldhagen, D. (1996) *Hitler's Willing Executioners: Ordinary Germans and the Holocaust*. London: Little, Brown.

Gottfredson, M., and Hirschi, T. (1990) *A General Theory of Crime*. Stanford: Stanford University Press.

Hayward, K. (2002) Crime and the Urban Experience. Ph.D. thesis, University of East London.

Katz, J. (1988) *Seductions of Crime: Moral and Sensual Attractions in Doing Evil*. New York: Basic Books.

Kelman, H., and Hamilton, V. (1989) *Crimes of Obedience*. New Haven, CT: Yale University Press.

Lemkin, R. (1944) *Axis Rule in Occupied Europe*. Washington, DC: Carnegie Endowment for International Peace.

Levi, P. (1986) *The Drowned and the Saved* (trans. Raymond Rosenthal). New York: Summit Books.

Lévinas, E. (1985) *Ethics and Infinity: Conversations with Philippe Nemo* (trans. Richard A. Cohen). Pittsburgh: Duquesne University Press.

Libaridian, G. (2000) The ultimate repression: The genocide of the Armenians, 1915–1917. In I. Wallimann and M. Dobkowski (eds.), *Genocide and the Modern Age*. Syracuse: Syracuse University Press, 203–36.

Matza, D. 1969 *Becoming Deviant*. Englewood Cliffs, NJ: Prentice Hall.

Morrison, W. 1995 *Theoretical Criminology: From Modernity to Post-Modernism*. London: Cavendish.

Newsweek (1971) Tony Clifton, *The Terrible Blood Bath of Tikka Khan*, June 28.

Pick, D. (1989) *Faces of Degeneration: A European Disorder, c.1848–c.1918*. Cambridge: Cambridge University Press.

Presdee, M. (2000) *Cultural Criminology and the Carnival of Crime*. London: Routledge.

Roshier, B. (1989) *Controlling Crime: The Classical Perspective in Criminology*. Milton Keynes: Open University Press.

Runnel, R. (1992) *Democide*. New Brunswick, NJ: Transaction.

Runnel, R. (1995) *Death by Government*. New Brunswick, NJ: Transaction.

Smith, R. (2000) Human destructiveness and politics: The twentieth century as an age of genocide. In I. Wallimann and M. Dobkowski (eds.), *Genocide and the Modern Age*. Syracuse: Syracuse University Press, 21–42.

Staub, E. (1989) *The Roots of Evil: The Origins of Genocide and Other Group Violence*. Cambridge: Cambridge University Press.

Steiner, G. (1977) *Language and Silence: Essays in Language, Literature and the Inhuman*. New York: Atheneum.

Sumner, C. S. (ed.) (1982) *Crime, Justice and Underdevelopment*. London: Heinemann.

Sumner, C. S. (ed.) (1997) *Violence, Culture and Censure*. London: Taylor & Francis.

Vahakn, D. (1995) *The History of the Armenian Genocide: Ethnic Conflict from the Balkans to Anatolia to the Caucasus*. Providence, RI: Berghahn Books.

Wetzell, R. (2000) *Inventing the Criminal: A History of German Criminology 1880–1945*. Chapel Hill: University of North Carolina Press.

Wilson, J. Q., and Herrnstein, R. (1985) *Crime and Human Nature*. New York: Simon & Schuster.

Young, J. (1999) *The Exclusive Society*. London: Sage.

Part II
Juvenile Delinquency and Justice for Youth

5

The Criminologists' Gang

Jack Katz and Curtis Jackson-Jacobs

Criminologists of the gang struggle with what may be the most frustrating of all challenges in crime research. When they look to standard sources of data on crime and criminals, what they find is disappointing. The police, who generate data on a variety of crimes as a by-product of their working routines, do not help much in this case. They use legislative categories that define crimes when making arrests and processing complaints, but, despite the proliferation of references to "street gangs" in US criminal statutes, police commonly use traditional categories like robbery and assault when filing charges against perceived gang members. With regard to gang crimes, the police fail to perform their usual role as unwitting assistants to social researchers.

What police agencies wittingly record about gangs and their crimes is no less problematic when treated as data for social research. Many develop departmental ways of keeping counts of gangs and gang members, but not all do. Those that do keep counts use inconsistent criteria (Maxson and Klein 1996). Those that use the same criteria apply them without discrimination to diverse ethnic groups in which gangs have radically different meanings (compare Chin 1996 with Horowitz 1983). Within any given jurisdiction, police descriptions may vary radically over time for institutional reasons independent of changes in street realities (Meehan 2000; Katz 2003).

Victim reports, another standard source of data on crime, are not likely to be systematically helpful for tracing gang activity. Reports made by victims who themselves are outside of gang life are dubious sources for attributing assailants' gang identities. With respect to insiders' reports, we have reason to suspect that such data will be unreliable if not downright delusional. Self-reports have been obtained neither through censuses nor random population surveys but through questionnaires administered primarily to adolescent school populations. If to any significant extent gang life means operating outside of or resisting conventional obligations, self-reports on gang membership obtained from school students are of questionable value.

In part because of problems in acquiring data, criminologists have not settled on a definition of gangs nor on standards for grounding analyses in data. A currently hot debate is over whether gangs have become instrumental and entrepreneurial, as opposed to the older view of gangs as expressive and turf-defending. The controversy may be an artifact of different samples of what are very diverse phenomena: those who see expressive street gangs and those who see entrepreneurial drug gangs may not be looking at the same thing. Gang researchers either follow idiosyncratic procedures when describing the evidentiary bases for their analysis or, as a simpler solution, make elaborate assertions without presenting data (see, e.g., Sanchez-Jankowski 1991).

At the individual level, being in a gang is hardly a clear-cut fact. Few gangs have formal payrolls, and even when they produce something like membership and accounting books, they do not read like standard ledgers (see, e.g., Venkatesh and Levitt 2000). The problem is not just that the researcher is an outsider. Gang membership is unclear to insiders as well. Fleisher, who studied the "Fremont Hustlers" of Kansas City, comments: "'Member', 'membership,' 'join,' and 'gang' are static notions which fit neither the natural flow of Fremont social life nor the perceptions of Fremont kids" (1998: 39).

To emphasize the point, one might say that gangs only exist to the extent that their existence is problematic. Gang life is a matter of struggling over issues of inclusion and exclusion, and about giving meaning to the obligations of membership. Everyday gang life is a matter of imaginatively incorporating past events within a gang's history, both by keeping alive the sense of continuous collective identity and by interpreting the actions of individuals as gang actions. The personal meaning of being in a gang is defined in situationally emergent actions that recognize and elaborate gang affiliation as penetrating, shaping, and disrupting school, work, intimate, and intergenerational family relationships.

We know that proving whether one is in the gang or not is often a motivating factor in such characteristic forms of gang violence as drive-by shootings (Sanders 1994). Much of the everyday reality of gang life consists of claiming gang membership and responding to coded demands to identify where one is "from" (Garot 2002). Leaving the gang is alternately reported by long-term observers of gangs as common, unproblematic, and the subject of myth (Klein 1995), and by self-defined gang members as "impossible" (Decker and Winkle 1996).

Some of the best gang studies have found that mythmaking is one of the central activities of males involved in gangs (Horowitz 1983; cf. Decker et al. 2001: 78–9). The central myth is that the gang exists. In many settings, gang life consists of recounting history-making events, celebrating resonant symbols, and posturing defiance against morally hostile forces. Fervent rituals professing commitments may be necessary because of the lack of any independent, objective reality of the gang. That the same paradox haunts and inspires religion – rituals of faith are necessarily specifically because of a lack of objective evidence for what is promised – indicates the need for some imaginative methodological thinking for gang criminology.

If measurements of gang life are untrustworthy when taken from a distance, they are vulnerable to powerful reactivity when they are attempted close up. Indeed, one of the most enduring findings in the history of gang research is that social interventions, of which close-up social research is a significant form, promote gang cohesion (Klein 1971). By conferring significance specifically on "gang" activity, social research activity inadvertently promotes the youth interaction that is then described as evidence of gang existence. When the police report that gangs are out there, one should not be too sure they are. And when researchers searching for gangs find that gangs cooperate in making an appearance, there is no less cause for suspicion and a new basis for ethical self-reflection.

Despite the challenges of studying gangs, American criminology has now been engaged in the effort since the 1920s and shows no sign of retiring. The response to the weaknesses of data has been investigative resolution: the special research challenges in studying gangs are grounds for funding ever-new inquiries. But while admitting weakness in the literature makes perfect sense in grant applications, there is one central problem that has not been acknowledged: we never have had a good basis for thinking that gangs cause crime.

Without the presumptive belief that gangs cause crime, gang research, at least the specialized field of gang criminology as it has developed, makes little sense. The idea that gangs cause crime at first seems obvious. After all, just about every time we see them, we see gangs because they have been doing crime. But on examination the causal proposition becomes highly suspect.

Consider the implications of the message, told both by police sources and by well-seasoned gang researchers who have devoted careful effort to the question, that gangs have been proliferating in number and growing rapidly in membership in the United States since the early 1980s. In 1983, US local police departments reported about 2,200 gangs; in 1997, over 30,000 (Curry and Decker 2003: 28). This pattern helped make sense of the rapidly rising rates of US youth violence rates in the 1980s. But the image of geometrically increasing gang life does not jibe with the sharp declines in criminal violence that came in the 1990s (Blumstein and Wallman 2000). Moreover, the dramatic rises and falls in urban crime rates since the 1980s have been essentially the same in cities with and without celebrated gang problems (Katz 2003).

Perhaps gangs recently have become more prudent in their use of force, more utilitarian, less wild. Perhaps, if we let theoretical imagination run freely, we can believe that the increase in gang membership has been perfectly mated with a transformation of gang violence toward greater control, resulting in similar violence rates for gang and non-gang cities. But if so, then gangs can impact crime rates either by increasing or decreasing criminal violence, depending on something important other than the gang itself.

The contingencies for positive or negative effects should be at the forefront of gang research. Whether there is any systematic relationship between gang life and rates of criminal violence should be a central issue in the field. But these questions are not resolved; they are barely even raised.

We suggest that the best way to understand the criminology of the gang is by appreciating that the field is structured on a quiet agreement not to press the causal question. Not focusing on that question is essential for sustaining the myth of gangs as a transcendent evil, a force responsible for social harm independent of the responsibilities of individual members. In this essay we do not deny that there are gangs out there, and that individuals acting in their names have long been responsible for significant amounts of criminal violence. What we mean to highlight is that criminology has systematically avoided taking seriously the challenge of showing that "the gang" makes an independent, positive contribution to the level of criminal violence in communities or legal jurisdictions. Neither popular culture nor the police, neither college students in criminology classes nor funding sources in private and public agencies, worry much about the causal issue. And neither have gang criminologists, at least not until recently, and then in a way that suggests a desire to be done with the pesky issue.

The silent agreement among gang criminologists to downplay the causal question has made possible three fundamental defects in the research agenda on gangs. First, the field has long lost the healthy comparative perspective in which it was born. Frederic Thrasher began gang research with a classic scientific curiosity to describe all the instances of the phenomena he could find, and he found 1,313 (Thrasher 1927).[1] His naturalist ambitions led to a comparative appreciation of gangs among various forms of youthful peer associations. Today the study of gangs proceeds largely outside of the study of youth culture.

In a second perversion of the field, criminologists have seen through the gang, using the gang as a window onto phenomena which are treated as far more important than documenting the everyday realities of gang members on their own turf and in their own terms. Like the politicians and journalists who shape popular culture, gang criminologists have been preoccupied with the gang as metonym, icon, or index. The central debate is over which summary image to invoke when thinking about gangs and which background realities to bring to mind when the gang image is invoked.

The third defect in the corpus of gang research is the failure to develop the causal issues fully. At least three causal questions about the relationship of gangs and crime should be investigated. Do individuals become more criminal by virtue of joining or being in gangs? Do gangs increase the level of criminal violence in society? Taking gangs as collective phenomena, what accounts for their emergence, decline, spread, and evolution toward greater or lesser violence?

Only the first of these three questions has been asked with a modicum of intensity, and even then the answer remains unclear. But it is the second question that is the most revealing, for without the assumption that rates of criminal violence would be lower were there no gangs, the field never would have developed; or at least it would not have developed along its now-familiar lines. If everyone assumed that gangs have no systematic effect on the level of criminal violence, research funding would dry up and what remains of the gang literature would be read very differently, to the extent that it would be read at all.

THE LOST NATURALISTIC AND COMPARATIVE PERSPECTIVE

The history of gang research can be divided into three periods. Thrasher's *The Gang*, published in 1927 and remembered for his "Chicago School" explanation, was a promising start to the first period. Thrasher found that gangs arose in areas that were "interstitial" in the social ecology of the city. Such areas, located between stable residential zones, were pressed by encroaching business development, marked by rapid population change, and displayed severe social disorganization.

But Thrasher's own work was more dedicated to documenting gangs than in arguing that social ecology explained gangs. Explaining why gangs exist was a relatively minor aspect of the effort to describe a great variety of groups. The social ecology perspective was not developed in his work but in other research projects, which he merely cited, invoking the prevailing ideational boilerplate as a narrative device to frame his inquiry.

Subsequent researchers criticized Thrasher's explanation as an instance of an increasingly discredited view of urban poverty as "social disorganization." The critique of the social ecology framework helped advance the sociological study of the city by encouraging a search for internal order in poverty, or "slum," areas (Suttles 1968). In the wake of broadscale disenchantment with social ecological theory, Thrasher's rich comparative description of forms of childhood social organization was ignored. Gang criminologists ridiculed the "play groups" that he abundantly described. Such innocent associations were absurdly innocuous in comparison with the seriously destructive gangs they studied.

When the naturalist impulse is killed, the opportunity to develop naturally occurring comparisons is an innocent victim. What sociology has remembered about the Chicago School has helped it forget that in its first incarnation, the field was self-consciously and vigorously tied to the discovery and descriptive thrusts of natural science inquiry. Darwin loomed larger than Marx, Weber, or Durkheim in early sociology textbooks. Quite apart from the appeal of evolutionary theory, Darwin's work represented meticulous description, the ideal of bringing nature back to the university laboratory in as much detail and with as much respect for ecological interaction as is possible (see Park and Burgess 1924). Today, virtually no researcher documents gangs in comparison with the various other social forms in which adolescents associate in a city.

With such comparative data in hand, criminologists might hesitate before explaining gang membership as motivated by low self-regard, a need for status, uncertainty about one's identity, the need for a substitute "family" outside of a broken biological family, etc. By comparing what the gang offers with what boys and young men can find in other forms of association, we might specify the attractions of gang life. Such data could be either synchronic/cross-sectional or diachronic/biographical. Gang members do not stay for life; they do not always leave on a stretcher or for prison terms. The very issue of what makes gangs seductive to their members has been obscured by the neglect of alternative associations outside the gang. We have no empirical basis for believing that gangs are the only way that adolescents can satisfy personal needs, make up for family failings, protest hierarchical domination, seek mobility, etc.

The second stage in gang criminology emerged after World War II with the proliferation of a national research community. In Chicago, New York, Los Angeles, and Boston, sociologists/criminologists developed portraits of gang life through their involvement in city-specific intervention programs. Primarily funded through private philanthropy and local government, these programs featured "detached workers" who variously sought to affect gang cohesion, develop community organizational resources independent of gangs, and link gang members, or would-be gang members, to community and employ-ment opportunities. The researcher/authors typically operated with one foot in university research departments and the other in intervention program administrations.

The studies emerging from the wave of intervention efforts of the 1950s and 1960s made gang criminology a notable field, even though the intervention programs were not primarily research projects. Several of the most celebrated studies were a mix of theoretical arguments geared to structuring future inter-ventions and the product of ad hoc efforts to collect data through the access to gang life developed by previous, independent programs. Perhaps the most highly regarded publication of the period, Cloward and Ohlin's *Delinquency and Opportunity* (1960), was almost completely devoid of data (see also the thin data in Albert Cohen's *Delinquent Boys*, 1955).

In some program efforts, the involvement of social scientists was more a matter of field supervision than writing up research findings. An example is Hans Mattick's involvement in the programs of the Chicago Youth Develop-ment Project (as discussed in Klein 1995). Others were the products of formal research designs (Short and Strodtbeck 1965). Some were intensive efforts to develop unprecedented measures of such matters as gang culture, gang cohe-sion, and careers in gang life and crime (Miller 1958; Miller et al. 1961; Klein 1971).

Overall, there appeared to be an inverse relationship between the richness of data in a publication and the recognition that the work received outside of the small corps of gang researchers, at least at the extremes (this pattern did not go unnoticed: Bordua 1961). Like Cloward and Ohlin's award-winning, book-length adaptation of the Mertonian theory of deviance to gang formation, Matza's *Delinquency and Drift* (1964) and Sykes and Matza's "Techniques of Neutralization" (1957), while advanced through writings devoid of data, never-theless became, respectively, a prizewinning book and one of the most widely cited journal articles in American sociology.

Thrasher's book had portrayed a diversity of youthful social life as a grounding for a single theoretical perspective. In neat contrast, one writer after another in the 1950s and 1960s stimulated an elaborate theoretical debate by presenting a summary view of gang life based on the model of a given program or city's experience. In the 1960s, national political life underwrote the appreci-ation of summary images of gang kids and gang life. During the Kennedy presidential administration, and as the precursor to the War on Poverty program that emerged in the subsequent presidency of Lyndon Johnson, social interven-tion programs in which Cloward and Ohlin had been active were taken as models for planning remedial national social policy (Moynihan 1969). In the face of such political clout, the institutions shaping academic prestige in social science did not insist on the tedious business of evidentiary grounding.

When American college populations expanded rapidly in the 1960s, the simplifying narrative structure of the monographs of this period made several of the books ideal teaching tools. Insofar as causal issues were addressed, they took the form of theorizing on the motivations for joining gangs and for the rise of gangs in inner-city areas. That gangs increased crime was taken for granted. The premise of most intervention programs was that gangs were bad for their members and their communities; neither the programs nor the research studies based on them were structured to gather evidence on the issue.

In a rare instance, one causal issue of overriding practical significance was clearly specified: the effects of intervention programs on the delinquent careers of gang members. While many intervention programs had not planned an evaluation phase, this issue was of undisputed relevance to all. And when evidence was organized around the issue, the results undermined general presumptions. After years of personal involvement in social research/social work with gang kids in Los Angeles, Malcolm Klein (1971) concluded that ameliorative social program interventions aimed at fighting gangs often unexpectedly increased gang cohesion, a result that had the expected further consequence of increasing the criminal activity of gang members. Later, Klein (1995) saw the same effects from programs of police repression.

A third stage of gang research has developed since the 1970s, based on a new mix of philanthropic, university, and federal government funding and conducted by researchers more firmly housed in university departments. This large wave of studies has been produced through intensive participant observation with gang members, through building interview data by snowballing to gang members, or, in an overlap with delinquency research methods, by surveying youth populations, primarily through their representation in schools. Gang research has thus remained largely separate from the quantitative, social-survey, and police data-set methodologies that came to dominate criminology in the 1960s.

Gang research has also remained separate from sociological studies of youth social life and culture outside of gangs. Gang studies refer primarily to other gang studies but not to studies of young male, or female, social life, violence or even criminality outside of gangs. In the broader literature, however, one can find evidence of attractions to violent versions of masculinity independent of gangs and crime (Wacquant 2000), peer groups that collectively engage in crime without the markings of street gang culture (West 1978; Sullivan 1989), and networks among youths who disproportionately and cooperatively commit crimes without generating gang identities (Sarnecki 2001).

Further undermining causal inquiry, writers on street gangs often set aside studies of skinheads, soccer hooligans, and drug gangs as not comparable (e.g. Klein 1995). Studies of adolescent life-cycle processes, social life in schools, and youth culture in general are almost completely ignored. Studies of inner-city, low-income, ethnic-minority social life that do not appear as "gang" studies (Anderson 1978; Liebow 1967) are left to other scholars to explore, even when they describe the same social milieu in which gangs are prominent.

Throughout the history of gang research, the lack of a comparative perspective has been at the root of a persistent embarrassment: the failure to define what a "gang" is. The problem has long been openly recognized, subjected to repeated agonizing, and used as a justification for national tours such as Walter Miller's (1975) effort to collect a broad-based sample of instances that might inform an authoritative definition. Definitions that do not include dimensions of criminality are deemed unattractive because they would capture as "gangs" social groups that are not contributing to crime rates, and because the background characteristics of non-criminal and criminal gangs would be confounded. But definitions that do include criminality in the group definition set up analyses for tautology when investigating the impact of gangs on crime rates: criminal youth groups by definition contribute to crime.

Developments in youth culture may finally point the way to resolving the definitional dilemma. Through "gangsta," "hip hop," and related forms of popular culture, street gang symbolism has spread rapidly across the United States since the 1980s; "gangs" have emerged in small and large communities where their presence was unknown or denied. "L.A." gang styles have emerged in communities coast-to-coast, and after initial suggestions that "Bloods" and "Crips" from Los Angeles were developing branches elsewhere, it has become apparent that youths across the nation were responding to mass-media images of performances that exploited Los Angeles gang styles (often by performers whose bases were in the East and Midwest).

By necessity now, researchers who would distinguish the backgrounds of violent offenders, stages in the process of forming violent gangs, and the discrete contributions of gangs to crime rates, must distinguish among various youth associations and culture movements. In a promising new twist, Malcolm Klein has conceptualized "tipping points" at which youths associated under gang-related symbols, like "break dancers" and "taggers" (graffiti writers), begin to see themselves as in a group that requires violence. A similar sensitivity to group transformation is evident in studies of street gangs that exploit public housing communities and drug markets (Venkatesh 1997).

What a gang is, who is in it, and what being in a gang means are not in the first instance problems for researchers; they are problems for young people who challenge each other to declare membership, who test each other's loyalty and commitment, and who are far more widely fascinated with clothing themselves in gang symbolism than in arming themselves for violence. Street gangs are inherently amorphous phenomena, and when they are not, when membership in a gang puts one on a payroll and is a matter for disciplined structuring over extended periods of time, it is likely that the group has become a drug marketing organization. An appreciation of the inherent, naturally occurring ambiguity of street gang identity should lead to a research agenda that exploits ambiguity as a central topic for comparative research rather than one that tries to resolve it by definitional fiat (on measurement by fiat, see Cicourel 1964).[2]

As a practical matter, the field still resists embracing the ambiguities of gang phenomena as a basis for shaping a broad research agenda. Journalists have taken a handful of inner-city youth, or the young people on particular inner-city blocks, and written about the variety of their associations and involvements in legitimate and illegitimate activities (Butterfield 1995). But gang researchers get funded to study gangs, and even the most data-rich and thoughtful investigations of the relationship of gang members to their families and communities start with samples biased toward individuals identified as criminally involved (Decker and Winkle 1996). As we explain in detail later, indications that gang members commit acts of violence at rates much higher than their peers do not speak with great authority about the effects of gangs on crime rates. And studies that develop evidence on the situational contingencies that move youth groups from flaunting gang symbolism into violent action (Sanders 1994; Fagan and Wilkinson 1998; Fagan 2000; Wilkinson 1998) are not incorporated into the theoretical discussion about the nature of the gang.

A vast array of alternative causal understandings of the significance of gangs in America has been essentially untouched by sustained research. Here are a few:

- gangs are so widespread, crime cannot be attributed to the gang itself but must lie in the contingencies that turn gangs violent;
- gangs are where violent offenders belong, such that where gangs exist, violent offenders disproportionately will want to be in them;
- by concentrating violence in expressive symbolism, gangs contribute to social control by drawing the attentions of law enforcement and enabling community youth and families to understand who they need to avoid;[3]
- by intensifying conflicts among violent youths, gangs reduce the level of criminal violence in the long run;[4]
- many social areas lacking gangs somehow produce crime rates from their youth population equivalent to those in "gang-infested" areas, indicating that the relationship of gangs and violence, where it exists, is spurious;
- the rise of gang violence is a response of the "demoralized poor" (see the discussion below) in a transitory historical period that heralds a coming decline in a population's social pathologies.

After 75 years of gang research in the United States, the proposition that gangs raise rates of criminal violence beyond what would obtain in their absence remains deeply problematic because of the narrowed research agenda in the field. Other critical causal issues have also been systematically obscured. Had Thrasher's example been honored, the conditions for the formation of gangs could have become a vigorous area of study. As it stands, gang criminologists explain gang formation with little more than a flourish of the explanatory wand in the direction of whichever social conditions happen to be in the background of their particular gang examples. If the gang is in the "rustbelt," then it must be "deindustrialization," the decline of social spending to rebuild older cities, and the flight of middle-class blacks from the inner city that is responsible (Hagedorn 1988). If the gangs are Mexican American and located in the booming Sunbelt's suburban and ex-urban areas as much as in the large cities, then it must be that "multiple marginalities" explain the flourishing of gangs (Vigil 1988).

Significant progress in explaining gang formation awaits a research agenda that would describe the myriad social formations within which gangs emerge. There are repeated indications in the gang literature that other social relations, networks, or latent ties are mobilized in the gang formation process: family connections, institutional ties to schools and perhaps jails, neighborhood boundaries defined by the physical structure of highways and housing projects. These are never sufficient conditions, and there are indications that historically critical events are additional necessary conditions. As is often noted, one-gang cities are rare. The explanation of gang formation will require the same multi-case, multi-stage processual explanation that has been developing in the field of social movements. What has stood in the way of developing the database for such theory development is not the lack of a model of inquiry, nor the lack of multiple social relations in the environments of youth lives. The major blockage has been the mesmerizing power of waving causal imagery at background conditions. It is time to disenchant that explanatory wand.

THE GANG AS WINDOW

After Thrasher, gang researchers have had little patience for describing the people they study. Some spend years becoming familiar with gang kids up close, only to find them "boring" as they pass hour after hour "hanging out," apparently they are too boring to describe (Klein 1971). Many researchers who have interviewed gang members do not bother to quote them, or if they do, they present aged ex-gang members who talk surprisingly like the social theorists conducting the study (Moore 1991). It is common for gang researchers to encourage gang members to summarize their lives, a shallow if convenient research strategy that dispenses with the need to describe what gang members do and say in their own milieu, outside of interview situations, when they are pressed to respond to immediate exigencies in their social worlds. Others devise multiple measures of gang members and their actions, but the resulting picture is of indicators of dimensions, not of the gang as a cultural form sustained by its members (Short and Strodtbeck 1965). Some of the most notable recent gang studies rely on members' memories. When such memories purport to recall the relatively recent formation of specific, originally small gangs (Hagedorn 1988), they are much more trustworthy than when they are offered as bird's-eye snapshots of the experiences of thousands of people who have lived in and around gangs during a 30-year period (Venkatesh 2000).

There are exceptions to the rule against description, among them:

- a study of gang violence as it is described in police records, supplemented by fieldnotes from police ride-alongs and interviews, all organized by the situated occasions of violent events (drive-bys, gang bangs, robberies, etc.) (Sanders 1994);
- an ethnographic sketch of Chicago's "Vice Lords" in the 1960s, which remains one of the few studies that conveys the local symbolic world that sustains gang members' involvement (Keiser 1967);
- Decker and Winkle's (1996) report of extensive, first-person, verbatim descriptions of gang life produced by 101 members of 29 St. Louis gangs who were contacted in high-crime neighborhoods and screened with the question "Are you claiming?"

There are also numerous gang studies that, despite their overriding concerns with explanatory language and/or standardized forms of measurement, illustrate their arguments with rich field data. Short and Strodtbeck's (1965) study is perhaps the most industrious, collectively conducted, elaborately organized effort to understand gang life; it reads as a wrenching, remarkably honest struggle to make inapposite theory and inelastic data manipulations fit with the close-up accounts of gang life created by participant-observing "detached workers." A more typical indicator of the stagnated methodological thinking in the field is Hagedorn's *People and Folks* (1988). Hagedorn packages invaluable gang histories as told by "top dogs" from 19 Milwaukee gangs in a boilerplate theoretical framing about the gang-institutionalizing effects of "deindustrialization." As noted by Walter Miller (1989), Hagedorn has no comparative data

about gang life before and during the supposed sea change of "deindustrialization," and such limited data as he does produce on the issue, most notably a list
of unemployment levels in various cities, run counter to his arguments by
showing relatively low unemployment rates for cities with large gang populations like Boston and Los Angeles.

It appears that no one has attempted to describe a "day-in-the-life," or what
gang members do with others continuously and in detail, over any significant
stretch of time (but see Fleisher's 1998 ethnography of Kansas City adolescent
social circles). The work of painstakingly reconstructing lived experience is
routinely bypassed in favor of summary recollections elicited in an interview. It
is a revealing paradox that gang life is at once a symbolic image sufficiently
powerful to justify study after study, and at the same time, never worth actually
describing. How could this be?

It has been so obvious that American gangs are terribly important to understand that it has been hard to justify spending the time describing individual
members in their routine activities. The problems that the gangs present are of
such gravity that to take the time to describe what they do, person by person, day
by day, has apparently seemed a foolish diversion from the need to comprehend
the phenomenon as a whole, understand what to do about it, and institute
reforms. Instead of building up a picture of gang life block-by-behaviorally-
situated-block, gang researchers become acquainted with one or a few groups,
summarize what they have found, and conclude by indicating how to change
society to reduce the gang problem. Sometimes the researcher's involvement
extends over many years and entails intense personal challenges in relations
with gang members, only to end in the urgent recommendation that what is
needed is not, ironically, more personal involvement by well-meaning gang
workers but structural change: ending segregation, reducing social inequality,
offering decent-paying jobs to the unemployed, providing childcare services for
working mothers, and perhaps, for good measure, prosecuting white-collar
crime in order to reduce grounds for cynicism.

After Thrasher, the criminologists' gang became a window, something to be
framed and seen through. As windows, gangs work two ways for criminologists.
From one side, the criminologist sees through gangs to the social conditions that
produce them. From the other side, the criminologist looks at the false stereotypes that society has produced about gangs. Throughout, the gang itself is
transparent. But windows can be dangerous tools, hiding what is on the other
side by fascinating the viewer with nothing more than a reflection of the gazing
perspective.

Treated as transparent openings onto pathological social conditions, the
American gang has been portrayed – one might justifiably say, exploited – by
one prevailing theoretical perspective after another. Beginning in the 1950s, and
continuing to date, wave after wave of newly outfitted theoretical perspective
has seized on the gang as a proving ground for:

- social class theory, which, in one form, analyzes gangs as an outgrowth of
  working-class culture (Miller 1958);
- Freudian-styled theories that construct gang culture as a reaction formation
  against the closed doors of middle-class society (Cohen 1955);

- psychiatric social work, which portrays gang kids as needing ties to multiple remedial resources (Bloch and Niederhoffer 1958);
- Merton's deviance theory which, combining a sense of social class injustice and a critique of popular culture from above, frames gangs as responses to the contradiction between materialistic values and arbitrarily limited opportunities (Cloward and Ohlin 1960);
- a perspective reflecting the American emphasis on legality in the 1960s, which imagines delinquents becoming committed to criminal ways as they see the irrationally different treatments that the criminal justice system imposes on them and their equally guilty friends (Matza 1964);
- a psychological theory holding that pathologically violent individuals are at the core of the gang problem (Yablonsky 1966);
- a post-civil rights movement perspective, which sees a combination of opening mobility doors for minorities and the loss of manufacturing jobs in the inner city as having created a new underclass (Wilson 1987);
- and most recently, a Merton-like characterization of gang members as perverse American mobility hustlers who know the sad score but don't lie down. Gang members are characterized as defiant individualists who, like the sharpest of America's legitimate hustlers, know the odds and respond as cold-eyed entrepreneurs, seizing opportunities where they lie, developing ties with local politicians for protection, and serving the local community's needs by offering jobs and redistributing wealth (Sanchez-Jankowski 1991).

The gang has been a rich resource for telling stories formatted as social theory. Yet gangs themselves never provide the origin of the theory. The gangs are the provinces, onto which theories developed at the theoretical center are imposed.

Although Thrasher's original finding that gangs originate in play groups has been confirmed repeatedly, and is even emphasized in some theory-heavy works (e.g., Hagedorn's), the idea that there might be something distinctively different in the world of the gang, something that might attract members to it independent of more widespread motivational frameworks, is neglected. Again and again, the gang is treated as a type of phenomenon that demonstrates the reach of theories first introduced in domains without reference to gangs, domains such as clinical psychotherapy, Merton's general analysis of American deviance, small-group analysis, and political-economic theory based on ideology or on quantitative studies of race, socioeconomic status, and population movements. One after another fashionable idea in academic centers is celebrated through its elaboration of gang topics, with little if any representation of native realities. If gang members think they have found a special source of motivation in their collective relations, a first cause for their commitments, an inspiration for action that exists for them but not for others of their background, it must be because they are confused.

This multi-theory interpretive feast has been made possible by a tacitly shared agreement to treat gangs as windows for seeing the troublesome structural conditions in their backgrounds. And once one has viewed the background realities through gang panes, it is a simple matter to walk to the other side and look back at the distorted stereotypes with which others have depicted gangs. Every theoretical narration of gang problems is part of a conflict within the theorizing class. Every new gang theory first sees through gangs to the root conditions that produce them, then turns around and criticizes other interpreters for projecting their own false images onto the gang screen. If gang members have needs for repairing multiple broken ties, then those who would focus on community organizing alone neglect them. If gangs are produced as part of an underclass which in turn is the upshot of historical forces that individuals cannot resist, then to focus on mending social ties is to further confound the matter. And if gang members are defiant individualists, then those who see them as defeated by their racial and class oppression convey insults that border on racism.

The criminologist's habit of seeing through gangs in the desire to explain them has had two significant unfortunate results. The first is staining the group as a whole with an image of deviance. It is a tricky business to link the minority poor with crime in order to plead for remedial intervention or, more radically, social justice. If the pleas fail, only the stigma may remain. The criminologists' gang has been a dominant image in what outsiders imagine about the population that gangs are taken to represent. This is especially true of the Mexican American population in the southwest. Since the mass prosecution of alleged gang members in the "Sleepy Lagoon" murder case in the 1940s (Moore 1988; Verge 1993), the gang has been a dominant image of a population growing toward majority status in the Los Angeles area. The size and internal diversity of the population should make any ethnic icon absurd. For decades grossly underrepresented in the area's political life, living in large numbers in the shadows due to illegal residency status, and, in comparison with African Americans, dispersed in residence around the region and relatively invisible when achieving middle-class status, the Mexican-origin population in southern California has long been grossly overrepresented by gang imagery in local popular culture (Katz 2003).

Not all communities are equally represented in the public mind by the gangs they produce. If the Mexican American population is at one extreme, the Chinese American population is at the other. Despite well-documented, sensationally violent, Chinatown gangs, the image of the Chinese in the United States is barely blemished. Consider the contrast in the Los Angeles area. Any impressions of youth chaos associated with immigrant-filled Chinatowns are overshadowed by a series of factors:

- young Chinese men are visible in restaurant service staffs, working under the discipline of Chinese families. Compare the shallower impression of ethnic social structure conveyed by "Mexican restaurant" workers. Young Mexican and Central American service personnel work in massive numbers in chain-run, national and multinational, corporate-owned "Mexican" restaurants. Chinese service workers are seen in settings that indicate the strength of Chinese social forms for social control; Latino workers work in conditions that indicate a perceived necessity for discipline by white and black owners and supervisors;
- offsetting the image of dense, chaotic, impoverished Chinatown populations is the simultaneous rise of affluent Chinese suburbs, such as Monterey Park east of Los Angeles. Compare the diffusion of the Mexican-origin population in low-income population pockets throughout the region and the residential dispersal and geographic invisibility of high-income Mexican Americans;

- overriding the image of the poor Chinese immigrant is the overrepresentation of Chinese students on university campuses and in scientific circles. Compare the underrepresentation of the Mexican-origin population in higher education.

The differential power of gang images in shaping the general public understanding of ethnic and regional populations points to a second destructive result of using the gang as a window onto general background conditions: the lost opportunity to develop a comparative understanding of how gangs differentially relate to the communities from which they emerge (for a partial exception, see Spergel 1964). Put another way, the failure of gang criminology to develop a comparative analysis of gang/community relations in different times and places is evidence of the strength of the tendency to look through gangs to background conditions conceived in the terms of general social theory. Reading the major works in gang literature of the 1950s and 1960s, one learns virtually nothing about these decades or the particular conditions in the cities in which the studies were made.

The third wave of gang research offers little more on local community background realities. Cloward and Ohlin (1960) theorized that local area differences would produce different kinds of gangs, but their analysis, although rooted in New York experiences, was both abstracted from geopolitical place and narrowly focused on opportunities for illicit gain. Ethnic culture and the history of ethnic community were essentially ignored. When a large-scale research project attempted to test delinquent opportunity theory in Chicago by working with service and police agencies with intimate knowledge of delinquency areas, the researchers failed to locate cases that would fit the three hypothesized types of gangs: criminal (innovative, rationally organized pursuit of criminal profits); retreatist (drug using, self-absorbed) and conflict (fighting). They noted: "[This] failure...is a 'finding' of some importance, for it casts doubt on the generality of these phenomena....We were led in the end to seek groups not primarily oriented around fighting, but with extensive involvement in the pursuit of 'kicks' or various forms of theft" (Short and Strodtbeck 1965: 13).

In the current phase of gang research, when background conditions are described, they are described in highly generalized demographic terms and refer only very broadly to socio-economic trends. Chin's (1996) study of Chinatown gangs is an exception that indicates the value of the research opportunities that have been lost. Chin provides a history of the rise of gangs and gang violence in New York's Chinatown since the 1960s. Groups that began as martial arts clubs became street gangs and then tools of tongs that organize and exploit commercial activity in the immigrant-receiving area. Here, gangs are understood in the web of social ecological relationships that tie together various forms of social organization in local Chinese society, including family structure, affiliation to groups based on originating districts in China, commercial needs, and the specialized law enforcement attentions of a variety of local policing and prosecution offices.

That Chin could portray gang context and activities with unusual richness was not due to an unusual ease of access. Notoriously hard to penetrate, and especially hostile to Americanized Chinese, underworld Chinatown offers a challenge to gang researchers that is equal or greater than those faced by researchers focused on other ethnic populations. While Chin ends by recommending reforms of immigration policy, community and business organization, and with a plea for removing the fraudulent "patriotic" image that has protected tongs from closer scrutiny, he is offering little more than a convenient way to end the book: the value of his study does not rest on those policy-oriented arguments.

The example of Chinatown gangs, and Asian American gangs more generally, is a sign that gang criminology will have to change to reflect the exploding ethnic diversity of the United States. Most of the gang literature of the last 50 years has been based on Midwestern and east-coast populations, mostly African American and, to a lesser extent, Puerto Rican and Mexican American. An understanding of black and Mexican-origin youth gangs should have long ago inspired a study of their respective relationships to segments of pop youth culture. The rise of gangs from different Asian-origin populations, and immigrant gangs from different cultures of the ex-Soviet Union, may make it harder to avoid a comparative analysis of ethnic history, culture, and social structure (Song et al. 1992; Vigil 2002).

In its narrative qualities, gang research is a unique field in criminology. In crime studies, the typical research strategy is to link variation in criminal conduct with variation in background characteristics of individuals, social settings, or historical periods. On the explanatory side, the units of analysis are individuals, areas, or epochs; on the side of the explanandum, individual actions or population rates. The central message is about responsible social structure and history. The image of the individual criminal – the kind of person the criminal is, his/her motives, outlooks, character – is only indirectly implied. Not so when the topic is the gang, for which metonymic resonances leap to prominence. The central argument in the gang literature is over iconography. After Thrasher, criminologists have essentially been engaged in a graffiti war, competing to tag the gang and the gang member.

As a collective noun, the "gang" appears to sum up something important about what membership means to members. The risks that members run by affiliating with the group's symbolic identity imply that something revealing must be at hand. Young men at times are willing to reduce all of the potential of their lives, and all of their relations with others, to honor the gang for a brief moment, and to make a fleeting gesture indicating something they presume essential about themselves.

Similarly for the gang criminologist. In its typical form, as a study of a given gang or of gangs in a given city or region, the gang criminologist's effort is to advance a summary image. Even if more than one type of gang is recognized in the study, typically there are only two or three types. It is taken for granted that for members, gangs summarize something important about their lives; the point of gang research is to provide a summary of that summary.

At a first level of metonymy, the individual's gang membership characterizes the individual. At a second level, the portrait of the individual characterizes the gang. At a third level of metonymy, the gang stands for all gangs. At a fourth level, studying gangs is appealing as a summary way of understanding youth criminality in general. And, at a fifth level, the gang is a trope for the low-income, young, inner-city, minority male. As they presume to conjure up some kind of profound generalization with their hand gestures, gang members seem aware of the heavy baggage their insubstantial symbols carry. That academics agree should give us pause. The weightiness that a slim gang monograph can have in academic discourse indicates that it is not only the author/researcher who is ready to generalize liberally from his or her case study. The metonymic resonances of gang research are built upon conventions used by a community of readers.

The deepest concern brought to the reading of gang criminology is that of defining the image of the low-income, minority male. Images matter. It is not an array of statistical correlations, but summarizing images, or, less politely, stereo-types, that go into the voting booth and that also haunt the shadows of policy making across all levels and branches of governmental power. This is why it matters whether we see the gang as psychopathologically violent men, expressive youngsters epitomizing lower-class culture, adolescents dependent on the respect of peers, ghetto youth hopelessly lost in self-destructive hedonism, unemployed labor frustrated with the boredom imposed by deindustrialization, entrepreneurs spreading L. A. gang organization across the country to control valuable drug markets, representatives of populations oppressed by racism and creating other-wise absent "social capital" to forge links to mobility routes, or as boys redefin-ing their maintenance of childish ways with violent dispositions until they mature out of the extended youth that American affluence now makes possible for an "underclass" that suits up for battle in designer-labeled clothes. Given the failure to describe the individually lived realities of gang social life, gang research, as it has developed in the United States, is essentially an argument over the correct description of a ghost.

GANGS, CRIME, AND CAUSAL ANALYSIS

The causal proposition that gangs significantly elevate levels of crime is essential to their metonymic power. If gangs were no more criminal than a random sample of the youth populations from which they emerge, why base theory and policy on images of gangs as opposed to the social dimensions of that larger popula-tion? Implicitly, gang criminology has been based on the claim that gangs are a strategic focus for crime research because gangs produce an overrepresentation of criminal individuals and activities.

After Thrasher (1927), gang criminologists began depicting gang members, without qualification, as more violent and delinquent than their non-gang counterparts. For decades, virtually the only evidence that gangs cause crime consisted of scattered qualitative descriptions and quantitative data in the form of correlations and cross-tabulations that describe the gang youth of some time and place as in more trouble than non-gang youth (see, e.g., Short and Strodtbeck 1965; Suttles 1968; Johnstone 1981; and the evidence critiqued in Zatz 1987). Only in the 1990s has the causal issue been given sustained atten-tion. Enough work has been done that it is appropriate to consider the strength of the evidence that gangs increase the level of criminal violence beyond what would exist without the presence of gangs. It is notable that nearly as soon as the results of these studies were published researchers began treating the issue as closed (see, e.g., Bjerregaard and Smith 1993; Klein 1995; Rosenfeld et al. 1997). Thus, without citing evidence, Decker and Curry claim: "Gangs facilitate the commission of crime. To ignore that is to ignore (or worse, to excuse) the violence gang members commit against each other and their communities" (1997: 514). We are warned that raising doubt about the causal nexus of gangs and crime is not only empirically wrong, it is morally irresponsible!

The idea that gangs cause violence has been understood on at least two levels. On the level of individual biography, it might be that individuals become more violent when they join gangs. On the collective level, it might be that the rate of violence would be lower were it not for the presence of gangs in the community. Both ideas appear to be confirmed by data that describe gang youth as more violent than non-gang youth, and youths as more violent during periods in which they are in a gang. But there are several plausible alternative understandings that indicate why the causal issue should not be laid to rest:

1 *Folk wisdom.* When surveyed in school, student respondents are biased toward reporting that gang members are criminal because that is conventional wisdom. They use folk ideas in perceiving peers and in defining their own lives.

2 *Sampling and data-elicitation biases.* Gangs are showy symbolic vehicles for professing criminality. Gang members are especially willing to express their criminality, thus especially likely to be known by their peers. Non-gang criminal youth are less inclined to indicate their criminality and are not as readily known to those who are sampled. Acts of violence carried out to honor the gang generate news stories, enhance police attention, and excite talk on the streets.

3 *Circular labeling.* The category "gang" is applied to individuals by youths in the community, by social scientists, and by the police only if those youths have been associated with crime, especially violent crime. Labeling someone as in a "gang" makes his violence comprehensible. The gang does not cause members to be violent; violence causes youth to be seen as gang members. When an interviewer asks "So the reason you call it a gang basically is why?," Money Love, a 20-year-old Insane Gangster Disciple, responds, "Because I beat up on folks and shoot them. The last person I shot, I was in jail for five years." Or, again, when Paul, an 18-year-old 107 Hoover Crip, is asked "What makes you all a gang?," it makes sense for him to respond, "The things we do. Fighting, shooting, selling drugs" (Decker and Winkle 1996: 64).

4 *Where violent youth belong.* The decision to join and stay in a gang is fueled by the desire to get involved in more violence. In gangs, violent youths who are often ostracized because of their violence, find a place to belong. And, because violence is attractive to them for reasons they do not understand, the gang is especially attractive as a context in which violence makes accepted sense to members and gang rivals, and even to outsiders who condemn gang violence but accept that it makes sense according to gang understandings. Through tortuous biographical journeys, individuals first come to appreciate violence as an attractive response to chaotic social environments because it insists on immediate, vivid, vertically structured social order. Gangs then

provide conventionally understood explanations for what otherwise might appear to be irrational, idiosyncratic, or even emotionally disturbed behavior. Gangs strut themes of dominance in heroic and collectively celebrated styles. "We grew up fightin', we just grew up fightin' and everybody hangin' around so they decided to call they self somethin'" (Decker and Winkle 1996: 56). Gangs shape the form but not the incidence of violence.

5 *A means and a protective habitat.* Youths who feel threatened and who expect to be in violent conflicts find gangs to be attractive vehicles for coping with risks that are endemic to their social areas. Thus violence causes gangs. Historically, a high level of violence in a social area is a precondition for gang formation. But gangs may as often provide a sense of security that makes violence unnecessary as they occasion outbreaks of violence. Gangs have the same ambivalent relationship to violence as do military organizations. Armies may be necessary for war but they are not sufficient causes of conflict. Indeed, by creating an organized group that risks getting killed in war militaries may limit the outbreak of violence, quite apart from the deterrent effects on enemies.

6 *Violence makes youth groups into gangs.* Young people associate in many different social forms. Violence is a critical "tipping point" for turning peer groups into gangs. Gangs do not make groups violent; violence makes groups into gangs.

It may well be that violence causes gangs much more powerfully than gangs cause violence. A few short-lived acts of violence can generate gangs that live over generations. Thus the causal impact of violence in constructing gangs is often far greater in temporal reach than the impact of gangs on violence. A rare act of violence makes a group into a long-lasting gang, while gangs only sporadically produce temporal concentrations of violent actions.

Indeed, following the analogy to the military and war, the very ongoingness of the gang makes it unlikely that gangs will be closely associated with the incidence of crimes. The critical causal contingencies are not likely to be "the gang" but short-lived conditions that mobilize gang members into criminal activity. A study in Chicago found that gang homicides were committed by just four, drug-marketing gangs (Block and Block 1995). The null hypothesis has many more supporters.

7 Alternatively, *crime may be necessary to the persistence of gangs.* If violence brings gangs into existence, gangs may cease to exist in the absence of criminality. We find a close association between the existence of gangs in a community and the level of criminal violence in that community, because gangs disintegrate when criminal violence declines.

8 *Self-fulfilling prophecy.* Gang members become criminal because they are treated by police and peers on the presumption that they are criminal. Someone styled as a gang member is especially likely to be solicited by a would-be drug buyer, attacked in a preventive defensive strategy by someone anticipating being attacked, and focused upon and then arrested by the police. Thrown into jail because of police responsiveness to gang symbolism, youth come to need strong ties with peers in order to mount an intimidating,

aggressive posture toward other peers. In this scenario, gangs do increase criminal violence, but the increase develops because of the general belief that gangs do increase criminal violence, a belief that gang criminology helps sustain.

9   *Regression to the mean.* As another reason that gang criminologists may have falsely perceived gangs as causing violence, the risk of "regression to the mean" looms large in the design of gang research. Researchers seeking to justify their investigations as illuminating serious gang problems are well-advised to search for violent gangs. As youth violence peaks, political calls for solutions get louder, intervention programs emerge, and funding expands for a research focus on violent gangs. When gang researchers tag along and stay for a short while, their data collection is biased toward recording acts of violence in a relatively unrepresentative phase of the cycle of gang life. No-one, after all, has suggested that gang violence is produced with systematic temporal regularity. When, after research is completed, gang violence recedes as part of its natural cycle, the gang researchers will have left the field. They are not around to record the lack of violence.

10   *Gangs reduce violence* in variety of ways. Gangs are so intimidating that where they exist, people may avoid starting conflicts for fear they will get out of hand (see note 4). By exaggerating their members' violent proclivities, gangs make it unnecessary for members to prove their aggressiveness individually. Gangs concentrate violent youth in places and under symbols that facilitate avoidance of violence by residents not committed to the gang world, and that guide police attentions, thus contributing to the repression of an area's crime rates over time. Gangs draw a variety of violent youth into relatively disciplined relations, facilitating control of the most violent over the less violent. And gangs intensify their members' violence, destroying members' lives more quickly than would otherwise be the case, thus lowering area crime rates over the long run.

Although each of these rival hypotheses is questionable, and although when presented together they are in many ways mutually inconsistent, their neglect indicates the ideological status of gang criminology. Various ways of combining these hypotheses could lead to a comprehensive modeling of the relationship of gangs and violence. In their interactions and cumulative effects, they point toward a research agenda far more demanding than the simplistic, unidirectional, gangs-to-violence, model. Several of these alternate views stress that the issue as a whole should be understood in a reflexive manner, that is, by taking into account not only the contingencies of violence but also the contingent effects of police and research attentions. That existing studies fail to take alternative views into account is indicated by their approach to matters of definition, their treatment of causal directionality, and their neglect to argue the effect of gangs on crime rates.

Defining gang membership

There is a widespread reluctance to rely on police definitions of gang membership, in part because it is known that departments vary in how they define gang

crimes (Maxson and Klein 1996), and in part because police actions are politically suspect (Hagedorn 1990). But despite this recognition, the research literature has failed to take seriously the problems of defining gang membership.
Henry et al. (2001), for example, rely on police records in combination with
self-reports. Youth who denied membership yet who had an arrest report indicating a "gang-related" incident were coded as members.

Curry and Spergel (1992) developed a scale of "gang-involvement" based on
behavior typical of gang members. Some of the items used to define gang
membership included activities that themselves often incite violence, such as
"flashing gang signs" and "attacking someone in a gang fight." Such definitions
bias the sample, selecting as gang members the most violent and dangerous
youth (Morash 1983). As a result, the relationship between gang membership
and criminality will likely be overstated.

Some studies use police reports to measure criminality and self-reports to
impute gang membership. Huff (1996), for example, compared the ages of
first arrest for gang and non-gang youth, finding a significantly younger median
age for gang youth. There was no control for the likely possibility that gang
youth, especially younger members, are more engaged in making their criminal
inclinations visible. Consider the implications of the possibility that, for many if
not all gang youth, what being in a gang means is primarily a matter of sustaining an ongoing stream of symbolic expression: a certain way to dress and use
clothing, a style of movement on foot and in cars, ways and places to "hang out,"
the display of a unique semiotics through gestures, car styling, and graffiti, etc.
While such youth may have an audience of peers in mind, they unwittingly
provide the grounds to be strategically targeted for arrest by police. Even if
gang youth commit crime at rates no greater than non-gang youth, they should
be expected to be overrepresented in police statistics.

Studies that employ self-reports have been the most common (Thornberry
et al. 1993; Dukes et al. 1997; Battin et al. 1998; Harper and Robinson 1999).
Although this method avoids some of the sampling biases described above, a
contingent process of applying the label "gang" is also at work when youth self-
report membership. These studies lack evidence to rule out the possibility that
youth involved in highly delinquent gangs will be more likely to report themselves as "gang members." Less subtle biases show the extent to which the gang/
crime causal nexus has not been seriously questioned. Esbensen and Huizinga
(1993), for example, asked youth directly if they belonged to a gang or not. Of
the 193 who claimed gang membership, 33 were coded as non-members because
the respondents did not report that their gangs were involved in enough gang
fights or other illegal activities.

Definitional issues have long plagued gang research and perhaps always will
(cf. Ball and Curry 1995), but research designs more open to null findings on the
gang/crime nexus might develop evidence that would improve the discussion.
Existing studies of police data usually compare gang and non-gang youth, not
gang youth and youth in other groups. In self-report studies, respondents typically have no choice to describe their peer groups other than by saying they are in
"gangs."

As another strategy for improving the evidence, sampling for self-reports
could be based on residential areas rather than on school populations. While

gangs are universally presumed to be negative phenomena in criminology, it is not coincidental that Thrasher's area-based study led to his statement "that the gang is a protean manifestation: no two gangs are just alike; some are good; some are bad; and each has to be considered on its own merits" (1927: 5). Notably, Suttles's (1968) area-based study similarly resisted the assumption that gangs are malevolent in their impact on crime. Suttles found that the youth in the slum he studied were equally delinquent, regardless of gang membership. In another neighborhood-focused field study, Horowitz (1987) found that non-gang local residents at times differentiate between good and bad gangs (cf. Venkatesh 1997).

Which came first?

The neglect of temporality is a major weakness in the research on the gang/crime connection. Whether the analysis is correlational (Morash 1983; Huff 1996) or employs more advanced statistical techniques (Curry and Spergel 1992; Dukes et al. 1997; Harper and Robinson 1999), data often have been drawn at one point in time. Although they present results in causal form, these studies give no basis for understanding which came first, the violence or the gang.

Several studies have attempted to model the temporal sequence of gang membership and criminality with longitudinal data (Esbensen and Huizinga 1993; Thornberry et al. 1993; Battin et al. 1998; Henry et al. 2001). They test whether gangs "facilitate" crime based on whether members are more violent when in gangs than when they are not. Without discussion, the question of the impact of gangs on crime levels is transformed into a question about individual biographies. But even if gangs make their members more violent than they otherwise would be, there are any number of interactively related processes that could offset the effect of members' activities on area crime rates: earlier termination of violent careers through death, injury, and incarceration; discouragement of gang membership at the entry point and acceleration of exits from the gang; decline in violence by non-gang youth, etc.

Thornberry et al. (1993) is currently the most frequently cited work in advance of the claim that gangs cause crime. Students in Rochester, New York were surveyed first in eighth- or ninth-grade classes, then the next year, then a year later. The final sample included 175 self-identified gang members; only 34 identified as gang members all three times, indicating the ephemeral nature of membership. The authors hypothesized that gang members would have significantly higher rates of delinquency and drug use when they are in a gang as compared to when they are not. Their results show that, for most types of crime, youth are indeed more criminal while in gangs than they were before they were gang members, and also that they are less criminal after leaving gangs (see also Thornberry 1998).

Even though these data are longitudinal in the sense that they describe the same person at different biographical moments, they do not describe the temporal ordering of the key variables, i.e., whether changes in propensity to commit crime preceded or came after defining oneself as affiliated with or independent of the gang. The suggestion is that adolescents become more likely to commit crime after they join, but many of the alternative readings, discussed above, could apply. For example, the results may indicate that doing violence increases the likelihood that young people will define themselves as in gangs. Put another way, the relationship of violence and membership may be spurious: before and as a motivation for gang membership, students may have become involved in the early stages of what will flower as an intensive spate of violence; and conversely with regard to leaving the gang. When gangs are not present in a community, the flowering of an especially violent phase of biography may still occur.

Note how the Thornberry reading, that gang membership precedes and causes crime, is more appealing if one forgets that adolescents who do not commit crimes also spend much time with peers. What specifically about the gang heightens criminality? Why should not the gang, which makes the criminality of each heighten the vulnerability of all, control, limit, even suppress otherwise wild, egocentric criminality? The commonsense reading of positive gang/crime correlations may be nothing more than an elaborate formulation of the universal parental wisdom, individually sensible but collectively tautological, that each individual's culpability is due to the bad kids he or she hangs with. Nobody is at fault if a Durkheimian malevolent spirit rises spontaneously from the *frisson* of gang interaction. (Compare the "contagion" idea that the gang milieu raises pre-existing violence, as stated in Curry and Decker 2003: 62.)

Since Shaw and McKay's classic study (1931), criminologists have long held that juvenile delinquency is a group phenomenon. But the pattern that young people do crime together rather than alone is not limited to "gang" associations (Zimring 1981). Hence, if we want to show that gangs as distinct organizational types cause crime, we should also want to know if they do so independent of the role of the delinquency of friendship groups.

The most influential study to take up the question (Battin et al. 1998) concludes strongly that gangs exert more criminogenic influence on youth than do similarly delinquent peer groups.[5] Battin et al. (1998) used structural equation modeling (SEM) techniques to test for relationships between variables, as did many others (Curry and Spergel 1992; Dukes et al. 1997; Harper and Robinson 1999; Henry et al. 2001). But SEMs do not rule out the alternative readings that we have proposed.

Most statistical procedures, such as correlations or regression procedures, aim to bolster a theorized relationship by negating competing views. SEMs do the reverse: they attempt to find models *that cannot be rejected by the data*. They show that a given hypothesis cannot be ruled out, but they do not show that other hypotheses can be discarded.

Of the studies identified here, whether they use regressions or SEMs, all but one made no mention at all of the possibility that gangs might in some way result from violence or crime. Using their evidence, we can, with equal logic, simply reverse the conclusion that gangs are the cause and that violence is the effect.

The exception is a study in which Curry and Spergel (1992) asked 439 Chicago students in the sixth through eighth grades whether they had partici-pated in a number of "gang-related" activities or held "gang-related" attitudes. These measures were modeled against self-, school, and police reports of delin-quency. Although this study has been taken as positive evidence that gangs cause delinquency, and not the reverse, we find reason to pause. Even putting aside limitations of the sample, which barely reaches into adolescence, the findings are, in a simplified form, that kids who identify with gangs also had been delinquent. Again, this can be plausibly read as a finding about popular discourse. As the dictionary tells us, a prominent meaning of "gang" includes delinquency, but not vice versa. Put another way, it is necessary to be delinquent before being in a gang, but it is not necessary to be in a gang to be delinquent. Read this way, the study supports the hypothesis that delinquency precedes and contributes to gang membership.

The weakness of the evidence that gangs cause crime is essentially due to a neglect of process. Thrasher's (1927) work provides a contrast. In a section entitled "Does the gang cause crime?," he suggests a number of potential mechanisms for understanding *how* gangs might cause crime (e.g., that they socialize youth to delinquent values, or that they increase the efficiency of delinquent activities by increasing numbers and opportunities). Recent studies do not consider even this simple framing of the process in which gangs might increase crime. After 75 years, the criminologists' gang has bullied the processual issue out of the discussion.

Gangs and crime rates

As noted, the studies of the gang/violence connection to date have been on the individual level. Joining a gang, it is argued, is bad because it increases the individual's criminality. But the field of gang criminology as a whole is also and perhaps more fundamentally based on the idea that gangs increase criminal violence in society. What crime rates fluctuate in relation to increases and decreases in the number of gangs and the size of their membership?

Police departments and popular culture can change perceptions of gangs for political, organizational and emotional reasons, but counts of dead bodies and other signs of victimization are less subject to political pressures and public mood. In 1995, Malcolm Klein, describing extensive, nuanced interviews he conducted with police and lay gang experts around the country, wrote of the dramatic "proliferation" of gangs that had been in progress since at least the mid 1980s. "This much is clear: The gang problem is exploding" (1995: 370). Another study published at about the same time found 16,000 gangs in 300 cities with half a million members (Curry et al. 1996). This seemed to make sense of the well-publicized rise in youth crime rates in the 1980s and early 1990s. But, late in 1995, evidence appeared to indicate that:

> what sociologists call a "moral panic" had set in . . . youth violence rates had peaked in 1993; the 1994 police data showing a decline from the peak, a decline that has continued every year since, did not become available until late in 1994. Thus youth violence had been in decline for nearly two years when concern about it reached its height. (Tonry and Moore 1998: vii)

For the public in general, an assumption that expanding gang membership will lead to an explosion of youth violence may be a matter of panic. For gang criminologists, presumably some other explanation must be sought.

Conclusion

The greatest challenge facing gang research is the narrative power of the topic. Criminologists and street kids share a fascination with the gang as a symbolically protean mythology. Gang members seem to have an infinite appetite for gathering around and retelling stories of the wounds they have received (Horowitz 1983). Particular episodes of conflict resonate so profoundly that narrator and audience can remain transfixed upon repeated re-livings even though no new information is imparted. Similarly, gang criminologists cannot resist going far beyond the limits of their data and speaking to the great issues of the day.

The narrative seductions of the gang genre are evident if one compares writings on gangs to the research literatures on youth violence, on guns and violence, on drug criminality, on career criminals, or on the relationship between age and crime. In other areas of criminology, writers hone in much closer to variations in their data. While criminology in general lives on journal articles, the sub-specialty of gang researchers more readily produces book monographs. In writings on gangs, there is a much stronger temptation to locate causes in background factors that figure prominently in culture wars and political debates but that do not vary in relationship to gang life, as least not so far as one can tell from the data presented. As an intellectual enterprise, gang writing risks being a reverse kind of mythmaking. In classic form, myths explain constants (e.g., why we see a mountain over there) by reference to changes that occurred beyond the reach of human observation: a past change, itself unobservable, explains a present constant. In gang writing, a present constant (e.g., an ongoing social inequality that we can readily see) explains unobserved changes (the emergence of gangs, entries into gangs, the rise of gang violence).

Thus virtually the entire Mexican American population fits some part of Diego Vigil's characterization of the "multiple marginalities" that account for Mexican American gang life. Are we then to see all Mexican American youths as gang members? If so, the link between gangs and violence must be weak. If not, what is missing from the explanation?

Even gang researchers who spend decades making carefully guarded statements that are drawn close around variations in their data find it irresistible, in the writings of their years of wisdom, to tell a story about the origins of gang life that, if heeded, would reshape national policy on the grandest scale. Thus Malcolm Klein, in what may be the crowning book of his career, leaps to explain gang life with the theories of William Julius Wilson and John Hagedorn on "deindustrialization," the decline of social programs in the 1980s, and the success of the civil rights movement in taking positive role models and other social supports out of the inner city; even though his own research was in booming southern California, not the Midwestern Rust Belt; even though his work covered Mexican-origin populations for which new immigrants have been much more relevant in shaping social structure than affirmative action paths toward mobility; and even though his distinguishing contribution, based on immersion in field research in the 1960s and 1970s, argued the causal power not of socio-economic conditions but of situationally contingent social processes, in this case, the positive effects of gang-intervention programs on group cohesion. And Hagedorn, who became prominent in gang research with his study of Milwaukee gang formation as a response to "deindustrialization," was soon adding a smorgasbord of social problems to the list of contributing causes: guns, drug markets, prison, the mass media's celebration of materialism, and – what the hell! – brutish masculinities and values indifferent to community service. One benefit of the smorgasbord is that it lures attentions from the unattractive feature of any one cause. In this case, readers who overindulge at the smorgasbord may fail to focus on Hagedorn's failure to specify deindustrialization in historical time and to relate it, or even unemployment levels, to rising gang formation, and to the variations over the last twenty years from rapidly rising to rapidly falling gang violence.

Why can't gang writers stick to their data? Why is it not obvious that it is gratuitous to refer to background conditions that do not vary in relationship with variations in the data about gang life? Why have gangs become such a clear window, in criminology and in the popular cultural forms of movies, newspaper journalism, and folk wisdom, for telling stories about what has gone wrong in American society and what should be done about American social policy? (Martin Scorsese's current movie, *Gangs of New York*, elevates the gang narrative to the level of a primordial myth about the founding of the American character.)

We suggest that the mystification of the field begins with a central act of evasion. Gangs make it unusually easy to finesse causal issues. As compared to guns, age, or even peer networks, gangs are mythical matters from the start. They exist, if they exist in a manner worth distinctive study at all, as transcending symbols, as collective phenomena that overarch, inspire, and give honor to their members. It is hard for researchers to know whether gangs exist and who is in them because of their ontology: they exist as matters whose existence is put repeatedly on the line, in ceremonies of claiming membership, in challenges that test loyalty, in everyday routines in which hanging out might, with a turn of a phrase, become the beginning of a collectively organized assault. To the extent that gangs do not have such transcendent status, then the criminality of the individuals involved may be studied in standard ways, with individual level measures alone.

We recommend a two-step process for reorienting the field. First, state clearly the various causal issues necessarily implicated in gang research. We see three: the production of gangs, or gang formation; the effects of gang membership on individual criminality and other biographical matters; and the impact of gangs on crime rates. Second, specify alternative hypotheses and distinguish the forms of data that will aid research on each of these issues.

With regard to the impact of gangs on crime rates, we need comparisons among communities. Within any one community, we need to follow the social histories of gangs and crime rates over time; and we need to consider how gangs interact with other parts of the youth population. With regard to the impact on individual biography, we need longer perspectives on individual lives, and we need measures that open up the ambiguities of gang "membership" and that can distinguish the temporal ordering of gang involvement, criminal activity, and other personal changes. We need more situationally specific data that include descriptions of how violence emerges in different social situations, and how, if at all, gang membership is used in the violence process.

The field is most promising with regard to the question of gang formation, essentially because in studying gang formation, one need not make presumptive codings of gang/non-gang youth; one can specify the emergence of gangs as meaningful groups in members' own distinguishing practices. There is a growing, lively debate on whether gang formation now is fundamentally different than it was in mid-century and whether, in turn, the early industrializing city gave rise to gangs in a still different manner. With refreshing echoes of the "natural history" emphasis in Thrasher's original work, several gang researchers have suggested that it might be possible to build a stage-theory to explain gang formation.

The ideas on gang formation currently floating around might be organized as follows. Youth play groups are shaped as part of the universal social organization of childhood but also as political and historical changes shape patterns of everyday proximity. Residential patterns structure childhood social relations around kinship; government policies build and destroy public housing, implement school busing, occasion immigration and residential movements within the region and the nation. These "macro" developments shape the demographics of youth and patterns of peer affinity.

At the same time, themes arise and go out of fashion in mass popular culture. Play groups or informal youth associations embrace and innovatively transform culture movements. Their innovations may emerge in the style of ethnic culture, in "crack" consumption, as a culture of marginality, within a youth fad like break dancing or surfing, or in the form of the "gangsta" fashion that is used to characterize a lifestyle lived through music, clothes, gestures, etc.

The transition from hedonistic creativity with a cultural style to gang organization requires opposition. Male adolescence is a fertile ground for paranoia, which may be variously stimulated by family cultures of conflict, by points of transition from neighborhood elementary schools to middle schools covering wider areas, and by any number of chance events, such as encounters with suspicious police, provocative and defiant peers, and anxious school authorities. Objective trends, such as the imprisonment of an increasing number of inner-city youth and the street marketing of a hot-selling drug, institutionalize budding gang affiliation, giving the seductions to gangs new self-protective and economic meanings. In all of these respects, which include cultural fads, social organizational changes, and repressive actions, the gang's existence depends not solely on the interests, values, and actions of gang members, but also on what many non-gang others do. The latter includes the sympathetic responses of many local area residents, whose pride in identifying with defiant youth is underwritten by the contribution that "slum" reputations make in keeping local rents down and resisting "gentrification." The gang's formation and persistence must be understood to be a collaborative act.

Note how studying gang formation settles the hoary issue of defining what a gang is. The meaning or meanings of gangs are empirically settled by finding the social processes that historically lead to different types. For this inquiry, we should not expect to have "a" definition of the gang. How to define a gang is discovered by uncovering members' meanings, which does not mean asking them to provide a definition but documenting how their social lives developed and the uses to which they put their relationships. Just as we discover multiple forms of violent criminality when we ground definitions of crime in subjects' meanings and actions, all of which may fit in the same legal category and receive the same label from the criminal justice system, so we should expect to come up with numerous types of groups. Each will have a different natural history, each will be used differently by members. We will come to set aside the dummy variable gang/non-gang youth that is employed by police.

If gang research to date has only in sketchy ways appreciated the contributions of others to gang formation and maintenance, the essential contribution of gang members themselves to gang formation has been completely missed. Given the massive immigrations and internal migrations in the last twenty years of US history, it is striking that the gang literature persists in using local economic conditions as explanatory factors. Literally millions of extremely poor, grade-school-educated immigrants have incurred large costs and run enormous personal risks to cross borders in search of improved economic opportunities. Many such migrants from Latin America have come as adolescents. At some point in the history of social thought, the neglect of this mobility evidence will become an embarrassment for the field. What sense does it make to invoke locally unattractive economic conditions like "deindustrialization," "unemployment," and "social inequality" to explain gang formation, without explaining why native-born residents facing limited local opportunity do not move toward greater opportunity, especially when they do not face the legal barriers to movement that impede border-crossing migrants, and especially when poorly educated migrants who have uprooted themselves are flooding into the very cities said to be stuck in a deindustrializing cul-de-sac? The issue is being addressed, albeit gingerly, in migration and labor studies, but in the gang literature, there is no recognition that, if limited local economic conditions are to have causal effect, as they may well have, there must be another part of the explanation that is missing, something that is necessary to give local conditions determining power.

It is just here that the sociological genius of gangs has been missed. Gangs make local attachments glorious. They transform what might be seen as the shameful maintenance of childhood ways into a matter of pride. An outsider might hear "homeboy" as perilously close to "momma's boy," but "homeboy" now is not an insult; in the gang world it is a badge of respect. If gangs do not raise the level of violence beyond what otherwise would obtain, they may still play a powerful role by emotionally and symbolically sustaining barriers to mobility. And, if recent gang research has it right, gangs appear to be increasingly able to make the maintenance of a childhood social world locally respectable well into adult life.

Thirty years ago, long before the phrases "deindustrialization" and "underclass" became common currency, David Matza (1966) wrote of the "demoralized poor." He was referring to those ethnics who remained in such areas as Hell's Kitchen and the Lower East Side of New York after huge portions of their ethnic peers had moved up and out. Such populations should be expected in all historical periods, *especially* when the economy is working *well* and there is rapid upward mobility. No process of mobility will work in one historical moment for an entire population, not unless a government institutes something like the migrations that Bismarck directed in order to push Germany into the industrial age. Those who remain behind have to make sense of being left behind in inner-city conditions. Gangs make local area attachments morally respectable. Violence and the fear it inspires make for heroic commitments and a blinding narrowness of vision. And in material terms, gangs serve local community populations by creating "ghetto" reputations that keep gentrifying forces out.[6]

Gang criminologists appear to have fallen for the same seductive fantasies that sustain gangs, the idea that local conditions by themselves could explain the careers of local youth. Members secretly collaborate across gangs, sustaining the affiliations of each by imagining enemies in mirror-image peers. Essentially identical young people face off against each other in the name of one or another local area, and the myth works even for gang members who do not live in the areas they "claim." Violence then transforms what might be seen as the childishly imaginary into undeniably real, serious, adult business. Likewise, gang members celebrate the fantasy of creating a high life through crime by imagining that drug profits will make them rich,[7] and the gang research community joins in by depicting gangs as entrepreneurial tools. It may be that it is the very absence of determining forces in local background conditions that explains the seductive magic of the gang. Put in other terms, gang affiliation offers an inspiring alternative to what might otherwise be a demoralizing view of one's historical situation. But it is not the gang members themselves whose employment prospects count. Their fascination with the gang starts so young as to indicate that they appreciate the defiant posture of the gang as a proud alternative to what they perceive lurking in the humbled shadows of their parents' generation.

Attempts to link background features to gang formation share a common problem. The background features exist beyond the awareness of the youths themselves. It speaks worlds about gang criminology, and sociological explanations of poverty more generally, that the problems of the parents are imputed to the children without explaining the linkage. It may be that high unemployment keeps young men affiliated with gangs in their twenties, but they typically do not first join at that age. At the age of entry, which in some studies is treated as young as 11–13 years, what would a strong job market mean? Gang writers struggle to suggest that the lack of summer jobs is a significant incentive to gang involvement. Without really addressing the matter, they imply that government should take over the structuring of early adolescence, creating occupational commitments through providing attractive jobs in order to create a more moral population.

As soon as one begins to think seriously about the linkage between adult realities and the worlds of childhood, the issues become extremely complex. If it is not actually the child's immediate economic opportunities that count but those of the adults in their families or neighborhoods, then in which phase of adult life should we measure the economic opportunities that shaped mobility outlooks? It is not obvious that the immediate present is the relevant phase.

And then, how do adult outlooks become translated into sensed backgrounds of childhood? This linkage is the key missing piece in explanations of gang life that refer to socio-economic conditions. The image of the demoralized poor portrays adults as realizing their own failure through witnessing the successes of peers. If these "loser" adults respond by developing a routine paranoia about disrespect, then the culture they generate may remain in a community's atmosphere even as generation after generation passes through and sees many get up and out. And that becomes a resonant background for the everyday paranoia of gang life.

Perhaps the distinctiveness of the American gang problem is due to the lack of barriers to labor and social mobility. Perhaps the aggravating problem is not the removal of positive role models ("old heads") but the vividly present awareness that ethnicity and original social condition do not determine one's fate. Perhaps deindustrialization is a blessing, not only for low-skilled, poor immigrants but also for the native-born who, compared to immigrants, have advantages ("cultural capital") for moving into managing positions in the service economy.

But we risk committing the very error we seek to warn against, over-theorizing. Our goal is to show that once the causal issues have been explicated and separated analytically, gang theory will have to be reformulated. It will then not be so easy for gang researchers to see through the gang in order to tell stories about relatively invariant background conditions. They will at least have to stop and clarify some of the links along the way.

A further implication is that the study of gang formation should develop as part of a larger sociology of youth, marrying with social movement and collective behavior studies, and creating collections of historically documented cases as a new research methodology. To get around the sampling problems that haunt the field, researchers can use analytic induction (Katz 2001), comparative qualitative analysis (Cress and Snow 2000), or the constant comparative method (Glaser 1965) for theory testing and development. Launched on these roads, the gang research literature may be able to break its addiction to shaping the prevailing imagery about the gang and leave the storytelling to the gang kids and the popular media, at least until the research literature is equipped to describe the natural histories of gang formation, the situational contingencies through which criminal attacks emerge, and the processes linking socio-economic background to the foreground of gang life.

Notes

1   Actually he did not. He found hundreds of gangs, but, according to Solomon Kobrin, whose career overlapped with Thrasher's, the 1,313 figure used in the book's famous subtitle apparently came from a joking reference by research assistants to the street address of a brothel, the joke perhaps also being a mocking of the pedantic effort to come up with a precise number (Geis and Dodge 2000).

2   The gang label is powerful not only for youth on the streets, but, increasingly in the United States, for anyone with a serious complaint about organizational conspiracies that facilitate crimes. The flexibility of the term is itself a powerful social fact. The federal RICO (anti-"racketeering" statute, first applied to organized crime of the "Mafia" variety, recently has been invoked to charge the Catholic Church with criminal conspiracy for covering up sexual abuse by priests. Faced with such stretched use, gang research needs a strategy to hold onto a distinctive field of social behavior. An initial step would be to reserve the term for collaborative activities that seduce members to criminal violence, quite apart from material gain. That is, while we should study drug gangs, organized crime directed by adults in Mafia and

Chinatown contexts, the criminal activities of CREEP (the committee to re-elect president Nixon), etc., we can focus the study of what are often called "street gangs" by focusing on collectivities whose transcendent qualities are built upon commitments to violence. It may be that drug gangs are utilitarian and that its members are indifferent to the charms of being members of an awe-inspiring group. Or it may be that many drug gangs grew out of street gangs, then became cold organizational tools, and then took on awe-inspiring identities which became collectively charismatic for their members. This is not a matter that will be settled by theory, definitional conventions, or by studies that never leave the discourse of the university long enough to show us the symbolic environment that is constructed by the people allegedly studied.

3   This is the implication of the Harvard Kennedy school anti-violence effort in Boston. It claims great success in reducing criminal violence by swarming gang leaders with zero-tolerance law enforcement (Kennedy 1997). The argument goes that while shotgun police-repression efforts may backfire by increasing gang cohesion, a sharp decline in a jurisdiction's rate of homicide can be achieved quickly if local and federal enforcement powers are pinpointed on the most egregious core offenders.

4   Here several mechanisms may be at work, both within the gang and without. Gangs may concentrate the violent careers of their members biographically, and gangs may discourage non-members from violence. The latter possibility is indicated by current research being conducted by Curtis Jackson-Jacobs on white youths in a southwestern city who regularly go out looking for fights in bars and in party scenes. The informality of the commitment to violence appears to be central to its persistence. When on occasion these young men encounter minority and prison gang members in provocative settings, many reflect on the meaning that violence would have in a gang context and quickly bow out. Gangs appear to shape the volume and the social location of youth violence in ways much more complex than have been considered. A relatively low rate of white youth violence seems at least partially produced by a high rate of minority youth violence, especially as expressed in dramatic gang forms.

5   Other studies that take up the question, Morash (1983) and Henry et al. (2001), find significant effects, but of small magnitude and in only specific types of delinquency. A more useful predictor of delinquency, they found, was whether the respondent had delinquent friends.

6   The anti-yuppie or anti-gentrification sentiment in many gang areas expresses a classic hostility toward the bourgeoisie, but not from progressive or bohemian sentiments. It may seem odd to understand gangs as socially conservative agents, but the characterization is worth contemplating. The symbolism and culture of gangs is a celebration of elitism, of the natural superiority of color (whether black and white, or red and blue) or native territorial origins, not a pride in the common humanity of downtrodden masses. Urban American gangs are much too quickly isolated in analysis from rural and European racist and fascist movements that attract youth to the call of resisting the uprooting effects of macro-level social changes through symbolisms that would honor threatened local attachments. American criminologists' efforts to make the city street gang into an agent of progressive social change are based on precisely the wrong understanding of the gang's attractions to its members (Katz 1988: 153–63).

7   On the economic earnings of street gangs involved in drug markets, compare MacCoun and Reuter (1992) with Levitt and Venkatesh (1999).

References

Anderson, E. (1978) *A Place on the Corner*. Chicago: University of Chicago Press.

Ball, R. A., and Curry, G. D. (1995) The logic of definition in criminology: Purposes and methods for defining "gangs." *Criminology*, 33(2), 225–40.

Battin, S. R., Hill, K. G., et al. (1998) The contribution of gang membership to delinquency beyond delinquent friends. *Criminology*, 36(1), 93–115.

Bjerregaard, B., and Smith, C. (1993) Gender differences in gang participation, delinquency and substance abuse. *Journal of Quantitative Criminology*, 4, 329–55.

Bloch, H. A., and Niederhoffer, A. (1958) *The Gang*. New York: Philosophical Library.

Block, C. R., and Block, R. (1995) Street gang crime in Chicago. In M. W. Klein, C. L. Maxson, and J. Miller (eds.), *The Modern Gang Reader*. Los Angeles: Roxbury, 186–99.

Blumstein, A., and Wallman, J. (2000) *The Crime Drop in America*. Cambridge: Cambridge University Press.

Bordua, D. J. (1961) Delinquent subcultures: Sociological interpretations of gang delinquency. *Annals of the American Academy of Social Science*, 338, 119–36.

Butterfield, F. (1995) *All God's Children: The Bosket Family and the American Tradition of Violence*. New York: Knopf.

Chin, K.-L. (1996) *Chinatown Gangs*. New York and Oxford: Oxford University Press.

Cicourel, A. (1964) *Method and Measurement in Sociology*. Glencoe, IL: The Free Press.

Cloward, R. A., and Ohlin, L. E. (1960) *Delinquency and Opportunity*. Glencoe, IL: The Free Press.

Cohen, A. K. (1955) *Delinquent Boys: The Culture of the Gang*. New York and London: The Free Press.

Cress, D. M., and Snow, D. A. (2000) The outcomes of homeless mobilization: The influence of organization, disruption, political mediation, and framing. *American Journal of Sociology*, 1054, 1063–104.

Curry, D., and Decker, S. (2003) *Confronting Gangs: Crime and Community* (2nd ed.). Los Angeles: Roxbury.

Curry, D., and Spergel, I. (1992) Gang involvement and delinquency among Hispanic and African-American adolescent males. *Journal of Research in Crime and Delinquency*, 29, 273–92.

Curry, G. D., Ball, R. A., and Decker, S. (1996) Estimating the national scope of gang crime from law enforcement data. In C. R. Huff (ed.), *Gangs in America*. Thousand Oaks, CA: Sage, 266–75.

Decker, S., Bynum, T., and Weisel, D. (2001) A tale of two cities: Gangs as organized crime groups. In J. Miller, C. L. Maxson, and M. W. Klein (eds.), *The Modern Gang Reader*. Los Angeles: Roxbury 73–97.

Decker, S., and Curry, G. D. (1997) What's in a name?: A gang by any other name isn't quite the same. *Valparaiso Law Review*, 312, 501–14.

Decker, S. H., and Winkle, B. V. (1996) *Life in the Gang: Family, Friends and Violence*. Cambridge: Cambridge University Press.

Dukes, R. L., Martinez, R. O., and Stein, J. A. (1997) Precursors and consequences of membership in youth gangs. *Youth & Society*, 292, 139–65.

Esbensen, F.-A., and Huizinga, D. (1993) Gangs, drugs, and delinquency in a survey of urban youth. *Criminology*, 31, 565–89.

Fagan, J. (2000) Contexts of choice by adolescents in criminal events. In T. Grisso and R. G. Schwartz (eds.), *Youth on Trial: A Developmental Perspective on Juvenile Justice*. Chicago and London: University of Chicago Press, 371–401.

Fagan, J., and Wilkinson, D. L. (1998) The social contexts and functions of adolescent violence. In D. Elliott, B. Hamburg, and K. Williams (eds.), *Violence in American Schools*. New York: Cambridge University Press, 89–133.

Fleisher, M. (1998) *Dead End Kids*. Madison: University of Wisconsin Press.

Garot, R. (2002) Unpublished ms., Department of Sociology, University of California, Los Angeles.

Geis, G., and Dodge, M. (2000) Frederic M. Thrasher 1892–1962 and *The Gang* 1927. *Journal of Gang Research*, 81, 1–49.

Glaser, B. G. (1965) The constant comparative method of qualitative analysis. *Social Problems*, 124, 436–45.

Hagedorn, J. (1988) *People and Folks: Gangs, Crime and the Underclass in a Rustbelt City*. Chicago: Lakeview Press.

Hagedorn, J. (1990) Back in the field again: Gang research in the nineties. In C. R. Huff (ed.), *Gangs in America*. Newbury Park, CA: Sage, 240–59.

Harper, G. W., and Robinson, W. L. (1999) Pathways to risk among inner-city African-American adolescent females: The influence of gang membership. *American Journal of Community Psychology*, 273, 383–404.

Henry, D. B., Tolan, P. H., et al. (2001) Longitudinal family and peer group effects on violence and nonviolent delinquency. *Journal of Clinical Child Psychology*, 30(2), 172–86.

Horowitz, R. (1983) *Honor and the American Dream: Culture and Identity in a Chicano Community*. New Brunswick, NJ: Rutgers University Press.

Horowitz, R. (1987) Community tolerance of gang violence. *Social Problems*, 34, 437–50.

Huff, R. C. (1996) The criminal behavior of gang members and nongang at-risk youths. In R. C. Huff (ed.), *Gangs in America*. Thousand Oaks, CA: Sage, 75–102.

Johnstone, J. W. C. (1981) Youth gangs and black suburbs. *Pacific Sociological Review*, 24(3), 355–73.

Katz, J. (1988) *Seductions of Crime*. New York: Basic Books.

Katz, J. (2001) Analytic induction. In N. J. Smelser and P. B. Baltes (eds.), *International Encyclopedia of the Social and Behavioral Sciences*. Oxford: Elsevier, 1, 480–4.

Katz, J. (2003) Metropolitan crime myths. In D. Halle (ed.), *New York and Los Angeles: Politics, Society and Culture*. Chicago: University of Chicago Press, ch. 6.

Keiser, R. L. (1967) *The Vice Lords: Warriors of the Street*. New York: Holt, Rinehart & Winston.

Kennedy, D. M. (1997) Pulling levers: Chronic offenders, high-crime settings, and a theory of prevention. *Valparaiso University Law Review*, 31, 449–84.

Klein, M. W. (1971) *Street Gangs and Street Workers*. Englewood Cliffs, NJ: Prentice-Hall.

Klein, M. W. (1995) *The American Street Gang: Its Nature, Prevalence, and Control*. New York: Oxford University Press.

Levitt, S., and Venkatesh, S. A. (1999) An economic analysis of a drug-selling gang's finances. Working Paper 9814. Chicago: American Bar Foundation.

Liebow, E. (1967) *Tally's Corner: A Study of Negro Streetcorner Men*. Boston: Little, Brown.

MacCoun, R., and Reuter, P. (1992) Are the wages of sin $30 an hour? Economic aspects of street-level drug dealing. *Crime and Delinquency*, 38, 477–91.

Matza, D. (1964) *Delinquency and Drift*. New York: John Wiley.

Matza, D. (1966) Poverty and disrepute. In R. K. Merton and R. A. Nisbet (eds.), *Contemporary Social Problems*. New York: Harcourt, Brace & World, 619–69.

Maxson, C., and Klein, M. (1996) Defining gang homicide: An updated look at member and motive approaches. In R. C. Huff (ed.), *Gangs in America*. Thousand Oaks, CA: Sage, 3–20.

Meehan, A. J. (2000) The organizational career of gang statistics: The politics of policing. *Sociological Quarterly*, 41(3), 337–70.

Miller, W. B. (1975) *Violence by Youth Gangs and Youth Groups as a Crime Problem in Major American Cities*. Washington, DC: US Department of Justice.

Miller, W. B., Geertz, H., and Cutter, H. S. G. (1961) Aggression in a boys' street-corner group. *Psychiatry*, 24(4), 283–98.

Miller, W. E. (1958) Lower-class culture as a generating milieu of gang delinquency. *Journal of Social Issues*, 4, Summer, 5–19.

Miller, W. E. (1989) Review of *People and Gangs*. *American Journal of Sociology*, 95(3), 784–7.

Moore, J. (1988) Introduction: Gangs and the underclass: A comparative perspective. In J. Hagedorn (ed.), *People and Folks*. Chicago: Lakeview Press, 3–17.

Moore, J. W. (1991) *Going Down to the Barrio: Homeboys and Homegirls in Change*. Philadelphia: Temple University Press.

Morash, M. (1983) Gangs, groups, and delinquency. *British Journal of Criminology*, 23 (4), 309–35.

Moynihan, D. P. (1969) *Maximum Feasible Misunderstanding: Community Action in the War on Poverty*. New York: The Free Press.

Park, R. E., and Burgess, E. W. (1924) *Introduction to the Science of Sociology*. Chicago: University of Chicago Press.

Rosenfeld, R., Bray, T. M., and Egley, A. (1997) Facilitating violence: A comparison of gang-motivated, gang-affiliated and nongang youth homicides. *Journal of Quantitative Criminology*, 15(4), 495–516.

Sanchez-Jankowski, M. (1991) *Islands in the Street: Gangs and American Urban Society*. Berkeley: University of California Press.

Sanders, W. B. (1994) *Gangbangs and Drive-Bys*. New York: Aldine de Gruyter.

Sarnecki, J. (2001) *Delinquent Networks: Youth Co-Offending in Stockholm*. Cambridge: Cambridge University Press.

Shaw, C., and McKay, H. (1931) *Social Factors in Juvenile Delinquency*. Washington, DC: National Commission on Law Observance and Enforcement.

Short, J. F., Jr. and Strodtbeck, F. L. (1965) *Group Process and Gang Delinquency*. Chicago: University of Chicago Press.

Song, J. H. L., Dombrink, J., and Geis, G. (1992) Lost in the melting pot: Asian youth gangs in the United States. *Gang Journal*, 1, 1–12.

Spergel, I. A. (1964) *Racketville, Slumtown, Haulburg: An Exploratory Study of Delinquent Subcultures*. Chicago: University of Chicago Press.

Sullivan, M. L. (1989) *Getting Paid: Youth Crime and Work in the Inner City*. Ithaca: Cornell University Press.

Suttles, G. D. (1968) *The Social Order of the Slum: Ethnicity and Territory in the Inner City*. Chicago: University of Chicago Press.

Sykes, G. M., and Matza, D. (1957) Techniques of neutralization: A theory of delinquency. *American Sociological Review*, 22, December, 664–70.

Thornberry, T. (1998) Membership in youth gangs and involvement in serious and violent offending. In R. Loeber and D. P. Farrington (eds.), *Serious and Violent Juvenile Offenders*. Thousand Oaks, CA: Sage, 147–66.

Thornberry, T., Krohn, M., Lizotte, A., and Chard-Wierschem, D. (1993) The role of juvenile gangs in facilitating delinquent behavior. *Journal of Research in Crime and Delinquency*, 301, 55–87.

Thrasher, F. M. (1927) *The Gang: A Study of 1,313 Gangs in Chicago*. Chicago and London: University of Chicago Press and Phoenix Books.

Tonry, M., and Moore, M. H. (1998) Preface. In M. Tonry and M. H. Moore (eds.), *Youth Violence*. Chicago: University of Chicago Press, vii–ix.

Venkatesh, S. A. (1997) The social organization of street gang activity in an urban ghetto. *American Journal of Sociology*, 1031, 82–111.

Venkatesh, S. A. (2000) *American Project: The Rise and Fall of a Modern Ghetto*. Cambridge, MA: Harvard University Press.

Venkatesh, S. A., and Levitt, S. D. (2000) *The Political Economy of an American Street Gang*. Chicago: American Bar Foundation.

Verge, A. C. (1993) *Paradise Transformed: Los Angeles During the Second World War*. Dubuque, IA: Kendall/Hunt.

Vigil, J. D. (1988) *Barrio Gangs: Street Life and Identity in Southern California*. Austin: University of Texas Press.

Vigil, J. D. (2002) *A Rainbow of Gangs: Street Cultures in the Mega-City*. Austin: University of Texas Press.

Wacquant, L. (2000) *Corps et Ame: Carnets Ethnographiques d'un Apprenti Boxeur*. Marseilles: Editions Agone.

West, W. G. (1978) The short-term careers of serious thieves. *Canadian Journal of Criminology*, 20(2), 169–90.

Wilkinson, D. L. (1998) *The Social and Symbolic Construction of Violent Events among Inner City Adolescents*. New Brunswick, NJ: Rutgers University Press.

Wilson, W. J. (1987) *The Truly Disadvantaged: The Inner City, The Underclass, and Urban Social Policy*. Chicago: University of Chicago Press.

Yablonsky, L. (1966) *The Violent Gang*. Baltimore: Penguin.

Zatz, M. S. (1987) Chicano youth gangs and crime: The creation of a moral panic. *Contemporary Crises*, 11(2), 129–58.

Zimring, F. E. (1981) Kids, groups and crime: Some implications of a well-known secret. *Journal Of Criminal Law and Criminology*, 72(3), 867–85.

6

Youth Crime and Crime Control in Contemporary Japan

MARK FENWICK

INTRODUCTION

In spite of what might reasonably be characterized as a general neglect of Asia within English-language criminology, Japan has proved to be a focal point for a significant amount of comparative criminological research. The main impetus for this has been the perceived uniqueness of Japan. This uniqueness might be programmatically characterized as "modernization without crime." Japan achieved the transition from feudal fiefdom to highly affluent, secularized, post-industrial society in a little over a century *without* a concomitant explosion in crime rates. As such, Japan is one of the rare examples (often mentioned alongside Switzerland) of a society that has avoided the modernization–crime nexus that has often been identified as axiomatic in criminology (see, for example, Shelley 1981). Accounting for this "anomaly" (Archer and Gartner 1981) – examining the reasons *why* Japan has enjoyed such low levels of officially recorded crime in spite of undergoing profound social change – has fascinated criminologists in search of a better understanding of the causes of crime and more effective forms of crime control.

This essay begins by briefly reviewing the main features of the extant criminological literature on Japan. It is suggested that although this work is extremely valuable it tends to create the slightly misleading impression that low crime rates equate with an absence of "crime talk." The various ways in which representations of crime are present in everyday life in Japan have received much less attention in the literature. The broader issue of the relationship between this kind of "crime talk" and the operation of criminal justice and crime control more generally has not been subject to sustained consideration. In making this observation, it is not being suggested that Japanese crime rates are much higher than normally supposed, but rather to point to the fact that what might appear to be low levels of crime from an international perspective may well be experienced altogether differently inside Japan.

In the remainder of the essay, this line of thinking is pursued through a discussion of youth crime. It will first be suggested that since the mid-1990s, Japan has experienced an acute "moral panic" surrounding youth crime. The pervasiveness of images of delinquent youth and the ensuing public debate somewhat belies the idea of a society unconcerned by crime. The discussion will then consider how one of the outcomes of this experience of youth crime, namely the recent reform of the juvenile justice system, is an event of some significance. The traditional concern with protection and rehabilitation has been supplemented by a new emphasis on punitiveness, the rights of the victim, and parental responsibility. The significance of these changes is further highlighted when considered in the light of other events that have been occurring in the field of crime control over recent years, as well as broader changes in Japanese society. A concern with the *presence* of crime can offer comparative criminologists an interesting case study for an analysis of the distinctive form that penal modernity has taken in a different cultural context, and the ensuing crisis that is occurring as a result of the pressures of late modernity.

Culture, Comparison, and Criminal Justice

From the point of view of a North American or European observer, Japanese crime rates are remarkably low (see Fukuyama 1999: 32–3 for a helpful general comparison). The "gap" was at its widest in the early 1990s. For example, the number of Penal Code offenses per 100,000 people in Japan was 1,324 in 1990, compared with 5,829 Crime Index violations in the United States in the same year (Miyazawa 1997: 195; see also Castberg 1990: ch. 1 for a comprehensive review). In 1993, the murder rate in Japan was 1.6 per 100,000 population. In the United States, it was 10.1 per 100,000 population (Ramseyer and Nakazato 1999: 175; for a more detailed and up-to-date analysis, see Finch 2001). And yet, perhaps even more remarkable than the relatively low levels of crime is the fact that for much of the postwar period Japanese crime rates actually declined (Fukuyama 1999: 34). A postwar high of 1.6 million Penal Code offenses known to the police in 1949 gradually declined to 1.2 million by 1973, in spite of a sharp increase in population (National Police Agency 2000: 53). Even though general levels of crime have subsequently started to rise, it is worth noting that the overall crime rate is still lower than it was in the late 1940s and early 1950s. Again, this is in marked contrast to the North American and European experience (Fukuyama 1999: 31–4). Understanding the causes of these low levels of crime has provided the primary impetus for English-language research. Two closely related themes dominate the literature on this topic, both of which identify certain distinctive features of Japanese society as the basis of an answer to Japanese "exceptionalism," namely a culture that cultivates conformity and community-based, reintegrative forms of crime control.

First, there is a body of criminological research that utilizes the findings of an earlier generation of social anthropologists to explain the low crime rates by reference to certain features of Japanese "culture" (for an up-to-date and authoritative version of this argument see Komiya 1999; see also Clifford 1976; Adler 1983; Fenwick 1985; Westerman and Burfeind 1991; Fujimoto 1978 offers an interesting discussion of this issue in the context of Japanese Americans). Although economic and demographic factors have received some attention (for example, Evans 1977; Merriman 1991), the abiding concern has been with the claim that Japanese culture is particularly effective at socializing individuals into law-abiding subjects. Heavily influenced by Ruth Benedict's *The Chrysanthemum and the Sword* (1946), criminologists have argued that Japanese cultural values have created an environment in which informal social controls exert a tremendously powerful pressure to conform. As such, this framework owes much to the insights of Travis Hirschi's (1969) control theory.

The broad pattern of this argument about Japan is well documented (on the anthropological literature see Benedict 1946; Nakane 1970; Reischauer 1978; Magasatsu 1982; Hendry 1987). It is suggested that Japanese culture ascribes a special value on the group as the source of personal identity. Self-control is strongly encouraged in the context of a social order where self-esteem requires the approval of others (Doi 1971: ch. 1). Because individuals are tied into these hierarchical groups their behavior is subjected to constant surveillance, and a failure to live up to the expectations of others has social and psychological consequences. Individuals constantly monitor themselves and tend not to engage in any deviant behavior. Everyone develops a deep stake in conformity and a desire to preserve the harmony of the "in-group" (Komiya 1999: 372–4). Clifford summarizes this view in the following way: Japan is a social world in which each person:

> [h]as a proper place, everyone fits into the hierarchy of a vertical society: everyone...has a recognized position to fill in the scheme of things, and he is expected to live up to it. The Japanese society is so constructed that if he does live up to it, then he will benefit; if he does not live up to it then he will be despised and bring shame on all those connected with him. (1976: 8–10)

In a society where the opinions of others provide the sole criteria for behavior, a failure to live up to these expectations produces an insufferable degree of shame. To be abandoned by the group is in an important sense to be robbed of one's identity. The desire to maintain a sense of self-worth produces conformity. Individualism is equated with selfishness and is hence discouraged. Consequently, those crimes that do occur tend to be group-based (most obviously, organized or politically motivated crime), where individuals in fact "conform to the non-conformity" (Clifford 1976: 31; see also Raz 1993). The low crime statistics simply reflect the social reality: a culture in which informal social controls exert a tremendously powerful pressure to conform.

This is not the occasion for a substantive review of this argument. However, it is worth pointing out that the continued pervasiveness of culture as the key explanatory variable within much of the criminological literature is noteworthy. Not least, because it is this kind of "culture-based" approach that has been questioned in other academic disciplines concerned with Japan (see Dale 1993 for an overview of this trend). In socio-legal studies, for example, the "myth of the reluctant litigant" – the idea that the Japanese have a deep-rooted cultural aversion to the law (Kawashima 1997 [1963]; Noda 1976) – has been challenged by a younger generation of mainly US scholars keen to point out the structural obstacles to litigation (Upham 1987; Haley 1991, 1999; Ramseyer and Nakazato 1999). Certainly, an emphasis on Japanese culture as the source of the low crime rates feeds into broader conceptions of Japanese "uniqueness" and provides some legitimacy for a nationalism that continues to exert influence. The problem is not the concept of culture *per se,* but rather the concept of culture that is utilized, namely as something that corresponds with national boundaries and is racially pure. Such an approach often ignores the hybrid nature of Japanese culture: the failure to broaden the argument out through comparisons with East Asian countries, most obviously South Korea, is particularly unfortunate. Moreover, there is little consideration of the historical dimension of the crime issue. Specifically, the fact that in the immediate prewar and postwar period, Japan had comparable (and in some cases higher) crime rates than the United States or the United Kingdom, in spite of the influence of the same Japanese culture that purportedly explains the subsequent decline in crime.

The second body of English-language criminological research on Japan consists of empirical studies of various criminal justice agencies, such as the police or penal system. It is argued that Japanese criminal justice agencies have adopted a very different (and effective) approach to the transgression of social norms, and that there is much that commentators and practitioners in the West could learn from such methods. These are variously labeled "reintegrative shaming" (Braithwaite 1989) or "benevolent paternalism" (Foote 1992), and through them criminologists have focused on the informal, community-based nature of crime control in Japan.

According to Braithwaite (1989: 100–1), reintegrative shaming is "shaming which is followed by efforts to reintegrate the offender back into the community of law-abiding or responsible citizens through words or gestures of forgiveness or ceremonies to decertify the offender as deviant." At various points in his book, Braithwaite suggests that Japan is a model of such an approach (see especially 1989: 61–5). In making this claim, he draws on the work of other scholars whose empirical research suggests that this focus on community and reintegration is what accounts for the peculiar effectiveness of Japanese criminal justice agencies. Bayley (1991 [1976]), for example, presents an upbeat and affectionate portrayal of the Japanese police in which he places great emphasis on their integration into local community life, the broad scope of their activities, and their routinized use of informal forms of social control as a means of maintaining social order. A focus on the pivotal role of the *koban,* or police box, in Japanese policing encouraged Bayley in the belief that such a community-style, preventive policing could be usefully transplanted to an American context. The novelty of this argument when the first edition of Bayley's book was first published in 1976 should not be underestimated. Elmer Johnson in his research on the Japanese correction service (1996, 1997; Johnson and Johnson 2000) presents a similar assessment of the penal system and its effectiveness (see also Shikata and Tsuchiya 1990). A "parsimony" in the use of prison, the "tranquility" and "orderliness" of life inside the prison, and the relative ease with which repentant offenders are reintegrated back into society are all linked to the "cultural heritage" of the Japanese (Johnson 1996: 292). In such accounts,

Japan is thus portrayed as a rare example of the successful implementation of various novel forms of community-based preventive policies. The distinctive feature of penal modernity in a Japanese context is the marriage of Western ideas of rehabilitation with an Asian concern for community control and more informal forms of reintegration. The low crime rates are thus interpreted as a function of culturally distinctive patterns of social control.

It is interesting to note that this work has, on occasion, been criticized by Japanese scholars on the grounds that it is too willing to accept official self-representations of criminal justice agents. Whereas Bayley (1991 [1976]) and to a lesser extent Ames (1981) portray police practice as a successful example of reintegrative shaming practices, Miyazawa's (1992) research on the police paints a rather different picture (see also Araki 1988; Yokoyama 2001). According to these more critical accounts, the police are less interested in reintegrating offenders through informal sanctions than manipulating their legal powers to detain offenders for the purposes of securing confessions. Miyazawa (1992: chs.12, 13) links this to the bureaucratic pressures placed on the police to maintain high clearing rates. This more critical view of police practice fits with the findings of various human rights organizations that have often been critical of the police, as have constitutional scholars concerned at the unwillingness of the Supreme Court to clamp down on police abuses (see Foote 1991; George 1996; Koyama 2000).

Other criminal justice agencies are perhaps less reintegrative than is sometimes suggested. Recidivism rates amongst former prisoners are consistently high, reflecting the genuine difficulties that convicted criminals have in achieving a normal life after release from detention (Miyazawa 1997: 201). The prison regimes themselves have also been criticized on the grounds that there is little in the way of treatment or vocational training, and the work that prisoners are forced to do is both menial and degrading (Amnesty International 1998). Moreover, it is a mistake to regard this as state-sanctioned implementation of a culturally specific policy of reintegration. Rather, many of the measures introduced in postwar Japanese criminal justice (i.e., the high levels of suspended prosecutions, the use of volunteer probation officers, and the frequent use of suspended sentences) can equally be interpreted as an effective means of limiting the burden on the state. Miyazawa (1997) suggests that such measures can be characterized by an unwillingness on the part of government to make a significant "investment" in criminal justice rather than in a strategic or culturally informed reintegrative project. However, the view persists within much of the literature in English that penal modernity has taken a relatively effective form in the Japanese case, and that this is linked to the considered use of culturally specific forms of reintegration. It has been suggested that this is the reason why Japan has not experienced exploding crime rates or the kind of generalized crisis of penal modernity that has disrupted criminal justice in a Western context over the last two decades.

In spite of some of the limitations already mentioned, it is important to emphasize that these two bodies of research have made an extremely valuable contribution to the question of Japanese crime rates and to the developing literature on comparative criminology. Highlighting the role of culture provides a powerful corrective to the view that the ascendance of capitalism necessarily weakens traditional pre-capitalist forms of social solidarity and somehow inevitably generates high levels of crime. Moreover, the literature on criminal justice agencies provides important empirical evidence of issues (such as the Japanese police), which are rarely discussed within criminology. Braithwaite, in particular, develops an innovative model that can provide the basis for a powerful critique of much contemporary criminal justice practice. In an important sense the empirical validity of his argument about reintegrative shaming in Japan is of less importance than its broader normative force. The work of writers such as Braithwaite and Bayley played an important role in contributing to the increased popularity of the idea in the 1970s and 1980s that crime control needs to be relocated in the community (see Garland 2001: 123–4).

And yet, much of the criminological discussion of Japan has tended to proceed from an overly positivist conception of a crime problem. That is to say, it takes the official statistics at face value, as an accurate index of the presence – or in this case, absence – of crime. Explaining the absence of crime in Japan came to dominate the English-language criminological research agenda. Now clearly, this is an important issue, and it would be naïve to suggest that Japanese crime rates are, in fact, as high as they are in a European or North American context or even that underreporting of crime can explain away much of the difference. What is equally clear, however, is that the extant literature has failed to offer a sustained discussion of the *presence* of images and experience of crime in everyday life and their relationship with the operation of criminal justice and crime control. Comparative criminologists need to adopt a method that is sensitive to the social representations of crime rather than simply assume that the relatively low crime *statistics* reflect the absence of crime from ordinary social experience. A more pluralistic conception of a crime problem would highlight what is rarely commented upon in the literature, namely the constant proximity and pervasiveness of images, fictions, and representations of crime in ordinary social life (see Schrieber 1996 for a journalistic take on this issue). To use the concept developed by Sasson in the context of the United States (1995), "crime talk" is pervasive in Japan. The idea that Japan is a "nation not obsessed with crime" (Adler 1983) in some sense misses this point, and reflects an international perspective on the crime statistics. From a Japanese point of view, the situation can sometimes appear rather different.

There are various ways that crime talk is present in everyday Japanese life. What follows will offer a more sustained comment on youth crime as an illustration of this claim. However, it might be useful to make a couple of general points about the various fora within which this concern with crime manifests itself. Firstly, there is the presence of crime in the mass media. As in the United States and Europe, crime forms the staple component of many TV dramas and films. Moreover, it is central to the world of the *manga* comic books that continue to be extremely popular. Crime also receives extensive coverage in the news media. In part, this is linked to the introspective nature of a media whose primary concern is with domestic, rather than international, affairs. However, the extent of the coverage given to crime is startling to anyone who comes to Japan expecting the low crime rates to be reflected in popular culture. The so-called "wide shows" daily, tabloid magazine programs also feature extensive coverage on crime-related stories. Relatively loose restrictions on what can be reported and the close links between journalists and the police, mean that a large amount of semi-officially sanctioned information is regularly leaked to the press. Moreover, the journalists often conduct their own investigations in the shadow of the police with witnesses being interviewed on camera and former police and prosecutors being called upon to comment on interesting aspects of a case.

Secondly, and perhaps more significantly, there is the presence of crime in social life. Again this is a topic that receives little attention (although see Ito 1993 for a discussion of the fear of crime), but as with the media, crime talk is prevalent in civil society and rather undermines the idea that the social reality corresponds to a Western criminological perspective on the statistics. To take just one example, community life in Japan is structured around a series of local committees comprising members of the immediate neighborhood who, on a rotation basis, take it in turns to manage various aspects of community life. These local committees perform a number of functions such as distributing information, organizing waste disposal, local festivals, and street cleaning, as well as, on occasion, mediating any low-level disputes that may arise. However, some of the most important tasks are directly related to crime. Local committees coordinate with local police and government officials to provide regular circulars on crimes that have occurred in the area or to report on the suspicious activities of strangers. They also produce posters that contain crime warnings as well as street patrols that police areas around local schools. Finally, they provide extensive information on crime prevention and security advice. This explains, in part, what might seem like an anomaly, namely the flourishing private security industry. Academics have suggested that these committees have played a crucial role in crime prevention (Kusuda-Smick 1990; Thornton and Endo 1992). More recently, commentators have argued that their effectiveness has diminished as a result of the long-term effects of urbanization. This may well be the case. In this context, however, I simply want to point to the activities of these local committees as one illustration of the pervasiveness of crime talk.

A focus on explaining the perceived absence of crime in Japan has meant that there has been a neglect of the multitude of ways that crime is actually present in everyday experience. Moreover, a focus on explaining the low rates of crime (which is understandably of interest to foreign observers) gives rise to a situation in which various developments important within a Japanese context are neglected. The remaining sections of the essay considers in more detail one particular example of how crime has been present in public and political life in recent years, namely the "moral panic" surrounding youth crime and the recent reform of the juvenile justice system.

THE MORAL PANIC OVER YOUTH VIOLENCE

In May 1997, in the port city of Kobe in the west of Japan, an 11-year-old boy named Jun Hase was reported missing after leaving home to visit his grandparents. Three days later his severed head was discovered in front of the main gate of a local school. With the head was a note – apparently written by the killer – expressing his hatred of the school and of society in general. Later the same day, a decapitated corpse was found close to the school. Within a few days the focus of the investigation was a 14-year-old boy from the same school who was known to have been bullying Jun. An analysis of the suspect's schoolwork was carried out and the handwriting matched the note found with the body. The next day, the police arrested the 14-year-old, whom the media came to refer to as *Shonen A* ("young person A"). The violent nature of the murder of Jun Hase and the fact that it was perpetrated by a fellow student shocked the nation. In that respect it can be compared with the murder of James Bulger in the United Kingdom: an individual tragedy that came to symbolize a more generalized societal malaise about youth crime and youth more generally. Along with the Sarin gas attack on the Tokyo subway, the Great Hanshin earthquake, and the collapse of the "bubble" economy, the Kobe murder was a defining moment of the 1990s.

In order to provide some context for the subsequent discussion, it is worth dwelling on the various elements that comprise the current moral panic. First, there is a widespread perception that youth crime, and particularly violent crimes, have increased. The official statistics provide some support for this claim. The National Police Agency, for example, recorded 2,237 "heinous crimes" committed by juveniles in 1999, as opposed to figures hovering around 1,200–1,300 for much of the earlier part of the decade (National Police Agency, 1999: 31–7). However, it is the nature of some of these crimes and the extensive coverage that they have received in the media that has further fueled public concern. In one case, for example, a 17-year-old boy who murdered a woman he had never met was reported to have told police that he did it out of a desire to "experience killing someone." In May 2000, another 17-year-old, unemployed youth hijacked an intercity bus with a large kitchen knife in Saga prefecture. He held a six-year-old girl hostage, killed one elderly woman, and wounded five others. The so-called "bus-jack" was shown live on television on a national holiday. The boy forced the driver to travel across the country for over 18 hours before police successfully stormed the bus and freed the hostages. Finally, there was the case of a 15-year-old boy who crept into a neighbor's house during the night and attacked a family. All six family members were stabbed, and three later died. It was widely reported that the one of the victims had earlier caught the boy spying on her whilst she bathed. A steady stream of similar meaningless crimes perpetrated by alienated, teenage boys have fueled public concern about violent youth.

The second element of this moral panic revolves around the activities of youth gangs, the so-called *bosozoku*. In an excellent ethnographic account of the activities of *bosozoku*, Ikuya Sato (1991) describes the main features of what he characterizes as these modern-day "kamikaze bikers." They are most famously associated with high-risk car and motorcycle driving. On weekend nights in the summer, the streets of many Japanese cities are disturbed as large numbers of cars, whose original appearance has been modified beyond recognition, drive at speeds well in excess of the legal limits. Carefully dressed in bizarre, "post-punk" costumes, they live for *boso*, high speed, high risk, and illegal driving. Although police figures suggest there are only around 40,000 "official" members throughout Japan, the disruption they cause and the apparent unwillingness of the authorities to actively do anything about what can be a serious public nuisance means that they exert a disruptive influence on many people's lives. However, the widespread belief is that these gangs engage in a range of other kinds of criminal activities. Certainly, there have been a number of violent attacks on members of the public who have complained about the noise and there are also several cases of inter-gang fights. These gangs also feed into other concerns, namely suggestions of connections with organized crime (Kersten 1993) and increased levels of drug use among teenagers (National Police Agency 2000: 42–6).

Third, there has been the rise of *enjo kosai*, a dating phenomenon involving teenage girls and older men (Kawai 1997). *Enjo kosai* literally means "dating for assistance," and the "assistance" in this context is invariably financial. In return for payments, young girls provide middle-aged men with their company. Although no one has any clear idea how many girls are engaged in *enjo kosai*, the 1999 Police White Paper on Crime reports that in 1998 4,510 girls received "guidance" (i.e., were taken into police custody) in connection with "sexual misconduct" (i.e., prostitution) (National Police Agency 2000: 33). Although in absolute terms this figure is low, it is worth noting that the figure in 1990 was 913. Again, though, it is the media-fueled public perception of this phenomenon that is perhaps more significant. Concern has focused on the fact that most of these girls seem to be motivated by financial reasons, in spite of levels of affluence that older generations could scarcely have imagined in the immediate postwar period. Moreover, a series of violent crimes involving these girls engaged in *enjo kosai* have focused public attention on the seemingly unregulated "telephone-dating clubs" that provide a forum for arranging these meetings (National Police Agency 1999: 44). In a particularly troubling recent case, a junior high school teacher is alleged to have thrown a 12-year-old-girl out of his car on the freeway, after arranging to meet her through such a telephone-dating service.

Finally, there is the problem of violence and a more generalized lack of discipline within schools. Acts of violence have been steadily increasing since the early 1990s. Or at least, that is the impression that is being generated by official statistics. In 1985, for example, the number of officially recorded acts of violence was 283 for senior high schools and 1,173 for junior high schools. The corresponding figures for 1999 were 1,726 and 3,572 (Ministry of Education, personal communication). Equally disturbing has been the increase in violent attacks against teachers. Hovering at around 500 since the 1980s, they have recently increased to over 2,000 per year (Ministry of Education, personal communication). Once again, the relatively low level of these numbers in international terms should not obscure the fact that from the Japanese perspective these are unprecedented increases over a relatively short space of time. As such, it links to a more general perception that the system of education is in crisis and in urgent need of reform. Schools seem increasingly incapable of producing the regimented, obedient subjects who, for much of the postwar period, have seamlessly moved into a labor market characterized by lifetime employment. Over the last decade, both sides of this system have come under increasing strain, with a worsening economic situation paralleling the kind of disciplinary problem mentioned above. An image of teenagers as sullen, disobedient, and lacking in self-discipline, may not strike Western observers as particularly startling, and yet in Japan, it has come to symbolize a broader set of concerns about the collapse of the stability and prosperity characteristic of the postwar order.

This sense of confusion and anger is further compounded by the lack of respect that many young people show to their social "superiors." To use Ralph Miliband's (1978) influential concept, "de-subordination" is becomingly increasingly prevalent. One potent example of this that has received extensive media coverage recently surrounds the annual school-reunion ceremonies that are organized by local governments for high school students two years after their graduation. Recently, at a number of these ceremonies local dignitaries have been subjected to heckling and fights have even broken out. In a society that places such an emphasis on social hierarchy and respect for seniors, such behavior is genuinely perplexing.

A "by-the-book" debate as to the causes of this crisis in youth has flourished in recent years. With causes attributed to everything from "bad" diet (the influence of junk food) to a more conservative emphasis on declining levels of discipline in the classroom and poor parenting, the task of understanding why large numbers of young people are seemingly out of control has become something of a national obsession. The extent to which this perceived increase in criminal and antisocial behavior among young people is a genuine trend is, however, much less clear. Criminologists have pointed to the fact that youth crime has actually been falling steadily since the 1960s. Moreover, the upsurge in "heinous crime" is not necessarily something particularly new either. Many more such crimes were committed in the immediate postwar period and in the 1960s. Aware of these historical parallels, many commentators in the media have focused on an interesting contrast between the current spate of violent crimes and earlier crime waves. The postwar period was characterized by a poverty and hunger that, although not justifying crime, at least go some way to explaining it. Equally, the crimes of the 1960s often had a different, and in some ways understandable, political dimension. For example, in 1960 Inejiro Asanuma, chairman of the Japanese Socialist Party, was stabbed to death, and in the following year an attack on the home of prominent businessman Shimanaka Hoji resulted in the death of his maid and serious injury to his wife. Teenage right-wing extremists were responsible for both of these crimes. However, with these crimes there was less questioning of the motives of the perpetrators: it at least made some sense to ascribe them to fervently held political views. After all, the 1960s were a period of extreme political upheaval (see Katzenstein and Tsujinka 1991; Katzenstein 1996). Political radicalism was at least something adults could identify with, even if the results of that radicalism were clearly undesirable. In contrast, however, the general view exists today that young people are profoundly different from their parents' generation (not least by virtue of their apoliticism). It is the apparently nihilistic nature of the current crime wave that is so deeply troubling to the older generation.

RECENT REFORMS

Some discussion about reforming the system of juvenile justice had occurred prior to the Kobe incident. However, it is clear that this event provided fresh impetus to reform efforts. In October 1997 the government established a committee to look into possible changes. In April 1998, this committee made a series of recommendations, which after a long and protracted process of negotiation and compromise between politicians, lawyers, prosecutors, and other interest groups resulted in the passing of Law no. 142 amending the Juvenile Law in November 2000. This section will briefly consider the resulting changes. It will be suggested that the new law can be understood, at least in part, as a partial response to the experience of youth crime discussed in the previous section, and that the new emphasis on punitiveness, victims' rights, and parental responsibility represents a significant break with previous policy.

The Japanese system of juvenile justice was established by the Juvenile Law of 1947, which was drafted under the influence of US occupational forces and was, until recently, widely regarded in Japan as one of the most successful aspects of penal policy (see generally Johnson 1996: ch. 7; Yokoyama 1997). The purpose of the law can be found in Article 1: "The object of the law is, with a view to the wholesome rearing of juveniles to carry out protective measures relating to the character, correction and environmental adjustment of delinquent juveniles." The system is based on notions of protection and tolerance toward the juvenile offender who is regarded as much as a victim as a criminal (on this point see Izumi-Tyson 2000). The system was designed, at least in principle, to protect juveniles from the stigma of crime and the environment that produced their delinquent behavior. In keeping with this principle, the law makes no mention of punishment: its primary aim was simply to rehabilitate the offender. This is particularly significant when one considers Article 2, namely that "the term juvenile shall mean any person under 20 years of age."

Once a juvenile has been arrested, the police can hold them for up to 48 hours before the case must be passed to prosecutor. Except in cases where it is "absolutely necessary" (which, in practice, rarely arise), the prosecutor must then refer the case to the Family Court within a further 24 hours. This procedure was designed to protect suspects from the kind of vigorous police and prosecutorial questioning described by Miyazawa (1992) and other commentators. A case is then transferred to the Family Court, where a single judge, assisted by a court-appointed investigator, examines the offender. An extensive search of the suspect's background, family and school life, and psychological condition is carried out before the judge decides whether to pursue the case. In 1951, 39.8 percent of cases referred to the Family Court were dismissed without a hearing. By the mid-1990s this figure was over 70 percent (Johnson 1996: 164). Whether this reflected a considered awareness of the stigmatizing effects of a formal hearing, or was simply a function of the heavy caseload of a small number of judges, the majority of cases were diverted out of the system without any formal sanction. In this regard, the system parallels the practice of adult criminal justice (see Haley 1999: ch. 6).

Hearings are not open to the public and must be conducted in a "cordial atmosphere" (Article 22). They tended to be relatively informal, at least in the sense that very few procedural restrictions are in place. The symbols of power so typical of adult criminal trials were dispensed with, as participants would sit around a table in a small room. Normally present at the hearings would be the judge, the court-appointed investigator, the suspect, and the parent or guardian. Under the original law, neither the prosecutor nor the victim or their families were entitled to participate in the hearing. And, for whatever reason, many suspects chose not have any legal representation.

In disposing of those cases that reach the hearing stage, the judge has a range of options. There are various forms of conditional or non-conditional discharge, which account for the largest number of cases. A custodial option is used in a very small number of cases (less that 5 percent of all cases in the mid-1990s; Johnson 1996: 164). What is of particular interest, however, is the option to refer a case back to the prosecutor with a view to prosecuting a juvenile in an adult criminal court (Article 20). Under the original law, this discretionary power only applied to particularly serious crimes committed by a juvenile aged between 16 and 20. However, this was an option that the judges were increasingly unwilling to take, even in the most serious of cases. In 1951, 5.6 percent of all cases were referred to the prosecutor, by 1990 this figure had declined to 0.5 percent (Johnson 1996: 164). According to Ministry of Justice officials, only 20–30 percent of underage murderers would receive any kind of criminal penalty in any given year.

The extent to which one might characterize this system as reintegrative is debatable. The limited use of custodial sentences, the clauses guaranteeing the anonymity of the suspect/offender, which until the Kobe case were strictly enforced, and the fact that an offender's record is erased at age 20 suggests at least the possibility of some form of reintegration. And yet, the social stigma associated with any suggestion of criminal wrongdoing should not be underestimated in a society such as Japan where "face" is so important. Certainly, until relatively recently the law was generally seen as highly effective. Soon after the Kobe murder, however, and in the broader context of the moral panic described above, there were increasing calls from politicians and media commentators to reform the law.

Various aspects of the system were identified as problematic. First, it was regarded as "unfair" in that it was oriented toward the offender rather than the victim. In fact, the exclusion of the victim from the process became one of the key issues in the ensuing debate. There were stories of parents of murder victims, receiving almost no information on the details of their child's death or of the murderer's identity or motive. Second, it was argued that the law was based on naive assumptions of childish innocence. Offenders were not forced to take responsibility for their actions. This is particularly significant when one considers the relatively high age of 20. Third, the fact that any criminal record was erased when the suspect reached the age of 20, combined with the guarantees of anonymity meant that many people felt the law failed to have any real value as a deterrent. On the contrary, the law was seen as providing an invitation to commit crimes safe in the belief that there would be minimal consequences. Finally, there was the absence of a punitive moment, symbolized by the limited use of custodial sanctions, the exclusion of the prosecutor from the hearings, and the unwillingness of the judges to exercise their discretionary power to refer cases back to the prosecutor for criminal prosecution. Critics of the law drew upon a widespread public outrage at the kind of cases mentioned above to discredit a law that was seen as out of touch with popular attitudes toward criminal wrongdoing. Other aspects of the law that might reasonably have been criticized, namely the extensive powers to detain youth who have not committed any criminal offense but may be "prone to do so" (Article 3(3)) and the lack of due process protection for suspects were rarely, if ever, raised.

The process of reform was long and protracted and a detailed review is beyond the scope of this essay. However, it is worth noting the extent to which discussion of reform of the law became a prominent issue in political debate. The Prime Minister at that time, Yoshiro Mori, and his ruling Liberal Democratic Party utilized the issue in an attempt to muster popular electoral support in both national and local elections. This was unusual in that the kind of politicization of crime so typical of the modern-day United States or United Kingdom is still relatively uncommon in Japan. Another feature of the debate was the extent to which the political class relied on popular support to discredit the concerns of lawyers, juvenile justice workers, and academics opposed to reform. Again, this displacement of criminal justice experts through an appeal to broader public support is less common in Japan, where such expertise is still accorded a great deal of respect.

The result of this process was Law no. 142, amending the Juvenile Law, which completed its passage through the Diet in November 2000. In the end the law was passed with the support of not only the government coalition parties, but also the two main opposition parties to the left of center, the Democratic Party (who had earlier opposed changes) and the right-wing Liberal Party. Only the Communist Party and Social Democratic Party voted against the bill, arguing that it would destroy the principles of protection and reintegration on which the system was based. The new law – which marked the first significant revision to the system since it came into force in 1949 – introduced a number of significant changes to the Juvenile Law.

The revised law lowered from 16 to 14 the minimum age at which juveniles can be held criminally responsible for their acts. It is now possible for a 14-year-old who has committed a serious offense to have their case referred to the prosecutor for criminal prosecution (Article 20 of the revised law). The most obvious consequence of this change is that the killer of Jun Hase – who was aged 14 at the time of the offense – would now at least face the possibility of a criminal prosecution. Moreover, the revised law requires that in principle the Family Court should send all juvenile murder suspects aged 16 or older to the prosecutor so that they can be put on criminal trial (Article 20(2) of the revised law). Although it still remains a discretionary power, the presumption would now appear to be firmly in favor of such referrals. Although Article 1 of the law was not changed, it seems clear that the revised law places a new emphasis on punitiveness and expressive justice. The rehabilitative ideal may not have been entirely displaced, but it has clearly lost its preeminent status.

This impression is further compounded by a number of other significant changes. First, Article 22 has been revised. The previous emphasis on the "cordiality" of the proceedings has also been supplemented by the requirement that juvenile offenders must engage in "soul-searching" over the crimes they have committed. Lawmakers seem to have accepted the criticism that unrepentant offenders were taking advantage of the informal nature of proceedings under the old system. Now the logic appears to be that protection and rehabilitation of offenders can only occur after the offender has recognized their criminal responsibility and feels remorse for their victims. Secondly, a newly added section (Article 22(2)(i)) gives the Court the discretionary power to allow the prosecutor to participate in the hearing. Again, it only applies to serious cases, but it does point to a change to a more adversarial type of hearing. The prosecutor was also given the right to petition a higher court in order to review the findings of the Family Court. Although not the full prosecutorial right of appeal enjoyed by Japanese prosecutors in adult criminal procedure, it still represents a significant power. Critics of these changes point to the fact that the mere presence of the prosecutor in the Family Court would disturb the delicate search for truth characteristic of the judge–court investigator relationship under the former system. Article 22(3), requiring that a lawyer for the defendant be present if a prosecutor is involved, reinforces this impression of a shift from a more welfare-oriented to legalistic style of proceedings. Finally, a series of complex procedural changes related to sentencing mean that any offender convicted for a serious crime will serve a longer sentence before being eligible for parole.

The amended law also strengthens the rights of the victims. Victims and their relatives have the right to be notified of the Family Court's findings (Article 31(2) of the revised law), and may be given access to copies of investigation records (Article 5 of the revised law). Victims or relatives will also be given an opportunity to present their views at any hearing that is held (Article 9(2) of the revised law). The law does not, however, go as far as many victims' groups wished. Victims will not be allowed to attend the hearings in their entirety, although such a measure was strongly urged. It seems that one of the government coalition members – the Buddhist New Komei Party – insisted that the privacy of the underage suspect would almost be inevitably violated if details of the trials were leaked, as they might be if victims were too involved. Notwithstanding this last point, the introduction of these measures related to victims marks an important change.

Finally, under the revised law (Article 25(2)) judges have been given the power to issue warnings and instructions to parents of juveniles falling under their jurisdiction. It is as yet unclear what form such admonitions might take, but this new emphasis on parental responsibility reflects broader concerns about socially irresponsible parenting as a possible cause of the current problem. A recent government-sponsored TV ad campaign has focused on the same issue. In one ad, a woman in her early thirties sits alone in a darkened room with a baby's dummy in her mouth. In another, a man of a similar age sits staring at the TV, also sucking a dummy. In both cases the caption reads: "Just because you have a child, it doesn't mean you are a parent." The changes to the law and such publicity campaigns send a clear message to parents that they need to take responsibility for their children's acts. Instead of simply addressing the crime in a direct fashion by means of a punitive sanction against the offender, this approach promotes a different kind of indirect action, which attempts to prevent crime through a new form of "governing at a distance."

The reformed law came into effect in April 2001 and within one year its impact – particularly in terms of the effect on how very serious crimes are treated – is clear. According to figures released by the Secretariat of the Supreme Court for the period April 2001–February 2002, there was a significant increase in the number of cases referred back to the prosecutor for criminal prosecution. In that period, there were 59 cases of serious crimes in the 16–20 age category: 9 murder cases, 8 cases of robbery resulting in death, and 42 cases of bodily injury resulting in death. Of these, 6 murder cases, all 8 cases of robbery resulting in death, and 28 cases of bodily injury resulting in death were sent back to prosecutors. This was a sharp rise from the average figures since the 1990s – 67 percent from 25 percent for murder, 100 percent from 42 percent for robbery resulting in death, and 67 percent from 9 percent for bodily injury resulting in death. Of the 59 cases, 21 were handled with three judges attending, 25 with prosecutors participating, and 6 with state-paid defense lawyers for the suspects. Interestingly, no cases involving young offenders aged 14–16 were returned to the prosecutor during this period.

It seems clear that the reform of the juvenile law is an important event in the postwar history of Japanese crime control. Not only because it represents the first substantive change to a law that has been in place for over fifty years, and has, until recently, been regarded as a great success. But, perhaps more importantly, because it reflects a profound change in the language and substance of youth justice policy. A traditional concern with protection and rehabilitation has clearly been displaced by a new emphasis on punitiveness, the rights of the victim, and notions of parental responsibility. As such, the new law marks an important break in the rhetoric and practice of Japanese crime control.

CONCLUSION

It is worth concluding by very briefly alluding to a number of other recent developments that have occurred in the field of criminal justice, and which indicate a possible broader shift in the form of Japanese crime control. Most notably, there have been a series of high-profile corruption scandals involving the police that have severely damaged public confidence. There has also been the emergence of a vocal victims' rights movement that elicits extensive public support. Anxiety over public security has struggled to recover from the Aum Shinrikyo cult's Sarin gas attack on the Tokyo subway. In addition, the violent murder of eight primary school children in Ikeda city, Osaka in 2002 by a man with a history of mental illness led to controversial proposals to reform procedure related to how mentally incapacitated offenders are dealt with in the criminal justice system. And there is increased concern over crime committed by foreigners (including US military personnel) and the impact of organized crime gangs from China. Finally, public criticism of judicial handling of high-profile criminal trials and sentencing practices has also become increasingly common. The government responded to these and other problems by creating a Justice System Reform Council whose recently published report (2001) attempted to address some of these concerns by recommending a series of significant reforms in the organization of criminal justice, most notably the introduction of a jury system.

This not the occasion for a detailed review of these developments, but what is striking is how – at one level – the themes of declining public confidence in the police, the emergence of victims' rights, the displacement of the rehabilitative ideal, and the increasing gap between judicial practice and the public mood echo similar developments in Europe and the United States. Moreover, one of the key lessons of the reform of the Juvenile Law would appear to be that the current political class are willing to resort to populist measures in the area of criminal justice policy in an attempt to secure their own fading fortunes. Certainly, if the opinion polls are to be believed, public support for the changes discussed in this essay seems widespread. The kind of crime talk discussed earlier has provided a context in which the protesting voices of academics and legal professionals have been drowned out by a population in despair over a series of violent, seemingly nihilistic crimes. Again, this is a trend which can be compared with similar developments in Western penality, notably the emergence of crime as an issue in electoral politics and the way that criminal justice policy-making is increasingly driven by individual high-profile cases rather than generalized trends or expert knowledge. Finally, many of the broader social changes associated with the transition to late modernity, and which are often identified as crucial factors in explaining the crisis of penal modernity, apply equally in the case of Japan (see Garland 2001). Most obviously these would include economic instability and changes in the form of family life, as well as the displacement of the nation-state as an actor capable of effectively managing increasingly complex globalized societies. Once again, the parallels are striking.

And yet, it is important not to push such comparisons too far. Clearly there is nothing like the generalized crisis of penal modernity that has so changed the criminological landscape in the United Kingdom and United States. Moreover, at a purely abstract level it is clearly dangerous to read into Japanese events a theoretical framework borrowed from a very different regional context. In fact, it was one of the virtues of the earlier generation of English-language criminological research that they remained so aware of the *distinctive* features of the Japanese experience. Perhaps they could be criticized for failing to develop a more sophisticated concept of culture or for failing to consider the Asian dimension of Japanese culture, but nevertheless they clearly recognized the crucial importance of a sensitivity to local difference. If the reform of the Juvenile Law can be interpreted as one element in a broader, and as yet nascent, crisis in Japanese penal modernity, it remains important that any such account also identifies the culturally distinctive as well as the common features of that reconfiguration. In pursuing this task criminologists would have to rely upon the earlier generation of writers. The challenge for the next generation of English-language criminologists interested in Japan is to combine the insights of these earlier writers with a new set of research questions that focus on the presence of crime, and the challenge of characterizing the contemporary reconfiguration of Japanese crime control.

References

Adler, F. (1983) *Nations not Obsessed with Crime*. Littleton, CO: Fred Rothman.

Ames, W. L. (1981) *Police and Community in Japan*. Berkeley: University of California Press.

Amnesty International (1998) Abusive punishments in Japanese prisons. Available online at http://www.amnesty.org/ailib/aipub/1998/SUM/32200498.htm

Araki, N. (1988) The role of police in Japanese society. *Law and Society Review*, 22, 601–29.

Archer, D., and Gartner, R. (1981) Homicide in 110 nations: the development of the comparative crime data file. In L. I. Shelley (ed.), *Readings in Comparative Criminology*. Carbondale: Southern Illinois University Press.

Bayley, D. (1991) [1976] *Forces of Order: Policing Modern Japan*. Berkeley, CA: University of California Press.

Benedict, R. (1946) *The Chrysanthemum and the Sword*. Tokyo: Tuttle.

Braithwaite, J. (1989) *Crime, Shame and Reintegration*. Cambridge: Cambridge University Press.

Castberg, D. (1990) *Japanese Criminal Justice*. New York: Praeger.

Clifford, W. (1976) *Crime Control in Japan*. Lexington, MA: Lexington Books.

Dale, P. (1993) *The Myth of Japanese Uniqueness*. London: Routledge.

Doi, T. (1971) *The Anatomy of Dependence*. Tokyo: Tuttle.

Evans, R. (1977) Changing labor markets and criminal behavior in Japan. *Journal of Asian Studies*, 16, 477–89.

Fenwick, C. R. (1985) Culture, philosophy and crime: the Japanese experience. *International Journal of Comparative and Applied Criminal Justice*, 9, 10–30.

Finch, A. (2001) Homicide in contemporary Japan. *British Journal of Criminology*, 41, 219–35.

Foote, D. H. (1991) Confessions and the right to silence in Japan. *Georgia Journal of International and Comparative Law*, 21, 415–88.

Foote, D. H. (1992) The benevolent paternalism of Japanese criminal justice. *California Law Review*, 80, 317.

Fujimoto, T. (1978) *Crime and Delinquency among the Japanese Americans*. Tokyo: Institute of Comparative Law.

Fukuyama, F. (1999) *The Great Disruption: Human Nature and the Reconstitution of Social Order*. New York: Simon & Schuster.

Garland. D. (2001) *The Culture of Control*. Chicago: University of Chicago Press.

George, B. J. (1996) The rights of the criminally accused. In K. Port (ed), *Comparative Law: Law and the Legal Process in Japan*. Durham, NC: Carolina Academic Press.

Haley, J. O. (1991) *Authority without Power: Law and the Japanese Paradox*. New York: Oxford University Press.

Haley, J. O. (1999) *The Spirit of Japanese Law*. Athens: University of Georgia Press.

Hendry, J. (1987) *Understanding Japanese Society*. London: Routledge.

Hirschi, T. (1969) *Causes of Delinquency*. Berkeley, CA.: University California Press.

Ito, K. (1993) Research on the fear of crime: perceptions and realities of crime in Japan. *Crime and Delinquency*, 39, 385–92.

Izumi-Tyson, M. (2000) Revising *Shonenho*: a call to a reform that makes the already effective Japanese juvenile justice system even more effective. Available online at http://www.vanderbilt.edu/Law/journal/33-3-5.html

Johnson, E. H. (1996) *Japanese Corrections: Managing Convicted Offenders in an Orderly Society*. Carbondale: Southern Illinois University Press.

Johnson, E. H. (1997) *Crimininalization and Prisoners in Japan: Six Contrary Cohorts*. Carbondale: Southern Illinois University Press.

Johnson, E. H., and Johnson, C. H. (2000) *Linking Community and Corrections in Japan*. Carbondale: Southern Illinois University Press.

Justice System Reform Council. (2001) Recommendations of the Justice System Reform Council: For a justice system to support Japan in the 21st century. Available online at http://www.kantei.go.jp/foreign/judiciary/2001/0612report.html

Katzenstein, P. J. (1996) *Cultural Norms and National Security: Police and Military in Post-war Japan*. Ithaca: Cornell University Press.

Katzenstein, P. J., and Tsujinka, Y. (1991) *Defending the Japanese State: Structure, Norms and the Political Response to Terrorism and Violent Social Protest in the 1970s and 1980s*. Ithaca: Cornell University Press.

Kawai, H. (1997) The message from Japan's schoolgirl prostitutes. *Japan Echo*, 24(2), 56–68.

Kawashima, T. (1997) [1963] Dispute resolution in contemporary Japan. In M. Dean (ed.), *Japanese Legal System: Texts and Materials*. London: Routledge.

Kersten, J. (1993) Street crime, Bosozoku, and Yakuza. *Crime and Delinquency*, 39, 277–95.

Komiya, N. (1999) A cultural study of the low crime rate in Japan. *British Journal of Criminology*, 39, 369–90.

Koyama, M. (2000) The public prosecutor, criminal law, and the rights of the accused in Japan: Yet to strike a balance? In S. Nagel (ed.)., *Handbook of Global Legal Policy*. New York: M. Dekker.

Kusuda-Smick, V. (ed.) (1990) *Crime Prevention and Control in the United States and Japan*. Tokyo: Transnational Jurist Publications.

Magasatsu, M. (1982) *The Modern Samurai Society: Duty and Dependence in Contemporary Japan*. New York: AMA.

Merriman, D. (1991) An economic analysis of the post-World War II decline in the Japanese crime rate. *Journal of Quantitative Criminology*, 7, 19–39.

Miliband, R. (1978) A state of de-subordination. *British Journal of Sociology*, 29, 299–309.

Miyazawa, S. (1992) *Policing in Japan: A Study on Making Crime*. New York: State University of New York Press.

Miyazawa, S. (1997) The enigma of Japan as a testing ground for cross-cultural criminological studies. In D. Nelken (ed.), *Comparing Legal Cultures*. Aldershot: Dartmouth.

Nakane, C. (1970) *Japanese Society*. Tokyo: Tuttle.

National Police Agency (1999) *White Paper on Police, 1998*. Tokyo: Japan Times.

National Police Agency (2000) *White Paper on Police, 1999*. Tokyo: Japan Times.

Noda, Y. (1976) *Introduction of Japanese Law*. Tokyo: University of Tokyo Press.

Ramseyer, M. J., and Nakazato, M. (1999) *Japanese Law: An Economic Approach*. Chicago: University of Chicago Press.

Raz, J. (1993) *Aspects of Otherness in Japanese Culture*. Tokyo: ISL.

Reischauer, E. O. (1978) *The Japanese*. Tokyo: Tuttle.

Sasson, T. (1995) *Crime Talk: How Citizens Construct a Social Problem*. New York: Aldine de Gruyter.

Sato, I. (1991) *Kamikaze Biker*. Chicago: University of Chicago Press.

Schrieber, M. (1996) *Shocking Crimes of Post-War Japan*. Tokyo: Tuttle.

Shelley, L. (1981) *Crime and Modernization: The Impact of Industrialization and Urbanization on Crime*. Carbondale: University of Southern Illinois Press.

Shikata, M., and Tsuchiya, S. (eds.) (1990) *Crime and Criminal Policy from 1926 to 1988*. Tokyo: Japan Criminal Policy Society.

Thornton, R. Y., and Endo, K. (1992). *Preventing Crime in America and Japan: A Comparative Study*. London: M. E. Sharpe.

Upham, F. (1987) *Law and Social Change in Postwar Japan*. Cambridge, MA: Harvard University Press.

Westerman, T. D., and Burfeind, J. W. (1991) *Crime and Justice in Two Societies: Japan and the United States*. Pacific Grove: Brookes Cole.

Yokoyama, M. (1997) Juvenile justice: an overview of Japan. In J. Winterdyk (ed.), *Juvenile Justice Systems*. Toronto: Canadian Scholars' Press.

Yokoyama, M. (2001) Analysis of Japanese police from the viewpoint of democracy. In S. Einstein and M. Amir (eds.), *Policing Security and Democracy: Theory and Practice*. Huntsville, TX: Office of International Criminal Justice.

7

Consumer Culture and Crime in Late Modernity

Keith J. Hayward

Introduction

New and distinct consumer-driven patterns of relationships and integrative transformations are forcing us to reconsider virtually every aspect of contemporary society, from the cultural logic of materialist historicism to (even more fundamental) issues surrounding the notion of personal/individual identity. Yet, despite these significant changes and reformulations, criminology, in all its many theoretical variants, seems to have developed something of a studied disregard toward the subject of late modern consumer culture, choosing instead to uphold a more traditional materialist reading of the relationship between commodification and crime. In a bid to address this shortcoming, this essay has two aims: first, to introduce to a criminological audience the key themes and debates associated with the burgeoning literature on consumer culture and consumerism; and second, to identify and explore some of the overlapping theoretical terrain that now exists between this body of research and certain branches of theoretical criminology, the intention being to formulate some tentative theoretical links between these two seemingly distinct fields of inquiry.

Late Modern Consumer Culture: A Short Review of Key Themes

To understand contemporary society, it is essential to understand the role of consumer culture (for a general overview of the literature in this area, see Lury 1996; Slater 1997; Miles 1998). For many social theorists, the culture of consumption is now the most distinctive feature of advanced Western societies (Lasch 1979; Baudrillard 1981, 1994, 1996; Campbell 1989; Featherstone 1994; Bauman 1998). Two major consequences flow from this situation. The first thing to recognize is the extent to which consumerism has permeated all levels of society. The vast majority of people in the West now live in a world in which their everyday existence is, to a greater or lesser degree, dominated by the pervasive triad of advertising/marketing, the stylization of social life, and mass consumption. As Phillip Sampson has commented: "Once established, such a culture of consumption is quite undiscriminating and everything becomes a consumer item, including meaning, truth and knowledge" (quoted in Lyon 1994: 61). Importantly, in characterizing contemporary society as a consumer culture, I am not referring to particular patterns of needs and objects – a particular consumption culture – but rather to a *culture of consumption* (see Fromm 1976; Lasch 1979). To talk in this way is to regard the dominant values of society as deriving from the activity of consumption.

At this point it is important to address the latent question that constantly overshadows discussions of late (or post-) modern consumerism: specifically, how is all this different from classic Marxist accounts of capitalist commodification and the increasing subjection of all aspects of life to mediation through the cash nexus? For example, long before terms such as "late" or "post" modernity were being popularized, Raymond Williams (1974) – echoing the classical tradition of the Frankfurt School (see Horkheimer and Adorno 1973) – was urging orthodox Marxists toward the study of culture, in particular, the way that society's needs were increasingly being drawn into the marketplace. One important answer can be found in the recent work of Ian Taylor (1999). In a typically succinct passage that speaks volumes about the increasing pervasiveness of consumer culture, Taylor asserts that the key difference now lies in the fact "that 'the market' is now a *fundamental* motor force in contemporary social and political discourse and practice, in a way that it was not in the 1970s. The market is *hegemonic* in the realm of discourse, and in very many practices (including some domains of that most resistant area of all, the public sector)" (1999: 54). Furthermore, Taylor is stating in no uncertain terms that currently there is no viable "oppositional culture" strong enough to challenge the inexorable rise of "market culture" (cf. Ferrell (2001) on various emerging forms of oppositional culture).

The second important thing to stress (again diverging from classic Marxist accounts) regarding the cultural significance of market culture is the continued move toward consumption as a *mode of expression*. Again, at one level, this may not seem intrinsically new; after all, conspicuous consumption has long-established antecedents (see Mukerji 1983 on fifteenth- and sixteenth-century Europe, McKendrick et al. 1982 on eighteenth-century England, and Veblen 1925 – the first to use the concept in a theoretical sense – on the nineteenth-century US leisure classes). However, what is unique about the last few decades of the twentieth century is the way that the creation and expression of identity via the display and celebration of consumer goods have triumphed over and above other more traditional modes of self-expression (on this point see also Baudrillard 1988: 19; Morrison 1995 ch. 13; Bauman 1998).[1] Anderson and Wadkins explain:

> In a culture of consumption, the collective focus is on self-definition through the purchase of goods. Status differentials are based less on one's role in the productive sphere than on one's ability to consume. Social relations are mediated through

objects. . . . As group affiliation at work is replaced by individual achievement, and the role of the family as a source of ascribed status is lessened, individuals attempt to differentiate themselves through their "lifestyles", a term which largely connotes consumption patterns. (1992: 149–50)

This relationship between consumer goods and the construction of self in late modernity is of great importance. So encompassing is the ethos of consumerism within (late) capitalist society that, for many individuals, self-identity and self-realization can now only be accomplished through material means. Thus, identity, as Christopher Lasch (1979) brilliantly pointed out, takes on the form of a consumption-oriented narcissism. Twenty years after Lasch's seminal monograph, the full force of his message is only now being felt. In the school playground, the pub or restaurant, the nightclub, and on the street corner, products and material possessions are now the primary indices of identity for virtually all strata of society, establishing status but, more importantly, imbuing individuals with a (narcissistic) sense of who they are. This is what it means to live in a consumer culture. More problematically, much street crime – from shoplifting to street robbery – should therefore be seen for exactly what it is: neither as a desperate act of poverty nor a defiant gesture against the system but as a nonetheless transgressive act that, at one level, enables a relative (or perceived) material deficit to be bridged, and, at another level, represents a form of identity construction – if it's true of shopping, then it's also true of shoplifting!

I wish to present a brief review of the main debate that surrounds contemporary consumer culture: namely, the extent to which the prevailing systems of consumption represent a positive or negative societal development. On one side of the debate there are those commentators who suggest that consumerism offers up potential social and economic benefits by engendering a sense of enhanced creativity, hedonism, and self-actualization. They point to the pleasurable and emotional dimensions of expressing identity, autonomy, and self-interest via the consumption and exhibition of goods and services. For example, for Campbell (1989), consumerism in Western society is simply an extension of (modernist) Protestant Romanticism – the belief that individuals are rarely satisfied with reality and instead constantly strive toward an intangible "other" self. Consequently, advertising (in all its related forms) should be understood simply as a function of this general feature of the culture. An even more "postmodern" reading of consumerism is provided by Featherstone (1994), who (also) sees the consumer as somewhat of a romantic figure – a postmodern *flâneur* if you will – relishing the diversity of commodities and the abundance of new sites and avenues of consumption (only now, they have become the observer of their own performance!). Featherstone claims that what is new and of importance in today's consumer society "is that the practices of dandyism (art) are no longer confined to the artistic or elite enclaves, but are increasingly widespread. This is the project of turning one's life into a work of art" (1994: 75). The key notion here seems to be that consumerism is now inextricably linked to an expanding culture of aesthetics wherein to look good is to be good – or as the mass media insist on telling us, "image is everything." For slightly different reasons, other commentators also see consumerism as a potentially liberating phenomenon. Michel de Certeau (1984), for example, has suggested that resistance and oppositional practices have a vital role to play in the consumption process. Consider the influence consumer lobby groups (or indeed the public more generally) had in bringing about recent changes in manufacturers' production and purchasing processes. One thinks immediately of the recent *volte-face* by major British supermarkets in response to widespread public opposition to genetically modified foods, the rise of organic and ecologically sustainable products, and, most recently, the emergence of the new "ethical eating" movement.[2]

Sharply contradicting this position is the more established classical view that casts consumerism in a more negative role. Here it is suggested that the prevailing ethos of consumerism will result only in the continued rise of individualism and the "death of the social." There is no room here for the idea that the so-called "postmodern consumer" might somehow represent the "hero of the age" (cf. even the supposed "consumer-led" economic recovery since September 11), capable of "transcending structural hierarchies" and "renegotiating class relations." In fact, such thinking is dismissed as little more than a theoretical abstraction. Instead, the point is stressed that many of the practices and processes associated with late modern consumer culture, by their very nature, must exclude as many (possibly even more) individuals than they include, thus creating an environment in which the distinction between the "haves" and the "have-nots" becomes ever sharper (see Bauman 1987: 149–69; Clarke and Bradford 1998). Furthermore, it is argued that theories of consumption that overplay the self-valorizing potential of consumer culture are deeply troubling in the sense that they focus myopically on the consumption practices of the so-called "new middle classes" or "new petite bourgeoisie" (middle-income earners who perpetuate shared values based around standard of living, expressive "lifestyles," and, importantly, consumption patterns: see Bourdieu 1984; Lash and Urry 1987), and thus tend to ignore other major demographic groups such as senior citizens and the unwaged (cf. Taylor et al. 1996).

It is this latter perspective that holds most sway in social theoretical circles where it is argued that, in most circumstances, the perceived benefits of consumerism are far outweighed by the cultivation of a more damaging and profound set of sensibilities. This is not to say that consumer culture is inherently bad in any simplistic sense. On the contrary, certain aspects of consumerism (in particular, the ability to chose from a globalized marketplace) can be both rich and invigorating. However, as Baudrillard (1981) noted, as the difference between commodities and signs becomes increasingly meaningless, and, as one might say, the distinction between the real and the fake becomes ever more redundant, ours will become a world of endless reproduction: a place, not simply where everything becomes relative, but where relativism itself becomes just another part of the outmoded way of thinking.[3]

From this perspective the romantic consumer is confounded. While the late modern subject might find initial solace through participation in the multiplicity of consumption practices associated with the consumer society, these are "escape routes" (Cohen and Taylor 1976) that are ultimately futile. Taken as promises, the fantasies and aspirations propagated within the individual by a consumer culture can never be fully realized. Thus, feelings of frustration, social strain, and futility abound, a point Lury expresses clearly:

Consumption expresses the romantic longing to become an other, however, whatever one becomes is not what one wants to be. This is because the actual consumption or use of goods becomes a disillusioning experience. The actuality of consumption fails to live up to the dream of fantasy thus we continue to consume endlessly. In the material world, it seems that one's desires can never be exhausted. (1996: 73)

The implications for crime of such a situation hardly need spelling out. Yet criminology seems reluctant to engage with the specific research concerning the various and distinct aspects of late modern consumer culture, preferring instead to operate with substantially underdeveloped modernist strain-theory models. By failing to consider the new (and often destructive) emotional states, feelings, and desires that are now characteristic features of Western consumer societies, criminology is neglecting a vital component of the contemporary crime equation. In what follows, this essay will explore this line of thinking by focusing on the particular relationships that currently exist between crime and consumerism under the social conditions associated with late modernity.

CRIME AND CONSUMER CULTURE: SOME TENTATIVE THEORETICAL LINKAGES

In the remainder of this essay, I intend to propose a series of suggestions as to how various features associated with contemporary consumerism are creating and cultivating – especially among young people – new forms of concomitant subjectivity based around desire, simultaneity, individualism, and impulsivity, that, in many instances, can find expression in certain forms of transgressive behavior. It should be stated at this juncture that the various themes discussed here are intended to be entirely heuristic and are in no way postulated as a positivistic set of factors. Rather, they should be seen as a tentative and explorative conceptual framework for undertaking future theoretical research into what I wish to call here the "crime-consumerism nexus."

Transcending Merton: Consumer expectation in late modernity

desire does not desire satisfaction. To the contrary, desire desires desire. (Taylor and Saarinen, quoted in Bauman 1998: 25)

The renewed interest in consumer culture inevitably forces us to revisit the material analyses of Merton, and, in particular, his classical strain theory (Merton 1938). Simply stated, strain theory suggests that crime and deviance occur when there is a discrepancy between what the social structure makes possible (i.e., the means and opportunities for obtaining success), and what the dominant culture extols (i.e., the social value of material accoutrements and the culture of consumption). Yet, despite the monumental impact of Merton's work, theorists have been somewhat reluctant to update early strain models in light of the particular cultural and economic changes associated with *late modernity* (cf. Cohen 1997; Passas 1997; and, in particular, the work of Robert Agnew, e.g. 1985, 1989, 1992). One notable exception has been Wayne Morrison (1995), who has argued for some time that we need more sophisticated analyses of the emotional states, the feelings, and the contingencies associated with strain/ anomie. He suggests we need to look more acutely at the way the self is being assailed by the various and competing cultural messages of late modern life:

> Criminology not only operates with underdeveloped models of desire, but also largely restricts itself to narrow interpretations of strain theories; wherein crime is the result of frustration by the social structure of the needs which culture identifies for the individual. Today, even in the most contemporary of mainstream criminological theory, ideas of positionality and status are underdeveloped. Instead ideas of needs and greed predominate. (1995: 317)

Whilst acknowledging the subtle differences that exist between theories of "strain" and the concept of "relative deprivation," there have, in recent years, been some interesting attempts made to revive Stouffer's (1949) original deprivation thesis, most notably within that variant of critical criminology known as left realism. Alas, it remains the case that left realists continue to operate with a vastly underdeveloped concept of relative deprivation that fails to recognize the full extent to which late modern consumerism has cultivated "new forms of consumer desire" that now extend far and beyond any simple Mertonian notion of culturally based strain. To understand this point, it is necessary to revisit the original concept of relative deprivation.

Relative deprivation was given considerable empirical validity in the UK by Peter Townsend's various classic studies into absolute levels of poverty. A dominant theme in this body of work was what one might call the discourse of poverty: Townsend was keen to promote the idea that "need" was in fact *culturally determined*. Prior to his research, poverty (and therefore need) was typically defined by semi-biological standards (i.e. poverty was related *inter alia* to starvation, disease, nutrients etc.). However, following the publication of Townsend's findings, notions of need became entwined with (more abstract) cultural considerations (e.g., in one report, much was made of the British need for tea!). Simply stated, need became defined by part of the cultural consensus. In the UK, of course, the cultural consensus was highly stratified (and therefore more constrained) by class factors; however, in the USA relative deprivation was more pronounced because of a culture with a more unified set of goals that all could aspire to (what Merton described as the "cardinal American virtue, 'ambition'" (1968)). This conception of relative deprivation has remained virtually undeveloped in criminology ever since. However, in his recent book *The Exclusive Society*, Jock Young is keen to extend the concept radically. He argues that, although relative deprivation persists in this "era of mass unemployment and marginalization," it is being "transformed": "It no longer involves comparison across the serried ranks of the incorporated; it becomes comparison across the division of the labor market and between those in the market and those excluded" (Young 1999: 48). Thus for Young, the transformation in relative deprivation stems from the fact that in contemporary society the "inequalities have widened" and "the prizes have also become more unequal." It is at this point that Young augments the concept of relative deprivation in a new and novel way that goes well beyond the Townsend Report. Relative deprivation, he argues, should now be thought of not just as a "gaze upwards," but also *as a troubled and anxious look toward the excluded of society*:

> Relative deprivation is conventionally thought of as a gaze upwards: it is the frustration of those denied equality in the market place to those of equal merit and application. But it is also a gaze downwards: *it is dismay at the relative well-being of those who although below one on the social hierarchy are perceived as unfairly advantaged*: they make too easy a living even if it is not as good as one's own. This is all the more so when rewards are accrued illicitly, particularly when the respectable citizen is also a victim of crime. (1999: 9; emphasis added)

This is unquestionably a very important statement that not only fits well with the overarching ethos of Young's monograph, but also goes some way to updating relative deprivation in light of the changing social formation and cultural dynamics of late modern society. However, if we set aside this important new take on relative deprivation, it appears to me that the main point of interest remains the changing nature of the "gaze upwards," and especially, *the expansion of need as a discourse of justification*. Young does not dispute this:

> [c]rime, whether street robbery or embezzlement, is rarely committed in order to reach the average median wage. The poor do not steal Beetles but Porsches, looters do not carry home a booty of baked beans but of camcorders, no one – outside of a tiny few – takes illicit drugs to feel normal. And the rich do not commit crimes in order to ensure a future retirement in comfort. That they already have; they do so in order to excel in their affluence and to exult in their edge over all comers. (1999: 53)[4]

While this insightful passage is highly important because it fully acknowledges the fact that the vast majority of crime within our cities is perpetrated, not by the extreme poor, the homeless, or the hungry, but by individuals whose motives are driven primarily by cultural determinants, it does not, in my opinion, fully explain what is happening to the idea of need within contemporary society. In short, the passage quoted above does not go much beyond the explanation of relative deprivation set out by Townsend. It is my contention that criminology must go further and develop new and more sophisticated "deprivation" models that specifically consider the phenomenal rise of consumer culture since the 1980s (a task that Young has clearly begun by adding a "gaze downward" to the concept of relative deprivation). For, without such models they will inevitably fall short of gaining a complete understanding of much contemporary criminality.

Since the 1990s, within most industrialized, consumer-orientated countries, the distinction between "having" and "being" has become somewhat confused as individuals continue to construct identity through the commodities they consume and display. Such a situation marks something of a break with what has gone before. Previously, a Cartesian view of identity held sway, at least in the West. Identity was conceived as unique, autonomous, and uninfluenced by other people or sociocultural surroundings, an "interior" self behind the mask. This view has been replaced by a more dislocated and fractured conception of identity as "life project" – a never-to-be-completed process of perpetual construction and reconstruction (Campbell 1989; Featherstone 1994). We now construct and display a self-identity chosen from the shop window of our pluralized culture. It is no longer a case of "I think, therefore I am" but rather, "I shop, therefore I am." In the light of such a situation, the important thing to recognize is that today *what people are now feeling deprived of is no longer simply the material product itself, but, rather, the sense of identity that products have come to bestow on the individual.*

This deprivation of identity appears to many individuals as a deprivation of a basic *right*, and thus consumption becomes not simply something that is culturally desirable, but something that is *fundamentally expected* – what one might describe as a changing rights discourse in relation to consumer practices. Consider, for example, how people (especially the young) in a consumer society believe they now have an implicit *right to consume*. A foreign holiday, for instance, is now seen by the majority of young people in Britain as an intrinsic right, even if its cost is prohibitive (indeed, life without such an annual break for many people would be inconceivable). Further evidence of this confusion between needs and desires is apparent in everyday modes of expression – "I need new shoes," "I simply must have a holiday." This being the case, it is imperative that the wishes and the dreams of the individual are afforded greater coverage within theoretical circles. For no longer is consumer need tied in any simplistic sense to rising standards of living or expanded cultural expectations (as in Merton or Young's reading). The current situation is far more intense. In late modern society, need and desire have transmogrified, and as a consequence, we now face a situation in which individual expectations are seen in terms of basic rights, and are therefore no longer fettered by traditional economic or social restraints. On the contrary, a new untrammeled, straightforward form of desire prevails which bears no relation to classical notions of need whatsoever. A desire that no longer needs to be excused, an unapologetic, unrepentant sense of desire that ensures individuals are now furious at the very idea of need – "Why should I have to justify my desire?" "Why can't I have what I want?" "If I want it, I need it!"

At this point it is possible to discern the basis for an important shift in explanatory frameworks in relation to the concept of relative deprivation. Specifically, one might suggest that what has been outlined above demands a move away from the *instrumentality* inherent in Merton's original strain theory, toward a concept predicated more on the *expressivity* associated with new (and distinctly late modern) forms of desire. Such a situation has massive implications for our understanding of crime, for this is "strain" on an unprecedented scale. It is interesting to evoke the psychoanalytical literature on desire (most obviously, the work of Jacques Lacan) which sees desire as being attached to the lost object – or the fantasy of self-completion. In other words, what is being discussed here is the thematics of attaining something that is by definition beyond our grasp. This, in a sense, is the essence of a consumer society – a constant sense of unfulfillment. Morrison emphasizes the tension that inevitably arises within a consumer culture when desire and fantasy become common currencies and when the individual sense of identity and meaning become inextricably linked with desire and the "lost affect":

Modernity gives us a series of expectations as to self-realization and personal growth – we are to become other than what we have been through the choosing of identities, employment roles and seizing opportunities – but actual human beings have not fully escaped being defined by their location in situations of enablement and restraint. Human beings will be disappointed – they wish to take control of their selves, they wish to realise their (future) self-potential, but are located in demeaning and restraining circumstances – a crisis of action develops. (1995: 301)

In many cases, the "crisis of action" Morrison refers to will be crime. Indeed, one might describe the situation outlined above as a recipe for criminality. This being the case, it is essential that any attempt to revamp the concept of relative deprivation takes into consideration *the concomitant forms of subjectivity* that are engendered by a fast-moving consumer culture, and attempts, when possible, to link this to criminal motivation. Simply stated, emotions, sensations, and consumer-orientated cognitions must now be located prominently on the crim-inological agenda. Interestingly, there is at least one commentator who has already recognized this fact, the American criminologist, Elliott Currie. Develop-ing the work of Willem Bonger, Currie shares with Merton and Young the belief that market society creates crime by promoting standards of consumption which the vast majority of people can never feasibly achieve. However, he goes consid-erably further, and points to the actual "psychological distortions" that are engendered within individuals by a fast-paced consumer society. Consider, for example, the following passage, which is worth quoting in full for all its tone of high moralism:

One of the most chilling features of much violent street crime in America today, and also in some developing countries, is how directly it expresses the logic of immediate gratification in the pursuit of consumer goods, or of instant status and recognition.... People who study crime, perhaps especially from a "progressive" perspective, sometimes shy away from looking hard at these less tangible "moral" aspects.... A full analysis of these connections would need to consider, for exam-ple, the impact on crime of the specifically psychological distortions of market society, its tendencies to produce personalities less and less capable of relating to others except as consumer items or as trophies in a quest for recognition among one's peers. (Currie 1996: 348)

In the following section I intend to follow the line of inquiry set down by Currie, albeit without lapsing into a simple moral critique of current social trends. In particular, the focus will be trained on the emerging forms of subjectivity being brought about – at both the individual and the cultural level – by unmediated consumerism.

"Sensation gatherers" and the "pursuit of the new": Impulsivity and instant gratification as features of late modern life[5]

Historically, the insatiability of desire has been regarded as a symptom of a certain moral pathology (be it sin or decadence) or as a sign of status amongst social elites. However, as set out above, a unique feature of late modern consumer culture is that insatiable desire – the constant demand for more – is now not only normal but essential for the continuance of the socio-economic order. From the expansion of credit facilities (see Ritzer 1995; Spiers 1995), to the emergence of digitized "sales loops"[6] we are, at a societal level, increasingly encouraged to eschew long-term conservatism and pursue instead a course toward individual gratification, plotted by materialistic desires and located as sources of pleasure and identity. In short, the "very essence" of modern consumption is that it is "an activity which involves an apparently endless pursuit of want." One of the central tasks consumer culture sets itself, therefore, is the production of subjects who are constantly on the look out for new commodities and alternative experiences – what Campbell (1989) refers to as "neophiliacs" or lovers of novelty. Consumerism is a culture of experimentation and, perhaps paradoxically, given the perceived "benefits" it brings, a culture of terminal dissatisfaction.[7] A world where the pursuit of the new (now combined with the ideology of "personal growth") is valued above a more cautious satisfaction with what one has or is (on this point see O'Malley 1993).

Zygmunt Bauman (1997: 146) coins the phrase "sensation-gatherers" to characterize this peculiarly "postmodern" form of subjectivity. Focusing on the deregulation and privatization of desire within contemporary culture, he describes how the "soldier-producer" of industrial capitalism has been supplanted by a different type of subject who constantly craves new experience. Bauman describes a series of emotions that might be seen as characterizing the "sensation-gatherers": impulsivity, dissatisfaction, narcissism, and spontaneity. Although Bauman does not specify any generational distinctions, it is clear that this desire for the new will be most acutely developed within younger members of society (not least because it is this group that is exposed to the most aggressive forms of so-called "lifestyle advertising").[8] This is an especially interesting point, given we know that the vast majority of crime is perpetrated by young males approximately between the ages of 14 and 25.

There is another feature of contemporary forms of desire that can help us understand why individuals tend to become separated from prevailing normative values. In addition to being insatiable, consumer culture also cultivates a desire for *immediate, rather than delayed gratification*. Again, this represents an historical shift of some importance. Consider Baudrillard's account of Victorian concepts of ownership:

> Objects once acquired were owned in the full sense, for they were a material expression of work done. It is still not very long since buying a dinner table and chairs, or a car, represented the end-point of a sustained exercise in thrift. People worked dreaming of what they might later acquire; life was lived in accordance with the puritan notion of effort and its reward – an object finally won represented repayment for the past and security for the future. (1996: 158–9)

Today a new "morality" exists where consumption has precedence over accumulation, where "forward flight, forced investment, speeded-up consumption and the absurdity of saving provide the motors of our whole present system of buying first and paying off later" (1996: 163).

Inevitably such a situation has significant implications for our experience of time, a point eloquently expressed in Harvey's account of "time–space compression" (1990: ch. 17), and Jameson's (1991) interpretation of postmodern culture in which he argues that our sense of history (both at the level of the public sphere and at the level of the individual personality) is being made redundant by the processes of capitalism in its late twentieth-century Western form to such an extent that society can now no longer effectively engage with its past. As Jameson sees it, this is the world of *simultaneity* (an "eternal present"); a world in which cultural and historical antecedents are unashamedly cannibalized, ransacked, and subjugated in a bid to *constantly stimulate the present*. In these memorable accounts it is stated that, whereas in the past, personal identity was forged through a "temporal unification of the past and the future with the present before me," the *privileging of the present* associated with consumerism cultivates instead "an inability to unify the past, present and future of our own biographical experience of psychic life" (1991: 26). Thus, experience is reduced to "a series of pure and unrelated presents," a series of "nows." As for the past, so for the future: the idea of saving, of any sort of postponement predicated on an expected future, becomes meaningless. This is not a moral issue (as for Elliott Currie) of those who choose to "flout" the long-term view. Rather, it is simply to suggest that, as a consequence of the bombardment of stimuli associated with today's postmodern spaces/cultures, the experience of the present (the immediate) becomes overwhelmingly vivid and intense.

Such a breakdown in temporality coupled with the concomitant search for instantaneous experience has real consequences, not least in terms of attitudes toward social norms (Morrison 1995: 309–10; Bauman 1997: 146). Certainly, if one thinks about the conjunction of these new forms of consciousness with the heightened sense of strain outlined in the previous section, then one is forced to consider questions about the particular relationships between expressive desires and normative regulation; not least the possibility that, with its particular emphasis on the search for new sensations and the "pursuit of the immediate," late modern consumer culture will inevitably separate a great many individuals from the consequences of their actions, making them more likely to engage in transgressive or reckless behavior (on this point see Hayward 2002). Following this line of inquiry, is it possible to identify any areas within the criminological enterprise which have already began to engage (albeit tangentially) with the some of the features outlined here? I intend to highlight a convergence in thinking currently taking place regarding notions of instant gratification (in all its various forms) within diverse branches of the social sciences. In particular, the focus will be on notions of "impulsivity" and its increasing currency within varied, often conflicting, theoretical perspectives.

For some time, instant gratification (at the individual level) has been recognized within psychological circles as a vital element in explaining antisocial and criminal behavior (e.g., Buss 1966; Maher 1966; Robins 1978). Despite often conflicting opinions regarding the nature of the category of "willpower," psychologists have continued to develop explanatory models and theories of delinquency and criminality that draw heavily upon the constructs of impulsivity, instant gratification, and the delay of gratification paradigm. Similarly, failure to delay gratification has long been seen as a central feature of the psychopathic personality (Blanchard et al. 1977; Widom 1977; Newman et al. 1992). Considerable work has also been undertaken into the way in which supposed deficits in impulse control can bring about delinquency by interfering with children's ability to control their behavior and to think of the future consequences of deviant acts (e.g., Farrington et al. 1990; White et al. 1994).

Most famously from a purely criminological perspective, Wilson and Herrnstein (1985) asserted that personality differences in traits such as impulsivity may be strongly related to the development of frequent and long-term antisocial behavior. Central to their reading of criminal behavior is the concept of "present orientation": the idea that a "rapid cognitive tempo" and "shortened time horizons" are responsible for impulsive, disinhibited behavior, and the behavioral short-termism so often associated with criminal acts. This line of thinking is extremely apparent in Right Realist criminology more generally (cf. Elliott Currie as quoted above). While, typically, when discussing Right Realism, much is made of both the cognitive strategies of rational choice and the emphasis placed on the causal influence of social conditioning, less is made of the converse, the fact that impulsivity and instant gratification are also central planks of Right Realist thought. On the face of it, Right Realists might appear to be agnostic about why someone sets out to commit a crime, but buried deep within these criminologies is an implicit concern with the emotional element of criminality – namely the conceptions of "self-expression" and "self-control." Consider for instance, James Q. Wilson's *Thinking About Crime* (1985), perhaps the cornerstone of Right Realist theory. Often neglected in this work is the great store Wilson places in the emotions that act on and effect "internalized commitment to self-control." For example, at one point, Wilson (1985: 237–8) asserts that, as a result of the erosion of the modernist moral order, two contrasting modes of self-expression have emerged: rampant individualism linked to immediate gratification and greed; and a more innovative and creative sense of individualism (what Ian Taylor (1999) – proceeding, of course, from a very different ideological position – might have described as "market entrepreneurship"). Given his overarching moral position, it is the former that is of most concern to Wilson (1985: 228–40). Consider this passage from his later collaboration with Richard Herrnstein (closely reminiscent of classic social control theory *à la* Travis Hirschi):

> broad social and cultural changes in the level and intensity of society's investment (via families, schools, churches, and the mass media) in inculcating an internalized commitment to self-control will affect the extent to which individuals at risk are willing to postpone gratification, accept as equitable the outcomes of others, and conform to rules. (Wilson and Herrnstein 1985: 437)

The problem is that Wilson's critique of immediate gratification, the rise of nouveau fully-fledged individualism, and the concept of self-control (and thus his theory of crime more generally) remains one-dimensional. Wilson can only frame his analysis in terms of a perceived loss of traditional (i.e., modern, or, more accurately, a mix of modern and traditional) forms – the erosion of the "Protestant work ethic" and, more importantly, the demise of community values (remember the centerpiece of Wilson's argument is that crime begets crime at a community level). By placing the concepts of impulsivity and immediate gratification so squarely within the context of a lack of social cohesion and disinvestment in society, Wilson presents us with a reading of these important aspects of criminality that is ultimately rooted to a set of conservative morals. By the same token, he chooses to ignore the fact that, in reality, these "impulsive," "disinvested" urbanites are simply the obvious end-products of an unmediated system of consumer capitalism. Consequently, Right Realists like Wilson are never able to *separate out* sociological descriptions of cultural change from their moral critique of these changes – nor, for that matter, can they rein in their moral contempt for those individuals who (for whatever reason) "are unable to assert a sense of self control" or sufficiently delay gratification, and thus are typically labeled by Right Realists as "lacking in moral fiber."

The development of an allegedly more "fully inclusive" concept of impulsivity is well underway elsewhere, albeit from a strictly non-criminological perspective and, not surprisingly, where one would most expect it, *the market*. In the fields of economic psychology and consumer research, traditional rational choice models of self-control and consumer decision-making are being significantly revised/reconsidered, as researchers factor in the important visceral and emotional factors that are seen by many as a major feature of what has been described as "hedonic consumption" (see Williams and Burns 1994).

Traditionally, in the field of consumer research, consumer choices and behavioral patterns have been understood in terms of rational choice models that explain purchases by weighing the costs and benefits of alternatives. In these normative models (much the same as in rational choice models of crime), consumers are viewed as "dispassionate information processors" (Katona 1975; Bettman 1979; Peter and Olson 1994). Yet such models have typically proved unable to answer the important question with which this literature concerns itself: why do consumers frequently act against their own better judgment and engage in spending they later regret?[9] Consequently, a new school of thought has emerged that concentrates instead on the role played by short-term *emotional* factors in the consumption process (see Hirschman and Holbrook 1982; Holbrook and Hirschman 1986; Mick and DeMoss 1990; Williams and Burns 1994). This division in the field of consumer research can be conceptualized as a tradeoff between "interests" (normative rational behavior) and "passions" (impulsive or *akratic* action: the word *akratia* originates in Aristotelian ethics – the weak-willed person) (Hoch and Lowenstein 1991: 493). Interestingly, this theoretical divide closely resembles the staunch opposition that exists within contemporary criminology between, on the one hand, theories of crime predicated on classical notions of rationality, and, on the other hand, etiological explanations that stress instead the centrality of individual emotions and existential concerns in the commission of the criminal act (as exemplified in the compelling work of Jack Katz (1988)). However, rather than pulling in different directions (as has so long been the case within criminological theory), research into consumer behavior is attempting to bridge the division between rationality and emotionality. New research is being undertaken that acknowledges the importance of *both* positions. Such an ethos is illustrated in this statement by Hoch and Lowenstein:

> Our economic-psychological model of self-control stands at the intersection of two broad currents in consumer behaviour research. One perspective views decision-making as rational and dispassionate; the other views it as visceral and emotional. Thus the desire-willpower framework provides an ideal arena for examining the interaction between rational and hedonic motives. These two types of psychological processes are normally compartmentalized into separate literatures. Although each perspective adequately describes a wide range of consumer behaviours, neither alone can provide an adequate account of the decision-making process. (1991: 504)[10]

There does appear, then, to be some mutual ground around the subjects of instant gratification and impulsivity on which very different theoretical perspectives can coexist and indeed flourish. If conscious impulsivity is becoming a characteristic feature of late modern society, then might it not be the case that further exploration of this line of inquiry could provide a possible way forward for criminology to reconcile some of its more polarized theoretical positions?

The commodification of crime and the marketing of transgression

A further aspect of the crime–consumerism nexus concerns the way the market is responding to the subjective emotions and cultural sensibilities outlined above by "commodifying crime" and marketing and promoting the concept of transgression. As outlined earlier, one of the main features of late modern consumer culture is its ability to permeate all aspects of society. It now appears this process has even extended to include the commodification of acts of crime and violence. Again, one might be tempted to suggest this tendency represents little that is new – crime has always been used as a means of selling product (one need only look at the various songs and publications that surrounded the Whitechapel Murders in London over a century ago to recognize this to be the case: see Curtis 2002). But, as I have asserted elsewhere, what has changed is both the force and range of the message: "Crime has been seized upon: it is being packaged and marketed to young people as a romantic, exciting, cool and fashionable cultural symbol. It is in this cultural context that transgression becomes a desirable consumer choice" (Fenwick and Hayward 2000: 44). Within consumer culture, crime is being aestheticized and stylized, presented in the mass media on a par with a fashion aesthetic. This is not to suggest any simple deterministic link between violent imagery and crime; rather, it is proposed that the distinction between representations of criminality and the pursuit of excitement – especially in the area of youth culture – are becoming extremely blurred:

> It is worth pausing to reflect on this "re-branding" of crime within contemporary culture. One obvious example of this process is the way in which "gangster" rap combines images of criminality with street gang iconography and designer chic to create a product that is immediately seductive to youth audiences. For instance, in recent years it has become very difficult to tell whether gangster rap imagery and styling is shaping street gang culture in the US or vice versa.... Stylized images of crime abound in many other areas of the mass media, sending mixed messages to a

young audience who often take their lead from popular and consumer culture. In film, violent crime and drug dealing are glamorized by slick production values and carefully selected soundtracks. The central characters in films such as *Pulp Fiction*, *New Jack City*, *Reservoir Dogs*, *True Romance* and *Natural Born Killers* are then lionized as cool popular culture icons. Likewise on television, crime is being packaged as entertainment. Shows like *America's Most Wanted*, *Justice Files*, *Cops*, *Top Cops* and *America's Dumbest Criminals* in the US...and *Police, Camera, Action*, *Crimewatch UK*, *Crimewatch Files* and *Crime Report* in the UK are little more than a mixture of dramatic case re-enactments and real life crime footage, cobbled together to provide audiences with a vicarious televisual cheap thrill. (Fenwick and Hayward 2000: 44–5)

Whether via the "vicarious televisual cheap thrill" of "real-crime" TV shows, the "Gothic" pleasure derived from membership of one of the many serial-killer "fan clubs" that abound on the Internet, or the fun experienced whilst traversing the type of "digital crime environment" associated with computer/console games such as *Kingpin* and *Grand Theft Auto III* (advertised as "the ultimate crime simulation game"), images of criminality are now firmly tied into the production of youth culture/identity and inscribed in numerous forms of related entertainment and performance. The full ramifications of such a situation are, of course, still unfolding, but, as articulated by Mike Presdee, we must now confront a situation in which

individualism, greed, destruction, dishonesty, fear and violence are woven, through the processes of production and consumption, inevitably into all our everyday lives. Now crime in the form of a commodity, enables us all to consume without cost as we enjoy the excitement, and the emotions of hate, rage and love that crime often contains. (2000: 58)[11]

CONCLUSION

This essay began by introducing and explaining the key themes and debates associated with the burgeoning literature on late modern consumer culture. It then went on to propose a series of tentative theoretical linkages between some of the cultural sensibilities and subjective emotions engendered (at both the social and individual level) by an unmediated consumer culture, and certain traits and characteristics that are considered by many theorists to be constitutive of criminality under late modern conditions. Finally, it considered various ways in which the market is increasingly choosing to celebrate and, importantly, commodify many of the very sensations and emotions outlined above as a means of selling product to young people. Inevitably the nature of many of the themes and ideas presented in this essay militates against any obvious solutions or social "quick fixes." Similarly, such a theoretical line of inquiry does not readily lend itself to the type of empirical investigation that currently preoccupies mainstream criminology on both sides of the Atlantic. Yet, given the centrality of these themes to late modern life – and by extension, late modern criminality – the need for criminology to engage with such matters becomes ever more pressing.

Notes

1 Consumer culture does not solely refer to expensive luxury or, more accurately, status goods. As Nava (1992) has pointed out, consumer culture also has much to do with the unprecedented cheapness of all sorts of commodities, even seemingly banal or oblique products.

2 Of course, from a Foucauldian perspective, this resistance itself might simply be seen as just another part of the very mechanisms of power (see Žižek on Butler's account of Foucault in Butler et al. 2000).

3 Consider, for example, the current situation regarding the marketing and packaging of commodities, and the way that many goods are subject to stylization and aggrandizement to such an extent that the inherent pleasure of consumption is transferred from consuming the product to "consuming the sign" (in the case of many foodstuffs, for example, one might even suggest that you now "eat the advert"!). In today's consumer society, the sign is no longer simply a promise or an expectation relating to the future, rather it is the immediacy ("the now") of the advert, wrapping, image or sign that is of fundamental importance. Bauman recognizes something similar when he suggests that "Goods acquire their lustre and attractiveness in the course of being chosen; take their choice away, and their allure vanishes without trace. An object 'freely chosen' has the power to bestow the distinction on its chooser which objects 'just allotted' obviously do not possess" (1998: 58–9).

4 Something similar was identified by Burney (1990: 63) in her report on street robbery in which she stresses the importance of cultural and stylistic factors in contemporary street crime.

5 An earlier version of this section appeared in Fenwick and Hayward (2000).

6 In a world increasingly reliant upon the Internet, the "sales loop" is getting ever tighter, creating what has been described as "the ultimate in instant gratification" (Kessler 1997: 86). On-line sales can now be completed in milliseconds, and every month new software packages are being developed that can speed up the order-taking process, forward information to customers on new products and sales, and even coordinate sales representative visits.

7 This dissatisfaction is superbly illustrated in Craig Thompson's (1994) article on the broad disparity that exists between the "idealized and actual benefits" (to consumers) of technological and electronic consumer products.

8 Lury estimates that the average British child sees 140,000 television advertisements between the ages of 4 and 18 (1996: 205).

9 In one recent survey of over 4,200 consumers, it was confirmed that over 60 percent of supermarket purchases and an amazing 53 percent of mass-merchandise purchases were "unplanned" (POP Advertising Institute 1995, cited in Wood 1998: 314).

10 A similar bipolar approach is also much in evidence in the psychological research into the mental mechanisms that underlie immediate gratification recently undertaken by Metcalfe and Mischel (1999).

11 It is also interesting to reflect on the possible desensitizing effects of many of these forms of "entertainment." Presdee again (note also the emphasis placed on instantaneity in the following quote):

> In its consumption, violence is simplified and reduced to a trivial act of instant enjoyment; it thereby becomes no different from, say, the eating of a chocolate biscuit or the drinking of a can of Coke. There is no moral debate, no

constraint, no remorse, no meaning. This is disposable violence that need not concern us or delay us in our journey through the week. It is violence without responsibility. (2000: 65)

References

Agnew, R. (1985) A revised strain theory of delinquency. *Social Forces*, 64, 151–64.

Agnew, R. (1989) A longditudinal test on the revised strain theory. *Journal of Quantitative Criminology*, 5, 373–88.

Agnew, R. (1992) Foundation for a general strain theory of crime and delinquency. *Criminology*, 30, 47–86.

Anderson, L., and Wadkins, M. (1992) The new breed in Japan: consumer culture, *Canadian Journal of Administrative Studies*, 9, 146–3.

Baudrillard, J. (1981) *For a Critique of the Political Economy of the Sign*. St. Louis: Telos Press.

Baudrillard, J. (1988) *America*. London and New York: Verso.

Baudrillard, J. (1994) *Simulacra and Simulation*. Ann Arbor: University of Michigan Press.

Baudrillard, J. (1996) *The System of Objects*. London: Verso.

Bauman, Z. (1987) *Legislators and Interpreters: On Modernity, Post-Modernity, and Intellectuals*. Cambridge: Polity.

Bauman, Z. (1997) *Postmodernity and its Discontents*. Cambridge: Polity.

Bauman, Z. (1998) *Consumerism, Work and the New Poor*. Buckingham: Open University Press.

Bettman, J. R. (1979) *An Information Processing Theory of Consumer Choice*. Reading: MA: Addison-Wesley.

Blanchard, E. B., Bassett, J., and Koshland, E., (1977) Psychopathy and delay of gratification. *Criminal Justice and Behaviour*, 4, 265–71.

Bourdieu, P. (1984) *Distinction: A Social Critique of the Judgement of Taste*. London: Routledge & Kegan Paul.

Burney, E. (1990) *Putting Street Crime in its Place*. London: Centre for Inner City Studies, Goldsmiths' College, University of London.

Buss, A. H. (1966) *Psychopathology*. New York: Wiley.

Butler, J., Laclau, E., and Zizek, S. (2000) *Contingency, Hegemony, Universality: Contemporary Dialogues on the Left*. London: Verso.

Campbell, C. (1989) *The Romantic Ethic and the Spirit of Modern Consumerism*. London: Blackwell.

Clarke, D. B., and Bradford, M. G. (1998) Public and private consumption in the city. *Urban Studies*, 35, 865–88.

Cohen, A. (1997) An elaboration of anomie theory. In N. Passas and R. Agnew (eds.), *The Future of Anomie Theory*. Boston: Northeastern University Press, n.p.

Cohen, S., and Taylor, I. (1976) *Escape Attempts: the Theory and Practice of Resistance to Everyday Life*. Harmondsworth: Penguin.

Currie, E. (1996) Social crime prevention strategies in a market society. In J. Muncie, E. McLaughlin, and M. Langan (eds.), *Criminological Perspectives*. London: Sage, 343–54.

Curtis, L. P. (2002) *Jack the Ripper and the London Press*. London and New Haven, CT: Yale University Press.

de Certeau, M. (1984) *The Practice of Everyday Life*. Berkeley, CA: University of California Press.

Farrington, D. P., Lober, R., and Van Kammen, W. (1990) Long-term criminal outcomes of hyperactivity-impulsivity-attention deficit and conduct problems in childhood. In L. N. Robins and M. Rutter (eds.), *Straight and Devious Pathways From Childhood to Adulthood*. Cambridge: Cambridge University Press, 62–81.

Featherstone, M. (1994) *Consumer Culture and Postmodernity*. London: Sage.

Fenwick, M., and Hayward, K., (2000) Youth crime, excitement and consumer culture: The reconstruction of aetiology in contemporary criminological theory. In J. Pickford (ed.), *Youth Justice: Theory and Practice*. London: Cavendish, 31–50.

Ferrell, J. (2001) *Tearing Down The Streets: Adventures in Urban Anarchy*. Basingstoke: Palgrave.

Fromm, E. (1976) *To Have Or To Be?* New York: Harper & Row.

Harvey, D. (1990) *The Condition of Postmodernity*. Cambridge, MA: Blackwell.

Hayward, K. J. (2002) The vilification and pleasures of youthful transgression. In J. Munice, G. Hughes, and E. McLaughlin (eds.), *Youth Justice: Critical Readings*. London: Sage, 80–93.

Hirschman, E. C., and Holbrook, M. B. (1982) Hedonic consumption: emerging concepts, methods and propositions. *Journal of Marketing*, 46, 92–101.

Hoch, S. J., and Lowenstein, G. F. (1991) Time-inconsistent preferences and consumer self control. *Journal of Consumer Research*, 14, 492–507.

Holbrook, M. B., and Hirschman, E. C. (1986) The experimental aspects of consumption: consumer fantasies, feelings and fun. *Journal of Consumer Research*, 9, 132–40.

Horkheimer, M., and Adorno, T. (1973) *Dialectic of Enlightenment*. London: Allen Lane.

Jameson, F. (1991) *Postmodernism or the Cultural Logic of Late Capitalism*. London: Verso.

Katona, G. (1975) *Psychological Economics*. New York: Elsevier.

Katz, J. (1988) *The Seductions of Crime: Moral and Sensual Attractions in Doing Evil*. New York: Basic Books.

Kessler, A. J. (1997) Instant gratification. *Forbes*, August 25.

Lasch, C. (1979) *The Culture of Narcissism: American Life in the Age of Diminishing Expectations*. New York: W. W. Norton.

Lash, S., and Urry, J. (1987) *The End of Organised Capital*. Cambridge: Polity.

Lury, C. (1996) *Consumer Culture*. Cambridge: Polity.

Lyon, D. (1994) *Postmodernity*. Buckingham: Open University Press.

McKendrick, N., Brewer, J., and Plumb, J. H. (1982) *The Birth of A Consumer Society: The Commercialization of Eighteenth-Century England*. London: Europa.

Maher, B. A. (1966) *Principles of Psychopathology: An Experiential Approach*. New York: McGraw-Hill.

Merton, R. (1938) Social structure and anomie. *Sociological Review*, 3, 672–82.

Merton, R. (1968) *Social Theory and Social Structure*. New York: The Free Press.

Metcalfe, J., and Mischel, W. (1999) A hot/cool system analysis of delay of gratification: dynamics and willpower. *Psychological Review*, 106, 3–19.

Mick, D. G., and DeMoss, M. (1990) "To me from me": A descriptive phenomenology of self gifts. *Advances in Consumer Research*, 17, 677–82.

Miles, S. (1998) *Consumerism as a Way of Life*. London: Sage.

Morrison, W. (1995) *Theoretical Criminology: From Modernity to Post Modernism*. London: Cavendish.

Mukerji, C. (1983) *From Graven Images: Patterns of Modern Materialism*. New York: Columbia University Press.

Nava, E. (1992) *Changing Cultures: Feminism, Youth and Consumerism*. London: Sage.

Newman, J. P., Kosson, D. S., and Patterson, C. M. (1992) Delay of gratification in non-psychopathic offenders. *Journal of Abnormal Psychology*, 101, 630–6.

O'Malley, P. (1993) Containing in our excitement: the limits to discipline in commodity-based societies. *Studies in Law, Politics and Society*, 13, 159–86.

Passas, N. (1997) Anomie and relative deprivation. In N. Passas and R. Agnew (eds.), *The Future of Anomie Theory*. Boston: Northeastern University Press, n.p.

Peter, J. P., and Olson, S. (1994) *Understanding Consumer Behaviour*. Burr Ridge: Irwin.

Presdee, M. (2000) *Cultural Criminology and the Carnival of Crime*. London: Routledge.

Ritzer, G. (1995) *Expressing America: A Critique of the Global Credit Society*. Thousand Oaks, CA: Pine Forge Press.

Robins, L. N. (1978) Sturdy predictors of adult antisocial behaviour: replications from longitudinal studies. *Psychological Medicine*, 8, 611–22.

Slater, D. (1997) *Consumer Culture and Modernity*. Cambridge: Polity.

Spiers, J. (1995) Watch out! A debt bomb is ticking. *Fortune*, November 27, 55–62.

Stouffer, S. A. (1949) *The American Soldier*. Princeton, NJ: Princeton University Press.

Taylor, I. (1999) *Crime in Context: a Critical Criminology of Market Societies*. Cambridge: Polity.

Taylor, I., Evans, K., and Fraser, P. (1996) *A Tale of Two Cities: Global Change, Local Feeling and Everyday Life in the North of England: A Study in Manchester and Sheffield*. London: Routledge.

Thompson, C. J. (1994) Unfulfilled promises: a post positivist inquiry into the idealized and experienced meanings of consumer technology. *Advances in Consumer Research*, 21, 104–8.

Veblen, T. (1925) *The Theory of the Leisure Class: An Economic Study of Institutions*. London: George Allen & Unwin.

White, J. L., Moffitt, T. E., Avshalom, C., Bartusch, D. J., Needles, D. J., and Stoutha-mer-Loever, T. E. (1994) Measuring impulsivity and examining its relationships to delinquency. *Journal of Abnormal Psychology*, 13, 192–205.

Widom, C. S. (1977) A methodology for studying non-institutional psychopaths. *Journal of Consulting and Clinical Psychology*, 45, 674–83.

Williams, L. A., and Burns, A. C. (1994) The halcyon days of youth: A phenomenological account of experiences and feelings accompanying spring break on the beach. *Advances in Consumer Research*, 21, 98–103.

Williams, R. (1974) *Television, Technology and Cultural Form*. London: Chatto & Windus.

Wilson, J. Q. (1985) *Thinking About Crime*. New York: Vintage.

Wilson, J, Q., and Herrnstein, R. (1985) *Crime and Human Nature*. New York: Simon & Schuster.

Wood, M. (1998) Socio-economic status, delay of gratification and impulse buying. *Journal of Economic Psychology*, 19, 295–320.

Young, J. (1999) *The Exclusive Society*. London: Sage.

8

The Politics of Youth Crime and Justice in South Africa

Elrena van der Spuy, Wilfried Schärf, and Jeffrey Lever

Introduction

The colonized youth of South Africa have long been at war with their society. Over the twentieth century, a modernizing state has responded, on the one hand, with the parsimonious apparatus of enlightened penal legislation and, on the other, with a much more generous regime of coercion. The social history of (white) justice toward black youth is one of almost unmitigated disaster throughout the twentieth century, figures such as Alan Paton notwithstanding. Recent moves to liberalize the legislative regime run the danger of producing, if not more of the same, then at least of ignoring the lessons of the past. This essay looks at successive attempts to tame South African youth within the confines of a rational–legal system.

The topic itself is of immense political relevance. A large youth constituency, as marginalized as the South African one, poses a considerable challenge to the country's democratic future. The so-called "crisis of youth," as the historian of youth movements in South Africa, Clive Glaser, recently put it:

> cannot be regarded as a peripheral social issue. The South African population is getting proportionately younger and, if anything the problems are deepening. The youth are at the heart of the most critical issues facing policy-makers: crime, education, and employment. What happens to South African youth will powerfully determine the country's future. (2001: 190)

On this score, the South African case study is of comparative interest to those concerned with the structural imperatives of underdevelopment, its effects on patterns of (male) criminality, and the prospects for social order in the near future. It forms part of a "criminology of the South," for similar conditions prevail in many African and Latin American countries such as Brazil, Colombia, Peru, and Kenya.

Since the early 1990s there has been a great deal of energetic lobbying of the South African government around reform of juvenile justice. Attempts are being made to develop an alternative youth justice paradigm and to overhaul the legal and administrative machinery. The spirit and letter of such developments are encapsulated in the most recent draft legislation before the South African parliament. A new Child Justice Bill has been strongly influenced by the recognition of children's rights on the one hand, and the restorative justice paradigm on the other. Heralded as an extremely enlightened and progressive piece of legislation, the prospects for its implementation will be shaped by both the legacies of the past and the notoriously deficient institutional capacities of the present.

Demographic Trends and Crime Patterns

The quest for valid general statistics of crime patterns in twentieth-century South Africa is not easily satisfied. Even a cursory examination of the available crime data reveals their inherent shortcomings. In the early part of the century it is almost impossible to extract crime information for juveniles other than for whites. For the first four decades after Union in 1910 only prosecutions and convictions were recorded. Only later in the century did crime statistics become more elaborate, with the inclusion of reported crime and sentencing data. From the 1940s onward crime recording was meticulously structured along racial lines. Such information, however, allows only for a rudimentary mapping of differential patterns of offending and sentencing.

Longitudinal comparisons are complicated by the fact that the legal definition of who is to be regarded a juvenile has not remained constant. The definition of "juvenile" also varied *within* the criminal justice system. For the prisons a juvenile has always been a person under 21, while for the police and courts it has been a person under 16 and, after 1937, 19 years of age. The apartheid homeland policy, from the 1970s, meant the exclusion of relevant crime data pertaining to the "self-governing homelands" or Bantustans, as they were popularly known, from the national statistics of the Republic of South Africa, until 1994.

Here are some summary points concerning the demographic correlates associated with the youth crime problem as currently experienced.

- By international standards, South Africa has high levels of violent crime. Schönteich, for example, points out that "every third crime in South Africa is violent in nature," compared with 15 percent of comparable US and 6 percent of UK recorded crime (2001: 97). The violent propensity embedded within local offending patterns also holds true for young offenders.
- Like most developing countries, South Africa has a very young population. According to the 1996 census, under-20s constitute 44 percent of a total population of 40.6 million (Statistics South Africa 1996). The cohort considered most at risk for committing violent crime, the 15–25 age bracket, made up 20.1 percent in 1996.
- The two provinces with the highest crime rates, namely Gauteng and Western Cape, are also the most urbanized: 97 percent and 88.6 percent, respectively.

- In 1998 the general unemployment rate was pegged at 37.5 percent (South African Institute of Race Relations 2000:1). The most vulnerable age group, 16–36, was calculated as experiencing unemployment at around 50 percent in 1996 (Chisholm et al. 1997: 217).

THE EMERGENCE OF URBAN YOUTH CRIME IN THE WHITE POLITY, 1900–1976

Like almost every social phenomenon in South Africa, youth and youthful deviance can be divided into four parts. "White" youth throughout our period of concern were the most favored recipients of a haltingly progressive system of youth justice built up from the inception of Union in 1910. Their incidence of delinquency remained comparatively low – one is almost tempted to say "normal." The lion's share of paternalist concern and Afrikaner academic study was directed at white youth. "Indian" youth offending profiles resembled those of their white compatriots, and offer an interesting counterpoint to the other groupings subordinated to the white-dominated polity. "Colored" and "African" youth, for most of the twentieth century, presented a very different picture.

The following figures from 1969 illustrate a pattern that has typified the whole of the period under review. Criminologists attached to the Afrikaner-dominated Human Sciences Research Council compiled for that year the first detailed statistics on juvenile crime along racial lines from a variety of sources (Strijdom and van der Colff 1975) Calculated per 10,000 of the population, the propensity to commit crime amongst juveniles within the 7–20 age category for the period 1969 varied from 69 for whites, to 83 for Indian South Africans, 125 for the black population, and 390 for colored youth. The most important offenses committed in order of importance amongst white juveniles were traffic transgressions (driving without a license for example), then property crimes; among colored and Indian youth, liquor/drugs and property crimes; and amongst African youth, violent crimes and property crimes. For all four groupings juvenile adults (17–20 years of age) were most at risk of offending.

Insofar as the delinquency of the young has a particular South African angle to it, it is on black and colored boys and adolescents (girls being predictably underrepresented) that any dispassionate observer would wish to concentrate, as this essay does. This fourfold way of dividing the youth of South Africa makes a coherent narrative tricky. Also, many might object to it on grounds of "essentializing" race. But as even a democratic government has found, the enduring patterns of endogamy, language, and the decades of enforced segregation, even among the dominated, make this division unavoidable.

Early days: Migrant adaptation in the urban cauldron

The urbanization of South African society from its agrarian origins was subject to sudden upsurges over an extended period. It began (to go with the somewhat arbitrary but conventional South African historiography) with the creation of a city *de novo* in the wake of the discovery of the immense gold reserves of the Witwatersrand in the 1880s. The rise of Johannesburg was a further catalyst for urban growth elsewhere, as the established coastal centers responded to the new opportunities created by the mining industry.

The result was an unprecedented concentration of all elements of the South African population around the new mining town. As the shafts drove ever deeper, with the technical advances of the 1890s, so the appetite of the gold mines for tens of thousands of unskilled hands waxed voracious. The supply was attracted, coaxed, and coerced from one source above all: the rural black regions only recently fully subjugated: Zululand, the Eastern Cape, Basutoland, and Mozambique. The ubiquitous figure of the *black migrant* had arrived, bringing both succor and social headaches for the dominant white administrators, entrepreneurs, and not least, the white trade unions.

Seminal work by La Hausse (1990) and Van Onselen (1982) has documented the way in which black migrant youth generated an underworld in the interstices of this economic transformation. Van Onselen, for example, has chronicled how an enterprising young Zulu migrant, Mzoozepi Mathebula, learnt from his apprenticeship with white robbers, and went on to put himself at the head of a motley group of compatriots. From their hideout in the hills south of Johannesburg, they preyed on the stream of fellow migrants passing by to the mines. Hence arose "the regiment of the hills" (*umkosi wezintaba*). In the course of his career Mathebula (now known as Jan Note) installed himself at the head of his followers with all the ritual of the rural society from which he was drawn. Here is an illustration of a common theme running through the exuberant and frequently illegal activities of the migrant youth in town: a creative syncretism harnessed to the new surroundings. Inevitably many of these youth found their way to the white man's prisons, where the organization forged on the outside mutated into the mosaic of prison gangs still operative today, the notorious number gangs such as the "28s" among them (Haysom 1981: 3).

Paralleling the rise of the *umkosi wezintaba* and later migrant gangs on the Reef were the *amalaita* gangs first recorded by white society in 1900 in Durban (La Hausse, 1990: 83) The base from which the *amalaita* operated was the backyard quarters of domestic workers in white residential areas. A considerable amount of the time of the *amalaita* was spent in stick fights with other gangs – a skill popular in a rural society in which this form of playful encounter as a preparation for more serious business as warriors was common. But they were also perceived as the source of a slowly climbing incidence of theft and violence in white suburbia and the central city.

In what has come to be a persistent thread in South African social commentary, the *amalaita* were denounced for disrespect for their elders, altogether against the grain of rural custom. This generational conflict in the making, which recurs time and again in the later decades, has been interpreted by many respected black and white observers as perhaps the single most disastrous impact of urbanization on African community life.

From tradition to township: Black urbanization and the tide that never turned

Early forms of youthful deviance and crime were transformed as the pace of urbanization quickened from the 1930s onward. For by then youth in their thousands who knew little and cared less for the forms of social life of their rural forebears were growing up in urban milieux.

Beginning in the 1930s, in the work of the social researcher Ellen Hellmann and her colleagues in the South African Institute of Race Relations (founded in 1929), a new and more sympathetic analysis of the etiology of youth deviance emerged. Based on intensive fieldwork in the "backyard" slums of downtown Johannesburg, Hellmann combined meticulous empirical observation with a skeptical approach to conventional white wisdom on the matter. Her seminal 1948 work, *Rooiyard: A Sociological Survey of an Urban Native Slum Yard*, deconstructed popular white notions of "detribalization" and "Westernization" item by item. Hellmann decisively rebutted what might be called the subtext of "cultural nudity" implicit in the notion of detribalization. Far from the loss of culture, Hellmann argued, the migrant forms of life were transmuting by select-ive absorption from the cultural resources of the dominant white section. A new "composite culture" was in the making, but it was being perversely contorted by the poverty, social exclusion and oppressive social control exerted in the urban surrounds (Hellmann 1948: 113–17). In particular, African kinship systems were under severe stress, mostly for economic reasons. It was a setting highly condu-cive for the generation of juvenile delinquency.

In the 1930s, influential white and black intellectuals also began to develop an understanding of urban youth crime on the Rand that was at the same time inextricably bound up with a critique of the prevailing political and economic structures. Overshadowing "culturalist" explanations was a matter-of-fact de-lineation of the economic circumstances of the mass of the urban black popula-tion. The most definitive statement of this position is to be found in the proceedings of the *Conference on Urban Juvenile Native Delinquency* held in Johannesburg in 1938 (Non-European and Native Affairs Department 1938). Convened by the Non-European and Native Affairs Department of the City of Johannesburg, the conference brought together 200 delegates to deliberate on "the alarming increase in juvenile delinquency among the Bantu population." Among them were many of the liberal luminaries of the time, Hellmann and Alan Paton included.

The causes of juvenile delinquency among urban African communities were firmly located in the social and material conditions of their existence. Poverty, inadequate housing, instability at home, and the lack of education and recre-ational facilities were identified as the most important criminogenic factors. In the spirit of pragmatism the conference concluded with a wide range of prevent-ive recommendations: the provision of educational and recreational facilities, the creation of employment opportunities for African youngsters, and the rapid expansion of social welfare services. Deeply critical of the double standards in the state's provision of a social safety net for white as opposed to black children, the delegates insisted on the extension of the social welfare approach to juvenile delinquency amongst all South Africans, regardless of race.

A liberal spirit similarly pervaded the proceedings of the *National Conference on Post-War Planning of Social Welfare Work* held at the University of Witwatersrand in 1944. There is a great deal of overlap with the findings of the 1938 Confer-ence. The retributive logic prevailing in the penal system was deplored and ways sought to remedy its imperfections. Economic upliftment and the social reconstruction of family and neighborhood were seen as the building blocks for crime prevention. The need for coordinating state intervention in pursuit of crime prevention was strongly emphasized (Union of South Africa 1946).

Thus it was not for lack of informed analysis that the issue of urban youth deviance hovered uneasily before the transfixed eyes of the South African political classes. In a prophetic statement in 1940, Ellen Hellmann noted how popular constructions concerning the "menace" of an undisciplined and criminal youth population growing up in the city's locations were gaining political momentum. The negative policies it would feed were, in her view, doomed to failure:

> But it can be asserted with the utmost confidence that increased repressive measures will prove useless and futile in combating this "menace". Only constructive measures will prove of any avail.... They are not deterred by the ineffective sanctions of their own society floundering in a chaotic transition period. The laws of the European they fear but by no means respect. Unless energetic and sympathetic action is rapidly taken, I believe that this rising generation will, in years to come, constitute an ever-growing problem to the whole community, both White and Black. (Hellmann 1940: 87, 141)

But, throughout the 1940s, the whole issue mutated to a higher level: if, as an increasingly powerful white political grouping argued, the flow of blacks to the cities could be halted and then reversed, then the problem of black youth – and adult – crime would simply disappear. In the meantime harsher measures were called for. The National Party (NP's) "total solution" of the fundamentals of South African racial conflict had arrived. It was premised on turning a tide that in the event never ebbed.

Crime control: The National Party's law and order counter-attack

From the 1940s onward the level-headed insight into the real conditions of black urban poverty characteristic of liberal analyses of the youth crime issue, and the necessity for a broad-based social crime prevention, were starkly juxtaposed with the law and order campaign of Nationalist Party politicians. In contrast to the liberal emphasis on state-sponsored reconstruction of the urban milieu as an antidote to the criminal potential embedded in conditions of abject poverty, the counter-discourse of repressive crime control prevailed in National Party circles. Rising crime rates in the urban areas in the World War II years led to the appropriation of the issue as a handy stick with which to beat the incumbent party of Smuts.

Despite the screeds devoted to Afrikaner nationalism and the genesis of apartheid, there is much that remains unexplained about this eruption of a backward-looking *volkische* racism, one of the iconic events of the twentieth century. What is notable, however, as Dirk Van Zyl Smit pointed out some years ago, is the extent to which "writings on criminological matters were part and parcel of the Afrikaner political ferment" (Van Zyl Smit 1989: 235). In the hands of C. R. Swart, the future National Party Minister of Justice, the specter of

African crime was central to the development of a militant law and order campaign in the run-up to the elections that were to transfer power to the Nationalists.

The new Afrikaner paradigm appeared highly persuasive to the white constituency for whom it was designed. In its radical consistency – a marked contrast to the often hapless inconsistency of the Smuts regime – apartheid thinking in the 1930s and 1940s seemed to offer a solution to practically all the social problems exercising the white electorate, crime included. Its elements were clear-cut and coherent. The National Party saw youth crime – the figure of the *tsotsi* (see later) had already appeared on the scene – and the "crime wave" as a direct consequence of the laissez-faire policy of its opponent, the United Party. The unrestricted urbanization of Africans, the resulting denationalization of urban Africans, and the unrestrained spread of communist ideas among black people in particular were the deep roots of the crisis. The answer was to contain crime through curbing the rate of African urbanization, curtailing the spread of Communist ideas about racial egalitarianism and, finally, more policing and harsher punishment. In sharp contrast to liberal sentiments and strategies, the drift toward an increasingly punitive discourse in the mid-1940s was to set the terms of reference for penal practice after 1948. In years to come the reduction of crime was intimately linked to the repressive control of the movement of African people into urban centers.

With the National Party in power after May 1948, the new Minister of Justice was able to put into practice his own ideas about the virtues of harsher punishment so as to contain the "crime wave." Time and again C. R. Swart argued strongly in favor of heavier sentences and the desirability of indeterminate sentencing (House of Assembly Debates, Cols. 999–1002, May 16, 1949; Col. 2078, May 17, 1949; Col. 5169, April 25, 1950). In addition, the nation was to be lashed into subjection. To Swart, an official beating was a cheap and salutary manner of dealing both with adult criminals and with wayward youngsters (*Hansard*, Cols. 4113–14, March 24, 1948). This policy caused one of the most eminent legal scholars of the time, Ellison Kahn of the University of the Witwatersrand, to exclaim, "What a change there has been from the low-water mark of 1940!" After a careful examination of both the crime and punishment statistics, Kahn went on to observe:

> Any hopes that with the rise of whipping would come a fall in serious crime have been dashed.... Even making the utmost allowance for extraneous factors such as changes in population and in the efficiency of the police forces and prosecuting authorities, it seems reasonable to conclude that the deterrent effect of compulsory whipping is nowhere to be seen. If this is so, its retention can only be attributed to some spirit of retribution or revenge. (1960: 211–12)

Kahn's remarks have a more general scope. Crime and juvenile delinquency among the subordinate masses increased during the 1950s as the Nationalists put their pre-1948 blueprints into action. By the mid-1950s the regime was forced to concede that the social conditions of the black urban youth were at the root of the matter. Two attempts were made on the Rand to set up employment schemes for them; none proved effective. By the late 1960s the writing was on the wall. For all its talk of law and order, and for all its repressive machinery, the crime wave which the NP had so lamented during their years of opposition had grown into an endemic feature of South African life. The National Party had not succeeded in either diminishing or eliminating youthful criminality but simply accommodated to it. The era of the *tsotsi*, the youth gangs and pervasive social disorder in the black areas in particular, had come to stay.

Ducktails, skollies and *tsotsis*: Afrikaner intellectual debates

Although terms such as social dislocation had featured in earlier analysis, it was only in Afrikaner intellectual circles grappling again with the social causes of crime that the Chicago School really came to the South African town, and was applied, *inter alia*, to delinquent youth. From the mid-1950s onward a new generation of Afrikaner criminologists turned their attention to the disturbing rates of juvenile delinquency. Working in close cooperation with their ethnic allies in government departments, they were at first mostly concerned with troublesome white youth. Various government and Dutch Reformed Church interventions probed the issue in the 1950s in particular. It was a decade when the "ducktail" problem first caught public attention. For conservative whites, these youths with Elvis-type haircuts (hence "ducktail") heralded a dangerous slide away from the *mores* of the *volk*, particularly as many if not most of the ducktails were Afrikaans-speaking.

Of more concern, and of much longer standing, were the phenomena of the *tsotsi* in urban African communities, and the colored "skollie" in the environs of Cape Town especially. In the emergent Afrikaner criminology, the phenomena of "ducktails," *tsotsis*, and "skollies" were conceptually linked. Ducktails have been mentioned above; "skollie" is an Afrikaner term meaning scoundrel, rascal, or rogue, with undertones of gangster; "tsotsi" is the Sotho equivalent of "skollie." In all three cases the intellectual and political diagnosis was based on the politically neutral notion of the disruptive effects of city life. In cruder versions of the thesis, each racial community was differentially affected by the exposure to the city. Afrikaner intellectuals argued that the problem with Africans in town was to be ascribed to denationalization and detribalization, the subversion if not destruction of rural African customary life. In contrast, the colored community was seen as a grouping without any culture of its own, defenseless in the urban maelstrom. In the case of whites, positioned at the top end of the stratification system, cultural erosion was a function of the exposure to materialist values and the cult of individualism that prevailed in middle-class urban society.

The dominant paradigm for explaining juvenile delinquency, which was to emerge from the new generation of Afrikaner criminologists, was thus a localized version of the Chicagoan notions of social disorganization and social disintegration. Referring to the phenomenon of gangs in African communities, Venter and Retief (n.d., ca.1955: 260) stated that "the living conditions of urban Natives are in the first place identified by social disorganisation and disintegration which result from the process of urbanisation, detribalisation and westernisation." Bothma (1951: 82), too, in his anthropological account of *tsotsi* gangs, portrays "gang formation as a symptom of a culture in transition." By the early seventies the thesis of social disorganization became more nuanced. As a slow critique of apartheid began to fester even within loyalist Afrikaner ranks, the fact that socially fractious youth groupings did not just arise as an automatic consequence of urbanization now received some recognition. That economic inequality, social exclusion, and coercive state control also played a role was conceded. In such writings an affinity surfaces with the liberal analyses of the 1930s, though the political conclusions to be drawn remained far apart.

A related contribution of Afrikaner academe to the topic of juvenile delinquency lay at the level of descriptive statistical analysis. Between the 1950s and 1970s, research institutions such as the National Bureau of Education and Social Research and the Human Sciences Research Council produced detailed statistical profiles involving cross-tabulations on juvenile delinquency. Through such work, trends in juvenile offending could be plotted and "risk profiles" for each of the officially designated race groups constructed. Given its emphasis on positivist, quantitative research and analysis, it simply ignored the larger political and social explanations for the racial divergence toward criminal propensity amongst South African youth.

Youth culture, gangs and politics

South African gangs have been relatively well documented over the years. Although they lack the empirical depth and methodological sophistication of comparable US and European work, local gang studies provide us with a grasp of the history of gang formation, the varying social milieux within which youth gangs arose, and at least some ethnographic insight into their operation. Reference has already been made to the earliest phase of urban gangs with their basis in the migrant experience of black youth. The largest contribution has come from historians, working from the safety of the archives rather than the danger of the streets. This work continues apace, as archival research deepens our understanding of urban dynamics throughout the twentieth century. These scholars underline the transformation of youthful group deviance into a city-based phenomenon and the creation of urban-born youngsters with distinctly urban tastes and aspirations.

Local ethnographic scholarship on gangs is much thinner on the ground. Some of it has been conducted behind prison walls for a privileged few researchers with access to inmates (Lötter and Schurink 1984). Far fewer are the studies based on work with gang members on the outside. For all its parochialism, the study by Bothma (1951) mentioned earlier appears to deserve some accolades as the first fieldwork investigation into gangs in the country. For a white-dominated academia, access to colored gangs proved easier, as they could use the lingua franca of Afrikaans. The main work here is by Pinnock (1984, 1998), with subsequent studies by Schärf (1984, 1990) and Mokwena (1991).

For Pinnock (1984), gang formation on the Cape Flats was a reaction to the loss of community and the fracturing of social cohesion in the wake of forced population removals brought about by the 1950 Group Areas Act. Through gangs a surrogate brotherhood was created. It embraced intricate social rituals and routinely engaged in violent turf battles in the hope of filling the existential void. Pinnock's analysis – as opposed to his ethnography – leant heavily on a kind of critical criminological slant in fashion in the UK. We have hardly any accounts of the "life-world" of youth gangs in the later 1980s and 1990s, at least in published form.

The most ambitious work on gangs – and the most recent – is that by historian Clive Glaser, whose book *Bo-Tsotsi – The Youth Gangs of Soweto, 1935–1976* (2001) attempts to chart the development of gang culture in one of the largest townships near to Johannesburg. Although conceding necessary points to the existing structural tradition, Glaser is also concerned with what might be termed the subculture of criminality that has grown "organically out of the social and economic dead ends that township youths faced throughout the 1930s, the 1940s and 1950s" (Glaser 2001: 402). To the young and marginal caught within the "furnace of a hostile urban environment" (p. 47), *tsotsi* gangs offered a powerful source of identification, a measure of security as well as a means of livelihood. To the community at large, however, they posed a threat of predation and intercommunal division – particularly of a generational and ethnic kind (Goodhew 1993). Glaser (2001) explores the distinctive subcultural styles associated with such gang formations and the complex interrelationship that developed between youth gangs and school-going youth.

By the late 1950s, youth culture in Soweto was dominated by "two associative networks," schools and gangs. Each embraced different political cultures and spawned "competing traditions of defiance." Attempts by the school-going youth to harness the gangs to the wider political cause met with only intermittent success, though it played some part in the Soweto Uprising of 1976 and the subsequent social disorder that reigned almost uninterruptedly in South Africa from that time into the 1990s. This work by Glaser, and similarly by researchers at the Centre for the Study of Violence and Reconciliation in Johannesburg, is an exciting new development in South African criminology. It attempts to go beyond political exculpation to an understanding of criminality as a way of life, or at least a way of earning a living (see Steinberg 2001).

The Evolution of the Legal Framework and Practices of Social Control

Beginning in 1911 with the Prisons and Reformatories Act, reformers such as the Transvaal and later Union civil servant, Jacob de Villiers Roos, attempted to introduce modern penological ideas into South Africa (Chisholm 1987). In terms of the Act, prison treatment was to be humanized, habitual criminals separated from those awaiting trial, a probation system introduced, road camps and prison farms created, and reformatories and industrial schools established. Like so much else in South Africa, this humane promise was scarcely fulfilled. Twenty years later the remarkable Afrikaner maverick judge, F. E. T. Krause, described the South African prison regime as "a barbarous, wrong and purposeless system" (Krause 1939: 119). Nevertheless, modern penal ideas were at least present at the birth of the newly unified country's punitive regime, and continued to make an appearance down the years. Intellectually at least, the road to a harsh colonial-type penal regime was not lacking in enlightened elements.

The 1911 Prisons Act was followed by the Children's Protection Act of 1913, which comprised the first national piece of legislation designed to deal with needy, abused, and neglected children. Through this Act child-saving ideas, very much in vogue in the international context at the time, were imported into South Africa. The promulgation of the Act took place in a context where politicians were alert to the growing social hazards of an urbanizing population. As a consequence, the provisions of the Act stressed the need to consider the social circumstances of the needy child. Furthermore, statutory provision was made for dealing with those guilty of neglecting and abusing children.

However, children still remained subject to the punitive provisions of the 1911 Act, together with the Criminal Justice Administration Act of 1914 amended shortly afterwards by the Criminal Procedure and Evidence Act of 1917. Thus the legal regime for the care and control of juveniles was bifurcated from the beginning of a unified South Africa. While this division might seem to be a trivial administrative matter there was a much more serious flaw in it. It prevented the child justice regime from being seen as an entirety, informed by principles specific to children and juveniles. After all, child abuse and child neglect and destitution, the key concerns of the welfarist legislation throughout the century, cannot be managed in isolation from juvenile offending. Those early statutory failures of vision or commitment were to set the tone (and structure) for the entire century until democratization in 1994.

None of the opportunities to correct this error were embraced when the child-saving legislation was amended in 1937, 1960, and 1983. In 1937 it was a very close call, but the liberals were outmaneuvered by the conservatives. Only after the first democratic elections, and only after South Africa signed and ratified the International Convention on the Rights of the Child in 1995, did the Law Commission initiate a process for the harmonization of the principles and laws affecting children's issues. It is still in process at the time of writing.

The Children's Act of 1937 brought about a major consolidation of the legislative framework regarding destitute and, to a lesser extent, delinquent children. The Act raised the maximum age up to which someone could be regarded as an infant from 7 to 10 years and that of a child from 16 to 19 years. It gave a children's court statutory powers, thus separating criminal proceedings with regard to children from adult criminality. Informal proceedings were to characterize the working of the children's court. The latter, however, had no original criminal jurisdiction. All criminal cases came to it via the criminal courts, known as juvenile courts (Midgley 1974: 65). Imprisonment of juveniles was to be a last resort, only to be used "in exceptional cases." Additional penal measures for young offenders included committal to reformatories and hostels, placement under probation officers, and a compulsion to take up apprenticeships.

The 1937 Act was widely regarded as a liberal and progressive piece of legislation, as it stressed that the treatment of juvenile offenders was an educational rather than a penal problem. Treatment of juvenile delinquency was cast in the discourse of prevention and rehabilitation. Administrative reshuffling further boosted the educational approach. In 1937 reformatories were transferred from the Department of Prisons to the Union Education Department. The punitive penal ethos that prevailed in the reformatories of earlier decades gave way to a more rehabilitative regime, epitomized by the approach instituted by Alan Paton during his years at Johannesburg's Diepkloof Reformatory (Paton 1993).

The 1937 Act provided the legislative framework for the state's regulation of both destitute and delinquent children for the next thirty years. In decades to come, various legislative and administrative changes were made (for example in the Children's Act of 1960), but the basic legislative pattern had been set.

Rhetoric and reality: The false promise of the law

In the event, the implementation of the 1937 Act tended to make a mockery of the legislature's flash of wisdom. One major reason was the recurring problem of insufficient resources and places of safety, and inadequately trained magistrates, police, and welfare officers. But another factor was to deepen the existing de facto bifurcation of the treatment of juveniles. After 1948, "the derailment of the liberal project" was underway (Chisholm 1989). Its demise meant the consolidation of racially bifurcated outcomes in dealing with juvenile delinquency. Over white youth, a haphazardly benevolent, white-dominated state apparatus presided. Judicial officers manifested the typical social schizophrenia of the white polity. White offenders were much more likely to be diverted into reeducation and reintegration efforts than their black counterparts. In practice this meant that while non-custodial options were quite frequently sought for young white offenders, young black offenders were routinely whipped, imprisoned, repatriated, or apprenticed.

Even for white youth the machinery never operated at the optimal level envisaged by the drafters of the Act. The Children's Court in particular was supposed to be the primary means for diverting youngsters away from the penal system. Its operation was little invoked. Instead, as the left-wing scholar Jack Simons demonstrated in his magisterial 1949 review of the operation of the law, for most black youth the penal system manifested a punitive and custodial disposition, and was in "a primitive stage of its development" (Simons 1949: 96). For young black offenders, the enlightened welfare provisions contained in the Child Care Act existed on paper only.

What took the place of diversion and humane treatment, as has already been noted, was the cane. In a way that was inconceivable to outside observers and totally unpalatable to penal reformers such as Judge F. E. T. Krause, the South African magistrate corps attempted to lash recalcitrant youth into submission. In contrast to developments in the West (ironically white South Africans' treasured reference group), flogging was extended in the first half of the twentieth century. Caught in the grips of a "moral panic" about crime in the early 1950s, the National Party government abolished the court's discretion through the enactment of mandatory whipping legislation for a wide variety of offenses. While flogging, as Kahn (1960: 207) observes, became "more merciful in the manner of its infliction," its use was extended. After 1952, with the enthusiastic backing of the Minister of Justice, "Blackie" Swart, there was an exponential increase in the use of corporal punishment by the courts. Juveniles in particular bore the brunt of the burning buttock.

Extra-legal practices of social control

Complicity in the differential administration of justice extended well beyond the courts and the sentences imposed. Throughout the twentieth century the subordinate population regarded the South African Police as instruments of brutal repression against a people who had "no civic rights" (Simons 1949: 76). The tightening vice of apartheid only intensified this situation after 1948, and particularly for youth hovering on the margins of the colonial society, but also for their elders, who found themselves helpless in controlling an upsurge of gangs and youth crime.

Communities responded to the problem of predatory gang crime with numerous self-help policing initiatives. Black urbanites for the most part gave up on the white-controlled police force in disgust. The stage was set for violent confrontations, as the black "locations" grew despite the best efforts of the National Party regime to "stem the tide of the Bantu":

> By 1950 the culture of youth gangs was one of the strongest currents running through the locations. Itself the offspring of instability, it profoundly dislocated location life, setting up rival poles of allegiance, antagonism and protection between gang and gang, between young and old, and above all between the fully and transitional urban (African). (Bonner 1988: 402)

But when the youth revolt broke out in 1976 the police (not for the first time) discovered the uses to which *both* self-help policing *and* gangs could be put. As in the past, they continued to turn a blind eye to rampant crime as long as it could be cordoned off from white areas by the spatial grid of the apartheid regime. The 1976 protest by school pupils in Soweto about the language of tuition proved to be a critical watershed in the country's history. Widespread protests in black schools across the country resulted in the political mobilization of school-going youth. Before long trade unions and civic organizations too were deeply engulfed in the events. By 1984, with the formation of the United Democratic Front, youth had become the central category in political opposition (Seekings 1993: 20).

For the post-1976 period it is thus not surprising that the bulk of the academic literature dealing with youth and children is not much concerned with the aspects of "conventional" youth criminality and juvenile justice. During this period attention is squarely focused on the youth as the foot-soldiers of a "people's war" against the apartheid state. Increasingly violent confrontations between mobilized youth and the apartheid police fueled an incipient militant consciousness amongst youth. The presence of children in detention without trial and in prison for committing political crimes became the launching pad for a strengthened children's rights movement.

DEMOCRATIZATION AND THE ONGOING REFORM OF JUVENILE JUSTICE

After the turmoil of the Soweto uprising moderated somewhat in the years after 1976, the National Party regime was forced, however reluctantly, to extend a measure of toleration to the growth of a foreign-funded human rights movement within civil society. This loose alliance of new groupings began to monitor rights abuses and to advocate progressive, rights-based reform. It also used the courts, where possible, to obtain judgments curtailing the excesses of the enforcement agencies. One of the early successes of their pressure was the reduction of the incidence of whipping by the early 1990s without any legislative amendments. Judges simply read the signs of the times and resorted to other punishments, often, ironically, reformatory or prison terms.

From the mid-1980s onward the international pressure on the state encouraged the first studies of prison conditions for juveniles (McClachlan 1985). Thereafter that wedge was driven deeper, so that by the late 1980s, when the demise of apartheid was imminent, a rapid growth of rights-based studies and initiatives took place. When South Africa's last white-elected president, F. W. de Klerk, announced the turn to negotiation in February 1990, (the *de facto*, if not *de jure*, end of apartheid), the children's rights groupings consolidated to promote major policy changes regarding juvenile justice.

Post-transition context

While the advent of majority rule, under the dominance of the African National Congress (ANC)-led Government of National Unity after the April 1994 elections, seemingly swept aside the obstacles to improved legislation for juveniles in trouble with the law, it also brought with it new and unforeseen challenges. The new democratic government of 1994, equipped with a very liberal constitution, and encouraged by the rights lobby, introduced three early changes to juvenile justice. First, the Constitutional Court ruled that whipping was unconstitutional and must be abolished (*S v. Williams and others*, 7 BCLR 861, 1995). The second was the ratification of the UN Convention on the Rights of the Child in 1994 (Skelton 1998: 3).

The third turned out to be a rather embarrassing saga. The children's rights lobby urged the newly elected President Mandela to act quickly. After his 27 years in prison he needed little prompting, and in 1994 he promoted legislative change to prevent juveniles from being held in police or prison cells for longer than 24 hours. Without proper planning this generous gesture proved to be highly problematic. Alternative appropriate facilities to house juveniles while awaiting trial were not available. Many children were simply released, to howls of public protest. This was one of the painful early lessons of the first flush of democratic enthusiasm and was reversed two years later (Sloth-Nielsen, 1996: 66–72). This bungle was also an early warning about how difficult and costly it was going to be to transform a justice system from top to bottom, as circumstances seemed to demand (and, alas, still demand at the date of writing).

Sensibly, the process of juvenile justice transformation was thereafter entrusted to the South African Law Commission (SALC), a statutory think-tank of the Ministry of Justice. After extensive research and consultation, the Law Commission produced a blueprint for a new and very ambitious system of juvenile justice (South African Law Commission 1998, 2000, 2001). But this proposed new juvenile justice dispensation was only one of many dramatic and far-reaching schemes for the transformation of the criminal justice system competing for resources and the favorable attention of the legislature. Progress from research to policy formulation to draft statute has been slow. In keeping with a new rationalization of the legislative process introduced in 1998, each new law has to be costed so that the legislature can be aware of cost and staffing implications. The intention is to ensure that new measures, however laudable in principle, will indeed be *implementable* and *sustainable*, even after the withdrawal of the assistance foreign governments often offer at the initial stages of implementation.

The post-apartheid redesign of children's legislation

In 2002 the seven-year effort to redesign comprehensively both the welfarist and criminal justice regimes for children saw its first results in the introduction of two statutes comprising an interlinked system of child justice. In broad brushstrokes, there are three notable features of the proposed new dispensation. First, the new measures are in full compliance with the international Convention on the Rights of the Child. There is therefore a strong emphasis on children being protected against excessive, state, punitive interventions by extensive due process provisions. But at the same time children who violate the law are expected to take responsibility for their actions and make good the harm they have caused, both to the victims and their community.

Second, the liberal ethos which pertained during deliberations on the 1937 child-care legislation is a strong leitmotiv. The purpose of any state intervention is, first, in the best interests of the child's development, and, second, aimed as far as possible to keep the child out of the criminal justice system. There is a tacit acknowledgment that custodial punitive institutions have not been at all helpful to the development of children, and to their reintegration into society. Therefore, diversion is the preferred option wherever it is in the interests of justice to use it. Custodial placement is the last resort.

Third, a new set of institutions and administrative arrangements are to be set up to minimize contamination of children by the adult or quasi-adult custodial institutions. Interdepartmental cooperation will become the key to child-friendly treatment and processing with a view to improving efficiency and efficacy. In this sense the legislative process has been unique in that the implementation machinery has been costed and administratively and educationally pre-planned. The hope is that the new child justice law will be implemented nationwide the moment it is promulgated. This would be in contrast to the previous position, where institutional structures would still need to be set up and staff would still need to be trained before implementation could take place (Skelton and Mbambo 2002: 1–4).

It is clear that what has been described are very ambitious and far-reaching innovations. If they work they will constitute a decided improvement on the status quo. They attack frontally the (tacit) assumption underlying the existing system that there is little, other than warehousing, that can be done for the children.

But, after all, these good intentions are not novel in South Africa, though some of the thinking is. The inevitable question is whether the already overburdened justice system will be able to cope with yet another major restructuring and the new infrastructure and staffing re-organization that will be necessary to make the system work. Already the halting implementation of the Domestic Violence Act of 1998 suggests that "transformation fatigue" may be setting in, as the complexities of social reform become apparent to the many officials concerned.

The costing which accompanied the legislative drafting process concluded that the new system will be significantly less expensive than the existing one. But it still requires wide-ranging changes to structures and procedures, improved or new working relationships between state structures, and a change in the existing professional power relations. For example, probation officers, currently occupying the lowest level in the justice hierarchy, will play a more important role.

The implementation difficulties are significantly complicated by the hardening of public opinion against crime. The legislature has already responded by pandering to public opinion in 1998 through the introduction of tougher bail laws and mandatory minimum sentences (Van Zyl Smit 2001). The public itself, in some of the more crime-affected areas had turned to a rough self-help justice by way of vigilantism. The incidence of youth crime remains high, and most troubling of all, so does the frighteningly violent nature of its manifestation. Even the most liberal of systems will struggle to process, secure, and rehabilitate many young offenders the nature of whose offenses seem in stark contrast to their years. Rapid economic development, the one panacea that commands the support of just about every constituency in South Africa, remains elusive, and its absence will continue to shape the life-world of our cohorts of youth negatively.

Criminal justice responses to young offenders continue to oscillate between the iron fist and the velvet glove. For example, despite recent efforts to reduce the number of children being sent to prison, the opposite has occurred. Although children under 18 constitute only 1.5 percent of the prison population (Muntingh 2001: 6), from January 1995 to July 2000 an increase of 158.7 percent took place in the under-18 age bracket, compared to only a 33.2 percent increase for the 18–20 year-old age-bracket. A parallel development is that their sentences last for a longer time (2001: 8). But it should also be noted that over the same period at least some fruits of the diversion efforts are also evident. As the capacity of the diversion infrastructure grew, so did the number of diversions to which the system resorted. In 1999 and 2000 the figures rose from 9,466 to 9,984.

All these problems place into harsh relief the challenges of large-scale transformation of a society and its justice system. The experience of comparable societies grappling with similar issues is not very encouraging. Eight years into the transformation of the South African criminal justice system, there is still a very long way to go, a decade perhaps, before it will be functioning at a level at which it deserves the title of a *justice* system. Until then, it can safely be predicted, youth justice too will lurch from crisis to crisis.

References

Bonner, P. (1988) Family, crime and political consciousness on the East Rand, 1935–1955. *Journal of Southern African Studies*, 14(3), 393–420.

Bothma, C. V. (1951) 'n Volkekundige ondersoek na die aard en ontstaansoorsake van Tsotsi groepe en hulle aktiwiteite soos gevind in die stedelike gebied van Pretoria.: MA verhandeling in Volkekunde, Universiteit van Pretoria.

Chisholm, L. (1987) Crime, class and nationalism: The criminology of Jacob De Villiers Roos, 1869–1918. *Social Dynamics*, 13(2), 46–59.

Chisholm, L. (1989) Reformatories and industrial schools in South Africa: A study in class, colour and gender, 1882–1939. Ph.D. thesis, University of the Witwatersrand.

Chisholm, L., Harrison, C., and Motala, S. (1997) Youth policies, programmes and priorities in South Africa: 1990–1995. *International Journal of Educational Development*, 17(2), 215–25.

Glaser, C. (2001) *Bo-Tsotsi – The Youth Gangs of Soweto, 1935–1976*. Cape Town: David Philip.

Goodhew, D. (1993) The people's police force: Communal policing initiatives in the western areas of Johannesburg, circa 1930–62. *Journal of Southern African Studies*, 19 (3), 447–70.

Haysom, N. (1981) *Towards an Understanding of Prison Gangs*. Cape Town: Institute of Criminology, University of Cape Town.

Hellmann, E. (1940) *Problems of Urban Bantu Youth: Report of an Enquiry into the Causes of Early School-Leaving and Occupational Opportunities Amongst Bantu Youth in Johannesburg*. Johannesburg: South African Institute of Race Relations.

Hellmann, E. (1948) *Rooiyard: A Sociological Survey of an Urban Native Slum Yard*. Oxford: Oxford University Press.

Kahn, E. (1960) Crime and punishment 1910–1960. *Acta Juridica*, 91–122.

Krause, F. E. T. (1939) Crime and its punishment. *South African Journal of Science*, 36, 104–31.

La Hausse, P. (1990) "The cows of Nongoloza": Youth, crime and Amalaita gangs in Durban, 1900–1936. *Journal of Southern African Studies*, 16(1), 79–111.

Lötter, J. M., and Schurink, W. J. (1984) *Gevangenisbendes: 'n Ondersoek met Spesiale Verwysing na Nommerbendes onder Kleurlinggevangenes*. Verslag S-115. Pretoria: Raad vir Geesteswetenskaplike Navorsing.

McLachlan, F. (1985) *Children in Prison: South Africa*. United Nations Center Against Apartheid. New York: United Nations.

Midgley, J. (1974) Corporal punishment and juvenile justice. *Crime Punishment and Correction*, 3(3), 16–26.

Mokwena, S. (1991) The era of the jackrollers: Contextualising the rise of youth gangs in Soweto. Paper presented at the Centre of the Study of Violence and Reconciliation, Johannesburg, Seminar 7, October 30.

Muntingh, L. (2001) Sentenced and diversion statistics, 1999–2000. *Article 40*, 3(3), 8.

Non-European and Native Affairs Department (1938) *Findings and Recommendations of a Conference on Urban Juvenile Native Delinquency held at Johannesburg in October 1938*. City of Johannesburg: Non-European and Native Affairs Department.

Paton, A. (1993) *Diepkloof: Reflections of Diepkloof Reformatory*. Cape Town: David Philip.

Pinnock, D. (1984) *The Brotherhoods*. Cape Town: David Philip.

Pinnock, D. (1998) *Gangs Rituals and Rites of Passage*. Cape Town: Sun Press.

S. v. Williams and others (1995) (7) BCLR 861 (CC).

Schärf, W. (1984) The impact of liquor on the working class with particular focus on the Western Cape. M.Soc.Sci. thesis, University of Cape Town.

Schärf, W. (1990) The resurgence of urban street gangs and community responses in Cape Town during the late eighties. In D. Hansson and D. van Zyl Smit (eds.), *Towards Justice? Crime and State Control in South Africa*. Cape Town: Oxford University Press, 232–64.

Schönteich, M. (2001) Security. In J. Kane-Berman (ed.), *South African Survey 2001/2.* Johannesburg: South African Institute of Race Relations.

Seekings, J. (1993) *Heroes or Villains: Youth Politics in the 1980s.* Johannesburg: Ravan.

Simons, H. J. (1949). The law and its administration. In E. Hellmann (ed.), *Handbook on Race Relations in South Africa.* Cape Town, London, and New York: Oxford University Press for the South African Institute of Race Relations.

Skelton, A. (1998) Juvenile justice reform: Children's rights and responsibilities versus crime control. Paper presented at the conference on "Children's Rights in a Transitional Society," University of Pretoria, October 30.

Skelton, A. and Mbambo, B. (2002) Working towards implementation. *Article 40,* 4(1), 1–3.

Sloth-Nielsen, J. (1996) Pre-trial detention of children revisited: Amending s.29 of the Correctional Services Act. *South African Journal of Criminal Justice,* 9(1), 60–72.

South African Institute of Race Relations (SAIRR) (2000) *Fast Facts,* 7, Braamfontein: SAIRR, 2.

South African Law Commission (SALC). (1998) *Discussion Paper no 79 – Project 106 – Juvenile Justice.* Pretoria: Government Printer.

South African Law Commission (SALC). (2000) *Juvenile Justice Report. Project 106.* Pretoria: SALC.

South African Law Commission (SALC).(2001) *The Review of the Child Care Act.* Discussion Paper, Project 110. Pretoria: SALC.

Statistics South Africa (1996) *Census 96.* Pretoria: Statistics South Africa. Available online at: www.statssa.gov.za/census96/HTML/CIB/Population/219.htm

Steinberg, J. (ed.) (2001) *Crime Wave: The South African Underworld and its Foes.* Johannesburg: Witwatersrand University Press.

Strijdom, H. G., and van der Colff, J. A. L. (1975) *'n Ontleding van Suid-Afrikaanse jeugmisdaadstatistiek, 1969–1970.* Pretoria: RGN Navorsingbevinding nr. S-N-55.

Union of South Africa (1946) *Report of the South African National Conference on the Post-War Planning of Social Welfare Work.* Pretoria: Government Printer. GPS. 4221–1946-2-2600.

Van Onselen, C. (1982) *Studies in the Social and Economic History of the Witwatersrand 1886–1914, vol.1 New Babylon, vol. 2 New Nineveh.* Johannesburg: Ravan.

Van Zyl Smit, D. (1989) Adopting and adapting criminological ideas: Criminology and Afrikaner nationalism in South Africa. *Contemporary Crises,* 13, 227–51.

Van Zyl Smit, D. (2001) Tough justice: South African style? In E. Fattah and S. Parmentier (eds.), *Victim Policies and Criminal Justice on the Road to Restorative Justice: Essays in Honour of Tony Peters.* Leuven: Leuven University Press.

Venter, H. J., and Retief, G. M. (n.d.; ca.1955) *Bantoejeugmisdaad: 'n Krimineel-Sosiologiese Ondersoek van 'n Groep Naturelleoortreders in die Boksburgse Landdrosdistrik.* Kaapstad: Haum.

Part III
Punishment and its Alternatives

9

Penal Policies and Contemporary Politics

PAT O'MALLEY

Over the past few years, the development of the "punitive turn" and a "penal regression" in contemporary penal policies (Radzinowicz 1991) – in short the erosion of the modernist reformist ethos – has become the subject of considerable theorization. Partially in response to calls to restore the sense of the irrational and emotional into our understanding of penal policy (e.g., Garland 1990), accounts are appearing that link these major shifts in penal policy to changes in the psyche and sensibilities of the populace, which in their turn are linked to transformations in modernity. While accounts vary, in each case certain "late modern" or "postmodern" conditions are held to create an individualistic society of exclusion, competition, fear, and excess, in terms of which the punitive turn in penal policy is understood (e.g., Bauman 2000; Garland and Sparks 2000; Pratt 2000a, 2000b; Simon 2000; Vaughan 2000a, 2000b; Young 1999).

Thus, Pratt and Vaughan both view the sociocultural and psychic "civilizing process" identified by Norbert Elias (1984) as being unevenly reversed by postmodern developments. Elias argued that state formation and the centralization of the means of violence were linked with changes in the division of labor that required more extensive interdependence and cooperation. These social relations in turn constrained spontaneous, emotional, and aggressive behavior, and increased the need for foresight and self-restraint. Such modernized shifts in popular sensibility and the concerns of governance were registered in the realm of penal policy. Effects included the disappearance of lethal and maiming sanctions, the substitution of corporal punishment by restrained and reason-based interventions, and the retreat of punishment behind prison walls (Spierenberg 1984). However, it is now argued that this process has been disrupted by postmodern conditions and that as a result punishments are becoming more emotional, humiliating, expressive, "excessive," and violent. For example, Pratt (2000a) sees postmodernity, particularly through the medium of globalization, as registered in a heightened consciousness of risk and danger, and in an increasingly competitive economy leading to cultures of rivalry, individualism, and increased social distance. For Vaughan (2000a), deindustrialization generated by the globalized economy, and the associated declining demand for unskilled labor, has meant that a new set of social divisions have opened up that have led to a contraction in the scope of mutual identification, and thus progressive "decivilization." These processes are linked by the respective authors with the creation of excluded groups and the erosion of popular and governmental empathy for their members (see also Young 1999). In turn this has released the social and psychic inhibitions against violent and excessive responses, and thereby created highly punitive and segregating penal policies associated with the alienating imageries of offenders.

For Bauman (2000), the rise of the "excluded" and of the penal policies directed at them also register what he sees as "a response to the postmodern social field" and the "logic of globalization." However, the critical process for Bauman is a reversal of the characteristically modernist trading-off of measures of individual liberty, in exchange for increased collective guarantees of security (a legacy that stretches from Hobbes to the welfare state). In the postmodern era, the process has become one of trading collective security for the removal of more and more restraints on personal choice. As individuals gain in autonomy, they become increasingly isolated from the security offered by membership of collectivities. In Bauman's view this creates generalized fear and anxiety – channeled by mass-media and government forces into greatly heightened concerns for law and order. These popular anxieties and concerns are given focus and direction by the existence of new dangerous classes created by industrialization. For this "surplus" and chronically unemployable sector of the population, however, a penal response based on modernist "industrial" penal reformism is now pointless and necessarily ineffectual (see also Simon 1994). The combination of these two pressures result in policies that consign larger and larger numbers of the excluded "underclass" to long-term and merely incapacitating penal practices.

It is not difficult to recognize evidence of many aspects of these accounts, particularly the exclusionary nature of current responses in social and penal policy (see especially Young 1999, Taylor 1999). However, in their identification of these shifts as effects of historic watersheds in social structure, these accounts join a venerable, considerable, and dubious lineage of what Colin Gordon (1986) called "semiologies of catastrophe." These are genealogies of climactic transformation and rupture, usually pessimistic, that imagine us to be on the brink of a fundamentally different future. Among the best known of these, the "risk society thesis" (Beck 1992, 1997) posits the wholesale shift in mass consciousness away from concerns with class and the distribution of wealth and toward risk consciousness, as the effect of the emergence of "modernization risks" – that is, environmental destruction, nuclear weaponry and contamination, global warming, and so on. In this hypothesized climate of generalized anxiety and insecurity, government turns to risk management as a means of allaying widespread popular fear and at least appearing to contain the dangers. This risk consciousness, in turn, is linked with diverse changes in penal policy – these include mass incarceration and incapacitation as discussed above, but also more specific responses such as public exposure and isolation of "at-risk" (former) sexual and violent offenders, and an actuarial justice that displaces proportional sanctions and individually based sentencing by mandatory sentencing said to be based on actuarial data (Hebenton and Thomas 1996; Ericson and Haggerty 1997; Simon 2000).

One set of arguments against these catastrophic accounts is that the connections they make between penal policy and social transformations are weakly grounded – for example, little evidence is provided about the existence and impact of mass risk-consciousness (Chambliss 1994a, 1994b; cf. Taylor 1999). But perhaps greater weight should be placed on the discipline's general record of making false predictions. We now find unconvincing the warnings about "crises of capital" – "legitimation crises," "fiscal crises," crises created by the fall in the rate of profit, and so on – that sociology and criminology diagnosed in the 1970s as representing the future and changing penal policy forever. At the broader level, the anticipated profound crises did not materialize – indeed, capitalism seemingly has gone from strength to strength while socialism experienced legitimation and fiscal collapse. At the specific level of penal policy these crises were supposed to generate "decarceration" (Scull 1975). On the eve of probably the longest period of sustained and massive increase in imprisonment in most of the English-speaking world, this thesis predicted the mass closure of prisons driven by the fiscal crisis of the capitalist state, and their displacement by cost-effective community corrections.

Just why sociology and criminology retain a love affair with catastrophic theorizations, in the face of such unambiguous and humbling lessons to the contrary, is a matter for speculation. But one of its principal effects has been to provide accounts that trivialize or minimize the authentic role of politics. By politics in this sense I mean not so much the minutiae of ephemeral political party maneuvering – which is rarely sociologically graspable – but more broadly the contests between and ascendancy of political rationalities or ideologies. The twin difficulty that catastrophic theories present in this respect, I suggest, is that as macro-societal accounts they are pitched at such a level that it is difficult to deploy them usefully in relation to a politics, and it is correspondingly difficult to see how a local or even national politics could affect the processes which they regard as determinative.

With respect to explaining penal policies, this apolitical character of the catastrophic accounts is surprising because most of their recent advocates recognize the peculiarly volatile, seemingly conflicted and diverse character of contemporary penal policies. Whereas in the 1970s there was a general acceptance of the reformist-correctional agenda, and punishment was regarded as marginal and often counterproductive, now there is no such consensus (Garland 1999). Instead we are witness to a wide array of penal philosophies, and linked with this an equally diverse, volatile, and contradictory array of sanctions. These include not only prison warehousing and electronic monitoring based on assumptions of prevention and deterrence, but also: strict disciplinary boot camps and intensive probation orders linked with mid-nineteenth-century correctional theories; victim restitution linked with contractual philosophies of civil responsibility; "enterprising prisoner schemes" founded on recent market philosophies of "empowerment"; harsh and humiliating sanctions such as the chain gang and the death penalty, deriving primarily from traditional retributive foundations; shame-based sanctions linked with new ideas on reintegrative criminology; decriminalizing policies based on harm-minimizing; and so on (O'Malley 1999).

For Jonathan Simon (1995), the scene is so volatile and contradictory that he more or less despairingly associates it with "postmodern nostalgia," in which the collapse of modernist rationality gives rise to a process in which obsolete and socially irrelevant sanctions are recycled and re-presented in kaleidoscopic fashion. The implied pessimism here leaves little space for politics, other than of a cynical or bewildered kind. But such an account also leaves unexplained the emergence of innovative and novel sanctions – such as the enterprising prisoner and reintegrative shaming schemes – alongside those capable of being interpreted as "nostalgic."

However, others have attempted accounts that – while still marginalizing politics – address this diversity of innovative and nostalgic, inclusive and exclusionary sanctions. For Pratt (2000a), alongside the "decivilizing" impact of globalization outlined above, are contradictory "civilizing" impacts such as those associated with the increased "global village," effects that bring into closer focus suffering in the Third World, stimulate global empathy, and increase toleration of difference. This civilizing effect is said to be reflected in the development of new forms of inclusive justice such as reintegration. The result is that the resurgent penality of emotionality, exclusion, and excess is co-present with a furthering of "civilized" punishment. For Vaughan (2000a), on the other hand, such diversity and volatility is an effect of the fact that the formation of excluded populations creates new dilemmas. Primarily this is because decivilization does not simply generate two clear and distinct categories, the included and excluded, but also many marginal categories – since many citizens have conditional or marginal status. This introduces a new dilemma for penal policy – to decide which populations are irredeemable and which are reformable. Volatility maps the working-out of these dilemmas: it is the "task of penality to assess who is being judged worthy of inclusion and how it is to be achieved" (Vaughan 2000a). Yet because of the focus on the universal and holistic processes of postmodernity and decivilization, these accounts imply a political process but provide no theoretical bridge that links highly abstracted, structurally generated dilemmas with the more mundane but more demonstrable nexus between political activity and penal policy. This distancing of such explanations of penal policy from the political processes that most immediately affect its course creates two closely related difficulties of major concern – the first more normative, the second more theoretical.

Normatively, those concerned with penal politics are entitled to ask of such approaches how they can or could contribute to the process of resisting, deflecting, or transforming emerging penal policies (Garland and Sparks 2000). Significantly, every one of the analysts noted above deplores or – at the very least regards as worryingly problematic – most of the changes they identify in penal policy. But to engage critically at this level requires precisely that we begin to ask political questions not developed by these theories: questions concerning how the changes can be understood or grasped in terms of current politics, how they are linked with broader policies and strategies of governance, and so on. In their turn, posing such questions has explicit theoretical implications.

Take the example of the risk society and actuarial justice. The analyses of Feeley and Simon (1992, 1994) and many others alert us to the multiple dilemmas and dangers of risk-based justice. These are important observations, and provide invaluable interpretations and insights. But what is to be done? Should we oppose all risk-based justice and penality, as sometimes seems to be implied? Surely a critical question to be raised concerns the precise forms risk takes, since actuarialism is only a technique and available to many forms of politics and policy. Thus, as Simon suggests (1987), the welfare state also was actuarial, working through insurance techniques to govern social problems. But the kind of actuarial interventions we now confront are manifestly at odds with this, being deployed primarily by those hostile to welfare regimes and – by implication – hostile to reformist "welfare sanctions." Current risk-based incapacitating sanctions, for example, do not so much reflect a move toward actuarialism per se, but rather a move toward a specific form of actuarialism. This form isolates the individual offenders from their social contexts (a specific rejection of the key, social concerns of welfare actuarialism) and renders them individually responsible for the risks or harms they create for others. Offenders thus appear as the deserving subjects of punishment, incapacitation, and deterrence. This form of actuarialism is, in turn, directly connected with political visions that identify welfarism as creating a "dependent population," and that exposes the members of such vulnerable populations to the cold winds of market forces in order to mobilize them into becoming "active on their own behalf" (O'Malley 1992; Rose 2000). Also, it is associated with ascendant forms of economic rationalism that have calculated the costs and benefits of imprisonment to indicate that correctional reform is not cost-effective, and that general incapacitation is highly cost-effective (e.g., Zedlewski 1985). It is also directly linked with a political strategy that renders potential *victims* individually responsible for their exposure to crime victimization and encourages them to purchase the means of security – ranging from security devices to homes in gated communities.

Risk-based justice and penal policies, in this view at least, are being given their particular shape by *neo-liberal politics*. We need to understand this theoretically in order to develop a normative political response – regardless of whether we theorize the emergence of the alleged global concern with risk and security in terms of modernization risks, civilization/decivilization, or global deindustrialization. Take, for example, strategies that target specific groups such as women, and render them responsible for their own safety, that urge them to purchase security commodities and to seek security by constricting their own freedom (e.g., Stanko 1996). At this level it is of comparatively little help, and arguably politically disempowering, to regard such developments as an effect of the "postmodern" turn against collective security (Bauman 2000). If, however, these developments are recognized as specific strategies of government that are linked with explicit political assumptions and governmental frameworks, then they can be identified as such, understood, and either supported or resisted. This is not to dismiss global theses out of hand, but it is to require that they be theoretically articulated with political processes, and political programs.

As this begins to indicate, thinking in terms of political changes rather than global transformations has theoretical as well as normative implications. These same neo-liberal political rationalities that can account for the forms of contemporary penality are articulated with the social polarization, individualistic competitiveness, and abandonment of the welfare-collective ethos that are associated with the rise of the "exclusive society," a society that excludes whole sectors of its populace from full participation in social, economic, and political life (e.g., Young 1999). In this way, the implied causal relationships become political relationships. It is not so much that postmodernism generates exclusion and that this then affects penal policies, but that political rationalities generate social exclusion and exclusionary penal policies as part of the same political practice. Of critical importance here is that rendering causes into politics, in this way, renders penality both contingent and contestable (Taylor 1999).

Such claims, however, need to confront those who have argued that as these political rationalities and the penal policies associated with them are generalized internationally and across almost the whole spectrum of contemporary political parties, they cannot be reduced to the level of "politics" (Bauman 2000). A political approach may respond to this in a way that allows a rather different interpretation of postmodern catastrophes than is implied in the above accounts. It may be argued that neo-liberal political rationality was put together from a diversity of political constructions of, and consequent responses to, very widespread "problems" of late modernity. Some of these include the "fiscal crisis" and the "legitimation crisis" believed to be confronting the welfare state. This is not to confirm the unproblematic "reality" of these crises. But we do know that both the political Left and Right over the last quarter of the twentieth century mobilized these ideas in arguments justifying radical change, and both sides used them to assault the welfare state (Rose 1996). Such arguments were gradually assembled together into a more or less consistent rationality that became neo-liberalism. These included fears of the fiscal crisis, being visible, for example, in its "economic rationalism" and its program to demolish welfare-state benefits and interventionist state regulation of the market. They also included fears of legitimation crisis, appearing in its hostility toward paternalistic domination by experts in the human sciences and its preference for valorized individual autonomy. In their turn, the neo-liberal pursuit of these policies generated the "predicted" collapse of the welfare state – which neo-liberals in their turn interpret as the outcome that resolved the "fiscal crisis." From this viewpoint, what matters is not whether the crises were ever real, but that those formulating the new neo-liberal politics identified them as real. Consequently, the fact that the "neo-liberal" or "advanced liberal" response was taken up by dominant economic nations (especially the United States and United Kingdom under Reagan, Thatcher, and others), and is currently promoted by organizations such as the World Bank, accounts in good measure for how and why neo-liberalism – and its effects – have become globalized (Rose 1996; O'Malley 1992). Such a position escapes the forms of determinism and naive realism implicit in catastrophic accounts, and gives some degree of autonomy to political process while not denying that there are major changes in the global environment. However, it no longer allows us to deny the relevance of politics to penal policies – no matter how "global" shifts in penal policy have become.

At this point, then, it becomes vital to reconcile the generalized pattern of volatile and contradictory penal policies with the "global" rationality of neo-liberal politics. Certainly this has been attempted in the literature. For example, restitution has been seen to reflect the ethic of individual responsibility, as envisaging the victim as the "customer" of justice, promoting quasi-contractual market-like relations and taking the state out of governance (e.g., White 1994). Reintegration is linked to the neo-liberal reaffirmation of individual responsibility and of the family and community – and in so doing it also expresses in law the faith of neo-liberals in the institutions of "private society" over those of government (Cohen 1985). Incapacitation is seen to reflect the urge for accountability, as it prioritizes victims as the customers of criminal justice, withdraws welfare practices from penal policy, and renders justice more cost-effective (Pratt 1995). The schemes that seek to create "enterprising prisoners" put into practice the neo-liberal affirmation of the entrepreneurial spirit, wedded with the emphasis on individual autonomy and responsibility (Garland 1997). Punitive and just-deserts penalties remove the welfare orientation of the previous penal regimes and bring to the fore the responsibility of individuals, while at the same time reducing correctional costs (O'Malley 1994). The strict discipline programs likewise center individual responsibility, while at the same time promoting values of self-reliance and application consistent with neo-liberal images of the active citizen (Simon 1995). Further, it has been argued that the neo-liberal stress on the small state and the privileging of the market, as well as on cost-effectiveness, can account for the shedding of many crime control functions (such as the operation of prisons) to the private sector and the community.

We have now constructed a theoretical bridge linking contemporary "catastrophes" with neo-liberal politics and thence to the trends in penal policies. Yet if neo-liberal models can in this way *prima facie* provide an account for many of the diverse policies and practices, the post hoc process of linking it to the particular sanctions is neither convincing nor useful. Seemingly it could be made consistent with almost any penal practice. Can the same political rationality usefully be deployed to explain the rise of subjugating boot camps *and* prisoner enterprise schemes? Surely, the blind obedience and self-denial of the boot-camp regimes are at odds with the model of the enterprising prisoner and of "enhanced autonomy." Likewise, retributive criminal stigmatization and exclusionary warehousing both seem to be at totally odds with reintegration. How can all of these be neo-liberal? Without an adequate account of this inconsistency within neo-liberalism, arguably we are no further advanced in explaining politically the original problem of the volatile and contradictory nature of contemporary penality.

Recently, Rose (2000) has tackled part of this question by suggesting that, despite their apparent complexity and heterogeneity, contemporary control strategies do show "a certain strategic coherence" in advanced liberal politics. Rose suggests that these diverse sanctions may be organized into two main families: those governing offending by "enmeshing individuals in circuits of inclusion," and those seeking to "act upon pathologies through...circuits of exclusion" (2000). Here the critical element is that, as Vaughan suggests above, penal policy is increasingly about deciding who shall be excluded and who included. For Rose, the answer is provided increasingly in terms of governmental deployment of risk profiles – indicators that register the capacity to reform oneself. Those judged reformable are subject to benign and inclusionary sanctions, those assessed as incapable are subjected to exclusionary sanctions.

Rose's account provides important insights, but perhaps at an unacceptable price, for while it can account for contradiction, can it explain volatility? In the contribution that started the debate over the volatility of contemporary penal policies, Garland (1996) argued that this reflected a volatility in the politics of the sovereign state in the present era. On the one hand, faced with the tenacity and consistency of high rates of offending, politicians abandon responsibility for crime's governance by treating the state of affairs as "normal." In consequence, citizens have to take on more responsibility for governing an environment that is now an irreducible commonplace. At the same time, the sheer normality of high crime rates is associated with the formation of "criminologies of the self" (i.e., criminals are ubiquitous, thus everyone could be a criminal, hence offenders are "like us"). A corollary is the devolution of responsibility to the community, coupled with integrative and mild penal policies. On the other hand, faced with the politically risky consequences of such abandonment of responsibility, politicians oscillate toward a repressive mode, cracking down on crime, protecting the public, and regarding criminals as villains and monsters ("criminologies of the other") who are deserving of the sternest governmental response. Rose's development of the "neo-liberal" model retains the precision of that account in relation to *the content* of current penal policies. But by assigning the contradictory forms to the governance of different categories of offender, his account cannot account for the *volatility* of penal policy that Garland's equally political account makes central.

Part of the problem is that Rose's account – like much other governmentality work – creates a policy field occupied by integrated political rationalities that are in consequence devoid of internal conflict and incoherence (Hindess 1997). While restoring a form of "politics" to the field, such a form of governmental analysis provides a consistency and seamlessness that deprives politics of any internal dynamic that could explain the shifting and uncertain nature of penal policy (Garland 1997). On the other hand, however, Garland's (1996) approach makes a good fist of explaining volatility, but compared to the models of neo-liberal penality, does a poor job of explaining the content of penal politics and can make nothing of their link with the content of broader government policies – the "neo-liberal" policies that also apply in such areas as unemployment, access to welfare benefits, and so on.

One solution to this conundrum is to recognize that "advanced liberal politics" or "neo-liberal politics" as dealt with in the literature is composed of two distinct elements formed in the Anglophone world as the New Right in the Thatcher–Reagan era. These are a "neo-conservative" *social authoritarian* strand, and a more narrowly defined "neo-liberal" *free-market* strand (see generally O'Malley 1999). The alliance between these strands is firmly bound by a shared faith in individual autonomy, and a belief in the marketplace both as the testing ground of individual character and fitness and as the optimal deliverer of goods. They also share a common and enduring hostility to welfare techniques and the welfare state. For these reasons, they form an enduring political alliance, but not without some contradictions and tensions.

Neo-conservatives operate with a vision of society that has very specific organic overtones which do not sit well with neo-liberals' radical, market individualism. Allegiance, loyalty to, and membership of, traditional collectivities such as the family, church, and nation, and subordination to universal moral schemata are paramount to neo-conservatism. Such obligations are in a sense given in the nature of being born into a society. They are morally required of subjects per se, rather than being formed contractually, self-interestedly, and voluntarily as neo-liberals would stress (Scruton 1984). For neo-conservatives, the state, in particular in its role as the preserver of order and the governor of the nation, is the privileged symbol and instrument of political rule. Their assertion of the sovereignty of the strong state in turn privileges law and moral order, even more so than the marketplace. Indeed, for neo-conservatives the market is by no means an unmixed blessing – for while they stress the work ethic and the economic play of "natural selection," they tend to regard with a more morally jaundiced eye unfettered consumerism, unbounded innovation, and libertarian freedom of choice (Hayes 1994).

This does not imply any necessary instability in the alliance. Not only did long-lived regimes such as Thatcher's manage such tensions, but organic intellectuals have incorporated almost polar opposite elements from each component into a rationalized whole. Hayek (1988), for example, amalgamates free-market individualism with an emphasis on the need for traditional institutions to provide social cohesion in a market economy.

What we are likely to find in such regimes is thus not necessarily instability of tenure, but a degree of potential for internal contradiction and a certain volatility and inconsistency in the face of governmental problems that straddle sensitive areas. One of these areas, as seen above, is likely to involve matters touching on the sovereignty of the state. In this perhaps we see one of the sources of the "oscillation" in penal policies noted by Garland (1996), but now interpreted as volatility between *neo-conservative* imageries of the strong authoritarian state governing morally good and evil subjects, and *neo-liberal* strategies of devolution of government to the public sector and a vision of subjects as rational-choice individuals. In this way both the oscillation and diversity of penal policy may now be brought together in a substantively political framework. While the repertory of policies is made intelligible in this approach, which policies are dominant at any time would depend on the genuine indeterminacy of politics, which is in a sense beneath the explanatory threshold of sociology or criminology (Hindess 1997).

There is a last issue to be raised in considering the accounts linking penal policy and contemporary politics. Not only does Rose's (2000) stable, advanced liberal model have difficulties accounting for oscillation, but also it can account only for limited aspects of the diversity of sanctions. It can draw together incapacitation, enterprising prisoner schemes, and even (though less convincingly) strict discipline boot camps, under advanced liberal utilitarianism. Each sanction performs its function relative to the type of "included" or "excluded" offender. But it will be recalled that a critical feature of contemporary penal politics has been held to be its abandonment of modernist penality (Radzinowicz 1991), its emotive and "excessive" character (Pratt 2000a), and in Vaughan's (2000b) view, its explicit abandonment of utilitarianism. Indeed, resort to Elias's

civilizing process was taken by such writers in order to understand the proliferation of penalties that humiliate and shame, of penalties that inflict the cruelty of
the chain gang and the death penalty. These are penalties that they see not only
as adding incapacitation to rational and reformative penal modernism (which
had always included some element of incapacitation and community protection
in any case), but as *reversing* penal modernism. While there is a degree of
exaggeration in such accounts they surely are picking up on the non-utilitarian
and moral-authoritarian component of the neo-conservative agenda. One aspect
of this, picked up by Garland (1996), is the "reversion" to sovereign techniques
of power and coercion. Another, linked and perhaps even more important, is the
foregrounding of *retribution*. Retribution makes no sense in the calculative and
utilitarian regime that Rose envisages. However, it makes a great deal of sense to
neo-conservatives, for whom the principal priority of punishment is neither
reform of offenders nor the protection of individuals – although these are
secondarily important. Rather, it is the assertion and vindication of a unified
moral order.

Conclusions

> The role of theory today seems to be just this: not to formulate the global
> systematic theory which holds everything in its place, but to analyze the specificity
> of mechanisms of power, to locate the connections and extensions, to build little by
> little a strategic knowledge. (Foucault 1980)

If there is one area of overlap between theories of catastrophe and the more
political interpretations favored in this essay, it is that the changes occurring
cannot be reduced to the level of party politics. Many of the changes associated
with the rise of the New Right in the 1970s have become generalized. Increasingly, governance – whether of crime, economy, or education – is mobilized in
terms of responsible individuals, active communities, market models, costs, and
benefits. As noted by others (e.g., Bauman 2000), this shift, whatever its origins,
is now no longer to be associated exclusively, or even perhaps primarily,
with governments of the "New Right." In the early 1990s, the former Keating
Labour government in Australia, for example, embraced many neo-liberal technologies both generally and in the governance of crime, while retaining a social
democratic profile. It was this Labour regime that oversaw the introduction of
market (or market-like) techniques, and related "neo-liberal" mechanisms, in to
almost every area of life from the funding of tertiary education to the provision
of unemployment relief (Dean and Hindess 1998). The era of "Rogernomics" in
New Zealand saw parallel – and perhaps more extreme – developments under
Labour regimes (Taylor 1999), and both demonstrably provided leads which
were subsequently taken up by the Blair "New Labour" government in Britain.
Correspondingly, in criminal justice there were also Labour-promoted moves
toward rendering offenders more individually responsible for their offenses, and
thus subject to punishment rather than correction. New Labour, under Jack
Straw's guidance, has extended programs rendering offenders personally responsible to victims, promoted reintegrative strategies, generated explicitly risk-

based interventions under the Crime and Disorder Act 1998, expanded imprisonment, and engaged extensively in punitive discourses (e.g., Morgan 1999). In such neo-liberal/Labour amalgams, then, similar room for diversity and incoherence may be detected, as has been characteristic of the New Right.

Such an apparently unlikely alliance between neo-liberalism and Labourism – perhaps better seen as the deployment of neo-liberal techniques and frameworks by Labour regimes – may not be so surprising. As pointed out above, the formation of neo-liberalism reflected criticisms of welfare-interventionist strategies from the political Left and Right. Meanwhile, some commentators on the Left are suggesting that certain neo-liberal techniques – such as market models – may be deployed "strategically" in the crime control field. Jock Young (1999), for example, has suggested the development of "radical meritocracy" as a social program for dealing with both broad social issues of relative deprivation and inequality, and the criminal offending they generate. In another example, following analysis of neo-liberal governance and criminal justice, Shearing has explored market techniques as a "strategic" approach to governing security in post-apartheid South Africa (Shearing 1995). This model adapted elements of the market by relocating taxation to provide blacks with the power to purchase the forms of security they desire at the local level. In many ways Shearing's work reflects neo-liberal governmental developments in local policing in Britain, where money may be diverted from formal policing to alternative security techniques where local demand is strong (O'Malley 1997).

The present essay is not the place to explore or evaluate the implications of Young's or Shearing's unsettling of the certainties of criminological politics (see O'Malley 1996). However, they make clear that old political certainties – of what is Left and what Right – have been destabilized (Garland and Sparks 2000). We are in an era in which neo-liberal techniques of government are being grafted and adapted to serve all manner of political agendas. The prognosis, I suggest, is for a prolonged period of continuing inconsistency and volatility in penality. This essay has argued that this would seem to have more to do with rationalities and techniques of government than with anything as catastrophic and fixed as the emergence of postmodernity. If such a case is accepted, then – with an eye to work such as that of Shearing and Young – the importance of a theory of contemporary penal politics becomes all the more clear: for it is required to guide the shaping of the new era.

References

Bauman, Z. (2000) Social issues of law and order. *British Journal of Criminology*, 40, 205–21.

Beck, U. (1992) *Risk Society*. New York: Sage.

Beck, U. (1997) *World Risk Society*. London: Polity.

Chambliss, W. J. (1994a) Profiling the ghetto underclass. *Social Problems*, 41, 177–84.

Chambliss, W. J. (1994b) Don't confuse me with facts – "Clinton just say no." *New Left Review*, 204, 113–28.

Cohen, S. (1985) *Visions of Social Control*. London: Polity.

Dean, M., and Hindess, B. (eds.) (1998) *Governing Australia*. Melbourne: Cambridge University Press.

Elias, N. (1984) *The Civilizing Process* (2 vols.). New York: Pantheon.

Ericson, R., and Haggerty, K. (1997) *Policing the Risk Society*. Toronto: University of Toronto Press.

Feeley, M., and Simon, J. (1992) The new penology. Notes on the emerging strategy of corrections and its implications. *Criminology*, 30(4), 449–70.

Feeley, M., and Simon, J. (1994) Actuarial justice. The emerging new criminal law. In D. Nelken (ed.), *The Futures of Criminology*. London: Sage, 173–201.

Foucault, M. (1980) Power and strategies. In C. Gordon (ed.), *Power/Knowledge. Selected Interviews and Other Writings*, Brighton: Harvester, 134–45.

Garland, D. (1990) *Punishment and Modern Society*. Oxford: Clarendon Press.

Garland, D. (1996) The limits of the sovereign state. *British Journal of Criminology*, 6(4), 445–71.

Garland, D. (1997) "Governmentality" and the problem of crime. *Theoretical Criminology*, 1, 173–215.

Garland, D. (1999) Punishment and society today. *Punishment and Society*, 1, 5–10.

Garland, D., and Sparks, R. (2000) Criminology, social theory and the challenge of our times. *British Journal of Criminology*, 4, 189–204.

Gordon, C. (1986) Question, ethos, event. *Economy and Society*, 15, 73–8.

Hayek, F. (1988) *The Fatal Conceit*. London: Routledge.

Hayes, M. (1994) *The New Right in Britain*. London: Pluto.

Hebenton, B., and Thomas, T. (1996) Sexual offenders in the community: Reflections of problems of law, community and risk management in the USA, England and Wales. *International Journal of the Sociology of Law*, 24, 427–43.

Hindess, B. (1997) Politics and governmentality. *Economy and Society*, 26, 257–72.

Morgan, R. (1999) New Labour "law and order" politics and the House of Commons Home Affairs Committee Report on Alternatives to Prison Sentences. *Punishment and Society*, 11, 109–14.

O'Malley, P. (1992) Risk, power and crime prevention. *Economy and Society*, 21, 252–75.

O'Malley, P. (1994) Neo-liberal crime control. Political agendas and the future of crime prevention in Australia. In D. Chappell and P. Wilson (eds.), *The Australian Criminal Justice System. The Mid 1990s* (4th ed.). Sydney: Butterworths, pp. 283–98.

O'Malley, P. (1996) Post-social criminologies. Some implications of current political trends for criminological theory and practice. *Current Issues in Criminal Justice*, 8, 26–39.

O'Malley, P. (1997) Policing, politics and postmodernity. *Social and Legal Studies*, 6, 363–81.

O'Malley, P. (1999) Volatile and contradictory punishment. *Theoretical Criminology*, 3, 175–96.

Pratt, J.(1995) Dangerousness, risk and technologies of power. *Australian and New Zealand Journal of Criminology*, 28(1), 3–32.

Pratt, J. (2000a) Emotive and ostentatious punishment. Its decline and resurgence in modern society. *Punishment and Society*, 2, 417–41.

Pratt, J. (2000b) The return of the Wheelbarrow Man. Or the arrival of postmodern penality. *British Journal of Criminology*, 40, 127–45.

Radzinowicz, L. (1991) Penal Regressions. *Cambridge Law Journal*, 50, 422–44.

Rose, N. (1996) Governing advanced liberal democracies. In A. Barry, T. Osborne, and N. Rose (eds.), *Foucault and Political Reason*. London: UCL Press, 37–64.

Rose, N. (2000) Government and control. *British Journal of Criminology*, 40, 321–39.

Scruton, R. (1984) *The Meaning of Conservatism*. London: Macmillan.

Scull, A. (1975) *Decarceration, Community Treatment and the Deviant – A Radical View.* New York: Spectrum.

Shearing, C. (1995) Reinventing policing. Policing as governance. *Privatisierungstaatliche Kontrolle: Befunde, Konzepte, Tendenzen.* Baden Baden: Nomos, 97–115.

Simon, J. (1987) The emergence of a risk society: Insurance, law, and the state. *Socialist Review*, 95, 61–89.

Simon, J. (1994) Doing time: Punishment, work discipline and industrial time. Unpublished paper, University of Michigan.

Simon, J. (1995) They died with their boots on: The boot camp and the limits of modern penality. *Social Justice*, 22(1), 25–49.

Simon, J. (2000) Entitlement to cruelty: Neo-liberalism and the punitive mentality in the United States. In K. Stenson and R. Sullivan (eds.), *Crime, Risk and Justice.* Cullompton: Willan, 125–43.

Spierenberg, P. (1984) *The Spectacle of Suffering.* Cambridge: Cambridge University Press.

Stanko, E. (1996) Warnings to women. Police advice and women's safety in Britain. *Violence Against Women*, 2, 5–24.

Taylor, I. (1999) *Crime in Context.* Cambridge: Polity.

Vaughan, B. (2000a) The civilizing process and the Janus-face of modern punishment. *Theoretical Criminology*, 4, 71–91.

Vaughan, B. (2000b) Punishment and conditional citizenship. *Punishment and Society* 2: 23–39.

White, R. (1994) Shame and reintegration strategies: Individual, state power and social interests. In C. Alder and J. Wundersitz (eds.), *Family Conferencing and Juvenile Justice.* Canberra: Australian Institute of Criminology, 57–71.

Young, J. (1999) *The Exclusive Society. Social Exclusion, Crime and Difference in Late Modern Society.* London: Sage.

Zedlewski, E. (1985) When have we punished enough? *Public Administration Review*, 45(5), 771–9.

10

Beyond Bricks, Bars, and Barbed Wire: The Genesis and Proliferation of Alternatives to Incarceration in the United States

Barry R. Holman and Robert A. Brown

Much of the discussion concerning corrections in US academia, press, and politics concerns incarceration. Less discussed is the fact that of the 6.5 million people under correctional control, two-thirds are not in prisons or jails. Most sentenced offenders are supervised in the community – 3.84 million on probation, another 725,000 on parole (United States Department of Justice 2001).

Probation, parole and their variant "alternative sentences" are the doorway between prison and freedom in the community.[1] This essay outlines the historical roots of alternatives to incarceration, examines the range of community-based sanctions imposed today, and explores the unintended consequences of these sanctions.

The Cobbler's Dream

To raise the fallen, reform the criminal, and so far as my humble abilities would allow, to transform the abode of suffering and misery to the home of happiness. (John Augustus 1984 [1852])

John Augustus, a successful bootmaker, sat in the gallery of Boston's Police Court in August 1841 observing the machinations of justice. The courts at that time were greatly influenced by the temperance movement. Augustus witnessed a succession of "common drunkards" uniformly sentenced to the House of Correction while outside of the courts "some that pretend to be very temperate drink the worst." He noticed a "ragged and wretched-looking man" and spoke with the drunk finding him "not yet past all hope of reformation, although his appearance and his looks precluded a belief in the minds of others that he would ever be a *man* again" (emphasis in original). Augustus approached the judge and offered to "bail" the drunk in lieu of his being sent to the house of correction. The judge agreed on the condition that in three weeks the man return to court for sentencing. During this period of "probation" the man, with the help of Augustus, became sober and presented himself to the court "changed and no one, not even the scrutinizing officers, could have believed that he was the same person." The judge, impressed with the former drunk and Augustus's work, sentenced the man to a fine of one cent plus court fees (Augustus 1984 [1852]).

As he continued to haunt the courts, Augustus saw women being brought before the court for drunkenness while young boys were sent into the same prisons as adult convicts. He soon took up their causes as well, telling the courts he could do better at rehabilitating them than the prison. He diverted many women from prison (some later led the temperance movement under which they had faced prison time) and his business employed numerous boys otherwise destined for prison. He enlisted friends, clergy, and philanthropists to help meet the costs of bail, to supervise the probationers and to provide other necessary social supports to aid in the reformation of offenders (Augustus 1984 [1852]).

Augustus established many practices, programs, and mechanisms taken for granted today. He influenced bail procedures, conducted risk-assessments of potential probationers, outlined conditions for probation, kept meticulous records, and reported to the court on an individual's progress; he provided intensive supervision, employment assistance, detoxification and substance abuse treatment, family therapy, and respite care. His work with young boys was the impetus for what 50 years later would become the juvenile court, and he also suggested specialized residential treatment for curing alcoholism as an alternative to prison.

John Augustus showed the court that alternatives to incarceration did exist, that incarceration is not the only correctional intervention that can change an offender's behavior (he believed incarceration less likely to change behavior), and that alternatives involve a commitment of personal, social, and financial resources. Most importantly, he argued that prisons be reserved for those who cannot be punished and supervised otherwise.

THE PROLIFERATION OF PROBATION

In 1878, Massachusetts passed the first statute mandating probation. Other states slowly passed similar legislation and by 1935 at least 30 states had probation for adults and 30 percent of all sentenced defendants were given probation. By 1965, every state had probation services, 25,000 probation officers were employed by the courts, and about half of those under correctional control were on probation (Cahalan 1986). In 1980 there were 1.1 million probationers, by 1990 almost 2.7 million (Petersilia 1997), and today there are 3.84 million on probation with another 725,000 on parole.

While probation was becoming standard criminal justice practice, the use of incarceration was also continually expanding. In 1860, 14 years after Augustus began his work, the rate of incarceration was 61 prisoners per 100,000 citizens.

It progressively increased until World War II. In the 1950s and early 1960s the rate rose to and stabilized at between 110 and 120 prisoners per 100,000. In the late 1960s the rate fell to below 100 but by 1974 it was rising rapidly. In 1980 the rate stood at 140 (Cahalan 1986). Over the next decade the rate more than doubled to 292 per 100,000 and today stands at 478 state and federal prisoners per 100,000 citizens. If those held in local jails are included in the rate it increases to nearly 700 (Beck and Harrison 2001). Clearly, the institutionalization and bureaucratization of alternatives expanded in their own right while simultaneously failing to quell the use of incarceration.

Transforming Alternatives into Intermediate Sanctions

Probation and parole came under attack during the 1970s and 1980s as the "nothing works" attitude concerning rehabilitation gained public and professional prominence (Wilson 1975). The rate of growth for probation slowed to roughly 2 percent per year and the caseloads of probation officers increased to unmanageable levels as funding for probation services fell precipitously relative to incarceration. Today, probation services receive less than 15 percent of corrections dollars while servicing two-thirds of those under correctional supervision (Center for Community Corrections 1997). Both an image makeover and operational redefinition were undertaken to save the beleaguered probation bureaucracy. Once perceived as passive and lenient, probation and its variants transformed from alternatives to prison into "intermediate sanctions" – punishments in their own right.

Intensive supervision (ISP)

Enhanced surveillance, control, and punishment of offenders beyond that provided through regular probation represent the backbone of intermediate sanctions. "Intensive supervision" probation [ISP] is now the most prevalent intermediate sanction" (Lurigio and Petersilia 1992: 6). While no two jurisdictions define intensive supervision the same way, all provide supervision that exceeds regular probation. In comparison with those on regular probation, ISP typically requires offenders to report more often on their whereabouts and behavior. Some are monitored more closely through telemetric equipment. Most are subject to frequent drug testing and most importantly, any violations of the conditions of their supervision are consequential.

Today, every state has some form of intensive supervision. The most notable distinctions between early intensive supervision programs and those established after 1980 involve a general de-emphasis of treatment and service delivery, a heightened emphasis on surveillance and offender accountability, and the establishment of a broader base of offenders to be supervised.

It is clear from the research on ISP that increased surveillance alone does not reduce recidivism – as typically measured by technical violations, new arrests, or reincarceration (see Gendreau et al. 1996; Fulton et al. 1997; MacKenzie 1997). Further, ISP does no better at reducing the recidivism of offenders sanctioned and supervised by other means, such as regular probation or incarceration (Fulton et al. 1997). The increased surveillance used in ISP typically results in frequent technical violations[2] for offenders – translating to higher revocation rates which are linked to higher rates of reincarceration (Latessa et al. 1997). However, there are indications that ISPs incorporating treatment and employment programming into their requirements can have a positive effect on recidivism (Fulton et al. 1997; MacKenzie 1997).

Boot camps

Boot camps attempt to change offenders' behavior by imposing a brief, intense, sentence of imprisonment (90 to 180 days), followed by a period of community supervision. While incarcerated, participants are subjected to a daily regimen of strict discipline, military drill, and physical labor. Some programs also offer vocational and educational training or services (Gowdy 1993).

Boot camps have an enticing appeal: they are perceived as giving a stiff punishment, promoting discipline, teaching respect, and saving correctional resources – because of their brief duration. Boot camp supporters believe that militaristic discipline and training are associated with law-abiding behavior, and that the lessons and experiences of the program are transferable to regular life (Stinchcomb 1999).

The research on boot camps, however, does not support these views. Comprehensive reviews of boot camp programs demonstrate no significant differences in recidivism between offenders who have completed boot camps and those who serve their sentence either on probation or in prison (MacKenzie 1997). In some instances, boot camp participation has been shown to actually increase recidivism (Peters et al. 1997). The research on traditional boot camps should signal a swift retreat from this form of the sanction.

Exploratory research on programs that devote more than three hours per day to counseling drug treatment, or education coupled with some type of follow-up in the community after participants left the boot camp, show positive results (MacKenzie 1997).

Community residential facilities (CRFs)

Originally called "halfway houses," community residential facilities, or CRFs, are an important part of the continuum of punishment, supervision, and treatment options (Dupont 1985). They are designed as transitional placements to facilitate the movement of the inmate from imprisonment to life in the community (Latessa and Travis 1992). For offenders leaving incarcerative settings, these facilities represent "halfway-out" houses. For those on probation they are "halfway-in" houses.

Lower costs than prison, the philosophy of reintegration, and the success of similar programs in the mental health field all contributed to the expansion and redefinition of halfway houses (Allen et al. 1978). This rise in the number of facilities, an expanding scope of services and supervision, and the increased diversity of clientele served by halfway houses necessitated a change in terminology to better reflect what these facilities are, and what they are not. Community residential facility is a broad term that more adequately describes the changing role of traditional halfway houses (Latessa and Travis 1992).

According to Rush, a residential facility is "a correctional facility from which residents are regularly permitted to depart, unaccompanied by any official, for the purposes of using community resources, such as schools or treatment programs, and seeking or holding employment" (2000: 284). Note that this definition makes no reference to incarceration or provision of services within the facility. Traditional halfway houses do fall under this definition, but are also joined by pre-release centers, restitution centers, community corrections centers (CCCs), and community-based correctional facilities (CBCFs) – all categorized as CRFs.

Early residential facilities provided a transitional setting to help offenders adjust to life in the community where provision of treatment and reintegrative services were the focus. Now, the facilities themselves are sanctions, and the emphasis on rehabilitating offenders has been replaced by a focus on custody and control (Hicks 1987).

Research on the effectiveness of residential facilities at reducing recidivism and increasing prosocial behavior among participants is mixed at best (Allen et al. 1976; Seiter et al. 1977; Latessa and Allen 1982). Results from studies indicate "halfway house residents having lower recidivism rates and at times showing no differences or that halfway house residents did worse on recidivism rates" (MacKenzie 1997). In general, residential facilities monitor and provide services to more high-need and high-risk offenders (Latessa and Travis 1991). Unfortunately, many residential facilities do not adequately assess offender risk with few distinctions made between offenders based on risk. Many halfway house programs are considered to be just a step above "three hots and a cot" (three hot meals and a bed to sleep on – the inadequate, bare minimum). Such custody-orientated facilities outnumber those attempting to meet all the needs of the offenders they serve (Latessa 1998).

Day reporting centers (DRCs)

In 1986, Massachusetts borrowed the concept of day reporting centers (DRCs) from Great Britain (McDevitt 1988; McDevitt and Miliano 1992). Under the Massachusetts program DRCs were designed as a mechanism for early release from prison and jail for prisoners approaching their discharge or parole date (Latessa and Allen 1999). Initially a backdoor solution to institutional crowding, the clientele served by DRCs expanded to pretrial detainees and offenders with state prison sentences. DRCs involve a mixture of intensive supervision and treatment in a community setting, are operated by public and private agencies, and are used to supervise offenders on pretrial release, those on probation or work-release, and offenders on parole (Parent 1990, 1996).

DRCs have common program elements – contact and monitoring on a daily basis, formalized scheduling, offender accountability for his or her whereabouts, and drug testing. The function and operation of DRCs across the country, however, is varied and in many ways each center is unique to its jurisdiction and population served (McDevitt and Miliano 1992).

Survey data indicate that certain characteristics of DRCs are correlated with higher rates of negative terminations. The term "negative termination" refers to offenders removed from DRCs for violating program rules, which can include rearrest for a new crime. The survey, however, did not provide specific information on the rearrest rates of program participants, so it is not possible to differentiate those who committed a new crime from those who violated the rules (Parent et al. 1995). Compared to programs operated by public agencies, DRCs operated by private agencies experience high negative termination rates. DRCs with curfews and those having strict policies concerning violation of center rules also have higher negative termination rates. Finally, DRCs that offer more services and those that experience high staff turnover have higher rates of negative terminations (ibid.).

Latessa et al. (1998) compared offenders in Ohio DRC programs to offenders released from prison, those under intensive supervision, and offenders under regular probation. Incarceration rates of the DRC group were higher than the regular probation comparison group, lower than the group under intensive supervision, and very similar to the group of offenders released from prison. The evaluation found the quality of treatment provided by the Ohio's DRCs to be poor and the use of increased surveillance coupled with little service delivery to be ineffective.

DRCs exemplify the potential advantages and pitfalls of intermediate sanctions. Both the strength and the weakness of the day reporting concept lie in its flexibility and adaptability to various community factors and clientele. DRCs are an easy sell as a "get tough" sanction and method of supervising offenders (Taxman and Byrne 2001). However, it is increasingly clear from the research on crime prevention and correctional intervention that punishment and intensive forms of supervision *alone* do not reduce recidivism, particularly when compared to interventions that involve proven treatment approaches (MacKenzie 1997). If DRCs (and other intermediate sanctions) embrace the principles of treatment *and* control of offenders – instead of strict surveillance and control – they could be an effective alternative to imprisonment.

Home detention and electronic monitoring

Home detention, also known as home confinement or house arrest, has a long history as a criminal penalty, but as an alternative to imprisonment it took flight in the mid-1980s when it became a front- and back-end attempt to alleviate institutional crowding (Renzema 1992; Tonry 1996). Through recurrent contacts by supervising agents (i.e., probation or parole officers, private agencies, telemetric monitoring equipment), the offender's residence is transformed into a place of confinement that restricts and regulates the offender's freedom and mobility in the community (MacKenzie 1997). Under home detention offenders are permitted to leave their residence for specific, authorized purposes, such as work, treatment, and community service. Absence from the residence for an unauthorized purpose, or at an unauthorized time, may result in a technical violation of the conditions of supervision, which in turn may result in imprisonment.

While home detention and electronic monitoring are separate sanctions, the two are frequently used in concert, typically with electronic monitoring used to enforce the conditions of home detention (Gordon 1991). In general, electronic monitoring is used to increase accountability for those being supervised in the community, as it is also commonly used as a component of sanctions or sentences involving intensive supervision. Electronic monitoring provides a technological link between punishment and supervision that makes sanctions such as home detention a practical and affordable option, particularly when the costs of monitoring are deferred to the offender. While home detention with electronic monitoring is generally used for low-risk transgressors, such as those convicted of driving while intoxicated, or property offenses, electronic monitoring has enhanced the ability to supervise more serious offenders in the community. Today, electronic monitoring is used in several points in the criminal justice system: pretrial release and detention, probation, halfway house settings, and prerelease for offenders returning to the community (Bureau of Justice Assistance 1989).

Electronic monitoring can be active or passive. Under active surveillance the supervising agent takes affirmative steps to monitor the offender. A transmitter attached to the offender's body (usually in the form of an ankle bracelet) sends a signal relayed by a home telephone to the supervising agent during the hours the offender is restricted to the residence. When the supervising agent telephones the offender, the transmitter must be placed in the monitoring equipment to confirm the offender's presence in the home. Under passive surveillance the offender is fitted with a transmitter that emits a continuous signal, which must be kept within range of a transmitter in the residence, that in turn sends a signal to the supervising agency. If the offender leaves the range of the connection between their anklet and the transmitter, the boundaries of the home itself, the monitoring system is alerted. Hybrid monitoring systems that try to reap the benefits of both systems are also used to monitor offenders (Schmidt 1994). Obviously, both the agency attempting to conduct electronic monitoring and the offender being sanctioned and supervised must have the resources necessary for such supervision. Agencies or jurisdictions must have access to the funds and appropriate technology necessary to electronically monitor offenders, and offenders must be able to provide their own technology and resources as well. No home or residence, no telephone or telephone access in the dwelling, means no option of electronic monitoring.

Widespread use of electronic monitoring as a sanction or enhancement to sanctions like home detention has occurred with little knowledge of its effectiveness on recidivism (Baumer and Mendelsohn 1992; Fabelo 2000). Research on the effects of house arrest with electronic monitoring for those convicted of driving under the influence of drugs or alcohol (DUI) indicates that this type of offender can be supervised in the community with recidivism rates comparable to similar offenders who are imprisoned (Courtright et al. 1997). It has also been suggested that electronic monitoring is a viable reintegrative sanction, but the key is its viability for appropriate offenders (Gainey et al. 2000). By and large, home confinement and electronic monitoring are not considered to be effective programs for reducing recidivism, particularly when used to intensify control and supervision of offenders. The positive effects on recidivism and increased public safety attributed to electronic monitoring may not lie with the sanction itself; rather, low recidivism and violation rates for the offenders placed on electronic monitoring may be more reflective of low-risk offenders typically placed under this form of supervision (MacKenzie 1997).

Day fines

Monetary fines are a common and widely used punishment, often in conjunction with other criminal sanctions (Gordon and Glaser 1991). In general, court-imposed fines are fixed sums defined by statute for a particular offense; the fine is governed by the nature of the crime, not by the offender's wealth or ability to pay (Gowdy 1993). Fines or financial penalties in criminal matters can themselves be punishment (Morris and Tonry 1990). As an intermediate sanction they can be self-sustaining and generate revenue (Hillsman and Greene 1992), they can serve as a means of reconciliation between offenders and their victims (Gilbert 2000), and they can be imposed without diminishing the offender's ties to the community. It appears, however, that the perceived lack of teeth attributed to the use of fines alone – in addition to potential inequities of such sanctions against the poor – dissuades policy makers and administrators from widespread implementation of day fines as an alternative to imprisonment (Tonry 1999).

Day fines differ from fixed-sum fining by approaching the issue of financial punishment in an individualized fashion. Under the day-fine approach, courts determine the amount of punishment based on the seriousness of the offense. This initial decision-making process is separated from considerations of what the offender can actually pay (McDonald et al. 1995). This amount is then translated into "punishment units," which are then put into monetary units based on the offender's daily income (Winterfield and Hillsman 1993). Typically, unit scales are developed by a planning committee consisting of judges, prosecutors, and defense counselors from the jurisdiction. These court professionals are familiar with local court sentencing practices (Winterfield and Hillsman 1993). For example, under the Staten Island (New York) Day-Fine Project punishment units range from 5 for minor offenses to 120 units for serious misdemeanors. The amount of the fine is determined by multiplying the number of punishment units by the offender's daily earnings, which is adjusted downward depending on family support responsibilities and personal needs (Gowdy 1993).

Day fines are infrequently used in the United States. This limits the empirical research on the viability of day fines as a supervision and crime prevention sanction. Existing research suggests that day fines (in conjunction with probation or other sanctions) can reduce recidivism relative to the number of technical violations and rearrests (Gordon and Glaser 1991; Turner and Petersilia 1996). Furthermore, day fines can be collected as successfully as regular fines, and the introduction of day-fine systems can occur without affecting offenses that typically went unfined, i.e., day fines do not automatically result in net-widening (Gowdy 1993).

Community service orders (CSOs)

Offenders sentenced to community service orders (CSOs) complete a pre-set number of hours of service to a public or charitable organization or agency. CSOs can involve anything from manual labor to a service that taps the personal skills of the offender. For example, an offender could be required to pick up trash in a public area, or they could be ordered to provide their technical expertise to programs for the disadvantaged. It is not uncommon for the community service to be explicitly tied to the offender's crime. Offenders convicted of driving under the influence of alcohol or drugs have received CSOs that put them in hospital emergency rooms or other facilities treating the seriously injured. Here the offender gains insight into the potential damage of his or her offense.

The use of community service as a sanction in the United States can be traced to several judges in Alameda County (California) Courts. In the mid-1960s, Alameda's judges began using CSOs to sanction poor people who committed minor crimes; the judges began sentencing poor women convicted of traffic violations to unpaid work at charities and public agencies in lieu of fines (which they could not pay) or imprisonment (which would remove them from their children and families) (McDonald 1992). For crimes not serious enough to warrant imprisonment, orders of community service are more appropriate than jail (von Hirsch et al. 1989).

Community service orders can serve both utilitarian and retributive goals of sentencing, be scaled to the seriousness of an offender's conduct, and be tailored to facilitate rehabilitative and reparative objectives (Morris and Tonry 1990; von Hirsch 1992; Bazemore and Maloney 1994; Tonry 1999). Furthermore, CSOs hold the potential to alleviate jail and prison crowding, be a cost-effective form of community supervision, provide labor and services for public and charitable agencies, and enhance the social consciousness of offenders and the public (McDonald 1992).

Unfortunately, community service is underused as an intermediate sanction, and, in general, when it is used it is often unwisely implemented (Tonry 1996). Only 6 percent of felons sentenced in state courts in 1996 were ordered to complete some form of community service (Brown et al. 1999). CSOs are often joined with other intermediate sanctions with no clarity as to their goal. This has led to the criticism that they appear to be imposed simply because they can be.

Conflicting, unclear, or undefined purposes of sanctions may occur when intermediate sanctions are "stacked," such as simultaneously imposing electronically monitored home detention and community service (Parent et al. 1997). When the purpose of community service orders are not clear, it potentially undermines the CSO and other components of the offender's sentence in the eyes of correctional administrators and the public (Smith 1999).

As they have been implemented to date, community service orders have not been shown to have any significant deterrent or rehabilitative effect on offenders (Parent et al. 1997). The most comprehensive examination of community service as a sanction in the United States was conducted by the Vera Institute of Justice in four of the five boroughs of New York City (McDonald 1986). Criminal court judges in the Bronx, Brooklyn, Manhattan, and Queens were provided the option of CSOs instead of 90-day or shorter jail terms for chronic property offenders. The project was designed to provide an alternative to a jail sentence and as a means to punish offenders who would otherwise escape supervision and punishment due to the pettiness of their offense. A sample group of those given CSOs and a sample of similar offenders given short jail sentences were compared after a six-month follow-up period. The proportion of rearrests (39–51 percent) was identical for both groups, which indicates that under this program community service orders did not rehabilitate offenders or deter them from future crimes more effectively than a short jail term (McDonald 1992). However, the return on punishment may have been greater for the CSO group, as instead of consuming tax dollars while jailed, they were contributing tax dollars to the community.

CLIENT-SPECIFIC PLANNING

As intermediate sanctions became mainstays in the array of criminal sanctions, one of the most important aspects of John Augustus's work had almost fallen by the wayside – offender-specific dispositions that strive to rehabilitate, not just supervise.[3] In the late 1970s and early 1980s, it was again outsiders who stood before a court asking for an alternative to common sentencing and correctional practices. While a handful of private practitioners and a few public defender offices were independently developing individualized sentencing recommendations to criminal courts, a small nonprofit organization, the National Center on Institutions and Alternatives (NCIA), successfully popularized the concept with the label "Client-Specific Planning" (Klein 1997: 35–6).

Client-specific planning (CSP) is not a criminal justice sanction. It is a methodology or approach to developing a set of sanctions and conditions imposed by the court. CSP, sometimes called defense-based sentencing, provides judges with a sentencing plan tailored specifically to the individual offender. The plan includes an extensive family, education, employment, and financial history. This is accompanied by an assessment of the client's ability to meet the demands of a community-based set of sanctions. Sentencing specialists use this information and analysis to recommend an alternative sentence that may include an array of the intermediate sanctions discussed previously and community services, including drug and alcohol treatment, psychological counseling, employment training, and restitution or victim–offender reconciliation where appropriate. The CSP approach calls for meaningful sanctions and punishments combined with treatment and constructive conditions.

Identification of the community resources necessary to enforce the proposed sentence and to change offenders' behavior is the linchpin of such plans. These may include employment, education, various mental health treatments, accountability circles (composed of community members who monitor the offender), and other supports. CSP services bring to the attention of the courts programs and services that it may not have been aware of or may not have had a relationship with. In this way CSP promotes both alternatives to prison and the reintegration of offenders in the community.

Client-specific planning has grown beyond a movement advocated by a few to a practice utilized by many. Today there are at least 200 CSP programs in 37 states, handling 22,000 cases per year (Sentencing Project 1995). The offenses for which the CSP approach has been successfully employed "run the gamut from homicide to housing code violations" (Klein 1997) with more than 70 percent of the plans presented to the courts accepted by judges in full or in part (Yeager 1992). Many public defender offices now have CSP units or sentencing specialists on their staff. *The National Association of Sentencing Advocates*, a professional association established by advocates and practitioners, provides training and sets standards for the profession.

However, as client-specific planning becomes absorbed into the corrections bureaucracy, there is concern that the proliferation of the CSP approach will result in unintended, negative consequences for offenders. Indeed, Herbert Hoelter, Director and co-founder of the NCIA, expresses concern about a state agency's ability to conduct client-specific planning and advocacy:

> We've trained a number of probation offices across the country in CSP. We find that existing bureaucracies often have little motivation, imagination or incentive to do individualized sentencing plans. In those few jurisdictions where we see good work, it results because the agencies are quasi-independent. They are funded by the state but run independently of existing probation or public defender offices and they have good leadership whose number one priority is advocacy for the client. (personal interview)

NET-WIDENING AND "ALTERNATIVE" PATHS TO PRISON

Our critical summary of intermediate sanctions should in no way be interpreted as support for the "nothing works, so lock 'em up and throw away the key" approach to corrections. Rather, the intent of our summary is to illustrate how institutionalized alternatives to incarceration in the United States provide more intensive, offender-specific supervision services than they do offender-specific treatment. Rutherford (1993) characterizes this model as "attack" probation where the goal is to "Trail 'em, Surveil 'em, Nail 'em, and Jail 'em." Miller (1996), whose "Augustus Institute" works with serious offenders in the community, called this sea change in image and operation "the demise of probation." These critics note that social problems such as drug abuse and mental illness have increasingly become issues dealt with by the police and the courts. This, they argue, results in an increase in the number of citizens capable of being placed under correctional control in the community – a net-widening effect which not only increases the number of people in community corrections but ultimately in prisons and jails.

Another pitfall lies in the revolving door between community-based sanctions and prison. Last year 600,000 prisoners left correctional institutions and returned to the community. Simultaneously, slightly more were admitted to prison. One-half of those entering prison come from probation and another one-third from parole. Of the 2 million people discharged from the ranks of probation, 300,000 (15 percent) were sent to prison; 42 percent of those discharged from parole were returned to prison, nearly 193,000. Yet only 20 percent of probationers and 26 percent of parolees sent to prison are convicted of a new sentence (United States Department of Justice 2001), leaving the majority returning to prison for technical violations of their community-based sanction.

It is becoming increasingly clear that intermediate sanctions that do not address the individual needs and risks of an offender through effective principles of treatment and offender management do not significantly deter future offending (MacKenzie 1997). They are, in effect, "setups" for failure as revocations of probation, intermediate sanctions, or other alternatives for non-criminal violations make it easier to imprison offenders alleged to be incorrigible or "untreatable." The resulting contradiction is that programs designed to be "alternatives to incarceration" and alleviate prison crowding lead nearly half a million people into American prisons each year.

Conclusion – The Augustus Conundrum

In his time, John Augustus's methods for keeping offenders out of prison were considered radical, even dangerous to public safety. In spite of the opposition, probation became standard practice in courts and corrections. Augustus's work eventually set the foundation from which other alternatives to incarceration were developed.

Alternatives to incarceration, particularly intermediate sanctions, were designed to alleviate America's reliance on incarceration while providing more humane and effective treatment of offenders. There exists for each of these goals a mixed bag of interrelated successes and failures. Intensive treatment aimed at rehabilitation largely gave way to intensive supervision and control. The use of alternatives can facilitate appropriate offender-based treatment yet can also widen the net of correctional control. Those supervised in the community today are likely to be housed in prison tomorrow. In sum, when punitive sanctions do not embrace the principles of effective correctional intervention *and* individualized treatment, criminal behavior is not deterred and the alternative to prison becomes a tool for the very prison expansion it was designed to alleviate.

Notes

1 Probation is a sentence served in the community, often in lieu of a prison term, contingent on compliance with court-ordered conditions. Parole is the release of a prisoner into the community during the last part of a prison sentence, also contingent on compliance with the terms of supervision.
2 Technical violations involve a failure to comply with the conditions of probation or parole that may result in a commitment or return to prison. Technical violations include: failure to report to the probation officer, failure to pay court costs or supervision fees, positive urinalysis for alcohol or drugs, changing residence/leaving the state without permission, failure to maintain employment, and other non-criminal acts.
3 A detailed discussion of the principles of effective correctional intervention is beyond the scope of this chapter. The knowledge-base on effective (and ineffective) methods of changing behavior is ever growing. For those interested in a comprehensive discussion and review of rehabilitation, the principles of effective correctional intervention and their use in community-based corrections see Cullen and Gendreau 2000; also see MacKenzie 1997.

References

Allen, H., Carlson, E., Parks, E., and Seiter, R. (1978) *Program Models: Halfway Houses*. Washington, DC: US Department of Justice.
Allen, H, R., Seiter, E., Carlson, E., Bowman, H., Grandfield, J., and Beran, N. (1976) *National Evaluation Program Phase I: Residential Inmate Aftercare, the State of the*

Art Summary. Columbus, OH: Ohio State University, Program for the Study of Crime and Delinquency.

Augustus, J. (1984) [1852] *A Report of the Labors of John Augustus, For the Last Ten Years, In Aid of the Unfortunate.* Boston: Wright & Hasty. Reprinted by the American Parole and Probation Association.

Baumer, T., and Mendelsohn, R. (1992) Electronically monitored home confinement; does it work? In J. Byrne, A. Lurigio, and J. Petersilia (eds.), *Smart Sentencing: The Emergence of Intermediate Sanctions.* Newbury Park, CA: Sage, 54–67.

Bazemore, G., and Maloney, D. (1994) Rehabilitating community service: Toward restorative service sanctions in a balanced justice system. *Federal Probation,* 58(1), 24–35.

Beck, A., and Harrison, P. (2001) *Prisoners in 2000.* Washington, DC: US Department of Justice, Bureau of Justice Statistics.

Brown, J., Langan, P., and Levin, D. (1999) *Felony Sentences in State Courts, 1996.* Washington, DC: Bureau of Justice Statistics.

Bureau of Justice Assistance (1989) *Electronic Monitoring in Intensive Probation and Parole Programs.* Washington, DC: US Department of Justice.

Cahalan, M. (1986) *Historical Corrections Statistics in the United States, 1850–1984.* Washington, DC: US Department of Justice.

Center for Community Corrections (1997) *Community Corrections: A Call for Punishments That Make Sense.* Washington, DC: Center for Community Corrections.

Courtright, K., Berg, B. L., and Mutchnick, R. J. (1997) Effects of house arrest with electronic monitoring on DUI offenders. *Journal of Offender Rehabilitation,* 24, 35–51.

Cullen, F., and Gendreau, P. (2000) Assessing correctional rehabilitation: Policy, practices, and prospects. In J. Horney (ed.), *Policies, Processes, and Decisions of the Criminal Justice System.* Washington, DC: National Institute of Justice, 109–75.

Dupont, P. (1985) *Expanding Sentencing Options: A Governor's Perspective.* Washington, DC: National Institute of Justice.

Fabelo, T. (2000) "Technocorrections": The promises, the uncertain threats. *Sentencing & Corrections: Issues for the 21ˢᵗ Century,* 5, May, 1–7. Washington, DC: National Institute of Justice.

Fulton, B., Latessa, E., Stichman, A., and Travis. L. (1997) The state of ISP: Research and policy implications. *Federal Probation,* 61(4), 65–7.

Gainey, R., Payne, B., and Poole, M. (2000) The relationship between time in jail, time on electronic monitoring, and recidivism: An event history analysis of a jail-based program. *Justice Quarterly,* 17(4), 733–52.

Gendreau, P., Goggin, C., and Fulton, B. (1996) Intensive supervision in probation and parole. In C. R. Hollin (ed.), *Handbook of Offender Assessment and Treatment.* Chichester: John Wiley, 194–204.

Gilbert, E. (2000) The significance of race in the use of restitution. In M. Markowitz and D. Jones-Brown (eds.), *The System in Black and White: Exploring the Connections between Race, Crime, and Justice.* Westport, CT: Praeger, 199–212.

Gordon, D. (1991) *The Justice Juggernaut: Fighting Street Crime, Controlling Citizens.* New Brunswick and London: Rutgers University Press.

Gordon, M., and Glaser, D. (1991) The use and effects of financial penalties in municipal courts. *Criminology,* 29, 651–76.

Gowdy, V. (1993) *Intermediate Sanctions.* Washington, DC: National Institute of Justice, *Research in Brief.*

Hicks, N. (1987) A new relationship: Halfway houses and corrections. *Corrections Compendium,* 12(4), 1, 5–7.

Hillsman, S., and Greene, J. (1992) The use of fines as an intermediate sanction. In J. Byrne, A. Lurigio, and J. Petersilia (eds.), *Smart Sentencing: The Emergence of Intermediate Sanctions*. Newbury Park, CA: Sage, 123–41.

Klein, A. (1997) *Alternative Sentencing, Intermediate Sanctions and Probation* (2nd ed.). Cincinnati, OH: Anderson.

Latessa, E. (1998) *Public Protection Through Offender Risk Reduction: Putting Research into Practice*. Washington, DC: National Institute of Corrections.

Latessa, E., and Allen, H. (1982) Halfway houses and parole: A national assessment. *Journal of Criminal Justice*, 10(2), 153–63.

Latessa, E., and Allen, H. (1999) *Corrections in the Community* (2nd ed.). Cincinnati, OH: Anderson.

Latessa, E. and Travis, L. (1991) Halfway houses or probation: A comparison of alternative dispositions. *Journal of Crime and Justice*, 14(1): 53–76.

Latessa, E. and Travis, L. (1992) Residential community correctional programs. In J. Byrne, A. Lurigio, and J. Petersilia (eds.), *Smart Sentencing: The Emergence of Intermediate Sanctions*. Newbury Park, CA: Sage, 166–81.

Latessa, E., Travis, L., and Holsinger, A. (1997) *Evaluation of Ohio's Community Corrections Act Programs and Community Based Correctional Facilities Final Report*. Cincinnati, OH: Division of Criminal Justice, University of Cincinnati.

Latessa, E., Travis, L., Holsinger, A., and Hartman, J. (1998) *Evaluation of Ohio's Pilot Day Reporting Program: Final Report*. Cincinnati, OH: Division of Criminal Justice, University of Cincinnati.

Lurigio, A., and Petersilia, J. (1992) The emergence of intensive probation supervision programs in the United States. In J. Byrne, A. Lurigio, and J. Petersilia (eds.), *Smart Sentencing: The Emergence of Intermediate Sanctions*. Newbury Park, CA: Sage, 3–17.

MacKenzie, D. (1997) Criminal justice and crime prevention. In L. Sherman, D. Gottfredson, D. MacKenzie, J. Eck, P. Reuter, and S. Bushway, *Preventing Crime: What Works, What Doesn't, What's Promising*. Washington, DC: National Institute of Justice, Office of Justice Programs, US Department of Justice, 436–520.

McDevitt, J. (1988) *Evaluation of the Hampton County Day Reporting Center*. Boston: Crime and Justice Foundation.

McDevitt, J., and Miliano, R. (1992) Day reporting centers: An innovative concept in intermediate sanctions. In J. Byrne, A. Lurigio, and J. Petersilia (eds.), *Smart Sentencing: The Emergence of Intermediate Sanctions*. Newbury Park, CA: Sage, 152–65.

McDonald, D. (1986) *Punishment Without Walls: Community Service Sentences in New York City*. New Brunswick, NJ: Rutgers University Press.

McDonald, D. (1992) Punishing labor: Unpaid community service as a criminal sentence. In J. Byrne, A. Lurigio, and J. Petersilia (eds.), *Smart Sentencing: The Emergence of Intermediate Sanctions*. Newbury Park, CA: Sage, 182–93.

McDonald, D., Greene, J., and Worzella, C. (1995) *Day Fines in American Courts*. Washington, DC: US Department of Justice.

Miller, G. (1996) *Search and Destroy: African-American Males in the Criminal Justice System*. Cambridge: Cambridge University Press.

Morris, N., and Tonry, M. (1990) *Between Prison and Probation: Intermediate Punishments in a Rational Sentencing System*. Oxford: Oxford University Press.

Parent, D. (1990) *Day Reporting Centers for Criminal Offenders: A Descriptive Analysis of Existing Programs*. Washington, DC: National Institute of Justice.

Parent, D. (1996) Day reporting centers: An evolving intermediate sanction. *Federal Probation*, 60(4), 51–4.

Parent, D., Byrne, J., Tsarfaty, V., Valade, L., and Esselman, J. (1995) *Day Reporting Centers, Volume 1: Issues and Practices*. Washington, DC: National Institute of Justice.

Parent, D., Dunworth, T., McDonald, D., and Rhodes, W. (1997) *Intermediate Sanctions. Key Legislative Issues in Criminal Justice*. Washington, DC: National Institute of Justice Research in Action.

Peters, M., Thomas, D., and Zamberlan, C. (1997) *Boot Camps for Juvenile Offenders Program Summary*. Washington, DC: US Department of Justice.

Petersilia, J. (1997) Probation in the United States, practices and challenges. *National Institute of Justice Journal*. Washington, DC: US Department of Justice.

Renzema, M. (1992) Home confinement programs: Development, implementation, and impact. In J. Byrne, A. Lurigio, and J. Petersilia (eds.), *Smart Sentencing: The Emergence of Intermediate Sanctions*. Newbury Park, CA: Sage, 41–53.

Rush, G. (2000) *The Dictionary of Criminal Justice* (5th ed.). Guilford, CT: Dushkin/McGraw Hill.

Rutherford, A. (1993) Book Review of Nils Christie, *Crime Control as Industry: Towards Gulags, Western Style?* (London: Routledge, 1993). *British Journal of Criminology*, Fall, 474–5.

Schmidt, A. (1994) Electronic monitoring in the United States. In U. Zvekic (ed.), *Alternatives to Imprisonment in Comparative Perspective*. United Nations Interregional Crime and Justice Research Institute. Chicago: Nelson-Hall, 363–83.

Seiter, R., Carlson, E., Bowman, H., Grandfield, H., Beran, N., and Allen, H. (1977) *Halfway Houses*. Washington, DC: Government Printing Office.

Sentencing Project, The (1995) *National Directory of Sentencing Advocacy Services, 1995*. Washington, DC: The Sentencing Project.

Smith, M. (1999) Noncustodial sentencing: Why individual characteristics and circumstances should be considered. In P. Harris (ed.), *Research to Results: Effective Community Corrections*. International Community Corrections Association. Arlington, VA: Kirby Lithographic Co., 75–104.

Stinchcomb, J. (1999) Recovering from the shocking reality of shock incarceration – what correctional administrators can learn from boot camp failures. *Corrections Management Quarterly*, 3(4), 43–52.

Taxman, F., and Byrne, J. (2001) Fixing broken windows probation. *Perspectives*, 25(1), 22–9.

Tonry, M. (1996) *Sentencing Matters*. New York: Oxford University Press.

Tonry, M. (1999) Parochialism in U.S. sentencing policy. *Crime and Delinquency*, 45(1), 48–65.

Turner, S., and Petersilia, J. (1996) *Work Release: Recidivism And Corrections Costs In Washington State*. Washington, DC: National Institute of Justice *Research in Brief*.

United States Department of Justice (2001) *National Correctional Population Reaches New High: Grows by 117,400 During 2000 to Total 6.5 Million Adults*. Washington, DC: US Department of Justice.

von Hirsch, A. (1992) Scaling intermediate punishments: A comparison of two models. In J. Byrne, A. Lurigio, and J. Petersilia (eds.), *Smart Sentencing: The Emergence of Intermediate Sanctions*. Newbury Park, CA: Sage, 211–28.

von Hirsch, A., Wasik, M., and Greene, J. (1989) Punishments in the community and the principles of desert. *Rutgers Law Journal*, 20, 595–618.

Wilson, J. Q. (1975) *Thinking About Crime*. New York: Basic Books.

Winterfield, L., and Hillsman, S. (1993) *The Staten Island Day-Fine Project*. Washington, DC: National Institute of Justice *Research in Brief*.

Yeager, M. (1992) Client-specific planning: A status report. *Criminal Justice Abstracts*, September.

11

Rehabilitation: An Assessment of Theory and Research

Mark W. Lipsey, Nana A. Landenberger, and Gabrielle L. Chapman

Introduction

Although criminal behavior is a social construction that varies across cultures and social systems, certain forms of antisocial behavior are almost universally proscribed. Offenders judged guilty of such crimes are subject to punishment or other sanctions under prevailing laws and norms. While one role of such sanctions is retribution, to ensure that offenders are punished for the harm they have caused, there are obvious social benefits if, after their experience with the justice system, the likelihood that they will commit subsequent offenses has been reduced. The topic of criminal rehabilitation deals with the programs and treatments used for this latter purpose, with particular attention to their effectiveness in reducing recidivism.

A full understanding of rehabilitative treatment for offenders would integrate three components. First, insight into the etiology of criminal behavior is required to provide the grounding for rehabilitative treatments. The most compelling rationale for any approach to rehabilitation is that it counteracts the factors that cause criminal behavior in ways that lead to desistance. Second, a diagnostic typology of offenders is needed that is relevant to their responsiveness to treatment. Criminal behavior has different proximal causes for different offenders and, if treatment is to be successful, it should address the issues appropriate to each offender. Finally, and most importantly, an understanding is needed of which rehabilitative treatments are most effective for which offenders.

Though there is a vast research literature on criminal behavior, it provides little integration of the themes relevant to rehabilitation. The causes of criminal behavior, differentiation of types of offenders, and the effectiveness of treatment have generally been studied as separate topics and, indeed, largely represent the interests of different networks of researchers. Thus, research on the causes of crime rarely addresses how intervention might counteract those causes.

Similarly, typologies and classification systems are typically developed to differentiate offenders according to risk for subsequent offense, institutional security, appropriate sentencing, and other such concerns without examination of their implications for treatment. Even the direct study of rehabilitative treatment is surprisingly impoverished in theory development around the issue of how offenders change and why various interventions bring about that change.

Despite the limitations of existing research, these three components of rehabilitation theory provide a useful framework for summarizing the major concepts and research findings that constitute the current state of knowledge about rehabilitative treatments for criminal offenders.

THE ETIOLOGY OF CRIMINAL BEHAVIOR

Theoretical criminologists often seem preoccupied with establishing which theory of the causes of crime is best, but no one explanation can realistically be expected to account for such a complex phenomenon. For understanding rehabilitation, the important matter is to determine what each of the pertinent theories contributes to identifying criminogenic factors that can potentially be mitigated by intervention. Those theories that have received significant support in criminological research and appear to have relatively direct implications for treatment fall into four broad families, differentiated by the causal factors to which they give primary emphasis.

Social control

Social control theories (e.g., Hirschi 1969; Sampson and Laub 1993) emphasize formal and informal controls on criminal behavior such as attachments to non-deviant others, belief in the validity of the rules and laws of the community, and commitment to conventional goals and normative activities (e.g., holding a job, getting married). These theories generally describe the causes of crime as weak social bonds at the micro level or social disorganization at the macro level. Correspondingly, these theories imply that effective rehabilitative strategies for criminal offenders would be those that strengthen relationships with non-deviant peers, family, prosocial organizations and activities (e.g., school, church, work), and the like, or increase motivation to succeed in conventional work, family, and community endeavors. Braithwaite (1989) expanded on the relationship of social control to deviant behavior by observing that community reactions to deviance often cause shame. His central thesis is that forms of social shaming that are reintegrative and reconcile offenders with the community, rather than being stigmatizing, are most effective in preventing future deviant behavior.

Social and economic disadvantage

Another group of theories about the causes of criminal behavior emphasizes the stresses resulting from the social structure, particularly those associated with a disparity of wealth and resources (e.g., Merton 1938; Quinney 1997). In this view, crime is a problem-solving strategy for those with limited economic and social opportunity. Opting to use illegal means to obtain goods and status not readily available by legal means can be seen as a rational choice if the likely benefits are perceived to be greater than the risks of adverse consequences (Cornish and Clarke 1986). The implications for criminal rehabilitation are straightforward. From this perspective, rehabilitative programs must help offenders expand their access to economic and social opportunities so that their chances of achieving conventional goals by conventional means are increased.

Deviant norms

The main theme of this family of theories is that deviant behavior results from alternative values to which individuals have been socialized (e.g., Sutherland and Cressey 1970; Akers 1978). These theories assume plurality and conflict among the different subcultures within society with individuals learning the norms of the groups to which they belong, or wish to belong. Perspectives that emphasize the learning of deviant group norms imply that changing an individual's deviant behavior may be best accomplished through social influence. Thus rehabilitation should give attention to the social ties offenders have with criminal associates, and the norms and values they hold as members of that deviant subculture. The corresponding treatment approaches might include attempts to resocialize offenders to mainstream values, promote affiliation with non-deviant others, and minimize exposure to the criminal subculture.

Predisposing psychological characteristics

This eclectic group of theories and concepts highlights those relatively enduring individual characteristics that increase the likelihood of antisocial responses to personal or social situations. Such characteristics include lack of self-control (Gottfredson and Hirschi 1990), sensation seeking (Gove and Wilmoth 1990), criminal thinking styles (Walters and White 1989), emotional deficits (Hare 1998), low intelligence, mental illness, or other manifestations of psychopathology or dysfunctional personality traits. Because the range of psychological anomalies that might promote criminal behavior is extensive, the implications of this perspective for rehabilitation are also broad. Generally, what follows from these theories is medical, psychiatric, or psychosocial therapy for the disorders or dysfunctions diagnosed for the offender or assumed to characterize offenders generally.

It should be noted that the theoretical perspectives identified above are not mutually exclusive. An individual offender might well be affected by more than one of the criminogenic factors they entail, and different offenders may be affected by different factors. In similar fashion, a rehabilitation program for offenders may address more than one criminogenic factor and these may reflect quite different theoretical perspectives on the causes of criminal behavior.

It should also be noted that many of the criminogenic factors delineated in contemporary theories about the causes of criminal behavior characterize the social ecology in which offenders reside rather than inherent personal traits of those offenders. Moreover, many of the personal traits that are related to criminal behavior are themselves largely products of the social environment. It follows that rehabilitation approaches which focus on treating the individual offender, as nearly all such approaches do, rarely touch the deeper social roots of much criminal behavior that are nourished by economic disadvantage and restricted opportunity for healthy social development. Thus, when examining the effects of rehabilitation, it must be kept in mind that even the most successful approaches will be undermined to greater or lesser extent by the criminogenic factors in the social environments to which offenders typically return upon release from the criminal justice system.

GENERAL EFFECTIVENESS OF DIFFERENT REHABILITATION APPROACHES

The large body of research on the effectiveness of rehabilitative treatment is uneven in quality and coverage. Moreover, most of it has been conducted in the United States, Canada, and Great Britain. The applicability of its findings outside these countries is largely unknown. Within the context of this research, *effectiveness* is defined almost exclusively in terms of officially recorded offenses. That is, rehabilitative treatments are considered effective when they decrease the proportion of offenders who are rearrested or reconvicted relative to control groups not receiving the treatment.

Because of the costs associated with criminal justice processing, as well as the harm to victims, reductions in official offenses of this sort are an appropriate outcome for rehabilitative treatment. They are not, however, a very complete indicator. Anonymous self-report studies show that offenders generally commit many crimes for which they are not arrested, so arrest and reconviction counts underestimate their actual levels of criminal behavior (Blumstein et al. 1986). In addition, reoffense data used as intervention outcome measures typically do not incorporate information about the severity of the offenses so that no effects are identified when treatment decreases the seriousness, but not the occurrence, of subsequent offenses. Furthermore, a narrow focus on reoffending may neglect other socially important treatment outcomes such as employment, improvements in mental health, and better social functioning. Although some research studies measure outcomes in these other domains, they have not received consistent attention and, as a result, currently available research is not sufficient to determine what effects rehabilitative treatment has on them.

With recognition of the relatively narrow view of effectiveness inherent in the studies of rehabilitative treatments undertaken to date, we will summarize the major findings presented by that body of research. For this purpose, we will rely primarily on systematic research syntheses using meta-analysis techniques. Carefully done, such synthesis provides a valid and discriminating approach to integrating the results of empirical research (Cooper 1998). In addition, these techniques have been rather widely applied to research on offender rehabilitation, with a small set of these syntheses being sufficiently comprehensive to allow the effectiveness of different intervention approaches to be directly compared. Because few treatment studies have been conducted with specialized samples, most of the available research is undifferentiated with regard to the offender population studied. Research findings on rehabilitation for general offenders will therefore be reviewed first, and what is known about treatments for selected types of offenders will be discussed in later sections.

Counseling and its variants

Within the counseling category we include those treatments centered on a relationship with a trained or lay helper whose primary role is to provide advice, problem-solving discussion, emotional support, or personal assistance. Among these treatments are the recognized varieties of counseling (e.g., individual, group, family), as well as general psychotherapy, social work, advocacy, and mentoring. Part of the appeal of this treatment approach is the presumption that a skilled counselor can help an offender deal constructively with virtually any of the factors that sustain criminal behavior, whether these are relationships with antisocial peers, economic stress, psychological problems, or whatever.

Studies of the effectiveness of counseling approaches with offenders have been examined in several research syntheses (MacKenzie 1997; Lipsey and Wilson 1998; Redondo et al. 1999). On average, counseling interventions have positive but rather modest effects on the subsequent criminal behavior of offenders. However, those effects show wide variability, which indicates that some counseling-based treatments are considerably more effective than others. Unfortunately, research is not yet sufficient to sort out which counseling approaches are most effective for which offenders under what circumstances. One strength of counseling is that it is often a component of relatively effective multimodal treatment programs (discussed later); thus it may be most appropriate as an adjunct to other treatment modes.

Training and skill-building

Included in this category of rehabilitation treatments are those that use relatively systematic didactic techniques to train offenders in some defined skill, behavior, or knowledge presumed related to the proximal causes of their criminal behavior. Research on this approach has mainly involved training related to interpersonal behavior, cognitive behavior, and academic and employment skills.

INTERPERSONAL BEHAVIOR

Several of the major etiological theories for criminal behavior highlight variables related to interpersonal behavior; for example, attachment to pro-social others, managing conflict with those from other social groups, and controlling anger and impulses that lead to interpersonal aggression. Correspondingly, research has been reported and reviewed on the effects of training offenders in interpersonal skills, empathy, conflict resolution, assertiveness, and related domains. For juvenile offenders, training in interpersonal skills is among the most effective interventions for reducing subsequent recidivism (Tolan and Guerra 1994; Lipsey and Wilson 1998). The research is insufficient to draw conclusions about the effectiveness of interpersonal skills training for adult offenders, but many of them are affected by the etiological factors these programs address.

COGNITIVE BEHAVIOR

From a psychological standpoint, one of the notable characteristics of chronic offenders is distorted cognition – self-justificatory thinking, misinterpretation of social cues, deficient moral reasoning, and the like (Walters and White 1989; Dodge 1993). Cognitive-behavioral treatments employ training regimens aimed at "cognitive restructuring" to develop new patterns of reasoning and reacting in situations that trigger criminal behavior. For instance, they may train offenders to monitor their patterns of automatic thoughts to situations in which they tend to react with violence. Various techniques are then practiced for assessing the validity of those thoughts and substituting accurate interpretations for biased ones. These therapies have consistently been found to be among the most effective rehabilitative strategies for both juveniles and adults (Andrews et al. 1990; Lipsey and Wilson 1998; Redondo et al. 1999).

ACADEMIC AND EMPLOYMENT SKILLS

As expected from etiological theories emphasizing social and economic disparity, most offenders are economically disadvantaged, poorly educated, and lack job skills. For those with such handicaps, a straightforward rehabilitative approach is training to increase their academic or employment skills and, hence, their prospects for economic stability in non-criminal lifestyles. Even if such training is successful at enhancing offenders' job skills, however, it will not provide alternatives to the economic benefits of crime unless there is a market for those skills. In highly stratified societies and tight labor markets where well-paying jobs are scarce, offenders with enhanced skills gain little advantage. Moreover, the discrimination against those with criminal records that is typical in employers' hiring decisions creates a disadvantage that is difficult for even well-trained offenders to overcome in any competitive labor market. Under these circumstances, it is not surprising that research on the effects of educational, employment, and vocational programs shows rather varied results that, on average, are positive and moderately large, but quite uneven (Lipsey 1992; MacKenzie 1997; Lipsey and Wilson 1998; Redondo et al. 1999; Wilson et al. 2000; Lattimore et al. 1990).

Behavioral control and supervision

An alternative to attempting to counteract the processes that produce criminal behavior is to control that behavior directly without any particular reference to what its sources are. If control can be exercised over an offender at large in the community that is sufficient to prevent criminal behavior, a form of rehabilitation has been attained. If that control is internalized so that it becomes part of the habit pattern of the offender, then the results constitute rehabilitation under any definition.

FORMAL SUPERVISION AND LEGAL SANCTIONS

Probation and parole supervision are the traditional methods intended to control the behavior of offenders who are under the authority of the justice system, but not incarcerated. There is little evidence that routine probation or parole supervision has significant effects on subsequent offense rates, so research has concentrated on various intensive supervision or reduced caseload programs. The findings have been somewhat mixed but, generally, indicate that these approaches by themselves are not effective in reducing the recidivism of the offenders under supervision (MacKenzie 1997; Lipsey and Wilson 1998; Petersilia 1999). In similar fashion, research on programs involving community restraints such as home confinement, electronic monitoring, and day reporting does not reveal any significant effects on recidivism (MacKenzie 1997).

An analogous behavioral control argument can be made for incarceration itself by way of "specific deterrence," the notion that released offenders will be deterred from further criminal behavior because they do not want to risk being sent back to prison. Methodologically sound research comparing imprisonment with suitable control conditions to determine the effects on recidivism is difficult to conduct and correspondingly rare. A research synthesis conducted by Gendreau et al. (1999a) found that both longer time served in prison and serving a prison sentence versus a community-based sanction were associated with slightly higher recidivism rates. Similarly, shock probation, shock incarceration, and other such programs that introduce offenders to the severity of criminal justice sanctions in an attempt to deter them from criminal activity do not decrease subsequent offending and, indeed, seem to exacerbate it (MacKenzie 1997; Lipsey and Wilson 1998; Petrosino et al. 2000).

CONTINGENCY MANAGEMENT

Contingency management programs are designed to shape and maintain appropriate behaviors until they are habitual and can be sustained. These approaches include behavior modification techniques, particularly behavioral contracting and token economies. Most of the effectiveness research has been conducted on juvenile offenders and demonstrates that these interventions are among the most effective in reducing recidivism (Gottshalk et al. 1987; Lipsey and Wilson 1998; Redondo et al. 1999; Greenwood and Turner 1993). Moreover, these programs appear to be effective in community residential settings, criminal justice institutional settings, and as an adjunct to probation supervision. Studies with adult offenders have shown positive effects, but are not yet sufficient in number or scope to support generalization.

INCULCATING SELF-DISCIPLINE

Still another variation on the theme of behavioral control is embodied in programs configured so that the offender experiences a strict disciplinary regimen or must undertake challenging tasks that require self-discipline to master. If self-discipline is learned and then sustained after the program ends, it is presumed to help the offender resist temptation to engage in criminal behavior and facilitate a stable, normative lifestyle. The interventions in this category include boot camps organized along paramilitary lines and physical challenge programs such as wilderness survival, rope courses, and the like.

Despite their intuitive appeal, programs of this type generally have not proven to be very effective in reducing reoffense rates. Research on paramilitary-style boot camps designed to expose offenders to stringent, intensive, short-term disciplinary programs has not found positive effects on recidivism for either juvenile or adult offenders (MacKenzie 1997). Challenge programs for offenders, usually involving wilderness experiences, have shown only somewhat more favorable effects (Wilson and Lipsey 2000). However, these positive results came largely from programs with a distinct therapeutic component, e.g., adjunct counseling, and not from programs oriented exclusively toward challenge and discipline.

Restorative and reintegrative programs

A rather distinctive approach to offender rehabilitation is organized around restorative justice themes (Bazemore 1998) and requires the offender to "help make things right" by providing restitution for the damage done or to engage with the victim and other stakeholders for purposes of reconciliation, mediation, or reintegration of the offender into the community. These approaches draw support from etiological theories emphasizing social bonds to family and community and have been influenced by Braithwaite's (1989) concept of reintegrative shaming – social processes that invoke moral regret in offenders while reinforcing their membership in the community of law-abiding citizens. Interventions in this general category include community service by offenders, restitution programs, victim–offender mediation and reconciliation programs, and family group conferences.

The main goal of many of these programs is not reducing offender recidivism but, rather, ameliorating some of the harm done to victims and increasing their satisfaction with the justice process. Nonetheless, these programs do include rehabilitative themes and their effects on the recidivism of participating offenders have been investigated. A small research synthesis conducted by Bonta et al. (1998) found modest effects on recidivism, as did Lipsey and Wilson (1998) for restitution programs. The limited number of controlled studies that have been conducted and the diverse nature of the programs in this category, however, make it premature to draw conclusions about their impact on recidivism.

Multimodal interventions

Offenders typically come from very poor segments of society, are often unemployed, and have limited literacy, high levels of family discord, family and friends who engage in antisocial behavior, and a high prevalence of drug abuse. Given this background, a rehabilitation program may need to have multiple components that target a variety of criminogenic factors in order to be very effective. Such a program, for instance, might involve cognitive-behavioral therapy, employment training, and drug treatment.

Though multimodal programs necessarily represent great variety, as a general category they are among the most effective at reducing recidivism in research syntheses that include them (Lipsey 1992; MacKenzie 1997; Benekos 1992; Lipsey and Wilson 1998). Positive results have also been reported for research on Germany's social-therapeutic prisons, an inherently multimodal program (Lösel 1995). Most of the individual treatment categories reviewed above, even those relatively ineffective by themselves (e.g., counseling, employment training, formal supervision) have been included in effective multimodal combinations.

Other dimensions of effective intervention

Rehabilitation programs are conventionally identified in terms of the type of intervention they represent, as in the review above. One of the more important revelations from discriminating syntheses of intervention research, however, is that other aspects of the programs are strongly related to their effects on recidivism. Chief among these are factors relating to the amount, intensity, and degree of implementation of the treatment provided (Gendreau et al. 1999b). Well-implemented, high-dosage programs generally show positive effects on recidivism even when they employ one of the less effective treatment modalities (Lipsey and Wilson 1998; Redondo et al. 1999). Of course, the programs that combine the strongest modalities with high implementation are the most effective.

Themes and outcomes that characterize effective rehabilitation programs

The relative similarity of the recidivism effects (for better or worse) of many types of interventions, coupled with the general importance of strength of implementation and other such cross-cutting factors, undermines any attempt to identify a "best" type of rehabilitation program. What emerges from the broad research syntheses that compare interventions is not one kind of program that trumps all the others as the most effective for reducing recidivism, but a few themes that differentiate the more effective intervention efforts from the less effective ones.

Four such themes can be readily induced from the review above and the most comprehensive syntheses of intervention research (cf. Andrews et al. 1990).

1 The more effective programs target for change either criminal behavior directly (as in contingency management programs) or specific proximal causes of criminal behavior (as in cognitive-behavioral programs), but they do not use fear-based or punitive approaches to do this (e.g., boot camps, intensive supervision).
2 The more effective programs involve rather structured regimens, such as training, as their primary component. This is reflected in the generally greater effectiveness of behavioral and skill-building programs for reducing recidivism than less structured interventions centered on building relationships, such as counseling, mentoring, and restorative programs.
3 Multimodal programs are generally more effective than programs that employ a single treatment strategy and, in particular, adjunct counseling, academic and employment training, and supervision appear to be more effective in multimodal combinations than as freestanding treatments.
4 Well-implemented programs that deliver a relatively high dose of treatment tend to be more effective. Because different types of programs provide

different services and use different kinds of service units, what constitutes a high dose varies with the type of intervention. Overall, the high end of the service range is something greater than about 25 weeks' program duration with 5–10 contact hours of treatment per week delivered in multiple sessions (Lipsey and Wilson 1998).

The question of what treatments are most effective in reducing the recidivism of offenders, therefore, is not answered by identifying some "magic bullet" intervention program that, by itself, represents best practice. Rather, the research indicates that, in general, the best programs are any of the many variations that embody the themes described above. Though this result supports many different program choices, it should be noted that most of the interventions tested in the research literature produced weak or negligible effects on recidivism, and some had negative effects. Despite the evidence that many programs, in principle, can be effective, actually configuring and implementing such a program appears to be relatively difficult.

When programs of the best sort are actually implemented, and implemented well, however, their effects on the reoffense recidivism of the offenders they treat can be quite significant in practical and policy terms. The recidivism rates for adults released from prison can be as high as 50–70 percent (Beck and Shipley 1989), with those for probationers and juvenile offenders running somewhat lower. The average effect on recidivism found for the best forms of intervention in the research syntheses cited in the discussion above was in the range of a 10–25 percentage point differential between treatment and control groups. For instance, if the recidivism rate of a control group receiving no intervention (or treatment as usual, e.g., probation supervision) was 55 percent, the best programs might reduce this by as much as 25 percentage points to about 30 percent. Viewed in terms of the harm done to victims and society by recidivistic offenses, and the cost to law enforcement and the criminal justice system of responding to new offenses (Welsh and Farrington 2000), these are socially and economically meaningful outcomes for a rehabilitation program.

DIFFERENT TREATMENT FOR DIFFERENT TYPES OF OFFENDERS

The development of diagnostic typologies for guiding the selection of appropriate treatment for criminal offenders is still in its infancy, and only limited insight on this matter can be gained from the available treatment research. Most studies use samples from a general offender population and rarely break out the results for different types of offenders. Thus, little is known about which treatments work best for which offenders. Nonetheless, a few quite distinct offender types have been identified, and some research is available about their response to treatment.

Offenders with severe and persistent mental illness

As many as 15 percent of prisoners in the United States may have severe and persistent mental illness (SPMI) (e.g., Lamb and Weinberger 1998). Among such offenders, those whose SPMI is accompanied by antisocial/psychopathic personality traits, sexual deviance, or substance abuse are at particularly high risk for violence (Monahan, 2001). Interventions that treat these offenders' mental illness without addressing their co-morbid dysfunctions are likely to fail.

In contrast, the criminal behavior of SPMI-only offenders is more likely to be disorganized and is often nonviolent, although certain acute psychotic symptoms (e.g., believing that others wish one harm, that one's mind is dominated by forces beyond one's control) indicate risk for violent behavior (Link et al. 1999). Pharmacotherapy is the first-line treatment for these offenders and anti-psychotic medications can often stabilize their symptoms (Kane 1999). Skill-building interventions, such as family/marital education to decrease hostility, criticism, and emotional over-involvement in the immediate social environment, and cognitive therapy focusing on medication compliance and coping skills, have been shown to reduce relapse and further improve functioning in SMPI patients (Butzlaff and Hooley 1998; Tarrier and Bobes 2000).

Community support and social work may also be necessary to divert SPMI offenders from the criminal justice system. According to US statistics, about half the SPMI defendants arrested for minor offenses were homeless (e.g., Martell et al. 1995). Supportive housing and assertive case management that provide structure, ongoing supervision, and prompt response to reemerging crises have been recommended to decriminalize the primary-SPMI group (Lamb and Weinberger 1998).

Psychopathic offenders

Among the antisocial personality disorders, a growing body of research suggests that psychopaths may be a distinct subgroup characterized by neuropsychological and affective abnormalities not typical of the "average" antisocial personality (Patrick 1994; Hare 1996; Newman 1998). These abnormalities may contribute to the relatively extreme criminal conduct and personality traits characteristic of psychopaths (e.g., egocentric, manipulative, devoid of empathy and remorse, impulsive). Psychopaths constitute about 15–25 percent of the US prison population and are often professional criminals who have led a pervasive antisocial lifestyle since early adolescence (Hemphill et al. 1998). They stand out not only because of a particularly high rate of crime and criminal versatility, but also because they are responsible for a disproportionate amount of violent crime (Cornell et al. 1996).

Psychopathic offenders are often considered untreatable, but the empirical support for this view is weak inasmuch as few studies have investigated treatment outcomes for these offenders. Unstructured approaches, such as insight-oriented group counseling, are unlikely to be effective as psychopaths are deficient in the self-analytical skills these treatments require and tend to deny responsibility for the harm they cause. Punishment and deterrence-oriented interventions are also unlikely to have an impact on psychopaths – clinicians have long described them as offenders who fail to learn from negative experience (Gray and Hutchinson 1964). Treatments that employ a combination of cognitive restructuring and interpersonal skill-building may be most appropriate for this group. These approaches have the potential to challenge the cognitive distortions that give psychopaths free rein to victimize others without remorse, as well as teach them impulse and anger-control techniques. The limited treatment research with psychopaths, however, leaves much uncertainty about the most effective rehabilitation programs for this difficult type of offender.

Sex offenders

Sex offenders are generally acknowledged to constitute a separate offender subgroup with distinct criminal motives, cognitive distortions, modi operandi, and treatment and supervision needs (Marshall and Barbaree 1990). There are significant differences between sex offenders who victimize children and those who victimize adults (Grubin and Kennedy 1991), but they are often treated jointly.

Child sex offenders may be pedophiles with an exclusive sexual interest in children or also maintaining sexual relations with adults, and they may be incest offenders or extra-familial child offenders, or both. Nonetheless, they show many commonalities in their cognitions and behaviors (Finkelhor and Araji 1986; Ward et al. 1999). These offenders can be described as master manipulators who hide behind a façade of "Mr. Nice Guy." They may lead seemingly conventional lifestyles, have successful careers, and often hold respected positions that engender trust (and easy access to children). These offenders may take months or even years to "groom" a child victim and the care-taker. Manipulating the victim into keeping the abuse secret is part of their cover-up for their crimes (Lang and Frenzel 1988).

Relative to child offenders, those who victimize adults are more criminally versatile, show more psychopathic traits, have lower socioeconomic status, are more likely to commit their offenses under the influence of drugs or alcohol, and are more likely to use excessive force (Bard et al. 1987; Scully 1990; Porter et al. 2000). The sexual deviance of the rapist is typically part of a larger criminal lifestyle and marked by a pattern of entitlement, power orientation, impulsivity, and anger (Polaschek et al. 1997). The notorious sadistic "serial killers" constitute a highly disturbed, but rare, subgroup of sex offenders (Douglas and Olshaker 1996).

Meta-analyses and research reviews have generally concluded that sex offenders are difficult to treat, but some forms of intervention have produced positive results (Hall 1995; Grossman et al. 1999; Polizzi et al. 1999; Lösel, 2000). The most promising approaches are multimodal, with cognitive restructuring and relapse prevention as centerpieces. Positive effects have also been found with pharmacological interventions using hormonal agents (anti-androgens) and antidepressants. The cognitive restructuring treatments aim to correct the characteristically distorted beliefs of sex offenders, e.g., that children benefit from sex or that "seductive" women are asking to be raped. Relapse prevention programs focus on identifying and managing risk factors that are the precursors to an individual's sex offending. Behavioral contracts (e.g., no contact with children) and intensive supervision may also be used to help offenders adhere to the necessary life changes for avoiding relapse.

Drug and alcohol offenders

The association between substance use and crime is well documented in the research literature (e.g., Roizen 1993). Over 70 percent of US prisoners have histories of substance abuse and about half report being under the influence of drugs or alcohol at the time of their offense (Bureau of Justice Statistics 2000). At least four types of drug- or alcohol-involved offenders can be identified: (a) *addicts* who commit crimes to support their habit; (b) *motor vehicle offenders* who drive under the influence; (c) *public order offenders* who are disruptive while intoxicated; and (d) *assault offenders*, including spousal assault offenders, whose rates of violence increase dramatically under the influence of drugs and alcohol. For purposes of reducing reoffense recidivism, interventions that specifically aim to reduce alcohol and drug use are most likely to be effective with these offenders. Surveys of individuals discharged from substance abuse treatment have found that the percentage reporting criminal activity declined by one-quarter to one-half between the five years before and five years after treatment (Schildhaus et al. 2000).

Studies of substance-abuse treatment with corrections and aftercare populations support the effectiveness of therapeutic community programs (which often include cognitive-behavioral therapy, relapse prevention, or 12-step programs) in reducing the recidivism of chemically dependent offenders (Pearson and Lipton 1999; Chanhatasilpa et al. 2000). Boot camps, group counseling, and increased supervision and monitoring (e.g., urine testing) have not been found effective with these populations. For alcoholic patients, a major clinical trial has shown equal results for 12-step facilitation, motivational enhancement, and cognitive-behavioral therapy, except that highly angry alcoholics drank less in motivational enhancement (Project MATCH Research Group 1998). The applicability of these findings to alcohol-involved offenders has not been investigated. For heroin users, research syntheses show that methadone maintenance has a moderate effect in reducing both drug use and income-producing crimes, especially when paired with contingency management using urine screens and immediate reinforcement (Marsch 1998; Griffith et al. 2000).

CONCLUSIONS

Linking etiological theories of criminal behavior to intervention for offenders can guide treatment toward goals that are relevant for rehabilitation and provide a starting point for developing a better understanding of why intervention is or is not effective. From this perspective, rehabilitative treatments can be conceptualized in terms of their service approach (e.g., counseling, job training) and the criminogenic factors those services attempt to address (e.g., deviant peers, economic stress). However, no one etiological theory accounts for all criminal behavior, and there is no one set of criminogenic factors that, if altered, can be expected to rehabilitate all offenders.

In light of the diversity of criminogenic factors and behavioral problems that characterize offenders, the most promising rehabilitative strategies are those that use one of the more effective treatment approaches as their centerpiece and supplement that with other treatment components, such as counseling and job training, to address more completely the factors related to criminal behavior. Similarly, in light of the diversity of offenders, it is not reasonable to expect any treatment package, even a well-developed multimodal one, to be optimal for every offender. Research about the response of different types of offenders to different treatments and, indeed, about what diagnostic categories to use for this purpose, is not well developed. Nonetheless, it is clear that such relatively distinct offender types as those with severe and persistent mental illness, psychopaths, sex offenders, and those with substance abuse as a primary factor in their criminal behavior are best treated with interventions tailor-made for their particular profiles.

Amid the diversity of etiological theories, intervention approaches, and offender types, two overriding features of the evidence from rehabilitation research should not be forgotten. First, nearly all intervention approaches produce at least modest reductions in reoffense rates, and the best interventions yield quite substantial reductions, even with serious offenders. In a phrase, "rehabilitation works," and the best rehabilitative treatments work rather well. Second, the critical practical questions of just what works best for which offenders in which circumstances and why has not yet been well answered in the research literature. While recent advances in treatment and research have provided a solid basis for confidence about the efficacy of rehabilitative efforts, there is still much to be learned before such efforts can reach their full potential.

References

Akers, R. L. (1978) *Deviant Behavior.* Belmont, CA: Wadsworth.

Andrews, D. A., Zinger, I., Hoge, R. D., Bonta, J., Gendreau, P., and Cullen, F. T. (1990) Does correctional treatment work? A clinically-relevant and psychologically informed meta-analysis. *Criminology,* 28, 369–404.

Bard, L. A., Carter, D. L., Cerce, D. D., Knight, R. A., Rosenberg, R., and Schneider, B. (1987) A descriptive study of rapists and child molesters: Developmental, clinical, and criminal characteristics. *Behavioral Sciences and the Law,* 5, 203–20.

Bazemore, G. (1998) Restorative justice and earned redemption: Communities, victims, and offender reintegration. *American Behavioral Scientist,* 41, 768–813.

Beck, A. J., and Shipley, B. E. (1989) *Recidivism of Prisoners Released in 1983.* Bureau of Justice Statistics, Special Report No. NCJ-116261. Washington, DC: US Department of Justice.

Benekos, P. J. (1992) Shock incarceration: The military model in corrections. In K. Humble and G. Eccleston (eds.), *Corrections: Dilemmas and Directions.* Highland Heights, KY: Academy of Criminal Justice Sciences, 121–33.

Blumstein, A., Cohen, J., Roth, J. A., and Visher, C. A. (1986). *Criminal Careers and "Career Criminals."* Washington, DC: National Academy Press.

Bonta, J., Wallace-Capretta, S., and Rooney, J. (1998) *Restorative Justice: An Evaluation of the Restorative Resolutions Project.* Ottawa: Department of the Solicitor General Canada (www.sgc.gc.ca).

Braithwaite, J. (1989) *Crime, Shame, and Reintegration.* Cambridge: Cambridge University Press.

Bureau of Justice Statistics (2000) *Correctional Populations in the United States 1997.* Report No. NCJ-177613. Washington, DC: US Department of Justice.

Butzlaff, R. L., and Hooley, J. M. (1998) Expressed emotion and psychiatric relapse: A meta-analysis. *Archives of General Psychiatry*, 55, 547–52.

Chanhatasilpa, C., MacKenzie, D. L., and Hickman, L. J. (2000) The effectiveness of community-based programs for chemically dependent offenders: A review and assessment of the research. *Journal of Substance Abuse Treatment*, 19, 383–93.

Cooper, H. (1998) *Synthesizing Research: A Guide for Literature Reviews* (3rd ed.). Thousand Oaks, CA: Sage.

Cornell, D. G., Warren, J., Hawk, G., Stafford, E., Oram, G., Pine, D., Weitzner, I., and Griffith, R. (1996) Psychopathy in instrumental and reactive violent offenders. *Journal of Consulting and Clinical Psychology*, 64, 783–90.

Cornish, D. B., and Clarke, R. V. (1986) *The Reasoning Criminal*. New York: Springer-Verlag.

Dodge, K. A. (1993) Social-cognitive mechanisms in the development of conduct disorder and depression. *Annual Review of Psychology*, 44, 559–83.

Douglas, J. E., and Olshaker, M. (1996) *Mindhunter: Inside the FBI's Elite Serial Crime Unit*. New York: Pocket Books.

Finkelhor, D., and Araji, S. (1986) Explanations of pedophilia: A four factor model. *Journal of Sex Research*, 22 145–61.

Gendreau, P., Goggin, C., and Cullen, F. T. (1999a) *The Effects of Prison Sentences on Recidivism*. Ottawa: Department of the Solicitor General Canada (www.sgc.gc.ca).

Gendreau, P., Goggin, C., and Smith, P. (1999b) The forgotten issue in effective correctional treatment: Program implementation. *International Journal of Offender Therapy and Comparative Criminology*, 43 180–187.

Gottfredson, M., and Hirschi, T. (1990) *A General Theory of Crime*. Stanford, CA: University of Stanford Press.

Gottshalk, R., Davidson, W. S., Mayer, J., and Gensheimer, L. K. (1987) Behavioral approaches with juvenile offenders: A meta-analysis of long-term treatment efficacy. In E. K. Morris and C. J. Braukmann (eds.), *Behavioral Approaches to Crime and Delinquency: A Handbook*. New York: Plenum, 399–422.

Gove, W. R., and Wilmoth, C. (1990) Risk, crime, and neurophysiologic highs: A consideration of brain processes that may reinforce delinquent and criminal behavior. In L. Ellis and H. Hoffman (eds.), *Crime in Biological, Social, and Moral Context*. New York: Praeger, 261–94.

Gray, J. A., and Hutchinson, H. C. (1964) The psychopathic personality: A survey of Canadian psychiatrists' opinions. *Canadian Psychiatric Association Journal*, 9, 452–61.

Greenwood, P. W., and Turner, S. (1993) Evaluation of the Paint Creek Youth Center: A residential program for serious delinquents. *Criminology*, 31(2), 263–79.

Griffith, J. D., Rowan-Szal, G. A., Roark, R. R., and Simpson, D. D. (2000) Contingency management in outpatient methadone treatment: A meta-analysis. *Drug and Alcohol Dependence*, 58, 55–66.

Grossman, L. S., Martis, B., and Fichtner, C. G. (1999) Are sex offenders treatable? A research overview. *Psychiatric Services*, 50, 349–61.

Grubin, D. H., and Kennedy, H. G. (1991) The classification of sexual offenders. *Criminal Behaviour and Mental Health*, 1, 123–9.

Hall, N. G. C. (1995) Sexual offender recidivism revisited: A meta-analysis of recent treatment studies. *Journal of Consulting and Clinical Psychology*, 63, 802–9.

Hare, R. D. (1996) Psychopathy: A clinical construct whose time has come. *Criminal Justice and Behavior*, 23, 25–54.

Hare, R. D. (1998) Psychopathy, affect, and behavior. In D. J. Cooke, A. E. Forth, and R. D. Hare (eds.), *Psychopathy: Theory, Research and Implications for Society*. Dordrecht: Kluwer, 105–38.

Hemphill, J. F., Templeman, R., Wong, S., and Hare, R. D. (1998) Psychopathy and crime: Recidivism and criminal careers. In D. J. Cooke, A. E. Forth, and R. D. Hare (eds.), *Psychopathy: Theory, Research and Implications for Society*. Dordrecht: Kluwer, 375–99.

Hirschi, T. (1969) *The Causes of Delinquency*. Berkeley: University of California Press.

Kane, J. M. (1999) Pharmacologic treatment of schizophrenia. *Biological Psychiatry*, 46 1396–1408.

Lamb, H. R., and Weinberger, L. E. (1998) Persons with severe mental illness in jails and prisons: A review. *Psychiatric Services*, 49, 483–92.

Lang, R. A., and Frenzel, R. R. (1988) How sex offenders lure children. *Annals of Sex Research* 1, 303–17.

Lattimore, P. K., Witte, A. D., and Baker, J. A. (1990) Experimental assessment of the effect of vocational training on youthful property offenders. *Evaluation Review*, 14(2), 115–33.

Link, B. G., Monahan, J., Stueve, A., and Cullen, F. T. (1999) Real in their consequences: A sociological approach to understanding the association between psychotic symptoms and violence. *American Sociological Review*, 64, 316–32.

Lipsey, M. W. (1992) Juvenile delinquency treatment: A meta-analytic inquiry into the variability of effects. In T. D. Cook, H. Cooper, D. S. Cordray, H. Hartmann, L. V. Hedges, R. J. Light, T. A. Louis, and F. Mosteller (eds.), *Meta-analysis for Explanation: A Casebook*. New York: Russell Sage Foundation, 83–127.

Lipsey, M. W., and Wilson, D. B. (1998) Effective intervention for serious juvenile offenders: A synthesis of research. In R. Loeber and D. P. Farrington (eds.), *Serious and Violent Juvenile Offenders: Risk Factors and Successful Interventions*. Thousand Oaks, CA: Sage, 313–45.

Lösel, F. (1995) Increasing consensus in the evaluation of offender rehabilitation? Lessons from recent research syntheses. *Psychology, Crime and Law*, 2, 19–39.

Lösel, F. (2000) The efficacy of sexual offender treatment: A review of German and international evaluations. In P. J. Koppen and N. Roos (eds.), *Rationality, Information, and Progress in Psychology and Law*. Maastricht: Metajuridica Publications, 145–70.

MacKenzie, D. L. (1997) Criminal justice and crime prevention. In L. W. Sherman, D. Gottfredson, D. L. MacKenzie, J. Eck, P. Reuter, and S. Bushway (eds.), *Preventing Crime: What Works, What Doesn't, What's Promising*. Washington, DC: National Institute of Justice, ch. 9.

Marsch, L. A. (1998) The efficacy of methadone maintenance interventions in reducing illicit opiate use, HIV risk behavior and criminality: A meta-analysis. *Addiction*, 93, 515–32.

Marshall, W. L., and Barbaree, H. E. (1990) An integrated theory of the etiology of sexual offending. In W. L. Marshall, D. R. Laws, and H. E. Barbaree (eds.), *Handbook of Sexual Assault*. New York: Plenum, 257–78.

Martell, D. A., Rosner, R., and Harmon, R. B. (1995) Baserate estimates of criminal behavior by homeless mentally ill persons in New York City. *Psychiatric Services*, 46, 596–600.

Merton, R. (1938) Social structure and anomie. *American Sociological Review*, 3, 672–82.

Monahan, J. (2001) Major mental disorder and violence: Epidemiology and risk assessment. In G. F. Pinard and L. Pagani (eds.), *Clinical Assessment of Dangerousness: Empirical Contributions*. New York: Cambridge University Press, 89–102.

Newman, J. P. (1998) Psychopathic behavior: An information processing perspective. In D. J. Cooke, A. E. Forth, and R. D. Hare (eds.), *Psychopathy: Theory, Research and Implications for Society*. Dordrecht: Kluwer and NATO Scientific Affairs Division, 81–104.

Patrick, C. J. (1994) Emotion and psychopathy: Startling new insights. *Psychophysiology*, 31, 319–30.

Pearson, F. S., and Lipton, D. S. (1999) A meta-analytic review of the effectiveness of corrections-based treatments for drug abuse. *Prison Journal*, 79, 384–410.

Petersilia, J. (1999) A decade of experimenting with intermediate sanctions: What have we learned? *Justice Research and Policy* 1, 9–23.

Petrosino, A., Turpin-Petrosino, C., and Finckenauer, J. (2000) Well-meaning programs can have harmful effects! Lessons from experiments of programs such as Scared Straight. *Crime & Delinquency*, 46, 354–79.

Polaschek, D. L. L., Ward, T., and Hudson, S. M. (1997) Rape and rapists: Theory and treatment. *Clinical Psychology Review*, 17, 117–44.

Polizzi, D. M., MacKenzie, D. L., and Hickman, L. J. (1999) What works in adult sex offender treatment? A review of prison- and non-prison-based treatment programs. *International Journal of Offender Therapy and Comparative Criminology*, 43, 357–74.

Porter, S., Fairweather, D., Drugge, J., Herve, H., and Birt, A. (2000) Profiles of psychopathy in incarcerated sexual offenders. *Criminal Justice and Behavior*, 27, 216–33.

Project MATCH Research Group (1998) Matching alcoholism treatments to client heterogeneity: Project MATCH three-year drinking outcomes. *Alcoholism: Clinical and Experimental Research*, 22, 1300–11.

Quinney, R. (1997) The social reality of crime. In P. A. Adler and P. Adler (eds.), *Constructions of Deviance* (2nd ed.). Belmont, CA: Wadsworth, 123–7.

Redondo, S., Sanchez-Meca, J., and Garrido, V. (1999) The influence of treatment programmes on the recidivism of juvenile and adult offenders: An European meta-analytic review. *Psychology, Crime, & Law*, 5, 251–78.

Roizen, J. (1993) Issues in the epidemiology of alcohol and violence. In S. E. Martin (ed.), *Alcohol and Interpersonal Violence: Fostering Multidisciplinary Perspectives*. Rockville, MD: National Institute on Alcohol Abuse and Alcoholism, 3–36.

Sampson, R., and Laub, J. (1993) *Crime in the Making: Pathways and Turning Points Through Life*. Cambridge, MA: Harvard University Press.

Schildhaus, S., Gerstein, D., Brittingham, A., Cerbone, F., and Dugoni, B. (2000) Services research outcomes study: Overview of drug treatment populations and outcomes. *Substance Use & Misuse*, 35, 1849–77.

Scully, D. (1990) *Understanding Sexual Violence: A Study of Convicted Rapists*. Boston: Unwin Hyman.

Sutherland, E., and Cressey, D. (1970) *Principles of Criminology*. New York: Lippincott.

Tarrier, N., and Bobes, J. (2000) The importance of psychosocial interventions and patient involvement in the treatment of schizophrenia. *International Journal of Psychiatry in Clinical Practice*, 4 (suppl. 1), 35–51.

Tolan, P., and Guerra, N. (1994) *What Works in Reducing Adolescent Violence: An Empirical Review of the Field*. Boulder: Center for the Study and Prevention of Violence, University of Colorado.

Walters, G. D., and White, T. W. (1989) The thinking criminal: A cognitive model of lifestyle criminality. *Criminal Justice Research Bulletin*, 4, 1–10.

Ward, T., Hudson, S., Johnston, L., and Marshall, W. L. (1999) Cognitive distortions in sex offenders: An integrative review. *Clinical Psychology Review*, 17, 479–507.

Welsh, B. C., and Farrington, D. P. (2000) Monetary costs and benefits of crime prevention programs. *Crime and Justice*, 27, 305–61.

Wilson, D. B., Gallagher, C. A., and MacKenzie, D. L. (2000) A meta-analysis of corrections-based education, vocation, and work programs for adult offenders. *Journal of Research in Crime and Delinquency*, 37, 347–68.

Wilson, S. J., and Lipsey, M. W. (2000) Wilderness challenge programs for delinquent youth: A meta-analysis of outcome evaluations. *Evaluation and Program Planning*, 23, 1–12.

12

Female Punishment: From Patriarchy to Backlash?

LAUREEN SNIDER

INTRODUCTION

This essay examines the punishment of women through the criminal justice system. It documents the surge of punitiveness that characterizes modern responses to certain types of female rulebreaking, measured most dramatically through rising incarceration rates. And it examines the sources and significance of increases in formal social control.

The bulk of the research on women's crime and punishment comes from feminist criminology, defined as the application of feminist approaches or perspectives to the subject matter of criminology (Naffine 1996:1–5). While there was never only one feminist approach, and feminism has become ever more fragmented with the advent of Foucauldian and postmodern approaches in the 1980s and 1990s,[1] feminist perspectives typically include the following knowledge claims or assumptions: gender is a social construction, not a biological fact; it "orders social life and social institutions in fundamental ways"; established gender orders assume male superiority and reflect and embody male dominance over women; and, finally, existing knowledge claims and systems reflect "men's views of the natural and social world" (Daly and Chesney-Lind 1988: 108). Feminist criminology, like feminism more generally, has always had a practical as well as a theoretical component, aiming to change the social, political, and economic structures responsible for the oppression of women, not just analyze them. Thus, feminist writings on the crimes and punishment of women have been policy-oriented, aimed at legal and correctional change and at transforming the institutions and personnel responsible for implementing systems of criminal justice.

Applied to criminological thought by feminist criminology, this perspective both justified and necessitated the rethinking of virtually all of criminology. It is front and center in this chapter because feminist criminology has essentially replaced the versions of criminology that preceded it, particularly in substantive areas focusing on lawbreaking by women and female incarceration. The old studies have been shown to be so flawed by unacknowledged and untheorized gender bias that no criminologist today ventures to discuss female crime without at least a footnote on gender (although still, far too often, there is little beyond this; Laberge 1991; Faith 1993; Howe 1994; Smart 1995; Naffine 1987, 1996; Belknap 1996, 2001; Cook and Davies 1999; Chesney-Lind and Faith 2001).

This essay is organized into three sections, aimed at answering the questions What?, How?, and Why? It looks at what has happened to the punishment of women, documenting increased levels of social control over women in systems of criminal justice. It goes on to examine the trajectory of formal control, tracing punishment from the nineteenth-century battles waged by first-wave feminists that created woman-centered practices and institutions, to their modern-day successors.[2] Finally, it asks why a 200-year struggle to improve conditions for women and establish humane institutions for criminalized females has paradoxically led to the very different realities we see today.

Increasing Punitiveness through Incarceration

One of the most pernicious and dramatic reversions in social policy in the modern age occurred in penal systems in the last quarter of the twentieth century. After generations of "civilizing" penal policy (Spierenburg 1984), followed by successful campaigns in the 1960s and 1970s to abolish torture, ban capital punishment, and institute minimal civil rights for inmates, a decivilizing spiral has stopped this process in its tracks. Prison conditions have worsened, and chain gangs, bread-and-water diets and 24-hour surveillance, along with capital punishment, have been reintroduced (Snider 1998). Punitive control of the "flawed consumer," the Other, those deemed dangerous, defective, or different, has become hallmark and symbol of the modern state. Increased punitiveness, reflected in surging rates of incarceration, appears in its starkest form, ironically, in the world's only superpower, its most powerful and envied nation, the United States. Between 1990 and 2000, the rate at which men and women were locked up, in federal, state, and local facilities, increased by 5.6 percent *per year* (Bureau of Justice Statistics 2000). In summer 2001, a total of 6.5 million Americans were under formal control, on parole or probation, under house arrest, or in electronic shackles. From somewhat under 500,000 inmates in 1980, the number of men and women incarcerated rose to "nearly two million" in 2000 and "numbers continue to rise" (Austin et al. 2001: 14). Those targeted for incarceration are sharply skewed by class, race, and gender, with poor, young, black men the most overrepresented group, and old, privileged, white women the least. "Approximately one third of all Black males will experience state prison in their lifetime" (ibid.).

The rates at which women are incarcerated, especially among African Americans, have jumped at an even greater rate. While the total number of incarcerated males increased by 303 percent between 1980 and 1999, it leapt by 576 percent for females. "The increase in the number of women in these facilities has outpaced the increase for men each year since 1995" (Austin et al. 2001: 15).

Between 1986 and 1991, African American women's incarceration rates for drug offenses rose by 828 percent, that of Hispanic women by 328 percent, and that of white women by 241 percent. In 1980 there were approximately 12,000 female inmates in US prisons; by 1996 there were approximately 75,000, a sixfold increase (Belknap 2001: 166–8). Female prisoners, who accounted for 3 percent of the US prison population in 1970 and 3.9 percent in 1980, jumped to 5.7 percent in 1990 and 6.7 percent by June 2000 (Bureau of Justice Statistics 2000). These figures depict a matrix of domination, one justly described as a "war on black women" (Chesney-Lind and Faith 2001: 297; see also Owen 1999).[3]

This increase in incarceration cannot be attributed to increased crime, since rates for both men and women have dropped continuously and dramatically from 1993 onward (Austin et al. 2001). And, despite media reports, there is no evidence that women have become more violent, greedy, aggressive, and dangerous. Statistically, the types of crimes women commit has remained constant in the 1980s and 1990s, with no spike in crimes of violence, bank robbery, or other serious offenses – and this in spite of ever-greater police vigilance, public fear, surveillance, and increased awareness and reporting of traditional, individual offenses of this sort.[4] Indeed, with more women arrested and processed through systems of criminal justice, "the proportion of women imprisoned for violent crimes has actually decreased" (Belknap 2001: 167, citing Immarigeon and Chesney-Lind 1992). This decline is most visible in California, the state with the largest prison system. While 37.2 percent of women admitted to the California prison system in 1982 were convicted of violent crime(s), by 1992 the proportion had dropped to 16 percent. What *has* increased is the number of women, especially black women, locked up on non-violent drug charges, typically for possession of crack cocaine.[5]

While the United States presents the most extreme example of surging punitiveness, other countries, with very different social, economic, and political realities and criminal justice histories, have followed in its wake (Cohen 1994). Despite its spectacular failures in criminal justice, the American model continues to be flavor of the month – indeed, unfortunately, of the era. This is particularly apparent in the Anglo-American democracies, where American cultural dominance (through everything from CNN and Rambo to Eminem) has reproduced American agendas, fears, and obsessions. Although policy makers and reformers in many countries have argued against the American model, they frequently face an uphill battle resisting get-tough pressure from politicians and from an increasingly fearful, crime-obsessed populace.

In Australia, for example, prison populations overall grew from 9,826 to 19,906 between 1982 and 1988, an increase of 102 percent. While males still comprise 95 percent of prisoners, women made up 5.3 percent of the total prison population in 1988. This increased to 5.7 percent in 1998, a statistically insignificant amount (Carcach and Grant 2000). All the same, omnibus figures such as these mask important trends. The number of females serving time for offenses against "government security and justice procedures" has almost doubled. This is the modern equivalent of the status offense (see note 5), in that "the overwhelming majority of prisoners counted in this category are charged – for breach of maintenance order and offenses against the enforcement of order" (Carcach and Grant 2000: n. 2). There are also differences by state: rates of female imprisonment in Victoria, a large state that includes the city of Melbourne, tripled from 1979 to 1985, standing at 6.7 percent in 1988–9, the highest rate since 1900 (Howe 1990: 43–8). Howe has also reported an increasing tendency for women in Victoria to be imprisoned for offenses of poverty such as welfare fraud, or for failing to pay (traffic and other) fines. This observation, published a decade ago, looks prescient indeed (Cook and Davies 1999).

In Canada overall adult incarceration rates jumped 17 percent from 1988 to1998 (Finn et al. 1999), with admissions to federal facilities rising by 3 percent in 1998–9 alone (Canadian Centre for Justice Statistics 2000).[6] Since 1977, the total number of women charged per year has increased by 54 percent, three-quarters of these for shoplifting, fraud, or drug and liquor violations (Boritch 1997). Looking at incarceration, women represented 9 percent of adults sentenced to custody, up from 7 percent in 1986 (Canadian Centre for Justice Statistics 1997; Finn et al., 1999). Women still make up "only" 5 percent of inmates (1,807 of Canada's 1996 prison population of 37,541). They are less likely than males to be incarcerated for violent crimes, particularly in provincial institutions, where most are serving time for theft and minor drug-related offenses such as possession, or variants of drunk and disorderly.

In the United Kingdom the number of women prisoners increased by 100 percent from 1993 to 1998, compared to a 45 percent increase for men. Almost 50 percent of this increase can be attributed to more women being convicted of drug offenses, although the most common crime for women is still shoplifting and other forms of theft (British Home Office 1999). Here too there is evidence of greater punitiveness, with more women getting custodial sentences, for longer periods. However, for all serious offenses, women are still less likely than men to be sentenced to incarceration (British Home Office 1999: 12).

In these countries too, it is impossible to examine incarceration without discussing race/ethnicity. Everywhere those most likely to be imprisoned are racial and ethnic minorities, especially people of color. In 1997 aboriginal people, who make up only 4 percent of the Canadian population overall, accounted for 17 percent of inmates overall, 22 percent of female prison inmates and 41 percent of those held in maximum-security facilities (Jackson 1999; Finn et al. 1999). Female aboriginals in federal custody (serving sentences greater than two years in length) were more likely to be charged with violent offenses, diagnosed as "high-need" inmates (which translates in correctional services into high-risk), and incarcerated in the most coercive conditions at high security facilities. In the United Kingdom, as of June 1999, women from minority ethnic groups comprise 6 percent of the British population but 25 percent of the female prison population (British Home Office 1999: 5). And in Australia, the number of indigenous prisoners increased from 1,809 in 1988 to 3,750 in 1998, a 107 percent increase, with aboriginal rates of incarceration still rising. Aboriginals, who make up less than 2 percent of the Australian population overall, represent 19 percent of prison populations (Carcach and Grant 1999, 2000). Few gender differences were noted: aboriginal males and females are equally overrepresented (Carcach et al. 1999).

PUNISHMENT REGIMES FOR INCARCERATED WOMEN

In the beginning

In traditional criminology, from classical versions to the positivists, women criminals were seen as a defective lot, the product of inbreeding, biologically and anatomically inferior ((Beccaria 1778; Goring 1913; Thomas 1923; Pollak 1950; Hooton 1939). Criminals in general were seen as weak minded, but criminal women were "more terrible than any man" – less intelligent, more passive, more "deficient in moral sense," but stronger in "sexual instincts" (Lombroso and Ferraro 1895). Feminist criminologists, reading this history as sexist (Bertrand 1969; Smart 1976; Leonard 1982; Morris 1987; Naffine 1987), joined the general attack on early positivism as scientifically defective. Samples were too small, they were not randomly selected, results were not interpreted properly, nor were they subjected to the proper statistical tests. But they also attacked the gender, race, and class blinders of these literatures. They pointed out that, for the Fathers of Criminology, only women had a gender, only women were programmed by nature to behave irrationally, only women were victims of their body, their sexuality, and their reproductive roles. And they alone questioned the ability of the privileged white, male, European criminologist to remove or transcend his gendered blinkers (Smart 1976; Messerschmidt 1993; Naffine 1996).

In histories of incarceration, on the other hand, women were conspicuous by their absence. In traditional, male-stream criminology, female prisoners were ignored, dismissed by male experts and penal authorities, in the United Kingdom, Canada, the United States, and Australia, as "too few to count" (Adelberg and Currie 1993). In modern societies, any group that cannot be counted does not, for the purposes of governance, exist (Haggerty 2001). In virtually every country, women have always comprised no more than 3–4 percent of prison populations, present in significant numbers in only a handful of offenses such as theft and fraud, and overrepresented only in sex-specific crimes such as prostitution, abortion, and infanticide (with welfare fraud a recent addition) (Boritch 1997; DeKeseredy 2000). Penitentiaries were conceived with the male offender in mind – the debates over the relative merits of the Auburn versus Pennsylvania models that consumed social reformers from 1780 to1850 hardly deigned to notice women. In the early years of the nineteenth century, female prisoners were an afterthought, held in a separate room, basement, or wing of institutions designed for men. Here they were crowded together with minimal provision for their safety, comfort, or health, targeted for abuse by staff and inmates alike. The dubious benefits of solitary confinement, silence, and congregate or solitary labor were not for them; they received, instead, "overcrowding, harsh treatment and sexual abuse" (Freedman 1981: 13).

Feminist criminology set out to discover, document, and reclaim female incarceration. It challenged the myth of progress presented by traditional historians, who saw the history of incarceration as a journey from a barbaric past to an enlightened present (Giallombardo 1966; Radzinowicz and Hood 1986). And it sought to correct the gender-blindness of revisionist or neo-Marxist histories

(Rothman 1971, 1980; Ignatieff 1978). Many feminist criminologists were intrigued by the centrality of nineteenth-century female prison reformers. At a time when women were excluded from roles in the public sphere, these women, largely middle class and privileged, succeeded in revolutionizing female incarceration and in influencing the course of prison reform world-wide. The most famous example was the Englishwoman and Quaker, Elizabeth Fry. While prejudice and patriarchy put many obstacles in her path, Fry and her successors and imitators justified the "interference" of women into the very male and public domain of incarceration by claiming that women had special expertise. Because of their gender, women had knowledge and nurturing abilities men lacked. Since women were the only sex that knew the temptations of womanhood, the demands of domesticity, and the difficulties of being obedient and pious, women were therefore better than men at transforming the immoral, licentious, and profane into God-fearing wives and mothers.

Harriet Freedman (1981), studying women's prisons in the United States from 1830 to 1930, examined attempts by early female reformers to mitigate the harsh treatment and abuse female inmates in male prisons received. Citing Fry's work and example, these women argued that female prisoners were sinners, lost souls who needed protection from male inmates and jailers, in addition to wise, maternal guidance and measured but kindly discipline. As mothers and wives themselves, they understood their sex and could succeed where institutions designed for men were bound to fail. In many areas these arguments were successful, and specialized institutions, called reformatories, were built. Reformatories were meant to reproduce the patriarchal family, with matrons standing in for the male head of household. Eight to ten inmates lived together in cottages under the care and control of female staff whose job was to civilize and educate the female offender, teaching her the habits of virtue and piety and the skills of housekeeping and child-care. Freedman argues that most matrons took their mission very seriously and, as a result, reformatories were better run and less cruel than many male prisons at the time. She recognized however, that the reformers' dual goals – rescue and discipline – were incompatible, and inevitably produced highly punitive regimes for those inmates deemed incorrigible.

Nicole Rafter (1985) paints a different picture of the reformatory. She argues that reformatories were reserved for a select, few offenders, typically the young, white, working-class girl charged with minor, often sex-related offenses.[7] Most women served time as they always had, in dank, traditional institutions run by and for men, emphasizing punishment, not rescue. Older women, black and native women, and all those convicted of felonies were never deemed eligible for admission. They received the same overcrowding and physical punishment as men, with sexual as well as physical abuse. Later criminologists have supported this point: reformatories were never established in the American South, where black women continued to serve long sentences for minor offenses such as resisting the advances of white males or stealing bread from employers' kitchens. They were always concentrated in a few states in the northeast, and never made it out west at all (Zedner 1998).

Rafter also casts a more critical eye on the motivations and achievements of the first-wave feminist reformers, those who established and oversaw the reformatories. She challenges the claim that reformatories were more humane than other total institutions, since inmates were subjected to exceptionally close supervision and frequent, repressive discipline. And those deemed sufficiently worthy to benefit from such regimes were not the most disadvantaged and marginalized groups – they were working class rather than lower class, whites rather than minorities. Nor was this a disinterested, benign movement. The benefits for reformers and matrons were considerable, in that they got to reproduce the gender and class order which legitimated their own role, status and social importance, and to bask in starring roles as benefactors and guardians of the (white) race. In some cases, they received free domestic labor from inmates as well.

Dobash et al. (1986) examined female incarceration in Britain. Although male prison reformers (such as John Howard, Jonas Hanway, and Jeremy Bentham) are briefly discussed, they focus on Elizabeth Fry and her quest to reform Newgate Prison. Fry was horrified by the half-starved, begging, swearing, card-playing, lewd female inmates she observed in 1813, and argued for a regime which would provide them with clean and sufficient food, healthful labor, scriptures, and education, thereby inculcating cleanliness, respect, and defer-ence. She was ultimately successful and, as these authors point out, conditions for women in British prisons actually did improve, for a time. Her belief that women needed productive rather than punitive labor saved them from the horrors of the treadmill and rock pile, dominant in male prisons in England at the time (McConville 1998). Over the course of the nineteenth century, separ-ation between male and female inmates was achieved, female wardens and matrons were appointed, and corrupt, dirty prisons were replaced by "austere fortresses of discipline and punishment" (Dobash et al. 1986: 59). As in the United States, there were pluses and minuses – the new female regimes subjected women to less sexual assault, but to greater disciplinary surveillance and harsh punishment for the recalcitrant.

In keeping with the Foucauldian perspectives that characterize recent feminist criminology,[8] this account emphasizes the fluidity of power, the fact that it is not a "thing" possessed by any one group, gender, or class. They point out that female staff were under control and surveillance almost as much as inmates (though presumably not subjected to the straitjacket, handcuffs, or restricted diet regimes). Dobash et al. also shift the spotlight onto the female inmate, beginning the search for the response of the Subject, the female inmate, to incarceration. Unfortunately, in these literatures "response" has often been equated with "resistance," which has been empirically narrowed even further to mean "defiance," an inadequate, libertarian concept which does not begin to capture the complexity of women's' responses to incarceration. For Dobash et al., there was little they could identify as resistance in the early years, a fact they attribute to the short sentences most inmates were then serving (typically for drunkenness or prostitution), and to the "mildness and kindness" (1986: 77) of the regime. This was the 1820s and 1830s, when Fry's influence was strongest, female guardians were newly empowered, and inmates were presumably grate-ful, since memories of the old regime would be very much alive. And conditions inside, for many women, were better than those that awaited them on release, with British cities in the throes of the Industrial Revolution. Later in the nineteenth century, however, when Fry's charisma had faded and her innovations had been bureaucratized, institutionalized, and therefore gutted, hunger strikes, incessant noise, knocking codes, and self-violence became common modes of defiance in women's prisons.[9]

To sum up, female prisoners were once seen, by traditional criminologies, state authorities, prison governors, and religious elites of the nineteenth and early twentieth centuries, as worse than any male – harder to handle, more resistant to reformation, more promiscuous and treacherous. Because the ideal woman of the time was docile, modest, pious, religious, maternal, and above all obedient to the patriarchal authority of father, husband, minister, or priest, the female offender was conceptualized as her dichotomous opposite. Given prevailing lower societal expectations for males, the female criminal had fallen further, departed more radically, from her social role. She was in every sense incomprehensible, an unknown and unknowable Subject who deserved punishment because she was outside the bounds. In contrast, nineteenth-century female reformers saw the female inmate, or at least a select sub-sample, as a pitiful fallen creature in need of rescue from sin and degradation, by women such as themselves. This would be done in cottage-style, family-like institutions serving only women, through religious instruction, supervision, guidance, and discipline. In such institutions women, removed from the corrupting influences of the world of men, would see the light. Punishment was seen by these reformers as a corrective tool to be reserved for the very few women (or so they theorized) who proved themselves incorrigible and unredeemable.

When feminist criminologists came on the scene in the 1970s, they argued that woman offenders had been doubly victimized, sanctioned by law and custom more harshly than any male. Women and girls were arrested and jailed for offenses that would be ignored or admired in a man, such as ungovernability, promiscuity, and prostitution. Such differentiation was viewed as legitimate at the time because men, viewed through the lenses of patriarchy, were not blamed for rape or what we would now call sexual assault. The male sex drive, it was believed, was innate and ungovernable, a biological urge men could not be expected to control. Women, on the other hand, lacked sexual urges unless they suffered from some pathological disorder, and were therefore obligated to behave in a modest, chaste manner to avoid arousing the insatiable male beast. Feminist criminologists pointed out that such practices and beliefs reek of bias, of patriarchy, of a learned and gendered inability to see women in their own right. For feminist criminologists, the failure of nineteenth- and twentieth-century criminologists, supposedly men of science, to notice this bias or comment on its implications, or on the fear of women, their bodies, sexuality and reproductive capacities that sustained these beliefs, demonstrates the total inability of mainstream criminology to transcend gender bias.

In recent decades

Studies of the female inmate today, and since the 1970s, have seen the female criminal and inmate as more needy than evil, more offended against than offensive. In Comack's memorable phrase, she is the Woman in Trouble (Comack 1996). Feminist criminologists argue that the physical and sexual abuse suffered by the majority of female offenders is an important explanatory fact, that women's crimes cannot be understood without taking abuse into account. Similarly, they argue, the social, political, and economic implication of class and race on systems of criminal justice must be analyzed to understand female incarceration. As I have already documented, women in prison are most often poor, uneducated, unemployed, and ethnically and racially different from the dominant group – disproportionately African American in the United States, of Caribbean origin in the United Kingdom, aboriginal in Canada, New Zealand, and Australia. Because most female crimes are nonviolent, prisons, particularly maximum security prisons, are seen as unnecessary – overkill, figuratively and often literally. Female inmates, it is argued, need healing and empowerment, not punishment and exclusion.

The female inmate is now portrayed as doubly disadvantaged, cast out because she has transgressed against domesticity (the term "patriarchy" is less often found) as well as law. In Carlen's phrase (1983), she is "outwith" gender norms, family norms and work norms, deemed a failure as wife/partner, mother, daughter, and employee. When incarcerated, she is still likely to be seen by prison authorities as more sick, more troublesome, and more difficult to control than any male. Her living conditions are frequently worse, because she is more likely to serve time at higher security levels than her offense and maturity level require. She is also more likely to lose her partner and all close personal relationships while incarcerated and, relatedly, to do time in a remote location far from her community. Fewer job, training, or educational programs will be available to her. Health care, particularly reproductive and sexual care, will be substandard (in the United States, the only developed country lacking universal health services, comparisons are more difficult because none but the privileged and well insured receive high-quality medical care). Many of these differences will be justified by prison authorities through economic rationality. Because women inmates are still "too few to count," it costs much more per inmate to provide opportunities and programs.

The female inmate will also suffer pains of imprisonment unique to her role as a mother. If she has children, as a third to half of female inmates do, she will likely lose all contact with them as well as custody over them (assuming she had custody when arrested). It will be hard to reestablish any of these relationships, harder yet to regain custody of any dependents. And she will be shamed and stigmatized, by herself and others, for being an inadequate mother – a level of punishment seldom visited on the inadequate, absent, or abusive father (overall, see Carlen 1983, 1988; Heidensohn 1985; Eaton 1986; Worrall 1990; Faith 1993; Shaw 1993; Bertrand 1999; Faith 1999; Jackson 1999; Owen 1999). In fact, the only way in which she will be better off than her male counterpart (a significant advantage even if it only applies to US prisons, given its disproportionately high incarceration rates) is that incarcerated women "appear to be far less likely – to be raped by fellow prisoners" (Belknap 2001: 195).

This summary of patterns and trends in female incarceration is underlined by a recent comparative study of 24 prisons for women in Canada, Denmark, England, Finland, Germany, Norway, Scotland, and the United States, between 1991 and 1996 (Bertrand 1999). Despite promises, Royal Commissions, and changes in some areas, conditions for inmates in the 1990s, in most jurisdictions and countries, have not improved, and in many places have deteriorated. The sexual double standard is alive and well, and living in women's prisons. Laws governing the rights of inmates, for example, are still "sexist, male and gendered" (Bertrand 1999: 57). Where inmates are allowed to file lawsuits against prison officials, or to protest prison conditions, female inmates are less likely to participate in them, or to benefit from any victories won (Belknap 2001).

One of the most striking (and worrisome) features to emerge from studies since the 1990s is the tendency for feminist-inspired reforms to backfire. Reforms such as mixed gender living units, co-corrections, and family leaves have all been found to "go sour when applied to women" (Bertrand 1999: 56). A meta-analysis of co-corrections found that women receive "few if any economic, educational, vocational and social advantages." Basically, "male prisoners and system maintenance," not women, benefit from co-corrections (Smykla and Williams 1996: 61). Similarly, home leaves with family members, a program found in a few progressive European states, have proved problematic. Most female inmates, after a few months inside, lose their partner and family. For them there is no wife holding the fort, maintaining the household, looking after the children, and waiting anxiously for their return. Of course this model was always peculiarly male, a fact seldom noticed. And it has become increasingly invalid even for men, with fewer women willing to remain celibate and keep the home fires burning. Prisons with mixed gender units, where men and women live in proximity under close supervision, often end up making life easier for male inmates, who benefit from the civilizing influence and maternal behavior of the females (female inmates are, on average, older than the males and tend to be cast in "big sister" or "little mother" roles). But life becomes more difficult for the women, forced to cope with higher levels of aggressive or infantile behavior and unrest. Even long-sought, much-heralded liberal reforms such as decarceration were criticized for "infantilizing discipline and supervision" (Bertrand 1999: 57). Mother and child programs, intended to allow women to spend time with their children and learn (better) parenting skills, were seen as domesticating women. They were also found guilty of promoting a "pronatalist and eugenic ideology" in which the only "good woman" was the biological mother providing full time care for her offspring (Bertrand 1999: 57–8).

This picture of "good intentions gone wrong" is found in many contemporary accounts. In one British study, Anne Worrall (1990) interviewed 29 probation officers, 8 solicitors, 12 magistrates, 7 psychiatrists, and 8 other court officials, along with 11 female lawbreakers. The book focuses on the ways in which experts, the social workers, psychiatrists, and magistrates of the criminal justice system construct the female offender, and the ramifications and implications of what could be termed "death by expertise." This Foucauldian-inspired approach asks how professionals and experts in the United Kingdom became authorized to define certain women (inmates) as inadequate beings in need of treatment, management, control and punishment. While Worrall never uses the language of "effectiveness," nor does she issue value judgments on the morality of, or need for, expert intervention, she points out that discourses of domesticity, sexuality, and pathology are employed to define, regulate, and manage women offenders (1990: 32). The result is that the rehabilitation of female lawbreakers comes to be centered around traditional notions of femininity. *Plus ça change....*

A later study by Bosworth (1999) looks at the effects of incarceration on the identity and self-esteem of female inmates. After interviewing 52 female inmates in 3 different prisons in Britain, she concludes, not surprisingly, that prison is still a corrosive experience. But while confinement erodes confidence, inmates were able to exercise a certain amount of independence and autonomy – not by participating in prison-sponsored programs and activities, but by resisting them. Different inmates chose different styles of resistance, but virtually all were individualist not collective, and involved the adoption of particular identities as identifying features and sources of personal pride. For some this meant valorizing themselves through spirituality, or sexual orientation, or through race or ethnic identity, as in "I *am* a Muslim or Rastafarian or lesbian." Some chose to valorize their role as mothers, an identity their great-grandmothers (and their great-grandmothers' keepers) would recognize and approve. This does not mean inmates refused to participate in prison-sponsored programs and activities, since such resistance would have been punished, directly or indirectly, by prison authorities. However, they refused to allow their own, personal identities to be colonized, or to choose identities seen as prison-sponsored and therefore suspect.

A recent Canadian study makes similar arguments and reaches similar conclusions. Focusing on federal incarceration, Kelly Hannah-Moffat (2001) examines the relations of power inside the Prison for Women. This institution was once Canada's only facility for women with sentences exceeding two years in length. Opened in 1934, it was finally shut down in June of 2000, more than ten years after its imminent closure was hailed in *Creating Choices* (Task Force on Federally Sentenced Women 1990). Through an intense and intelligent analysis of women's incarceration, Hannah-Moffat concludes that feminist-inspired strategies of empowerment have been translated by the Correctional Service of Canada into "responsibilizing strategies." Similarly, feminist emphasis on "meeting inmates' needs" has been translated into classifications which sort inmates according to categories of risk. The definition of "risk" is an institutional one, where "risk of escape" (an event which embarrasses penal authorities) trumps all. Thus, while some female inmates have benefited from the new regional institutions and the aboriginal healing lodge set up in response to feminist demands through *Creating Choices*, many have not.[10] And it is ironic indeed that aboriginal women, whose overrepresentation in criminal justice drove the reform process, remain overrepresented – not in the healing lodge intended to serve them, but in the ranks of maximum-security inmates.

Is a "responsibilizing strategy" more or less punitive than the techniques that preceded it? Hannah-Moffat, like all good Foucauldians, does not say – her interest is in tracing the pastoral, maternal, disciplinary, and empowerment strategies of governance that have animated female incarceration for the last two centuries. However it is clear from this and from similar analyses that, while women's punishment has changed in response to feminist critiques, it has not been transformed in the humanitarian sense envisaged by reformers (Shaw 1993; Hayman 2000; Hannah-Moffat 2001). The "therapeutic" programmes found in some prisons are critiqued as pathologizing, individualizing, and disempowering (Balfour 2000; Kendall 2000; Pollack 2000). Thus, as O'Malley (1996) says, a (new) spiral of resistance has been created, a resistance that is now (re)inscribed into patterns of governance. But what does this mean to female inmates? Are prisons organized around therapy "better" for inmates than those (probably still the majority) organized around punishment? How do these such changes affect their lives, their futures? Surely this is the most important question, but it is neither posed nor answered in these literatures.

However, feminist-inspired studies to improve the lot of criminalized women have not disappeared. In social work, psychology and criminology (though seldom in theoretical or Foucauldian sociology), practitioners and academics are working within systems of criminal justice to "improve" conditions and "help" the female offender. Thus there are feminist criminologists developing new programs and disciplinary regimes, instituting "successful gender-responsive programming" (Bloom 2000: 1–2). They are studying how to make prison programs more "effective," overcome program failure, and "meet women's needs" – defined as achieving drug-free status, avoiding recidivism, and becoming responsible employees, mothers, and/or wives (Teplin et al. 1996; Bloom and Steinhart 1993; Brennan and Austin 1997; Rice et al. 1999; Reed 1987; Koons et al. 1997; and many more). These are the very approaches and techniques, however, that are critiqued by critical and Foucauldian academics, who see them as adding to systems of domination, as part of the problem, not the solution. And it is not at all clear how criminalized women, if their voices could be disentangled from the feminist and other discourses that now constitute the debate, and if they could be assumed to speak with one voice (which they do not), would place their votes.

Explaining Punitiveness

The final section of this essay asks why the cycles of reform and the ocean of arguments and claims on female incarceration, the bulk of it seeking better conditions and less punitiveness, has instead produced more social control, more incarceration and intensified punitiveness. At the most general level of analysis, decreased tolerance for nonconforming behavior has been a central component of the backlash against progressive social movements that began around 1980. Feminism, environmentalism, civil rights, affirmative action, and equal opportunities movements were all targeted. Critics of feminism began publicly claiming, variously, that equal opportunity for women had already been achieved, that feminists were man-hating publicity-seekers out to destroy the family, that discrimination against men was the real social problem, and much else. The backlash itself has been linked to neo-liberal regimes, particularly to the determination of corporate and political elites to reverse what they saw as dangerous, destabilizing trends that emerged in welfare states in the 1960s and 1970s. Demands for a higher minimum wage, the right to refuse unsafe work, abortion rights, equal pay for equal work, paid maternity and paternity leaves, were seen as harmful to the polity, the economy, and the status quo. Women, employees, and citizens were becoming much too independent, patterns of deference between authority figures and subordinates (workers and bosses, men and women, teachers and students) were declining, and elites were confronting increasingly militant demands from groups whose subordination had always been taken for granted.

Thus the 1980s and 1990s saw massive cuts in social projects of all kinds, from after-school programmes to legal aid, from welfare to unemployment insurance. Government grants to progressive movements engaged in rights struggles, from environmentalists to aboriginals, were cut. Government services were downsized or privatized. Unemployment and income inequality rose, while levels of corporate taxation declined, dramatically, as corporate tax rates were repeatedly slashed. Changes in statutory law and the appointment of more conservative judicial officials (and more conservative political/ideological climates) led to legal defeats or reverses for workers and unions (where rights to organize, collect dues, or strike were removed), for inmates, and for women (Boyd 1997; Boyer and Drache 1996; Fudge and Cossman 2001; Ehrenreich 2001; Schrecker 2001). This picture is a general one, the specifics vary by nation-state and within it, but all Anglo-American democracies, regardless of the political stripe of the government in power, experienced some measure of government downsizing, privatization, and loss of equality. In Canada, for example, by the late 1980s "it took between 65 and 80 hours of work each week for a family to earn what it took a single breadwinner, who was typically a man, to earn in a 45 hour work week in the mid 1970s" (Fudge and Cossman 2001: 15).

Feminist criminologies were poorly positioned to resist this onslaught. Unlike criminologists in Right Realist schools (e.g., Wilson and Herrnstein 1985; Gottfredson and Hirschi 1990), who constructed for government and public consumption the evil offender, the rational, calculating criminal of the neo-liberal state, the offender constituted by feminist criminology was not culpable but victimized. This central conceptual claim is "at the heart of – [female] lawbreaking and – best explains women's involvement in crime" (Chesney-Lind and Faith 2001: 299). Female offenders have been seen not as evil predators but as victims of abuse, sexism, racism, heterosexism, and classism. Politically this offender is aligned with progressive, counter-hegemonic voices; addressing her needs calls for extensive, expensive, revolutionary, and destabilizing change. However, taking the high poverty and unemployment levels of marginalized women, aboriginals and women of color seriously is not on the agenda of governments keen to offer tax cuts to corporations and tax rebates to high earners. In any case, in the smaller meaner gaze of neo-liberalism, "victims" were those who suffered from crime, not those who committed it – and the higher their social class, the more traditional their sexual habits and lifestyles, and the lighter their color, the more legitimate their victim status became. Thus some female rape victims – the chaste teenager or faithful wife – were recognized in law and policy reform. Others – the abused prostitute or native girl – were not. In the real lower-class worlds where most of the criminalized reside, offenders are victims and victims are offenders, but this inconvenient social fact was not something policy-makers and their political masters wanted to hear. These arguments and statistics, therefore, have been ignored by these elites.

A second component of backlash was made possible, ironically, by feminist-inspired discourses of equality, employed in legal and other ways to disadvantage women. This is "equality with a vengeance," in Smart's memorable phrase (Smart 1995: 42). In criminology, this led to a protracted debate called the "chivalry hypothesis," which centered around the claim that female criminals benefited from patterns of lenience generated by chivalrous male officials in criminal justice. The null hypothesis was that, compared to male offenders, women were less likely to be charged by police, more likely to be found not guilty when charged, and less likely to receive punitive sanctions. This formulation of the lenience problem, which sees "crime" as a fact which is objectively knowable, was not one many feminist criminologists would accept. For many feminists, crime is a social construction whose meaning varies socially, culturally, and historically, not something that can be known through measurement (Cain 1990; Smart 1995; Naffine 1996). It also takes male crime rates, conditions, and male-based theories as the norm against which women must be compared.

Despite such epistemological and ontological flaws, many studies, quantitative to a fault, were carried out. The central question was not whether men were punished too much, but whether women were punished too little. The issue was "lenience," defined as the extraction of fewer pounds of flesh per defendant than law and judicial discretion allowed. Evidence from the United States, where the chivalry hypothesis was pursued with most vigor and methodological rigor (fittingly, since it houses the most fervent believers in positivist criminology), indicated that some women defendants in the 1970s, particularly white, older, familied women seen as playing caregiver familial roles, were indeed receiving less severe sentences than the equivalent male defendant, albeit only in some jurisdictions for some offenses (Steffensmeier 1978, 1980, 1983; Moulds 1980; Kruttschnitt 1981, 1984; Daly 1987, 1989; Morris 1987). Similar studies of female prisons indicated that conditions there were sometimes better than in male institutions, with less violence, more conviviality and informality, less inmate/staff antagonism, and regulations allowing only female guards in living areas (Daly and Chesney-Lind 1988).

In any event, once attention was drawn to the existence of "lenience," once it was constituted as real by criminological experts (Bagley and Merlo 1995), it quickly disappeared. Apparently, once criminal justice officials discovered that the systems they administered were actually favoring women, they changed their behavior in a hurry. Laws and administrative directives were also changed.[11] In the United States, and in all Anglo-American countries where this phenomenon was identified, it was gone by 1990 (Naffine 1989; Carrington 1993; Daly 1994; Boritch 1997).[12]

Two points must be noted here. First, it is significant that lenience arguments were only ever heard in ways that legitimated punishing women more, never as rationales for punishing men less. Punishing up, not "leniencing" down;[13] equal opportunity oppression, not equal opportunity clemency, dominated the debate. This illustrates the importance, for those who would understand increased punitiveness, of examining how arguments are heard, how expert knowledge claims are interpreted. It requires looking at dominant cultural climates, and how they are constructed and maintained, or challenged and resisted. This in turn requires analysis of major players, parties, and interests, not just description of dominant discursive themes.

Second, and relatedly, the institutional sites where women receive more intensive surveillance, discipline, and punishment than men – in the family, at work, through media objectification and commodification, through psychiatry and body images – were not deemed problematic (McRobbie 1978; Hudson 1984;

Nava 1984). New, blatantly unequal, initiatives aimed specifically at women continue to mount, through campaigns to criminalize pregnant women who smoke, drink alcohol, or give birth to babies addicted to crack cocaine (Tong 1996). As juveniles girls have always received longer and more punitive sentences than boys, particularly for behaviors such as sexual acting-out, behaviors ignored or even admired in boys (Chesney-Lind 1981, 1987, 1988). Black and aboriginal women never benefited from lenience, and have often received longer sentences and harsher prison conditions, than comparable males (Kruttschnitt 1981; Spohn et al. 1987). Neoliberal "reforms" in the 1980s and 1990s exacerbated this, a fact which causes no media flurry or political angst. Expert arguments that legitimate differential but less punitive treatment for female offenders are either not heard (as in many American states) (Immarigeon and Chesney-Lind 1992), or heard in ways that legitimate expanded surveillance, repression, and control (as in Canada and Australia) (George 1999; Hannah-Moffat 2001). Asymmetries such as these are not probed or problematized in the media or in political debate. In the many American states which now prosecute pregnant women addicted to cocaine, for example, it is apparently in the best interest of "healthy babies" to incarcerate their mothers. But free medical care, day care, or public education are apparently not in their interests, since all of these have been cut back or eliminated over the last 20 years (Fudge and Cossman 2001; Schrecker, 2001).

At the level of legal change, backlash has been facilitated and institutionalized through judicial "reform." Changes in sentencing that eliminate judicial discretion make it impossible for judges to accommodate sentences to individual circumstances, or bend rules to exercise mercy. Vengeance thereby becomes the policy norm (Schichor and Sechrest 1996). Equal opportunity statutes have increased the length of time women serve in prison, removed much of the informality from female prisons, and mandated the inclusion of women on chain gangs (Daly and Chesney-Lind 1988; Smart 1989). Mandatory "zero-tolerance" laws on spousal assault have resulted in more women being hauled into court to face contempt of court charges (Snider 1994, 1998). More women now are charged with assault in domestic disputes, for acts that boil down to no more than self-defense (Comack et al. 2000). These developments illustrate the perils of good intentions: in a culture of punitiveness, arguments will be heard, and policy changes will be instituted, in ways that reinforce rather than challenge dominant political and economic agendas.

However, backlash, while a useful concept in some ways, is curiously unsatisfactory in others. The changes wrought by neo-liberalism have occurred in democratic states and, unlike cuts in Medicare or raises for politicians, measures to increase punitiveness in criminal justice enjoy widespread public support. They were not imposed on an unwilling populace by an out-of-touch elite; quite the reverse. The officials in government ministries of corrections and most of the academic experts, at least in countries such as Canada and Australia, have been mildly to vehemently opposed to many of these measures, such as Three Strikes laws or the abolition of parole (Welch et al. 1998; Hannah-Moffat 2002). Even in police forces, traditionally the most hardline of criminal justice officials (along with correctional officers), support has been concentrated in the rank and file, with those at the top far more skeptical or resistant. The key question then changes: why did substantial proportions of citizens demand and/ or support changes to "crack down on criminals"?

There is no easy answer. Rising levels of immiseration and inequality (Fudge and Cossman 2001; Schrecker 2001), cutbacks in basic government services, and job losses certainly play a part. When people feel threatened and helpless, when their ability to pay mortgages or put high-quality food on the table is jeopardized, there is less sympathy for the deviant, the refugee, or the poor. Declines in lifestyle and life chances cause anger, and that anger has been channeled down the social scale. As historical examples illustrate, scapegoating those below rather than those above one's social station does not "naturally" occur (Ignatieff 1978). In the 1980s and 1990s institutional elites in media, business, and government were quick to deflect blame for unpopular decisions and cutbacks. The need to be economically competitive, the inexorable forces of international capital or the irresistible requirements of globalization were all invoked, and widely publicized, as causal factors. These were presented not as the intended results of decisions made by high-placed elites in bodies such as the World Bank, but as "facts of life." Meanwhile, social programs were denounced as overly "generous," costly frills which benefit the undeserving, lazy, and profligate, the "ne'er do wells," and bankrupt the "average, hard-working, taxpaying citizen." Those on the bottom were and are regularly denigrated in mainstream media – the black welfare mother with 6 children, each with a different father, the drunken aboriginal accosting passersby on the streets of Winnipeg, the bogus refugee claimant, the job-stealing immigrant, the "scrounger" on the dole. The fact that it is always possible to find someone, however atypical, who can be made to fit the stereotype, lends credibility to such accounts.

In the case of crime, the media play an increasingly important role. While the majority of inmates are convicted of nonviolent offenses, typically more guilty of poverty, addiction, and inadequacy than of violence and evil, here too there are exceptions. And the exceptions have become the mainstay of popular culture. On talk shows and call-in radio, in fiction and news, in the tabloid and the establishment press, the criminal occupies center stage. As the central folk devil of our time, demonizing him [sic] is the one thing people can agree on. In societies driven apart by fragmentation, mobility, technological change, individualism, and diversity, this is a unifying factor, a rallying cry. The huge increase in crime coverage driven by the explosion in media outlets, with satellite and cable outfits and 24-hour news stations all engaged in a competitive, incessant search for material to fill the hours and pages, is an exacerbating factor. Crime news is perfect media fodder – it is cheap (police departments, Justice and Corrections have paid staff providing copy), always available, uncomplicated, and dramatic. The demonized are unlikely to sue for libel, or even write letters of protest to editors (and "criminals" have no legitimacy if they do object). In addition to delivering audiences to advertisers, the fear of the evil criminal sells everything from cellphones and burglar alarms, to insurance and Mace. With crime coverage up an average of 300 percent since the 1990s, it is not surprising that fear of crime has sharply increased as well (Sacco 1995, 2000; Cayley 1998).

While rates of violent crime are down, and citizens in Western societies face fewer physical risks than ever before, more and more people are terrified of going to the corner store after dark. They buy fortified homes in gated communities (an oxymoron if ever there was one) and lie awake listening for intruders. Children as well as possessions are bar-coded, and taught to fear "the stranger" (though they are always at most risk from parents and relatives). No one knows the name of the executives or corporation that killed thousands of people in Bhopal, India, but everyone knows the story of photogenic victims such as Jamie Bulger, and the names of serial killers such as Ted Bundy and Paul Bernardo. Of course serial killers too are real – and they justly evoke fear. But present-day levels of fear, and preoccupation with risk and danger, are way out of proportion. They impede civility and threaten public space. However fearmongering is a highly profitable enterprise – and implementing the kind of changes that would produce less desperate citizens and safer societies, is not (Osborne 1995; Kidd-Hewitt 1995; Sacco 1995, 2000; Snider 1998; Surrette 1998; Bailey and Hale 1998).

However, this cannot fully explain increased punitiveness toward women. Most public fear is fear of the male, particularly the adolescent male, the male in groups, the ethnically different male. Fear of the rogue female, even in a group or "gang," is not (yet) a central component of folk history or urban myth. Such fear may be rising, as every new case of violence or assault by women receives massive media attention, but even this is speculative. Increased punishment of women can probably be traced, more accurately, to anger, spillover, and fear of change. Fear that women are refusing to fill traditional roles, that they might become more violent, and media-fanned moral panic are factors explaining the nonstop coverage every violent or aggressive female act receives (Pate 2000). In addition, attitudes that "a criminal is a criminal" and "equality with a vengeance" mean female offenders get swept up in legal changes originally aimed at, for example, the young black male. With equality now enshrined in civil rights codes in most Anglo-American democracies, it is no longer possible (whether or not it was ever desirable) to particularize laws by gender. And then there is always the symbolic female criminal, the demonized but very real woman who represents what many fear as the female criminal of the future, the end result of decades of feminism and "lenience." In Canada this is Karla Homolka, charged with her partner/husband Paul Bernardo in the sadistic, videotaped sexual torture and murder of three young women in 1995. The fact that Homolka "got off lightly," with a sentence plea-bargained down to 12 years, still inflames public anger – and is sure to be mentioned in every classroom discussion on the characteristics of women, or the need for ameliorative reform in female prisons.

CONCLUSION

This essay has looked at female crime and punishment, and at those who have measured, documented, and interpreted it. It has illustrated how complex and overdetermined patterns of punishment can be. However, the recent intensification of punishment for women, it is argued, must be viewed in the light of changes in political economy, particularly the pace of change, the widening gap between rich and poor (between and within the nation-state), and the increasing obsession with "risk factors" that characterizes the modern state.

Notes

With thanks to Janet Gwilliam, research assistant extraordinaire.

1   This fragmentation is not unique to feminist criminology: it characterizes all aspects of the discipline – see studies in Nelken 1994, particularly Ericson and Carriere.

2   I agree with Howe that studies of punishment need "to break out of the confining claustrophobia of penology's narrow, positivistic obsession with competing treatment programmes and penal ideologies" (Howe 1994: 3). The social control of women and girls has always been achieved more through institutions like the family and the church than through criminal justice. This has not changed, except that medicine (especially psychiatry) and the market (commodification, media, the body) have supplemented earlier modes of control.

3   It is true, as Laberge (1991) has pointed out, that large percentage increases may be misleading. When the absolute number of offenders is small, a 100 percent increase may mean a rise from 5 to 10 inmates! However this is not a danger in this instance, because the number of black women incarcerated in the United States is small only in relation to the number of black men.

4   This contrasts sharply with the deregulation, decriminalization, and downsizing of enforcement personnel that characterize societal response to corporate crime during this same period (Snider 2000).

5   While this chapter is on adult females, similar developments have taken place in the censure and criminalization of girls in the United States. Here, however, the explicit focus on girls' sexuality and control reflected in high rates of "status offenses," such as uncontrollability or promiscuity, has shifted. Laws governing juveniles were rewritten during the 1980s and 1990s and many status offenses were eliminated. Today's rhetoric emphasizes legal equality between girls and boys, with an official emphasis on violent crimes, drug offenses, and theft. However, many would argue that the age-old focus on female sexuality and obedience to patriarchal agendas has been disguised, not eliminated (Chesney-Lind 1987, 1988; for British examples see Gelsthorpe 1989; for Canadian, Chunn 1992).

6   Overall, the total number of adult admissions to custody declined in 1998–9, a fact hailed by the Centre for Justice Statistics, a division of Statistics Canada, as a stunning turnaround (see Haggerty 2001 on the politics of Statistics Canada). Admissions to provincial and territorial prisons declined by 3 percent in 1998–9. Since these jurisdictions process the vast majority of inmates, a 3 percent decline here produced an overall rate decline despite an increased number of federal offenders.

7   In fact, in many institutions of the time, being charged with a criminal offense was not necessary. At the Magdalen Asylum in Toronto, for example, women "in need of rescue" were urged to admit themselves, for "voluntary incarceration" (Minaker 2001). Many apparently did – but once inside they often could not get out. Other relatives, particularly parents, were also empowered to sign in daughters or other young females deemed promiscuous or in danger of becoming so.

8   There is great variation by nation-state. The bulk of the Foucauldian/critical analyses come from Europe, including the United Kingdom, Canada, Australia, and New Zealand. There appear to be few pure Foucauldian analyses of incarceration in US criminology, which is still dominated by quantitative empirical approaches. Critical criminology there adopts a variant of left realism; traditional is deeply ensconced in Right Realism (see Naffine 1996 for details on the Left/Right Realism distinction). Henry and Milovanovich's (1999) almost incomprehensible (to me, at least) constitutive criminology is perhaps the closest to a Foucauldian approach.

9 In the US reformatories for women, the most common response (documented by Rafter, 1985, in letters from former reformatory inmates to matrons) was acquiescence and gratitude, not rebellion. Of course, it is unlikely that those who resisted matrons' efforts would write to tell them about it later, and nineteenth-century records of what we would now call recidivism were abysmal by twenty-first-century standards.

10 The implementation of feminist recommendations in *Creating Choices* was anything but straightforward. Several of the new institutions were not built in urban centers, as recommended, but in more remote areas, in face of citizen opposition and political debt-settling. And security levels have been upgraded in all of them, resulting in prisons less open to the community and more prison-like in structure and philosophy. Many feminists and aboriginal activists saw this as total betrayal.

11 This is a striking example of the power of hegemonic cultural forces to shape and change behavior. Compare the ease and speed with which "lenience" was erased with the century-old struggle to achieve counter-hegemonic change in, for example, the attitudes of police toward female victims of physical or sexual assault. Or look at struggles to get prison officials or police to obey laws granting civil rights to defendants, or to get judges to eliminate lenience when sentencing corporate executives for corporate manslaughter (Pearce and Tombs 1998).

12 This is not yet the case worldwide. Note exceptions in Poland (Platek 1999) and Israel (Erez and Hassin 1997).

13 We have no verb to describe the act of being lenient, while there are many verbs, nouns, adjectives and adverbs to describe punishment. The poverty of conceptualizations to denote the act highlights the dominance of punishment as a cultural theme.

References

Aldelberg, E., and Currie, A. (1993) *In Conflict with the Law*. Vancouver: Press Gang Publishers.

Austin, J., Bruce, M., Carroll, L., McCall, P., and Richards, S. (2001) The use of incarceration in the United States. *The Criminologist*, 26 (3), 14–16.

Bagley, K. and Merlo, A. (1995) Controlling women's bodies. In A. Merlo and J. Pollock (eds.), *Women, Law and Social Control*. Boston: Allyn & Bacon, 135–54.

Bailey, F., and Hale, D. (1998) *Popular Culture, Crime and Justice*. Toronto: Nelson.

Balfour, G. (2000) Feminist therapy with women in prison: Working under the hegemony of correctionalism. In K. Hannah-Moffat and M. Shaw (eds.), *An Ideal Prison? Critical Essays on Women's Imprisonment in Canada*. Halifax: Fernwood Press, 94–102.

Beccaria, C. (1778) *Essays on Crime and Punishment*. Edinburgh: A. Donaldson.

Belknap, J. (1996) *The Invisible Woman: Gender, Crime and Justice*. Belmont: Wadsworth.

Belknap, J. (2001) *The Invisible Woman: Gender, Crime and Justice* (2nd ed.). Belmont: Wadsworth.

Bertrand, M.-A. (1969) Self-image and delinquency: A contribution to the study of female criminality and women's image. *Acta Criminologica*, 2, 70–144.

Bertrand, M.-A. (1999) Incarceration as a gendering strategy. *Canadian Journal of Law and Society*, 14(1), 45–60.

Bloom, B. (2000) Successful gender-responsive programming must reflect women's lives and needs. *Women, Girls and Criminal Justice*, 1(1), 1–3.

Bloom, B., and Steinhart, D. (1993) *Why Punish the Children: A Reappraisal of the Children of Incarcerated Mothers in America*. Washington, DC: National Council on Crime and Delinquency.

Boritch, H. (1997) *Fallen Women: Female Crime and Criminal Justice in Canada*: Toronto: ITP Nelson.

Bosworth, M. (1999) Agency and choice in women's prisons: Towards a constitutive penality. In S. Henry and D. Milovanovic (eds.), *Constitutive Criminology at Work: Applications to Crime and Justice*. Albany: State University of New York Press, 205–36.

Boyd, S. (1997) *Challenging the Public/Private Divide: Feminism, Law and Public Policy*. Toronto: University of Toronto Press.

Boyer, R., and Drache, D. (1996) *States Against Markets: The Limits of Globalization*. London: Routledge.

Brennan, T., and Austin, R. (1997) *Women in Jail: Classification Issues*. Washington, DC: National Institute of Corrections.

British Home Office (1999) Aim 4: The government's strategy for women offenders. Available online at http://www.hmprisonerservice.gov.uk/filstore/189–190

Bureau of Justice Statistics (2000) *Prison and Jail Inmates at Mid-Year 2000*. Washington, DC: US Department of Justice, # 185989.

Cain, M. (1990) Towards transgression: New directions in feminist criminology. *International Journal of the Sociology of Law*, 18(1), 1–18.

Canadian Centre for Justice Statistics (1997) *Uniform Crime Reporting Survey*. Ottawa: Statistics Canada.

Canadian Centre for Justice Statistics (2000) *Juristat: Adult Correctional Services in Canada, 1998–99*. Ottawa: Statistics Canada, 20(3).

Carcach, C., and Grant, A. (1999) *Imprisonment in Australia: Trends in Prison Populations and Imprisonment Rates*. Canberra: Australian Institute of Criminology, 130, October, 1–6.

Carcach, C., and Grant, A. (2000) *Imprisonment in Australia: The Offence Composition of Australian Correctional Populations, 1998 and 1988*. Canberra: Australian Institute of Criminology, 164, July.

Carcach, C., Grant, A., and Conroy, R. (1999) *Australian Corrections: The Imprisonment of Indigenous People*. Canberra: Australian Institute of Criminology, 137, November.

Carlen, P. (1983) *Women's Imprisonment: A Study in Social Control*. London: Routledge.

Carlen, P. (1988) *Women, Crime and Poverty*. Milton Keynes: Open University Press.

Carrington, K. (1993) *Offending Girls: Sex, Youth and Justice*. North Sydney: Allen & Unwin.

Cayley, D. (1998) *The Expanding Prison: The Crisis in Crime and the Search for Alternatives*. Toronto: Anansi Press.

Chesney-Lind, M. (1981) Juvenile delinquency: The sexualization of female crime. *Psychology Today*, July, 43–6.

Chesney-Lind, M. (1987) Girls and violence: An exploration of the gender gap in serious delinquent behavior. In D. Corwell, I. Evans, and C. O'Donnell (eds.), *Childhood Aggression and Violence*, New York: Plenum, 207–30.

Chesney-Lind, M. (1988) Girls and status offenses: Is juvenile justice still sexist? *Criminal Justice Abstracts*, 20, 145–65.

Chesney–Lind, M. and Faith, K. (2001) What about feminism? Engendering theory-making in criminology. In R. Paternoster (ed.), *Criminological Theories*, Los Angeles: Roxbury Press, 287–302.

Chunn, D. (1992) *From Punishment to Doing Good: Family Courts and Socialized Justice in Ontario 1880 to 1940*. Toronto: University of Toronto Press.

Cohen, S. (1994) Social control and the politics of reconstruction. In D. Nelken (ed.), *The Futures of Criminology*. London: Sage, 63–88.

Comack, E. (1996) *Women in Trouble*. Halifax: Fernwood Press.

Comack, E., Chopyk, K, and Wood, L. (2000) *Mean Streets? The Social Locations, Gender Dynamics, and Patterns of Violent Crime in Winnipeg*. Ottawa: Canadian Centre for Policy Alternatives, December, 1–23.

Cook, S., and Davies, S. (1999) Will anyone ever listen? An introductory note. In S. Cook and S. Davies (eds.), *Harsh Punishment: International Experiences of Women's Imprisonment*. Boston: Northeastern University Press, 3–12.

Daly, K. (1987) Discrimination in the criminal courts: Family, gender and the problem of equal treatment. *Social Forces*, 66(1), 152–75.

Daly, K. (1989) Gender and varieties of white-collar crime. *Criminology*, 27, 769–94.

Daly, K. (1994) *Gender, crime and punishment*. New Haven, CT: Yale University Press.

Daly, K., and Chesney-Lind, M. (1988) Feminism and criminology. *Justice Quarterly*, 5 (4), 101–43.

DeKeseredy, W. (2000) *Women, Crime and the Canadian Criminal Justice System*. Cincinnati: Anderson.

Dobash, R., Dobash, R., and Guttridge, S. (1986) *The Imprisonment of Women*. Oxford: Basil Blackwell.

Eaton, M. (1986) *Justice for Women? Family Court and Social Control*. London: Open University Press.

Ehrenreich, B. (2001) *Nickel and Dimed: On (Not) Getting By in America*. New York: Metropolitan Books.

Erez, E. and Hassin, Y. (1997) Women in crime and justice: The case of Israel. *Women and Criminal Justice*, 9(2), 61–85.

Ericson, R., and Carriere, K. (1994) The fragmentation in criminology. In D. Nelken (ed.), *The Futures of Criminology*. London: Sage, 89–109.

Faith, K. (1993) *Unruly Women: The Politics and Confinement of Resistance*. Vancouver: Press Gang Publishers.

Faith, K. (1999) Transformative justice versus re-entrenched correctionalism: The Canadian experience. In S. Cook and S. Davies (eds.), *Harsh Punishment: International Experiences of Women's Imprisonment*. Boston: Northeastern University Press, 99–122.

Finn, A., Trevethan, S., Carriere, G., and Kowalski, M. (1999) Female inmates, aboriginal inmates, and inmates serving life sentences: A one-day snapshot. *Juristat*, 19(5), 1–14.

Freedman, E. B. (1981) *Their Sister's Keepers: Women's Prison Reform in America, 1830–1930*. Ann Arbor: University of Michigan Press.

Fudge, J., and Cossman, B. (2001) Introduction: Privatization, law and the challenge to feminism. In B. Cossman and J. Fudge (eds.), *Privatization, Law and the Challenge to Feminism*. Toronto: University of Toronto Press, 3–37.

Gelsthorpe, L. (1989) *Sexism and the Female Offender*. Aldershot: Gower.

George, A. (1999) The new prison culture: Making millions from misery. In S. Cook and S. Davies (eds.), *Harsh Punishment: International Experiences of Women's Imprisonment*, Boston: Northeastern University Press, 189–210.

Giallombardo, R. (1966) *Society of Women: A Study of a Women's Prison*. New York: Wiley.

Goring, C. (1913) *The English Convict: A Statistical Study*. London: His Majesty's Stationery Office.

Gottfredson, M., and Hirschi, T. 1990: *General Theory of Crime*. Stanford: Stanford University Press.

Haggerty, K. (2001) *Making Crime Count*. Toronto: University of Toronto Press.

Hannah-Moffat, K. (2001) *Punishment in Disguise: Penal Governance and Canadian Federal Women's Imprisonment*. Toronto: University of Toronto Press.

Hannah-Moffat, K. (2002) Governing through need: The hybridizations of risk and need in penality. Paper presented to Annual Meetings, *Canadian Law and Society Association*. Vancouver, BC, May 31.

Hayman, S. (2000) Prison reform and incorporation: Lessons from Britain and Canada. In K. Hannah-Moffat and M. Shaw(eds.), *An Ideal Prison? Critical Essays on Women's Imprisonment in Canada*. Halifax: Fernwood Press, 41–52.

Heidensohn, F. (1985) *Women and Crime: The Life of the Female Offender*. New York: New York University Press.

Henry, S., and Milovanovich, D. (eds.) (1999) *Constitutive Criminology at Work: Applications to Crime and Justice*. Albany: State University of New York Press.

Hooton, E. A. (1939) *The American Criminal: An Anthropological Study*. Cambridge, MA: Harvard University Press.

Howe, A. (1990) Sentencing women to prison in Victoria: A research and political agenda. *Law in Context*, 8(2), 32–53.

Howe, A. (1994) *Punish and Critique: Towards a Feminist Analysis of Penality*. New York: Routledge.

Hudson, B. (1984) Femininity and adolescence. In A. McRobbie and M. Nava (eds.), *Gender and Generation*. London: Macmillan, 31–53.

Ignatieff, M. (1978) *A Just Measure of Pain: The Penitentiary in the Industrial Revolution*. New York: Pantheon.

Immarigeon, M., and Chesney-Lind, M. (1992) *Women's Prisons: Overcrowded and Overused*. San Francisco: National Council on Crime and Delinquency.

Jackson, M. (1999) Canadian aboriginal women and their "criminality": The cycle of violence in the context of difference. *Australian and New Zealand Journal of Criminology*, 32(2), 197–208.

Kendall, K. (2000) Psy-ence fiction: Governing female prisons through the psychological sciences. In K. Hannah-Moffat and M. Shaw (eds.), *An Ideal Prison? Critical Essays on Women's Imprisonment in Canada*. Halifax: Fernwood Press, 82–93.

Kidd-Hewitt, D. (1995) Crime in the media: A criminological perspective. In D. Kidd-Hewitt and R. Osborne (eds.), *Crime and the Media: The Postmodern Spectacle*. East Haven, CT: Pluto Press, 1–24.

Koons, B., Burrows, J., Morash, M, and Bynum, T. (1997) Expert and offender perceptions of program elements linked to successful outcomes for incarcerated women. *Crime and Delinquency*, 43(4), 512–25.

Kruttschnitt, C. (1981) Social status and sentences of female offenders. *Law and Society Review Madison Wisconsin*, 15(2), 247–65.

Kruttschnitt, C. (1984) Sex and criminal court dispositions. *Journal of Research in Crime and Delinquency*, 21(3), 213–32.

Laberge, D. (1991) Women's criminality, criminal women, criminalized women? Questions in and for a feminist perspective. *Journal of Human Justice*, 2(2), 37–56.

Leonard, C. (1982) *Women, Crime and Society: A Critique of Criminology*. New York: Longman.

Lombroso, C., and Ferraro, W. 1895: *The Female Offender*. London: Fisher Unwin.

McConville, S. (1998) The Victorian prison: England, 1865–1965. In N. Morris and D. Rothman (eds.), *The Oxford History of Prison*. New York: Oxford University Press, 117–50.

McRobbie, A. (1978) Working-class girls and the culture of femininity. In Women's Studies Group (ed.), *Women Take Issue: Aspects of Women's Subordination*. London: Hutchinson, 96–108.

Messerschmidt, J. (1993) *Masculinities and Crime: A Critique and Reconceptualization of Theory*. Boston: Roman & Littlefield.

Minaker, J. (2001) Voluntary prisoners? "Fallen women", "wayward" girls and the Toronto Magdalene Asylum, 1852–1917. Paper presented at the Canadian Sociology and Anthropology meetings, Quebec City, May 27–31.

Morris, A. (1987) *Women, Crime and Criminal Justice*. London: Blackwell.

Moulds, E. F. (1980) Chivalry and paternalism: Disparities of treatment in the criminal justice system. In S. K. Datesman and F. R. Scarpitti (eds.), *Women, Crime and Justice*. New York: Oxford University Press, 277–99.

Naffine, N. (1987) *Female Crime: The Construction of Women in Criminology*. Philadelphia: Temple University Press.

Naffine, N. (1989) Towards justice for girls: Rhetoric and practice for the treatment of status offenders. *Women and Criminal Justice*, 1, 3–20.

Naffine, N. (1996) *Feminism and Criminology*. Philadelphia: Temple University Press.

Nava, M. (1984) Youth service provision, social order and the question of girls. In A. McRobbie and M. Nava (eds.), *Gender and Generation*. London: Macmillan, 1–30.

Nelken, D. (ed.) (1994) *The Futures of Criminology*. London: Sage.

O'Malley, P. (1996) Indigenous governance. *Economy and Society*, 21(3), 310–26.

Osborne, R. (1995) Crime and the media: From media studies to post-modernism. In D. Kidd-Hewitt and R. Osborne (eds.), *Crime and the Media: The Postmodern Spectacle*. East Haven, CT: Pluto Press, 25–48.

Owen, B. (1999) Women and imprisonment in the United States: The gendered consequences of the US imprisonment binge. In S. Cook and S. Davies (eds.), *Harsh Punishment: International Experiences of Women's Imprisonment*. Boston: Northeastern University Press, 81–98.

Pate, K. (2000) Why do we think young women are committing more violent offences?. In J. Roberts (ed.), *Criminal Justice in Canada*. Toronto: Harcourt Brace, 195–206.

Pearce, F. and Tombs, S. (1998) *Toxic Capitalism*. Aldershot: Ashgate/Dartmouth.

Platek, M. (1999) On the margin of life: Women's imprisonment in Poland. In S. Cook and S. Davies (eds.), *Harsh Punishment: International Experiences of Women's Imprisonment*. Boston: Northeastern University Press, 160–71.

Pollack, S. (2000) Dependency discourse as social control. In K. Hannah-Moffat and M. Shaw (eds.), *An Ideal Prison? Critical Essays on Women's Imprisonment in Canada*. Halifax: Fernwood Press, 72–81.

Pollak, O. (1950) *The Criminality of Women*. Philadelphia: University of Philadelphia Press.

Radzinowicz, L,. and Hood, R. (1986) *History of English Criminal Law and its Administration from 1750: The Emergence of Penal Policy*. London: Stevens.

Rafter, N. (1985) *Partial Justice: Women in State Prisons, 1900–1935*. Boston: Northeastern University Press.

Reed, B. G. (1987) Developing women-sensitive drug dependence treatment services: Why so difficult? *Journal of Psychoactive Drugs*, 19(2), 151–8.

Rice, A. F., Smith, L. L., and Janzen, F. (1999) Women inmates, drug abuse, and the Salt Lake County Jail. *American Jails*, 13(3), 43–55.

Rothman, D. (1971) *The Discovery of the Asylum: Social Order and Disorder in the New Republic*. Boston: Little, Brown.

Rothman, D. (1980) *Conscience and Convenience: The Asylum and Its Alternatives in Progressive America*. Boston: Little, Brown.

Sacco, V. F. (1995) Media constructions of crime. *The Annals*, 539 (May), 141–54.

Sacco, V. F. (2000) News that counts: Newspaper images of crime and victimization statistics. *Criminologie*, 33(1), 203–23.

Schichor, D., and Sechrest, D. (1996) *Three Strikes and You're Out: Vengeance as Public Policy*. Thousand Oaks, CA: Sage.

Schrecker, T. (2001) From the welfare state to the no-second-chances state. In S. Boyd, D. Chunn, and R. Menzies (eds.), *(Ab)Using Power: The Canadian Experience*. Halifax: Fernwood, 36–48.

Shaw, M. (1993) Reforming federal women's imprisonment. In E. Adelberg and C. Currie (eds.), *In Conflict with the Law: Women and the Canadian Justice System.* Vancouver: Press Gang Publishers, 50–75.

Smart, C. (1976) *Women, Crime, and Criminology: A Feminist Critique.* London: Routledge & Kegan Paul.

Smart, C. (1989) *Feminism and the Power of the Law.* London: Routledge.

Smart, C. (1995) Feminist approaches to criminology, or postmodern woman meets atavistic man. In C. Smart (ed.), *Law, Crime and Sexuality.* London: Sage, 32–48.

Smykla, J., and Williams, J. (1996) Co-corrections in the United States of America, 1970–1990: Two decades of disadvantages for women prisoners. *Women and Criminal Justice,* 8(1), 61–76.

Snider, L. (1994) Feminism, punishment and the potential of empowerment. *Canadian Journal of Law and Society,* 9(1),75–104.

Snider, L. (1998) Towards safer societies: Punishment, masculinities and violence against women. *British Journal of Criminology,* 38(1), 1–39.

Snider, L. (2000) The sociology of corporate crime: An obituary. *Theoretical Criminology,* 4(2): 169–206.

Spierenburg, P. (1984) *The Spectacle of Suffering.* Cambridge: Cambridge University Press.

Spohn, C., Gruhl, J., and Welch, S. (1987) The impact of the ethnicity and gender of defendants on the decision to reject or dismiss felony charges. *Criminology,* 25, 175–91.

Steffensmeier, D. (1978) Crime and the contemporary woman: An analysis of charging levels of female property crime, 1960–1975. *Social Forces,* 57(2), 566–84.

Steffensmeier, D. (1980) Sex differences in patterns of adult crime, 1965–1977: A review & assessment. *Social Forces,* 58, 1080–108.

Steffensmeier, D. (1983) Organizational properties and sex-segregation in the underworld: Building a sociological theory of sex. *Social Forces,* 61 (June), 1010–32.

Surrette, R. (1998) *Media, Crime and Criminal Justice: Images and Realities.* Toronto: Nelson.

Task Force on Federally Sentenced Women (1990) *Report of the Task Force on Federally Sentenced Women: Creating Choices.* Ottawa: Ministry of the Solicitor General.

Teplin, L. Abram, K., and McClelland, G. (1996) Prevalence of psychiatric disorders among incarcerated women. *Archives of General Psychiatry,* 53, 505–21.

Thomas, W. (1923) *The Unadjusted Girl.* Boston: Little Brown.

Tong, R. (1996) Maternal–fetal conflict: The misguided case for punishing cocaine-using pregnant and/or postpartum women. In C. Sistare (ed.), *Punishment: Social Control and Coercion.* New York: Peter Lang, 153–78.

Welch, M., Fenwick, M., and Roberts, M. (1998) State managers, intellectuals and the media: A content analysis of ideology in expert's quotes in feature newspaper articles on crime. In G. Potter and V. Kappeler (eds.), *Constructing Crime: Perspectives on Making News and Social Problems.* Prospect Heights, IL: Waveland Press, 87–110.

Wilson, J. and Herrnstein, R. (1985) *Crime, Human Nature.* New York: Simon & Schuster.

Worrall, A. (1990) *Offending Women: Female Lawbreakers and the Criminal Justice System.* London: Routledge.

Zedner, L. (1998) Wayward sisters. In N. Morris and D. Rothman (eds.), *The Oxford History of Prison.* New York: Oxford University Press, 294–324.

Part IV
Gender and the Masculinity of Crime

13

Beyond Bad Girls: Feminist Perspectives on Female Offending

Meda Chesney-Lind

Contemporary criminology has just begun to consider the topic of girl and women offenders. Most often, though, the consideration of women's crime is reduced to the notion that gender can be a variable plugged into theories generated to explain male offending. Elsewhere, I've called this the "add women and stir" approach to thinking about girls' and women's crime (Chesney-Lind 1988). What is really needed to understand the lives of girls and women who come into the criminal justice system is to *theorize* gender in the same way that time-honored theories of crime have theorized class (and less frequently race). That is, to make explicit the fact that all crime (female and male) occurs in the social context of patriarchy, is shaped by that system of male privilege and is inextricably affected by that system (as well as by systems of class and race privilege).

What would criminology look like if women's crime and victimization were at the center rather than the periphery of scholarly inquiry? Suddenly, men have a gender, not just women; and male behavior is no longer normalized. Male violence against women, in particular, takes on a very different meaning if women's relative nonviolence were the normal response to life, and men's aggression the aberration. The violence, fear, and victimization that are so much a part of many women's lives (that is, the other side of male violence) are suddenly important areas of study and research. One can immediately see why feminist perspectives have so invigorated criminology and criminological theory. The progress, though, has been uneven.

In the United States, for example, the construction of woman as victim has made the greatest headway. The recognition of women's victimization, while long overdue, had some effects unanticipated by feminist activists and scholars. Specifically, the discovery of "domestic violence" supplied mainstream criminologists and criminal justice policy makers with "new" crimes to study, new moral behaviors to regulate (e.g., pornography), and new men to jail (particularly men of color). Most importantly, centrist (and some right-wing) approaches to these problems did not fundamentally challenge androcentric criminology. Its appeal is, in part, a product of the fact that the victimized woman does not challenge core notions of patriarchal ideology; she – the plundered waif – after all, needs male protection and assistance. None of these comments should be taken to mean that women's victimization is not horrific, but rather that the study of women's victimization (long considered, in some circles, to be coextensive with feminist criminology) caused the least resistance in the field itself.

The study of women in conflict with the law and out of control, as noted above, has not developed as fully (for exceptions to this generalization, see Chesney-Lind and Faith 2001: 6). Perhaps the existence of these women suggests that male domination is not as complete as it might be? These women were certainly trouble for theories of male criminality which were long described as theories of crime. So the "offending" women were ignored, and those who studied them, until recently, did so from the very edges of the field.

This has meant, of course, that the lives of women on the economic margins, who were the overwhelming victims of this control, were left largely undocumented and unexplained. Their race and class simply placed them outside of a slightly modified criminology where men (assumed to be poor and nonwhite) are criminals and women (assumed to be docile, good, and white) are victims.

The relative paucity of scholarship on the topic of "unruly" women (Faith 1993) has permitted two troubling trends to develop, particularly in the United States and Canada. First, the lack of solid scholarship has permitted the occasional discovery of "bad" women during periods when this would serve patriarchal interests. In the 1970s, the female offender was touted in the media as a byproduct of the then emerging social movement which was seeking legal and social equality for women (Chesney-Lind 1986). In more recent years, the discovery of female aggression and violence, particularly girls' violence, has again been blamed on the women's movement (see Chesney-Lind 1999; DeKeseredy 2000).

More importantly, the lack of a robust body of scholarship about women and crime has meant that when the women's prison population in the United States soared in the waning decades of the twentieth century, there was virtually no information about the women being jailed, with the exception of media hype about violent, drug-dependent women of color in conflict with the law.

While women's crime was overlooked almost completely by criminologists, the state had no such hesitancy about criminalizing large numbers of adult women, particularly in the United States. For criminologists, the time-honored defense of this posture was that there were so few women in the system that accounting for gender was not necessary. Now that is clearly not the case, either for girls or women.

As an example, for most of the twentieth century, we imprisoned about 5,000–10,000 women, but in mid-2000, there were nine times that amount (92,688) doing time in US prisons (Beck and Karberg 2001: 5). Another 70,000 women were being held in the nation's jails. Both women's prison and jail populations expanded at rates far in excess of those seen in male facilities; since 1990, women's prison populations expanded at an average annual rate of 8.1 percent (compared to 6.2 percent for men) and women's jail populations increased by 6.6 percent compared to 4 percent for males (Beck and Karberg 2001: 5, 7).

As a result, the number of women incarcerated in prisons and jails in the United States is now approximately ten times more than the number of women incarcerated in Western Europe. This despite the fact that Western Europe and the US are roughly equivalent in terms of population (Amnesty International 1999: 15).

Given the recent shift in these patterns, there is an urgent need to "locate women's criminalization and imprisonment in broader historical and social contexts" (Cook and Davies 1999: 4). That is the intent of this essay. Moreover, since girl's problems are inextricably linked with not only their involvements in the juvenile justice system but also later in life with the adult system, we will examine shifts in both girls' and women's offending as well as detailing a few issues that have surfaced around their treatment in the criminal justice system.

GIRLS AND DELINQUENCY: RISING NUMBERS, RISING VIOLENCE?

Shortly after the American Association of University Women's study documented the dramatic and widespread drop in the self-esteem of girls during early adolescence (1992), a curious thing happened in the media. There was a dramatic surge of journalistic interest in girls, often girls of color, engaged in nontraditional, masculine behavior – notably joining gangs, carrying guns, and fighting with other girls.

The fascination with a "new" violent female offender is not really new, however. In the 1970s, a notion emerged that the women's movement had "caused" a surge in women's serious crimes. But this discussion focused largely on an imagined increase in crimes of adult women – usually white women (see Chesney-Lind 1997). The current discussion, though, has settled on girls' commission of violent crimes, often in youth gangs. Indeed, there has been a veritable siege of these news stories with essentially the same theme – today girls are more violent, they belong to gangs, and their behavior does not fit the traditional stereotype of girls' delinquency as simply "minor" and often "sexual" delinquency (see Chesney-Lind and Shelden 1998).

On August 2, 1993, for example, in a feature spread on teen violence, *Newsweek* had a box entitled "Girls will be Girls" which noted that "some girls now carry guns. Others hide razor blades in their mouths" (Leslie et al. 1993: 44). Explaining this trend, the article noted that "The plague of teen violence is an equal-opportunity scourge. Crime by girls is on the rise, or so various jurisdictions report" (Leslie et al. 1993: 44). More recently, the *Boston Globe Magazine* ran a cover story on girls and violence. Against a backdrop of large red letters reading "BAD GIRLS," read a text saying "girls are moving into the world of violence that once belonged to boys" (Ford 1998).

The recent surge in girls' arrests initially seems to provide support for the notion that girls have become more delinquent and even more violent. Between 1990 and 1999 in the United States, girls' arrests increased by 31.8 percent compared to only 4.7 percent for boys (Federal Bureau of Investigation 2000: 217)). Concomitant with these arrest increases are increases in girls' referral to juvenile courts; between 1988 and 1997, the number of delinquency cases involving girls increased by 83 percent compared to a 39 percent increase for males (Office of Juvenile Justice and Delinquency Prevention 2001: 25). Finally, there was a "surge" in the number of female delinquency cases involving detention during the same period (a 65 percent increase compared to a 30 percent increase for males) (Porter 2000).

Apparently responsible for many of these trends has been the rising number of arrests of girls for "violent" offenses. Adolescent female arrests for serious violent offenses increased by 39.8 percent between 1990 and 1999; arrests of girls for "other assaults" increased by more – 92.6 percent (Federal Bureau of Investigation 2000: 217). The Office of Juvenile Justice and Delinquency Prevention (1998) found that the female violent crime rate for 1997 was 103 percent above the 1981 rate, compared to 27 percent for males. This prompted them to assert that "increasing juvenile female arrests and the involvement of girls in at-risk and delinquent behavior has been a pervasive trend across the United States" (p. 2). Discussions of girls' gang behavior and, more recently, girls' violence, have also been extremely prevalent in the media (see Chesney-Lind 1999 for a review).

Similar patterns have also been observed in other countries. In Canada, between 1991 and 1995, the number of girls placed in secure custody increased by 55 percent. DeKeseredy (2000: iv) describes the situation as that of sweeping up young women "in an imprisonment binge" similar to that in the United States. The Canadian Centre for Justice Statistics (2001) and the Police Services Division of the British Columbia Ministry of the Attorney General reported (Police Services Division 1998) that the violent crime rate for both male and female youth increased steadily during the 1980s and mid-1990s. For male youth, the rate rose from a level of 8.5 per 1000 in 1988 to a peak in 1994 at 16.2 per 1000 and began, in 1995, to decline. The rate for females rose from a level of 2.2 per 1000 in 1988 to a peak in 1996 of 5.6 per 1000, remained at approximately 5.3 per 1000 over the next two years, and began to decline only in 1999 (see Chesney-Lind et al. 2001 for a full discussion of these issues).

Are girls closing the gap with boys in the area of serious delinquency, and more specifically, are girls becoming more violent? Certainly, if girls' delinquent behavior was dramatically more serious, this might account for the surge in the social control of girls that is accompanying this increase.

A review of the facts presents, though, a very different picture. Indeed, it is probably extremely likely that the run-up in girls' arrests for "violence" involves processes long present in the juvenile justice system rather than a change in the behavior of girls – processes of relabeling (or "bootstrapping"), as well as criminalizing minor forms of aggression and violence that were always present in girls' behavior (rediscovery).

A couple of examples will suffice here (for a full discussion, see Chesney-Lind and Okamoto 2001).

"DISCOVERING" GIRL'S AGGRESSION AND VIOLENCE

With reference to what might be called girls' "nontraditional" delinquency, it must be recognized that girls' capacity for aggression and violence has historically been ignored, trivialized, or denied. For this reason, self-report data, particularly from the 1970s and 1980s, has always shown higher involvement of girls in assaultive behavior than official statistics would indicate. As an example, Canter (1982) reported a male-versus-female, self-reported delinquency ratio of 3.4:1 for minor assault and 3.5:1 for serious assault. At that time, arrest statistics showed much greater male participation in aggravated assault (5.6:1, Federal Bureau of Investigation 1980) and simple assault (3.8:1, Canter 1982). Currently, arrest statistics show a 3.54:1 ratio for "aggravated assault" and a 2.27:1 ratio for "other assaults" (Federal Bureau of Investigation 2000). Taken together, these numbers suggest the gap is closing between what girls have always done (and reported, when asked anonymously) and arrest statistics, rather than a course change in girls' participation in serious violence.

To further support this notion, other research on trends in self-report data of youthful involvement in violent offenses also fails to show the dramatic changes found in official statistics. Specifically, a matched sample of "high-risk" youth (aged 13–17) surveyed in the 1977 National Youth Study and the more recent 1989 Denver Youth Survey revealed significant *decreases* in girls' involvement in felony assaults, minor assaults, and hard drugs, and no change in a wide range of other delinquent behaviors – including felony theft, minor theft, and index delinquency (Huizinga 1997).

Finally, there are the trends in girls' lethal violence. While girls' arrests for all forms of assault skyrocketed in the 1990s, girls' arrests for murder actually fell by nearly 40 percent (Federal Bureau of Investigation 2000). If girls were in fact closing the gap between their behavior and that of boys, would not one expect to see the same effect across all the violent offenses (including the *most* violent offense)? That simply is not happening.

Further reinforcement of this notion comes from recent research on girls' violence in San Francisco (Males and Shorter 2001). They analyze vital statistics maintained by health officials (rather than arrest data) and conclude that there was a 63 percent drop in fatalities among teenage girls in San Francisco between the 1960s and the 1990s. They also indicate that hospital injury data show that girls are dramatically underrepresented among those reporting injury (including assaults). Girls make up 3.7 percent of the population, yet constituted only 0.9 percent of those seeking treatment for violent injuries (Males and Shorter 2001: 1–2).

RELABELING STATUS OFFENSES

But what about dramatic increases, particularly in arrests of girls for "other assaults"? Relabeling of behaviors that were once categorized as status offenses (noncriminal offenses like being a "runaway" and a"person in need of supervision") into violent offenses cannot be ruled out in explanations of arrest-rate shifts, nor can changes in police practices with reference to domestic violence. A review of over two thousand cases of girls referred to Maryland's juvenile justice system for "person-to-person" offenses revealed that virtually all of these offenses (97.9 percent) involved "assault." A further examination of these records revealed that about half were "family-centered" and involved such activities as "a girl hitting her mother and her mother subsequently pressing charges" (Mayer 1994).

More recently, Acoca's study of nearly one thousand girls' files from four California counties found that while a "high percentage" of these girls were charged with "person offenses," a majority of these involved assault. Further, "a close reading of the case files of girls charged with assault revealed that most of these charges were the result of nonserious, mutual combat, situations with parents." Acoca details cases that she regards as typical, including: "father lunged at her while she was calling the police about a domestic dispute. She (girl) hit him." Finally, she reports that some cases were quite trivial in nature, including a girl arrested "for throwing cookies at her mother" (Acoca 1999: 7–8).

In essence, when exploring the dramatic increases in the arrests of girls for "other assault," it is likely that changes in enforcement practices have dramatically narrowed the gender gap. As noted in the above examples, a clear contribution has come from increasing arrests of girls and women for domestic violence. A recent California study found that the female share of these arrests increased from 6 percent in 1988 to 16.5 percent in 1998 (Bureau of Criminal Information and Analysis 1999). African American girls and women had arrest rates roughly three times that of white girls and women in 1998: 149.6 percent compared to 46.4 percent (ibid.).

Relabeling of girls' arguments with parents from status offenses (such as being "incorrigible" or a "person in need of supervision") to assault is a form of "bootstrapping," has been particularly pronounced in the official delinquency of African American girls (Robinson 1990; Bartollas 1993). This practice also facilitates the incarceration of girls in detention facilities and training schools – something that would not be possible if the girls were arrested for noncriminal status offenses.

Simply stated, the current trends in juvenile justice suggest that social control of girls is once again on the criminal justice agenda – this century justified by their "violence" just as in the past century it was justified by their sexuality.

Women's Lives, Women's Crime

Is the dramatic increase in adult women's imprisonment a response to a women's crime problem spiraling out of control? If so, other indicators give little evidence of this. As an example, the total number of arrests of adult women, which might be seen as a measure of women's criminal activity, increased by only 14.5 percent between 1990 and 1999, while the number of women in prison increased by 105.8 percent (Federal Bureau of Investigation 2000: 217; Beck and Mumola 1999: 6).

What does explain the increase? A recent study by the Bureau of Justice Statistics indicates that growth in the number of violent offenders was the major factor for male prison growth, but for the female prison population "drug offenders were the largest source of growth." One explanation, then, is that the "war on drugs" has become a largely unannounced war on women.

In 1979, one in ten women in US prisons were doing time for drugs. In 1998, it was over one in three (33.9 percent) (Beck 2000: 10). Finally, while the intent of "get-tough" policies was to rid society of drug dealers and so-called kingpins, many of the women swept up in the war on drugs are minor offenders. The war on drugs also explains the fact that, despite media images of hyperviolent women offenders, the proportion of women doing time in state prisons for violent offenses has been declining steadily from about half (48.9 percent) in 1979 to just over a quarter (28.5 percent) in 1998 (Bureau of Justice Statistics 1988; Beck and Mumola 1999: 10).

Likely the most powerful factor in the increase in women's imprisonment has come from mandatory sentences for drug offenses, which all states have at least in some form. Estimates are that these policies have increased the likelihood of being imprisoned for a drug offense by 447 percent between 1980 and 1992 (Mauer 1999). Initially, these mandatory sentences appear to be gender-blind, but in practice, many suspect that women are at considerable disadvantage in plea negotiations that are permitted. Essentially, one of the few ways that the mandatory sentences can be altered is if the alleged defendant can provide authorities with information that might be useful in the prosecution of other drug offenders. Since, as noted earlier, women tend to be working at the lowest levels of the drug hierarchy, they are often unable to negotiate plea reductions successfully. Such was the case in one of the most high-profile of these cases, that of Kemba Smith, who was initially sentenced to 24 years in a federal penitentiary for a drug offense; she was later pardoned by President Clinton (Copeland 2000).

Is it fair and just to sweep large numbers of women with drug problems into US prisons – imprisoning them as if they were men? Research on women's pathways into crime clearly disputes this, and suggests that *gender matters* in the forces that propel women into criminal behavior. For this reason, gender must be specifically taken into account as we attempt to construct useful theories of both juvenile and adult female offending (see Heimer 2000).

Hints about the critical importance of gender can come from a national survey of imprisoned women in the United States. That research found that women in prisons have far higher rates of physical and sexual abuse than their male counterparts. Forty-three percent of the women surveyed "reported they had been abused at least once" before their current admission to prison; the comparable figure for men was 12.2 percent (Snell and Morton 1994: 5).

For about a third of all women in prison (31.7 percent), the abuse started when they were girls, but it continued as they became adults. A key gender difference emerges here. A number of young men who are in prison (10.7 percent) also report abuse as boys, but this does not continue to adulthood. One in four women reported that their abuse started as adults compared to only 3 percent of male offenders. Fully 33.5 percent of the women surveyed reported physical abuse, and a slightly higher number (33.9 percent) had been sexually abused either as girls or young women, compared to relatively small percentages of men (10 percent of boys and 5.3 percent of adult men in prison) (Snell and Morton 1994: 5).

Girls are, it turns out, more likely than boys to be the victims of child sexual abuse, with some experts estimating that roughly 70 percent of the victims of child sexual abuse are girls (Finkelhor and Baron 1986). Not surprisingly, the evidence is also suggesting a link between this problem and girl's delinquency – particularly running away from home (see Chesney-Lind and Shelden 1998). Since studies of adult women in prison clearly indicate the role that girlhood victimization has played in their lives, these suggest that society's failure to address adequately girls' serious problems (and, in fact, the criminalization of girls' survival strategies, such as running away from home) is inextricably linked not only to girls' delinquency but also to latter criminal behavior in adult women.

A look at the offenses for which women are incarcerated further puts to rest the notion of hyperviolent, nontraditional women criminals. "Nearly half of all women in prison are currently serving a sentence for a nonviolent offense and have been convicted in the past of only nonviolent offenses." By 1998, over half of all women in the nation's prisons were serving time either for drug offenses or property offenses (Beck 2000: 10).

Even when women commit violent offenses, gender plays an important role. Research indicates, for example, that of women convicted of murder or manslaughter, many had killed husbands or boyfriends who repeatedly and violently abused them. In New York, for example, of the women committed to the state's prisons for homicide in 1986, 49 percent had been the victims of abuse at some point in their lives and 59 percent of the women who killed someone close to them were being abused at the time of the offense. For half of the women committed for homicide, it was their first and only offense (Huling 1991).

But what of less dramatic, and far more common offenses among women? Kim English (1993) approached the issue of women's crime by analyzing detailed self-report surveys she administered to a sample of 128 female and 872 male inmates in Colorado. Her research provides clear information on the way in which women's place in male society colors and shapes their crimes.

She found, for example, that women were far more likely than men to be involved in "forgery" (it was the most common crime for women and fifth out of eight for men). Follow-up research on a subsample of "high-crime"-rate female respondents revealed that many had worked in retail establishments and therefore "knew how much time they had" between stealing the checks or credit cards and having them reported. The women said that they would target "strip malls" where credit cards and bank checks could be stolen easily and used in nearby retail establishments. The women reported that their high-frequency theft was motivated by a "big haul," which meant a purse with several hundred dollars in it as well as cards and checks. English concludes that "women's overrepresentation in low-paying, low-status jobs" increases their involvement in these property crimes (English 1993: 370).

English's findings with reference to two other offenses, where gender differences did not appear in participation rates, are worth exploring here. She found no difference in the "participation rates" of women and men in drug sales and assault. However, when examining the frequency data, English found that women in prison reported significantly more drug sales than men, but this was not because they were engaged in big-time drug selling. Instead, the high number of drug sales was a product of the fact that women's drug sales were "concentrated in the small trades (i.e., transactions of less than $10)." Because they made so little money, English found that 20 percent of the active women dealers reported 20 or more drug deals per day (English 1993: 372).

A reverse of the same pattern was found when she examined women's participation in assault. Here, slightly more (27.8 percent) of women than men (23.4

percent) reported an assault in the last year. However, most of these women reported only one assault during the study period (65.4 percent), compared to only about a third of the men (37.5 percent).

In sum, English found that both women's and men's crime reflected the role played by "economic disadvantage" in their criminal careers. Beyond this, though, gender played an important role in shaping women's and men's response to poverty. Specifically, women's criminal careers reflect "gender differences in legitimate and illegitimate opportunity structures, in personal networks, and in family obligations" (English 1993: 3, 74).

Finally, careful research on the role of the worsening economic situation facing women on the economic margins is necessary to understand what forces, if any, are propelling changes in women's crime. Women, and particularly women of color who are increasingly heads of households, certainly did not participate in the boom economy of the later part of the last century in meaningful ways.

Indeed, in a very careful assessment of the role of economic marginalization in women's crime, Heimer argues that what narrowing has occurred in the gender gap (the gap between male and female participation in crime) in the last few decades is likely caused by the confluence of three disparate trends: "dramatic changes in the composition of the family," "persistent wage inequality across gender," and finally, "increasing inequality or dispersion in income among women and men" (Heimer 2000: 455). Heimer links women's deteriorating economic conditions to an increase in women's participation in property crimes (including both traditionally female crimes like larceny and embezzlement, as well as some relatively nontraditional offenses such as motor-vehicle theft, burglary, and stolen property) and some crimes of violence (particularly assault) but, notably, not murder. To this list, one might be tempted to add drug arrests, since increases in women's arrests for these offenses have also increased while other women's arrests – particularly those for violent crimes – decreased in recent years (Federal Bureau of Investigation 2000: 217).

Since crime has been declining rapidly in the United States, by almost any measure (arrests or victimization data), most careful researchers would suggest that most of the run-up in women's imprisonment is *not* due to a change in women's crime, so much as a change in how the society handles drug offenses. However, Heimer's argument still merits further exploration. She marshals powerful evidence that *some* women's economic circumstances, particularly those of women who are single heads of households, have deteriorated considerably over the past few decades (particularly in communities of color). Such trends must be systematically examined when attempting to theorize women's crime. Beyond this, she correctly notes that recent mean-spirited changes in welfare policies (and, I would add, draconian laws prohibiting those found guilty of drug offenses from accessing welfare, public housing, and many other federal programs) may well encourage economically marginalized girls and women (particularly those who have already been convicted of crimes) to seek to survive through crime in much the same fashion that their male counterparts have long done.

One cannot leave the topic of adult women's offending without returning to the haunting figures that opened this essay. Specifically, in the waning decades of the last century, the number of women being held in US prisons increased eightfold and the women's imprisonment boom was born. There is an urgent need to both document and theorize the sources and consequences of the US pattern of mass imprisonment – for women and men. While its impact on women (and increasingly girls) is undeniable (as we noted at the beginning), it is less clear why the United States is such an international outlier on imprisonment policies (with the possible exception of Great Britain) (see Stern 2001).

To explain this phenomenon, it must be understood that crime in the United States has increasingly emerged as a code word for race. "Violence in our streets" was a catchphrase originally crafted by Barry Goldwater (the unsuccessful 1964 Presidential candidate) as a way to attack the civil rights movement by linking it to "violence" and "civil disorder." This focus was later expanded by President Nixon in his campaign for "law and order," and finally by Presidents Reagan and Bush, who launched and waged both the "war on crime" and the "war on drugs" (Chambliss 1999). By now, all in the United States understood that this "war" was to be waged more or less specifically on communities of color as the country moved away from attempting to address inequality and poverty to a policy that emphasized the use of the police, courts, and prisons to control economically and racially marginalized populations.

The consequences for communities of color are undeniable; nearly two-thirds of US prison and jail inmates are African American and Latino, numbers that have been rising dramatically both in absolute and proportional terms since the 1950s. Among young adults the figures for confined individuals are truly staggering – one of every eight black males in his twenties and early thirties is in prison or jail on any given day. At current rates of imprisonment, 29 percent of black males born today can expect to serve a sentence of at least a year in a state or federal prison in their lifetime. (Mauer and Chesney-Lind 2001). The impact on communities of color is exacerbated by the rapidly rising imprisonment of women – a trend which is also deeply racialized since African American women are incarcerated at three times the rate of Hispanic women and six times the rate of white women (Beck and Harrison 2001: 11). To the degree that the rest of the world negotiates racial diversity and inequality differently, they avoid the US pattern of mass imprisonment. If, however, they are tempted to deploy the criminal justice system to control and contain people of color rather than addressing racial inequality, they run the risk of following the United States into carceral apartheid.

CONCLUSION

Most feminists approach theory-making in the area of women's offending with a great deal of trepidation (see Chesney-Lind and Faith 2001). The early literature on women and crime, in particular, is littered with grandly terrible theorizing. We also tend to be hesitant to make global statements about the situation of all girls and women, since we, as criminologists, are keenly aware of the complex ways that race, gender, and class intersect to affect the female experience.

Clearly, the understanding of women's experience of crime, victimization, and justice requires thinking about and theorizing gender and crime – explicitly linking what we know about the lives of girls and women, particularly those who are economically marginalized, to the established literature on lawbreaking. There is also a critical need (not discussed here in detail) to place the official reactions to women's lawbreaking in their patriarchal context.

Much work lies ahead. The crucial questions that haunt all research and theorizing on gender will eventually also haunt criminology and criminological theory. How do we explain the vast differences in the involvement of women and men in criminal behavior – particularly violent behavior? How do we explain discriminatory criminal justice policies? When do we focus on theories that explore *similarities* between women and men, and when do we probe *difference*? Finally, can we theorize in ways that also capture the differences *between* women?

There is a certainly an urgent need for criminologists to engage in solid research and theory-building to challenge the crime myths that are played out in the media regarding women's crime and crime generally. Racism is clearly at the heart of much which passes as "truth" about crime, and the consequences of this misinformation on communities of color in the United States are devastating. Beyond this, the backlash against abundant solid research on the dimensions of girls' and women's victimization continues unabated (see Roiphe 1993; Wolf 1993). It is essential that feminist criminologists not be intimidated by such attacks, and that we continue to do work on this vital issue, both empirically and theoretically.

Finally, there is the responsibility of feminist criminology to research and theorize girl's and women's crime as well as official responses to that behavior. Howe discusses the value of Pat Carlen's work (1983, 1985, 1988, 1990), which stresses the importance of applying research findings to policy-making. "Academics must not let 'theoretical rectitude' deter them from 'committing themselves *as academics* and *as feminists*' to campaigns on behalf of women lawbreakers" (Carlen 1990: 111–12; Howe 1994: 214).

Research consistently documents that victimization is at the heart of much of girls' and women's lawbreaking, and that this pattern of gender entrapment, rather than gender liberation, best explains women's involvement in crime. That is, although most women who are victimized do not become criminals, the vast majority of imprisoned girls and women have been the victims of severe and chronic abuse. We have also seen, particularly in the United States, an increased willingness to incarcerate women and girls, often deploying the rhetoric of "equality" to justify this response. Good, clear thinking on both the theoretical and policy level will be necessary for us to respond to the unique questions that an understanding of gender poses for the field of criminology. So, for feminist criminologists, the "to do" list is quite long, and while activism to improve the situation of girls and women is clearly necessary, it is also necessary that we continue to build feminist theories and use these insights to improve the situation for all – girls and women as well as boys and men.

References

Acoca, L. (1999) Investing in girls: A 21st-century challenge. *Juvenile Justice*, 6(1) 3–13.
American Association for University Women (AAUW) (1992) *How Schools are Short-changing Girls*. Washington, DC: AAUW Educational Foundation.

Amnesty International (1999) *Not Part of My Sentence: Violations of the Human Rights of Women in Custody* Washington, DC: Amnesty International.

Bartollas, C. (1993) Little girls grown up: The perils of institutionalization. In C. Culliver (ed.), *Female Criminality: The State of the Art*. New York: Garland, 469–82.

Beck, A. (2000) *Prisoners in 1999*. Washington, DC: Bureau of Justice Statistics, US Department of Justice.

Beck, A., and Harrison, P. M. (2001) *Prisoners in 2000*. Washington, DC: Bureau of Justice Statistics, US Department of Justice.

Beck, A., and Karberg, J. C. (2001) *Prison and Jail Inmates at Midyear 2000*. Washington, DC: Bureau of Justice Statistics, US Department of Justice.

Beck, A., and Mumola, C. (1999) *Prisoners in 1998*. Washington, DC: Bureau of Justice Statistics, US Department of Justice.

Bureau of Criminal Information and Analysis (1999)) *Report on Arrests for Domestic Violence in California, 1998*. Sacramento: State of California, Criminal Justice Statistics Center.

Bureau of Justice Statistics (1988) *Profile of State Prison Inmates, 1986*. Washington, DC: Bureau of Justice Statistics, US Department of Justice.

Canadian Centre for Justice Statistics (2001) *Children and Youth in Canada*. Ottawa: Statistics Canada.

Canter, R. J. (1982) Sex differences in self-report delinquency. *Criminology*, 20, 373–93.

Carlen, P. (1983) *Women's Imprisonment: A Study in Social Control*. London: Routledge.

Carlen, P. (ed.) (1985) *Criminal Women*. Cambridge: Polity.

Carlen, P. (1988) *Women, Crime and Poverty*. Milton Keynes: Open University Press.

Carlen, P. (1990) *Alternatives to Women's Imprisonment*. Milton Keynes: Open University Press.

Chambliss, W. J. (1999) *Power, Politics, and Crime*. Boulder, CO: Westview.

Chesney-Lind, M. (1986) Women and crime: The female offender. *Signs*, 12, 78–96.

Chesney-Lind, M. (1988) Doing feminist criminology. *The Criminologist*, 13(1), 16–17.

Chesney-Lind, M. (1997) *The Female Offender: Girls, Women, and Crime*. Thousand Oaks, CA: Sage.

Chesney-Lind, M. (1999) Media misogyny: Demonizing "violent" girls and women. In J Ferrel and N. Websdale (eds.), *Making Trouble: Cultural Representations of Crime, Deviance, and Control*. New York: Aldine, 115–41.

Chesney-Lind, M., Artz, S., and Nicholson, D. (2001) Girls and violence. Unpublished paper in preparation for L. Rapp-Paglicci, A. R. Roberts, and J. S. Wodarski (eds.), *Handbook on Violence*. New York: John Wiley, 40pp.

Chesney-Lind, M., and Faith, K. (2001) What about feminism? Engendering theory-making in criminology. In R. Paternoster and R. Bachman (eds.), *Explaining Criminals and Crime: Essays in Contemporary Criminological Theory*. Los Angeles: Roxbury Press, 287–302.

Chesney-Lind, M., and Okamoto, S. (2001) Gender matters: Patterns in girls' delinquency and gender-responsive programming. *Journal of Forensic Psychology Practice*, 1(3), 1–28.

Chesney-Lind, M., and Shelden, R. G. (1998) *Girls, Delinquency and Juvenile Justice* (2nd ed.). Belmont, CA: Wadsworth.

Cook, S., and Davies, S. (eds.) (1999) *Harsh Punishment: International Experiences of Women's Imprisonment*. Boston: Northeastern University Press.

Copeland, L. (2000) Kemba Smith's hard time. *Washington Post*, February 13, FO1.

DeKeseredy, W. (2000) *Women, Crime and the Canadian Criminal Justice System*. Cincinnati, OH: Anderson.

English, K. (1993) Self-reported crime rates of women prisoners. *Journal of Quantitative Criminology*, 9, 357–82.

Faith, K. (1993) *Unruly Women: The Politics of Confinement & Resistance*. Vancouver: Press Gang Publishers.

Federal Bureau of Investigation (1980) *Crime in the United States 1979*. Washington, DC: Government Printing Office.

Federal Bureau of Investigation (2000) *Crime in the United States 1999 Uniform Crime Reports*. Washington, DC: US Department of Justice.

Finkelhor, D., and Baron, L. (1986) Risk factors for child sexual abuse. *Journal of Interpersonal Violence*, 1, 43–71.

Ford, R. (1998) The razor's edge. *Boston Globe Magazine*, May 24, 13, 22–8.

Heimer, K. (2000) Changes in the gender gap in crime and women's economic marginalization. In *Criminal Justice 2000: Vol. 1, The Nature of Crime: Continuity and Change*. Washington, DC: National Institute of Justice, 428–83.

Howe, A. (1994) *Punish and Critique: Towards a Feminist Analysis of Penality*. London: Routledge.

Huizinga, D. (1997) *Over-time changes in delinquency and drug-use: The 1970's to the 1990's*. University of Colorado: Research Brief.

Huling, T. (1991) Breaking the silence. Correctional Association of New York, March 4, mimeo.

Leslie, C., Biddle, N., Rosenberg, D., and Wayne, J. (1993) Girls will be girls. *Newsweek*, August 2, 44.

Males, M., and Shorter, A. (2001) *San Francisco Girls: Acting Better, Treated Worse*. San Francisco: Center for Juvenile and Criminal Justice.

Mauer, M. (1999) *Drug Policy and the Criminal Justice System*. Washington, DC: The Sentencing Project.

Mauer, M., and Chesney-Lind, M. (eds.). (2001) *Collateral Consequences: The Social Impact of Mass Incarceration*. New York: The New Press.

Mayer, J. (1994) Girls in the Maryland juvenile justice system: Findings of the female population taskforce. Presentation to the Gender Specific Services Training. Minneapolis, MN, July.

Office of Juvenile Justice and Delinquency Prevention (1998) What About Girls? Females in the Juvenile Justice System (flyer). Washington, DC: Department of Justice.

Office of Juvenile Justice and Delinquency Prevention (2001) *OJJDP Research 2000*. Washington, DC: US Department of Justice.

Police Services Division (1998) *BC Crime Trends: Youth Crime*. Victoria, BC: Ministry of the Attorney General, November, Issue No. 2.

Porter, G. (2000) *Detention in Delinquency Cases, 1988–1997*. OJJDP Fact Sheet #17. Washington, DC: US Department of Justice.

Robinson, R. (1990) Violations of girlhood: A qualitative study of female delinquents and children in need of services in Massachusetts. Unpublished doctoral dissertation, Brandeis University.

Roiphe, K. (1993) *The Morning After: Sex, Fear and Feminism on Campus*. Boston: Little, Brown.

Snell, T. L., and Morton, D. C. (1994) *Women in Prison*. Washington, DC: Bureau of Justice Statistics, Special Report.

Stern, V. (2001) The international impact of US policies. In M. Mauer and M. Chesney-Lind (eds.), *Collateral Consequences: The Social Impact of Mass Incarceration*. New York: The New Press.

Wolf, N. (1993) *Fire with Fire*. New York: Random House.

14

Managing "Men's Violence" in the Criminological Arena

Adrian Howe

Introduction

When men's violence against women and children is made an object of analysis – say, the focus of scholarly attention or the focus of an undergraduate criminology module – all hell breaks loose. Even calling men's violence "men's violence," thereby pushing home responsibility for that violence to men, can provoke uproar. It has even led to some sections of the academy in the United States, and now in the United Kingdom, to argue that, contrary to feminist claims, women are equally if not more violent than men and that there is a "sexual symmetry in marital violence" (Dobash et al. 1992). One thing's for sure – naming men as the main perpetrators of most forms of violence, especially violence against women and children, is still not culturally permitted in non-feminist forums. Saying, without qualification, that men have responsibility for most forms of serious violence in Western jurisdictions is tantamount to declaring war on the civilized discourses of erasure and denial in which criminology and related disciplines couch the question of men's pervasive violence against women and children. At least, that's my experience, but where I come from, the declaration of an experiential basis for an assertion is the beginning, not the end, of a conversation about men's violence.

For over ten years – now there's a bid for experientially based credibility – I have taught in the field of sexed violence. In these modules "experience," along with every other conceivably relevant concept, including "men," "women," "violence," "crime," "abuse," "sex," and, of course, "sexual violence," are relentlessly problematized. As for the discipline of criminology and its management of the "rediscovery" of men's pervasive "domestic" violence, that is subjected to a scathing critique. Actually, very little effort is required to expose criminology as inherently incapable of providing insights into any sexed question, especially the question of sexed violence. In no time at all, students come to see how positivistic criminology,

whether in its psychological or sociological manifestations, operates as an elaborate set of apologies for various forms of men's violence. Nor does it take long to see
that most varieties of "new" or critical criminology also fail to meet feminist
challenges on the man question. The new criminologies might purport to make
an epistemological and political break with positivistic paradigms. Yet when faced
with the issue of pervasive men's violence, they soon retreat into victim-blaming
etiologies and antediluvian conceptualizations of "gender" reminiscent of the old-
order criminology they claim to have supplanted. Of course, pointing all this out
can get you into trouble with the criminological industry, even, or perhaps especially, with those sections claiming to be "critical." Getting into trouble acts as a
deterrent to subversive speech for some folk. For others, it is a provocation, a red
rag to a bullish determination to give witness to a pervasive and devastating social
problem – men's violence against women and children.

This essay explores some of the key management strategies deployed by
criminological apologists for men's violence to counter insistent feminist naming
practices. It is concerned, more precisely, with managerial discursive strategies,
and not with the non-discursive finalities of institutional silencing regimes. For
when all else fails, governing academic bodies can simply refuse to fund research
on men's violence or abolish it as a teaching area. I have experienced that too.
Within weeks of my resignation from an Australian university in 2001, my
undergraduate criminology module, "Sex, Violence and Crime" (SVC), was
withdrawn from the syllabus at what was once an internationally renowned
school of social-legal studies. From a managerial perspective, the coupling
of "sex and "violence" with "crime" had spelt trouble from the beginning. It
signaled feminism. It oozed dissent. It was read, accurately, as code for an
avowedly counter-hegemonic reading of criminological accounts of criminal
violence. Ultimately, though, I find such brute force, manifest here as a gleeful
abolitionist coup, less interesting than the ongoing discursive struggles between
masculinist, or overtly antifeminist, managerial perspectives and still emergent
feminist modes of teaching and research.[1] Accordingly, this essay explores the
discursive responses of criminological apologists for men's violence to feminist
naming of men as the perpetrators of violence. These responses include the
tactics of denial, equivocation, and, crucially, victim-blaming, deployed in
the criminological arena whenever "men's violence" is on the agenda.

FEIGNING DEFENSIVENESS, HONING THE TARGET

In view of the well-documented fact that being called "anti-male" is a common
fate for any woman – no matter how happily hegemonized into heterosexuality
she might be – who refers to men's violence as "men's violence," it is well to
begin with assurances that there is no anti-male agenda here. On the contrary,
the following critique applies to any apologist for men's violence, whatever their
sexed identity. After all, the worried self-identified feminist woman beset by
concerned hesitancy around a "sensitive" male colleague might resort to an
apologist strategy as quickly as the defensive old-school male criminologist,
when confronted by one of those irascible feminist sisters hell-bent on calling
men's violence "men's violence." Witness the senior woman academic, one well

published in feminist criminology, rushing to defend a junior male colleague and close off discussion when a feminist critique is on foot in a seminar on "gender issues" in criminology. Witness the feminist lawyer dismissing out of hand a close feminist reading of the provocation defense as a profoundly sexed excuse for men who murder women. Feminist legal activists can be as quick as the most masculinist criminal lawyer to condemn feminist argument against provocation as a reactionary attack on defendants' rights (Howe 2002). Finally, witness the feminist academic who believes that modules focusing on men's violence against women and children are too fraught, too "emotional." Clearly, they would be for her. Clearly, some feminist women have a problem with feminist women who talk too openly about men's violence.

In view of these sensitivities, it might pay to at least feign defensiveness when raising the question of men's violence. So readers, be assured, this essay is not, heaven forbid, "anti-men." The target – and target there is, I'm sorry to say – is the array of apologies for men's violence, whoever speaks them, in the criminological arena. After all, what matter who's apologizing; really, what matter who's apologizing?[2] What matters is how men's violence is "put into discourse" (Foucault 1979: 11), as Foucault might have put it if he had ever turned his mind to the place of men in criminological inquiry.

Backs Against the Walls, Boys – Un-naming Men's Violence

Since the 1970s, feminist researchers have amassed a great deal of evidence relating to men's pervasive violence against women and children in all Western societies. The question here is how this evidence has impacted on criminology. Given the discipline's ostensible interest in addressing crime in all its manifestations, the response of most unreconstructed masculinist and ostensibly reconstructed feminist-touting male criminologists to the voluminous texts testifying to men's routine violence, has been, on the whole, tortuous at best. Indeed, the lengths that criminologists, whether of a critical or positivistic ilk, will go to un-name the pervasive problem of men's violence frequently strain credibility. At least, they would defy the belief of anyone who had not actually familiarized themselves with criminology texts, as Foucault had when he asked, in feigned or genuine puzzlement: "Have you read any criminology texts? They are staggering. And I say this out of astonishment, not aggressiveness, because I fail to comprehend how the discourse of criminology has been able to go on at this level" (1980: 47). Little has changed to make non-feminist criminology less astonishing or simply more credible when it comes to accounting for violent crime. Not that this would have bothered Foucault. He had no interest in the question of men's violence against women and children. Child sexual assault? Why, that's nothing more than one of life's "inconsequential bucolic pleasures" to the famous historian of sexuality (Foucault 1979: 31). Rape of adult women? Why, that's hardly a punishable offense in the eyes of the philosopher who waxed eloquent about subjugated knowledges of struggle and conflict; about the impact of power at the "local" level, say, in the family; and who, in his final work, focused on the care of the self – the masculinist self to the last. No wonder Foucault could afford to be merely "astonished" by criminology. Only those outraged by men's violent criminal acts care enough to condemn the discipline's staggeringly inadequate and defensive response to the unassailable evidence unearthed by feminist activists and researchers about intolerable levels of men's sexual and homicidal violence.

As examples of criminology's failure to come to grips with the sheer scale of men's violence against women abound, this critique is confined to some examples from my SVC undergraduate teaching materials. These texts, taken at random from criminology journal textbooks, now have the status of classics in the genre of erasing men's violence. The name of the game is to spot the "discursive maneuvers," a method adapted from Hilary Allen's brilliant analysis, now canonical in SVC, of how the discursive maneuvers deployed in professional reports on women charged with serious offenses work to erase their guilt, responsibility, and dangerousness, thereby "rendering them harmless." As Allen observes, these kinds of discursive strategies are "absent or untypical in cases involving males" (Allen 1987: 82). But different forms of discursive erasure work for men, none more blatantly than the victim-blaming narratives routinely invoked in criminal courts and the media to excuse men who kill "provocative" women.[3] Criminological texts, too, are littered with discursive strategies that are most effective in erasing men's responsibility for their own violence. Foremost among them are the "strategies of recuperation" which channel resistant voices into "nonthreatening outlets," notably by labeling feminist speech about men's violence as "extreme" (Alcoff and Gray 1993: 268). Spotting these discursive strategies is good sport for SVC students. After the hard work of grappling with Foucauldian discourse analysis as well as with the Master's own frailties in the field of sexed crime, they are up for the challenge of rereading criminology in what is – for all but those most deeply hegemonized into psychologically based criminology – a refreshing, new, post-positivist light.

We begin with "Violence: Criminal psychopaths and their victims" (Williamson et al. 1987), an analysis of the police reports on 101 incarcerated men in Canada. The men are divided into two groups, comprising 55 "psychopaths (Group P)" and 46 "nonpsychopaths (Group NP)," selected on the basis of a 22-item psychopathy checklist. The study supports the authors' hypothesis that "psychopaths seldom commit violent crimes colored by intense emotional arousal, and their victims are likely to be strangers." Of more interest, however, are the findings on the Group NP men. As predicted by the analysts, most of the murders they committed occurred "during a domestic dispute or during a period of extreme arousal" (Williamson et al. 1987: 454). Moreover, whereas the violence of the Group P men was "callous and cold-blooded" and committed against male strangers, the Group NP men had "understandable motives" for violence and knew their victims, most of whom were women. The difference is explained by the fact that Group P men, being nomadic and without long-term attachments, were "less likely to *find themselves* in violent domestic disputes, most of which involved females." While the authors feel that this makes "theoretical sense" (ibid., 460–1, my emphasis), a critical reading of the study's discursive maneuvers reveals just how problematic it all is. Translated into plain English, the ordinary Joes, or Non-Ps, bashed their women partners and some killed them. But they were understandably angry – they lived with a woman.

Finding themselves in violent situations with women and children seems to be a rather common experience for family men. While researching their response to the Cleveland child abuse scandal in the late 1980s, MacLeod and Saraga discovered a case study in a book by a pioneer of the use of therapy with "abusive" families. They quote it verbatim: "Brian...when playing hide and seek with his daughter's friend of four years of age...*found himself* sexually abusing her, and during the act was convinced the little girl was encouraging him, unlike his wife" (1988: 18; emphasis in the original). McLeod and Saraga draw the obvious parallel: "I found myself robbing a bank, and during the act was convinced that the bank teller was encouraging me." Bank tellers do not encourage violence, but women and children do, and they are so powerful and manipulative that they leave men without the ability to stop themselves. They continue:

> There is, we are aware, quite a long history to this way of talking about male sexuality – as driven and uncontrollable. It is surely not too much to ask that people theorizing about sexual violence – above all against children – should begin to examine their assumptions about male sexuality, and respond to the research that is available. (1988: 18)

Unfortunately, it has been too much to ask. Positivists have not learnt to examine their assumptions about sexed questions; they still respond defensively to research on men's violence, and they still talk about men's sexual violence and other forms of violence in ways that deny men agency. Not that they consciously try to conceal the reality of men's violence. There is no need to invoke a conspiracy of silence or denial on the part of non-feminist commentators who shift the focus from male perpetrators to their victims (Howe 1998: 30). What matters are the effects, intended or not, of editing out men and masculinity from analyses of sexed violence.

Next up is O'Brien's (1988) exploration of the so-called "intersexual nature of violent crimes" in the United States. The avowed aim is to "determine the extent to which violent crimes occur within or between the sexes." Two hypotheses are tested. One is that "men commit violent crimes against other men more often than (statistically) expected." That is, male offending is an "in-group phenomenon." The second hypothesis is that "F-M" violence (women's violent acts against men) occurs relatively more often than "M-F incidents" (men's violent acts against women). O'Brien is hell-bent on finding that women's violence is "less of an in-group phenomenon than male offending" (1988: 154), or, in plain English, that women are more violent toward men than men are toward women. But it's a very convoluted path he follows. Most notably, he has to put to one side, or "control," what even he acknowledges to be "the greater propensity of men to commit violent crime" (1988: 154). Using his preferred "Model 2," which assumes that there is "no propensity for men or women to be the victims of criminal homicides" (1988: 126), he finds support for his bizarre hypotheses. This is somewhat surprising, given that men committed 85.49 percent of the 11,410 homicides in his sample. As for aggravated assault, 88.85 percent of the 5,119 offenders were men. No wonder O'Brien needs to control men's greater propensity to commit violence.

Lest the reader assume that this is yet another lumpen positivist,[4] merrily testing hypotheses and applying baseline models in a delirious state of agenda-free empiricism, Brien's conclusions bear close examination. What he finds most "interesting" is that "females" use violence in simple assaults against men "less often than expected," but for aggravated assaults they resort to violence against men "more often than expected" – that is, of course, if you control for men's greater propensity to commit violence. So for women, "intersexual violence is associated with more serious forms of violence, but for men, intersexual violence is associated with less serious forms of violence." What is the point of all this? It soon becomes clear. Men, he speculates, "threaten women into compliance with minor assaults," and as long as women "comply," men "may not need to escalate violence." Women, on the other hand, will not be able to threaten men with "minor" violence and so may be forced to end the "cycle of violence" by resorting to serious violence. A lone footnote gives the game away – O'Brien is responding to feminist research on battered women who kill their husbands. His concern, however, is not with exposing, let alone condemning, the violence endured by women forced to kill in self-defense. It is to confirm his hypotheses that serious violence is mostly an "out-group phenomenon" for women and mostly "in-group" for men. That men may use "minor threats to gain compliance from women" is as unproblematic for this researcher as the "routine activities of males and females" that structure the rates of intersexual violence in Western societies. After all, men spend more time away from home, interacting with same-sex rather than opposite-sex individuals, while "women spend more time at home, where there is less segregation on the basis of sex, and where a large proportion of violent incidents occur" (1988: 165–7).

Thus does the criminologist un-name the pervasive social problem of men's violence against women. Transform the lived experience of women who are battered by and too frequently die at the hands of male partners into aggregate data and then translate the data into a location – "home," a place where violent "incidents" occur. Women who do not "comply" with and "submit" to men's demands spark off a "cycle of violence" – a perennial favorite with positivists – and end up receiving "minor" violence. Women then end the cycle by resorting to "serious" violence (1988: 166–7), and men's responsibility for their own violence against women disappears down a deep tunnel of aggregate data, base models, and reality-defying verbal gymnastics.

Paradoxically, O'Brien ends up desexing and degendering the very "intersexual" violence he set out to explore. As we shall see, desexing sexed violence is an occupational hazard for criminologists who never stray across disciplinary boundaries to discover "new" theorizations of sexed subjectivities and sexed violence developed over the last twenty years. This is so even when criminologists are asked to research violence at the national level, as they were in Australia in the late 1980s. The brief given to the National Committee on Violence, headed by the Director of the Institute of Criminology, was to examine "the contemporary state of violent crime in Australia," including "related social, economic, psychological and environmental aspects" and "gender issues in violence" (National Committee on Violence 1990: xxi). Replete as they are with the full panoply of tried-and-true discursive tactics for decentering men from the analysis of violence, the Committee's discussion papers and final report are particular favorites with SVC students who, by the time we get to them, are well-versed in detecting positivist ways of putting men's violence into discourse. In its "Domestic Violence" discussion paper, men are named as the "main perpetrators" on the basis of evidence indicating that 95 percent of calls to police in one state related to men's assaults on women partners. Yet just one sentence later, the paper describes "highly controversial" findings from a US national study of "family violence," indicating that "within the family women are about as violent as men" (Mugford 1989: 2, citing Straus and Gelles 1986). Very soon we are in the throes of the "cycle of violence" – the one based on the man's experience of frustration exploding in violence. In the "Violence Against Children" discussion paper men appear just once, but it is a telling appearance: "A survey of Australian tertiary students found that 1 in 4 girls and 1 in 11 boys had been the victim of child sexual abuse by *a male* more than five years their senior" (Dwyer 1989: 2; my emphasis).

Men then drop out of the picture. Sexual assault almost does too, except for a brief paragraph in the section on causes – always a happy hunting ground for reliable agent-deleting discursive meanderings. Here we learn that "abusive parents" can have trouble "controlling their impulses" and that, moreover, physical abuse is an "interactive phenomenon and there is evidence to suggest that there are factors in the child as well as the parent which may result in the abusive behavior." One key "factor in the child" is being born prematurely. The "higher than expected number of premature babies among the victims of abuse" means that there is a very early onset indeed of factors in the child causing parents to abuse them. These include neurological problems, failure to bond with the mother, and disabilities. In the case of sexual abuse, however, "completely different factors seem to be operating." Perpetrators have been "studied very little" – (the study of Australian tertiary students is already forgotten) – but we do know that many of them are … men? No, "themselves victims of child sexual abuse." So much for the diagram in the report indicating, in graphic tabular fashion, that in one study of child maltreatment in New South Wales, the number of cases of child sexual assault soar above cases involving neglect and physical and emotional abuse (Dwyer 1989: 3–5).

If pinning the responsibility on premature babies and small children for their own abuse seems rather extreme even by positivistic standards, what are we to make of the section on prevention of child abuse where young, single, working-class mothers bear the brunt of the responsibility for child abuse in Australia? Here "predictive factors," which are most marked in "abusive families," move further back, from the child to the womb. In criminological accounts of male violence, the "cycle of violence" usually manages to make its way back from the man's moment of explosive fury, be it an assault on a wife or a serial murder, to the man's mother – always already a bad mother. Here, however, the downward etiological spiral path ends up locating the problem in the mother's childhood and her "experiences" during pregnancy and the perinatal period (Dwyer 1989: 6). While these experiences are unspecified in the discussion paper, they are described in the Committee's final report, *Violence: Directions For Australia* (1990), as "peri-natal difficulties" which can be "naturally occurring or caused by illness, injury or lifestyle." The resulting damage can be "amplified by unfavorable family circumstances" (National Committee on Violence 1990: 64).

In all this, there is not a word on the missing link, dads, now known to be a more common cause of harm to their pregnant wives than medical conditions screened for in pregnancy.[5] Focusing on men goes against the natural bent of the positivist criminologist who, when explaining the root cause of all forms of violence, always looks to the mother. So, setting up perinatal screening (read: more surveillance) for young working-class mums in public hospitals (1990: 130) is a perfect solution to the problem of child abuse.

What is happening here? The Committee began its final report by stating that violent offenders in Australia are "overwhelmingly male" and, moreover, that "Victims of violence most commonly fall into two broad categories: men who become engaged in altercations with other men; and women and children who suffer at the hands of men with whom they have been living" (1990: 4). As the report proceeds, however, men disappear behind an increasingly dense agent-deleting veil. For example, foremost amongst the "considerable number of violent crimes" which never come to police attention are "the majority of sexual assaults and incidents of domestic violence." Translation: men's violence at home against "their" women and children is greatly underestimated in official surveys. By the time we get to the chapter "Explaining Violence," the report is in disarray. Important factors are listed in "descending order of relative importance" (1990: 65), but they soon get out of order. Biological factors, relegated to fifth place behind child development and the influence of the family, cultural factors, personality factors, and substance abuse, catapult to first place in the discussion section. So-called biological factors have always displayed a gravity-defying prowess in positivistic accounts of crime. The brief section on "Sex" shows why. It begins by declaring that in Australia, "men are at least ten times more likely than women to be charged with violent offences." While that might seem to be a biological factor to be reckoned with, psychology texts are quickly hauled out to dilute the harshness of the statistic. It takes only three paragraphs for the spotlight to shift from men, the ten-times-more-likely sex, to a study of 11- and 12-year-old children which purports to show that the girls were more aggressive than the boys. The girls, it is surmised, were "practising for the social life of adults" (1990: 67) – code, presumably, for learning to become provocative adult women. Hey presto, unpalatable criminal statistics highlighting men's violence miraculously disappear in a whiff of positivist smoke, leaving prepubescent girls holding the etiological candle.

If young girls can be made to carry the weight of criminological concern about the asymmetry of criminal assault statistics, all bets are off for who or what will bear the brunt of the socio-psychological explanations of violence in Australia – "abusive homes," the cycle of violence turning abusive children into abusive parents, single-parent families and, of course, bad mothers. According to one study cited in the report, "[A]ggression among young boys resulted from a combination of the boys' temperament and the extent to which his mother was hostile, rejecting, cold or indifferent towards him" (1990: 77). There are no case studies of hostile dads. As for "gender," it receives a brief mention at the very end of the explanatory section. This is somewhat surprising given that "gender issues in violence" was ranked third in the Committee's terms of reference, thereby giving the impression that they would be central to the analysis. It is also surprising to find cultural factors bringing up the rear, given that they were listed

as the second most important cluster of factors in explaining violence. We might
ask, too, why "gender" is listed as a "cultural factor," separate from "sex," listed
as a "biological factor," after a decade of Australian feminist research dismantling the sex/gender distinction (Howe 1998: 4–5). For positivists, gender signifies
women (or more usually, "females"), which in turn signifies feminist. Accordingly, some of the feminist literature is reviewed in the section on gender, but not
enough to prevent the Committee from asserting, in ostensibly gender-neutral
language, that "Attitudes of gender inequality are deeply embedded in Australian culture, and both rape and domestic assault can be viewed as violent
expressions of this cultural norm" (1990: 62). Also, it hastens to assure us that
"it would be unwise to suggest that a single cause – patriarchy – is the reason for
all violence" (1990: 102). Translation: in a misogynist society like Australia,
men's violence against women is so widespread as to be normative. Or: men's
violence against women is culturally sanctioned and thus routine in Australia as
in other Western jurisdictions (but we wish feminists would shut up about it).

Variations of these discursive strategies still saturate criminology journals and
textbooks today. In the standard textbook, "masculinities" but not "men" may
appear in the index, but they are not discussed in the chapter on violent crime.
Expect men's violence against women and children to be reclassified as "spouse
or partner abuse," a safely un-gendered sub-category of similarly un-gendered
"violent offenses." Unsurprisingly, spouse or partner abuse can take up less than
two pages, and men do not even need to be mentioned when you have "controlled studies" revealing that a majority of "abusers" have "experienced violence in childhood or witnessed violence between their parents" (Jones 1998:
377). This is what passes as objective analysis in mainstream criminology.
Putting men's violence into discourse in this way, deleting the agents who are
the bearers of masculinity and rendering spouses and partners genderless,
remains *de rigueur* for non-feminist criminologists tackling the vexed problem
of men's violence against women and children.

FIGHT BACK – WOMEN (AND FEMINISTS) ARE WORSE

Feminist scholars have been alert to these kinds of discursive strategies for some
time. Consider, for example, what Mary McIntosh had to say about the formulation of the question of child sexual abuse in the public domain in Britain in the
late 1980s:

> Perhaps its most remarkable feature is the absence of the perpetrator as a recogniz-
> able character in the drama. There are "parents", ungendered and acting in cou-
> ples, readily endowed with all the rosy lineaments of the myth of modern classless
> parenthood, and there are "children", also often ungendered, and of indeterminate
> age. (1988: 6)

For MacLeod and Saraga, the failure to discuss the gender of the perpetrators of
child abuse "amounts to a deceit" (1988: 18). They provide, by way of example,
the notion of a "cycle of abuse" that is transmitted from one generation to the
next. In this "theory," the abusers are parents rather than adult men, and usually

problem or "deviant" families. As we have seen, the notion of a "cycle of abuse" or "cycle of violence" is also used to describe the man's experience in an abusive relationship. His anger builds up until he explodes violently. Then he is remorseful and a quiet phase ensues until the "cycle" starts again. In both versions of "the cycle of violence" the abuser is a victim of forces beyond his control and he usually ends up disappearing altogether behind a cloud of obfuscation. In some criminological quarters, however, he has reemerged, repackaged as a victim, not simply of the genderless cycles of violence ruling his life, but of women's violence.

While the women-are-more-violent-than-men school of thought is predominantly a North American development, its foundation texts, Straus and Gelles's (1986) family conflict studies suggesting that women's assaults on their husbands constitute a social problem comparable in nature and magnitude to that of men's assaults on their women partners, have been cited favorably elsewhere. Recently, for example, their findings have been taken up and developed by a small but vocal publicity-seeking group of researchers in the United Kingdom.[6] SVC students delight in dismantling the array of mind-numbing ellipses required to "emphasize causal influences that are common to both men and women" in a "meta-analysis" of "partner violence" (Archer 2000a: 651). Unpacking the painstaking positivistic distinction made between aggressive actions and their consequences in order to equalize the number of aggressive acts committed by men and women against each other (Archer 2000b: 697–8) is good, clean fun for undergraduates. Less amusing is the fact that it is women's and not men's violence that is the new hot item on the criminological agenda in Britain today. Postgraduate programs in some leading universities are encouraging doctoral students to write dissertations "proving" that the feminists were wrong to focus on men's violence because women are as violent, if not more violent than men. In the near future, expect to see the publication of British dissertations taking a similar tack to a North American study of "gay and bisexual male domestic violence victimization" presented as a "challenge to contemporary feminist domestic violence theory." With its "doctrine of male victimizers and female victims," this theory, it is argued, has "contributed to the invisibility of gay and lesbian domestic violence because it precludes the possibility of such violence occurring" (Letellier 1994: 95).

Among other problems, well documented elsewhere (e.g., Dobash et al. 1992), this kind of feminist-bashing analysis makes for bad history. Its advocates would do well to brush up on genealogies of the discovery and rediscovery, by first- and second-wave feminist activists in the United States, United Kingdom, and Australia, of widespread domestic and sexual violence committed by men in the private realm (see, e.g., Genovese 2000). Blaming feminism for obscuring violence within queer relationships is like blaming feminist campaigns against men's sexual assaults of girls for obscuring men's sexual assaults of boys. Let the historical record stand: throughout the late nineteenth and twentieth centuries, it has been feminist campaigners who have exposed men's violence in the home against women and children of both sexes. By bringing those issues into the public arena in the face of immense obstacles, notably male-dominated legislatures and the legal profession (Smart 1999), feminist activists have given a voice and a discourse – "survivor discourse" (Alcoff and Gray 1993) – to *all* victims of sexed violence.

I have neither the space nor the will to engage with the women-are-more-violent-than-men thesis mounted on behalf of the "invisible legion of assaulted husbands" (Dobash et al. 1992: 74). Suffice it to say that it beggars belief that researchers could pursue this line of research in the face of national surveys, medical records of pregnant women, and the accounts of so many survivors, men as well as women, testifying to the massive and incalculable physical and psychic harm inflicted by violent men on women and children. It is incredible too that, in 2000, family violence researchers could rely on such a spectacular array of naive binaries – science/politics; empirically-based or evidence-based analysis/"politically-motivated analysis" (Archer 2000b: 697) – and there are no prizes for guessing on which side of these great divides feminist research falls. The recent British amplification of the "family conflict" strain of thought is also remarkable for its well-drilled ignorance of theoretical developments in feminism since the 1980s. How could a researcher maintain, again in 2000, that there are "two conflicting viewpoints about partner violence" – the "family conflict" view and "*the* feminist view" – and that the latter "regards partner violence as a consequence of patriarchy" (Archer 2000a: 651; my emphasis)? Thanking research assistants for their literature search doesn't quite cut it. Had the researcher read the literature himself, he might have found that there is more than one feminist view on men's violence and that feminist invocations of "patriarchy" are hard to find after 1980. Had he been informed about any minority or Third World feminist critique of universalizing and essentializing white feminisms, he might have paused before concluding that in modern secular liberal Western nations where women are "emancipated," there will be "a greater impact of the norm of disapproval of men's physical aggression toward women and a lesser impact of patriarchal values" (Archer 2000a: 668). Women and children who are subjected to men's violence in Western societies have yet to register this "norm of disapproval" – they are too busy surviving the far greater impact of men's physical assaults, sexual assaults, and homicidal fury, never mind supposedly declining "patriarchal values."

If psychology-based victimology studies arguably lie outside of the parameters of criminology proper, how about a chapter on violent crime in a criminology handbook? It doesn't take long for "violent crime" to meet some definitional hitches here. Should rape and indecent assault be included as violent crime when criminal statistics classify them as "sexual" rather than "violent" crimes? Focusing on "the risks of non-domestic 'sexual' and 'non-sexual' (in form) violence" (Levi 1997: 843) does not really assist. Levi seems to be oblivious to Deborah Cameron's damning account of how "sex," and especially the "sex" of "sex crime," spells trouble for lumpen positivists, be they criminal investigators or criminologists (1994: 152). Also, why would anyone wanting to understand violent crime want to emphasize "non-domestic" violence? The idea that men are more likely than women to be victimized by partner violence gets short shrift. But what would drive a criminologist aware that the British Crime Survey does not measure domestic violence accurately to want to find that the existing data suggests that "*in England and Wales as a whole, actual* violence in the home is *not* a common experience for a large *proportion* of women" (Levi 1997: 852; his emphasis)? And why place almost the entire sentence in italics? The specters of "female on male violence" and "feminists" rear their heads suspiciously throughout the chapter, but it is only at the end that the antifeminist animus of this non-feminist analysis of violent crime becomes clear. By focusing on risks and fear of crime, feminist researchers and campaigners have led criminology astray. First, the discipline has lost sight of the causes of violence. Second, and connected, the feminist-forced etiological focus on masculinities has led not only to an over-emphasis on men, but a failure to account for "the non-violence of all males most of the time," and "the non-violence of the majority of adult working-class and middle-class males all of the time" (Levi 1997: 880–1).

The sisters are powerful indeed. Without avid gatekeepers like Levi, they might have derailed the criminological enterprise altogether, with their irritating practice of naming the perpetrators of most forms of violence and making "nonviolent" working-class and middle-class men feel bad in the process. The question is: who will come forward to defend upper-class men from feminist allegations of widespread men's violence against women and children? The advertisement could be brief: "Apologist required, apply within."

"Critical" Criminologies – "Advancing" the Feminist Cause?

Ingrained masculinist fears of feminist criticism of men and uninformed beliefs about *the* feminist agenda of research on men's violence die hard in the crimino-logical arena. They can even be found in the work of those who would claim the mantle of "critical criminologist." I have discussed elsewhere the peculiar brand of critical criminology which parades under the banner of "postmodern," noting its many unpostmodern and decidedly uncritical moments (Howe 2000b). Most notably, lionizing Jack Katz's *Seductions of Crime* as a dazzling new postmodern text shows just how far self-defined critical criminologists will go to celebrate men's violence. Getting caught up in the "wonderful attractions within the lived experience of criminality," losing yourself to "the seductive appeal" of violence, and grasping the "magic in the criminal's sensuality" can so deplete your re-sources that you overlook the dead bodies of the victims (Katz 1988: 3–4). Tellingly, sex killings and sexual assaults are omitted from Katz's list of "tran-scendent" criminal projects, perhaps to prevent his claim about the universality of the sensual magic of violent crime collapsing in the face of the massive numerical imbalance of male and female sex killers and rapists. And look how Katz's followers, would-be critical criminologists to a man, react to feminist criticism. Responding to a feminist critique of their theory of edgework or voluntary risk-taking which highlights how it ignores questions of class, race, ethnicity, and gender, the postmodern criminologists deploy what might be called an incorporatist strategy. The excluded groups are simply brought into the masculinist fold. Girls, too, can have fun. African American sex workers can enjoy "edgework" just like excitable transcendent boys jumping out of planes. After all the Katzian account of emotionality and fun is a "general account for all people," if we can just leave aside the small matters of "double standards and the extra jeopardy women face in sexual relations" (read: sexed violence). Happily, too, "gender roles" are becoming androgynous under the impact of consumerism (O'Malley and Mugford 1994: 206–8).

If the unreflective reference to "gender roles" betrays a spectacular ignorance of three decades of feminist work on sex/gender questions, what are we to make of the casual dismissal of men's violence against women as "extra jeopardy" by these "critical" non-feminist criminologists? Add yet another discursive erasure of men's violence to the list and note that the incorporatist strategy fails for want of an informed critical and ethical sensibility? Elsewhere, critical criminologists are trying out different gatekeeping strategies against feminist intruders. A favorite ploy is to dismiss feminist work on men's violence and masculinities as simplistic, theoretically naive and not as "advanced" as it should be. The least advanced, apparently, are the early radical feminists who are berated for still dominating "the rape debate" with their outdated notions of "male power" (Jefferson 1997: 456). To make this claim it is necessary to drop into a footnote an enormously influential poststructuralist feminist text which challenged the terms of that debate over a decade ago (Smart 1989). Good to see that the masculinist footnote fetish, always a handy device whenever complex theoretical feminist work threatens masculine sensitivities, is still alive and well.

With the radical feminists – the folk who put men's violence on the criminological and political agenda all those years ago – relegated to the lowest ranks on the hierarchy of scholarly achievement in the field and the poststructuralist feminists tossed into a footnote, the path is opened to celebrate the most "advanced," those who frame the problem of men's violence and masculinity in "socially literate" psychoanalytic terms. This entails learning to appreciate the ambivalent feelings, the anxieties and defensive projections of, say, the rapist or the serial killer. The way forward is to focus on the social and psychic dimensions of criminal violence. For example, case studies in masculinity should look at the individual violent offender, checking for "an emotionally impoverished and rejecting background," and understanding his attempts to "build up a more powerful sense of masculine identity" (Jefferson 1997: 547). These will show the radical feminists were wrong – men's violence is not about male power. The picture of the rapist or pedophile that emerges is of a weak and inadequate man. Moreover, girls can be murderously violent too, which warns against "pinning everything on gender difference" (1997: 548), as feminists tend to do.

Focusing on the individual violent man, however, does have its drawbacks. Most obviously, it sounds like old-fashioned positivism, listing background factors such as childhood experiences and parenting (read: mum), although, as this is a critical, "socially literate" account, the killer's mother is transformed into a long-suffering working-class mum. We would not want to overemphasize gender, but why is it that mum still ends up representing the killer's despised "feminine" part which must be annihilated? Why could not the killer have annihilated his brutish masculine part (represented by his violent dad) and given the girls (the past and projected despised feminine) a break? Do the social and psychic dimensions of deep-seated misogyny in Western culture need more emphasis? Would this critical criminologist have benefited from reading some poststructuralist feminist work undertaken outside of the criminological arena? After all, some of it is quite advanced, especially that showing how representations of violence are themselves violent and, moreover, "inseparable from the notion of gender" because their meaning is dependent on the gender of the violated object depicted. It follows that violence is always already "engendered in representation" (de Lauretis 1987: 32–3). Then there is Elisabeth Bronfen's searching reading of men's paintings of dead women as a form of violence that "stages the absence of violence" and permits "a blindness toward the real" (1992: 50). If this is all going too far astray from the question of masculinity and violence, there's Henrietta Moore's (1994) complex analysis of the problem of explaining violence in the social sciences. Moore manages to theorize the engendered subjectivities of thwarted violent men without losing sight of the violence they inflict on women. She, too, seems to be advancing our understanding of men and masculinity remarkably well – for a girl.

MANAGING MEN'S VIOLENCE IN PUBLIC POLICY

The launch of the Blair government's domestic violence awareness campaign in January 1999 has given a new urgency to the politics of naming and un-naming men's violence in Britain. The government would have us believe that "tackling domestic violence on every front" (Home Office 2001a: 1) is now a policy priority. With the Home Office assuming the policy lead on the new strategy on violence against women, the question of men's violence, while not named as such in the flurry of policy documents or in the descriptions of local projects funded under the Violence Against Women Initiative, is now firmly on the public agenda. So, too, is the vexed question of "prevalence," a question inextricably associated with the equally vexed question of agency, that is, of who is doing what to whom. While noting that there are attacks by women on men and within same-sex relationships, the Home Office recognizes that heterosexual women are "more likely to experience domestic violence at some point in their lives, more likely to experience repeat victimization, more likely to be injured and to seek medical help, more likely to experience frightening threats and more likely to be frightened and upset" (2001a: 2). Men might be missing agents here, but it is recognized that women are twice as likely as men to be injured by a partner and much more likely to be killed by a male partner. Well-publicized homicide statistics indicate that nearly half of women homicide victims are killed by male partners in the United Kingdom, whereas less than 10 percent of male homicide victims are killed by their partners. So much for "symmetry" in marital violence. But statistics, as we have seen, lend themselves to discursive twists and roundabouts when it comes to measuring the impact of men's violence. Commenting on the 2001 British Crime Survey recording that domestic violence decreased significantly by 34 percent between 1999 and 2000, the Home Office advises interpretative caution, given the small size of the statistical samples and the findings of self-report surveys indicating that prevalence rates for domestic violence are about three times higher for women and ten times higher for men (Home Office 2001b: 29).

The stage is now set for more discursive battles between, on the one hand, feminist activists and scholars who have fought for so long to make men's violence against women and children a public issue and, on the other, all those non-feminist apologists who have strived so voraciously to recuperate for men all the ground lost to criticism. While non-feminists are sure to query the twice-as-likely to-be-injured-figure for women and to pounce on the ten-times-higher prevalent rate for men, feminists will continue to point out that men's violence against women is still greatly underestimated in official surveys, especially in the United Kingdom (Walby and Myhill 2001). Still, feminists are used to things going awry when campaigns against men's violence are translated into policy initiatives. Negotiating the visibility of private violence in the public forum is well understood within the movement as a management issue. Feminist strategists are highly skilled in the art of "looking after" representations of domestic violence, "*managing*" them as they get translated into government policy (Mason 2000: 83; original emphasis). To get domestic violence rhetoric recognized as a public discourse in the 1970s, Australian feminists had to accept "the good graces of a masculinist public," but it did so "*knowingly*," making do with benign terms like "domestic violence" rather than "criminal assault in the home," let alone "men's violence against women" (Genovese 2000: 124; original emphasis). British feminists should be congratulated on getting "Violence Against Women" onto the public agenda at the turn of the new millennium. Naming the main agents – as in "*Men's* Violence Against Women" – can wait a while longer. The task at hand is to combat the discursive wizardry of the apologists as they try to flee again from the overwhelming evidence of men's widespread and extraordinarily brutal violence against women in the "civilized" world. Then we who work in the criminology arena and related sites can all get on with the larger task of dealing with this massive social problem head on, without employing any discursive maneuvers whatsoever.

Notes

1   I have written elsewhere (Howe 2000a) about the new conservative attacks on feminist pedagogy in the context of the retreat from theory and a social contextual approach to law and legal studies in the Australian university.
2   Can I get away with putting yet another spin on Foucault's parody of Samuel Beckett's "what matter who's speaking; really, what matter who's speaking"? For previous incarnations see Howe 1994, 2000a.
3   See Allen's (1988) superb analysis of law's spectacular betrayal of a sex-neutral standard in the operation of the provocation defense, a betrayal favoring male defendants; see also Howe 2002.
4   "Lumpen positivist" and much more are borrowed from Deborah Cameron's blisteringly beautiful critique of "expert" accounts of serial killers (Cameron 1994).
5   See, e.g., Laurence (2001), reporting a study undertaken in the United Kingdom by the Royal College of Obstetricians that found that a third of assaults on women took place for the first time when they were pregnant.
6   Women-are-more-violent-than-men research has been reported in the Australian, British, and US press (see, e.g., Zuger 1998, Goodchild 2000).

References

Alcoff, L., and Gray, L. (1993) Survivor discourse: Transgression or recuperation? *Signs*, 18(2), 260–90.
Allen, H. (1987) Rendering them harmless: The professional portrayal of women charged with serious violent crimes. In P. Carlen and A. Worrall (eds.), *Gender, Crime and Justice*. Milton Keynes: Open University Press, 81–94.

Allen, H. (1988) One law for all reasonable persons? *International Journal of the Sociology of Law*, 16, 419–32.

Archer, J. (2000a) Sex differences in aggression between heterosexual partners: a meta-analytic review. *Psychological Bulletin*, 126(5), 651–80.

Archer, J. (2000b) Sex differences in physical aggression to partners: A reply to Frieze, O'Leary and White, Smith, Koss and Figueredo. *Psychological Bulletin*, 126(5), 697–702.

Bronfen, E. (1992) *Over Her Dead Body*. Manchester: Manchester University Press.

Cameron, D. (1994) St-i-i-ll going...the quest for Jack the Ripper. *Social Text*, 40, 147–53.

de Lauretis, T. (1987) *The Technology of Gender*. Bloomington: Indiana University Press.

Dobash, P., Dobash, R. E., Wilson, M., and Daly, M. (1992) The myth of sexual symmetry in marital violence. *Social Problems*, 39(1), 71–91.

Dwyer, K. (1989) Violence against children. *Violence Today*, 3, 1–6.

Foucault, M. (1979) *The History of Sexuality*, Vol.1. London: Allen Lane.

Foucault, M. (1980) Two lectures. In C. Gordon (ed.), *Power/Knowledge: Michel Foucault*. Brighton: Harvester Press, 78–108.

Genovese, A. (2000) The politics of naming: 70s feminisms, genealogy and "domestic violence." In R. Walker, K. Brass, and J. Byron (eds.), *Anatomies of Violence: An Interdisciplinary Investigation*. Sydney: Research Institute of Humanities and Social Sciences, 115–29.

Goodchild, S. (2000) Women are more violent, says study. *The Independent*, November 12.

Home Office (2001a) Government Policy Around Domestic Violence. Available online at http://www.homeoffice.gov.uk/cpd/cpsu/domvio198.htm

Home Office (20001b) The 2001 British Crime Survey. First Results, England and Wales. Available online at http://www.homeoffice.gov.uk.rds.bcs1.html

Howe, A. (1994) *Punish and Critique: Towards a Feminist Theory of Penality*. London: Routledge.

Howe, A. (ed.) (1998) *Sexed Crime in the News*. Sydney: Federation Press.

Howe, A. (2000a) Law out of context (or: who's afraid of sex and violence in legal education). *Alternative Law Journal*, 25(6), 274–8.

Howe, A. (2000b) Postmodern criminology and its feminist discontents. *Australian and New Zealand Journal of Criminology*, 33(2), 221–36.

Howe, A. (2002) Provoking polemic – provoked killings and the ethical paradoxes of the postmodern feminist condition. *Feminist Legal Studies*, forthcoming.

Jefferson, T. (1997) Masculinities and crimes. In M. Maguire, R. Morgan, and R. Reiner (eds.), *The Oxford Handbook of Criminology*. Oxford: Clarendon Press, 535–59.

Jones, S. (1998) *Criminology*. London, Butterworths.

Katz, J. (1988) *Seductions of Crime*. New York: Basic Books.

Laurence, J. (2001) Murder is biggest cause of death in pregnancy. *The Independent*, March 21.

Letellier, P. (1994) Gay and bisexual male domestic violence victimization: challenges to feminist theory and responses to violence. *Violence and Victims*, 9(2), 95–106.

Levi, M. (1997) Violent crime. In M. Maguire, R. Morgan, and R. Reiner (eds.), *The Oxford Handbook of Criminology*. Oxford: Clarendon Press, 841–89.

MacLeod, M., and Saraga, E. (1988) Against orthodoxy. *New Statesman and Society*, July, 15–19.

Mason, G. (2000) Managing homophobia. In R. Walker, K. Brass, and J. Byron (eds.), *Anatomies of Violence: An Interdisciplinary Investigation*. Sydney: Research Institute of Humanities and Social Sciences, 74–86.

McIntosh, M. (1988) Family secrets as public drama. *Feminist Review*, 28, 6–15.

Moore, H. (1994) The problem of explaining violence in the social sciences. In P. Harvey and P. Gow (eds.), *Sex and Violence*. New York: Routledge, 138–55.

Mugford, J. (1989) Domestic violence. *Violence Today*, 2, 1–8.

National Committee on Violence (1990) *Violence: Directions For Australia*, Canberra: Australian Institute of Criminology.

O'Brien, R. M. (1988) Exploring the intersexual nature of violent crime. *Criminology*, 26 (1), 151–70.

O'Malley, P., and Mugford, J. (1994) Crime, excitement and modernity. In G. Barak (ed.), *Varieties of Criminology*. Westport, CT: Praeger, 189–211.

Smart, C. (1989) *Feminism and the Power of Law*, London: Routledge.

Smart, C. (1999) A history of ambivalence and conflict in the discursive construction of the "child victim" of sexual abuse. *Social and Legal Studies*, 8(3), 391–409.

Straus, M., and Gelles, R. J. (1986) Societal change and change in family violence from 1975 to 1985 as revealed by two national surveys. *Journal of Marriage and the Family*, 48(3), 465–79.

Walby, S., and Myhill, A. (2001) New survey methodologies in researching violence against women. *British Journal of Criminology*, 41(3), 502–22.

Williamson, S., Hare, R. D., and Wong, S. (1987) Violence: criminal psychopaths and their victims. *Canadian Journal of Behavioral Science*, 19(4), 454–62.

Zuger, A. (1988) A fistful of hostility is found in women. *Science Times*, New York, July 28.

15

Masculinities and Crime: Rethinking the "Man Question"?

Richard Collier

Introduction

The relationship between men, masculinities, and crime has, over the past decade, assumed an increasing prominence within criminology. Indeed, it is arguably a now well-established feature of the criminological landscape; if not the "very stuff" of the discipline then at least a visible presence in both mainstream journal and criminological textbook (Carlen and Jefferson 1996; Jones 2001; Maguire et al. 1997; Walklate 1995). The issue of how the gender of men – understood as their masculinity or, more recently, masculin*ities*[1] – might connect to crime has been described as a "new direction" and "new frontier" (Maguire et al. 1997) for criminology to discover. It has been acclaimed as something without which "there will be no progress," the study of which is "vital" (Heidensohn 1995: 80–1: see also Walklate 1995: 160–84). This question of how masculinity connects to crime, criminality, and understandings of social (dis)order has not only become a pressing issue within academic criminology, however. It has also informed a range of concerns and debates bearing directly on the substance and direction of criminal justice policy and practice. For both academic criminologists, those working with male offenders in the diverse fields and contexts of criminal justice and for governments themselves in seeking to develop gender-relevant policies, the integration of a sensitivity to "the masculinity of crime" has been increasingly foregrounded within debates about criminality and criminal justice. The core assumption throughout has been that there is some analytic gain to be made for criminology by seeking to "take masculinity seriously." It is an assumption that, in this essay, I wish to question many aspects of.

The aim of what follows is threefold. I shall, first, introduce and overview some of the core themes within criminology's recent "masculinity turn" (Collier 1998). I then proceed to (re)assess the merits of two of the main sociological and social-psychological approaches to the study of masculinities and crime which have emerged within (broadly) Anglo-American criminology. That is, the "accomplishing masculinities" and "psycho-social" perspectives associated most closely, and respectively, with the North American writer James Messerschmidt (2000, 1999, 1997, 1993) and the British criminologist Tony Jefferson (1994a, b; 1996a, b; 1997a, b). Having traced this criminological shift from "structures to psyches" (Hood-Williams 2001), conclusions then seek to consider to what extent, if at all, the culturally (and criminologically) ubiquitous concept of masculinity might itself be seen as a product of a particular historical and cultural moment – and whether this association between masculinities and crime is one which can itself be questioned once a broader international and historical perspective, and rather different theoretical framework, are adopted.

THE NEW RESEARCH AGENDA OF MASCULINITIES AND CRIME

The starting point for criminology's recent engagement with masculinities and crime rests on a paradox at the heart of the discipline. The historical problem for criminology has not been that it has failed to recognize that the object of its analysis has been, largely, the relationship between men and crime. Criminologists of diverse persuasions have long-recognized sex-status, along with youth, to be one of the strongest predictors of criminal involvement. Indeed, it is perhaps something of a truism within criminology to state that the vast majority of conversations and debates about crime have historically (although certainly not exclusively) been largely about the actions of men. Rather, the target of the now well-established feminist critique of criminology which developed from around the mid-1970s (Smart 1977), and which has been taken up, at least to degrees, by recent proponents of the study of masculinities and crime, has been with *the way in which* the sex-specificity of crime is conceptualized. Criminology, it is argued, has been fundamentally flawed in (at least) two senses. First, it has failed to account in anything like an adequate manner for the nature of women's offending and, related to this, the treatment of women within criminal justice systems. And, secondly, criminology has failed to address the gender of crime; that is, it has failed to tackle the masculinity or maleness of crime, the crimes of men *as men* (that is, as gendered beings). What it might be about men, in Grosz's oft-cited words:

> not as working-class, not as migrants, not as underprivileged individuals but *as men* that induces them to commit crime? Here it is no longer women who are judged by the norms of masculinity and found to be "the problem". Now it is men and not humanity who are openly acknowledged as the objects and subjects of investigation. (quoted by Walklate 1995: 169)

Addressing the former issue – the failure to account for the crimes of women – has been the concern of a now well-established, diverse and extensive, if epistemologically and politically contested, body of feminist criminological scholarship (see, for example, Brown 1986; Cain 1990a, 1990b; Carlen 1988, 1983; Carlen and

Worrall 1987; Carrington 1993; Daly 1997, 1993; Daly and Chesney-Lind 1988; Gelsthorpe 1989; Gelsthorpe and Morris 1990, 1988; Hahn Rafter and Heiden-sohn 1995; Heidensohn 1994, 1989, 1985; Leonard 1982; Morris 1987; Naffine 1995, 1987; Smart 1977; Stanko 1995; Walklate 1995; Worrall 1990; on the possibility of a "feminist criminology" see further Naffine 1997; Smart 1990; Young 1996). Explicitly addressing the interconnections between *masculinities* and crime – from a perspective informed by this feminist critique of the gender blindness of the discipline – is a project of more recent origin.

The literature I am referring to as criminology's "masculinities and crime" debate has developed since the early 1990s and, in particular, following the publication of James Messerschmidt's influential book *Masculinities and Crime: Critique and Reconceptualization of Theory* (1993). In the intervening years a growing number of books, articles and research projects have sought to explore the relationship between men and crime via recourse to the idea that the gender of men (their masculinity/ies) is either interlinked to, is a cause of, or is in some other way associated with crime and criminality (see, generally, Carlen and Jefferson 1996; Collier 1998; Jefferson 1997a, 1994a; Messerschmidt 2000, 1997, 1993; Newburn and Stanko 1994a). Throughout these accounts what is seen as uniting men is, relative to women, their overwhelming propensity to-wards criminality, as testified to, across jurisdictions, by official criminal statis-tics, victimization and self-report studies and the everyday "lived experience" of both women and men (see, for example, and on the gendering of violence in the British context, Stanko et al. 1998).

It is important to consider what has been seen as potentially at stake here for criminology. For some, the specter of the unanswered "sex question" – the recognition that crime is almost always committed by men – has become a litmus test for the viability of the discipline *per se* (Allen 1989). If criminology cannot explain the cross-cultural gender-ratio of crime (why do men commit so much more crime than women?), if it cannot address its own generalizability problem (do theories designed to account for men's offending necessarily apply to women? Daly and Chesney-Lind 1988), what is the social and political significance of such a "gender blindness"? (Gelsthorpe and Morris 1988; Smart 1977). What does a historical failure to engage with [the] gender [of men] tell us about the relative success(es) or failure(s) of criminology in seeking to account for and/or control crime?

In such a context it is unsurprising that the all-encompassing nature of the concept's potential relevance has been such that both criminology's "Lombro-sian" and "governmental" strands or projects (Garland 1994) have, in different ways, embraced the emerging masculinities agenda. For those concerned with the development of an etiological, explanatory science (Garland 1985), a rich literature has emerged, spanning diverse political perspectives, concerned with the psychology of men's offending and the nature of a distinctively "masculine" criminal motivation. In terms of the "efficient and equitable administration of justice," meanwhile, masculinity has assumed an increasingly prominent pos-ition within debates about what might be termed the day-to-day practices of criminal justice systems, where there is evidence to suggest that governments are seeking to take gender, and in particular, masculinity, "seriously" in a number of respects in the development of criminal justice policies.

Taking these strands together, and to give no more than a flavor of the considerable body of criminological work which has taken place in this area, the concept of masculinity has recently been utilized in studies of topics as diverse as:

- the formation of the nation-state (Liddle 1996; Scraton 1990; Sumner 1990), the dynamics of "cop culture," policing practice and the identification of – and development of strategies aimed at challenging – pervasive sex discrimination within the legal and criminal justice systems (Fielding 1994; Ryder 1991; Sheptycki and Westmarland 1993; Westmarland 1997;
- in accounts of persistent offending by male youth, the dynamics of urban disorder and the relationship between crime, multiple deprivation, and family breakdown (a context in which the concept has been utilized, notably, within both neo-conservative, political-economic and feminist investigations of the idea of the underclass: compare, for example, Campbell 1993; Muncie et al. 1996; Murray 1990; Taylor 1999, 1994; Walklate 1995);
- in an interdisciplinary literature concerned with delinquency, schooling, and the educational underachievement of boys (Collier 1998: ch. 3; Messerschmidt 1994; O'Donnell and Sharpe 2000: ch. 1) and in accounts of men and boys' experiences of the fear of crime (Goodey 1997, 1998b);
- in discussions of victimology (Newburn and Stanko 1994b; Young 1995); of men in prison (Britton 1999; Carrabine and Longhurst 1998; Knowles 1999; Newton, 1994; Potts 1996; Sim 1994; Thurston 1996; Thurston and Beynon 1995; Wincup 1995), the practices of probation officers (Holland and Scourfield 2000; Scourfield 1998), the interconnections of race, ethnicity, and crime (Bourgois 1996; Gibbs and Merighi 1994; Goodey 1998a), sport and culture (Jefferson 1998, 1997a, b, 1996a) and issues of peace (Breines et al. 2000);
- in accounts of violent crime (Jones 2000: 96–101); men's apparently random violence (Collier 1997) and environmental crime (Groombridge 1998); drug use (Collinson 1996) and media representations of crime (Sparks 1996); car crime (Chapman 1993; Groombridge 1993); drinking cultures (Canaan 1996; Thomsen 1997); sex offending (Collier 2001); and white-collar crime (Beirne and Messerschmidt 1991: 54; Levi 1994);
- in relation to the censure of homosexuality (Collier 1998; Groombridge 2000; Thomsen 1998; Bernstein's chapter 16 in this volume) and the use of biographical accounts in criminology (Goodey 2000);
- and, perhaps with more resonance and in greater volume than any other topic, in relation to the seemingly intractable problem of men's violence against women, children, and other men (Alder and Polk 1996; Dobash et al. 2000; Gadd 2000, 2002; Hearn 1998; Kersten 1996; Polk 1994a, b; Snider 1998; Stanko 1994; Stanko and Hobdell 1993).

"Masculinity" has encompassed, variously, such attributes as the psychological characteristics of men, the possession of a range of gendered (as masculine) experiences and identities, both psychoanalytic and power-based readings of gendered practice, as well as analyses of men's gendered behavior within specific institutional settings (Hearn 1996: 203; see also McMahon 1993: 690). To extrapolate any unity to such a wide-ranging literature is, of course, difficult.

Yet notwithstanding the heterogeneity of issues being addressed in this work, and recognizing the diversity of methodological approaches and epistemological assumptions therein, it is possible to identify a recurring theme within these attempts to unpack "the isomorphism of certain forms of masculine desire and crime: the near perfect fit between the mortise of masculinity, and the tenon of crime" (Jefferson 1994b: 80).

It is a theme which can be depicted in both "weak" and "strong" forms. Underscoring the above scholarship is, at the very least, the increasing political and cultural resonance, certainly since the early 1990s, of the idea that there exists some kind of relation between the "masculinities" of men (whatever these may be or involve) and the changing nature and extent of men's criminality (and, in particular, the criminality of *young* men). And in what can be posited as a stronger form of this argument – one which has, importantly, transcended political perspectives and paradigms – what is seen as connecting these developments within criminal justice policy, criminology and public debate is a belief that the shifting experience of crime in late-modern societies is itself bound up, not simply with changing masculinities, but with the phenomenon of masculine *crisis* (Connell 1987; Brittan 1987; Kimmell 1987; and see, e.g., Sunley 1996). From this perspective the debate about masculinities and crime is itself, in effect, seen as emblematic of wider concerns and anxieties around the meaning of social, economic, cultural, and political changes since the 1980s, not least those between men and women (and importantly, I would add, children: Beck and Beck-Gernsheim 1995).

What has resulted, therefore, has been a cultural and political problematiza-tion of masculinity which would, at times, seem to have left no aspect of social life unaffected (as the diverse list of topics above testifies). In effect, the phenom-enon of crime has a powerful, symbolic significance at the very moment that this crisis of masculinity discourse has itself become a cipher for broader transitions and tensions, most notably in relation to a perceived relativizing of hitherto normative ideas about men's achievements and social status (what does it mean to be "a man"?). And, crucially, in this process many familiar features of what might be termed traditional "law and order" discourse – for example, in relation to the iconic figure of the "hooligan" or "yob" (Pearson 1983) – have themselves transformed or mutated into something else; a concern with issues, or, indeed, specific individuals, to be explained and assessed no longer (or solely) in terms of class, poverty, race, ethnicity, and/or disadvantage, but increasingly through the language of *gender* and social change – the idea that *something* is happening to men and their shifting "masculinities" and that this relates to crime.

What marks this recent literature on masculinities and crime as different from earlier criminological accounts is the extent to which it has sought to go beyond the broadly functionalist, positivist framework which marked earlier crimino-logical engagements with masculinity (see further Naffine 1985). This has in-volved a shift in conceptual terrain marked, initially, by a rejection of the once influential individualized theories of sex roles (Kimmell 1987) and subsequently, and importantly in seeking to understand the contours of present debates, by what was to become an at times seemingly wholesale adoption within much criminological scholarship of the concept of "hegemonic masculinity" (Connell 2002; Hall 2002).

STRUCTURES, PSYCHES, AND HEGEMONY

Structured action theory

HEGEMONIC MASCULINITY

It is not overstating the case, perhaps, to see the publication by the Australian sociologist R.W. Connell of *Gender and Power* (1987) as having "kick-started" the new engagement with masculinity in criminology (see also Connell 1995; Carrigan et al.1985). Certainly, the concept central to this wide-ranging and justly celebrated study – hegemonic masculinity – has become a ubiquitous presence in the debate about men and crime.[2]Hegemonic masculinity is used by Connell in such a way as to address what had, by 1987, become a pressing question within the then emerging critical study of men and masculinity in the social sciences and humanities (Carrigan et al. 1985; Hearn 1987; Hearn and Morgan 1990). How might it be possible to "conceptualise relations among men, especially when class and ethnic and generational relations are included?" (Jefferson 1994a: 15). How, that is, can the diversity of men's lives be addressed whilst at the same time recognizing the existence of a culturally exalted form of (heterosexual) masculinity? For Connell (1987: 183) the answer lay in hegemonic masculinity, something which "is always constructed in relation to various subordinated masculinities as well as in relation to women" (see also Maudsen 1993).

Central to hegemonic masculinity is the idea that masculinities can be ordered hierarchically and that gender relations are themselves constituted through three interrelated structures: what Connell terms labor, power, and cathexis. What orderliness exists between them is not that of a system but, rather, a "unity of historical composition"; and what is produced is a gender order, "a historically constructed pattern of power relations between men and women and definitions of femininity and masculinity" (Connell 1987: 98–9). Central to Connell's thesis, therefore, is a belief that a politics of masculinity cannot be confined to the level of the personal (be it matters of choice, conditioning, human nature, and so forth). They are embedded in the gender regime of society at any historical moment, always in a dynamic process of constitution: "structures identified by analysis . . . exist only in solution, they are not absolutely prior to the subject but themselves are always in process of formation. Social and personal life are practices" (Middleton 1992: 153). As Segal concisely puts it, masculinity is thus understood:

> as transcending the personal, as a heterogeneous set of ideas, constructed around assumptions of social power which are lived out and reinforced, or perhaps denied and challenged, in multiple and diverse ways within a whole social system in which relations of authority, work and domestic life are organised, in the main, along hierarchical gender lines. (Segal 1990: 288)

Following Gramsci (1971), any resulting hegemony is always incomplete (Connell 1987: 184), the politics of gender arising from the *always contested* nature of men's power and the ever-present possibility of resistance and contestation (see, for example, on men in prison, Sim 1994: 111). It is central to Connell's argument, in short, that hegemonic masculinity is never finally closed, fixed, or resolved.

The potential implications of Connell's work for a discipline struggling to address its own "sex question" in the light of the sustained feminist critique outlined above soon became obvious. And, in the work of James Messerschmidt, hegemonic masculinity was to receive its most thought-out and sophisticated development in the field of criminology.

THE "ACCOMPLISHING" OF MASCULINITY

Connell himself warmly (if, perhaps, not fully: Connell 1993: vii) endorsed the arguments of Messerschmidt's book *Masculinities and Crime* (1993). However, Connell's work is just one of the influences underscoring Messerschmidt's attempt to (in his own words) "reconceptualize" crime as a situational resource for the "accomplishing" of masculinity. As Jefferson (1996b, 1997a) and others have noted, the work is also influenced by Giddens (1991, 1976), from whom we find a concern with social structure based on practice "both constituted by human agency and yet at the same time the medium of that constitution" (Giddens 1976: 121, quoted in Messerschmidt 1993: 77); by Acker (1990, 1989), a recognition that gender, race, and class are implicated simultaneously in any such practice; by phenomenology and ethnomethodology, the idea that gender is "situationally accomplished," performed to or for particular social audiences according to normative codes (West and Zimmerman 1987; Fenstermaker et al. 1991; Goffman 1979); and by Connell, as above, "the notion of a multiply-structured field of gender relations and [of] hegemonic and subordinated masculinities" (Jefferson 1996b: 340). Following Connell, Messerschmidt argues that men exist in different positions in relation to the dominant hierarchies of gender, race, class, and sexuality and, as a result, their resources for the accomplishment of masculinity vary. In a manner which is not dissimilar to Mertonian strain theory, as Hood-Williams observes (2001), it is when these class and race relations combine to reduce conventional opportunities for the accomplishment of hegemonic masculinity that crime is seen by Messerschmidt as a ready replacement – not so much a "delinquent solution" (Downes 1966) for a minority but a potential solution for *all* men in their struggle to become (to be) masculine. As Messerschmidt puts it, crime is "a behavioral response to the particular conditions and situations in which we participate" (Messerschmidt 1994: 88). All men "do" masculinity. They just do it in different ways.

Masculinities and Crime presents a rich account of men's crime as a way of "doing" gender (see also Messerschmidt 2000, 1997) and has been rightly heralded as an "extremely important" (Hood-Williams 2001: 53) "significant advance" (Jefferson 1996a: 340) in theorizing masculinity and crime. It has, without question, made a major contribution to the criminological debate on masculinities. As an attempt to integrate the complexities of race, class, gender, and sexuality, and to take structural patterns of inequality seriously, it paved the way for further studies adopting a broadly similar approach in viewing crime as a way of accomplishing masculinity (see, for example, the Australian-based studies of interpersonal male violence by Polk 1994a, 1994b; and, in the UK context, the account of urban disorder by Campbell 1993). Nonetheless, as soon became clear, there are a number of problems with Messerschmidt's approach.

ASSESSMENT

Perhaps of greatest significance, not least in view of the fact that the theory is attempting to develop a politically useful engagement with the gender of crime, critics noted a marked failure in Messerschmidt's account to theorize the subjectivity of *individual* men. That is, the question of why some men "turn to" crime and others do not; "as is now widely recognized most crime is committed by *highly specific sub-groups of the category 'men'*" (Hood-Williams 2001: 43, original emphasis), men who are themselves often the principal victims of crime (Collier 1998; Hall 2002; Jefferson 1992; Walklate 1995). What is not asked is "why only *particular* men from a given class or race background (usually only a minority) come to identify with the crime option, while others identify with other resources to accomplish their masculinity" (Jefferson 1996a: 341). If masculinities are "offered up" for all men within a sociocultural, structural location, why do men choose one, and not another, masculine identity? And who, in any case, is doing the "offering up" (Walklate 1995: 180)? It can be argued that most men, regardless of their socioeconomic group, "do" a masculine gender without resorting to (at least certain) crimes. Yet it is difficult to see in structured action theory any account of *why* this should be the case (Jefferson 1994a, 1996b, 1997a); nor, importantly how individual life-history and biography impact on any such "choice" (see below). In the reproduction of the normative hegemonic masculine ideal, therefore, we find a certain rigidity in how men are seen to accomplish the attributes of dominant masculinity. Structure, in effect, constrains practice to such a degree that, at the very least, it is difficult to see where the contestation and resistance central to Connell's original thesis fit in here.

The above issue relates to the way in which Messerschmidt deploys a particular notion of the masculine social subject; a man conceptualized as a reflexively rational, self-interested being and whose social action, we have seen, relates in a distinctly deterministic way to the cultural norms of hegemonic masculinity (whatever these may be: Collier 1998; Hood-Williams 2001; Jefferson 1994a, 1997a). Yet what is not explained is precisely what it *is* in hegemonic masculinity that causes crime (or, at least, some crimes). Nor, importantly, why the criminal-*ized* are nearly always poor and overly black. The idea that "most crime" is committed by men is "a highly generalized notion which puts together disparate practices and invites us to treat them as if they were similar" (Hood-Williams 2001: 43). Men, for Messerschmidt and those who have broadly followed his analysis, are seen as "doing" their gender (masculinity) through engaging in crimes as diverse as burglary, rape, the sexual abuse of children, the taking of motor vehicles without consent, corporate crime, football hooliganism, state terrorism, traffic offences, road rage, violence toward others, and so on (each, it is to be remembered, the subject matter of recent analyses). To account for such diversity in terms of men "accomplishing" a gender identity is asking a great deal of the concept of masculinity, however. Is it the case that *all* crime is to be explained in this way? Or is it only to be those crimes which are violent and/or destructive which bespeak their origins in masculinity? Men, we have seen, dominate nearly all crimes, though some crimes appear to escape being gendered *as* masculine in ways in which others do not (which begs rather different questions about structure, discourse, and power). Masculinity is depicted as both primary and underlying *cause* (or source) of a social effect (crime); and, simultaneously, as something which itself *results from* (after all, it is accomplished through) recourse *to* crime. As Walklate observes, "not only does this reflect a failure to resolve fully the tendency towards universalism, it can also be read as tautological" (Walklate 1995: 181).

Hegemonic masculinity appears, ultimately, an unambiguously positive attribute for men in the sense that it is, for a host of (unexplored) psychological imperatives, something which is desired, to be achieved, to be accomplished. Yet leaving aside the fact that the qualities presently associated with manhood are not necessarily considered negative (or positive) in all cultural contexts, and that crime itself does not *necessarily* require strength, toughness, aggression, violence, and so forth,[3] critics have taken issue with Messerschmidt's underlying assumption that the experience of being masculine is itself premised on the domination of women and children. The cultural valorization of hegemonic masculinity certainly correlates strongly with – if it is not inherently interlinked to – various destructive, violent ways of "being a man." Yet, Hearn suggests, what is really depicted as negative about men here is itself, in effect, a description of culturally masculine traits (Hearn 1996: 207). These, certainly, conjure up powerful images about men and crime and speak to an empirical reality inasmuch as, as we have seen, most crime is almost unimaginable without the presence of men (Jefferson 1992: 10). However they remain, ultimately, popular ideologies of what constitutes the ideal or actual characteristics of being a man at particular historical moments and cultural contexts (Hearn 1996). Messerschmidt's account seems to open up an analysis of the diversity of masculinities. Yet it would appear to do so in such a way as to simultaneously *hold in place* a normative masculine gender to which is then assigned a range of (usually undesirable/negative) characteristics. As such it imposes: "an a priori theoretical/conceptual frame on the psychological complexity of men's behavior. What continues to be evaded...are the ways in which each act of aggression or kindness, sensitivity or independence, self-sacrifice or selfishness is itself encoded at particular moments and locations as a 'masculine' or 'feminine' attribute" (Collier 1998: 22).

The fact that the political, cultural, and ethical qualities of the "acceptable masculine" may be far removed from this hegemonic form within late modern gender regimes – or that they are, at the very least, more psychologically complex than this model would allow (Wetherell and Edley 1999: see further below) – is an issue which tends to be effaced in Messerschmidt's account.[4] And, notwithstanding the continued "salience" of the accomplishing masculinity thesis for criminology (Goodey 2000: 489), it is this issue of the complexity and multi-layered nature of the masculine social subject with which a "third stage" in thinking about masculinities has been primarily concerned (Jefferson 1996a: also Hood-Williams 2001).

Later developments: The (masculine) psycho-social subject

In the work of Tony Jefferson, either writing alone (1994a, 1996a, 1996b, 1996c, 1997a, 1997b, 1998) or with Wendy Hollway (Hollway and Jefferson 1996, 1997, 1998, 2000), a concerted effort has been made to move thinking about masculinity and crime onto a "different level" (Jefferson 1996b). Jefferson's work constitutes, first and foremost, an attempt to explore the tensions between the *social* and *psychic* processes which inform men's experience of masculinity. It is presented as an explicit challenge to etiological criminology to take the "psychic dimensions of subjectivity" seriously (Jefferson 1994a). It is not possible to do justice here to either the complexity of the substantive analyses which have been produced on this topic (for example, in relation to the boxer Mike Tyson, on date rape, sexual harassment, and the fear of crime: Jefferson 1996b, 1997b, 1998; Hollway and Jefferson 1996, 1997, 1998); nor the complex groundings of this work within contemporary psychoanalysis (on which see further Adams 1996; Chodorow 1994; Elliot 1994, 1996; Hood-Williams 1997; Hood-Williams and Cealey Harrison 1998). It is possible, however, to briefly trace some of the key characteristics of this development in the masculinities and crime literature with a view to establishing how it differs from, as well as what it shares with, Messerschmidt's account.

The psychosocial approach is based on a fusing of aspects of poststructuralist and psychoanalytic theory. From the former it is the concept of discourse, rather than that of social structure, which is utilized (cf. Pease 1999). In contrast to traditional psychoanalysis, what is placed center-stage is an attempt to engage with the presentational forms of "masculine" performances, identities, corporeal enactments, and so forth (cf. Butler 1993, 1990; also Bell and Valentine 1995; Gatens 1996; Grosz 1994, 1990; Grosz and Probyn 1995). At the same time, the approach rejects the idea of the unitary rational subject which Jefferson argues is implicit within Messerschmidt's determinist structured action model, as above. The focus of analysis shifts, in contrast, to the way in which a non-unitary and "inherently contradictory" subject comes [himself] to invest – whether consciously and unconsciously – in what are seen as empowering social discourses around masculinity (Jefferson 1996b, 1998). Jefferson's subsequent work in this area has been made up, accordingly, of a series of analyses which have sought, in different ways but utilizing a broadly similar theoretical framework,[5] to develop a *social* understanding of the masculine *psyche* which might, it is argued, then shed some light on the relationship between men, masculinities and crime (Jefferson 1996a: 341–2).

ASSESSMENT

By engaging with the notion of a dynamic unconscious this perspective recognizes, Jefferson suggests, the complexity of male subjectivity in such a way as to "prize open" the possibility "of making sense of the contradictions and difficulties that particular men experience in becoming masculine" (Jefferson 1994a: 28–9). That is, by integrating questions of individual biography and life-history (Hollway and Jefferson 1997, 2000), and addressing the lived experience and contradictions of "being masculine," a handle is given on the important question, noted above, of why some men do, and others do not, engage in certain crimes: "Placing the individual's biography within social structural forces [in this way] recognizes the *reality*, and not simply the theoretical *rhetoric*, of relative power and powerlessness experienced by different men throughout their lives" (Goodey 2000: 489, my emphasis).

It is no longer an overarching, all-encompassing social structure or gender norm which is seen as accounting for the crimes of men. It is within the complex interaction between the social realm and the individual psyche that the disposition or motivation of particular men toward particular actions is located (see, e.g., the readings of Mike Tyson: Jefferson 1998, 1997a, 1996b, 1996c). Crime is depicted, in effect, as the product of a range of biographically contingent anxieties and desires; the "choice" to commit crime is, like the fear of crime itself, not necessarily exercised or experienced rationally or logically. The psyche is, rather, understood as constantly defending itself against unconscious and powerful anxieties and desires producing psychological defenses which "are not only produced but are necessary. Necessary, but not without contradictions" (Walkerdine 1995: 327).

This would appear to be a great advance politically on the (always, already) empowered masculine subject implicit in Messerschmidt's work. Jefferson does not ignore the all-too-real social costs of men's crimes, be it for women, children, or other men, but seeks, rather, to "appreciate" the contradictory nature of social experience; for example, the coexistence of feelings of empowerment and powerlessness on the part of men (see, by way of illustration, the readings of domestic violence produced by Gadd 2002). What then emerges, it is suggested, is the possibility of developing a progressive politics of change which might recognize how the psychodynamic dimensions of social experience can be pervaded as much by emotional ambivalence and contradiction as any straightforward hegemonic masculine identification (Connell 1995; Goodey 2000, 1997; Jackson 1990; Thurston 1996; see further Hollway and Jefferson 1997; Edley and Wetherell 1997; and cf. Messerschmidt 2000). As such, this is an argument which would appear to resonate with themes in existing accounts of male offenders themselves (Graef 1992), as well as having clear implications for criminal justice policy; for example, in questioning many assumptions underlying the cognitive-behavioral frameworks which have, to date, tended to underpin many governmental strategies in dealing with male offenders across a range of spheres (see further Gadd 2000; on the fear of crime, Hollway and Jefferson 2000).

Notwithstanding what some have seen as the clear advantages of this approach over and above structured action theory, however, such a "merging" of poststructuralist and psychoanalytic theory has not escaped criticism. The charge that this is an approach which (to put it mildly) sits uneasily with the sociological moorings of criminology is one which advocates of the psychosocial approach might easily dismiss. The very *point*, indeed, is that sociogenic criminology has failed to engage with the "inner life" of a complex male subject. The well-established broader critique of psychoanalysis, however, remains pertinent in this context. The relation of these accounts to *other* psychoanalytic traditions, non-psychoanalytic psychology or, indeed, the idea that there might be multiple psychological mechanisms of subjective "positioning" is, at best, uncertain. Leaving aside the question of whether the particular strand of Kleinian psychoanalysis and object relations theory invoked in Jefferson's work is itself premised on an unduly mechanistic model of personality formation, the argument remains that, although psychoanalysis (of whatever form) might offer a rich story for describing the emergence of fantasies of sexual difference, these remain, at the end of the day, just that: stories. It is difficult to see, for example, how the kinds of readings produced by Jefferson of individual men (say, Mike Tyson) can ever be tested or proven in any meaningful way. Is what we are left with, ultimately, no more than a reflection of the researcher's own projection (no more, or less, plausible than any other reading) (Frosh 1997, 1994)? Or are we reduced, effectively, to an "all is discourse" position which, in disavowing an outer reality, embraces a wholly semiotic account in which "with so much emphasis on the signifier, the signified tends to vanish" (Connell 1995: 50–1)? Is it only the trained psychologist, counselor, or academic expert who is able to ascertain what is "really" behind an individual's actions? It is open to question whether the linear "third-stage" thinking presented by Jefferson is not equally as androcentric as the social structure theory it claims to supersede in the way in which it betrays a profoundly positivistic notion of progression (from first, to second, to third stage . . .) in depicting what is, ultimately, a "grand theory" of the crimes of men (cf. Smart 1990). As Hood-Williams (2001) notes, it is very difficult to maintain simultaneously that, on the one hand, psychoanalysis is just one of many "discourses of subjectification" whereby gendered identities become attached to individuals; and, on the other hand, to maintain that the claims it is making are grounded in real, historically specific, and *irreducible* psychological processes which result from the contingent dynamics of (in this case) pre-Oedipal attachment.

The implications in terms of policy and practice are similarly uncertain. Even *if* it is accepted that it is psychoanalysis, and not some other approach, that is necessary to theorize the subject, it remains unclear how theorizing subjectivity at the level of the individual can ever be an effective strategy in facilitating social change in a broader sense (for example, in reducing the incidence of crime in general, or in relation to certain crimes). The potential policy implications are, taking on the methodological difficulties and logic of the approach to their conclusion, arguably so far-reaching as to appear unmanageable. By what criteria is one offender to be chosen for intervention or analysis over and above another? Both offender and prosecutor, prison inmate and officer, policeman and young offender, government minister and "hooligan," criminology student and teacher each appear locked, albeit in different ways, in a complex matrix of defenses and projections, splitting, and introjections. Given that this always-defended masculine subject is constituted in a complex interaction with other individuals, at what point does it become necessary to engage with the accounts of others in order to obtain anything like a "complete" picture of an individual, and with a view to "appreciating" their biography? Or is it the case that what we are left with here is, ultimately, simply a call to engage with a gendered (masculine) culture and a certain form of (hegemonic) masculinity – something which is not dissimilar, in effect, to that found within structured action theory?

THE LIMITS OF MASCULINITY

Although "certainly provisional" in nature (Hood-Williams 2001: 54), it has been from outside of the discipline of criminology (or, at the very least, on its fringes) that a rather different set of questions about the relationship between men and crime has emerged. Coming from the interface of feminist, queer, materialist, and postmodern theory, within this recent sociological scholarship (work depicted as potentially "gate-crash[ing]...the criminological party", Groombridge 1999: 532) there has occurred a growing questioning of the concept of masculinity which has involved (amongst other things) a reappraisal of what it means to speak of, perform, or (in Messerschmidt's account) "do" a masculine gender (Collier 1998; Hearn 1996; MacInnes 1998; McMahon 1999; Pease 1999). Such a development can be seen, on one level, as part of a broader concern within the social sciences to develop a self-reflective "science of the subject" (Hood-Williams 2001: 54); to take seriously, that is, how a particular social experience (let us say, of being a man) might be "offered to thought in the form of a problem requiring attention" (Rose and Valverde 1998: 545; cf. Smart 1989: ch. 1; see also Rose 1994). And such a questioning of the analytic status of masculinity can be seen to chime in certain respects with the broadly Foucauldian-inspired engagement with the role of mechanisms, arenas, functionaries, forms of reasoning, and so forth in late modern societies which is itself a tradition well represented within contemporary criminological thought (Rose and Valverde 1998: 546; cf. Naffine 1997; Rose 1999, 1994, 1989, 1987). Nonetheless, what we have here is a development which does raise important questions about what criminology is seeking to achieve in "taking masculinity seriously."

Both the structured action and psychosocial perspectives discussed above do engage, in different ways, with this question of how *ideas* of masculinity become problematized at particular historical moments and contexts. Yet both approaches stand in an uneasy relation, as we have seen, to some essentialist conceptualizations of masculinity itself – whether it is in the tendency of structured action theory to depict a mechanistic relation between masculinity, culture, and crime or in the psychosocial grounding of gender difference in irreducible psychic processes. It is open to question, ultimately, just how adequate the concept of masculinity is when seeking to explain, understand, or otherwise account for the crimes of men. The general use of masculinity in this context has been seen as premised on "heterosexist" and heterosexual assumptions (Groombridge 1999: also Collier 1998), as "an ethnocentric or even a Eurocentric notion," a product of a particular historical moment which is, in some cultural contexts, at best "irrelevant or misleading" (Hearn, 1996: 209; cf., e.g., Connell 1995: 30–4; Gilmore 1993; Mangan and Walvin 1987; also MacInnes 1998; Pease 1999). And it has been depicted as analytically imprecise; "it is as if this concept exemplifies [a] field of concern and even, possibly, distils the aggregation of activity of men in the social world into one neat word" (Hearn 1996: 202; see, by way of response, to these charges Connell 2002). Criminological conceptualizations of masculinity have themselves, as Judith Allen suggested back in 1989 (predating the largely male-dominated current masculinity turn),[6] tended to perpetuate a "stranglehold grip of Cartesian-style dualisms by trading in uneven oppositions around the mind and the body, the real and the romantic, the scientific and the fantastic" (Murphy 1996: 57; note also Cousins 1980).[7] Both the structured action and psychosocial perspectives, in "categoriz[ing] . . . a vast range of activities and treat[ing] . . . them as if they were all subject to the same laws" (Smart 1990: 77; in effect, laws of gender), can be seen to be framed by, and as seeking to develop, a criminological project premised on giving "primacy to one form of explanation rather than another" (Smart 1990: 77). Yet it is this very kind of thinking for which, some critics have suggested, the time has "[itself] now passed" (Hood-Williams 2001: 53; also Collier 1998; Groombridge 1999).

Beyond this issue of conceptual ambiguity, the *political* consequences of focusing an analysis of men, gender, and change on the concept of masculinity have been called into question. Both the psychosocial readings and structured action accounts are clearly concerned with social practice and questions of politics and power. Yet both, we have seen, tend to presume the existence of normative masculine practices, cultures or identities; things which exist to be accomplished (in Messerschmidt's account) or performed (in Jefferson's more poststructuralist approach). Whether embedded within and reproduced through the interaction of social structure and practice, or else discursively constituted via the contingencies of psyche and society, masculinity continues to be deployed as "a reference point" against which a range of behavior and identities might be evaluated (Hearn 1996: 203). In each approach, however, while aspects of men's practices may be criticized, the focus of analysis is on the gender category masculinity; it is this which is to be challenged, transcended, or "changed." What remains open to question in such a line of thinking, McMahon (1999) suggests, is the extent to which this argument depicts men's gender as something which "floats free" from what men *do*. That is, male personality appears "a reification . . . of men's practices (and, of course, the practices of women that support them). [This] reification is then employed to explain these same prac-tices" (McMahon 1993: 689). What is then effaced, McMahon (1999, 1993) argues, is the question of whether men should change their behavior, of men's social *power* relative to women, and of men's individual and collective *interest* in maintaining present gender relations (compare, on the issue of freeing men of the responsibility for seeking to change, Frosh 1994; MacInnes 1998). As a material practice gender cannot be detached from increasingly global(ized) struggles around power and interest (Marchland and Runyon 2000). And "changing men," as Connell has long argued (1995, 1987), cannot be reduced to such individual or collective projects of self-actualization.

This is an argument which recasts the question of what criminology is ultim-ately trying to achieve in "taking masculinity seriously." I do not wish to argue that the concept of masculinity has proved ineffective in reconceptualizing the "problem of men" in relation to crime. It is increasingly rare, at the level of academic criminology at least, to find a collapsing of the politics of crime into familiar questions of class, capital, and/or race in such a way that the "question of gender" is totally effaced. In the very act of naming men, the subject matter of criminology has (to varying degrees) been transformed. A question remains, however. What, ultimately, is the aim of criminology's masculinity turn? Is it to "complete" an understanding of crime (Walklate 1995: 180), to provide, as it were, an ultimate Truth, the final piece of the (modernist) jigsaw? Is it to make mainstream criminology aware of feminism and gender perspectives, reeducating (presumably male?) criminologists to the inequalities of sex/gender? If so, then it is to misread Connell's (1987) original point about the ways in which *all* men are empowered by hegemonic masculinity:

> How can we expect democratic reform of gender relations from an institution that is dominated by those who benefit from the present gender order? What kind of reform process could possibly transform the gendered character of the state, without being trapped by the politics of social control in which the state is enmeshed? (Connell 1993: xvi)

Notwithstanding the (re)discovery of masculinity by criminology, the masculinity *of* criminology remains profoundly suspect (cf. Rock 1988, 1994). And in such a context, and bearing in mind the disciplinary research imperative to seek out new subject matters, new disciplinary terrains – to boldly go where no criminologist has gone before – whether the discipline of criminology will ever adequately address the sexed specificity of crime in the way that some of the protagonists within the masculinity debate hope is perhaps open to question – certainly for as long as criminology itself remains trapped in ways of thinking which make it so difficult to "see" the interconnections between men, gender, and power in the first place (Collier 1998: ch. 1; see also Naffine 1997; Young 1996).

What of the future? By the mid-1990s masculinity and crime was a topic being described within Anglo-American criminology as an area in which "much more...work needs to be done" (Walklate 1995: 181), a "barely started project" (Jefferson 1996a: 342; see also *Masculinity and Crime* (1993)). Less than a decade on it may well be that the ebb and flow of academic fashion – and commissioning editors' perceptions of commercially viable topics – has moved on. It is surely significant, however, that the vast majority of criminological scholarship, of whatever political or theoretical hue, continues to feminize a consciousness of "gender issues" via the routine association of sex/gender with aspects of the still-pervasive "woman question" – albeit that it might increasingly be doing so in an ostensibly pro-feminist form. "Gender" continues to be about women. It is all too rarely about questions of men and what men *do*. Far from rendering contingent the historically specific male subject of criminological discourse, whether it is in terms of methodological prescriptions or epistemological assumptions which surround tackling the "man question," men arguably remain the unexplored, desexed norm of criminology. A range of cultural discourses are, certainly, problematizing the relationship between men and crime in far reaching ways. They are doing so, however, in such a way that, behind a purportedly progressive rhetoric of equity, issues of power and material interest continue to be systematically marginalized and depoliticized.

To address issues of gender and power in relation to the production of criminological knowledge is not to deny that certain groups of men, rather than men in general, can be seen to benefit (all too clearly) from present social arrangements (Hall 2002). For as long as the "man question" is silenced at the point of criminological knowledge production, however, then notwithstanding the growing cultural salience of a desire to speak about the "maleness" of crime, perhaps what we will continue to be left with is, regardless of approach adopted, just the same old story of "boys' doing [criminological] business" (Newburn and Stanko 1994a).

Notes

1   In keeping with broader developments within the sociology of gender, recent studies have tended to stress the plurality of masculin*ities* rather than the singular masculinity, in so doing moving away from a fixed model and toward an understanding of the complexity, fragmentation, and differentiation existing between (as well as the continuities which unite) the diverse lives of men.

2   See, for example, Newburn and Stanko (1994a: 3), who remark on the influence of Connell at the time: "indeed this is illustrated by the number of references to his work throughout the chapters in this book."

3   What men are not seen as "doing" is a masculinity which might in any sense be interpreted as "positive;" not so much in the sense of the undoubted seductions of crime (Katz 1988; Jefferson 1992), but in terms of an engagement with the complexity of the ways in which the taking on of a masculine subjectivity is itself constituted through reference to relationships to women as well as other men. As Walklate (1995: 181) notes, raising such a question is not to imply that women are to blame for men's behavior. It is, rather, to suggest the need to recognize a subject for whom the meanings of masculinity cannot be confined to any generally oppressive and negative list of traits. Values more traditionally associated with the feminine may, in certain instances, be associated with specific crimes (qualities such as cunning, patience, deceit, an ability to empathize). The suggestion that men unproblematically aspire to the (oppressive) qualities of the hegemonically masculine, therefore, is one which serves to override an investigation of the complexity of the behavior of men in terms of their everyday relations with women and other men.

4   There are issues which Messerschmidt himself sought to explore in the later book *Nine Lives: Adolescent Masculinities. the Body and Violence* (2000). Yet here, again, we find within an attempt to integrate an appreciation of the specificities of individual life-history, structured action theory being used in such a way as to hold together an account of a diverse range of men's behavior as masculine phenomena.

5   This work seeks to locate individuals within an array of "discursive positionings." Breaking with the traditionally asocial subject of psychology, and following on from the earlier work of Henriques et al. 1984 and Hollway 1989, the psychoanalytic model engaged with draws on the work of Melanie Klein. Here, the emergence of distinctive "masculine" subjectivities are understood as being constituted through reference to a range of relational defense mechanisms (such as splitting, projection, and introjection) interlinked to the contingent processes of early-life "object relating."

6   A curiously overlooked and under-cited yet important article. Allen's work was in many ways to prefigure later developments.

7   To seek to question the male subject of criminology – criminology's "Man" – is not to reduce everything to discourse, but to recognize that the term man can itself no longer be "regarded as essentially dominant and self-contained; that, in truth, it takes its meaning from the term 'woman' that can now no longer be regarded as outside the concept of man, but utterly central to it" (Naffine 1997: 85; see also Daly 1997).

References

Acker, J. (1989) The problem with patriarchy. *Sociology*, 23(2), 235–40.

Acker, J. (1990) Hierarchies, jobs, bodies: A theory of gendered organization. *Gender and Society*, 4(2), 139–58.

Adams, P. (1996) *The Emptiness of the Image: Psychoanalysis and Sexual Differences*. London: Routledge.

Alder, C., and Polk, K (1996) Masculinity and child homicide. *British Journal of Criminology*, 36(3), 396–411.

Allen, J. (1989) Men, crime and criminology: Recasting the questions. *International Journal of the Sociology of Law*, 17(1), 19–39.

Beck, U., and Beck-Gernsheim, E (1995) *The Normal Chaos of Love*. Cambridge: Polity.

Beirne, P., and Messerschmidt, J (1991) *Criminology*. San Diego: CA: Harcourt, Brace Jovanovich.

Bell, D., and Valentine, G. (1995) The sexed self: Strategies of performance, sites of resistance. In S. Pile and N. Thrift (eds.), *Mapping the Subject: Geographies of Cultural Transformation*. London: Routledge, 143–58.

Bourgois, P. (1996) In search of masculinity: Violence, respect and sexuality amongst Puerto Rican crack dealers in East Harlem. *British Journal of Criminology*. 36(3), 412–27.

Breines, I., Connell, R. W., and Eide, I. (eds.) (2000) *Male Roles. Masculinities and Violence: A Culture of Peace Approach*. Paris: UNESCO.

Brittan, A. (1987) *Masculinity and Power*. Oxford: Blackwell.

Britton, D. K. (1999) Cat fights and gang fights: Preference for work in a male-dominated organisation. *Sociological Quarterly*, 40(3), 455–74.

Brown, B. (1986) Women and crime: The dark figures of criminology. *Economy and Society*. 15, 355–402.

Butler, J. (1990) *Gender Trouble: Feminism and the Subversion of Identity*. London: Routledge.

Butler, J. (1993) *Bodies That Matter: On the Discursive Limits of Sex*. London: Routledge.

Cain, M. (1990a) Realist philosophy and the standpoint epistemologies or feminist criminology as successor science. In L. Gelsthorpe and A. Morris (eds.), *Feminist Perspectives in Criminology*. Milton Keynes: Open University Press, 124–40.

Cain, M. (1990b) Towards transgression: New directions in feminist criminology. *International Journal of the Sociology of Law*, 1, 1–18.

Campbell, B. (1993) *Goliath: Britain's Dangerous Places*. London: Virago.

Canaan, J. E (1996) "One thing leads to another": Drinking, fighting and working-class masculinities. In M. Mac an Ghaill (ed.), *Understanding Masculinities*. Buckingham: Open University Press, 114–25.

Carlen, P. (1983) *Women's Imprisonment*. London: Routledge & Kegan Paul.

Carlen, P. (1988) *Women. Crime and Poverty*. Milton Keynes: Open University Press.

Carlen, P., and Jefferson, J. (1996) *British Journal of Criminology: Special Issue – Masculinities and Crime*, 33(6).

Carlen, P., and Worrall, A. (1987) *Gender, Crime and Justice*. Milton Keynes: Open University Press.

Carrabine, E., and Longhurst, B. (1998) Gender and prison organisation: Some comments on masculinities and prison management. *Howard Journal*, 37(2), 161–76.

Carrigan, T., Connell, R. W., and Lee, J. (1985) Toward a new sociology of masculinity. *Theory and Society*, 14, 551–604.

Carrington, K. (1993) *Offending Girls: Sex. Youth and Justice*. St. Leonards, Australia: Allen & Unwin.

Chapman, T (1993) Toys for the boys: Gender and car crime. In *Masculinity and Crime: Issues of Theory and Practice*. Conference Report, Brunel University, Centre for Criminal Justice Research, 143–50.

Chodorow, N. (1994) *Femininities. Masculinities. Sexualities*. Lexington: University Press of Kentucky.

Collier, R. (1997) After Dunblane: Crime, corporeality and the (hetero)sexing of the bodies of men. *Journal of Law and Society*, 24(2), 177–99.

Collier, R. (1998) *Masculinities, Crime and Criminology*. London: Sage.

Collier, R. (2001) The paedophile, the dangerous individual and the criminal law: Reconfigurations of the public/private divide. In C. Brants and P. Alldridge (eds.), *Personal Autonomy. The Private Sphere and the Criminal Law: A Comparative Study*. London: Hart, 223–45.

Collinson, M. (1996) In search of the high life: Drugs, crime, masculinities and consumption. *British Journal of Criminology*, 36(3), 428–43.

Connell, R. W. (1987) *Gender and Power*. Cambridge: Polity.

Connell, R. W. (1993) Foreword. In J. W. Messerschmidt, *Masculinities and Crime: Critique. and Reconceptualization of Theory*. Lanham, MD: Rowman & Littlefield, vii–xv.

Connell, R. W. (1995) *Masculinities*. Cambridge: Polity.

Connell, R. W. (2002) On hegemonic masculinity and violence: A response to Jefferson and Hall. *Theoretical Criminology*, 6(1), forthcoming.

Cousins, M. (1980) Mens rea: A note on sexual difference, criminology and the law. In P. Carlen and M. Collinson (eds.), *Radical Issues in Criminology*. Oxford: Martin Robertson, 109–22.

Daly, K. (1993) *Gender. Crime and Punishment*. New Haven, CT: Yale University Press.

Daly, K. (1997) Different ways of conceptualising sex/gender in feminist theory and their implications for criminology. *Theoretical Criminology*, 1(1), 25–53.

Daly, K., and Chesney-Lind, M. (1988) Feminism and criminology. *Justice Quarterly*, 5 (4), 498–538.

Dobash, R. E., Dobash, R. P., Cavanagh, K., and Lewis, R. (2000) *Changing Violent Men*. London: Sage.

Downes, D. (1966) *The Delinquent Solution*. London, Routledge & Kegan Paul.

Edley, N., and Wetherell, M. (1996) Masculinity, power and identity. In M. Mac an Ghaill (ed.), *Understanding Masculinities*. Buckingham: Open University Press,97–113.

Edley, N., and Wetherell, M. (1997)[1999?] Jockeying for position: The construction of masculine identities. *Discourse and Society*, 8(2), 203–17.

Elliot, A. (1994) *Psychoanalytic Theory: An Introduction*. Oxford: Blackwell.

Elliot, A. (1996) *Subject to Ourselves*. Cambridge: Polity.

Fenstermaker, S., West, C., and Zimmerman, D. (1991) Gender inequality: New conceptual terrain. In R. L. Blumberg (ed.), *Gender, Family and Economy*. Newbury Park, CA: Sage, 289–307.

Fielding, N. (1994) Cop canteen culture. In T. Newburn and Stanko, E. A., *Just Boys Doing Business*. London: Routledge, 46–63.

Frosh, S. (1994) *Sexual Difference: Masculinity and Psychoanalysis*. London: Routledge.

Frosh, S. (1997) *For and Against Psychoanalysis*. London: Routledge.

Gadd, D. (2000) Masculinities, violence and defended psycho-social subjects. *Theoretical Criminology*, 4(4), 429–49.

Gadd, D. (2002) Masculinities and violence against female partners. *Social and Legal Studies*, 11(1), 61–81.

Garland, D. (1985) *Punishment and Welfare*. Aldershot: Gower.

Garland, D. (1994) Of crimes and criminals: The development of criminology in Britain. In M. Maguire, R. Morgan, and R. Reiner (eds.), *The Oxford Handbook of Criminology*. Oxford: Clarendon Press, 17–68.

Gatens, M. (1996) *Imaginary Bodies: Ethics, Power and Corporeality*. London: Routledge.

Gelsthorpe, L. (1989) *Sexism and the Female Offender*. Aldershot: Gower.

Gelsthorpe, L., and Morris, A. (1988) Feminism and criminology in Britain. *British Journal of Criminology*, 28(2), 93–110.

Gelsthorpe, L., and Morris, A. (1990) (eds.) *Feminist Perspectives in Criminology*. Milton Keynes: Open University Press.

Gibbs, J. T., and Merighi, J. R. (1994) Young black males: Marginality, masculinity and criminality. In T. Newburn and E. A. Stanko (eds.), *Just Boys Doing Business? Men, Masculinities and Crime*. London: Routledge, 64–80.

Giddens, A. (1976) *New Rules of Sociological Method*. London: Hutchinson.

Giddens, A (1991) *Modernity and Self-Identity*. Cambridge: Polity Press.

Gilmore, D (1993) *Manhood in the Making: Cultural Concepts of Masculinity*. New Haven, CT: Yale University Press.

Goffman, E. (1979) *Gender Advertisements*. New York: Harper & Row.

Goodey, J. (1997) Boys don't cry: Masculinities, fear of crime and fearlessness. *British Journal of Criminology*, 37(3), 401–18.

Goodey, J. (1998a) Understanding racism and masculinity: Drawing on research with boys aged eight to sixteen. *International Journal of the Sociology of Law*, 26, 393–418.

Goodey, J. (1998b) Doping research on "fear of crime, boys, race and masculinities": Utilising a feminist standpoint epistemology. *International Journal of Social Research Methodology: Theory and Practice*, 1, 137–51.

Goodey, J. (2000) Biographical lessons for criminology. *Theoretical Criminology*, 4(4), 473–98.

Graef, R. (1992) *Living Dangerously: Young Offenders in Their Own Words*. London: HarperCollins.

Gramsci, A. (1971) *Selection From the Prison Notebooks*. London, Lawrence & Wishart.

Groombridge, N. (1993) Car crime: Is joyriding a male driving disorder? In *Masculinity and Crime: Issues of Theory and Practice*, Conference Report, Brunel University, Centre for Criminal Justice Research, September, 25–35.

Groombridge, N. (1998) Masculinities and crimes against the environment. *Theoretical Criminology*, 2(2), 248–67.

Groombridge, N. (1999) Perverse criminologies: The closet of Doctor Lombroso. *Social and Legal Studies*, 8(4), 529–48.

Grosz, E. (1990) A note on essentialism and difference. In S. Unew (ed.), *Feminist Knowledge. Critique and Construct*. London: Routledge, 332–44.

Grosz, E. (1994) *Volatile Bodies: Towards a Corporeal Feminism*. St. Leonards, Australia: Allen & Unwin.

Grosz, E., and Probyn, E. (1995) (eds.) *Sexy Bodies: Strange Carnalities of Feminism*. London: Routledge.

Hahn Rafter, N., and Heidensohn, F. (1995) (eds.) *International Feminist Perspectives in Criminology: Engendering a Discipline*. Buckingham: Open University Press.

Hall, S. (2002) Daubing the drudges of fury: Men, violence and the piety of the "hegemonic masculinity" thesis. *Theoretical Criminology*, 6(1), forthcoming.

Hearn, J. (1987) *The Gender of Oppression: Men, Masculinity and the Critique of Marxism*. Brighton: Harvester Wheatsheaf.

Hearn, J. (1996) Is masculinity dead? A critique of the concept of masculinity. In M. Mac an Ghaill (ed.), *Understanding Masculinities*. Buckingham: Open University Press, 202–17.

Hearn, J. (1998) *The Violences of Men*. London: Sage.

Hearn, J., and Morgan, D. (eds.) (1990) *Men, Masculinities and Social Theory*. London: Unwin Hyman.

Heidensohn, F. (1985) *Women and Crime*. London: Macmillan.

Heidensohn, F. (1989) *Crime and Society*. London: Macmillan.

Heidensohn, F. (1994) Gender and crime. In M. Maguire, R. Morgan, and R. Reiner (eds.), *The Oxford Handbook of Criminology*. Oxford: Clarendon Press, 997–1039.

Heidensohn, F. (1995) Feminist perspectives and their impact on criminology and criminal justice in Britain. In N. Hahn Rafter and F. Heidensohn (eds.), *International Feminist Perspectives in Criminology: Engendering a Discipline*. Buckingham: Open University Press, 63–85.

Henriques, J., Hollway, W., Urwin, C., Venn, C., and Walkerdine, V. (1984) *Changing the Subject: Psychology, Social Regulation and Subjectivity*. London: Methuen.

Holland, S., and Scourfield, J. B. (2000) Managing marginalized masculinities: Men and probation. *Journal of Gender Studies*, 9(2),199–211.

Hollway, W. (1989) *Subjectivity and Method in Psychology: Gender, Meaning and Science*. London: Sage.

Hollway, W., and Jefferson, T. (1996) Date rape. Paper presented to the American Society of Criminology Conference, Miami., November.

Hollway, W., and Jefferson, T. (1997) Eliciting narrative through the in-depth interview. *Qualitative Inquiry*, 3(1), 53–70.

Hollway, W., and Jefferson, T. (1998) "A kiss is just a kiss": Date rape, gender and subjectivity. *Sexualities*, 1(4), 405–23.

Hollway, W., and Jefferson, T. (2000) *Doing Qualitative Research Differently: Free Association. Narrative and the Interview Method*. London: Sage.

Hood-Williams, J. (1997) Stories for sexual difference. *British Journal of Sociology of Education*, 18(1), 81–99.

Hood-Williams, J. (2001) Gender, masculinities and crime: From structures to psyches. *Theoretical Criminology*, 5(1), 37–60.

Hood-Williams, J., and Cealey Harrison, W. (1998) Trouble with gender. *Sociological Review*, 46(1), 73–94.

Jackson, D. (1990) *Unmasking Masculinity: A Critical Autobiography*. London: Routledge.

Jefferson, T. (1992) Wheelin' and stealin'. *Achilles Heel*, Summer, 10–12.

Jefferson, T. (1994a) Theorizing masculine subjectivity. In T. Newburn and E. E. Stanko (eds.), *Just Boys Doing Business? Men, Masculinities and Crime*. London: Routledge, 10–31.

Jefferson, T. (1994b) Crime, Criminology, Masculinity and Young Men. In A. Coote (ed.), *Families, Children and Crime*. London: IPPR.

Jefferson, T. (1996a) From "little fairy boy" to "the compleat destroyer": Subjectivity and transformation in the biography of Mike Tyson. In M. Mac an Ghaill (ed.), *Understanding Masculinities*: Buckingham, Open University Press, 153–67.

Jefferson, T. (1996b) Introduction. In T. Jefferson and P. Carlen (eds.), *British Journal of Criminology*, 35(1), 1337–47.

Jefferson, T. (1996c) "Tougher than the rest": Mike Tyson and the destructive desires of masculinity. *Arena Journal*, 6, 89–105.

Jefferson, T. (1997a) Masculinities and crime. In M. Maguire, R. Morgan, and R. Reiner (eds.), *The Oxford Handbook of Criminology* (2nd ed.). Oxford: Clarendon Press, 535–57.

Jefferson, T. (1997b) The Tyson rape trial: The law, feminism and emotional truth. *Social and Legal Studies*, 6(2), 281–301.

Jefferson, T. (1998) "Muscle", "Hard Men" and "Iron" Mike Tyson: Reflections on desire, anxiety and the embodiment of masculinity. *Body and Society*, 4(1), 103–18.

Jones, S. (2000) *Understanding Violent Crime*. Buckingham: Open University Press.

Jones, S. (2001) *Criminology* (2nd ed.). London: Butterworths.

Katz, J. (1988) *Seductions of Crime: Moral and Sensual Attractions in Doing Evil*. New York: Basic Books.

Kersten, J. (1996) Culture, masculinities and violence against women. *British Journal of Criminology*, 36(3), 381–95.

Kimmell, M. (1987) The contemporary "crisis" of masculinity. In H. Brod (ed.), *The Making of Masculinities*. New York: Allen & Unwin, 121–53.

Knowles, G. J. (1999) Male prison rape: A search for causation and prevention. *Howard Journal*, 38(3), 267–82.

Leonard, E. (1982) *Women, Crime and Society: A Critique of Criminological Theory*. London: Longman.

Levi, M. (1994) Masculinities and white-collar crime. In T. Newburn and E. A. Stanko (eds.), *Just Boys Doing Business? Men, Masculinities and Crime*. London: Routledge, 234–52.

Liddle, M. (1996) State, masculinity and law: Some comments on English gender and English state formation. *British Journal of Criminology*. 36(3), 361–79.

MacInnes, J. (1998) *The End of Masculinity: The Confusion of Sexual Genesis and Sexual Difference in Modern Society*. Buckingham: Open University Press.

Maguire, M., Morgan, R., and Reiner, R. (1997) [1994] *The Oxford Handbook of Criminology* (2nd ed.). Oxford: Clarendon Press.

Mangan, J., and Walvin, J. (1987) (eds.) *Manliness and Morality: Middle-Class Masculinity in Britain and America 1800–1940*. Manchester: Manchester University Press.

Marchland, M. H., and Runyan, A. S. (2000) *Gender and Global Restructuring: Sightings. Sites and Resistances*. London: Routledge.

Masculinity and Crime: Issues of Theory and Practice (1993) Conference Report, Centre for Criminal Justice Research, Brunel University, September.

Maudsen, M. (1993) What is hegemonic masculinity? *Theory in Society*, 22, 643–57.

McMahon, A (1993) Male readings of feminist theory: The psychologisation of sexual politics in the masculinity literature. *Theory and Society*, 22(5), 675–96.

McMahon, A (1999) *Taking Care of Men*. Cambridge: Cambridge University Press.

Messerschmidt, J. W. (1993) *Masculinities and Crime: Critique and Reconceptualization of Theory*. Lanham, MD: Rowman & Littlefield.

Messerschmidt, J. W. (1994) Schooling, masculinities, and youth crime by white boys. In T. Newburn and E. A. Stanko (eds.), *Just Boys Doing Business? Men, Masculinities and Crime*. London: Routledge, 57–82.

Messerschmidt, J. W. (1997) *Crime as Structured Action: Gender, Race, Class and Crime*. Thousand Oaks, CA: Sage.

Messerschmidt, J. W.(1999) Making bodies matter : Adolescent masculinities, the body and varieties of violence. *Theoretical Criminology*, 3(2), 197–220.

Messerschmidt, J. W, (2000) *Nine Lives: Adolescent Masculinities, the Body and Violence*. Boulder, CO: Westview Press.

Middleton, P (1992) *The Inward Gaze: Masculinity and Subjectivity in Modern Culture*. London; Routledge.

Morris, A. (1987) *Women, Crime and Criminal Justice*. Oxford: Basil Blackwell.

Muncie, J., McLaughlin, E., and Langan, M. (eds.) (1996) *Criminological Perspectives: A Reader*. London: Sage.

Murphy, T. (1996) Bursting binary bubbles: Law, literature and the sexed body. In J. Morison and C. Bell (eds.), *Tall Stories? Reading Law and Literature*. Aldershot: Dartmouth, 57–82.

Murray, C. (1990) *The Emerging British Underclass* (with responses by Frank Field, Joan C. Brown, Nicholas Deakin, and Alan Walker). London: IEA Health and Welfare Unit.

Naffine, N. (1985) The masculinity–femininity hypothesis. *British Journal of Sociology*, 25(4), 365–81.

Naffine, N. (1987) *Female Crime: The Construction of Women in Criminology*. Sydney: Allen & Unwin.

Naffine, N. (1995) (ed.) *Gender, Crime and Feminism*. Aldershot: Dartmouth.

Naffine, N. (1997) *Feminism and Criminology*. Cambridge: Polity.

Newburn, T., and Stanko, E. A. (eds.) (1994a) *Just Boys Doing Business? Men, Masculinities and Crime*. London: Routledge.

Newburn, T., and Stanko, E. A. (1994b) When men are victims: The failure of victimology. In T. Newburn and E. A. Stanko (eds.), *Just Boys Doing Business? Men, Masculinities and Crime*. London: Routledge, 57–82.

Newton, C. (1994) Gender theory and prison sociology: Using theories of masculinities to interpret the sociology of prisons for men. *Howard Journal of Criminal Justice*, 33 (3), 193–204.

O'Donnell, M,. and Sharpe, S. (2000) *Uncertain Masculinities: Youth, Ethnicity and Class in Contemporary Britain*. London: Routledge.

Pearson, G. (1983) *Hooligan: A History of Respectable Fears*. London: Macmillan.

Pease, B. (1999) *Recreating Men: Postmodern Masculinity Politics*. London: Sage.

Polk, K. (1994a) Masculinity, honour and confrontational homicide. In T. Newburn and E. A. Stanko (eds.), *Just Boys Doing Business? Men, Masculinities and Crime*. London: Routledge.

Polk, K. (1994b) *When Men Kill*. Cambridge: Cambridge University Press.

Potts, D. (1996) Why do men commit most crime? Focusing on masculinity in a prison group. Wakefield, UK: West Yorkshire Probation Service.

Rock, P. (1988) The present state of criminology in Britain. *British Journal of Criminology*, 28, 188–99.

Rock, P. (1994) The social organisation of British criminology. In M. Maguire, R. Morgan, and R. Reiner (eds.), *The Oxford Handbook of Criminology*. Oxford: Clarendon Press, 125–48.

Rose, N. (1987) Transcending the public/private. *Journal of Law and Society*, 14(1), 61–75.

Rose, N. (1989) *Governing the Soul*. London: Routledge.

Rose, N. (1994) Expertise and the government of conduct. *Studies in Law, Politics and Society*, 14, 359–97.

Rose, N. (1999) *Powers of Freedom: Reframing Political Thought*. Cambridge: Cambridge University Press.

Rose, N., and Valverde, M. (1998) Governed by law? *Social and Legal Studies*, 7(4), 541–53.

Ryder, R. (1991) The cult of machismo. *Criminal Justice*, 9(1), 12–13.

Scourfield, J. B. (1998) Probation officer working with men. *British Journal of Social Work*, 28(4), 581–99.

Scraton, P. (1990) Scientific knowledge or masculine discourses? Challenging patriarchy in criminology. In L. Gelsthorpe and A. Morris, *Feminist Perspectives in Criminology*. Milton Keynes: Open University Press, 10–25.

Segal, L. (1990) *Slow Motion; Changing Masculinities, Changing Men* London. Virago.

Sheptycki, J., and Westmarland, L. (1993) Metaphors, masculinity and the reproduction of manliness in policing discourse. In *Masculinity and Crime: Issues of Theory and Practice. Conference Report*. Centre for Criminal Justice Research, Brunel University, 114–28.

Sim, J. (1994) "Tougher than the rest"? Men in prison. In T. Newburn and E. A. Stanko (eds.), *Just Boys Doing Business? Men, Masculinities and Crime*, London: Routledge, 100–17.

Smart, C. (1977) *Women, Crime and Criminology*, London: Routledge & Kegan Paul.

Smart, C. (1989) *Feminism and the Power of Law*. London: Routledge.

Smart, C. (1990) Feminist approaches to criminology or postmodern woman meets atavistic man. In L. Gelsthorpe and A. Morris (eds.), *Feminist Perspectives in Criminology*. Buckingham: Open University Press, 70–84.

Snider, L. (1998) Towards safer societies: Punishment, masculinities and violences against women. *British Journal of Criminology*, 38(1), 1–39.

Sparks, R. (1996) Masculinity and heroism in the Hollywood "blockbuster." *British Journal of Criminology*, 36(3), 348–59.

Stanko, E. A. (1994) Challenging the problem of men's individual violence. In T. Newburn and E. Stanko (eds.), *Just Boys Doing Business? Men, Masculinities and Crime*. London: Routledge, 32–45.

Stanko, E. A. (1995) Gender and crime. *Criminal Justice Matters*, 19, 3–4.

Stanko, E. A., and Hobdell, K. (1993) Assault on men: Masculinity and male victimisation. *British Journal of Criminology*, 33(3), 400–15.

Stanko, E. A., Marian, L., Crusp, D., Manning, R., Smith, J., and Cowan, S. (1998) *Taking Stock: What Do We Know About Violence?* Uxbridge: ESRC Violence Research Programme, Brunel University.

Sumner, C. (1990) Foucault, gender and the censure of deviance. In L. Gelsthorpe and A. Morris (eds.), *Feminist Perspectives in Criminology*. Buckingham: Open University Press, 26–40.

Sunley, R. (1996) *Criminal Justice and the "Crisis of Masculinity."* Leicester: Scarman Centre for the Study of Public Order, University of Leicester.

Taylor, I. (1994) The political economy of crime. In M. Maguire, R. Morgan, and R. Reiner (eds.), *The Oxford Handbook of Criminology*. Oxford: Clarendon Press, 469–510.

Taylor, I. (1999) *Crime in Context*. London: Sage.

Thurston, R (1996) Are you sitting comfortably? Men's storytellings, masculinities, prison culture and violence. In M. Mac an Ghaill (ed.), *Understanding Masculinities*. Buckingham, Open University Press, 139–52.

Thurston, R., and Benyon, J. (1995) Men's own stories, lives and violence. In R. E. Dobash, R. P. Dobash, and L. Noaks (eds.), *Gender and Crime*. Cardiff: University of Wales Press, 181–201.

Thomsen, S. (1997) A top night: Social protest, masculinity and the culture of drinking violence. *British Journal of Criminology*, 37(1), 90–102.

Thomsen, S. (1998) "He had to be a poofter or something": Violence, male honour and heterosexual panic. *Journal of Interdisciplinary Gender Studies*, 3(2), 44–57.

Walkerdine, V. (1995) Subject to change without notice: Psychology, postmodernity and the popular. In S. Pile and N. Thrift (1995), *Mapping the Subject: Geographies of Cultural Transformation*. London: Routledge, 309–31.

Walklate, S. (1995) *Gender and Crime: An Introduction*. Hemel Hempstead: Prentice Hall/Harvester Wheatsheaf.

West, C., and Zimmerman, D. H. (1987) Doing gender. *Gender and Society*, 1(2), 125–51.

Westmarland, L (1997) Uniformed bodies of men. Paper presented at the *SLSA Conference* "Crossing Boundaries," University of Cardiff, April.

Wetherell, M., and Edley, N. (1999) Negotiating hegemonic masculinity: Imaginary positions and psycho-discursive practices. *Feminism and Psychology*, 9(3), 335–56.

Wincup. E. (1995) Gender and imprisonment. *Criminal Justice Matters*, 19, Spring, 18–19.

Worrall, A (1990) *Offending Women: Female Lawbreakers and the Criminal Justice System*. London: Routledge.

Young, A. (1996) *Imagining Crime*. London: Sage.

Young, K. (1995) Why do men want to be victims? In T. Lloyd and T. Wood (eds.), *What Next for Men?* London: Working With Men, 211–18.

16

"Abominable and Detestable": Understanding Homophobia and the Criminalization of Sodomy

Mary Bernstein

In 1986, the US Supreme Court found no constitutional right to engage in "homosexual" sodomy and thus upheld a Georgia anti-sodomy law in its now-infamous *Bowers v. Hardwick* decision. The case involved a gay man arrested in his own bedroom for having sex with another consenting adult male. In its trek through the lower courts, judges ruled that the case could not be combined with a case of consensual sodomy between different-sex adults, thus ruling only on laws restricting the sexual activity between adults of the same sex. In his concurrence with the *Hardwick* decision, Chief Justice Burger claimed: "Condemnation of [homosexual] practices is firmly rooted in Judeo-Christian moral and ethical standards.... To hold that the act of homosexual sodomy is somehow protected as a fundamental right would be to cast aside millennia of moral teaching."[1] In fact, history and anthropology both tell us that same-sex erotic desire has existed in diverse forms throughout the millennia and in different cultural contexts (Greenberg and Bystyrn 1982; Greenberg 1988; Fone 2000). While love between two men or two women and other forms of same-sex eroticism have sometimes been embraced and even exalted, at other times same-sex desire is harshly condemned.

The degree to which same-sex erotic relations have been accepted or sanctioned varies over time and across societies. Today, laws against consensual sexual acts between adults in private – the so-called sodomy statutes – are often equated with homophobia and state condemnation of homosexuality. In seeking to understand the relationship between homophobia and the criminalization of sodomy, this essay will examine the symbolic and material meanings attached to the sodomy statutes and explore contemporary explanations of homophobia and its related concepts, heteronormativity and heterosexism (Adam 1998).

Sodomy Statutes

The sodomy statutes appear to constitute the bedrock of homophobia apparently criminalizing lesbians and gay men themselves. Opposition to sodomy stems initially from objections to nonprocreative sex; sodomy statutes condemned such acts between different-sex as well as same-sex partners (Greenberg 1988), although sodomy was often understood to refer to acts between men. From the Fall of Rome to the beginning of the Renaissance, the sodomy laws were codified in the canon law of the Roman Catholic Church and sodomites were burned at the stake. "By the Renaissance, the definition of sodomy had expanded. Once only sexual, the sin had now become conflated with all kinds of social deviance. Sodomites were accused of being heretics, traitors, sorcerers, or witches, the cause of plagues and civil disaster" (Fone 2000: 8). As repression of sodomites increased in the late eighteenth and early nineteenth century, communities of sodomites formed and developed a shared sense of identity. For the "mollies," this identity was based on cross-dressing as well as on sexual behavior.

Cross-dressing and homosexual relations were commonplace among many indigenous peoples in the Americas (see, e.g., Terl 2000). European colonizers exported their views on such practices to the Americas as they worked to eradicate sodomy among indigenous people through terror and extermination. Viewed as an offense to their Christian God, the colonizers embarked on a campaign of mass destruction and appropriation of Native land, carried out partially in the name of abolishing sin (Fone 2000: 319–21).

From the late nineteenth to the twentieth century, psychologists and sexologists in Europe and the United States began to classify people in terms of their sexual object choice[2] and to define "homosexuals" as a separate group of people, distinct from heterosexuals (Fone 2000: 4). Although sexuality continued to be defined as sinful and amoral, it began to take on medical meaning, defined in psychological terms as a pathology or mental illness. In the hands of the medical establishment, the cure was often worse than the "disease," as homosexuals were forcibly detained in mental institutions and given shock therapy or drug treatment (Fone 2000: 10). Whether homosexuality was viewed as a sin, a crime, or a sickness gave one group or another authority over its definition, and thus the power to control it (Foucault 1978). To this day, competing groups continue to vie for definitional power over homosexuality. The shifting discourse would ultimately help relax strictures against sodomy and homosexuality, as legal authorities conceded that "mental illness" should be treated by medical experts, not punished by the judicial system (Bernstein 2001).

In contrast to viewing gays and straights as two separate species, Freud suggested that infants were born with a potential for bisexuality, but he maintained that heterosexuality was the "mature" resolution of the Oedipal complex and that society would run amok if all forms of sexual desire were gratified (Freud 1961 [1930]). In 1948, Alfred Kinsey and colleagues published *Sexual Behavior in the Human Male*. Known as the Kinsey report, this controversial book found that by the age of 45, 37 percent of all men had had a homosexual encounter that culminated in orgasm. Kinsey suggested that rather than representing two types of species, straight and gay, homosexuality and heterosexuality should be viewed as part of a continuum of sexual behavior, with "exclusive" heterosexuals and homosexuals at opposite ends of the spectrum and everyone else in between. Thus Freud and Kinsey provided a conceptual framework and empirical evidence that could be used to challenge the pathologization of homosexuality, but hostility to homosexuality, nonetheless, remains rampant. Today, "[h]omosexuality is illegal in 85 countries; it is punished with death in eight of them, and draws a prison term of ten years to life in seven, three to ten years in eleven nations, and up to three years in ten others" (Ungar 2001: 236). What accounts for changes in the sodomy laws? In this section, I focus on the US case, and then I suggest some general ways to understand the decriminalization of sodomy and homophobia more generally.

Although laws against sodomy are commonly associated with homosexuality, they often apply to different- as well as same-sex couples. The British North American colonies in the 1600s and 1700s took language from English common law and prohibited the "abominable and detestable crime against nature, either with mankind or with beast" (Leonard 1993: 66). Just exactly what is covered by such laws has changed over time. In English common law, such archaic terminology once referred to anal intercourse, or what the British call "buggery." The US states codified prohibitions against sodomy into law after Independence.

Over time, through either express statutory language or judicial interpretation, the breadth of such laws has been expanded to include any form of oral–genital contact in addition to anal sex. Often such codification came in response to challenges that the statutes should be voided for vagueness (Leonard 1993). In some states, it was unclear whether sexual acts between women were covered (Halley 1994). Punishments in the United States varied from short-term incarceration to life in prison (Apasu-Gbotsu et al. 1986). Although what have come to be termed "sodomy statutes" were originally intended to forbid any nonprocreative sexual activity,[3] and many state laws forbade such acts between different-sex as well as same-sex couples, they are now popularly associated with homosexuality, despite the fact that heterosexual couples have sometimes been prosecuted under the sodomy laws (e.g., *People v. Onofre*; *Commonwealth v. Bonadio*).[4]

To understand the contemporary significance of the sodomy statutes, it is important to understand their symbolic and material implications, the relationship between culture and power, and the relationship between sodomy and lesbian and gay identity. Sodomy laws have come to be associated almost exclusively with lesbians and gay men, in part through the medical categorization of homosexuality, and also through the lesbian and gay movement which has often relied on the idea that homosexuality is innate (Bernstein 2002a). Why do the sodomy statutes continue to remain important for lesbians and gay men?

Prohibitions that criminalize private, consensual sodomy between adults have been, and continue to be, used to justify legal discrimination against lesbians and gay men (Copelon 1990; Cain 1993). Historically, these statutes have been used to deny basic rights of association to lesbians and gay men, making, for example, lesbian and gay bars illegal and banning lesbian and gay student groups (Boggan et al. 1975). In a rally against Georgia's sodomy law, activist Sue Hyde declared: "We make a particular demand today that the seven states [that criminalize only same-sex sodomy] . . . not only repeal these odious statutes, but also apologize to us for the unpardonable offense of defining us as a sexually criminal class of citizens" (quoted in Ross 1990). By effectively equating lesbians and gay men with the commission of illegal acts, the sodomy statutes continue to be used to justify denying employment to lesbians and gay men, removing children from lesbian mothers, and a host of other injustices (Rubenstein 1993). In one notorious case (*Ward v. Ward*), a Florida court awarded custody of a child to the father who had been previously convicted of murder rather than leave the child with the mother who was a lesbian. During the 2000 presidential election, the American Family Association tried to prevent Arizona Republican Representative Jim Kolbe from speaking at the Republican National Convention because he was openly gay. The Association claimed that because Arizona's sodomy statute was still on the books (it was overturned one year later), Kolbe was a criminal in his own home state and thus should not be allowed to speak (American Civil Liberties Union 2000). Although few people are actually arrested under the sodomy statutes, the collateral damage remains great.

Symbolically, laws against sodomy signify state disapproval of sexual conduct considered by many to be sinful, sick, or morally repugnant, giving the state's official stamp of approval to heterosexual behavior. Even more profoundly, such laws signify support for a heteronormative order that posits distinct gender roles for men and women and thus supports a strict sex/gender system (Rubin 1984). This hegemonic masculinity equates penetration with femininity and hence with emasculation. In this view, men should be the agents of sexual encounters, not their object (Connell 1995). Like homophobia, opposition to sodomy is rooted in firm beliefs about gender and heterosexuality.

Whether or not sodomy laws are overturned is determined by cultural and political factors. Based on an analysis of both judicial and legislative decision-making, I have argued elsewhere (Bernstein 2001) that sodomy-law repeal in the United States was possible because the state could maintain its condemnation of sodomy, while simultaneously disavowing responsibility for punishing every moral transgression. After all, immorality need not be equated with criminality. Secondly, the right to privacy was also used to justify removal of sanctions on the basis that no one would have to know about the gender/sexual transgressions taking place. The sodomy statutes directly challenge heteronormativity. Sexual contact between persons of the same sex fundamentally challenges hegemonic views of masculinity and femininity with their attendant views of sexuality. The rubric of the right to privacy allows laws to change while leaving dominant norms unchallenged (Bernstein forthcoming). Furthermore, when activists engage with the state, they must circumvent the challenge to heteronormativity symbolized by the laws. This occurs not only in the area of criminal law, but in family and civil rights law as well.

In addition, Backer (1993) contends that pursuing change through privacy constitutes a "liberal bargain of tolerance" so that the deviant status of homosexuality remains intact, as secrecy is the price to be paid for being left alone by the state. Cole and Eskridge contend that sodomy is criminalized because of the message it communicates. They claim that "Public expression of same-sex intimacy is as important a critique of gender assumptions and gender roles in American society as any published treatise" (1994: 328); therefore, it is expressive and should be subject to strict scrutiny under the first amendment. "Because lesbians, gay men, and bisexuals explore and develop their sexual identity through private sexual conduct, that 'private' conduct is critical to their ability to take part as lesbians, gay men, and bisexuals in public life" (1994: 329). This policy is enshrined in the military's "don't ask, don't tell" policy which allows lesbians and gay men to serve in the military as long as their homosexuality is not made public. Echoing Backer, Cole and Eskridge claim that by allowing lesbians and gay men to serve silently in the armed forces, "the military seeks to regulate not homosexuality itself, but its public acknowledgment and expression, that is, its communicative content" (1994: 333).

Activism to repeal sodomy laws varies over time, sometimes challenging the sex-phobic culture, at other times sticking to dominant gender norms. Over time, as opposition to repeal became more vocal and coalesced around the issue of homosexuality rather than privacy rights, activists emphasized cultural change rather than employing conservative rhetoric strategically in order to change laws. For example, in 1985, when Wisconsin, by special legislative bill, omitted sanctions for private, consensual-sex acts between adults, it stated explicitly that the state did not encourage sex outside of marriage and supported the institution of marriage (Apasu-Gbotsu et al. 1986). Thus the dominant sex/ gender system was left intact, despite the decriminalization of sodomy. Yet, in early 1990, Georgia activists staged a demonstration that "included gay couples lying down together in the road and embracing" (Walston and Usdansky 1990). According to the *Atlanta Journal and Constitution*, Representative Cynthia McKinney, one of the bill's sponsors, "thought some House members were frightened off by mentions of homosexuality associated with the bill and that others harbored resentment stemming from a demonstration against the state sodomy law" (Walston and Usdansky 1990). At times, activists emphasize the importance of challenging the cultural meaning attached to the sodomy statutes, and at other times they focus on changing the law in any way they can (Bernstein forthcoming).

Cultural and political factors also explain broader patterns of decriminalization across the United States and cross-nationally. Nice (1988) argues that cultural conservatism, particularly as exhibited through conservative religious views on sexuality, account for the maintenance of sodomy laws. He finds that the size of the Baptist population and the cultural conservatism of the state, as well as the ideology of the state's democratic party, account for both the presence of sodomy laws and for the length of sentence associated with the law. Nice found that neither political-party competition nor education explained changes in these laws. Today, 15 American states retain their sodomy statutes. Of those, 9 can be found in the conservative south or Southwest[5] and the rest are located in the Midwest, West, and Northeast.[6] Current challenges to the remaining sodomy laws in both the US Supreme Court and in several state courts increase the likelihood that the status of these laws will change. In their cross-national comparison of the decriminalization of sodomy, Frank and McEneaney (1999) test whether a "cultural opportunity structure" which consists of cultural individualism marked by a commitment to individual human rights, social movement activity, gender equality, and linkages to world society explains cross-national variation in legal change, controlling for institutionalized state religion. They found that social movement activity influenced the liberalization of policies regarding sex between men and between women, but state religion only influenced laws about sex between women. When the model was run without the measure of social-movement activity, gender equality and world linkages also explained decriminalization of sex between women. Their findings suggest that individualism strongly affected the formation of gay and lesbian social movements, while gender equality affected the liberalization of state policies.

Homophobia

For many, the key to understanding the continued criminalization of sodomy lies in understanding "homophobia," a term coined by psychologist George Weinberg in 1967 (Britton 1990: 423). Weinberg described the typical (male) homophobe in no uncertain terms:

> Most men who loathe homosexuals have a deathly fear of abandonment in the direction of passivity. The surrender of control signifies to them a loss of masculinity, and their demand for control produces narrowness.... The person I am describing usually feels under tremendous pressure to be the aggressor in sex, and he expects conformity and passivity on the part of his woman.... If a son is homosexual, he goes berserk... he might take a punch at the boy.... But why his assault?... One assaults him because one is mortally afraid of him. (1972: 3–4)

The word homophobia was quickly adopted by the gay liberation movement of the 1970s in order to lessen the opprobrium associated with homosexuality and place the onus of self-justification on those opposed to homosexuality, rather than on homosexuals themselves. In this way, homophobes were put on the defensive, obligated to explain their opposition to homosexuality, rather than forcing lesbians and gay men to account for their very existence (Cruikshank 1992: 93).

Although Weinberg claimed that the homophobe does not really want homosexual experiences (1972: 2), others claimed that deep down, those who are most homophobic fear their own latent homosexual desires. The tongue-in-cheek appropriation of Shakespeare's "The lady doth protest too much, methinks" has come to embody much of the psychological research on homophobia (e.g., Moss 1997). Thus many psychologists argue that homophobia stems from repressed erotic desires, as a reaction-formation defense against admitting "homosexual tendencies" (Herek 2000).

Embedded in Weinberg's description of the homophobe is a commentary on what Connell (1995) later termed "hegemonic masculinity," referring to the dominant form of masculinity in Western societies that defines itself in opposition to "femininity," and as not homosexual. Lesbians who are stereotyped as mannish, and gay men as effeminate, thus violate traditional gender roles and norms. Fear that one cannot live up to gender-role expectations – that is, fear or panic that one could be mistaken for being gay or lesbian – could lead to homophobia. Given the primacy placed on masculinity by Western cultures, men are more homophobic than women, and hold more negative attitudes toward gay men than toward lesbians. By exhibiting antigay/lesbian attitudes, heterosexuals who are afraid of being labeled deviant prove that their gender is appropriately masculine or feminine (see discussions in Britton 1990; Kite and Whitley 1998).

Adam points out that queer theory is a more sophisticated version of the traditional "gender-panic" theory. "Heterosexual masculinity builds itself precisely through the simultaneous exploitation and denial of homosexuality" (1998: 395). Here, homophobia is understood as "heteronormativity" and the source of these norms are located in culture, texts, and the structure of language. After all, without the homosexual, the "heterosexual" cannot exist. Each half of this binary opposition requires the other in order to achieve coherence (Seidman 1997).

The parallel between queer theory and psychological explanations for homophobia is not surprising, given the former's reliance on psychoanalysis (Adam 1998). Whereas psychology suggests that clinical or therapeutic interventions are needed to alleviate homophobia, queer theory emphasizes that disrupting the representation of binary oppositions between heterosexuality and homosexuality would expose heteronormativity. So, for queer theorists, eradicating the binary categories of gay/straight becomes the important political intervention. Yet as Seidman (1993) argues, when cultural practices are reduced to textual analysis, social critique is limited as social structures, institutions, and politics are ignored.

Nonetheless, both culture and law reflect gender-panic theory and psychological understandings of homophobia. In the United States, for example, a perpetrator could claim that a physical assault on a gay man was justified under the "fighting words" doctrine by alleging that the victim had made a pass at him (such a situation was far less likely to occur among women). Cultural norms support the "he-made-a-pass-at-me" excuse for gay-bashing. Karen Franklin found that three out of ten college students who had not actually attacked a homosexual "reported a likelihood to assault or harass a homosexual who flirted with or propositioned them [which] suggests a cultural permission to engage in violence based on homosexual innuendo" (2000: 354). Although it is less justifiable today as a legal defense, gender panic remains an important aspect of homophobia.

Much of the opposition to lesbian and gay rights stems from conservative religious denominations (Herman 1994; Scott 1998; Adam et al. 1999),[7] but the reasons for this opposition are open to debate. Biblical prohibitions against homosexuality may provide one explanation (Nyberg and Alston 1976). For many, the story of Sodom and Gomorrah represents the founding text of religious opposition, detailing God's destruction of these cities as punishment for homosexuality. But other religious scholars interpret this text to be about denial of hospitality rather than about sodomy or homosexuality (Greenberg 1988: 135–6). The other biblical foundation of religious opposition to homosexuality stems from Leviticus, which commands "thou shall not lie with mankind as with womankind; it is an abomination" (quoted in Greenberg 1988: 190–1). Of course Leviticus also recommends death for people who work on the Sabbath, among other arcane dictates. Nonetheless, those who adhere to literal interpretations of the Bible commonly invoke Leviticus in order to claim that homosexuality is immoral and violates God's will (Bernstein 2002b). Religion and homophobia may also be linked through psychological mechanisms. Presumably, those who attend religious services more often are also more conservative and adhere to rigid gender roles. Adherence to gender-role norms could explain the relationship between religion and homophobia (Britton 1990: 436).

Much of the research on homophobia is also guided by contemporary under-standings of the "contact hypothesis," which asserts that more contact between individuals belonging to antagonistic social groups helps to undermine negative stereotypes, thus minimizing prejudice and maximizing intergroup cooperation. Because, in the psychological view, any prejudice is fundamentally irrational (e.g., Allport 1954), exposure to real lesbians and gay men will likely dispel stereotypes and educate heterosexuals about homosexuality.

Contact-theory research, however, has two main problems: The first is one of causality. Does contact increase favorable attitudes, or do lesbians and gay men come out to those who already hold favorable attitudes? Differences in attitudes toward lesbians and gays can only be attributed to differences in contact if the high- and low-contact groups are initially similar in all relevant aspects except their contact with lesbians and gays. In these studies (Young 1992; Herek and Glunt 1993; Herek and Capitanio 1996; Jordan 1997; Yang 1998), the inde-pendent variable, contact may actually be the result of, rather than the cause of, attitudes toward lesbians and gays, since lesbians and gays are more likely to disclose their sexual identity to persons who already hold positive attitudes toward them (Wells and Kline 1986). Less homophobic people are also more likely to engage in activities and social interactions with people that they know to be lesbian or gay, thus increasing their contact. The second problem with existing tests of contact theory is that they provide little theoretical guidance as to why some groups hold more favorable attitudes than others, beyond their demographic correlates and the psychological functions served by homophobia. Contact theory also cannot account for differences within groups. In examining the effect of contact based on race and ethnicity, Forbes (1997) suggests that pressure toward assimilation can actually increase conflict based on both situational factors such as job scarcity and the resulting competition for jobs.

To date, psychologists have dominated the study of homophobia. Most of these studies are atheoretical (Britton 1990: 426) or suffer from a variety of methodological flaws (Britton 1990; Herek and Glunt 1993). The psychological research on homophobia focuses predominantly on examining the demographic correlates of negative attitudes toward lesbians and gay men, including sex, age, education, race, marital status, and number of children. These studies have found that those who are older, less educated, single, or male tend to be more homophobic than those who are younger, more educated, married, or female (Britton 1990; Yang 1998; Estrada and Weiss 1999). Anti-gay hate crimes, though, are more often the purview of younger men asserting their manhood through violence (Franklin 2000). Until recently, most studies of homophobia have been limited by their reliance on single measures of homophobia that are not necessarily reliable or valid. Second, most employ convenience samples of college students, limiting their generalizability to the larger population. Third, most studies only examine attitudes toward gay men that are not necessarily related to attitudes toward lesbians (Britton 1990: 426–7; Herek and Glunt 1993; Herek and Capitanio 1996; Kite and Whitley 1998).

Theoretically, psychological explanations tend to reduce explanations for homophobia to individual psychological states, failing to recognize the ways in which constructions of lesbians and gay men have changed over time and not situating it within institutions, politics, and practices. "Like racism, [homophobia] is more damaging as a disease of institutions than as an individual's failing" (Cruikshank 1992: 16). Similarly, Adam argues that attributing homophobia to individual psychological states ignores "the politics and practices of the state, capital, or family, and their derivative institutions in producing and reproducing structured gendered and sexual relations" (1998: 395). Often referring to anti-gay sentiment and practices as heterosexism, the sociological literature attempts to make clear the analogy with other forms of prejudice, such as racism and sexism, and to emphasize that heterosexism is something both structurally and materially based and can change over time.

Sociological Understandings

Sociology provides a more structural way to understand homophobia while also recognizing the importance of local meanings attached to homosexuality. According to Fone, "Another source of homophobia is the fear that the social conduct of homosexuals – rather than homosexual behavior alone – disrupts the social, legal, political, ethical, and moral order of society, a contention supposedly supported by history and affirmed by religious doctrine" (2000: 5). This view provides an alternative to the psychological interpretation of the relationship between religion and homophobia. Using literalist interpretations of the Bible as a jumping-off point, homophobia is intertwined with reactions against modernity. Lesbians and gay men (and feminists as well) are scapegoated for the demise of "family values" represented by high rates of divorce, a decline in traditional gender roles, and an increase in single-parent families (Bernstein and Reimann 2001).

Sociocultural models of prejudice claim that negative cultural views are socially learned and embedded in individual psyches (Allport 1954). Negative stereotypes of out-group members go unchallenged because of a lack of contact with minority-group members, even though the negative stereotypes often have little or no objective basis in reality. This was particularly apparent in my study of the 1992 passage of Vermont's statewide bill to protect lesbians and gay men from discrimination in a variety of areas including housing, employment, and public accommodations (Bernstein 1997; 2002b). In testifying against the bill, for example, attorney Duncan Kilmartin (1992) claimed that the bill "could give a preferred status to practising homosexuals given to no other category of human beings. S.131 affirms and approves criminal conduct, immoral conduct and high risk conduct for the individuals involved and society at large." For the opposition, that "practice" consisted of alleged sexual behavior (both public and private) with no less than 500 partners per year, as well as with animals. The opposition depicted these images in lurid, graphic detail during the hearings (e.g., Kilmartin 1992) and claimed that lesbians and gay men were out to recruit the state's children into "homosexuality."[8] Other opponents expressed fears that half of San Francisco (portrayed as menacing men in leather) would move to Vermont upon the bill's passage. The opposition also quoted scripture to justify their opposition to the bill.

Adorno et al.'s *The Authoritarian Personality* (1993 [1950]) provides a socio-logical variation on the psychology of the homophobe. In this work, the authors associated homophobia with anti-democratic or fascist potential (Moss 1997: 201), while also recognizing the importance of societal conditions. For example, the Nazi regime arrested tens of thousands of homosexuals for their consensual sexual activity and placed them in concentration camps where many died or were exterminated (Plant 1986). The Nazis forced Jews to wear yellow stars and homosexuals to wear pink triangles to identify them. The symbol of the inverted pink triangle has been reappropriated by contemporary lesbian and gay activists as a sign of pride and survival. Harkening back to the Nazi era, lesbians and gay men were associated with communism and purged from government jobs during the McCarthyism of 1950s America. According to Johnson, "Like Communism itself, [the growth in state] bureaucracy raised the specter of a face-less, gender-less, family-less welfare state. Homosexual civil servants were seen as the natural conclusion of this frightening trend" (1994–5: 51). In the case of both Nazism and McCarthyism, homosexuality stood in for a variety of societal anxieties that fascist regimes purported to cure.

Cruikshank (1992) characterizes institutions such as the military, Roman Cath-olic, and fundamentalist churches as authoritarian. These institutions "base their objections to homosexuality on their *authority* to condemn, not upon evidence" (1992: 14, original emphasis). So in addition to being linked through psycho-logical mechanisms, religious institutions use homophobia as a way to maintain their own status and position. The link between authoritarianism and homopho-bia has been extended to explain individual orientation toward religion – whether individuals pursue religion as a means to some other goal or simply as an end in itself is thought to correlate with homophobia (Fulton 1997).

In linking homophobia to material interests, Britton contends that homopho-bia serves an identity-maintenance function for those who prefer homosocial interactions (1990) or who are located in homosocial institutions, such as the military (Britton and Williams 1995). "Men homosocial in outlook prefer other men's company and also work to maintain all-male institutions. The relationship to homophobia lies in maintaining the boundary between social and sexual interaction in a homosocially stratified society," where those in all-male insti-tutions reap a disproportionate amount of society's desired goods (Britton 1990: 425). Because homosexuality could harm prevailing social relations, men who prefer homosocial environments could lose concrete benefits. Although Britton's explanation does not account for changes in outlook over time or differences among men in homosocial institutions, it provides a useful starting point for conceptualizing homophobia as being materially and socially rooted in a desire to maintain access to cherished goods or statuses, rather than a result of individ-ual psychological states.

Others argue that homophobia, particularly against lesbians, is simply an extension of sexism embedded in patriarchal societies (Rich 1980; Rubin 1984). That women could, and even worse prefer to, live apart from men shakes up the foundation on which male dominance rests. While sexism and notions about gender clearly underlie homophobia, cultural feminist approaches that posit misogyny as an explanation for anti-lesbian sentiment do not explain homophobia against gay men (Adam 1998).

Elsewhere, Kostelac, Gaarder, and I (Bernstein and Kostelac 2002; Bernstein et al. forthcoming) build on Blumer's model of group position (1958a, 1958b) as elaborated by Lawrence Bobo and colleagues (Bobo 1983, 1999; Bobo and Zubrinsky 1996; Bobo and Hutchings 1996) to incorporate discursive, institutional, and structural elements into a more dynamic explanation for heterosexism. Drawing on Adam (1998) and Omi and Winant (1994), we utilize the concept of sexual project to explore the extent to which civilian employees and sworn officers employed by a police department have different stakes in maintaining sexual inequality as a result of the disparate status between the two groups and the relationship of masculinity to that status.

So rather than focusing solely on the irrational psychological states of individuals or their rational material calculations, Blumer's group position model locates "the sense of group position" in the discursive and political struggles of concrete groups. In other words, by themselves, neither prejudice nor self-interest can explain interracial or, in this case, sexual hostility. Instead, perceptions of group position are dynamic, historically contingent, and contested. The group-position model provides a sociological, rather than psychological, explanation of the impact of religion on sexual prejudice. As powerful institutions, religious organizations may influence heterosexism through the propagation of discourse that situates heterosexuals above lesbians and gay men. Dynamic interactions between diverse groups that have a stake in maintaining sexual prejudice influence a group's sense of its proper position. In societies or historical eras where sexual object choice is not a relevant axis of delineation, then opposition to homosexuality, if it exists at all, would not stem from the fact that sexual partners were of the same sex, although it might be a function of a general opposition to non-procreative sexuality or to sexual pleasure more generally (Greenberg 1988). This analysis allows for variations in the social construction of the homosexual, as well as the extent to which the homosexual is considered deviant, to change over time and across different societies.

In an in-depth ethnography of the Oregon Citizen's Alliance, an antigay/lesbian organization responsible for placing numerous anti-gay referenda on the ballot in Oregon, Arlene Stein argues (2001) that class as well as religion plays a role in anti-gay/lesbian activism. According to Stein, the white working class adopts conservative rhetoric that attributes its decline in social and economic status to external sources, such as government-sponsored welfare for "undeserving minorities." Stein argues that religion and conservatism address, but ultimately fail to alleviate, the psychological pain arising from external forces over which her subjects have no control. She detects a sense of shame in these anti-gay activists akin to "the hidden injuries of class" (Sennett and Cobb 1972), resulting from personal hardship, exacerbated by an individualist ideology and a religious worldview which constructs "a sense of self based upon submission and self-control" (Stein 2001: 99). Conservative ideology helps them avoid the psychologically untenable conclusion that they are to blame for their own failures. Crusading against homosexuals allows them "to repair themselves, to construct a positive sense of themselves and their families as strong and independent, in contrast to weak, shameful others" (Stein 2001: 101).

Historical and sociological studies show that homophobia and heterosexism are socially constructed, meaning disparate things in different times and places.

"Invented, fostered, and supported over time by different agencies of society – religion, government, law, and science – [homophobia] tends to break out with special venom when people imagine a threat to the security of gender roles, of religious doctrine, or of the state and society, or to the sexual safety and health of the individual" (Fone 2000: 6–7).

Conclusion

As in previous eras, opposition to homosexuality is more about the meanings attached to homosexuality than about homosexuality itself. Today, many developing countries construct homosexual identity as a sign of Western decadence or an example of cultural imperialism. This stems, in part, from the expansion of identities based on sexual object choice, an identity associated with the West, as opposed to other forms of same-sex eroticism (Adam et al. 1999; Fone 2000) that do not in themselves constitute an identity. In these countries, opposition to the West can become opposition to homosexuality. Yet others claim "the thesis that homosexuality is Western and therefore by definition decadent constitutes itself a peculiarly Western power discourse, because it denies the richness of cultural and human experience" (Palmberg 1999: 284). Studies suggest that homophobia has declined in many countries (Scott 1998), but constructions of homosexuality that are less than auspicious for lesbian and gay rights continue to retain their cultural, political, and legal power. This essay has suggested that in addition to psychological factors, researchers must attend to the ways in which social structure, institutions, and cultural practices discursively define the "homosexual" and give powerful groups a stake in supporting or opposing lesbian and gay rights in order to understand homophobia and the prospects for decriminalizing sodomy.

Notes

1 *Bowers v. Hardwick*, 487 US 186 (1986).
2 I am not arguing that individuals did not define themselves previously in terms of sexual orientation. I am only outlining the ways in which developments in psychology affected the legal status of sodomy and ultimately of lesbians and gay men.
3 A complete discussion of the origins of the sodomy statutes is beyond the scope of this research. For further information, see Greenberg 1988 and Fone 2000.
4 *People v. Onofre*, 51 N.Y. 2d 476, 434 N.Y.S. 2d 947, 415 N.E. 2d 936 (1980); *Commonwealth v. Bonadio*, 415 A. 2d 47 (Pa. 1980).
5 Alabama, Florida, Louisiana, Mississippi, North Carolina, South Carolina, Virginia, Oklahoma, and Texas (American Civil Liberties Union 2001).
6 Kansas, Missouri, Idaho, Utah, Michigan, and Massachusetts. Currently, the legal status of the laws in Massachusetts and Michigan is unclear (American Civil Liberties Union 2001).
7 It should be noted that many religious denominations have been supportive of lesbians and gay men and of lesbian and gay rights. As early as the 1960s, lesbian

and gay rights activists and gay-friendly clergy worked together to promote tolerance of homosexuality (D'Emilio 1983).

8   For a thorough discussion of these myths about lesbians and gay men, see Herek 1991.

References

American Civil Liberties Union (ACLU) (2000) Calls for arrest of openly-gay GOP convention speaker reveal danger of sodomy laws, nationwide, ACLU says. Internet press release July 31. Available online at http://www.aclu.org/2000/n073100b.html

American Civil Liberties Union (ACLU) (2001) "Crime"and punishment in America: State-by-state breakdown of sodomy laws. Internet press release, July. Available online at http://www.aclu.org/issues/gay/sodomy.html

Adam, B. D. (1998) Theorizing homophobia. *Sexualities*, 1(4), 387–404.

Adam, B. D., Duyvendak, D. W., and Krouwel, A. (1999) *The Global Emergence of Gay and Lesbian Politics: National Imprints of a Worldwide Movement.* Philadelphia: Temple University Press.

Adorno, T. W., Frenkel-Brunswick, E., and Levinson, D. J. (1993) [1950] *The Authoritarian Personality.* New York: W. W. Norton.

Allport, Gordon W. (1954) *The Nature of Prejudice.* Reading, MA: Addison-Wesley.

Apasu-Gbotsu, Y., Arnold, R. J., DiBella, P., Dorse, K., Fuller, E. L., Naturman, S. H., Pham, D. H., and Putney, J. B. (1986) Survey on the constitutional right to privacy in the context of homosexual activity. *University of Miami Law Review*, 40(1), 521–657.

Backer, L. C. (1993) Exposing the perversions of toleration: The decriminalization of private sexual conduct, the model penal code, and the oxymoron of liberal toleration. *Florida Law Review*, 45(5), 755–802.

Bernstein, M. (1997) Celebration and suppression: The strategic uses of identity by the lesbian and gay movement. *American Journal of Sociology*, 103(3), 531–65.

Bernstein, M. (2001) Gender, queer family policies and the limits of law. In M. Bernstein and R. Reimann (eds.), *Queer Families, Queer Politics: Challenging Culture and the State.* New York: Columbia University Press, 420–46.

Bernstein, M. (2002a) Identities and politics: Toward a historical understanding of the lesbian and gay movement. *Social Science History*, 26(3), 531–81.

Bernstein, M. (2002b) The contradictions of gay ethnicity: Forging identity in Vermont. In D. Meyer, N. Whittier, and B. Robnett (eds.), *Social Movements: Identity, Culture, and the State.* New York: Oxford University Press, 85–104.

Bernstein, M. (forthcoming) Nothing ventured, nothing gained? Conceptualizing success in the lesbian and gay movement. *Sociological Perspectives.*

Bernstein, M., and Kostelac, C. (2002) Lavender and blue: Attitudes about homosexuality and behavior towards lesbian and gay men among police officers. *Journal of Contemporary Criminal Justice*, 18(3), 302–28.

Bernstein, M., Kostelac, C., and Gaarder, E. (forthcoming) Understanding heterosexism: Applying theories of racial prejudice to homophobia using data from a southwestern police department. *Race, Gender, and Class.*

Bernstein, M., and Reimann, R. (eds.) (2001) *Queer Families, Queer Politics: Challenging Culture and the State.* New York: Columbia University Press.

Blumer, H. (1958a) Race prejudice as a sense of group position. *Pacific Sociological Review*, 1, 3–7.

Blumer, H. (1958b) Recent research on race relations: United States of America. *International Social Science Bulletin*, 10, 403–77.

Bobo, L. D. (1983) Attitudes toward the black political movement: Trends, meaning, and effects on racial policy preferences. *Social Psychology Quarterly*, 51(4), 287–302.

Bobo, L. D. (1999) Prejudice as group position: Microfoundations of a sociological approach to racism and race relations. *Journal of Social Issues*, 55(3), 445–72.

Bobo, L., and Hutchings, V. L. (1996) Perceptions of racial group competition: Extending Blumer's theory of group position to a multiracial social context. *American Sociological Review*, 61(6), 951–72.

Bobo, L., and Zubrinsky, C. L. (1996) Attitudes on residential integration: Perceived status differences, mere in-group preference, or racial prejudice? *Social Forces*, 74(3), 883–909.

Boggan, E. C., Haft, M. G., Lister, C., and Rupp, J. P. (1975) *The Rights of Gay People: The Basic ACLU Guide to a Gay Person's Rights* (An American Civil Liberties Union Handbook). New York: E. P. Dutton.

Britton, D. M. (1990) Homophobia and homosociality: An analysis of boundary maintenance. *Sociological Quarterly*, 31(3), 423–39.

Britton, D. M., and Williams, C. L. (1995) "Don't ask, don't tell, don't pursue": Military policy and the construction of heterosexual masculinity. *Journal of Homosexuality*, 30 (1), 1–21.

Cain, P. A. (1993) Litigating for lesbian and gay rights: A legal history. *Virginia Law Review*, 79, 1551–641.

Cole, D., and Eskridge, Jr., W. N. (1994) From handholding to sodomy: First amendment protection of homosexual (expressive) conduct. *Harvard Civil Rights-Civil Liberties Law Review*, 29(2), 319–51.

Connell, R. W. (1995) *Masculinities*. Berkeley: University of California Press.

Copelon, R. (1990) A crime not fit to be named: Sex, lies, and the Constitution. In D. Kairys (ed.), *The Politics of Law: A Progressive Critique* (rev. ed.). New York: Pantheon Books, 177–94.

Cruikshank, M. (1992) *The Gay and Lesbian Liberation Movement*. New York: Routledge.

D'Emilio, J. (1983) *Sexual Politics, Sexual Communities: The Making of a Homosexual Minority in the United States 1940–1970*. Chicago: University of Chicago Press.

Estrada, A. X., and Weiss, D. J. (1999) Attitudes of military personnel toward homosexuals. *Journal of Homosexuality*, 37(4), 83–97.

Fone, B. (2000) *Homophobia: A History*. New York: Metropolitan Books.

Forbes, H. D. (1997) *Ethnic Conflict: Commerce, Culture and the Contact Hypothesis*. New Haven, CT: Yale University Press.

Foucault, M. (1978) *The History of Sexuality: An Introduction* (vol. I). New York: Vintage.

Frank, D. J., and McEneaney, E. H. (1999) The individualization of society and the liberalization of state policies on same-sex sexual relations, 1984–1995. *Social Forces*, 77(3), 911–44.

Franklin, K. (2000: Antigay behaviors among young adults: Prevalence, patterns, and motivators in a noncriminal population. *Journal of Interpersonal Violence*, 15(4), 339–62.

Freud, S. (1961) [1930] *Civilization and its Discontents* (ed. James Strachey). New York: W. W. Norton.

Fulton, A. (1997) Identity status, religious orientation, and prejudice. *Journal of Youth and Adolescence*, 26(1), 1–11.

Greenberg, D. F. (1988) *The Construction of Homosexuality*. Chicago: University of Chicago Press.

Greenberg, D. F., and Bystryn, M. H. (1982) Christian intolerance of homosexuality. *American Journal of Sociology*, 88(3), 515–48.

Halley, J. E. (1994) Reasoning about sodomy: Act and identity in and after *Bowers v. Hardwick*. *Virginia Law Review*, 79, 1721–80.

Herek, G. M. (1991) Myths about sexual orientation: A lawyer's guide to social science Research. *Law & Sexuality*, 1, 133–72.

Herek, G. M. (2000) The psychology of sexual prejudice. *Current Directions in Psychological Science*, 9(1), 19–22.

Herek, G. M., and Capitanio, J. P. (1996) "Some of my best friends": Intergroup contact, concealable stigma, and heterosexuals' attitudes toward gay men and lesbians. *Personality and Social Psychology Bulletin*, 22(4), 412–24.

Herek, G. M., and Glunt, E. K. (1993) Interpersonal contact and heterosexuals' attitudes toward gay men: Results from a national survey. *Journal of Sex Research*, 30, 239–44.

Herman, D. (1994) *Rights of Passage: Struggles for Lesbian and Gay Legal Equality.* Toronto: University of Toronto Press.

Johnson, D. K. (1994–5) "Homosexual citizens": Washington's gay community confronts the civil service. *Washington History*, Fall/Winter, 45–63.

Jordan, K. C. (1997) The effect of disclosure on the professional life of lesbian police officers. Doctoral dissertation, City University of New York. Dissertation Abstracts International, 58–05A, 1927.

Kilmartin, D. (1992) "Testimony." Testimony before the Vermont Senate hearing on S. 131. Courtesy of Susan Sussman.

Kinsey, A. C., Pomeroy, W. B., and Martin, C. E. (1948) *Sexual Behavior in the Human Male.* Philadelphia, PA: W. B. Saunders.

Kite, M. E., and Whitley, Jr., B. E. (1998) Do heterosexual women and men differ in their attitudes toward homosexuality? A conceptual and methodological analysis. In G. M. Herek (ed.), *Stigma and Sexual Orientation.* Thousand Oaks, CA: Sage, 39–61.

Leonard, A. S. (1993) *Sexuality and the Law: An Encyclopedia of Major Legal Cases.* New York: Garland.

Moss, D. (1997) On situating homophobia. *Journal of the American Psychoanalytic Association*, 45(1), 201–15.

Nice, D. C. (1988) State deregulation of intimate behavior. *Social Science Quarterly*, 69 (1), 203–11.

Nyberg, K. L., and Alston, J. P. (1976) Analysis of public attitudes toward homosexual behavior. *Journal of Homosexuality*, 2(2), 99–107.

Omi, M., and Winant, H. (1994) *Racial Formation in the United States* (2nd ed.). New York: Routledge.

Palmberg, M. (1999) Emerging visibility of gays and lesbians in Southern Africa: Contrasting contexts. In B. D. Adam, D. W. Duyvendak, and A. Krouwel (eds.), *The Global Emergence of Gay and Lesbian Politics: National Imprints of a Worldwide Movement.* Philadelphia, PA: Temple University Press, 266–92.

Plant, R. (1986) *The Pink Triangle: The Nazi War Against Homosexuals.* New York: Owl Books (Henry Holt).

Rich, A. (1980) Compulsory heterosexuality. In A. Snitow, C. Stansell, and S. Thompson (eds.), *Powers of Desire: The Politics of Sexuality.* New York: Monthly Review Press, 177–205.

Ross, S. Associated Press Writer (1990) Collection 7301 (National Lesbian and Gay Task Force), box 126, folder '90 Georgia. Cornell University Library, January 9.

Rubenstein, W. B. (1993) *Lesbians, Gay Men, and the Law.* New York: New Press.

Rubin, G. (1984) The traffic in women. In A. Jaggar and P. Rothenberg (eds), *Feminist Frameworks: Alternative Theoretical Accounts of the Relations Between Women and Men.* New York: McGraw-Hill, 155–71.

Scott, J. (1998) Changing attitudes to sexual morality: A cross-national comparison. *Sociology*, 32(4), 815–45.

Seidman, S. (1993) Identity and politics in a "postmodern" gay culture: Some historical and conceptual notes. In M. Warner (ed.), *Fear of a Queer Planet: Queer Politics and Social Theory*. Minneapolis: University of Minnesota Press, 105–42.

Seidman, S. (1997) *Difference Troubles: Queering Social Theory and Sexual Politics*. Cambridge: Cambridge University Press.

Sennett, R., and Cobb, J. (1972. *The Hidden Injuries of Class*. New York: Knopf.

Stein, Arlene. (2001) *The Stranger Next Door: The Story of a Small Community's Battle Over Sex, Faith, Civil Rights*. Boston: Beacon Press.

Terl, A. H. (2000) An essay on the history of lesbian and gay rights in Florida. *Nova Law Review*, 24, Spring, 793–853.

Ungar, M. (2001) Lesbian, gay, bisexual, and transgendered international alliances: The perils of success. In J. M. Bystydzienski and S. P. Schacht (eds.), *Forging Radical Alliances Across Differences: Coalition Politics for the New Millennium*. London: Rowman & Littlefield, 235–48.

Walston, C., and Usdansky, M. L. (1990) House vote kills sodomy issue for session. *Atlanta Constitution*, Feb. 3, A10. Collection 7301 (National Gay and Lesbian Task Force), box 126, folder '90 Georgia. Cornell Library.

Weinberg, G. (1972) *Society and the Healthy Homosexual*. Garden City: Anchor Books.

Wells, J. W., and Kline, W. B. (1986) Self-disclosure of homosexual orientation. *Journal of Social Psychology*, 127(2), 191–7.

Yang, A. S. (1998) *From Wrongs to Rights: Public Opinion on Gay and Lesbian American's Moves Toward Equality*. Washington, DC: National Gay and Lesbian Task Force Policy Institute.

Young, J. (1992) Attitude functions and political behavior: The issue of gay civil rights. MS thesis, Portland State University, Portland, OR.

17

The Gendering and Racializing of Criminalized Others

Elizabeth Comack

To criminalize, according to the standard dictionary definition, means to "turn a person into a criminal." Among its vast repertoire, this act stands out as one of law's most significant accomplishments. That law takes its work (and itself) seriously is indisputable. As Ngaire Naffine has noted, the official version of law is that it is an "impartial, neutral and objective system for resolving social conflict" (1990: 24) Law's task is to discern the truth of any matter placed before it. In criminal cases, truth is reached by extracting the legally relevant facts of a case to determine the guilt or innocence of the accused. In the process, law imposes an order; it imputes reason and sensibility to the messiness of everyday life. Crime categories constitute key components of law's method. The Criminal Code contributes to the appearance of consistency, precision, and uniformity. For instance, crimes against the person (like assault, assault with a weapon, assault causing bodily harm, and aggravated assault) are hierarchically ordered on the basis of their seriousness, with corresponding sanctions attached. When violence breaks out, it becomes a matter for law to impose its definition onto the event – to render a judgment on *who* is to be criminalized.

This business of criminalizing, however, is far more complicated than it might first appear. As critical legal theorists remind us, far from being an impartial, neutral, and objective enterprise, law deals in ideology and discourse – in the meanings and assumptions embedded in the language it uses, in its ways of making sense of the world, and in its corresponding practices (see, e.g., Davies 1996; Hunt 1993; Bell 1993; Kerruish 1991). Law's concern is ostensibly with making judgments on legal matters (culpability, reasonableness, admissibility, due process). But there is more at work. Extracting the facts of a case from the messiness of people's lives involves a deciphering or translation. It also involves making judgments on the legal subjects themselves – not only in terms of what they have done, but who they are and the social settings and spaces in which they move. The end result of this process is not simply the determination of a guilty party, but the creation of a criminalized Other – one who is separate in identity from, and in opposition to, the law-abiding majority.

Criminologists and sociologists of law have offered a number of ways to approach this process of creating criminalized Others. In his classic study of plea negotiation, David Sudnow (1965) used the concept of "normal crimes" to examine the activities of the court. Sudnow argued that over time, prosecutors and defense lawyers developed proverbial characterizations of offenses which encompassed features beyond the statutory conception of an offense. These included the typical manner in which offenses are committed, the social characteristics of the persons who regularly commit them, the features of the settings in which they occur, and the type of victim often involved. In a more recent work, Anne Worrall suggests that criminal cases undergo a process of normalization, "whereby an illegal action and the person who commits that action are represented as 'typical'.... The circumstances surrounding that action, the characteristics and motives of its perpetrator, the consequences for the victim, all have to be located within categories that are already known and recognized" (1990: 21).

While research on the courts (such as Sudnow's) has not typically been attuned to an analysis of gender, feminist writers have proposed differing ways of approaching the role of gender in the operation of law. Initial formulations viewed law as either "sexist" (Sachs and Wilson 1978) or "male" (MacKinnon 1982, 1983). More recently, however, Carol Smart (1992: 34) has argued that law be approached as a "gendering practice," as "one of the systems (discourses) in society that is productive not only of gender difference, but quite specific forms of polarized difference. Law is seen as bringing into being both gendered subject positions as well as ... subjectivities or identities to which the individual becomes tied or associated." In other words, law is "a mechanism for *fixing* gender differences and constructing femininity and masculinity in oppositional modes" (Smart 1995: 218; original emphasis).

Intersecting with the relation between law and gender is law's role as a racializing strategy. Writers like Marlee Kline (1994) locate law as one of the discourses in which racism is constructed and reinforced in society. More specifically, she elaborates on how certain "ideological representations of Indianness" have historically been reproduced in judicial reasoning, and their import in the encounters between First Nations people and Canadian law. In a similar vein, Sherene Razack (1998: 60) talks of the "culturalization" of racism, whereby the inferiority of certain groups is attributed to "cultural deficiency, social inadequacy and technological underdevelopment."

While the notion of law as a gendering and racializing strategy coincides with the idea of the normalization of criminal cases, the *process* by which this occurs remains unclear; that is, in the construction of normal crimes, how does law "do" gender and race? In what ways are criminalized Others gendered and racialized? One way of attending to such questions is to explore criminal cases involving violence. As Colin Sumner (1997: 1) has noted, "even a serious matter like violence is not a simple fact which speaks loudly for itself." What counts as violence is culturally and historically variable; it is "subject to the acculturated or political understandings and standpoints of the viewer" (Sumner 1997: 3). Following Sumner's lead, we can surmise that how law constructs violence in a particular case will be informed by culturally specific understandings. The question is whether and in what ways these understandings of violence are gendered and racialized.

RESEARCHING LEGAL DOCUMENTARY REALITY

The discussion which follows is based on a qualitative analysis of legal documents found in Crown attorneys' case files[1] on 45 women and 45 men who appeared before the Manitoba Court of Queen's Bench on charges of violent crime.[2] The case files included a variety of documents: police incident reports, police notes, notes written by the Crown, correspondence with the defense, pretrial memos to the Senior Crown, transcripts of preliminary hearings, presentence reports, medical reports, relevant case law, and appeal-court decisions. What can be learned from the study of these documents?

Some time ago, Dorothy Smith (1974) wrote on the social construction of documentary reality. Smith's interest was in the social organization of knowledge, how "socially organized practices of reporting and recording work upon what actually happens or has happened to create a reality in documentary form" (Smith 1974: 257). Such documents are based upon the construction of factual statements (as opposed to "facts") which give a temporal order or structure to events and assemble an account of "what actually happened." As products of a formal organization, they are produced with a particular context of reading and a particular practical purpose in mind.

Smith's analysis has relevance for the present study. Police incident reports, for example, have a distinct formulaic quality to them. Presiding officers are given the task of detailing the legally relevant facts of the case which establish the basis on which the criminal charge rests. Typically included are statements made by the accused, complainant(s), and bystanders, as well as comments by police on the demeanor of the accused. These reports form the starting point for the Crown attorney in building a case against the accused beyond a reasonable doubt.

The majority of cases which reach the Court of Queen's Bench have a preliminary hearing, the purpose of which is for the judge to determine whether there is sufficient evidence to warrant committing the accused to trial. As Marin (1995: 115) notes, the preliminary hearing is used by the defense "to test the strength and credibility of the evidence of the Crown witnesses and to take advantage of the hearing as a 'dry run' for the trial." In this respect, transcripts of the hearing offer a unique lens into the legal process. As a "dry run" for the trial, the preliminary hearing becomes a site where the strategies used by defense lawyers to undermine the case against the accused are revealed. These strategies often involve the construction of alternative accounts or plausible scenarios. Given the standard of reasonable doubt, they also entail attacks on the credibility of the Crown's key witnesses in the case.

One document found in virtually all of the Crown case files is a memo written by the Crown attorney in charge of the case to the Senior Crown. The memo typically includes factual statements about the case, the legal defenses which might be raised by defense lawyers, and descriptions of Crown witnesses (with special attention to their credibility). Also, the Crown will often comment on what are perceived to be the strengths or weaknesses of the case against the accused.

If a case goes to trial (plea bargaining often occurs after the preliminary hearing), the files may also include court transcripts of sentencing submissions, judges' reasons for sentence, pre-sentence reports, and the like. It is at the point of sentencing where competing accounts of the defendant are most likely to surface, as the Crown and defense put forward their justifications for a particular sentence, and the judge makes a determination.

Each of these documents is designed for a specific purpose and with a specific audience in mind. In combination, however, these "socially organized practices of reporting and recording" reveal the discursive practices involved in creating criminalized Others. Studying this legal documentary reality, then, can tell us a great deal about the normalization of criminal cases. We learn what is considered noteworthy or remarkable about a particular case – and what is not. In the process, the gendered and racialized presuppositions which inform law's construction of violent crime also come into view.

"Guys Will Be Guys"

Sumner (1997: 3) makes the point that "aggression and violence are not the same. Aggression is an action we accept, violence is an action we do not normally condone." The difference between the two lies not in physical action but in the meanings we attribute. Following Sumner, to the extent that aggression is acceptable behavior, it is culturally taken for granted as normal. This raises the issue of what constitutes "normal" aggression (and "normal" violence?) within a particular culture at a particular historical point in time.

In reading the case files on violent crime, it becomes clear that aggression is behavior associated with the actions of men. This coupling of aggression with masculinity is in part a feature of *who* are the subjects that the court deals with on a routine basis. The vast majority of defendants who appeared before the Court of Queen's Bench on violent crime charges were male. Only 7 percent of the 727 cases heard by the court between 1996 and 1999 involved female defendants; of these cases, 69 percent involved male co-accused. Given that the court is so accustomed to dealing with men accused of violent crime, it should not be surprising that law would come to see aggression in male terms. But the encoding of aggression as male runs much deeper than mere numbers. It is also embedded in the understandings which defendants, complainants, and witnesses bring with them into the courtroom.

Several of the files we examined involved cases of male-on-male violence – of men taking it outside at a party, getting into fights at a local bar, or retaliating over unpaid debts. Statements made to police by the participants in these events reveal their understandings of "what actually happened." One case (case 219), for instance, involved a charge of aggravated assault after two men who had been drinking together got into an argument. The complainant was hesitant to press charges, despite the fact that he was stabbed eight times with a pocket knife. As he explained to police, they had just gone outside to "duke it out." The accused similarly reasoned: "I just got into a fight. I was just defending myself." In these terms, fighting is not simply rationalized by the participants, it is normalized at the same time. Describing the aggressive mood of the assailants after a fight outside a house where some 200 people were attending a party, one witness remarked to police: "The whole group of guys sounded like a football team, like they had just won the game" (case 220).

Whether we interpret them as "contests of honour" (Polk 1994), expressions of "hegemonic masculinity" (Messerschmidt 1993, 1997) or significations of "normative heterosexuality" (Collier 1998), such displays of male aggression have an all-too-familiar ring to them. Men settle their disputes by "duking it out"; those who are victorious celebrate much like any sports team would. In short, that men engage in aggression is culturally taken for granted. As one accused commented to police on his arrest for assault: "That's just what happens when guys mess around. Guys will be guys" (case 234).

Yet this familiarity can be deceptive. For while it may appear to the inquiring researcher that these men's actions were steeped in masculinity, this was not something that drew law's notice. From reading the files, it would appear that male aggression has become such a normalized feature of social life that when such cases reach the court, gender is not marked. As Alison Young puts it, "forms of law-breaking have become such a naturalized feature of representations of masculinity that no gender interpretation is required" (1996: 42). Indeed, law's history of gender amnesia when it comes to male defendants charged with violent offenses is reflected in legal doctrine. The law on self-defense in Canada, for instance, has historically been premised on the paradigmatic case of the "one-time barroom brawl" (R. v. Lavallee 1990). The "typical persons" and "typical situation" envisioned by law were two male strangers who encountered one another at a local bar. If it could be shown that an accused's use of force in defending himself in a like situation was reasonable, then he would not be held culpable.

While the coupling of aggression with masculinity informs the construction of "normal crime," this is not to say that all men's actions are simply accepted or condoned by law. It is in the process of censuring some men's behavior as violence that law embraces particular constructions of the Violent Man. More often than not, these understandings are framed by the discourse of the "psy" professions. Two of the case files studied involved male defendants charged with murder. One of these cases (232) involved a Filipino man who confessed to stabbing his victim (an elderly woman acquaintance) 53 times with a knife. He had visited her home with the intention of borrowing money to support his cocaine addiction. In a court-ordered assessment, the psychiatrist offered a way of making sense of the defendant's actions:

> [T]his woman's death occurred while this man's ability to deal with frustration and to organize his emotions and his thinking in a reasonable manner, was profoundly shattered by his abuse of cocaine. The inability to control his impulses, resulting in a violent murderous rage, was directly related to the impact of this drug upon this man's central nervous system.... It is my opinion that, without the use of this drug, it is highly unlikely, if not remote, that anything of this nature would have occurred. (psychiatric report; case 232)

The second case (233) involved a 43-year-old man who was charged with second-degree murder in the shooting death of his mother (approximately 15 shots were fired at her). Four separate psychiatric reports were included in the Crown file on the case. One assessment noted: "This is not a man who has a history of being easily provoked to anger or violence." Nevertheless, other reports deemed the defendant's behavior to have "occurred within the context of a delusional state of a persecutory nature" and diagnosed him as suffering from "either paranoid schizophrenia or depression with psychotic features" (psychiatric report; case 233).

In several respects, these two cases are out of step with others recorded in the Crown files. As both cases involve the brutal killing of elderly women, they diverge from the normal situations in which men's aggression occurs. Because they are so atypical, they prompt the need for an explanation. By deferring to the "psy" professions, law makes sensible that which seems in-sensible. Men who kill their mothers "for no apparent reason" (bail hearing transcript; case 233) can be understood as being in a psychotic state at the time of the murder. Men who "tragically" become addicted to cocaine find themselves "out of control" and "compelled to violent urges" (psychiatric report; case 232). Either way, such men are easily cast as criminalized Others;[3] it is their identities as sick or addicted that separates them from the rest of us – and especially from other men.

Not all men who aggress against women are so readily pathologized. The most frequent charges against male defendants involved sexual assaults against women; of the 711 cases involving male defendants heard by the Court of Queen's Bench over the four-year period, 43 percent (302) involved charges of sexual assault. What is noteworthy in reading these case files are the ways in which men's sexual aggression is so routinely normalized during the legal process. This is in part a function of the fact that sexual assault cases are ones where the focus is squarely on the woman complainant: did she consent to the act which forms the basis of the charge? Despite decades of legal reform in Canada, rape myths continue to invade the practice of law (Busby 1999; Roberts and Mohr 1994; Snider 1985), as defense strategies regularly involve efforts to undermine complainants' credibility by casting them as "liars," "sexually promiscuous" or "asking for it." It is only when the woman complainant conforms to the image of the "real" victim – she is sober and sensible – that the legal gaze begins to shift to the types of man who engage in sexual violence. Up to that point, we get very little sense of who he is, other than perhaps a glimpse of the proverbial Everyman who is unable to resist the sexual opportunities ostensibly placed before him.

BETRAYING HER GENDER?: THE VIOLENT WOMAN

> Within the notion of conformity, there is inscribed a system of gender differentiation which enables defendants to be judged for their identity as much as for or instead of the crime that they may have committed. To that extent, the question must be asked whether defendants are found guilty of the crime charged or of the betrayal of their gender. (Young 1996: 43)

Our review of Crown files suggests that when cases of male aggression reach the court, gender is not marked. This is not the case, however, when the defendant is a female. Given the equation of aggression with masculinity, women who are charged with violent offenses rupture the proverbial characterizations of normal crime. These women are an anomaly; they pose a challenge to the already known and recognized categories used in the legal construction of a case. As Alison Young notes above, they also betray their gender. When women defendants appear before the court, therefore, some form of explanation is required. It is then when the typifications of the Violent Woman come into view.

One case (137) which stands out in the files involved a young woman charged with aggravated assault after stabbing a bouncer at a local bar with a paring knife. During his testimony in court, the complainant (who is described by the Crown as "built like the proverbial brick outhouse") revealed his surprise at being assaulted by a woman: "I was yelling, 'I got stabbed, the bitch stabbed me.' I couldn't believe it. I was in shock really." When asked about the long-term impact of the event, he noted: "I'm paranoid about girls in bars now. When I have to tell a girl to leave, it, it's more scary than guys, for me, now, 'cause I don't trust girls at all in a bar anymore" (preliminary hearing; case 137). What made the event even more puzzling for the participants was the "super-female" strength of the accused, who was described as a 5 feet 2 inches tall, 120-pound woman with a "petite frame." A second bouncer testified to kicking the woman in the back five times with steel-toed boots and then stomping on her hand ten times to release the knife from her grip. He stated to the court: "I know the strength of my kicks and there's no way she should have been able to withstand the kick that I gave." In short, aggression by women is unexpected; it breaches gendered expectations of what "girls in bars" do. Similarly, a woman's ability to withstand violence begs explanation. The only one offered, however, was that she must have been "strung up on heroin or something."

The Crown in this case engaged in a particular reading of the testimony presented in court to cast the accused as a Violent Woman. He noted, for example, that "despite her size, [she] is capable of causing great injury." The claim that she was "obviously under the influence of alcohol or drugs" is taken as evidence which "magnifies the potential seriousness of her actions." The force which was used to restrain her is cited by the Crown as evidence of "the extent of her rage." The judge subsequently imposed a 20-month prison sentence.

Other constructions of the Violent Woman are evident in the files. Another case involved aggravated assault charges which emerged from an incident at a house party when the accused slashed another woman across the face with a broken beer bottle. Much was made of the fact that the victim was an "aspiring model" who required 45 sutures to close the wound on her face.[4] While the Crown called the incident an "unprovoked" and "brutal" assault, the defense endeavored to construct a different account: given that the accused had recently terminated a pregnancy, the violence was an "isolated incident" brought on by a "medical situation" (defense's sentencing submission, case 110).

Despite pleas that "biology is destiny" (the hormones made her do it), a woman whose actions mar the beauty of her "aspiring model" victim is less likely to receive the sympathy of the court. So, too, are those women who plot to kill their husbands. One case (107) involved a woman charged with counseling to commit murder. Engaged in a custody battle with her estranged husband, she had arranged to have him killed as "she did not know what else to do to keep her child." In the Crown's estimation, however, the accused was a "cold" and "calculating" woman who "wasn't thinking of the child – just herself." Another case (117) involved a "highly-educated" woman charged with second-degree murder in the death of her husband. In the Crown's view, she is also cold and calculating as she "stood to gain a large sum of money from her husband's trust account." "Cold" and "calculating" are not adjectives which appear in the Crown files on cases involving male defendants. When applied to female defendants, they readily conjure up images of the Evil Woman, one who not only ruptures the proverbial characterizations of normal violent crime, but also the female script of the nurturing and supportive wife earmarked for women.

While this analysis suggests that law's construction of criminalized Others is indeed gendered, it would be a mistake to focus only on this element. Overlapping and intersecting with law's gendering practices are the ways in which race and racialization make their way into the practice of law. Race informs law's construction of cases not only in terms of who the legal subjects are, but the spaces from whence they come.

The Racialization of Violent Crime

The overrepresentation of Aboriginal people in the criminal justice system is a subject which has drawn the attention of criminologists not only in Canada but other countries as well (Monture-Angus 1999; Tyler 1998; Homel et al. 1999; La Prairie 1995; Silverman and Nielsen 1992). A recent Australian report, for instance, notes that the percentage of Aboriginal and Torres Strait Islander (ATSI) defendants in New South Wales is more than five times than would be expected given their numbers in the general population, and ATSI defendants are more likely to be convicted of violent offenses (Baker 2001). In the Canadian context, while Aboriginal people comprised 2 percent of the total population in 1991, they made up 24 percent of prison populations across the country (Jackson and Griffiths 1995: 235–6). Aboriginal people in the prairie provinces are particularly at risk of criminalization. A one-day snapshot of prisoners conducted in 1998 found that 61 percent of those in custody in Manitoba were Aboriginal, while Aboriginal people made up only 9 percent of the province's population (Robinson et al. 1998).

In terms of the present study, two-thirds of the women and 39 percent of the men in the sample of Crown files were Aboriginal; 78 percent of the Aboriginal women and 54 percent of the Aboriginal men were unemployed or on social assistance at the time of their arrest. Like many Aboriginal people in Canada, their files tell stories of economic hardship and social marginalization. Several of the events which form the basis of the criminal charges occurred on isolated reserves in the northern part of the province, where colonization has left deep scars (York 1990). Many occurred along what is known as the "Main Street Strip," an impoverished area located in the core of the province's main urban center. While alcohol, drug use, and violence have become all-too-common themes of life on the reserve or in the city, so too has criminal justice intervention into the lives of Aboriginal people.

Race has become an important signifier in the proverbial characterization of violent crime, to the point where police make the assumption (as in case 209) that an Aboriginal male running down the street is the likely culprit in a recent robbery. While it would be an easy route to argue that Aboriginal people's overrepresentation in the criminal justice system is the work of racist police (or lawyers or judges), such an approach is far too reductionist and simplistic. Rather, understanding how racism works in law involves attending to more complex and complicated processes. Marlee Kline, for instance, argues that racism flows from the ideological form of law rather than the isolated acts of individuals:

> Judges like other members of dominant society operate within discursive fields in which racist ideology helps constitute what is and is not to be taken for granted as "just the way things are". The appearance of racist ideological representations within judicial discourse may be more of a reflection of the power and pervasiveness of such dominant ideology in the wider society and the particular susceptibility of legal discourse to it, than individual racial prejudice on the part of judges. (1994: 452)

Along these same lines, Sherene Razack (2000) suggests that violence in Aboriginal communities has been "culturalized"; it has come to be viewed as a naturally occurring – and inevitable – feature of places inhabited by Aboriginal people. According to Razack (2000: 117), violence is "an event that is routine when the bodies in question are Aboriginal."

The "Usual Sort of Difficulty"

Racist ideological representations make their way into legal discourse at a number of entry points. Given the role of Crown witnesses in determining the strength of the case against an accused, attorneys regularly make assessments on the credibility of their key witnesses. In cases involving Aboriginal defendants, attorneys will comment on their difficulties in securing "good" witnesses. Commenting on a murder case which occurred on a northern reserve, one Crown attorney noted: "The case presents the usual sort of difficulty in that the witnesses are all either: drunk; related to one or both of the accused and victim; reluctant to talk; inarticulate; or all of the above" (memo to the Senior Crown; case 103). The presumption that Aboriginal people make poor witnesses in court is so prevalent that a Crown will remark: "[the complainant] was a strong witness and was a pleasant surprise from the usual difficulties that we have from witnesses in that locale" (memo to the Senior Crown; case 205).

Witnesses' reluctance or inability to testify in court is posed as a problem "of" Aboriginal people. There is little sensitivity to the difficulties they might encounter in participating in the legal process. In one case (211) involving a charge of sexual assault, for instance, the complainant (a young Aboriginal woman) did not appear at the preliminary hearing and was subsequently subpoenaed. It was only later determined that she had no way of getting to the city on that day. Also, Aboriginal witnesses are asked to participate in proceedings where the language used (English) is not their own (most Aboriginal languages, for example, have no word for "guilt"). Their reluctance to testify against an accused who is more often than not a member of their community only adds to their general discomfort.

The legal documents also reveal that defense lawyers will play on racist and class-based stereotypes to undermine the credibility of Crown witnesses. One case (134) involved a Caucasian cab driver who was charged with assaulting her customer, an Aboriginal woman. In some respects, this case was the antithesis of normal crime, as the proverbial characterization is one in which an Aboriginal passenger is charged with assaulting a cab driver.[5] The defense's strategy, however, was to attempt to discredit the complainant's testimony by drawing on stereotypes of welfare recipients who use the state's money to pay for cab fares (ostensibly, a luxury expense):

> *Defense*: Who paid for the cab?
> *Witness*: I did.
> *Defense*: You weren't working at the time, were you?
> *Witness*: No.
> *Defense*: So you were using this money from welfare to pay for this cab?
> *Witness*: Yes. (transcript of preliminary hearing; case 134)

Also, defense lawyers will endeavor to normalize the violence encountered by Aboriginal complainants. Two of the cases studied (239 and 241) involved older Caucasian men who were charged with multiple counts of sexual assault and procuring for the purposes of prostitution. The victims were all Aboriginal boys and girls who were defined as "runaways" and "street kids." The defense strategy involved Othering the complainants, describing them as "uneducated and unsophisticated" individuals, none of whom "were dragged, kicking and screaming, to become involved in this lifestyle."

While Crown attorneys express their frustrations with what they perceive to be the "usual sort of difficulty" encountered in cases involving Aboriginal complainants, and defense lawyers play on stereotypes of welfare recipients and street kids to undermine the credibility of Aboriginal witnesses, racialization also enters into the legal process at other points.

RACIALIZED SPACES

In Razack's (2000) terms, violence and violent people have come to be associated with the racialized spaces of inner-city communities and northern reserves. This presumption informs the legal construction of a case in a variety of ways.

One of the cases (103) occurred on a Native reserve during a wedding reception, when one woman fatally wounded another with a knife. Medical documents in the file suggest that the victim would likely have survived had she been located in an urban center where medical facilities were available. While the defense raised the lack of medical facilities as a mitigating factor, the Crown responded with the argument that the members of [the reserve] are well aware that should somebody, an individual, be stabbed that they very well might not be able to receive the kind of treatment that is required on the nursing station reserve and they may very well die from whatever wounds are inflicted prior to their being able to receive medical treatment. (Crown sentencing submission; case 103)

In short, a systemic issue relating to the historical colonization and displacement of Aboriginal people onto isolated and impoverished spaces is simply translated into a problem "of" Aboriginal people: they should have known better.

Despite the fact that the offense occurred during a wedding reception, the case is referred to in the legal documents as a "drinking party." By way of comparison, another case (110) involving an aggravated assault charge occurred when some seventy teenagers gathered at a house party in a white middle-class neighborhood to celebrate an eighteenth birthday (the mark of the legal drinking age in the province). As discussed earlier, one young woman slashed another across the face with a beer bottle. Even though the participants had all been drinking beer when the assault occurred, the event is referred to in the legal documents as a "birthday party." Clearly, violence in white middle-class neighborhoods is constituted as different from that in other racialized spaces.

The drinking party provides the context for the "typical situation" in which violent crime charges emerge for Aboriginal defendants, so much so that Crown attorneys will comment in cases where an accused was not drinking: "surprisingly, alcohol was not a factor in the offending behaviour" (Crown correspondence with the Assistant Deputy Attorney General; case 141). Defense lawyers will also utilize the drinking party context to normalize their client's actions. One case (120), for example, involved an Aboriginal woman convicted of aggravated assault for slashing a man with a carpenter knife during a "drinking party." In her sentencing submission, the defense explained the woman's actions as follows: "It's the circumstances of the lifestyle that resulted in this type of offence. We're dealing with poor people, with substance abuse issues, in very volatile situations where there's drinking parties, and we hear about them every day. [Accused] was living this lifestyle." What defense counsel is suggesting is that it is a certain type of situation (drinking parties) and a certain type of people (Aboriginal and poor) who commit violent offenses. What is considered normal in terms of criminal justice cases is abnormal for the rest of us; we only hear about it. Further, violence is the result of a lifestyle choice – not a feature of systemic poverty and racism.

LEGISLATING EQUALITY?

Recognition of the overrepresentation of Aboriginal people in the criminal justice system has prompted Canadian legislators to address the issue through statute law. Specifically, a 1996 Criminal Code amendment (section 718.2(e)) requires judges to consider "all other sanctions other than imprisonment that are reasonable in the circumstances . . . with particular attention to the circumstances of Aboriginal offenders."

Section 718.2(e) surfaced in several of the cases studied. One of these cases was heard shortly after the amendment was passed. It involved an Aboriginal woman charged with robbery. The position of the defense was that the complainant had hired the accused as a prostitute and the dispute which followed was merely the result of a "trick gone bad." In a memo to the Senior Crown, the Crown attorney notes:

> There is certainly room for suspicion here that this theory might be correct however, the victim steadfastly denies this and claims to be a religious man and a tea todler [sic]. . . . The credibility of our victim is excellent and the credibility of the accused is nil because she has a lengthy record for crimes of violence and failing to comply to recogs. and failing to appear in court. She has one listing on her record as a prostitute. (memo to Senior Crown; case 135)

The woman was convicted on the charge. On sentencing, the judge gave consideration to the woman's status as an Aboriginal, but concluded that "there are no sanctions other than imprisonment that are reasonable in the circumstances" (reasons for sentence; case 135). It was evident that the Crown considered such special considerations for Aboriginal defendants as an affront to the official version of law:

> And let's make this all clear, My Lord, whether one is black or white or Aboriginal, whatever one's racial origin, we are all Canadians and this book, this Criminal Code, governs everyone regardless of race or color or creed. . . . they say that justice is blind, so with regard to racial origin, I submit, whether or whatever racial origins, we must obey the law of the land. (court transcript; case 135)

An interesting paradox emerges here. On the one hand, the Crown makes an appeal to the rule of law to argue that the defendant should be treated on an equal footing as other Canadians who appeared before the court. On the other hand, the Crown's position on the case suggests that the defendant's status as a prostitute contributes to her *in*credibility in the eyes of the law – especially when held up against the claims of a religious teetotaler. Apparently, then, not all Canadians are treated on an equal footing.

The goal of section 718.2(e) was to address the overrepresentation of Aboriginal people in Canada's prisons. As Dioso and Doob (2001) note, the provision has been criticized on two counts. First, it suggests that there are two sets of principles of sentencing, one for Aboriginal people and one for other offenders. To this extent, the provision has been read as advocating more lenient treatment of Aboriginal people compared with other offenders. Second, the amendment is premised on the view that the overrepresentation of Aboriginal people in prison is a result of harsh sentencing decisions by judges – not the more fundamental problem of social and economic oppression. If the problem is one of poverty, then addressing it at the sentencing stage does not attend to the reasons for the case coming to court in the first place. It also "ignores that there are other people, and groups, who share this disadvantage" (ibid.: 406).

While such criticisms are valid, the analysis offered here suggests that the problems encountered in efforts to legislate equality run much deeper. Legal discourse and practice are infused with racist ideological representations that find their origins in discursive fields prevailing in the wider society. These representations inform the construction of normal crime used in the creation of criminalized Others. So long as such constructions remain unquestioned or taken for granted as "the way things are," law will continue to work as a racializing practice.

CONCLUSION

Contrary to law's image of itself as a neutral, impartial, and objective system, criminologists and sociologists of law have located it as a gendering and racializing strategy. By wedding this approach to the normalization of criminal cases, the intent of this essay has been to gain insights into how gender and race figure in the process of creating criminalized Others. The examination of legal documents on cases involving women and men charged with violent crime has provided one window into this complex and complicated process.

Clearly, law does not operate in a vacuum. In the process of seeking the legal truth of a matter – of imposing an order onto the messiness of people's lives – law draws upon and reproduces cultural understandings that are hegemonic in the wider society. Men's aggression, be it male-on-male or sexual aggression against women, falls within the realm of the normal or expected; in part because of the commonness of its occurrence, but also because of the meanings which participants bring with them to court. That which is abnormal or unexpected can readily be understood by deferring to the "psy" discourses; the Violent Man is one who is sick or addicted. Women's aggression, on the other hand, poses a challenge to the conceptions of normal crime. Women who appear before the court on violent crime charges constitute an anomaly not just in terms of their small numbers relative to men, but also in their breaching of gendered norms and expectations. Just as the identities of men who appear before the court are informed by stereotypes which hold purchase in the wider society, the Violent Woman is variously cast as "cold," "calculating," "vicious," "callous" – or a "bitch." The antithesis of the caring, nurturing wife and mother, she has betrayed her gender.

Overlapping and intersecting with the gendering of criminalized Others are the ways in which racist ideological representations make their way into the legal process. In the same way that the "law is sexist" formulation is too simplistic and reductionist to be of much value in understanding the legal process, the claim that "law is racist" does not take us very far. Analysis of the legal documents suggests that racism and racialization are deeply enmeshed in the legal process. Racialized presuppositions of credible witnesses and culpable defendants infuse the proverbial characterizations of normal violent crime. Racialized spaces set the context in which the actions of complainants and defendants are read and then reduced to "lifestyle choices." Recognition of the pervasiveness of these ideological representations leads to skepticism about the ability of "special considerations" legislation to solve the overrepresentation of marginalized populations in the criminal justice system. Nevertheless, while law does not operate in a vacuum, neither is it simply a mirror image of the wider society. By gaining deeper insights into this business of criminalizing, we open up spaces for articulating alternative visions and possibilities.

Notes

The research on which this essay is based was made possible by a grant from the Social Sciences and Humanities Research Council of Canada. The author would like to express her deepest appreciation to Vanessa Chopyk and Linda Wood for their hard work and attention to detail during the data collection process. In addition, Wayne Antony, Gillian Balfour, Cynthia Devine, Glen Lewis, and Colin Sumner offered their support at various stages.

1   In addition to the Crown files, court transcripts of sentencing submissions and reasons for sentence were ordered for several of the cases. This data collection produced over a thousand pages of detailed summaries and verbatim quotes on the 90 cases.
2   The 45 women represented 83 percent of the women who appeared before the Court of Queen's Bench on a violence charge over a four-year period (1996–9). A random sample (stratified by offense type) of 45 men was drawn for comparative purposes. This sample represented 8 percent of all men who appeared before the court on violence charges.
3   It is noteworthy that case 232 took only five months from the time of the offense to the rendering of a decision. The file on this case was also much slimmer than others we examined.
4   A newspaper clipping found in the file carried the headline: "Model's face slashed: Teen guilty of attack."
5   Indeed, the presumption that Aboriginal people are the typical offenders operated in the present case, as the Aboriginal woman was the one initially arrested and charged. The police incident report indicates: "Subsequent investigation revealed that the victim was indeed the victim in this incident and that details related to police by the accused were fabricated" (case 134).

References

Baker, J. (2001) The scope for reducing indigenous imprisonment rates. *Crime and Justice Bulletin*, 55. New South Wales Bureau of Crime Statistics and Research.

Bell, V. (1993) *Interrogating Incest: Feminism, Foucault and the Law.* London: Routledge.

Busby, K. (1999) "Not a victim until a conviction is entered": Sexual violence prosecutions and legal "'truth." In E. Comack (ed.), *Locating Law: Race/Class/Gender Connections.* Halifax: Fernwood, 260–88.

Collier, R. (1998) *Masculinities, Crime and Criminology.* London: Sage.

Davies, M. (1996) *Delimiting the Law: "Postmodernism" and the Politics of Law.* London: Pluto.

Dioso, R., and Doob, A. (2001) An analysis of public support for special consideration of Aboriginal offenders at sentencing. *Canadian Journal of Criminology*, 43(3), 405–12.

Homel, R., Lincoln, R., and Herd, B. (1999) Risk and resilience: crime and violence prevention in Aboriginal communities. *Australian and New Zealand Journal of Criminology*, 32, 182–96.

Hunt, A. (1993) *Explorations in Law and Society: Toward a Constitutive Theory of Law.* London: Routledge.

Jackson, M. A., and Griffiths, C. T. (1995) *Canadian Criminology: Perspectives on Crime and Criminality* (2nd ed.). Toronto: Harcourt Brace.

Kerruish, V. (1991) *Jurisprudence as Ideology.* London: Routledge.

Kline, M. (1994) The colour of law: ideological representations of First Nations in legal discourse. *Social and Legal Studies*, 3, 451–76.

La Prairie, C. (1995) *Seen But Not Heard: Native People in the Inner City.* Ottawa: Minister of Public Works and Government Services Canada.

MacKinnon, C. (1982) Feminism, Marxism, method, and the state: An agenda for theory. *Signs,* 7, 515–44.

MacKinnon, C. (1983) Feminism, Marxism, method and the state: Toward feminist jurisprudence. *Signs* 8, 635–58.

Marin, A. (1995) *The Guide to Investigations and Prosecutions.* Aurora: Canada Law Book.

Messerschmidt, J. W. (1993) *Masculinities and Crime: Critique and Reconceptualization of Theory.* Lanham, MD: Rowman & Littlefield.

Messerschmidt, J. W. (1997) *Crime as Structured Action: Gender, Race, Class and Crime in the Making.* London: Sage.

Monture-Angus, P. (1999) Standing against Canadian law: naming omissions of race, culture, and gender. In E. Comack (ed.), *Locating Law: Race/Class/Gender Connections.* Halifax: Fernwood, 76–97.

Naffine, N. (1990) *Law and the Sexes: Explorations in Feminist Jurisprudence.* Sydney, Australia: Allen & Unwin.

Polk, K. (1994) *When Men Kill: Scenarios of Masculine Violence.* Cambridge: Cambridge University Press.

R. v. Lavallee (1990) Supreme Court Reports, 852.

Razack, S. (2000) Gendered racial violence and spatialized justice: the murder of Pamela George. *Canadian Journal of Law and Society,* 15(2), 91–130.

Razack, S. (1998) *Looking White People in the Eye: Gender, Race, and Culture in Courtrooms and Classrooms.* Toronto: University of Toronto Press.

Roberts, J. V., and Mohr, R. (eds.) (1994) *Confronting Sexual Assault: A Decade of Legal and Social Change.* Toronto: University of Toronto Press.

Robinson, D., Porporino, F. J., Millson, W. A., Trevethan, S., and MacKillop, B. (1998) A one-day snapshot of inmates in Canada's adult correctional facilities. *Juristat,* 18(8), 1–14.

Sachs, A., and Wilson, J. H. (1978) *Sexism and the Law: A Study of Male Beliefs and Legal Bias in Britain and the United States.* Oxford: Martin Robertson.

Silverman, R., and Nielsen, M. (eds.) 1992) *Aboriginal Peoples and Canadian Criminal Justice.* Toronto: Butterworths.

Smart, C. (1992) The woman of legal discourse. *Social and Legal Studies,* 1(1), 29–44.

Smart, C. (1995) Proscription, prescription and the desire for certainty?: Feminist theory in the field of law. In C. Smart (ed.), *Law, Crime and Sexuality: Essays in Feminism.* London: Sage, 203–20.

Smith, D. (1974) The social construction of documentary reality. *Sociological Inquiry,* 44 (4), 257–68.

Snider, L. (1985) Legal reform and social control: the dangers of abolishing rape. *International Journal of the Sociology of Law,* 13(4), 337–56.

Sudnow, D. (1965) Normal crimes: sociological features of the penal code. *Social Problems,* 12, 255–70.

Sumner, C. (1997) Introduction: the violence of censure and the censure of violence. In C. Sumner (ed.), *Violence, Culture and Censure.* London: Taylor & Francis, 1–6.

Tyler, W. (1998) Race, crime and region: the socio-spatial dynamics of Aboriginal offending. *Journal of Sociology,* 34, 152–69.

Worrall, A. (1990) *Offending Women: Female Lawbreakers and the Criminal Justice System.* London: Routledge.

York, G. (1990) *The Dispossessed: Life and Death in Native Canada.* London: Vintage.

Young, A. (1996) *Imagining Crime.* London: Sage.

Part V
Capital, Power, and Crime

18

White-Collar Crime

AMEDEO COTTINO

The subtitle of a recent publication on white-collar crime (Lindgren 2000), "A social problem with obstacles," hits the target: dealing with this issue implies coping with obstacles. These obstacles are of various kinds: some are of a conceptual nature (how do we define this crime?), some others of theoretical nature (what are the causes?), some others of a penal policy nature (what can be done to prevent it?).

What I attempt to do here, in the first place, is to keep the different levels of analysis apart by being more clear about the variety of motivations inspiring the research within the field and the existing stereotypes about crimes and criminals. Thus, there are scholars interested in explaining the impunity of people highly ranked within the social hierarchy, in particular these people's capacity to keep themselves out of reach of the penal system (see, e.g., Levi 1989; Wheeler et al. 1982). Other scholars observe that the fact of not criminalizing certain behaviors that damage society – both in economic and human terms – constitutes more than just a theoretically challenging question; they will argue that it is a hot issue today more than it has ever been, since the process of globalization entails, among other things, an even stronger hold of the world market over the nation-state. Also, there is much concern about the seriousness of such misconduct. It has been said that "white-collar criminals cause more pain and death than all 'common criminals combined'" (Rosoff et al. 1998: viii). At the same time, the idea that so called "ordinary" people, people who have an occupation, more so if it is a prestigious one, may be criminals is somehow counter-intuitive. The stereotyped image of the criminal fits badly into the shape of a white collar – whether that of a politician or a clerk. The more so when the reference point is the enterprise. The notion of "moral capital" underscores a phenomenon that seems to have increased since the 1980s, namely that "business has literally been granted a moral status, as intrinsic to the well being and health of societies" (Tombs 2001: 21). And the social scientists themselves are part of this dominant culture. Yet the difference between bankers and pharmacists on the one hand and usurers and dope pushers on the other is far from being clear-cut. Sometimes the criminals themselves can unveil better than most of us the fictional character of our stereotypes and distinctions. This is the case, for example, with John Allen, professional robber and pimp, when he explains the difference between white-collar and blue-collar criminals by saying: "Some steal with a gun, others with a pen" (Allen 1977: xxv).

In the second place, we know that the interconnections between the legal system on the one hand and the structure of power relations within society on the other imply that the latter affect both the definitions of what has to be considered deviant and the way laws are applied. In other words, laws are legal constructions and, consequently, crimes are also. Therefore, the fact that the line varies between what can be considered illegal and what cannot, makes it of primary importance to look at power and at its related mechanisms, in particular at those that tend to blur this line and those which preserve it. All these and other related questions reflect the difficulty – or the ambiguity (Aubert 1952; Nelken 1994a) – of treating the issue within the realm, and with the instruments, of criminology and sociological theory. A further sign of the difficulties that one meets in this field is the variety of terms used to cover the notion of white-collar crime: corporate, economic, occupational, or organizational crime are used to describe various types of misconduct related to the economic sphere. For my purpose I will use the terms white-collar and economic crime interchangeably. However, I will not show disdain for the term "corporate crime" because of the particular theoretical and political significance of unlawful behaviors carried out by individuals and by collective actors ranking high within society.

POWER, CLASS, AND CRIME

The impunity of the rulers, that is, the fact that what counts in matters of law and justice is the individual's social standing rather than his or her misconduct, has been an open secret among the ruled for centuries. However, this is an insight that we find among an increasing number of intellectuals only from the mid-nineteenth century. Engels (1945 [1848]) is one of them. He not only denounces the devastating violence which early British capitalism wreaked upon the working masses, but emphasizes the interaction between crime and power. The crimes of London's poor against person and property cannot be understood separately from the daily violence of the economic system carried out in total and open disregard of the law and of basic human needs. The disrespect of the law is not only a crime in itself but it is also a criminogenic factor: it is itself a main cause of the crime of the working class.

Marx (1954 [1890]), in his weighty study of the consequences of bourgeois capitalism, explains the substantial impunity of producers and shopkeepers who ignore or circumvent the new labor laws (e.g., on working hours) by observing that the members of the courts which are supposed to enforce the law belonged to the same class as the offenders. Even a conservative scholar such as Vilfredo Pareto points out the damage in terms of consensus that the ruling elite inflicted upon itself by evading the law (1991 [1901]). Max Weber, with the ideal type of an ascetic entrepreneur in mind, is very worried about what he named "adventurers' capitalism": people "oriented to the exploitation of political opportunities and irrational speculation" (Weber 1984 [1904–5]: 76, in Lindgren 2000: 112). And Thorstein Veblen (1992 [1899]) expresses analogous worries about the new business class. Directly concerned with the issue of criminality in general and with the crime of the powerful in particular are Tarde (1886) and Bonger (1969 [1916]). The former develops a conception of the criminal which is particularly interesting for the issue at stake in the sense that he "regarded murderers... swindlers and thieves as individuals who served a long apprenticeship in just the same way as doctors, lawyers, farmers and professional craftsmen" (Lindgren 2000: 115). Bonger, in his turn, writing from a basically Marxian perspective, highlights the class nature of the legislation and the structure of opportunities favoring the occurrence of those he labels the "great criminals."

SUTHERLAND

In spite of these contributions, several decades elapse before what has been rightly viewed as the breaking point in criminological theory appears – Sutherland's *White-Collar Crime* (1949, 1983). To be more precise, it is in December 1939 that the term white-collar crime is introduced by Sutherland himself in his presidential address to the American Sociological Association. Sutherland defines white-collar crime as "a crime committed by a person of respectability and high social status in the course of his occupation" (Sutherland 1949: 9). These social attributes stress a specificity which we do not find among the so-called predatory crimes (crimes against persons and property) almost exclusively carried out by subjects belonging to the lower strata.

Sutherland, whose aim is to elaborate a general theory of crime, not only wants to provide a general hypothesis at the individual level; also he strives to give some hints as to those specific societal traits that favor the occurrence of white-collar crime. At the individual level he stresses the role played by those who make our social environment: a positive prevailing attitude toward the violation of the law does significantly contribute to the individual decision to violate it. Naturally, the prevailing attitude has a different impact, depending on the frequency and intensity of interaction. In this sense, the process of communication which is most relevant occurs primarily in intimate relationships. Anthropologically speaking, it is culture – or more precisely, the subculture of the reference group – that "teaches" us how to violate the law, providing justifications both as motives and rationalizations. This "learning" process, often taking place with one's associates, does not differ from the usual learning processes where other people's expectations can play a key role. This is how a young college graduate interviewed by Sutherland explains why, after having lost two previous jobs because of his unwillingness to be involved in unethical activities, he has accepted that he has to "play the game": "I argued that I did not have much chance to find a legitimate firm. I knew the game was rotten, but it has to be played – the law of the jungle and that sort of thing" (Sutherland 1983: 241–2).

As to the societal level, Sutherland claimed, two phenomena – anomie and norm conflicts – create social disorganization which in its turn brings about economic criminality. Both lack of norms guiding the individuals in their choices and rivalries between different social groups, each claiming to be the exclusive bearer and interpreter of the legal system, might very well affect the level of law compliance. This is particularly true in those cases where there is no immediate perception of individual physical harm. Yet, as Sutherland himself recognizes, the question is open as to which are the factors underlying social disorganization.

Sutherland's theory of differential association was tested by Cressey, Sutherland's student. His study of embezzlement (1971 [1953]) reveals the specific "techniques" which embezzlers learn and use in order to justify their unlawful behavior. Cressey finds a set of rationalizations, vocabularies of motive (Mills 1940), which – far from being ex post facto – constitute a strategic element of motivation. In other words, embezzlers need "to use a verbalization which would permit the commission of a crime while the ideal of honesty was maintained" (1971 [1953]: 142). Cressey's contribution is certainly important for being one of the few empirical investigations following Sutherland's theoretical indications. It is, however, debatable to what extent he has been able to provide them with an empirical support. Cressey himself admits that "the statement of the differential association process is not precise enough to stimulate rigorous empirical test, and it therefore has not been proved or disproved" (1960: 57). Nevertheless, both the idea that criminality has much to do with the number of associations favorable to crime (Braithwaite 1989), and Cressey's emphasis on the motives and excuses that people use to justify their misconduct, represent an important acquisition.

Sutherland has been criticized on several grounds. To begin with, he has been accused of including within the same category both criminal actions and violation of administrative and civil laws. He has replied that several among these behaviors were akin to white-collar crimes. For example, false advertising is basically fraud. More generally, some scholars have been critical of the idea of abandoning the legal definition of crime, instead of restricting the analysis to those behaviors that fall under the penal law. Some (e.g., Tappan 1947) have gone so far as to require that a criminal conviction has occurred. At the same time we cannot ignore the fact that, because of changes in the political and economic balance, certain misconducts are no longer treated as crimes. According to Snider, this is the case with corporate crime: "corporate crime can 'disappear' through decriminalization (the repeal of the criminal law), through deregulation (the repeal of all state laws, criminal, civil and administrative), and through downsizing (the destruction of the state's enforcement capacity)" (Snider 2000: 172, in Tombs 2001: 21).

A further question raised by many scholars concerns the problem of whether the social characteristics of the individual should belong to the definition. Sutherland's choice to include this requirement in the definition was certainly motivated by the need to challenge the dominant notion of crime as a phenomenon typical of the working class. However, as has been pointed out (cf. e.g., Nelken 1994a: 361–5, 1994b; Ruggiero 1996: 17–23), his choice has led to a basic ambiguity: crime confused with the criminal, the norms that have been violated with the social characteristics of the perpetrator (Vidoni Guidoni 2000: 9). In other words, two analytically independent questions have been mixed up: the question of how to define the crime and the question of how to explain it. Instead, "features of the offender such as social class or the position within the organization should be consequential to the definition of white-collar crime, rather than being a component" (Croall 1992: 10).

Other scholars have objected that Sutherland's theory assumes the existence of norms on whose basis misconducts are carried out; but nothing is said about how values and norms are created. As Clinard and Yeager (1980) have pointed out, this process of values and norms creation occurs within the culture of the corporation; it is this specific culture that discourages – or encourages – deviant behavior.

And then a further problem emerges: is white-collar crime a misconduct carried out on behalf of the organization, or at its expense? The distinction between corporate and occupational crime suggested by several scholars has been an attempt to clarify this ambiguity.

Another related question concerns whether or not there is congruence between levels of analysis and the empirical data. Sutherland argues that companies do violate the law; however, companies are collective actors, while the theory of differential association refers to individual behaviors. If the corporations should be considered accountable as individuals are (Fisse and Braithwaite 1988; Cressey 1988), one may have to assume that corporations think, act, and behave as individual actors do.

Also, it has been pointed out that to equate white collar with high status overemphasizes the latter at the expense of the former. Therefore it would be more appropriate to label white-collar crime as any crime committed during a legitimate activity implying an abuse of the occupational role (Braithwaite 1986; Hagan 1988; Shapiro 1990). If we do so, then, almost inevitably, we are going to find that most offenders do not significantly differ from the everyday person (Weisburd et al. 1991). As Nelken observes, "the problem of definition cannot be put aside . . . because it determines the findings of any investigation" (1994a: 363).

All these criticisms have led some scholars to conclude that Sutherland's attempt "to shift the criminological gaze upwards rather than simply downwards" (Tombs 2001: 28) has been a failure. Consequently, the same author wonders: "how can criminologists in general, and perhaps even policy-makers, take seriously the findings of a particular area of research where there remains such fundamental disagreement even on the definition of the object of inquiry" (2001: 29)?

EXPLANATIONS OF WHITE-COLLAR CRIME

In spite of the unresolved question of what is white-collar crime, attempts to explain its causation have been made – often concentrated upon specific offenses. Anomie, strain and structure of opportunities, social control, rational choice, organizational theory, and culture have provided the various theoretical frames of reference and analysis. Each suggestion – with its related terminology – has emphasized the explanatory power of at least one factor.

One line of research has drawn upon Merton's notion of anomie. This notion (Merton 1957) describes the condition of those individuals who are unable to reach the prescribed societal goals because society does not provide them with legitimate means to do so. Some of them may just give up their ambitions; others instead may look for alternative deviant solutions. They may, in the wording of Merton's typology, innovate (for a further development of this notion see Waring et al. 1995). And this can be precisely the case with economic crime. In other words, as Leonard and Weber (1970) have tried to show in their study of car dealers, strain can be the cause of deviance. Many car dealers, to survive economically, "must" cheat their clients. Crime becomes the more or less inevitable response to a condition where the respect of the law has become incompatible with economic activity. To what extent Leonard and Weber's conclusions can be generalized is doubtful. For example, there is now extensive evidence that arguments of the "I had to break the law to preserve my economic activity" sort were instrumentally used by many managers involved in the Italian "clean hands" (*mani pulite*) scandal. Huge amounts of money paid to various key figures on the national scene (members of the political establishment, in particular the Socialist Party and its secretary Bettino Craxi, local control authorities, etc.) were portrayed as a necessity and not, as it became clear during the trials, a profitable solution for all the parties involved (Della Porta 1992; Vannucci 1997). Thus the question is how much should be imputed to strain and how much to (illegal) opportunities. The size of the firm has probably much to say in this connection. Recently (Meštrovic 1991), the notion of anomie has been used to describe and explain much of what has happened within the economic sphere (from the Wall Street crash to the changes taking place in professional ethics). Anomie is viewed as the result of a widespread postmodern phenomenon, namely, decreasing legal control over economic activities, so-called deregulation.

To cope with strain, as Sykes and Matza (1957; Matza 1959)[1] have shown in their investigation of young delinquents, lawbreakers recur to what these authors have labeled *techniques of neutralization*. It is by learning these techniques that "the juvenile becomes delinquent, rather than by learning moral imperatives, values or attitudes standing in direct contradiction to those of the dominant society" (Sykes and Matza 1957: 668). The authors have identified five major techniques such as, for example, the *denial of victim* (we weren't hurting anyone) or the *condemnation of the condemners* (they're crooks themselves). As I will try to show later on, the fact that illegal acts are often performed by neutralizing rather than by negating values of respectability and norms of legality does not constitute a specific trait of juvenile delinquency, nor of economic crime (Coleman 1995); neutralization mechanisms reflect general cultural traits which operate not only as motivations for violating the law, but also as justifications and legitimizations of behaviors that could be treated as criminal. What remains to be explained, however, is why not everybody under strain violates the law. As Vaughan (1996) has suggested, misconduct may be the result of other factors: incompetence, disagreement with regulations, and so on.

New trends within economic sociology (Granovetter 1985; Swedberg 1990) have shown the importance of the larger structural, political, cognitive, and cultural context within which economic behavior takes place. Embeddedness (Polanyi 1994 [1957]) is the overall notion expressing the importance of social relations for the occurrence of economic transactions. Now if we assume that the difference between legal and illegal activities is not in their way of functioning but in their legal status (Smith 1975), then "how a network of contexts embeds individual actions has much to do in explaining processual twists and turns that a given criminal career... may take" (Morselli 2000: 46).

Another theoretical approach stresses the role of social control in promoting crime. In the case of corporations, crime can be viewed as the result of the fertile encounter between individual deviant values and organizational needs (Finney and Leiseur 1982). In other words, the probability for misconduct is high when the organization is looking or has to look for deviant solutions and there are individuals who are bearers of deviant values.

Several investigations have concentrated specifically on corporate crime. Among its causes, the degree of market concentration, the size of the firm, and the role of profitability have been signaled (Clinard and Yeager 1980; Jenkins and Braithwaite 1993). The conclusions, however, have been often contradictory; apparently, the only correlations that have been confirmed are those between low or decreasing profit of the firm and probability of unlawful behavior. Recently, adopting a rational-choice perspective, Simpson and colleagues (1998) have explored the macro–micro link, that is, the role played by individual and corporate characteristics in causing crime. At the micro-level career benefits constitute an important motivational factor, while at the macro-level, what counts are the culture of the firm, together with external constraints of legal and financial character.

That crime in general and corporate crime in particular are the result of rational choice – in the sense that decisions to violate the law are based upon judgments, albeit imperfectly, of costs and benefits of respectively legal and illegal paths, is of course an open question. One may argue that instruments and opportunities to commit crime are largely provided by the structure itself. For example, the notion of criminogenic industries (the specific reference is to the American automobile industry (Rosoff et al. 1998) introduced to cover all the factors – economic, legal, organizational, and normative – that facilitate corporate crime stresses precisely elements unrelated to individual motivation. From this angle, criminal activity is generated within the system "independently at least to some degree from the criminal's personal motives" (Needleman and Needleman 1979: 517). The idea that deviant behavior is intentional is clearly challenged in Vaughan's reconstruction of the *Challenger* disaster (1996), where she shows that it was the NASA culture that "normalized" (Simpson et al. 1998) the deviant decisions, making them fit criteria of conformity. It is not difficult, however, to find examples of cynical calculations: Ford knew very well that the car engine they were producing was dangerous; however, they calculated that the costs of recalling the cars were higher than the potential costs of repaying the damage (Dowie 1988).

Another factor central in understanding corporate crime is the organizational factor of illegal opportunity. According to this approach, which partly incorporates elements of rational choice, an illegal opportunity

is strongly influenced by the individuals' perception of how likely they are to be caught, how severe the punishment will be if they are, and of course how large the take. Each opportunity is judged in comparison to the other available options. The fewer the legitimate opportunities an actor has, the more attractive a particular crime is likely to appear. (Coleman 2001: 65)

Opportunities, in their turn, are related to trust, and this factor is differentially distributed along the occupational hierarchy. The oldest among the staff enjoy more trust and more opportunities to abuse it (Shapiro 1990).

A more general, structural, explanation is provided by those who, within a Marxist perspective, look upon economic criminality as the consequence of more or less unavoidable contradictions within capitalistic society:

> free enterprise – the pursuit of fair profit, the generator of wealth and employment, the backbone on which social welfare is possible – can be viewed, at least by corporate officials, as the primary ethics for and of an industrial society and conformity to this neutralizes any obedience to the law merely because it happens to be the law. (Box 1983: 57)

In particular, corporate crime is considered endemic to capitalism since it is rooted in

> the contradiction between capital accumulation and substantive democracy in advanced Western societies. Democratic calls for the establishment of broader participation of the subordinate classes in the direction of society create obstacles to the actions of profit-seeking corporations. Corporations bypass these obstacles through illegal maneuvers which, today, are made possible by the transnational nature of their activities. (Bonanno et al. 1997: 63)

The idea that capitalism itself is criminogenic, however, postulates a monolithical system, a cohesive structure. It ignores, in other words, that there are conflicts within it, such as the one between the short-sighted profit-seeking behavior of the individual capitalist and the long-term interests of the capital as a whole. Therefore, without denying that there is more than a grain of truth in this approach, one should not forget "to add that all organizations can be criminogenic in so far as they tend to reward achievement even at the expenses of the outer environment" (Nelken 1994a: 372). Moreover, as the very serious cases of pollution and corruption in many "state communism" countries have shown, the absence of market and competition is no safeguard against these types of misconduct.

A general theory of deterrence, with important consequences for a general theory of crime, has been put forward by Braithwaite. His "crime, shame and reintegration" is a theory of social control "achieved by integrating control, subcultural, opportunity and labeling theory into a cognitive learning theory" (1989: 53). Braithwaite argues that crime rates vary depending on the different processes of shaming wrongdoing. In Japan, where shaming exercises an extraordinary power on citizens, crime rates are low. This preventive power is due to the fact that in this society there are characteristics such as communitarianism and interdependency which reduce exposure to white-collar crime as well as common crime. Shaming, however, when it stigmatizes the deviant, that is, fails to include a reintegrative moment, becomes counterproductive. In this sense labeling becomes, if not *the* cause, a cause of deviance. The crux is that for shaming to function as an instrument of deterrence one must assume a large societal consensus on what should be viewed as deviant. And, as we well know, this is not really the case with white-collar crime. Therefore, the theory "is best reserved for the domain where there is strong consensus, that of predatory crimes (crimes involving victimization of one party by another)" (1989: 14).

A CONCLUSION AND A SUGGESTION

Hopefully, this sketchy review of the main contributions may be sufficient to come to a conclusion and to put forward a suggestion. The conclusion is pessimistic; the "relative incommensurability" of the research on white-collar crime (Tombs 2001), largely the result of the fact this crime is still an "unidentified object," extremely sensitive to economic, political, and social changes, leads me to share the opinion according to which "criminology as a discipline is inadequately constructed to grasp those phenomena Sutherland attempted, albeit imperfectly, to mark out by his term 'white-collar crime'" (Tombs 2001: 28). My suggestion in its turn is the child of this conclusion. It is an invitation to transcend the disciplinary boundaries and to pay attention to the recently explicitly raised question (Vidoni Guidoni 2000), of how high-status people succeed in *not* becoming classified as deviant. To do so, I will look very concretely at those factors both of a legal and extralegal nature that allow them to keep themselves out of the penal system. Although all these factors are known, some of them have not been put into the larger context to which they rightly belong. In particular, we are going to locate the techniques of neutralization and other similar mechanisms in the larger cultural context that provides them.

It is a truism to state that in our societies strategically relevant goods, such as health, education, and income, are unequally distributed. This unequal distribution affects, in many ways, how the individual copes with the law. There are those who are in the position to use the law for their own purposes, or to ignore it, or even to change it in their favor (as many independent observers have shown to be the case, when the Italian Parliament has passed laws clearly favoring the Prime Minister, Silvio Berlusconi). Similarly, there are people who enjoy, as it were, a sort of immunity when they violate the law. Their misconduct, because of the nature of their professional activity, of their organizational setting, tends to be invisible. Invisibility in its turn permits them to enjoy protection and therefore to run a low risk of detection (Vaughan 1992). The privileges of this privacy contrast fiercely with the costs of visibility, especially when the latter happens to be itself a cause of suspicion and a risk of being arrested and tried. It is a known fact that, in the United States blacks driving cars are stopped more frequently than whites. As a black Chicago academic and journalist tells a reporter: "I was getting stopped by the police so much that I used to compute the time of my stop into my travel time" (*International Herald Tribune*, March 30–31, 1996).

When high-status people are involved in criminal proceedings, status, education, and income again play a central part all the way through the various instances of the process: from the initial contact with the police to the trial

(Cottino 1986) and to prison. It is in this phase that access to a private attorney instead of a public defender can make all the difference (Cottino 1998).

This is not to deny that the "disparity of the outcomes may be also related to the social distance between judges and defendants" (Black 1998: 67). Tillman and Pontell, while discussing the well-known case of Medicaid provider fraud, suggest instead that this disparity "can be attributed to the traditional attitudes of the prosecutors that health care professionals such as doctors should not be sentenced to jail or prison for first-time property offences" (1992: 569).

The net of protections that members of the higher social strata enjoy finds its logical counterpart in what Pepinsky (1991) has aptly called the myths about white-collar crime. It is therefore not surprising that the idea that most crime is committed by the poor is deeply rooted among the general public. The high-status people who are locked up are few and their imprisonment seems to have, beyond the punitive one, a double symbolic function: on the one hand to provide evidence that "justice is blind" (people are all equal vis-à-vis the law), on the other to show that misconduct within higher social layers is rare.

Secondly, it is also said that white-collar crime harms nobody. Illegal financial operations, unfair advertising, may affect the market, but no individuals are hurt, as is often the case with predatory crime. Price-fixing is often not viewed as a crime because, as a Westinghouse executive on trial for this offense put it, "Illegal? Yes, but not criminal. I assumed that a criminal action meant damaging someone, and we did not do that" (Coleman 1989: 213). This view both expresses and strengthens the conviction that what makes a behavior criminal is its being an offense against a person and/or individual property. The view that collective interests are endangered, or that values such as trust – an essential fuel for the proper functioning of the market – are threatened by such misconduct, is definitely not the prevailing one in public opinion. Even less dominant is the idea that white-collar crimes can be extremely violent (Box 1983) – one reason for that could be due to the fact that violence, as Ralph Nader has put it, is "postponed." However, it is easy to find evidence showing that this is not the case. Thus, the effects of violations of safety measures or even of elementary precautions can be lethal: it may be sufficient to recall the explosion of the chemical plant in Bhopal or the Chernobyl's nuclear disaster. Incidentally, research carried out on these so called "accidents" "may be thought of as a strategy for revealing aspects of social structure and large organizations, including white-collar crime, which are normally hidden in the everyday functioning of society" (Poveda 1994: 80).

My thesis is that the dominant culture not only provides motives, excuses, and the like which contribute to the perpetuation of white-collar crimes (Vidoni Guidoni 2000), but also hides the real nature of behaviors which are in fact causing damage to society. My argument runs as follows: there are many events and situations which in most people's eyes neither fall under the heading "violence" nor are considered crimes. Children are deprived of their childhood, adults of their rights to have a healthy life, entire groups or populations may be condemned to starvation and death, not to mention all war victims. One may also think of less extreme situations, for example, those where individual or collective actions are not perceived as deviant because of the social standing of the people who commit them. The point here is that the ordinary person does not actually see violent actions take place because their very violent nature is often made invisible or neutralized. This is due to the fact that culture – i.e., language, science, law, religion and art – just to name its main components – provides notions which individual or collective subjects can use to negate their or other people's responsibility for a deviant deed. Neutralization in its turn helps one "to withdraw from the universe of obligations" (Fein 1979). These are patterns which find a fertile ground within bureaucratic apparatuses and hierarchical structures. The army and the corporations are good instances of contexts where, typically, the emphasis on values such as obedience and loyalty vis-à-vis the organization may play such a role. Yet one may ask if there is any common denominator between murder and theft on the one hand and economic crimes like fiduciary frauds and insider trading on the other. And what about social injustice and genocide?

It is nevertheless possible to reconcile these apparent inconsistencies – this seemingly odd mixture of deviant acts and situations – by placing them all under a common heading. Such a heading is the definition of violence as "avoidable insults to basic human needs, and more generally to life, lowering the real level of needs satisfaction below what is potentially possible" (Galtung 1990: 292). This definition comes to cover not only conventional notions of crime (direct violence), but also actions and situations which are currently not considered violent (structural violence), such as, for example, social injustice: "There may be no person who directly harms another person in the structure. The violence is built into the structure and shows up as unequal power and consequently as unequal life chances" (Galtung 1969: 114). From this definition of violence follow two fundamental implications:

1   the legal definition of crime is no longer the criterion according to which one judges whether or not a given behavior or situation is criminal; instead, violence is the new and only criterion;
2   any given fact or situation can be considered violent and therefore criminal, regardless of whether the "perpetrator" is a consciously acting physical subject or not, provided that the action or the situation satisfies the conditions stated in the definition, namely, that basic human needs are threatened or offended.

Moreover, on the basis of these two points, it follows that not only corporations and states are liable for the offenses they may commit, but entire social systems can be held responsible for their actions. Recently Cohen (1996), drawing on Braithwaite and Fisse (1990), has argued that corporations, as well as states, are rational, goal-oriented actors able to intentionally carry out criminal acts. However, direct and structural violence do not exhaust the concept of violence: there are aspects of the hegemonic culture that can be used to make invisible, justify, and legitimize direct and/or structural violence. These aspects are what Galtung (1990) has called "cultural violence." Thus cultural violence affects reality in two different (but not mutually exclusive) manners: by changing people's perception of it and by changing its definition. In the following discussion, however, I will mainly deal with this second aspect.

The effect of cultural violence on perception is simple and straightforward: reality is made "opaque" (Galtung 1990: 292) so people do not see the violent nature of an act or a fact. Language aspects are very important in this connection: this is what happens when prisons are "facilities" where inmates are "treated," any act of war as bombing is presented as a "surgical strike," and the killing of civilians "collateral damage." The second effect of cultural violence is more complicated and indirect, but not less powerful, since it changes the definition of reality. What was considered unacceptable, being a violation of legal and/or ethical codes, is now accepted. In other words and more generally, what a violent culture does here is to lift the moral and/or legal ban upon given violent practices. The redefinition of the situation is often indispensable if individual and/or collective subjects have to be involved in violent deeds. For many of these subjects it may be very difficult, if not impossible, to carry out these behaviors unless they perceive that relevant prohibitions (whether moral or legal or both) are not violated. However, cultural violence also represents an important element in the consensus-producing machinery. Therefore, one can say that the full implications of cultural violence are not limited to its significance for those who are involved in violent actions. Cultural violence also concerns those who are not involved, that is, the category to which most people belong. All are affected because the very definition of reality has been altered.

Let me now go back to the patterns of neutralization. Drawing on Matza (1959: 67), and on our previous definition of cultural violence, I conclude that the ways in which "delinquents" and people in general subtly evade "nonetheless accepted standards of behavior" can be brought under three main headings. These headings correspond to the three social mechanisms through which cultural violence operates: *darkening* (the media), *legitimization* (law and science), and *justification* (morals). To state that people in position of power largely enjoy some or all these mechanisms is a platitude; nevertheless, I believe it is worth reiterating.

REMAINING CONCERNS

Can we draw any lesson from this excursus into the "world of negation"? My first concern is with the direction that future research in cultural violence should take. Clearly, we have to know more about the structural conditions that make cultural violence possible. Some authors have already provided insights into this issue. Bauman (1989), for example, has shown in his analysis of the Holocaust how cultural violence was not only tied – as we all well know – to the racist ideology of Arian supremacy and the authoritarian structure of the Nazi state, but also was rooted in specific traits of modernity such as bureaucracy. However, one should not concentrate unilaterally on cultural violence. To grasp the explanatory factors behind the cultural variations in "rates" of violent traits requires that direct, structural, and cultural violence be considered parts of the same whole and that their links are explored.

My second concern is with the current legal notion of crime which, I think, can and should be challenged. This may appear to be a marginal matter, but I believe it to be peculiarly significant in representing a profoundly mistaken emphasis accepted by the courts, and also by the public and by the individuals involved: a concept whereby responsibility has been limited to momentary and often isolated actions...what is decisive in law, and therefore in the whole conduct of human affairs, is what a man does rather than what he is. (Sereny 1974: 124)

My third concern is with the implications of this methodological and theoretical approach for the field of criminology. This essay strongly emphasizes the view that the universe of wrongdoings does not necessarily coincide with the content of the penal law and, more precisely, that by and large the notoriously "dangerous classes" are not in fact the most dangerous ones. This point implies in its turn the recognition of what popular wisdom[2] has always painfully experienced, namely that "the big thieves hang the small ones," and "steal a coin, go to prison: steal a million, become a baron." So far, cultural violence has prevented most people and too many criminologists from hearing these voices. It is now time to listen to them.

Fourth, one may ask what may be gained through this approach. To begin with, the partition of violence into three analytically independent spheres throws some light on ties that are not visible and therefore often overlooked, or at least not adequately emphasized, given the fictitious nature of the line separating legality from illegality. Also, it points out some of the mechanisms that favor the negation of an act of misconduct both at the normative and at the individual levels. Finally, it allows a theoretical perspective able to unify both these levels. In conclusion, it seems to me that substituting the notion of crime with this tripartite notion of violence allows a comprehensive view of the intertwining of normative and empirical aspects: values and conducts, norms and social representations. Of course, this approach implies abandoning the principle according to which it is not our duty as scholars to debate normative questions. However, today, when the corporations are successfully trying to obtain the decriminalization of their activities (Tombs 2001) at the same time as predatory crime is presented as one of the major problems of our cities, and public spaces are increasingly militarized (e.g., Forni 2002), abandoning this principle is more important than ever.

Notes

1 In this connection, I will pay no attention to the considerable amount of research that has been carried out following Sykes and Matza's original contribution. A recent review of the literature and an excellent test of neutralization theory can be found in Agnew (1994).

2 Following the Gramscian tradition, I use the term "popular wisdom" to indicate the vision of the world that informs the life of the subaltern classes (Cirese 1976). An important component of popular wisdom is represented by proverbs, which not only provide "interpretations of specific actions or events in terms of a general, shared model...[but] are...concerned with morality, with evaluating and shaping courses of action and thus are frequently used in contexts of legal and moral argumentation" (White 1987:151).

References

Agnew, R. (1994) The techniques of neutralization and violence. *Criminology*, 32, 555–80.

Allen, J. (1977) *Assault With a Deadly Weapon*, New York: Pantheon Books.

Aubert, V. (1952) White-collar crime and social structure. *American Journal of Sociology*, 58, 263–71.

Bauman, Z. (1989) *Modernity and the Holocaust*. Cambridge: Polity.

Black, D. (1998) *The Social Structure of Right and Wrong*. San Diego: Academic Press.

Bonanno, A., Constance, D. H., and Lyman, K. L. (1997) Corporate crime in the global era. *Critical Sociology*, 2, 63–88.

Bonger, W. (1969) [1916] *Criminality and Economic Conditions*. Bloomington: Indiana University Press.

Box, S. (1983) *Power, Crime and Mystification*. London: Tavistock.

Braithwaite, J. (1986) Retributivism, punishment and privilege. In W. B. Groves and G. Newman (eds.), *Punishment and Privilege*. Albany, NY: Harrow & Heston, 264–303.

Braithwaite, J. (1989) *Crime, Shame and Reintegration*. Cambridge: Cambridge University Press.

Braithwaite, J., and Fisse, B. (1990) On the plausibility of corporate crime theory. In F. Adler and W. S. Laufer (eds.), *Advances in Criminological Theory (2)*. New Brunswick, NJ: Transaction, 15–38.

Cirese, M. (1976) Intellettuali, Folklore ed istinto di classe. Turin: Einaudi.

Clinard, M., and Yeager, P. (1980) *Corporate Crime*. New York: The Free Press.

Cohen, S. (1996) Manskliga raettigheter och statens brott. In M. Akerstroem (ed.), *Kriminalitet, kultur och kontroll*. Stockholm: Carlsson, 164–91.

Coleman, J. W. (1989) *The Criminal Elite. The Sociology of White Collar Crime*. New York: St. Martin's Press.

Coleman, J. W. (1995) Motivation and opportunity: Understanding the causes of white-collar crime. In G. Reis, R. Meier, and L. Salinger (eds.), *White-Collar Crime* (3rd ed.). New York: The Free Press, 360–81.

Coleman, J. W. (2001) The causes of white-collar crime and the validity of explanation in the social sciences. In S-Å. Lindgren (ed.), *White-Collar Crime Research. Old Views and Future Potential*. Stockholm: National Council for Crime Prevention, 55–68.

Cottino, A. (1986) Peasant conflicts in Italy. *Journal of Legal Pluralism and Unofficial Law*, 24, 98–131.

Cottino, A. (1998) The big thieves hang the small ones. Equality before the law in an unequal society. In V. Ruggiero, N. South, and I. Taylor (eds.), *The New European Criminology, Crime and Social Order in Europe*. London and New York: Routledge, 136–45.

Cressey, D. (1988) The poverty of theory in corporate crime research. In W. S. Laufer and F. Adler (eds.), *Advances in Criminological Theory*, vol. I. New Brunswick, NJ: Transaction, 31–55.

Cressey, D. R. (1960) Epidemiology and individual conduct: A case from criminology. *Pacific Sociological Review*, 3, 47–58.

Cressey, D. R. (1971) [1953] *Other people's money*. Belmont, CA: Wadsworth.

Croall, H. (1992) *White-Collar Crime. Criminal Justice and Criminology*. Buckingham: Open University Press.

Della Porta, D. (1992) *Lo scambio occulto*. Bologna: Il Mulino.

Dowie, M. (1988) Pinto madness. In L. Hills Stuart (ed.), *Corporate Violence: Injury and Death for Profit*. Totowa, NJ: Rowman & Littlefield, 213–57.

Engels, F. (1945) [1848] *Die Lage des Arbeitenden Klassen in England*. Leipzig: Wigand.

Fein, H. (1979), *Accounting for Genocide: National Responses and Jewish Victimization during the Holocaust*. New York: The Free Press.

Finney, H. C., and Lesieur, H. R. (1982) A contingency theory of organizational crime. In S. B. Bacharach (ed.), *Research in the Sociology of Organization*. Greenwich, CT: JAI Press, 255–99.

Fisse, B., and Braithwaite, J. (1988) The allocation of responsibility for corporate crime: Individualism, collectivism and accountability. *Sidney Law Review*, 11, 277–97.

Forni, E. (2002) *La città di Batman. Bambini, Conflitti, Sicurezza Urbana*. Turin: Bollati Boringhieri.

Galtung, J. (1969) Violence, peace and peace research. *Journal of Peace Research*, 3, 167–91.

Galtung, J. (1990) Cultural violence. *Journal of Peace Research*, 3, 291–305.

Granovetter, M. (1985) Economic action and social structure: The problems of embeddedness. *American Journal of Sociology*, 91, 481–510.

Hagan, J. (1988) *Structural Criminology*. Cambridge: Polity.

International Herald Tribune (1996) March 30–31.

Jenkins, A., and Braithwaite, J. (1993) Profits, pressure and corporate law-breaking, *Crime, Law & Social Changes*, 20, 221–32.

Leonard, W. N., and Weber, M. G. (1970) Automakers and autodealers: A study of criminogenic market forces. *Law and Society Review*, 4, 407–24.

Levi, M. (1989) Fraudulent justice? Sentencing the business criminal. In P. Carlen and D. Cook (eds.), *Paying for Crime*. Milton Keynes: Oxford University Press, 86–108.

Lindgren, S-Å. (2000) *Ekonomisk brottslighet. Ett samhällsproblem med förhinder*. Lund: Studentlitteratur.

Marx, K. (1954) [1890] *Capital. A Critical Analysis of Capitalist Production*. (English ed. of 1887, ed. F. Engels). Moscow: Foreign Language Publishing House.

Matza, D. (1959) *The Moral Code of Delinquents: A Study of Patterns of Neutralization*. Princeton, NJ: University Press.

Merton, R. K. (1957) *Social Theory and Social Structure: Towards the Codification of Theory and Research*. Glencoe, IL: The Free Press.

Meštrovic, S. (1991) *The Coming Fin de Siècle. An Application of Durkheim's Sociology to Modernity and Postmodernity*. London: Routledge.

Mills, C. W. (1940) Situated actions and vocabularies of motives. *American Sociological Review*, 5, 904–13.

Morselli, C., (2000) *Contacts, Opportunities and Crime: Relational Foundations of Criminal Enterprise*. Ecole de Criminologie, Université de Montréal.

Needleman, M. L., and Needleman, C. (1979) Organizational crime: Two models of criminogenesis. *Sociological Quarterly*, 20, 517–28.

Nelken, D. (1994a) *The Futures of Criminology*. London: Sage.

Nelken, D. (1994b) The future of comparative criminology. In D. Nelken (ed.), *The Futures of Criminology*. London: Sage, 220–43.

Pareto, W. (1991) [1901] *The Rise and Fall of the Elites. An Application of Theoretical Sociology*. New Brunswick, NJ: Transaction.

Pepinsky, H. E. (ed.) (1991) *Rethinking Criminology*. Beverly Hills: Sage.

Polanyi, K. (1994) [1957] *The Great Transformation*. Boston: Beacon Press.

Poveda, T. G. (1994) *Rethinking White Collar Crime*. Westport, CT: Praeger.

Rosoff, S. M. et al. (1998) *Profit Without Honor – White-Collar Crime and the Looting of America*. Englewood Cliffs, NJ: Prentice Hall.

Ruggiero, V. (1996) *Organized and Corporate Crime in Europe*. Aldershot: Dartmouth.

Sereny, G. (1974) *Into that Darkness. From Mercy Killing to Mass Murder*. New York: McGraw-Hill.

Shapiro, S. (1990) Collaring the crime, not the criminal: Reconsidering the concept of white-collar crime. *American Sociological Review*, 55, 346–65.

Simpson, S., Paternoster, R., and Leeper Piquero, N. (1998) Exploring the micro–macro link in corporate crime research. In J. W. Coleman and L. L. Ramos (eds.), *Research in the Sociology of Organizations*. Greenwich, CT: JAI Press, 237–66.

Smith, D. (1975) *The Mafia Mystique*. New York: Basic Books.

Snider, L. (2000) The sociology of corporate crime: An obituary (or: whose knowledge claims have legs?). *Theoretical Criminology*, 4(2), 69–206.

Sutherland, E. (1949) *White Collar Crime*. New York: Dryden.

Sutherland, E. (1983) *White Collar Crime: The Uncut Version*. New Haven, CT: Yale University Press.

Swedberg, R. (1990) *Economics and Sociology*. Princeton, NJ: Princeton University Press.

Sykes, G. M., and Matza, D. (1957) Techniques of neutralization: A theory of delinquency, *American Sociological Review*, 22, 664–70.

Tappan, P. (1947) Who is the criminal?, *American Sociological Review*, 12, 96–102.

Tarde, G. (1886) *La criminalité comparée*. Paris: Alcan.

Tillman R., and Pontell, H. N. (1992) Is justice "collar-blind"? Punishing Medicaid provider fraud. *Criminology*, 30(4), 547–73.

Tombs, S. (2001) Thinking about "white-collar" crime. In S-Å Lindgren (ed.), *White-Collar Crime Research. Old Views and Future Potentials*. Stockholm: National Council for Crime Prevention, 13–34.

Vannucci, A. (1997) *Il mercato della corruzione*. Milano: Società Aperta.

Vaughan, D. (1992) The macro–micro connection in white-collar crime theory. In K. Schlegel and D. Weisburd (eds.), *White-Collar Crime Reconsidered*. Boston: Northeastern University Press, 124–48.

Vaughan, D. (1996) *The Challenger Launch Decision*. Chicago: University of Chicago Press.

Veblen, T. (1992) [1899] *The Theory of the Leisure Class*. New Brunswick: Transaction Publishers.

Vidoni Guidoni, O. (2000) *Come si diventa non devianti*. Torino: Trauben Edizioni.

Waring,, E., Weisburd, E., and Chayet, E. (1995) White-collar crime and anomie. In F. Adler and W. S. Laufer (eds.), *The Legacy of Anomie Theory, Advances in Criminological theory (6)*. New Brunswick, NJ: Transaction, 207–25.

Weber, M. (1984) [1904–5] *The Protestant Ethic and the Spirit of Capitalism*. London: George Allen & Unwin.

Weisburd, D. et al. (1991) *Crimes of the Middle Classes: White Collar Offenders in the Federal Courts*. New Haven, CT and London: Yale University Press.

Wheeler, S. Weisburd, D., and Bode, N. (1982), Sentencing the white-collar offender: Rhetoric and reality. *American Sociological Review*, 44: 641–59.

White, G. M. (1987) Proverbs and cultural models: An American psychology of problem solving. In D. Holland and N. Quinn (eds.), *Cultural Models in Language & Thought*. Cambridge, MA: Harvard University Press, 151–72.

19

"Dance Your Anger and Your Joys": Multinational Corporations, Power, "Crime"

Frank Pearce and Steve Tombs

Dance your anger and your joys
Dance the military guns to silence
Dance their dumb laws to the dump
Dance oppression and injustice to death
Dance the end of Shells ecological war of 30 years
Dance my people for we have seen tomorrow
and there is an Ogoni star in the sky
– Ken Saro-Wiwa, "Dance"[1]

Introduction: Neo-Liberalism, Globalization and the Rise and Rise of the MNC

Though Multinational Corporations (MNCs) are hardly a new phenomenon (Gill and Law 1988: 192), the past quarter of a century has witnessed their rise to the status of a *dominant* actor within a key series of economic, social, and political trends emergent on an international scale – trends usually summed up in the catchall shorthand of "globalization." Key processes encapsulated within this term are well-known: government controls over capital movements have become steadily less effective, with the emergence of a global capital market; states have declined in power vis-à-vis productive capital, being forced into a global competitive process in order to attract or retain capital investment; capital, notably in its multinational forms, increasingly holds the advantage over states, operating in a "footloose" fashion, being able to dictate terms under which such investment will take place; and governments must embrace policies of deregulation, low taxation, and declining expenditures – diminishing their ability to retain or develop autonomous economic, public, and social policy. Increasingly, under pressure from the world's stock markets, from the dominance of US neo-liberal ideology, via the institutions of the global economy such as the International Monetary Fund (IMF), the World Bank, and the World Trade Organization (WTO), and, crucially, subject to the power of multinational capital, the price of nation-state integration into this "global economy" is a significant relinquishing of control over domestic policy agendas, facilitating an international convergence of such policies along neo-liberal lines (Leys 2001: 8–37).

Now, such claims are problematic: they are fraught with hyperbole, conflate the empirical and the normative, and usually fail to examine globalization in actual empirical contexts (Alvesalo and Tombs 2001). This is not to deny that real shifts of some kind in the international organization of economic activity *have* occurred, but it is to argue that what is most significant are the *discourses* of globalization, which have assumed the status of a hegemonic truth, a new orthodoxy (Pearce and Tombs 2001: 198–202). The "perceived dictats" (Goldblatt 1997: 140) of this orthodoxy are invoked by governments as they seek to attract or retain private capital through various forms of de- and re-regulation, impose massive cutbacks in the social wage, and more generally reproduce the "political construction of helplessness" (Weiss 1997: 15); and it is this orthodoxy to which multinational capital points as it seeks to increase its leverage over national states, and both intra- and inter-national sources of resistance.[2]

Certainly the internationalization of neo-liberalism has been accompanied by a dramatic growth in the size of some MNCs. In the United States, for example, each year since 1996 has seen a new record level of merger and takeover activity. Both Europe and Japan also found themselves in the midst of a further wave of "merger mania" at the end of the twentieth century (Pearce and Tombs 2001: 192–5). This merger mania continues: "2000 beat out 1999 – the previous record holder – for both the number and the value of mergers and acquisitions. In all, there were 38,292 transactions, totaling nearly $3.5 trillion.... A little more than half of that was in the U.S." (*Fortune*, 2001).

Many economic sectors and markets are highly concentrated – "monopolistic markets are now the norm in automotive, airline, computing, aerospace, electronics and steel" (Snider 2000: 189). In five industries crucial to the agricultural economies of developing countries – coffee, corn, wheat, pineapples, and tea – just five multinationals control 90 percent of world exports (Coates 1999). More generally, a comparison of the GDP of all 30 OECD member-states[3] with the annual revenues of the world's largest corporations is instructive: on the basis of such data, of the 50 largest economies, 24 are states, 26 are corporations; ExxonMobil, in 2001 the world's largest corporation, has a revenue greater than the GDP of fourteen OECD states.[4] Within the oil industry in particular are some of the world's largest, most powerful multinational actors: three of the seven largest multinationals by sales in 2000 were oil companies. An industry of immense economic and geopolitical significance (Whyte and Tombs 1998), and historically dominated by the so-called "Seven Sisters" (Sampson 1988), the oil sector has become even more concentrated following a flurry of merger activity – not least that between Exxon and Mobil. This merger took place in 1999 – reuniting "the two largest remnants of John D. Rockefeller's Standard Oil, which was broken up by anti-trust regulators in 1911" (Corporate Watch 1999). Over $200 billion in industry mergers between 1998 and1999 have created a "top echelon" of super majors – ExxonMobil, Royal Dutch/Shell, BP, and Total Fina Elf (Energy Intelligence Group 2001; Parker 2000).

There was little hyperbole, then, in a speech to representatives of the oil industry by the then Governor of the Bank of England, Eddie George, when he emphasized the economic *and* political power of the international oil industry:

> [t]he annual value of world oil output works out at something like $55 billion. But to put it into perspective, $50 billion is more than the annual gross domestic product of any country in the world outside of the G7. On that basis, I think that you might just find that you are entitled to a permanent seat on the UN Security Council! (cited in *Petroleum Review*, March 1997: 106)

In this essay, we consider the extent to which it is plausible to speak of a relationship between MNCs and crime. We do so largely through focusing upon one company, ExxonMobil, and one industry, that of international oil. We begin by addressing some of the key ways in which legal agreement has been used to facilitate an international regime within which MNCs and powerful states can operate in a relatively unopposed fashion. We then turn to consider further aspects of MNCs that render it unlikely that their activities will be labeled criminal – both in terms of the power that follows from their very structure, and then in respect of their relationships with investment-hungry, often non-democratic, local states. However, we then document that, despite all the legal, political, and economic advantages that MNCs enjoy, criminal activity on their part remains almost routine. We conclude by noting the extent to which the forms of analysis contained herein are compatible with criminology as currently constructed.

THE CONSTRUCTION OF A CORPORATE FRIENDLY INTERNATIONAL LEGAL REGIME

One of the weaknesses of the globalization orthodoxy is the claim that nation-states are necessarily becoming less powerful vis-à-vis corporate capital in general and MNCs in particular. While this is clearly the case in some respects, the reality is much more complex. In particular, it rather obscures the fact that in creating the conditions within which MNCs can operate both more freely and on an increasingly international scale, advanced capitalist states have been crucial actors. In other words, states, through law, have been facilitating the activities of international capitalist organizations just as they have always played a key role in developing and sustaining national capitalisms (Pearce and Tombs 1998: 3–82).

While criminal law polices the boundaries of capitalism and plays a key role in disorganizing its potential opponents (Pearce 1976), civil law is essential to its functioning (Pashukhanis 1978). Legal regulation of economic transactions depends upon the acknowledgment that actors are in some specific senses legal subjects. In the case of the modern business corporation, it also plays a key role in its very constitution as a legal subject and in its organization. The limited liability business corporation is a trading company construed as having its own legal personality, independent of its members. It has directors legally empowered to determine its business goals and the use of its assets and managers to organize specific profit-making activities. Its shareholders usually play some role in selecting its directors and are entitled to a share of its profits – but other than the monies that they have invested in the company, they are immune from the consequences of its actions or debts (Perrott 1981: 83–4). It is this last feature, in particular, that means that this organization is built upon a structure of irresponsibility (Pearce 1995). The generalization of this legal form, with its attendant privileges, and other elements of the advanced capitalist legal model, is one of the key and underemphasized aspects of the process of globalization. Furthermore, it is in the transnational context that we find the development of civil law in a direction that not only re-creates many elements of (pre-democratic) British common law but goes significantly beyond these. The most useful way to understand this is by a brief digression into aspects of the history of some key international institutions.

During World War II it became clear to those opposing the Axis Powers that it was necessary to set up a series of organizations to regulate political, social, and economic relations between and within states. Thus the United Nations (UN) gradually emerged over a four-year period from 1941. Also, during the Bretton Woods Conference of 1944, the International Monetary Fund (IMF) and the World Bank were created. These institutions were initially mandated to end world poverty and were placed under the control of the UN's Economic and Social Council. In 1947 a new body was proposed, the International Trade Organization (ITO), also under UN control and subject to its social mandate. American pressure prevented the creation of the ITO and also, in 1947, led to the creation of a new organization, the General Agreement on Tariffs and Trade (GATT), with a more restricted mandate not directly answerable to the UN. In 1947, the IMF and the World Bank were reconfigured so that their mandate and decisions were more controllable by the wealthiest nations, particularly the United States (Barlow and Clarke 2001: 54–9).

Since 1951, European trade barriers have been increasingly attenuated, so that the European Union (EU) integrates politically and economically a substantial number of European nation-states. Since 1994, the United States, Canada, and Mexico have become significantly more economically integrated through the North American Free Trade Agreement (NAFTA). In 1995, GATT was effectively replaced by the WTO which, although nominally democratic, is also effectively under the control of the wealthiest nations (Wallach and Sforza 1999; Barlow and Clarke 2001).[5] The policies of these countries, in turn, are largely dictated by the interests of the major corporations active within them – although this by no means guarantees a total coincidence of interests between the wealthiest nations, nor between these individually or collectively and specific corporations.

For our purposes, what is most significant about these changes is that in the name of "free trade" there have been and continue to be moves to develop international law in a way that significantly limits the ability of national governments to determine the nature of their social, political, legal, and economic systems. For example, Chapter 11 of the NAFTA agreement has been used to challenge directly a number of decisions made by governments concerning environmental and safety and health regulations. It allows corporations to sue the government of a NAFTA member-country for any lost profit resulting from that government's actions. This "has already been used successfully by Virginia-based Ethyl Corp. to force the Canadian government to reverse its legislation banning the cross-border sale of its product, MMT, a gasoline additive that has been outlawed in many countries and which Jean Chrétien once called a 'dangerous neurotoxin'" (Barlow and Clarke 2001: 119). In 1998 the case was settled out of court, with the Canadian government paying Ethyl Corp. US$13 million. Such moves are not restricted to NAFTA. In 1994 the US Environmental Protection Agency (EPA) had issued a rule implementing Congress's 1990 Clean Air Act amendments requiring reduction in gasoline contaminants. Subsequently the Venezuelan and Brazilian governments challenged this rule, claiming that it effectively discriminated against their oil industries. The WTO, in its very first ruling, declared the regulation to be an illegal trade barrier and the EPA replaced it with new, weaker rules, "identical to an industry proposal that the EPA had previously contended was unenforceable and too costly" (Wallach and Sforza 1999: 30). Such examples are, unfortunately, numerous (Barker and Mander 1999).

Further, these judgments are made by secret tribunals and are premised on an assumption, made explicit in the WTO's Agreement on Technical Barriers on Trade, that environmental standards must be both "necessary" and least "trade restrictive" (Barlow and Clarke 2001: 80). Clearly these "criteria" are based on the neo-liberal dogma that increased trade *per se* is intrinsically good. Furthermore, the rationale for damages lies in another doctrine developed by right-wing American lawyers. This is the doctrine of "takings" which provides an expansive new definition of property rights. Epstein (1989) argued that regulations "are takings under the Fifth Amendment ('nor shall private property be taken for public purpose without just compensation'), so government must pay those businesses or individuals whose property values is in some way diminished by public actions" (cited in Greider 2001: 4). The logic of this position is relatively clear: if there is a conflict between property rights and other social values – claims for the common good, and the rights of those who own little or nothing – the minority who own the bulk of the wealth will see their rights secured. This will even be true when the government intrudes into the "private sphere" in order to protect society's general health and welfare. A blatant attempt to demand such a legal regime might prove politically problematic in most democratic countries – hence its use as a legal rationale in such arm's-length decision-making bodies as the tribunals of NAFTA and the WTO is both a sly way to achieve similar goals, as well as providing a basis for claiming that it is external pressure, not an internal political demand, that leads to their national implementation. Right-wing politicians and the US Council for International Business were already discussing these ideas in the mid-1980s, well before the NAFTA negotiations and before the creation of the WTO (Greider 2001: 5). Clinton's Democratic administration proved a willing participant in such discussions (MacArthur 2001). Once again, then, we have a clear example of an unholy alliance between right-wing politicians, academics, and business leaders. At the same time, of course, there is a large and growing opposition to these policies.

POWER AND THE MULTINATIONALS

While the activities of MNCs are *facilitated* through international legal frameworks, these corporations continue to do a great deal of work to reframe constantly international and national-based regulatory regimes, both to avoid legal restriction upon their activity and to insulate themselves from critical legal scrutiny. The power of such companies clearly works in a myriad of ways at a variety of levels.

One obvious, highly direct, manifestation of multinational corporate power is to be found in their direct lobbying of international economic and political organizations, such as the WTO, and of governments and other policy-makers (Barker and Mander 1999). MNCs seek to prevent the development of regulations which would limit their activity, to remove existing law that has such an effect, or to render such law innocuous through challenging interpretations of it or by undermining the possibility of it being enforced. Direct lobbying is thus a key MNC activity, one to which such companies devote a great deal of time, money, and effort.

Through its myriad of lobbying organizations, its institutional and interpersonal links with US (and other national) governments, and its pervasive presence throughout research and teaching activities in higher education, Exxon clearly engages in direct – and, it is fair to assume, indirect – lobbying activities. That is, it both lobbies in order to win out where there is manifest political conflict (see Lukes 1974: 11–15), while also operating at a different level of power, which incorporates covert actions, non-decision-making and the mobilization of bias, whereby power works to organize certain issues off political agendas rather than simply involving conflict over issues which appear on such agendas (Lukes 1974).[6] For example, ExxonMobil has been labeled as the "King of Global Warming Denial" (Mokhiber and Weissman 2001),[7] its public position typified by its CEO Lee Raymond, who, while admitting that there could "conceivably be a global warming" problem, raises the lack of clear scientific evidence as a warning against the "considerable economic harm to society that would result from reducing fuel availability to consumers by adopting the Kyoto Protocol or other mandatory measures that would significantly increase the cost of energy" (ibid.). But this is not simply a position it promotes in public. While evidence of covert activity is always, by definition, difficult to uncover, this does, at times, surface. Thus in April 1998 the *New York Times* published a leaked memo, prepared in part by Exxon staff on behalf of the American Petroleum Institute (API), which set out a draft strategy on climate change. In terms that might have been lifted from a political science discussion of agenda manipulation, the memo stated that the API's opposition would be successful when "climate change becomes a non-issue meaning that the Kyoto protocol is defeated and there are no further initiatives to thwart the threat of climate change" (cited in Lewis 2000).

Not surprisingly, ExxonMobil devotes considerable resources to lobbying in Washington. Before the merger of Exxon and Mobil, the *New York Times* reported that Mobil and Exxon spent $5.3 million and $5.2 million respectively on lobbying. In 1999 it was estimated that ExxonMobil spent $11,695,800 on lobbying (Corporate Watch 2001b). Further, ExxonMobil Board members are senior figures in a range of interest and lobbying groups, and/or ExxonMobil supports financially a range of trade associations, pressure groups, and think-tanks, including the API, the US Council for International Business, the European Chemical Industry Council (CEFIC), the Centre for European Policy Studies (CEPS), the Global Climate Coalition (GCC), the Heritage Foundation, the American Enterprise Institute for Public Policy Research, the American Legislative Exchange Council, the Center for the Study of Carbon Dioxide and Global Change, the Citizens for a Sound Economy Educational Foundation, the Foundation for Research on Economics and the Environment, the Heartland Institute, the Hoover Institution, the Manhattan Institute for Policy Research, and the Political Economy Research Center. The company is represented on higher-education research councils and governing bodies throughout the world (ibid).

In 2000, ExxonMobil gave $1.2 million to the Republican Party; only Enron, the now infamous energy corporation, made a higher amount of political donations that year (Corporate Watch 2001b). Bush's cabinet turned out to contain several people with links and interests to the oil industry and ExxonMobil – not to mention the fact that Bush is of Texan oil stock himself, a fact of no little consequence (BBC2 2001).[8] The Bush administration subsequently withdrew US commitment to the Kyoto agreement to reduce carbon emissions.[9] ExxonMobil had been a major contributor to a $13 million US advertising campaign against the Kyoto agreement under the slogan: "It's not global and it won't work" (Campaign ExxonMobil 2001).

Such activities render multinational "crime" less likely, through the ability of MNCs to affect the legal framework within which they operate. But more significant still than these overt and covert activities is a third form, or level, of power, which we can for brevity's sake here call "structural" power. To appreciate the significance of structural power, we need to return briefly to a consideration of the significance of "globalization." Thus, for our considerations, the key implication of the hegemony of discourses of globalization is that governments can exert less political control over economies – economic management is relegated to the task of overseeing the operation of "free" markets – and over the key actors in these economies, namely corporations and, most significantly, MNCs. Having accepted – more or less willingly – the dictats laid down through the discourses of globalization, governments *discipline themselves* to the extent that they either eschew, or at best exercise supreme caution in imposing, additional "burdens" – that is, regulation – upon business.

Thus the utilization and development of the idea of globalization has profound implications for those who would seek to improve protective regulation and place constraints upon the operation of capital. As the legitimacy of business organizations has increased, so has the legitimacy of their control declined (Slapper and Tombs 1999: 85–109; Snider 2000). If one sets these processes in the context of the difficulties that have been historically attached to labeling the illegal activities of corporations as criminal – not least, if most regrettably, due to the support of a succession of academics (Pearce and Tombs 1990, 1991) – it is no surprise that this task has become much more difficult since the 1970s. Neo-liberalism has also raised the naked pursuit of profit to the status of almost moral exigency, which has the effect of legitimating virtually any activity because it is engaged in by business, and delegitimating opposition and resistance – the bases of pro-regulatory forces – for its very "anti-business" rhetoric and practice. All in all, the structural power of capital has greatly increased (Gill and Law 1993).

MNCs and the Avoidance of "crime"

MNCs avoid legal scrutiny in other ways, not least through their very structure. While it is clear that MNCs are not an homogeneous group, they share three basic characteristics: they control economic activities in more than one country; they have the potential to take advantage of geographical differences between countries in "factor endowments" – which include government policies; and they enjoy a geographical flexibility, being able to shift resources and functions between locations at an international level (Dicken 1992: 47). These features indicate the ways in which MNCs enjoy particular advantages in preventing the application of the label "crime" to their activities.

First, the international character of MNCs affords them enormous opportunities to circumvent nationally based legal systems. There are few, if any, enforceable bodies of law that operate at the international level to *restrict* (rather than facilitate) the activities of MNCs. Thus a peculiar advantage of the multinational form is that the MNC can seek out less rather than more regulated contexts in which to operate, often leading them to relocate activity in the developing world, where the power and willingness of national states to impose regulation is relatively low, as investment is eagerly sought, a phenomenon frequently labeled "regime-shopping." Through this phenomenon, multinationals have classically been able, for example, to "export hazard" (Castleman 1979; Jones 1984; Ives 1985; Michalowski and Kramer 1987) – that is, to use production methods or sell products in host countries that would be illegal in their home state (and, indeed, in other developed economies).

Second, and a further consequence of "regime-shopping," is the ability of MNCs to impose "investment conditions" upon states, under threat that investment will not otherwise take place. The very structure of multinationals renders the threat to relocate, disinvest, or invest in another country a forceful one, particularly where the marketization of former state-socialist states, and the waves of privatizations and deregulation across the world, have vastly augmented the terrain within which private capital may operate.

Third, where MNCs are suspected of illegality in a host country, the multinational form – the establishment of legally independent entities within the host country, albeit actually under the direction and control of senior management in the multinational's home country headquarters – has enabled them to cloud issues of responsibility and financial liability. This strategy was used most infamously by Union Carbide when, following the Bhopal "disaster," it (successfully) argued that Union Carbide India Ltd. was an independent company, thus restricting liability to the Indian subsidiary, and ensuring that any legal action would be faced in India, rather than the US, where civil awards were likely to be much reduced (Pearce and Tombs 1998: 194–219).

Fourth, the structure of MNCs makes them inappropriate objects of criminal law, given that most bodies of criminal law have historically been constructed around the individual and, crucially, the concept of *mens rea*. Criminal law does not easily apply to the fictional individual that is the corporate person, in effect a complex entity, consisting of layers of managements and employees, where decision making (and knowledge of this) may appear to be institutionally and geographically diffuse, communication and knowledge seems compartmentalized, various parts of the company are established as legally independent companies or subsidiaries, and where contracting out relationships and various forms of joint ventures and cross-corporate alliances are legion and complex. Indeed, there is no little irony in that fact that the very organizational structures that help to produce corporate crime on such a regular basis are the same structures which render legal systems relatively inefficient instruments for subjecting these corporations to scrutiny or calling them to account (Tombs 1995).

Given these structural features, it is hardly surprising that, for some, MNCs *necessarily* create impoverishment and uneven development, having the effect of redistributing wealth from the "Third" to the "First" world as profits are repatriated from host to home countries, concentrating poverty and generating widening inequalities, and requiring governments to suppress labor demands and other forms of unrest, thereby promoting "stability." Thus, there are numerous documented instances of MNCs maximizing profits through the exploitation of employers, consumers, and local peoples (Forsythe 2000). But we should emphasize that the *particular forms* of illegality or human rights abuses in which particular companies are likely to be implicated is greatly dependent upon the nature of the business in which they are engaged. Oil exploration and extraction involves massive costs for companies, and requires unrestricted access to large masses of land or water. Host countries are keen to provide the conditions whereby oil companies can explore, drill, and exploit reserves: such reserves promise much for host governments, yet cannot be exploited by governments themselves – they lack the technology, skills, and capital. In this sense, states are dependent upon capital to release the valuable resource. Thus it is unsurprising to find that, most infamously, oil companies have been charged with complicity with various states in recent investigations into human rights abuses. As many human rights observers have noted, state–corporate relationships which result in the generation of oil revenues often fail to improve living standards in the host country – where benefits do accrue locally, these tend to be enjoyed by ruling elites in host states rather than being more widely dispersed. Thus the peoples of host states may be subject to a double form of exploitation – that is, being subjected to various abuses in order to allow multinationals to operate while clearly seeing any benefits of such operations being repatriated to richer nations and/or retained by ruling elites, one effect of which is to bolster the relative power of these elites.

In fact, oil companies have been particularly implicated in human rights violations that involve, first, environmental destruction, secondly, violence used against local resistance (including relationships with local paramilitaries/ employment of mercenaries, and so on), and thirdly, displacement and cultural genocide (Davis and Whyte, 2000). The need for access to enormous masses of land can lead to enforced depopulation of massive areas, with the destruction of indigenous livelihoods, homes, and environments. Governments and oil companies have frequently been complicit in taking the measures to "stabilize" the unrest that such measures predictably cause. This complicity can range from governments using oil revenues to arm themselves, to corporations providing arms to death squads working on behalf of the state (ibid.).

It was precisely such a context – the threatened destruction of Ogoniland by Shell with the support of the Nigerian military dictatorship – that led to one of the most infamous sequences of events in the history of human rights and state crime related to the oil industry. In November 1995, following several years of opposition by MOSOP (see note 1) to the activities of Shell and the Nigerian dictatorship in the Ogoniland, Ken Saro-Wiwa and eight other MOSOP activists were hanged by the military government. Shell infamously rejected international governmental and nongovernmental pressures to intervene to prevent the planned executions – pressures it resisted on the grounds that it would not interfere in the politics of a sovereign state, a claim that would be laughable had its consequences not been so gruesome (Human Rights Watch 1999).

If the level of opprobrium heaped upon Shell following the deaths of the MOSOP activists has led it to reassess some of its activities in so-called developing states, this "reassessment" hardly extends to all oil majors (Campaign ExxonMobil 2001). Thus, for example, ExxonMobil continues to act as the lead contractor in the World Bank-backed Chad–Cameroon pipeline, a project which "threatens to replicate the devastating experience of Shell's operations in the Niger Delta, where money flowed to a corrupt, brutal and repressive national government while local communities saw their livelihoods destroyed by pollution" (Mokhiber and Weissman 2001). Allegations against ExxonMobil of complicity in human rights abuses are hardly restricted to the Chad–Cameroon pipeline. The company has been the subject of consistent allegations of complicity in some of the mass atrocities committed by the Indonesian military in Aceh Province, North Sumatra, while further allegations link ExxonMobil with human rights abuses and state crimes in Angola, Colombia, Ecuador, Nigeria, Peru, Russia, and Turkmenistan (Campaign ExxonMobil 2001; Corporate Watch 1999, 2001a, 2001b; Human Rights Watch 1999, 2000, 2001).

CORPORATE CRIME AND THE OIL INDUSTRY

Thus the emergence to dominance, and the very structure, of MNCs have clear implications for our ability to identify multinational corporate "crime." On the one hand, where external controls (both material and ideological) on profit maximization are weakened, then we can reasonably expect to see an increased incidence of illegal corporate activity (Pearce and Tombs 1998; Tombs 1990, 1996). Yet, on the other hand, there are some senses in which it is nonsensical to speak of the increasing incidence of corporate crime under conditions of a neo-liberal hegemony – for the increasing structural power and social credibility of capital may affect the legal category of corporate crime *per se*:

> [B]ecause its survival as an object of study is contingent on the passage and enforcement of "command and control" legislation, corporate crime can "disap-pear" through decriminalization (the repeal of criminal law), through deregulation (the repeal of all state law, criminal, civil and administrative), and through down-

sizing (the destruction of the state's enforcement capacity). All three have been used. (Snider 2000: 172)

Notwithstanding the force of Snider's claims, and in spite of the highly favorable legal regimes within which MNCs increasingly operate, it remains the case – perhaps remarkably – that much MNC activity can *still* be labeled illegal, even criminal. We have argued elsewhere for a utilizable and relatively inclusive definition of corporate crime (Pearce and Tombs 1998: 107–10; see also Slapper and Tombs 1999: 16–19). This definition rejects distinctions between what are conventionally constructed as separate categories of law – criminal, civil, regulatory – since, following Sutherland, such distinctions are both partly contingent and an effect of class-based power (Sutherland 1945). Yet this definition does maintain a clear reference to existing (that is, bourgeois) legal categories – thus it does not extend the term "crime" to socially harmful activities that are entirely legal. Using this definition it is possible to demonstrate clearly the extent to which, despite the fact that we are discussing bourgeois legal categories that corporations do much to help construct, *capitalist corporations routinely violate them*.

There is, in fact, a great deal of evidence of crime by ExxonMobil in particular and throughout the oil industry in general. Thus, for example, the directors of Standard Oil, the company famously broken up in 1909 via antitrust legislation in the United States – and out of which Exxon was formed, via Standard Oil of New Jersey – were labeled at the time by President Roosevelt as "the biggest criminals in the country" (cited in Yergin 1991: 108). Standard Oil of New Jersey – the immediate forerunner of Exxon – was infamously castigated by a 1942 Congressional Committee for its intimate business relationships with the Nazis and I. G. Farben, sustained during the war in some respects directly contrary to the war interests of the United States and Britain, to the extent that Senator Harry Truman "publicly excoriated Standard Oil's arrangements as 'treason' and an 'outrage'" (Black 2001: 337–8). It is perhaps no surprise, then, given this pedigree, to find that Exxon was listed as a "recidivist" company in the *Multinational Monitor*'s list of the worst 100 corporations of the 1990s. This was based largely on two celebrated convictions. The first saw Exxon Corporation and Exxon Shipping plead guilty to federal criminal charges in connection with the March 24, 1989 *Exxon Valdez* oil spill. Approximately 11 million gallons of crude oil spilled from the *Valdez*, fouling 700 miles of Alaska shoreline, killing birds and fish, and destroying the way of life of thousands of Native Americans. The company was fined $125 million (Mokhiber 1999). The second conviction followed Exxon Corporation pleading guilty to federal charges in connection with an oil spill of 567,000 gallons of domestic heating oil into Arthur Kill, a narrow waterway which separates New York from New Jersey. Exxon entered the plea as part of a $15 million settlement with local, state and federal governments, which included a fine of $200,000, the maximum allowed by law, and payments in restitution (ibid.).

Beyond these, other high-profile instances of convictions include the following. Esso Australia was recently convicted in Australia of 11 charges linked to a 1998 explosion at a gas-processing plant which killed two people (Mokhiber and Weissman 2001). A New Orleans jury in May 2001 ordered ExxonMobil to pay a Louisiana judge and his family $1 billion for contaminating their land with radioactivity. Exxon is appealing the verdict. Nor are these a few isolated incidents (ibid.). The US Public Interest Research Group (Manuel 2001) has documented a series of recent successful legal actions against ExxonMobil, which include the following:

- In an ongoing case, the State of Texas filed a suit against ExxonMobil, in January 2001, for extracting oil and natural gas from state land without permission. The state is seeking "tens of millions of dollars" in compensation.
- ExxonMobil was part of a $282-million agreement reached by 10 oil companies for underpaying the government by hundreds of millions of dollars in drilling royalties on federal land in the western United States. ExxonMobil agreed to pay $7 million to settle claims that it underpaid royalties for oil it extracted from federal lands in 2000.
- A Montgomery County jury awarded the State of Alabama $87.7 million in compensatory damages and $3.42 billion in punitive damages in December 2000, having found that Exxon defrauded the state on royalties from natural gas wells in state waters.
- Illegal exposure to chemicals of Lockheed Corporation workers in Burbank, California, resulted in Exxon paying $252 million as part of a $760-million punitive damage award in August 1998.
- Found to have discharged selenium, a carcinogen, into San Francisco Bay, Exxon and Tosco agreed to pay $4.8 million in damages and for environmental restoration in August 1998.
- After residents of Grand Bois, Louisiana, sued Exxon and Campbell Wells, alleging that the waste exceeded limits on toxins such as benzene, a known carcinogen, Exxon was ordered to pay $35,000 to four plaintiffs as part of the Campbell Wells oilfield waste suit (August 1998).
- In February 1998, the Department of Justice filed a civil complaint accusing Exxon of nearly 200 Clean Air Act violations and demanding $4.7 million in fines.
- Following the dumping of almost two billion gallons of chemical wastewater from their Baytown, Texas refinery, Exxon agreed to pay $600,000 to the Texas Natural Resource Conservation Commission in 1996.
- Violations of the Clean Air Act at its Baton Rouge, Louisiana, refinery resulted in Exxon paying a civil penalty of $20,000 in October 1996.
- In October 1996, Exxon paid a civil penalty of $73,000 for violating the Resource Conservation and Recovery Act and $116,000 for Clean Water Act violations at its Baton Rouge, Louisiana, refinery.
- The bypassing of air pollution-control equipment led to Exxon paying $1 million in air-pollution fines for its Bayway refinery in Linden, New Jersey, in October 1993.
- Exxon was fined $125,000 by the EPA in 1991 for discharging contaminated fluids from service stations into or directly above underground sources of drinking water.
- An admission by Exxon that its leak-detection system had not worked properly for 12 years, highlighted by a spill of 567,000 gallons of oil from an Exxon pipeline into the Arthur Kill waterway between Staten Island and

New Jersey in January 1990. The City of New York sued Exxon for submitting false pipeline-safety reports. Exxon settled out of court, agreeing to spend $10–15 million on environmental improvements.

This is a remarkable level of recidivism for operations in *one* country. This country, the United States, is also the originator of the infamous "three strikes and you're out" laws – laws which have never, of course, been extended to apply to corporate offenders (Geis 1996). Yet Exxon is hardly a uniquely rogue oil company. The oil industry has been a consistent focus of both qualitative and quantitative work that has sought to document the scale of corporate offending and the reasons for regulatory failure (Carson 1982; Coleman 1985; Molotch 1973; Woolfson et al. 1996; Whyte and Tombs 1998). Moreover, sectors closely allied to the oil industry have also provided a focus for corporate crime research. Most notable here are: a collection of articles examining the automobile industry as a criminogenic industrial structure (Farberman 1975; Leonard and Weber 1970; Nader 1965; Seib 1978); a recent political economy of corporate crime associated with the chemical industries (Pearce and Tombs 1998); and a series of texts and papers on crimes in and of the pharmaceutical industry (Braithwaite 1984, 1993; Finlay 1996; Peppin 1995). Moreover, beyond such qualitative, case-study research, Clinard and Yeager (1980: 119–22) had found in their *quantitative* analysis of violations that the industries in which companies were most likely to violate the law were oil, pharmaceuticals, and motor vehicle manufacturing.

CONCLUSIONS: POWER, CRIME, CRIMINOLOGY AND RESISTANCE?

We have sought in this essay to consider the extent to which it is possible to view the socially harmful activities of MNCs through a category of "crime." A key consideration has been the ability of multinationals to be protected from critical legal scrutiny via their access to power – a power augmented with the international spread of neo-liberalism and the emergence to orthodoxy of the discourses of globalization. We have also indicated how the structure of MNCs is associated with their involvement in a myriad of activities in which they produce socially harmful consequences, though these activities remain either formally legal, or evade any form of detection, investigation, enforcement, or prosecutorial activity.

These points being made, we should beware of exaggerating the power of MNCs and thus underestimating the extent to which their power can be challenged. Although discourses of globalization have the status of an almost unquestioned truth, they are far from entirely secure – no form of hegemony ever is – and obscure a much more complex reality (see Pearce and Tombs 2001). Thus, for example, while they may enjoy relative advantages vis-à-vis states, even the largest MNCs still require states to do a good deal of work for them, through erecting and maintaining national and international legal regimes in which their activities are facilitated, and through undermining resistance to their activities, both ideologically and materially.

Further, while many host states are often cowed into submission by MNC threats not to invest or to relocate, some states exaggerate such threats to allow them to do that which they would have done anyway. Thus, while "regime-shopping" is a real phenomenon, and investment and productive activity seeks out less over more regulated contexts, other considerations are clearly crucial – for example, access to markets, the scale of sunk costs, the availability of "human capital" and general infrastructure, a corporation's historical and cultural affiliations, and so on; thus we must pay attention to the specifics of industries and markets. In the oil industry, the relationship between states and corporations shifts once the process of exploration and drilling have begun; at that point, massive financial costs on the part of the MNC are, quite literally, sunk in a host state, requiring the MNC to extract as much oil as possible, shifting the balance of power toward the host state. Such specificities indicate that states have room for maneuver, even where they claim otherwise – which in turn means that pressure on states and corporations can result in very different forms of capitalist–social relations and forms of economic management across different nation-states. In short, politics – and resistance – matter. Particularly significant here is the rise of international pressure, challenging not simply states but those bodies to which states have subcontracted the construction of an international economy, including the WTO.[10] Neither the abilities of MNCs to act within the law whilst wreaking social havoc, nor the reality, possibilities, and limits of national and international resistance, can be captured adequately within the discipline of criminology, with its focus upon "crime" and "crime control."

We have also demonstrated that, notwithstanding advantages of size, structure, and power, MNCs routinely engage in crimes – by which we mean cases in which there have been formal verdicts of guilt or liability reached following some form of judicial process. Yet if corporate harm is (more understandably) marginalized by criminology, so too are corporate (and related state) *crimes* (Tombs and Whyte 2003). This is even more the case where such crimes involve MNCs, since criminology tends to remain nationally based, or at best looking through the world from an Anglo-American perspective. More generally, from its very emergence – as a discipline born out of a concern on the part of the medical and psychological professions with pathological individuals – criminology has been constructed in a way that does not lend itself easily to addressing *organizational* (corporate or state) crime. Even more significantly, criminology has always had close, indeed intimate, relationships to power – to the state and to criminal justice systems – which render this discipline likely to view the "problem" of crime in a way almost synonymous with state and criminal justice systems' own explicit definitions of that "problem."

Definitions of "the crime problem" can of course be challenged – and indeed, relatively successfully so, as feminists have demonstrated through their academic and political efforts in forcing recognition of sexual assault and domestic violence upon criminal justice systems. But in the case of corporate crime, particularly on the part of MNCs, there is little to suggest that criminology will provide empirical, conceptual, or theoretical supports for the social movements engaged in such challenges.

Notes

Thanks go to Dave Whyte, who brought to bear his considerable knowledge of the political economy of the oil industry on an earlier draft of this chapter.

1   http://www.mosopcanada.org/, the website for the Movement for the Survival of the Ogoni People (MOSOP).
2   Some recent studies have documented how the discourses of globalization may be used by already-powerful companies at moments when they seem most vulnerable to greater state and pro-regulatory scrutiny (Woolfson et al. 1996; Whyte 1999; Whyte and Tombs 1998). These studies indicate that corporate power is not simply an issue for peoples of developing economies.
3   The OECD includes almost all of the world's largest economies.
4   It has been calculated that "the top 500 transnational corporations are responsible for 30% of the world's gross product, 70% of world trade, and 80% of world investment" (Smith et al. 1999: 212).
5   And parallel to the WTO and regional agreements such as NAFTA-run industry-based agreements, including the Energy Charter Treaty, which seeks the extension of WTO rules to non-WTO countries (Project Underground 2001).
6   There are well-known limitations with Lukes's typology (see, e.g., Clegg 1989).
7   Thus it has been "singled out" by environmental organizations via the international StopEsso campaigns (see www.stopesso.com).
8   The Bush–Cheney Energy Plan, urging that local regulations not be allowed to interfere with profit maximization of oil companies, is a key element of the administration's trade policy (Project Underground 2001).
9   At the time of writing (2002), the administration was supporting the passage of legislation through Congress to open up the Arctic National Wildlife Refuge to oil drilling, threatening the ecology of the largest designated wilderness area in the US National Wildlife Refuge System.
10 These issues are addressed in detail in Pearce and Tombs (2001).

References

Alvesalo, A., and Tombs, S. (2001) The emergence of a "war" on economic crime: The case of Finland. *Business and Politics*, 3(3), 239–67.

Barker, D., and Mander, J. (1999) *Invisible Government*. San Francisco: International Forum on Globalization.

Barlow, M., and Clarke, T. (2001) *Global Showdown*. Toronto: Stoddart.

BBC2 (2001) The toxic Texan. *The Money Programme*, June 4.

Black, E. (2001) *IBM and the Holocaust*. London: Little, Brown.

Braithwaite, J. (1984) *Corporate Crime in the Pharmaceutical Industry*. London: Routledge & Kegan Paul.

Braithwaite, J. (1993) Transnational regulation of the pharmaceutical industry. In G. Geis and P. Jesilow (eds.), *White Collar Crime. The Annals of the American Academy of Political and Social Science*, Vol. 525, January, 12–30.

Campaign ExxonMobil (2001) *Can We Save the Tiger From ExxonMobil?* www.campaignexxonmobil.org/learn/misinform.shtml, accessed March 2002.

Carson, W.G. (1982) *The Other Price of Britain's Oil*. Oxford: Martin Robertson.

Castleman, B. (1979) The export of hazard to developing countries. *International Journal of Health Services*, 9, 569–606.

Clegg, S. (1989) *Frameworks of Power*. London: Sage.

Clinard, M., and Yeager, P. (1980) *Corporate Crime*. New York: The Free Press.

Coates, B. (1999) Time to shatter "free trade" myth. *Observer*, November 21, Business Section, 6.

Coleman, J. S. (1985) Law and power: the Sherman Anti-Trust Act and its enforcement in the petroleum industry. *Social Problems*, 32, 264–74.

Corporate Watch (1999) *OIL: A selection of stories from the world's dirtiest Industry*. http://www.corporatewatch.org.uk/magazine/issue8/cw8oil1.html, accessed March 2002.

Corporate Watch (2001a) *Corporate Crimes. Company Profiles/Oil & Gas/Exxon Mobil & Esso UK*. http://www.corporatewatch.org.uk/profiles/oil_gas/exxon_mobil/exxon_mobil5.html, accessed March 2002.

Corporate Watch (2001b) *Company profiles/Oil & Gas/ExxonMobil & Esso UK*. http://www.corporatewatch.org.uk/profiles/oil_gas/exxon_mobil/exxon_mobil1.html, accessed March 2002.

Davis, C., and Whyte, D. (2000) The adequacy of human rights claims as a challenge to corporate violence and environmental destruction: A case study of the international oil industry. Paper presented at *State Crime and Corporate Violence: Human Rights Violations in the New World Order. The Conference of the European Group for the Study of Deviance and Social Control*, April 25–27, University of Bangor, Wales.

Dicken, P. (1992) *Global Shift*. London: Paul Chapman.

Energy Intelligence Group (2001) *Ranking the World's Top Oil Companies*, 2001. http://www.energyintel.com/ResDocDetail.asp?document_id=50195, accessed March 2002.

Epstein, R. (1989) *Takings: Private Property and the Power of Eminent Domain*. Cambridge, MA: Harvard University Press.

Farberman, H. A. (1975) A criminogenic market structure in the automobile industry. *Sociological Quarterly*, 16 (Autumn), 438–57.

Finlay, L. M. (1996) The pharmaceutical industry and women's reproductive health. In E. Szockyi and J. G. Fox (eds.), *Corporate Victimisation of Women*. Boston: Northeastern University Press, 59–110.

Fortune (2001) *Global 500. The World's Largest Corporations*. http://www.fortune.com/indexw.jhtml?channel = list.jhtml&list_frag = list_global500.jhtml&list =19, accessed March 2002.

Forsythe, D. P. (2000) Transnational corporations and human rights. In D. P. Forsythe (ed.), *Human Rights in International Relations*. Cambridge: Cambridge University Press, 191–213.

Geis, G. (1996) A base on balls for white-collar criminals. In D. Shichor and D. K. Sechrest (eds.), *Three Strikes and You're Out. Vengeance as Public Policy*. Thousand Oaks, CA: Sage, 244–64.

Gill, S., and Law, D. (1988) *The Global Political Economy*. Baltimore: Johns Hopkins University Press.

Gill, S., and Law, D. (1993) Global hegemony and the structural power of capital. In S. Gill (ed.), *Gramsci, Historical Materialism and International Relations*. Cambridge: Cambridge University Press, 93–124.

Goldblatt, D. (1997) At the limits of political possibilities: The cosmopolitan democratic project. *New Left Review*, 225 (September/October), 140–50.

Greider, W. (2001) The Right and US trade law: Invalidating the 20th century. *The Nation*, October 15, 21–9.

Human Rights Watch (1999) *World Report 1999*. http://www.hrw.org/worldreport99/europe/turkmenistan3.html, accessed March 2002.

Human Rights Watch (2000) *Awakening: The Role of the Oil and Banking Industries in Angola's Civil War and the Plunder of State Assets*. http://www.hrw.org/press/2000/06/ango-0623–back.htm, accessed March 2002.

Human Rights Watch (2001) *Human Rights Backgrounder on Indonesia*. http://www.hrw.org/backgrounder/asia/indo-bck-sept.htm, accessed March 2002.

Ives, J., ed. (1985) *The Export of Hazard. Transnational Corporations and Environmental Control Issues*. Boston: Routledge & Kegan Paul.

Jones, K. (1984) Everywhere abroad but nowhere at home: The global corporation and the international state. *International Journal of the Sociology of Law*, 12, 85–103.

Leonard, W. N., and Weber, M. G. (1970) Automakers and dealers: A study of criminogenic market forces. *Law and Society Review*, 4 (February), 407–24.

Lewis, S. J. (2000) Comments on the proposed settlement regarding the ExxonMobil merger. *Letter to the Federal Trade Commission*, 31 January, http://www.campaign-exxonmobil.org/learn/pdf/comments.pdf, accessed March 2002.

Leys, C. (2001) *Market-Driven Politics*. London: Verso.

Lukes, S. (1974) *Power. A Radical View*. London: Macmillan.

MacArthur, J. R. (2001) *The Selling of "Free Trade"*. Berkeley: University of California Press.

Manuel, A. (2001) *The Dirty Four: The Case Against Letting BP Amoco, ExxonMobil, Chevron, and Phillips Petroleum Drill in the Arctic Refuge*. US Public Interest Research Group.

Michalowski, R. J., and Kramer, R. C. (1987) The space between the laws: The problem of corporate crime in a transnational context. *Social Problems*, 34, 34–53.

Mokhiber, R. (1999) The top 100 corporate criminals of the 1990s. *Multinational Monitor*, 20(7/8), http://www.multinationalmonitor.org/mm1999/99july-aug/crime1.html, last accessed March 2002.

Mokhiber, R., and Weissman, R. (2001) Corporations behaving badly: The ten worst corporations of 2001. *Multinational Monitor*, 22(12), http://63.111.165.25/01december/dec01corp1.html, accessed March 2002.

Molotch, H. (1973) Oil in Santa Barbara and power in America. In W. J. Chambliss (ed.), *Sociological Readings in the Conflict Perspective*. Reading, MA: Addison-Wesley, 297–323.

Nader, R. (1965) *Unsafe at Any Speed. The Designed-in Dangers of the American Automobile*. New York: Grossman.

Parker, R. G. (2000) *Solutions to Competitive Problems in the Oil Industry. Prepared Statement of the Federal Trade Commission Before The Committee on the Judiciary United States House of Representatives*. March 29.

Pashukhanis, E. (1978) *Law and Marxism*. London: Ink-Links.

Pearce, F. (1976) *Crimes of the Powerful: Marxism, Crime and Deviance*. London: Pluto.

Pearce, F. (1995) Accountability for corporate crime. In P. Stenning (ed.), *Accountability for Criminal Justice*. Toronto: University of Toronto Press, 213–38.

Pearce, F., and Tombs, S. (1990) Ideology, hegemony and empiricism: Compliance theories of regulation. *British Journal of Criminology*, Autumn, 423–43.

Pearce, F., and Tombs, S. (1991) Policing corporate "skid rows": Safety, compliance, and hegemony. *British Journal of Criminology*, Autumn, 415–26.

Pearce, F., and Tombs, S. (1998) *Toxic Capitalism: Corporate Crime and the Chemical Industry*. Aldershot: Ashgate.

Pearce, F., and Tombs, S. (2001) Crime, corporations and the "new" world order. In G. Potter (ed.), *Controversies in White-Collar Crime*. Cincinnati, OH: Anderson, 185–222.

Peppin, P. (1995) Science, law and the pharmaceutical industry. In F. Pearce and L. Snider (eds.), *Corporate Crime: Contemporary Debates*. Toronto: University of Toronto Press, 87–108.

Perrott, D. (1981) Changes in attitude to criminal liability – the European experience. In T. Orhnial (ed.), *Limited Liability and the Corporation*. London: Croom Helm, 81–96.

Project Underground (2001) *Oil, the World Trade Organization, & Globalization*. http://www.moles.org/ProjectUnderground/oil/ wto2001_nov_b.html, accessed March 2002.

Sampson, A. (1988) *The Seven Sisters. The Great Oil Companies and the World they Created*. London: Coronet.

Seib, G. F. (1978) Dallas ordinance against car repair frauds. In J. M. Johnson and J. D. Douglas (eds.), *Crime at the Top*. Philadelphia: J. B. Lippincott, 319–22.

Slapper, G., and Tombs, S. (1999) *Corporate Crime*. London: Addison Wesley Longman.

Smith, J, Bolyard, M., and Ippolito, A. (1999) Human rights and the global economy: A response to Meyer. *Human Rights Quarterly*, 21, 207–19.

Snider, L. (2000) The sociology of corporate crime: An obituary (or: whose knowledge claims have legs?). *Theoretical Criminology*, 4(2), 169–206.

Sutherland, E. (1945) Is "white-collar crime" crime? *American Sociological Review*, 10, 132–9.

Tombs, S. (1990) Industrial injuries in British manufacturing. *Sociological Review*, 38(2), 324–43.

Tombs, S. (1995) New organizational forms and the further production of corporate crime. In F. Pearce and L. Snider (eds.), *Corporate Crime: Contemporary Debates*. Toronto: University of Toronto Press, 132–46.

Tombs, S. (1996) Injury, death and the deregulation fetish: The politics of occupational safety regulation in UK manufacturing. *International Journal of Health Services*, 26 (2), 327–47.

Tombs, S., and Whyte, D. (2003) Scrutinising the powerful? Crime, contemporary political economy and critical social research. In S. Tombs and D. Whyte (eds.), *Unmasking the Crimes of the Powerful: Scrutinising States and Corporations*. New York: Peter Lang, n.p.

Wallach, L., and Sforza, M. (1999) *The WTO: Five Years of Reasons to Resist Corporate Globalization*. New York: Seven Stories Press.

Weiss, L. (1997) Globalization and the myth of the powerless state. *New Left Review*, 225 (September/October), 3–27.

Whyte, D. (1999) Power, Ideology and the Management of Safety in the UK Offshore Oil Industry. Unpublished Ph.D. manuscript, Liverpool John Moores University.

Whyte, D., and Tombs, S. (1998) Capital fights back: Risk, regulation and profit in the UK offshore oil industry. *Studies in Political Economy*, 57 (September), 73–101.

Woolfson, C., Foster, J., and Beck, M. (1996) *Paying for the Piper? Capital and Labor in the Offshore Oil Industry*. Aldershot: Mansell.

Yergin, D. (1991) *The Prize. The Epic Quest for Oil, Money and Power*. London: Simon & Schuster.

20

Globalization and the Illicit Drugs Trade in Hong Kong

K. Joe Laidler

Introduction

June 30, 1997 marked a historic moment in Chinese–British relations when Hong Kong ceased to be a British colony and became a Special Administrative Region (SAR) of China. From that day forward, Hong Kong would operate under the principle of "one country, two systems." In the period running up to and just after the 1997 handover, policymakers and law-enforcement officials in the United States, Australia, the United Kingdom, and Canada expressed concerns about the potential impact of this historical change on organized crime. In particular, international authorities feared that Hong Kong crime syndicates would regroup and move their operations, particularly in the heroin trade, overseas to cities where they had already established legitimate and illegitimate business links. In doing so, Hong Kong crime groups would supposedly avoid being subjected to the uncertainties of the Chinese law and punishment system. This line of reasoning made some sense as the popular press continually highlighted Hong Kong citizens' feelings of political uncertainty and the exodus of many Hong Kong residents overseas.

But why should this be so? Why would Hong Kong crime groups want to risk moving their "headquarters" overseas? Would overseas locales enable these crime groups to expand their drug trade, and, via money-laundering, their legitimate businesses? Drug trafficking and its related crimes had by 1997 already developed into a global industry. Hong Kong drug syndicates were already participants in this international industry. So would their movement represent another stage in the development of globalization and drug trafficking? The purpose of this essay is to examine this issue of globalization in relation to the illicit drugs trade in the Hong Kong context. It draws upon data gathered in both the United Nations Drug Control Program's (UNDCP) study of the global drug market and the study of the rise of the psychotropic drug-use problem in Hong Kong conducted for the Hong Kong Government Narcotics Division (see Laidler et al. 2000, 2001). The data was collected using official statistics, interviews, and focus groups with outreach workers, police, corrections officers, social workers, and treatment staff, and in-depth interviews with 60 drug users.

GLOBALIZATION: THE LOCAL AND THE GLOBAL

Globalization is presently one of the "hottest" issues of scholarly discussion and debate. Many in the social sciences including sociologists, anthropologists, economists, and political scientists have developed numerous perspectives on what exactly is meant by globalization. Depending on one's definition, further questions are raised as to how globalization operates, and what its implications are on modernity (Giddens 1990; Waters 1995; Robertson 1992; Gilpin 2000). A complete review of the debate is beyond the scope of this essay (see Guillen 2001 for an extensive review).

The perspective adopted here draws from Findlay's discussion on globalization and crime and is particularly concerned with addressing one of the many paradoxes of globalization. As he aptly points out, "it is paradoxical in the way it unifies and delineates, internationalises and localises" (1999: 3). Across the world, culture is universalizing. For example, dance music and the club scene associated with it has emerged in many corners of the world, from London to New York, to Toronto to Sydney, to Singapore and Beijing, and is experienced and appreciated by today's youth. This common experience is part of contemporary global youth culture. At the same time, individuals are not passive recipients but actively construct and negotiate culture and identity. Consequently, what is "global" becomes, through a process of negotiation, local. Global culture becomes localized, adapting to the particular features of a community or society. So, although dance music and the club scene are a reflection of a global youth culture, distinctive forms of music and venues develop in relation to local culture in communities like New York, London, Singapore, and Beijing.

In this essay, I examine this globalization paradox by examining the local and global dimensions of the drug market in Hong Kong. Hong Kong provides an ideal example of this paradox as its origins lie in the opium trade and colonial powers. Given its strategic position to Guangzhou, the access port to China at the time, Hong Kong became one of the principal business centers for opium importation into China. Opium became a lucrative and essential commodity for the big trading companies who established Hong Kong as their base. Because of its free-port status, the colonial government seized legal control of the domestic opium market to generate revenues for its administration. Despite international pressures in the late 1800s, the British continued to view opium as a primary source of revenue, accounting for 46 percent of total colonial government income in 1918 (Miners 1983; Traver 1992). Hong Kong's introduction to opium, then, was largely shaped and driven by colonial and capitalist expansion. By the late 1920s, Hong Kong was following the lead of China, Europe, and America such that heroin and morphine came to dominate – because they were viewed as cures and alternatives to opium. The decline of opium and the rising popularity of heroin gradually took hold over the next several decades as users found legal support for it rescinded, as well as the ease and safety of the use of heroin compared with opium (Traver 1992). Heroin came to dominate until recent times and came under the control of local organized crime groups. In the discussion that follows, the paradox of the global and local dimensions of the illicit drug trade resurfaced in the late 1990s as Hong Kong has followed and accommodated itself to the global trend of the stimulant drug market, especially with methylenedioxy-N-methamphetamine (MDMA), or ecstasy.

DENG'S CALL TO ALL: TO GET RICH IS GLORIOUS

As we examine the contemporary drug scene in Hong Kong, I raise the question again as to why organized crime groups in Hong Kong would want to move their "operations" abroad in 1997. There is, in fact, no good reason for them to move abroad. Hong Kong, long established as one of the premier examples of the Asian economic miracle, had already seized the opportunity to serve as a facilitator to China in market liberalization. China has turned away from the economic principles of communism and has embraced laissez-faire capitalism.

Deng's call for China to venture onto the road of capitalism has become the guiding principle of legitimate and illegitimate activities and has been embraced by those on the mainland, as well as those beyond its borders in its special administrative regions of Hong Kong and Macau. The police have observed:

> The level of triad crime has remained relatively stable in the past two to three years. 1997 has not affected the traditional forms of triad related crimes in Hong Kong. What has changed is the increase in loan-sharking and in connection with this, the quest to make fast semi-legal as well as illegal activities." (Detective Chief Inspector, Royal Hong Kong Police, personal interview, 1999)

Hong Kong's role in drug trafficking locally, regionally, and internationally can only be understood in the context of the Hong Kong's more general economic interdependence with China since the open-door policy began in 1978. From 1978 through to 2000, visible trade between Hong Kong and China climbed an average of 24 percent per annum in value terms (Hong Kong Government 2000: 49). China has become Hong Kong's largest external direct investor, having invested US$105 billion principally in businesses, banking, transport, and warehousing, but also in property, hotel, manufacturing, financial services, and infrastructure development (Hong Kong Government 2000: 51).

Cross-border investments have increased and shifted from industrial processing to a broader range of businesses and services including hotel, property, and infrastructure developments. In fact, Hong Kong has been the biggest direct investor in China, with its realized direct investment amounting to US$171 billion by the close of 2000 (Hong Kong Government 2000: 50). Hong Kong's realized direct investment in Southern China's Guangdong province approximated to US$64 billion at the end of 1999. The role of Hong Kong in this province's economy is significant as it represents nearly 75 percent of all inward direct investment.

Hong Kong's role in the Chinese economy is not solely as an investor. Long before 1997, Hong Kong served as a "middleman" for foreign investors wanting to position themselves in China. Economists predict that foreign direct investment will continue at an unprecedented rate as China's economy restructures in accordance with market liberalization (Sung 1998). Given this trend, Hong Kong's role as a conduit for China will continue. In light of this interdependence, I now turn to the contemporary drug market in Hong Kong. In particular, I highlight the ways in which drug consumption is a reflection of the global and local, as well as the ways in which Hong Kong traffickers have adapted to the local and global drug market.

THE LOCAL AND GLOBAL DIMENSIONS OF THE DRUG MARKET FROM THE HONG KONG EXPERIENCE

As noted above, Hong Kong has had a longstanding association with opiates dating back to the 1800s, and this pattern has continued through much of the 1990s. This association has been in relation to both consumption and trafficking. With regard to consumption, opiate use has generally been linked to lower-class adult males who did not present any immediate problems or threats to the community. Opiates' calming effects reduced the potential for violent crimes. Drug-related crime typically involved petty offenses that could be relatively contained. The potential for opiate addiction "spreading" to other populations, especially the young, was hampered by the social stigma of "hitting the bottom with heroin" within the drug community itself and in Hong Kong culture more generally. Many potential problems associated with opiate addiction were further impeded with the Hong Kong government's successful development of a comprehensive rehabilitation program that moves an addict from detoxification, to methadone maintenance, and to medical and social treatment.

This longstanding pattern of opiate use, however, has rapidly changed in the last few years. Today, heroin consumption among young persons under the age of 21 has dropped. At the same time, Hong Kong's local drug scene is following the lead of other countries and has experienced a dramatic increase in the use of amphetamine-type stimulants (ATS). In particular, ecstasy, ketamine, and to a lesser extent, methamphetamines, or "ice," prevail as the substances of choice in this age group. This trend has taken place in the context of a burgeoning and lucrative nightclub scene, an eclectic mix of local and global music, a Hong Kong–China cross-border system of manufacturing and a local system of selling in and around entertainment venues.

Hong Kong's role in the trafficking of heroin was domestic as well as international. With one of the world's largest cargo-container terminals, it has had a longstanding role as a "business center" for heroin distribution, and from 1987 until very recently, was known as a transit point for heroin going to other countries like the United States, Canada, and Australia. In November 2000, the US government removed Hong Kong from the "blacklist" of countries playing a major role in the transshipment of drugs internationally (Narcotics Division Press Release, November 2, 2000). According to the US government, the removal of Hong Kong from the "blacklist" was due to its decreased role as a transit point and its establishment of strong cooperative law-enforcement ties and extradition agreements with other countries. From the Hong Kong perspective, this removal from the "blacklist" is recognition of its longstanding efforts to address the international trafficking of heroin. According to local authorities, Hong Kong's role has been on the decline since 1992.

There are, however, other factors to consider in Hong Kong's changing role in the drug market internationally and locally. The demand for Southeast Asian heroin in some of the countries historically associated with Hong Kong as a transit point has changed, for example, UK consumers are showing a preference for the comparatively cheaper price and smokeable quality of Southwest Asian heroin. The United States, where heroin use is on the decline, has diversified sources for heroin, with many regions showing preference for brown tar smuggled across the Mexican border. Canada is a notable exception, with its rise in heroin use. In addition, the rising demand for ATS locally, regionally, and internationally has presented opportunities for market diversification. Hong Kong has experienced the "global shift" witnessed in other parts of the world in relation to the demand for ATS.

Trends in drug consumption

The rise in ATS use in Hong Kong is not surprising, as similar patterns have emerged across the world, from the United Kingdom and Europe to North America, Australia, and throughout many Asian countries. Mainland China also has witnessed a dramatic rise in the consumption of ice and ecstasy. Importantly, ATS use surfaced much earlier in many countries like Japan, Thailand, and the Philippines. Considering the epidemiological trends across the globe in ATS use, it is perhaps surprising that ATS use in Hong Kong is a relatively recent phenomenon and has not attained the prevalence rates found in other places.

Although it is impossible to determine the precise number of drug users, there are several methods to access the trends in the types of drugs being used and the characteristics of users. One source of information derives from the Central Registry of Drug Abuse database (CRDA) which, since 1972, has documented those users who come to the attention of law-enforcement and social welfare agencies, hospitals, clinics, and treatment centers. This database holds enormous monitoring potential as it is capable of linking an individual's reported use pattern over time via the Hong Kong Identity Number. The CRDA has been viewed as a relatively consistent indicator of patterns of opiate use. It has also enabled us to document the recent surge in particular psychotropic drugs.

Table 20.1 provides an overview of drug-use trends from 1995 until the first half of 2001 by age and drug type. In general, there has been a notable drop in reported heroin users. This drop in the number of reported heroin users is largely among younger users as the percentage of reported heroin users aged 21 years and over has remained relatively stable from 1995 (93 percent) to the first six months of 2001 (87 percent).

During this period, the most significant change has been the decline in heroin use among reported younger users, dropping from 72.5 percent in 1995 to 14 percent by the first half of 2001. This decline in opiate use among reported

Table 20.1   Reported individuals by age and by type of drug abused, Hong Kong, 1995–mid-2000 (%)

	1995	1996	1997	1998	1999	2000	2001 (first half)
Under 21							
Heroin	72.5	66.6	64.3	58.4	49.1	21.6	14.2
Opium	*	–	–	–	–	–	–
Morphine	*	–	–	–	–	*	*
Physeptone/Methadone	0.4	0.5	0.5	0.2	0.3	0.2	–
Amphetamines	1.8	8.0	15.8	19.4	29.2	61.9	62.9
MDMA	–	*	1.7	2.0	13.1	56.2	56.6
Ice	1.5	7.6	14.4	17.3	17.3	11.0	10.6
Cocaine	*	0.1	0.1	0.1	0.3	0.3	0.3
Methaqualone	0.1	0.5	0.2	*	0.1	0.3	*
Cannabis	20.2	21.0	21.8	26.6	30.2	21.2	14.3
Ketamine	–	–	–	–	0.6	36.9	56.4
Diazepam	0.1	–	0.2	0.2	2.0	2.3	0.3
Flunitrazepam	4.8	4.1	1.6	0.7	0.8	0.3	0.1
Triazolam/Midazolam	2.0	1.9	2.5	2.0	1.5	1.2	0.6
Cough medicine	9.7	7.8	7.4	5.2	4.5	2.6	1.1
Organic solvents	1.5	4.7	4.8	4.3	4.5	1.8	1.5
Number of persons with type of drug reported	3581	3363	2887	2551	2219	3466	2143
21 and over							
Heroin	93.0	90.8	91.4	91.7	91.8	88.3	86.6
Opium	0.4	0.4	0.3	0.2	0.4	0.4	0.2
Morphine	0.1	*	*	*	–	0.1	*
Physeptone/Methadone	1.3	1.2	1.1	0.7	0.7	0.5	0.3
Amphetamines	0.7	1.9	3.3	4.0	5.4	7.3	7.6
MDMA	–	*	0.1	0.1	0.4	3.0	3.7
Ice	0.7	1.8	3.1	3.8	4.9	4.5	4.1
Cocaine	0.1	0.1	0.1	0.1	0.1	0.2	0.2
Methaqualone	0.1	0.1	0.1	0.1	0.1	0.1	*
Cannabis	4.8	5.8	5.1	5.5	4.8	5.4	4.2
Ketamine	–	–	–	–	0.1	2.5	5.3
Diazepam	*	*	0.2	0.1	0.2	0.2	0.2
Flunitrazepam	0.9	1.0	0.6	0.2	0.3	0.3	0.2
Triazolam/Midazolam	2.6	3.5	6.7	6.4	6.9	6.7	5.4
Cough medicine	1.2	2.0	1.8	1.1	1.4	1.7	1.4
Organic solvents	*	*	*	0.1	0.1	0.2	0.1
Number of persons with type of drug reported	14425	15265	13609	13195	12984	12957	8369

Note: *Multiple answers are possible, so totals may not equal 100 percent.
Source: Central Registry of Drug Abuse, 2001.

young users has been met with a dramatic and rapid rise in psychotropic drug use, especially of ATS. The proportion of reported young persons using ATS – MDMA and ice – grew from less than 2 percent to 63 percent in six years. Since 1999, ketamine has also surfaced as a drug of choice among younger users. Among all reported older users, there also has been an increase in MDMA and ice use, but the proportion and the rise over the last few years have been much more modest compared to their younger counterparts.

This shift in the drug preferences among younger persons is even more pronounced when we consider those young persons who have been newly reported to the registry over the past six and a half years. As Table 20.2 shows, the number of newly reported young heroin users dropped from 63 percent in 1995 to 8 percent in the first half of 2001. A complete reversal has occurred in drug preferences, as

Table 20.2 Newly reported individuals by age and by type of drug abused, Hong Kong, 1995–mid-2001 (%)

	1995	1996	1997	1998	1999	2000	2001 (first half)
Under 21							
Heroin	63.3	51.3	48.0	38.9	29.4	10.6	8.1
Amphetamines	1.9	9.2	20.8	24.6	36.5	67.6	57.2
MDMA	–	0.1	2.3	3.6	19.1	62.9	52.1
Ice	1.5	8.7	18.5	21.0	18.8	9.7	7.8
Cannabis	27.6	29.3	31.2	39.8	39.8	20.0	13.2
Ketamine	–	–	0.1	–	1.1	44.4	59.5
Cough medicine	10.7	8.3	8.4	5.1	5.2	1.7	0.9
Tranquilizers	6.4	5.8	4.0	2.9	4.8	3.4	0.4
Cocaine	–	–	–	–	0.2	0.4	0.3
Total	1772	1617	1333	1210	1120	2252	1178
% with multiple drugs reported	11.9	11.8	14.7	13.8	21.1	42.6	36.6
21 and over							
Heroin	61.9	55.1	56.5	58.1	58.7	50.4	36.2
Amphetamines	2.9	7.5	11.4	12.0	14.6	21.6	22.6
MDMA	–	0.2	0.9	0.4	2.4	14.4	17.2
Ice	2.7	7.0	10.3	10.8	12.3	7.6	5.8
Cannabis	8.5	29.3	27.0	28.4	23.2	19.4	17.1
Ketamine	–	–	–	–	0.3	12.3	28.3
Cough medicine	5.6	9.4	7.8	4.2	5.2	3.8	3.5
Tranquilizers	4.2	3.4	3.5	2.6	5.3	2.7	2.8
Cocaine	0.5	0.5	0.3	0.5	0.3	0.3	0.8
Total	1565	1917	1479	1371	1242	1660	964
% with multiple drugs reported	5.5	5.8	7.4	7.5	9.2	12.3	13.2

Note: Multiple answers are possible, so totals may not equal 100%.
Source: Central Registry of Drug Abuse 2001.

the percentage of newly reported young amphetamine users grew quickly from 1996 onward and in the first half of 2001 accounted for two-thirds of all newly reported young users. In the first few years, this appeared to be due to an increase in ice use, but quite rapidly MDMA took the lead.

Among newly reported older users, amphetamine use increased from 1995 to mid-2001, but this increase was proportionately lower than for their younger counterparts. Moreover, most of the increase up to 2000 was largely attributable to the consumption of ice rather than MDMA. Ketamine was also being used among those in this age group but at significantly lower levels than newly reported young users. According to CRDA data, then, the most significant trend has been among younger users who are showing increasing preferences for ice, MDMA, and ketamine.

Who are Hong Kong's ATS users?

ICE OR CRYSTAL METHAMPHETAMINE

Ice typically appears in Hong Kong in the form of powder or fine crystals and began to surface in small quantities since at least the early 1970s. During this period, Filipino entertainers and musicians who found that the drug provided a source of energy for late-night work in Hong Kong principally consumed ice. From the 1980s until the early 1990s, local consumption of ice remained low and according to treatment workers, police officials, and our interviews with ice users, ice was sometimes combined with heroin to make speedballs. Speedballs can be found in Hong Kong today, but are largely confined to particular districts. During this period, the majority of ice seizures involved shipments from China en route to Japan and the Philippines where demand has been consistently high (Royal Hong Kong Police 1996).

From 1996 onward, Hong Kong witnessed an increasing number of reported ice users. This rise was especially apparent among female users –they accounted for approximately half of all reported ice users. There are a number of reasons for the increase in ice use reported by users, including the belief that ice is not addictive, and that it is a "cure" for getting off heroin. It is claimed to be a useful method for coping with and transcending evening and long work hours, and more generally, a source of energy, sociability, and, ironically, aggressiveness. Ice is typically smoked or fume-inhaled, occurs as an episode (from one to seven days), and is shared among a small group of users in a rented room, guesthouse, or flat. Unlike other drugs used and sold within Hong Kong, ice is a relatively private affair with use and transactions occurring in prearranged, private settings. As Table 20.3 shows, the average retail price of ice per kilogram grew from approximately US$38 in 1996 to US$65 in 1998 and dropped to US$38 per gram by 2001.

ECSTASY

Ecstasy use differs considerably from the patterns of ice consumption. While ice is used and bought in a private setting, ecstasy use and purchase generally occurs in public venues. Ecstasy normally comes in the form of tablets. The average

Table 20.3 Drug retail prices, Hong Kong, 1995–2001 (US$)

	1995	1996	1997	1998	1999	2000	2001
Heroin	46	52	54	55	49	48	48
Herbal cannabis	–	–	6	6	6	7	8
Cocaine	135	154	173	173	173	147	143
Ice	–	38	43	65	56	45	38
MDMA (per tablet)	–	–	32	32	29	27	23
Ketamine	–	–	–	–	–	23	51

Note: Prices are per gram, unless otherwise indicated. Based on an exchange rate of HK$7.8 to US$1.
Source: Royal Hong Kong Police 2002.

retail price since 1997 has ranged from US$23 to US$32 per tablet, based on police reports. User interviews suggest a retail price of far less, at US$13 per tablet. The Government Chemist documented 60 types in 2000 and cautioned that very likely there are more types on the market than have been examined. The Chemist also indicates that the majority of ecstasy tablets from seizures are not pure in MDMA content and contain adulterants like amphetamine, methamphetamine, ketamine, phenobarbitone, caffeine, and even chalk.

Ecstasy first appeared in Hong Kong in 1993 and, until 1996, was principally found in the occasional organized rave party, popular among expatriates. At that time, small quantities of tablets were brought in, usually by expatriates. In 1997, an increasing number of local residents began frequenting rave events. The popularity of these organized party events began to diminish by 1998 as many Hong Kong entrepreneurs recognized the potential profits of converting existing karaoke bars and restaurants into permanent venues for dancing and clubbing. From 1998 until the present, there has been a tremendous growth in the number of dance clubs and discos in traditional entertainment districts as well as outlying areas, and these have attracted the ranks of working- and middle-class youth and young adults.

Ketamine has been gaining ground in the Hong Kong drug market since at least 1998 and is likely to become as popular, if not more so, than ecstasy. It is typically used when going to discos and dance clubs and is believed to enhance the "head-shaking" dance experience. Ketamine is relatively easy to use in dance-club settings and is either snorted or dissolved in alcoholic beverages. It is normally sold in the form of white, crystalline powder, wrapped in small colored paper packets. The Government Laboratory analysis of seized ketamine shows that there is usually little adulteration of this drug, but occasionally paracetamol and caffeine have been found. According to the Hong Kong Police, the average retail price grew from US$23 to US$51 between 2000 and 2001.

Many local observers believe that growing popularity of these substances is due to factors like peer pressure, family stress, and the importation of Western culture into Hong Kong via Hong Kong returnees and expatriates. There are several other reasons to account for the growing popularity of MDMA and ketamine among young persons which are consistent with reports from other countries. First, users perceive MDMA as not addictive and as having few immediate and no long-term side effects, even with the knowledge that they are not consuming "pure" MDMA.

A second reason for the increase in ecstasy and ketamine use lies in their association with a distinctive, fashionable, and trendy social scene. These are characteristics of a youthful and "hip" culture which are in complete contrast to heroin. Heroin use is culturally understood to be part of the "older generation," and users are seen as having "hit the bottom" when they move into heroin. From the users' point of view, club drugs like ecstasy and ketamine are not associated with the negative identity or stigma of heroin users.

A third factor accounting for this rise is users' awareness, however vague, of the legal consequences of MDMA and ketamine. Most users report that while the police conduct routine license-checks of discos and organized raves, few people are arrested. In the event of unannounced license-checks, consumers can simply dump their supply onto the floor, and if it is not in their possession, there is little the police can do, except confiscate the dumped drugs. Some users report buying and using before entering discos to lessen the potential for police intervention. However, our field observations indicate that ecstasy and ketamine are openly used in some discos. In either case, users who have either been arrested or have had friends arrested are well aware that the penalties are relatively lenient.

One other reason is worthy of mention There has been a proliferation of venues for dancing and using. From our interviews with users, it is clear that different types of venues attract different types of user groups (e.g., social class, etc.). It is in this popular venue that buying and using are relatively easy. And it is relatively inexpensive. Normally half a tablet is taken shortly before or on arrival at a disco, and topped off by the other half-tablet or with ketamine several hours later.

It is clear that the drug scene in Hong Kong has been rapidly changing over the last few years for young people. Clearly, the globalization and subculture of the dance drug scene has moved into Hong Kong. Locally it has taken on a life of its own, shaped by its own youth culture and the entrepreneurial spirit of triad groups.

Hong Kong and Its Role in the Local and Global ATS Economy

Ice and Hong Kong

Ephedrine, the precursor chemical for methamphetamine, is readily and easily accessible in China as it is a stimulant found in the plant ephedra, native to China and used in Chinese medicines (Royal Hong Kong Police 1996). Given its proximity to Hong Kong, members of the 14K triad society, who were known to be an active syndicate in ice trafficking, smuggled the synthetics used to make ice (in cooperation with a crime group in Guangzhou) into Hong Kong for final processing. The police believed this was the first local manufacturing center for the production of ice and seized 22 kg in 1994. It is likely that the ice was destined for export as ice use was relatively low during the early part of the 1990s.

Also, in that year, the police seized a total of 100 kg of ice that was imported overland from China and suspected to be destined for the Philippines. A lorry

Table 20.4 Average wholesale and retail drug prices, Hong Kong, 1995–2001 ($US)

	1995	*1996*	*1997*	*1998*	*1999*	*2000*	*2001*
Heroin							
Wholesale (kg)	26,474	229,487	19,688	19,089	19,696	20,615	24,457
Retail (gm)	46	52	54	55	49	48	48
Herbal cannabis							
Wholesale (kg)	1,314	1,570	1,228	1,089	1,183	1,789	2,252
Retail (gm)	–	–	6	6	6	7	8
Cocaine							
Wholesale (kg)	–	–	46,154	40,385	41,346	41,667	31,410
Retail (gm)	135	154	173	173	173	147	143
Ice							
Wholesale (kg)	5,577	4,679	5,139	6,202	6,111	5,641	5,496
Retail (gm)	–	38	43	65	56	45	38
MDMA (per tablet)							
Wholesale (tablet)	–	–	13	13	13	13	12
Retail (tablet)	–	–	32	32	29	27	23
Ketamine							
Wholesale (kg)	–	–	–	–	–	4,188	4,776
Retail (gm)	–	–	–	–	–	23	51

Note: Based on an exchange rate of HK$7.8 to US$1.
Source: Royal Hong Kong Police 2002.

driver and an electrical worker were arrested while unloading the ice in bags labeled "duck feed" from a truck in a car park. The High Court judge imposed a 20-year prison term (although a life term was possible). This was based on the fact that they were not the main traffickers, and that the driver was to make about US$577 for a consignment worth between US$3,846,254 million and US $6,410,256 million (*South China Morning Post* 1994). At that time, police indicate that most of the ice imported into Hong Kong was ultimately destined for other Asian countries, including Japan, the Philippines, and Korea. Importantly, in that year, the wholesale and local retail price ranged between US$3,846 and US$6,410 per kilogram, and $US11.4 per gram and US$14 per gram, respectively. While the wholesale prices are consistent from 1995 onward, the retail price in 1994 and 1995 are considerably lower than the costs from 1996 onward. It is unclear what impact the complete move of manufacturing and production to the mainland had on the rise of local retail prices.

From 1996 onward, it appears that ice for local consumption in Hong Kong has been completely manufactured in China (there has been no evidence of recrystallizing it in Hong Kong). It is likely that the risks of manufacturing in Hong Kong were perceived to be too high, particularly in light of the compactness and density of Hong Kong. Interviews with officials and observations from news reports indicate that clandestine laboratories had emerged, scattered throughout China, but particularly, in Yunnan, Guangdong, and Fujian provinces. Compared with Hong Kong, the availability of locales in a vast area makes China a more suitable and less risky venue for manufacturing. Still, the potential legal consequences of manufacturing and trafficking in China are comparatively more severe than in Hong Kong. Chinese officials have responded to the emergence of these laboratories by stepping up their aggressive anti-drugs campaign, using the death penalty for ice traffickers, and introducing regulations on the management, as well as the export of, ephedrine. In 1997, a ceremonial burning of 150 kg of ice took place at the site of the Opium War in Guangdong (*South China Morning Post* 1997). In 1999, mainland Chinese authorities seized 16.059 tons of ice (People's Republic of China, National Affairs Office, 2002). Chinese authorities have not hesitated to impose the death sentence. In November 2000, five men were executed in Yunnan province for trafficking ice, and another eleven were given sentences ranging from three years in prison to a suspended death sentence (*South China Morning Post* 2000a).

More recently, in 1998, there were a number of unusually large seizures in Hong Kong, which appear to have been destined for other countries. For example, seizure figures for 1998 reached a record 233.7 kg, which was largely attributable to a 160-kg seizure of ice worth HK$82 million (along with 7 kg of heroin worth HK$17 million) arriving on a container vessel from Foshan in Guangdong Province, believed to be headed for the Philippines or Indonesia. Two Hong Kong males (one a hawker and one unemployed) were arrested in a Shamshuipo car park along with two mainland Chinese after police located the drugs in the trunk and rear passenger seat of the car (*South China Morning Post* 1998). According to police, "Statistics tell us that we are not a transit point, but this case...yes, it could be that Hong Kong is becoming one" (*South China Morning Post* 1998).

Since then, smaller quantities have been found. In April 2000, 20 kg, worth HK$10 million, was found packed and hidden underneath boxes of tissue in cartons, being loaded onto a container and headed for Australia (*South China Morning Post* 2000b). A 19-year-old male, boarding a flight for Tokyo, was arrested during the same week when authorities found HK$29 million-worth of ice packed on his body (*South China Morning Post* 2000c). A few days later, an 18-year-old male, casual laborer was arrested at the airport when customs officials found 1.4 kg of heroin and 2.3 kg of ice, worth a total of HK$2.3 million (*South China Morning Post* 2000d).

The method for importing ice for local consumption is understood to be the same as for heroin. According to several police officers, the organization is typically the same, involving three to four tiers, from purchasing to moving the supply into Hong Kong. The shipments are normally in crystalline form. Because of the heavy daily traffic (especially goods vehicles) across the Hong Kong and Shenzhen border, authorities indicate that truck drivers are a good source of importing drugs into the locale. Larger quantities can be brought in by truck, compared with a courier crossing the border on foot. Drivers usually conceal the package somewhere in their load, for example, under baskets of vegetables. Once the supply enters Hong Kong, larger quantities, brought in by drivers, are normally delivered to a car park and transferred to a car or taxi and taken for packaging and storage. With such larger quantities (e.g., 10 kg), some of the ice is destined for the local market but the remainder is to be exported to Southeast Asian countries such as Thailand.

Couriers are often young males (but not exclusively) who are unemployed, seek quick money to pay off mounting debts to loan sharks, and sometimes drug users themselves. Despite the risks and severe penalties for possession of ice, the amount of money made as a courier is relatively small, estimated as from US $256 to US$641. Comparatively, possession of 1 kg of ice or heroin results in at least 18- and 20-year sentence respectively.

Diversification not substitution

The police indicate that the majority of MDMA imported for local consumption is manufactured in China and brought into Hong Kong via ship, speedboats (*dai fei*), or walked across the border. It is not clear who the principal stakeholders are, nor whether they are connected to syndicates dealing in heroin, ice, or cannabis. However, some police believe that traffickers at the wholesale and retail levels are shifting to dealing in ecstasy and ketamine as these drugs are associated with less severe sanctions and generate better profits. Given the stability of the heroin scene over the last several years, it is likely that ecstasy and ketamine have resulted in a diversification rather than a substitution or replacement for heroin. There has been, for a long period, a consistent and stable demand for heroin. At the international level, as we saw from yesterday afternoon's discussion, some Hong Kong traffickers have been involved in moving ecstasy from mainland China to Los Angeles, Australia, and Canada. In the latter two cases, these shipments also included heroin.

The emergence of MDMA and ketamine have significantly altered the market of drugs in Hong Kong. This is due to a variety of factors, ranging from the growing popularity of dance music (although clearly dance music does not equate with ecstasy and ketamine use), and public perceptions that these are neither addictive nor dangerous drugs. In terms of the emergence of a market, however, the MDMA and ketamine markets are distinctive from those of other drugs.

Since 1999, Hong Kong has witnessed the emergence of dance clubs or *fing tao* bars (literally, head-shaking clubs). These are distinct from organized rave parties with promoters renting warehouses. Instead, *fing tao* bars are often established and licensed karaoke clubs (popular in the mid-1990s, but not associated with drug use) or tea-dance clubs (designed for businessmen and office workers) until around 11:00 P.M. or 12:00 A.M., at which time they are converted into smoke-filled (machine-generated) dancefloors for "shaking one's head" to the dance music.

Dance clubs typically contain at least a few private rooms for rent so that groups can enjoy the club in a semi-private setting (making consumption easier). Tables near the dance floor can also be reserved and "rented" for large groups. Importantly, there have also been a number of new clubs, some with substantial investments of over HK$10 million, which have opened for rave dancing. Clubs vary in size, smaller ones having a capacity of about 200 and larger ones having a capacity for approximately 1,200 dancegoers. These dance clubs or discos are found principally in areas that have traditionally been centers for night-time entertainment. There are also a few discos in outlying areas for those residents. These dance venues compete with each other through a variety of means – inviting celebrities, offering discounts and "freebies" on drinks and entrance fees, hosting particular disc jockeys, using sophisticated sound systems, and decorating the interior with sophistication or with illusory effects.

Some police report that the Internet is serving as a method for the local purchase of ecstasy and ketamine as several local websites have emerged. Most users, however, report buying directly on the premises from retail dealers, although transactions are sometimes conducted outside the club on the street to avoid police detection within the club. In the district with the largest and most diverse types of dance clubs (entrance fees from US$19 to US$64), retail dealers normally work in one club. In smaller districts, where there are fewer dance clubs, dealers normally patrol from one club to another.

Lockers are sometimes located within the premises, and are sometimes used to store the retail dealer's supply. Sales are essentially conducted in the club in open view with direct exchange of cash for the tablets or powder packet. Sometimes users report picking up their purchase in the toilet. Users who frequent a regular club are known to the agent and have no difficulty in securing tablets for the evening. Potential customers who are not known by the agent are usually approached and asked, "Do you want to play?"

From a business point of view, the opening and operation of dance clubs makes good financial sense. Why? Dance music and being part of the dance-music scene is seen as trendy and fashionable. Celebrities are often seen at these clubs (usually at the invitation of the managers to attract patrons). Entrance fees from US$19 to US$64 provide guaranteed revenue. Water and drinks are another sure source of revenue, with bottled water priced at US$6 to US$19 and beer priced at US$6. Given that a good percentage of the dancegoers are using MDMA and ketamine, revenue from refreshments is also guaranteed. There are a stable supply of customers.

According to police and users, local organized crime groups or triad groups operate the vast majority of *fing tao* bars in the following manner. Managers are typically associated with a particular triad group, and in some cases, but not always, may be one of the "investors" in the club. The "investors" themselves may include a collection of legitimate and triad businessmen. Among the most important staff are the doormen/bouncers, who belong to a security group (usually with the same triad affiliation as the manager) that normally provides protection for several clubs on one street or area (territory). The bouncers are employed as staff and are given either a wage or a one-off payment each month. The bouncers are accountable to their *dai lo* (a leader who also gets a "fee"). In the event of trouble, the bouncers on site call for assistance as their triad group provides "protection."

In another district, there also appears to be a "fluid" style of operations. Retail sellers are affiliated with the security group (triad-operated) of the disco, and either work as a team or as independent sellers. Because sellers work and are accountable to the security group, there is no competition for sales. Users confirm that the price for ecstasy and ketamine does not fluctuate. Moreover, they do not report aggressive sales by sellers in discos. The security group ensures that there is no internal or external competition. Triad groups seem to have established territories. Retail-level sellers obtain their supply through their triad affiliation (including within the security group) and are able to generate an estimated 40–50 percent profit.

The operation of these clubs operates in symbiosis with the ecstasy and ketamine markets. In many ways, the ecstasy and ketamine scene has provided a new market for making money as the profitable real-estate boom (and its associated activities) has gone bust. Importantly, the police note that the disco itself does not have an "investment" nor does it operate the retail sale of ecstasy and ketamine. While the "investors" and managers of the disco generate revenue from entrance fees and refreshments, the security group affords protection and generates revenue from the sale of drugs. Undoubtedly, however, managers must be taking a percentage of the retail sales proceeds. In other words, the dance club/drug enterprise does not exhibit a distinct and clear hierarchy but rather represents a network of entrepreneurs with the same triad affiliation. It is the newest capitalist venture. They have not had such an opportunity since pirated VCDs (video compact discs).

Yet there is a very clear need for investors, managers, and the security group to strike a balance. Triad bouncers must try to keep the operation "respectable" to avoid potential violence among triad groups who want to gain a foothold or get into trouble while partying. Clearly triad bouncers and investors do not want violence on or near their establishment for at least two reasons. First, investors and managers do not want "trouble" (competition, violence) because this brings unwanted police intervention and pressure (e.g., stepping up license-checks, undercover operations). Ultimately authorities have the ability to close down the dance club. Second, they also recognize that certain customers will be turned away or frightened off if there are competition and violence. Their clientele is not restricted to other triad members. Importantly, some of the users interviewed reported staying away from particular dance clubs because of fights between triad members.

CONCLUSION

The government has responded to the rising use of ecstasy and ketamine with educational campaigns, the formation of a psychotropic substance-abuse sub-committee to assess the problem, and funded research, and has proposed legis-lation for stiffer penalties for ketamine and a code of practice for organized events. District-level police conduct weekly license-checks of *fing tao* bars to keep pressure on the operators and managers of these clubs.

But there does not seem to be any immediate signs of a decline in ATS use among young people. In fact, the use of ecstasy, ketamine, amphetamines, cannabis, and other club drugs, over the course of the last decade, has become firmly entrenched in global and local youth and music culture. The trends in other countries also suggest that ATS use has become increasingly problematic as ecstasy users search for the sensation of their original high, and resort to a cocktail of illicit substances. In California, ecstasy euphoria-seekers have moved away from poor-quality MDMA tablets to intensity-driving crystal methamphetamine. In Scotland, ec-stasy users are reportedly taking five or more tablets in a single session and combining them with sleeping pills like Temazepam. Certain club scenes in England have witnessed a shift away from ecstasy toward increasing use of cocaine and cannabis. The combination of these two drugs "creates a sensory intensification without euphoria, tinged with nerve jangling paranoia" which fits with the mood of post-rave music sub-genres (Reynolds 1998: 85).

The experiences of other countries suggest, then, a transition to a "post-rave" culture. This transition reflects a diversification in the types of music appearing in dance venues and partially accounts for the emergence of new "cocktails" of drugs being consumed (the effects of particular combinations being conducive to particular moods of music). This transition also reflects a diversification in venues for dancing and drug use (although one should not presume that all dancegoers use dance drugs). In the UK, for example, the "rave scene" first flourished in the mid-1980s in large-scale venues like warehouses and open fields. The music and venues began to diversify and grow, resulting in an extremely lucrative industry (Morris 1998).

This transition is emerging in Hong Kong. There are signs of increasing numbers of psychotropic drug users and increasing numbers of poly-drug users. Large-scale warehouse dance events in Hong Kong happen only occasionally, with the real attraction being the ever-increasing number of permanent dance and disco clubs. The government most recently has become concerned about the large number of youths crossing the border into China to party and obtain ecstasy and ketamine. Because production sites are situated principally in Southern China, the costs of ecstasy and ketamine are believed to be relatively cheaper than in Hong Kong, and provide added incentive for partying across the border. In addition, there are reports of a small but growing number of "private and underground parties" as users seek out new experiences in new environments and desire less public scrutiny by the police. This pattern should not be surprising, as similar observations have been reported in the United States and the United Kingdom. These recent changes in Hong Kong's drug market reflect not solely the accommodation of the local drug culture but also the influence of the global trends in the style and use of contemporary drugs. The Hong Kong experience in relation to its domestic drug market and its participation in regional and international drug trafficking suggests that global culture is surely in the making, but that it is fundamentally operating in a dialectical process with the local.

References

Central Registry of Drug Abuse (CRDA) (2001) 48th Report (1992–2001). Narcotics Division. Government Secretariat. Hong Kong: Hong Kong Government.

Findlay, M. (1999) *Globalisation and Crime*. Cambridge: Cambridge University Press.

Giddens, A. (1990) *The Consequences of Modernity*. Stanford, CA: Stanford University Press.

Gilpin, R. (2000) *The Challenge of Global Capitalism*. Princeton, NJ: Princeton University Press.

Guillen, M. (2001) Is globalization civilizing, destructive or feeble? A critique of five key debates in the social sciences literature. *Annual Review of Sociology*, 27, 235–60.

Hong Kong Government (2000) *Hong Kong 2000*. Hong Kong: Hong Kong Government.

Laidler, Joe K., Day, J., and Hodson, D. (2001) *A Study on the Psychotropic Substance Abuse Problem in Hong Kong*. Final Report to the Action Committee against Narcotics, Hong Kong Government, Hong Kong Centre of Criminology.

Laidler, Joe K., with Hodson, D., and Traver, H. (2000) *The Hong Kong Drug Market*. A Report for UNICRI on the UNDCP Global Study in Illicit Drug Markets. Hong Kong: Centre for Criminology.

Miners, N. (1983) The Hong Kong government opium monopoly. *Journal of Imperial and Commonwealth History*, 1, 295–6.

Morris, S. (1998) *Clubs, Drugs and Doormen*. Police ResearchGroup – Crime Detection and Prevention Series, no. 86. London: Home Office.

People's Republic of China, National Affairs Office (2002) White Paper on Anti-Narcotics in China. Beijing:PRC Press Office.

Reynolds, S. (1998) Rave culture: Living dream or living death? In S. Redhead et al. (eds.), *The Club Cultures Reader*. Oxford: Blackwell, 84–93.

Robertson, R. (1992) *Globalization: Social Theory and Global Culture*. London: Sage.

Royal Hong Kong Police (1996) Personal communication with Narcotics Bureau.

Royal Hong Kong Police (2002) Personal communication with Narcotics Bureau.

South China Morning Post (1994) Judge warns of designer drug's "social cachet." September 13, 6.

South China Morning Post (1997) Drug haul goes up in smoke. June 16, 3.

South China Morning Post (1998) Record ice haul brings hub fears. October 16, 1.

South China Morning Post (2000a) Five ice traffickers executed in Yunnan amid crackdown. November 18, 7.

South China Morning Post (2000b) HK$10 million "ice" haul seized. April 21, 4.

South China Morning Post (2000c) Untitled. General news, April 23, 2.

South China Morning Post (2000d) Drugs charge. General news, April 25, 3.

Sung, Y. W. (1998) *Hong Kong and South China: The Economic Synergy*. Hong Kong: City University of Hong Kong Press.

Traver, H. (1992) Opium to heroin: Restrictive opium legislation and the rise of heroin consumption in Hong Kong. *Journal of Policy History*, 4(3), 307–24.

Waters, M. (1995) *Globalization*. New York: Routledge.

21

Trafficking in Human Beings and Related Crimes in West and Central Africa

ALEXIS A. ARONOWITZ AND MONIKA PERUFFO

INTRODUCTION

The exploitation and human rights abuses resulting from the smuggling and trafficking of human beings have become one of the most critical issues of modern times. They have been described as a modern form of slavery. Each year hundreds of people lose their lives trying to enter closed borders in other countries. This phenomenon has recently gained international attention through such catastrophes as the death of 58 Chinese nationals trying to enter Dover, England,[1] or the disappearance of the Nigerian vessel, the *Etireno*,[2] allegedly carrying child slaves in West Africa. Nongovernmental organizations (NGOs) are concerned with the design and implementation of prevention, victim protection, and repatriation projects. Law enforcement is focused on the investigation and arrest of individuals and criminal networks involved in the smuggling and trafficking phenomenon. Governments are attempting to define and implement legislation to allow for the protection of victims and the prosecution of offenders.

Trafficked victims and exploitation patterns differ throughout the world. Even within West and Central Africa,[3] the trafficking situation varies widely. This essay will examine some general concepts related to the trafficking of human beings and will later focus on the situation specific to a number of countries in West Africa.

We begin by providing general definitions of trafficking, smuggling, slavery and crimes related to the phenomenon. We continue by examining the historical development and contemporary forms of slavery in West and Central Africa. In representing the relationship between capital and crime, the illicit markets profiting from trafficking in persons will be a focus of attention. The factors contributing to trafficking in the region, as well as migratory and trafficking patterns, will be discussed. We then look in detail at three West African countries and close with a discussion of government and civil society approaches to the prevention and suppression of trafficking in the region.

TRAFFICKING IN HUMAN BEINGS AND OTHER RELATED CRIMES: DEFINITIONS[4]

In spite of the fact that the illicit movement and trade in human beings occurs in almost every nation in the world, definitions and legislation prohibiting its practice are varied, fragmented, and sometimes nonexistent. Any comparative studies or large-scale data collection are made more difficult by the fact that organizations are defining different phenomena.[5] This particular problem may be alleviated with the signing and impending ratification of the recent United Nations Convention against Transnational Organized Crime,[6] and the two supporting Protocols on the smuggling of migrants and the trafficking of human beings, in particular, women and children. According to the Convention and the two related Protocols:

> Smuggling of migrants shall mean the procurement, in order to obtain, directly or indirectly, a financial or other material benefit, of the illegal entry of a person into a State Party of which the person is not a national or a permanent resident. (United Nations Protocol against the Smuggling of Migrants by Land, Sea and Air, supplementing the UN Convention against Transnational Organized Crime, art. 3, Use of terms)
>
> Trafficking in persons shall mean the recruitment, transportation, transfer, harboring, or receipt of persons, by means of the threat or use of force or other forms of coercion, of abduction, of fraud, of deception, of the abuse of power or of a position of vulnerability or of the giving or receiving of payments or benefits to achieve the consent of a person having control over another person for the purpose of exploitation. Exploitation shall include, at a minimum, the exploitation of the prostitution of others or other forms of sexual exploitation, forced labour or services, slavery or practices similar to slavery, servitude or the removal of organs.[7] (UN Protocol to Prevent, Suppress and Punish Trafficking in Persons, especially Women and Children, Supplementing the UN Convention against Transnational Organised Crime, art.3, Use of terms)

In essence, smuggling involves the illegal movements of migrants across international borders, whereas human trafficking often involves smuggling plus coercion or exploitation. Exploitation of the victim is the key element in the trafficking of human beings. Consent of the victim is negated in cases where coercion or deceit is used to obtain consent.

The borders between smuggling and trafficking are sometimes blurred. Often both smuggled and trafficked individuals leave a country of origin willingly, possibly, however, under different pretenses. They may be exposed to similar cases of danger or discomfort during long journeys. However, upon arrival in the destination country, smuggled individuals are usually free to apply for asylum or look for work on the black market. Trafficked persons are, upon arrival, put in a situation of debt bondage and forced into slavery-like practices in the sex or labor market. Exploitation usually occurs over a long period of time, during which interdependency may develop between the trafficked persons and the (organized crime) group(s) that traffic them. This interdependency often leads to further networking, extended exploitation, and possible recruitment for criminal purposes (Bajrektarevic 2000: 16).

Types of criminality linked to the trafficking in human beings

One can view the trafficking of human beings as a process rather than a single offense. It begins with the abduction or recruitment of a person and continues with the transportation and entry of the individual into another country.[8] This is followed by the exploitation phase, during which the victim is forced into sexual or labor servitude. A further phase may occur, which does not involve the victim, but rather the offender. Depending upon the size and sophistication of the trafficking operation, the criminal (organization) may find it necessary to launder the criminal proceeds. There may be further links to other criminal offenses, such as the smuggling of weapons or drugs.

During this process, instrumental criminal activities may be perpetrated by the criminals involved in direct furtherance of the trafficking activity (Europol 2000). Examples of these crimes are procurement and violence associated with maintaining control over victims. Other crimes, such as money-laundering and tax evasion, are secondary, and occur as a result of the trafficking activity.

A typology can be created to understand further the nature of these offenses related to the trafficking process. The perpetration of crimes can be characterized according to the victim (the individual victim or the state) or in terms of the phase of the trafficking process, e.g., recruitment, transportation, and illegal entry of the trafficked person, the exploitation phase, or the subsequent phase of profit-laundering. The numbers and types of offenses are often contingent upon the sophistication of the smuggling and trafficking operation and the criminal groups involved therein. These operations can be as simplistic as the smuggling and subsequent trafficking of an individual by another individual over a border without proper documentation by transport vehicle or foot, or sophisticated operations moving large numbers of persons, using forged documents and generating huge profits which must subsequently be laundered. Trafficking may involve offenses against the state, such as abuse of immigration laws, document forgery, corruption of government officials, money-laundering, and tax evasion. Other violations are directed against the victims: unlawful coercion or threat, extortion, aggravated and/or sexual assault, rape, or even death. Table 21.1 shows the various offenses perpetrated at different stages of the trafficking process, while indicating whether the "victim" is the state or the individual who has been trafficked.

Seldom is violence exercised during the recruitment phase, except in cases where victims have been kidnapped. During this stage, fraudulent promises are often made to secure the willingness of the victim to leave. It is sometimes during the transportation phase, but much more commonly during the exploitation phase after having entered the destination country, that threats and violence are commonly perpetrated against victims. In cases of both labor and sexual exploitation, threats or actual violence are often used to maintain control and prevent the escape of the victim.

Table 21.1 Trafficking in human beings as a process and other related crimes

Recruitment	Transportation/ Entry	Exploitation	Criminal proceeds
Document forgery	Document forgery	*Unlawful coercion	Money-laundering
*Fraudulent promises	Abuse of immigration	*Threat	Tax evasion
*Kidnapping	laws	*Extortion	Corruption of
	Corruption of	*Procurement	government
	government	*False imprisonment	officials
	officials	*Theft of documents	
	*Assault	*Sexual assault	
	*False imprisonment	*Aggravated assault	
		*Rape	
		*Death	
		Corruption of	
		government	
		officials	

Note: * Offenses perpetrated against the individual victim.

We have examined the offenses perpetrated by the traffickers in furtherance of the trafficking scheme. However, the networks which smuggle and traffic human beings, as well as the victims themselves, have been linked to other criminal activities. Criminal groups have been known to make use of existing contacts, routes, corrupt government officials, and networks in order to expand their operations. A criminal organization may develop "horizontal interdependencies" (Adamoli et al. 1998: 17), by establishing connections among different activities. The criminal organization is thus able to diversify and expand its markets. Intelligence sources at Interpol reveal that trafficking in human beings supplements more traditional criminal activities such as drug trafficking, vehicle theft (Kendall 1999), trafficking in arms (Savona et al. 1995; Jantsch 1998), and money-laundering. Traffickers have been linked to moneylending to repay debts, extortion for protection money, and physical violence. Furthermore, traffickers have been known to coerce their victims into prostitution (a criminal offense in some countries), into selling drugs (Gunnatilleke 1994; Richard 1999), organized begging, and pickpocketing (Kendall 1999).

The previous discussion focused on trafficking from a legal and criminological perspective. However, human rights violations perpetrated against the victims during the exploitation phase are at the core of the trafficking issue. So we now turn to the historical development of slavery and current practices involving trafficking in West and Central Africa.

SLAVERY: HISTORICAL DEVELOPMENT AND CONTEMPORARY FORMS

Slavery has been defined

> as a state marked by the loss of free will where a person is forced through violence or the threat of violence to give up the ability to sell freely his/her own labour

power. In this definition, slavery has three key dimensions: control by another
person, the appropriation of labour power, and the use or threat of violence. (Bales
and Robbins 2001:16)

Traditional slavery, an inhumane way to obtain "free" labor, often involved the
kidnapping, buying, or trading of human beings. In existence in various parts of
the world since the beginning of humanity, European enslavement of Africans to
facilitate their colonization of the Western world dates back to the 1400s
(Synopsis of the Transatlantic Slave Trade website). West Africa supplied 60
percent of slaves for export between 1701 and 1810.

Colonialism in Africa embodied the search for the large profits made possible
through the payment of "exceptionally low wages": "[C]onsequently, the preservation of the rural peasantry was often functional for imperialism. It removed
the need for capital to pay wages which fully covered the cost of reproducing the
labour power of workers" (Sumner 1982: 23). The demand for African slaves
arose "from the development of plantation agriculture . . . and the demand for
miners" (Francis 1995). It continued from the early 1400s through the 1800s.
Although the abolition of the slave trade among the colonizers began in 1802, it
did not, however, put an end to slavery. It was not until November 10, 1903,
with the decree on "Native Justice," that French West Africa was on the path to
abolition. This, however, did not impede the growth of state-sanctioned (or at
least state-tolerated) slavery in parts of Africa itself. At the turn of the century,
the government of what was then Southern Rhodesia, in an effort to support the
mining industry, tolerated massive human rights abuses of laborers forced to
work the mines, and passed laws to punish severely those trying to escape (Van
Onselen 1976, discussed in Sumner 1982). In spite of the formal abolition of
traditional slavery, trafficking in West Africa has remained a modern-day form
of slavery.

Slavery had a relevant role in the economies of many societies. As Bales (1999:
102) observes: "it was one of the first forms of trade to become truly international." It was a special economic institution, able to overcome revolutions,
changes in political structures, and adapt to a changing world. It continues to do
so today. While in the past, slavery found justification in racial and ethnic
differences, today more often the common denominator is poverty, not color
or religion. "Behind every assertion of ethnic difference is the reality of economic
disparity. Modern slaveholders are colour blind, but they are acutely perceptive
to weakness. This colour-blindness is part of slavery's rapid adaptation to the
new global economy" (Bales 1999: 104).

Two factors have been identified as the most important in the emergence of the
new slavery: the dramatic increase in the world population since World War II,
and the social and economic change, caused in part by the population explosion,
which created the global conditions that make new forms of slavery possible
(Bales 1999). The population explosion radically increased the supply of potential slaves, lowering their price, especially in those areas where slavery was still
practiced or had been part of the historical culture. While the process of modernization created wealth, in developing countries only the elite profited from
these benefits, which remained unavailable to the poor majority. In those countries, mainly in Africa and Asia, civil war and the massive despoilment of

resources by homegrown dictators have further impoverished the increasing number of poor people: "[T]he forced shift from subsistence to cash-crop agriculture, the loss of common land, and government policies which suppress farm income in favor of cheap food for the cities have all helped to bankrupt millions of peasants and drive them from their land, and sometimes, into slavery" (Bales 1999: 104–5).

TRAFFICKING AND THE SHADOW ECONOMY: ILLICIT MARKETS PROFITING FROM TRAFFICKED PERSONS

The increasing number of migrant workers from poor countries and their exploitation can be understood as a supply-and-demand phenomenon: "where the supply of workers available for export is a function of specific economic conditions in the poorer country, and the demand for their services is a function of economic and social processes elsewhere within the world" (Taylor and Jamieson 1999: 5).

The process of trafficking – the buying, selling, and exploitation of – persons is, in itself, an illicit activity that generates economic gain for the individuals involved. Trafficking in human beings is characteristic of an illegal market "within which goods and services are exchanged whose production, sale and consumption are forbidden or strictly regulated by the majority of national states and/or by international legislation" (Arlacchi 1998: 203). While the actual trade or trafficking and subsequent exploitation of persons is illicit, the activities in which the victims of trafficking are exploited, however, may fall within either the licit or illicit sector.

Unrecognized, undocumented, and thus unregulated economic activities are the basis for the informal sector which is known by various names: clandestine, illegal, underground, black, or "shadow" economy (Fleming et al. 2000). The shadow economy, or the markets in which trafficked victims are forced to work, can be divided into four general sectors: the informal, the criminal, the irregular, and the household (Fleming et al. 2000). The informal sector has been defined (Feige 1990: 992) as "economic activities that circumvent the costs and are excluded from the benefits" of law. Micro-enterprise, such as selling food and vegetables on the street, is an example of an activity within the informal sector. The criminal sector concentrates on illegal goods and services, such as the production and sale of illicit drugs or forced prostitution. In the irregular sector, legally produced goods and services evade legal requirements. Tax evasion is an example of an activity within this sector. The household sector is concerned with domestic servitude (Fleming et al. 2000).

There are three basic (il)legal markets which are profiting from trafficked migrants. These are the legitimate or conventional market economies (restaurants, factories, farms, etc.), the legitimate domestic service economy (households which employ maids), and the criminal economies of the forced-sex industry, the foremost being prostitution (Ruggiero 1996, 1997).[9] Forced labor on farms, plantations, or factories, in which many West African male children are forced to work, often involves deplorable working, living, and sanitary conditions (Taylor and Jamieson 1999; Bales 1999; *Business Week* 2000). Within the domestic service economy, in which young female children are forced to provide service, employers profit from the children's exploitation by underpaying (or failing to pay them at all). The domestic servants are often mistreated, both psychologically and physically. In addition to the problem of forced child labor prevalent in most of West and Central Africa, forced prostitution of adolescent females and young women is a serious problem in Nigeria.

There is a symbiotic relationship between the legal and illegal economies in the shadow economy markets. (Il)licit companies which use forced labor often subcontract with legitimate corporations, which in turn profit from the forced labor (*Business Week* 2000). Profits generated by the sex industry are often reinvested in the legitimate economy through money-laundering operations and thus there is a profit nexus between the illicit and legitimate business worlds (Aronowitz 2001).

FACTORS CONTRIBUTING TO THE TRAFFICKING OF CHILDREN IN WEST AND CENTRAL AFRICA

The phenomenon of trafficking, particularly in women and children, is intrinsically related to the difficult socioeconomic environment and deep-rooted, abject poverty, regional inequalities, and inadequate programs for the creation of employment or revenue-generating activities, particularly for youth, in rural areas (Salah 2001). The massive debt of these countries and the failure of the structural adjustment programs to regulate the economic situation has resulted in economic decline, placing millions below the poverty line, and making children and their families more vulnerable to trafficking and other forms of exploitation (Talens 1998). The trafficking of children goes hand in hand with poverty and child labor. Africa has the highest rate of child labor in the world: 41 percent of 5–14-year-olds work (Robinson and Palus 2001). Further complicating the situation in much of Central and West Africa is political instability, and a lack of accountability of government institutions which have been either under military regimes or under one-party rule (Talens 1998).

In addition to devastating economic conditions and political instability, the trafficking of children is fostered by West and Central African nations' historical and cultural patterns of migration and the placement of children outside of the home (Salah 2001). Movement and the placement of children, based on cultural values, is done to foster extended family solidarity and to further the educational and vocational training of the child (Bazzi-Veil 2000). Difficult financial situations within the family often are the basis for the placement. Children are introduced to work at very young ages and it is believed that through this work they are taught social values. It is also believed that the life and education of a child is the responsibility of the extended family. It is not uncommon for children to grow up in the family of relatives, or third persons, if they are living in better circumstances and can thus provide the child with better educational and work opportunities (Bazzi-Veil 2000; Verbeet 2000). In part, the voluntary placement of children (which often leads to their trafficking) is driven by poverty, and in part by the desire to provide a better life for their children (Verbeet 2000).

Salah (2001) blames other factors, such as ignorance on the part of families and children of the risks involved in trafficking; the high demand for cheap and submissive child labor in the informal economic sector; the desire of youth for emancipation through migration; and institutional lapses such as inadequate political commitment, nonexistent national legislation against child trafficking, and the absence of a judicial framework allowing the perpetrators and accomplices of trafficking to be held responsible and punished for their acts. These institutional lapses may be explained by radical criminology theory, which holds that those in positions of wealth and power create (or fail to enact) laws to protect their interests.[10]

In conclusion, the causes or factors contributing to the trafficking of persons in West and Central Africa can be classified as both "intermediate" and "deep structural." Intermediate causes, such as the failure of parents to recognize the dangers to their children, children's desire for more freedom, or the lack of job opportunities in rural areas, can be more easily and quickly addressed than deep structural causes. The latter, such as the colonial practice of slaveholding, the historically accepted practice of child placement outside of the home, regional inequalities, and countries' massive structural debt, as well as the common practice of those in power to protect their interests, require long-term approaches and will continue to make it difficult, but not impossible, to eradicate trafficking and modern-day slavery in this part of the world.

MIGRATORY AND TRAFFICKING PATTERNS IN WEST AND CENTRAL AFRICA

Trafficking patterns mirror migratory flows. The shift is always from more economically disadvantaged countries (countries of origin) to those more economically secure (destination countries). The (il)legal displacement of persons – within and across borders – is a fast growing, informal-sector activity in West Africa, affecting in particular women and children.

Studies have indicated clearly defined trafficking routes involving Benin, Burkina Faso, Cameroon, Gabon, Ghana, Guinea, Côte d'Ivoire, Mali, Niger, Nigeria, and Togo (Salah 2001). In cross-border trafficking, Benin, Ghana, Nigeria, and Togo are the main countries of origin from which child domestic labor is exported to the main urban centers in countries such as Congo, Equatorial Guinea, Côte d'Ivoire, Gabon, and Nigeria (UNICEF 1998a). In spite of these patterns, it is not uncommon for a country to supply and receive children while also serving as a transit country.

There is some indication of a link between sending and receiving countries. These links are influenced by a number of factors, such as the ease of crossing borders (Kelly and Regan 2000), the traffickers use of the local customs, key locations, or weaknesses in border or migration control (IOM 2000), or expatriate populations in the destination country. Other determining factors are the historical/colonial links between countries, or the presence and tolerance of an extensive sex industry (Kelly and Regan 2000).

Figure 21.1 indicates major trafficking flows in West and Central Africa.

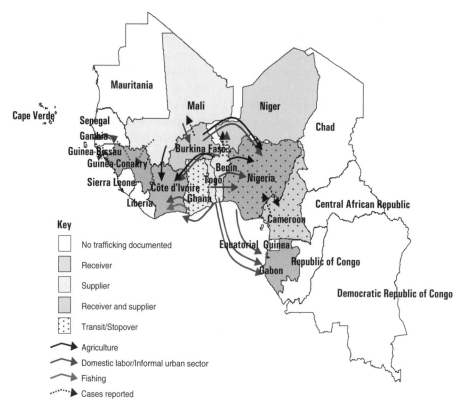

Figure 21.1   The flow of child trafficking in West and Central Africa (based on current knowledge)
Source: Bazzi-Veil 2000.

Two major trafficking patterns can be witnessed here. One involves intraregional trafficking flows with respect to the exploitation of children for the domestic service and labor market; the other, the trafficking and exploitation of girls and young women for forced prostitution to destinations in Europe, the Middle East, and the United States.

The exploitation of child labor is prevalent throughout the region (ILO 2002). UNICEF estimates that approximately 200,000 children are trafficked each year in West and Central Africa (Robinson and Palus 2001; UNICEF, News Notes). Male children are trafficked predominantly for labor on coffee or cocoa plantations or in the fishing industry, while female children are trafficked for work as market vendors or domestic servants. Children are also forced into soliciting and begging (ILO 2002). Female children are more frequently the victims of child trafficking than males. In a study of child trafficking between Benin and Gabon, 198 (86 percent) of the 229 children interviewed were female and more than 50 percent were under the age of 16 (Anti-Slavery International 1994). This has been attributed to the fact that emphasis is placed on the education of male children. In families that can only afford to educate one child, it is the male child who will be sent to school while the female child is placed in a family to work.

Internal trafficking of children occurs more frequently than trans-border trafficking. This is followed by trafficking of children within the region. Some children, however, are sent as far away as Europe and the Middle East.

While the focus of trafficking in the region is on the exploitation of child labor, and government officials report limited involvement of children in the sex market (ILO 2002), in a study of seven West African nations, ECPAT International (End Child Prostitution, Child Pornography, and Trafficking of Children for Sexual Purposes) reports a growing involvement of the commercial sexual exploitation of children in the region (ECPAT 2001).

The traffickers of children are "largely women and in some cases they are relatives. In some cases it is organized crime, but in West Africa they are often small rings abusing traditional systems" (Herzfeld 2001).

The second trafficking pattern in West and Central Africa involves the trafficking of adult women for exploitation in two different sectors. The first entails trafficking for the purpose of forced domestic service (an example of this can be found in the trafficking of Malian women to Saudi Arabia and Kuwait; IOM 2001). The second example involves the trafficking and sexual exploitation of young women, such as that of trafficking of Nigerians to destinations in Western Europe and beyond.

MEASURING THE PROBLEM

The United Nations estimates that four million people are trafficked within or between countries and that trafficking generates US$5–7billion annually (Raymond 2001). The true magnitude of the problem, however, is difficult to gauge. In part this is due to the varying definitions used, but it is also due to other factors, such as the accepted practice of the placement of children with relatives or other families both within and outside of the country, and the hidden economies in which the children work. Other reasons for the lack of accurate data include a lack of anti-trafficking legislation in many countries, the reluctance of victims to report their experiences to the authorities, and the lack of government priority given to data collection and research (IOM 2001). Statistics are generated by NGOs, governmental and international organizations, law enforcement (statistics on interceptions), and embassies (statistics on repatriations). These statistics often include estimates and portray only the tip of the iceberg: for example, although 535 trafficked women were returned to Ghana between 1999 and 2000, the Ghana Immigration Service estimates that between 1998 and 2000 some 3,582 women were trafficked (IOM 2001).

Indicators of child trafficking

With the exception of Nigeria, most of the research carried out in the field of trafficking and smuggling in those countries has focused primarily on children (Kekeh 1997; UNICEF 1998a, 1998b, 2000; ESAM 1998, 1999; Entraide Universitaire Mondiale du Canada 1999; Bazzi-Veil 2000; Verbeet 2000). This is due to the fact that the discovery and awareness of trafficking situations came about through research on child employment and the living conditions of working children.

Studies on child labor called attention to the phenomenon of child trafficking through the analysis of their method of entry into the labor market. According to a study carried out in Nigeria in1992 among children living in five states, it was found that 54–70 percent of children living in the street were migrants and that 40 percent of the children in domestic service came to town with a third party or non-family member (Bazzi-Veil 2000). In another survey carried out on 173 children living in the street in four Nigerian cities, it was discovered that 15 percent came with their parents, whereas 67 percent came in the company of other adults (friends of the family or strangers); 43 percent said that they had been victims of trafficking (Bazzi-Veil 2000).

A similar indicator of trafficking is when a child is in a situation of placement working outside of his immediate family unit and living with his employer (Talens 2000). In a study conducted in Benin on child labor, from 760 children in 3 cities, it was discovered that 73 percent lived with another person other than their parents, and 70 percent were working outside of the parental home. A large number of them were in situations of placement and likely to be exploited (Bazzi-Veil 2000).

Other factors which may indicate that a child has been a victim of trafficking is when the child worker is unpaid and lives with his employer with whom he has no family ties. In a study carried out on 59 Malian children who had been trafficked to Côte d'Ivoire, 63 percent said they received a salary, while 23 percent received no remuneration (Kouakou 1998). In the aforementioned survey of 173 children living and working in four Nigerian cities, 47 percent of children said that their employers paid their wages directly to the person who brought them, and 35 percent were ignorant of the arrangements made, while 19 percent said there was no monetary arrangement at all (Bazzi-Veil 2000).

Exploitation and Trafficking Patterns in Three Countries

Returning to the model we provided earlier, patterns of child trafficking in Central and West Africa differ from patterns of trafficking in other parts of the world. Reports from NGOs as well as government officials in Benin, Togo, and Nigeria indicate that kidnapping rarely occurs and violence is seldom if ever used against children in recruitment. Document forgery is rare, as children are smuggled by vehicle or on foot over the often porous borders. They are, however, often exposed to dangerous and sometimes life-threatening experiences during the voyage to neighboring countries; a voyage that at times has subjected the children to starvation, dehydration, and sometimes death. During the exploitation phase, children are commonly forced to work long hours, and not properly fed, clothed, or educated. There have also been documented cases of children being severely abused and sexually assaulted while in indentured slavery. Nigerian adolescents and young women are subject to similar physical and sexual abuses during the exploitation phase to those experienced by other young women trafficked throughout the world for the purpose of commercial sexual exploitation.

In the remainder of this section we will focus in more detail on three countries in the region. These have been selected to portray the situation in a source country, Benin, and a destination country, Côte d'Ivoire. Nigeria has been selected to illustrate the particular problem of organized trafficking of adolescent females and young women for forced prostitution.

Benin

More than half (3,109,000) of the total population of Benin (5,781,000) is under the age of 18 (Global March website). In a sample of child domestic workers researched by the UNICEF West and Central Africa Regional Office (UNICEF 1998a), 19.2 percent were below the age of 10, 72.4 percent were between the ages of 10 and 14, and only 8.4 percent were over the age of 14.

Trafficking of children within Benin is prevalent. Further, it is a source, transit, and destination country. Beninese children are trafficked to Gabon, Ghana, and Nigeria for farm labor, indentured or domestic servitude, and prostitution. Between 1995 and 1998, 1,363 children (117 in 1995, 413 in 1996 and 694 in 1997) were intercepted at the Beninese borders (UNICEF 1998a). These children were being taken abroad to work. Children from Burkina Faso, Niger, and Togo, and have been trafficked to Benin for indentured or domestic servitude (US Department of State 2001b).

Fueled by widespread poverty in rural areas and porous borders, trafficking flourishes in Benin because it bears a close resemblance to the West African practice of child apprenticeship, known as *vidomegon* ("putting a child in a home"). Poor, rural families often place a child, commonly a daughter, with a wealthier family. The children work, but the arrangement is voluntary between the two families. Children are forced to perform domestic services or may be made to sell goods on the street, often without pay and under conditions of hardship.

This custom of placement has dissolved into the practice of child trafficking. Those who come into the villages to recruit children with promises of an apprenticeship or education are often known to the families, and are often either friends or other family members. A trafficker may be able to trade three or four children a month and earn about US$30 for each child recruited (Sheil 2001).

Among others, UNICEF is collaborating with the Beninese authorities to make the practice of sending a child to work abroad socially unacceptable, by training members of village committees to watch out for evidence of child trafficking and to warn parents of the dangers their children face abroad.

Côte d'Ivoire

More than half (7,340,000) of the total population of Côte d'Ivoire (14,292,00) is under the age of 18 (Global March website). Trafficking within the country is prevalent. As a source country, Ivorian women and children are trafficked to African, European, and Middle Eastern countries. It serves as a destination country to women who are principally trafficked from Nigeria, Ghana, Liberia, and Asian countries (US Department of State 2001b). Children are trafficked from Mali, Burkina Faso, Guinea, Ghana, Benin, and Togo to Côte d'Ivoire for farm labor, indentured or domestic servitude, and sexual exploitation. A study (WAO Afrique 1999) showed that children were trafficked from Togo to Côte d'Ivoire for use as domestic servants, market traders, child beggars, and prostitutes, while children trafficked from Mali were forced to work on plantations.

UNICEF estimates that 15,000 children may be working on Ivorian cocoa plantations. Thousands of Malian children have been trafficked to Côte d'Ivoire and sold into indentured servitude on Ivorian plantations under abusive conditions (US Department of State 1999). It is believed that the sale of children for forced labor is organized around networks, which bring children from rural areas to urban centers to work for individual employers in domestic services, or in commercial activities such as in restaurants (Diop 1994). Immigrant farmers and traders in the cocoa-growing south-west of Côte d'Ivoire say teenagers and adults are trucked in each year from impoverished villages in neighboring Mali to work on the harvest. Most come from areas with established links to migrant communities.

A sharp fall in recent years in world prices for cocoa – as well as many of the region's other main agricultural commodity exports such as coffee, rubber, and cotton – has heightened demand for free or cheap labor both among small shareholders and in larger-scale agro-industries. Accusations appearing in British media that 90 percent of the former French colony's cocoa output was contaminated by child slavery caused the government to mount a full-scale counteroffensive. Border checks have been tightened, particularly with Mali and Burkina Faso, whose nationals form, by far, Côte d'Ivoire's two biggest migrant communities and account for two-thirds of workers in cocoa and coffee plantations. Ivorian authorities have repatriated more than 350 alleged child slaves in 2001.

Nigeria

Nigeria's population is the largest on the African continent. Half the total population (106,409,000) is under the age of 18 (Global March website). Nigeria is rated as one of the 20 poorest countries in the world. An estimated 40 percent of the total population in Nigeria is living below the poverty line. Women and girls from the rural areas seem to be the most affected by this situation. Many families unable to meet the costs of schooling will take girls out of education, resulting in the illiteracy of two-thirds of the female population. Today, 70 percent of women contribute to the domestic economy, as farmers, petty traders, domestic workers, and homemakers. Their work is undervalued and their lack of training and education make them an easy target of recruiters for trafficking.

Nigeria is a source, transit, and destination country for trafficked persons. The majority of trafficking from Nigeria involves females for the purpose of commercial sexual exploitation destined for Europe (Italy, the Netherlands, Belgium, the Czech Republic, Spain, and France) and the Middle East. Nigerians, primarily women and children, are also trafficked to work on plantations in other African countries, including Benin, Cameroon, Equatorial Guinea, and Gabon. Nigeria also serves as a transit hub for trafficking in West Africa and, to a lesser extent, a destination point for young children from nearby West African countries. There is also evidence of trafficking of children and women within Nigeria (US Department of State 2001b).

Child trafficking in Nigeria is mainly an internal problem but is slowly beginning to take on cross-border dimensions (UNICEF 1998b). Young boys from the age of five or six, may be entrusted by their families to serve as a religious leader, or *marabout*. In addition to performing various household tasks, the child is often, as part of the learning process, forced to beg (Anti-Slavery International 1994). Young children are forced to work as domestics, petty traders or hawkers, beggars, bus conductors, car washers, or on farms (UNICEF 1998b). This problem, however, receives less attention than the trafficking of young women for commercial sexual exploitation.

The commercial sexual exploitation of young women usually occurs when the young women are between the ages of 15 and 25. They are usually recruited by an older woman, a Maman or Madam, who acts as go-between for the women and girls and the organization preparing their migration. The recruiters enact rites originating in Voodoo practices binding the young women to the traffickers. Intermediaries provide girls and women with travel documents and tickets, and then create a debt–bondage relationship, based on economical and psychological subordination. Another Maman in the destination country[11] supervises, controls, and organizes the groups (comprising 10–15 girls or women), coordinates their activities, and collects their profits. Most Mamans started as prostitutes themselves and, once their debt[12] has been paid to their Maman, they, in turn, use the same method to make money.

In Benin City, one of the poorest states in the country and one of the major sources of trafficked women to Italy, this trade has become so lucrative that it has created a kind of industry:

> [A]n astonishing variety of small enterprises now depends on trafficking: forgers; phony lawyers who establish "contracts" between traffickers and girls; self-styled evangelists who pray for the girls from charismatic churches; traditional doctors who use voodoo to hold the girls to their promise; customs and immigration officials who take bribes to look the other way. (WOCON 2000: 6)

Where women are trafficked for commercial sexual exploitation there is evidence of highly sophisticated international networks involved in recruitment, the provision of travel documents, transportation, accommodation, and the exploitation of the women in the receiving countries. There is evidence to suggest that the trade is highly organized and syndicated. Traffickers working at local levels are being sponsored by criminal groups based in Europe. Victims have alleged that Nigerian immigration officials are actively complicit with, or may operate as part of, trafficking syndicates (US Department of State 2001b). Criminal networks corrupt immigration officers, who provide traffickers with false documentation (passports and visas) (Ojomo 1999).

The Nigerian president reported that 1,178 women and children who were believed to be the victims of trafficking were repatriated into the country between March 1999 and December 2000 (IOM 2001). According to the Nigerian Embassy in Rome,[13] Italy is the main destination country for trafficked women from Nigeria. The Embassy of the Federal Republic of Nigeria has collaborated with the Italian government to repatriate over 500 illegal immigrants in 1999 alone, most of whom are trafficked women.

OFFICIAL AND CIVIL SOCIETY APPROACHES TO THE PREVENTION AND SUPPRESSION OF TRAFFICKING IN THE REGION

Many countries in the region are dealing with a lack of resources, severe financial restraints, and porous borders. Most governments, however, recognize that the trafficking in women and children is a problem, and have taken measures to address it.

Legislative and legal approaches

Many countries are lacking adequate legislation to punish trafficking in human beings. Other offenses, linked to the trafficking process, such as forced prostitution, abandonment, slavery or child labor violations, may be punished. Many of these provisions are covered in countries' penal, civil, administrative, or labor codes.[14] There is a quadripartite agreement between the governments of Benin, Gabon, Nigeria, and Togo which focuses on border control and the repatriation of trafficked victims. A bilateral agreement exists between Mali and Côte d'Ivoire to cooperate against the trafficking in children. Furthermore, there are a number of international instruments addressing the problem of exploitation of children. These include the International Labour Organization (ILO) Convention 182 concerning the Prohibition and Immediate Action for the Elimination of the Worst Forms of Child Labour, and the Protocol to the Convention on the Rights of the Child, on the Sale of Children, Child Prostitution and Child Pornography.

The UN Protocol on Trafficking of Human Beings encompasses numerous approaches to dealing with the phenomenon in countries of origin, transit, and destination. Its far-reaching approach provides a framework for countries to criminalize trafficking; provide victim rehabilitation, and in appropriate cases, victim protection and assistance; address the status of the victim in the receiving state; repatriate trafficked victims; implement law enforcement measures against the traffickers; strengthen border controls; provide security and verify the validity of (travel) documents; and prevent trafficking through public information campaigns (US Department of State 2001a).[15]

Victim protection and assistance

Local, regional, and national governments, as well as NGOs within the West and Central African region, assisted by governments of other countries and international organizations, have introduced numerous measures to prevent and suppress trafficking in the region and overseas. Intergovernmental agencies (UNICEF, the IOM, and the ILO) and local and international NGOs are active in a number of countries to provide educational prevention programs, and repatriation of and assistance to trafficked children. UNICEF has organized numerous seminars on the trafficking of children and provides technical and financial support to local NGOs.

The ILO's International Program on the Elimination of Child Labour (ILO–IPEC) initiated a project to rescue approximately 9,000 children trafficked for labor exploitation and prevent the trafficking of other children in the countries of Benin, Burkina Faso, Cameroon, Côte d'Ivoire, Gabon, Ghana, Mali, Nigeria, and Togo. The project began with a study of the nature and scope of the problem in the countries involved and resulted in strategies for national and regional actions to address the problem. The second phase will address the trafficking problem at both the national and regional level through

> awareness raising campaigns; mobilization/capacity building/coordination of social partners and key actors; provision of multi-disciplinary preventive/ rehabilitative programs for child victims, children at risk and their parents; development of multilateral/bilateral agreements to prevent trafficking; and through the organization of sub-regional meetings to review regulations/ enforcement practice against trafficking in children. (Bureau for International Narcotics and Law Enforcement Affairs 2001: 3)

The IOM, over a two-year period, will provide assistance to roughly 2,000 Malian children who have been trafficked for labor exploitation to Côte d'Ivoire. It will further support the Malian Government's Plan of Action to combat cross-border child trafficking. The IOM, in cooperation with the Malian and Côte d'Ivoire governments, UNICEF, and local NGOs, plans to identify trafficked children, transport them to safe shelters in Mali, help identify their parents, and provide rehabilitative and reintegrative services (US Department of State 2001a). The IOM, working together with the Nigerian national and two state governments, is further involved in a project in Nigeria aimed at reintegrating and assisting women and minors who have been trafficked to Europe for sexual exploitation.

USAID is supporting and promoting a local NGO in Nigeria to place anti-trafficking on the legislative agenda, while in Cameroon, Côte d'Ivoire, Guinea, Ghana, and Nigeria, it is working together with trade organizations, industry, and government bodies to end child trafficking and indentured labor in the cocoa industry (Bureau for International Narcotics and Law Enforcement Affairs 2001).

Government initiatives include the following: In January 2001, the government of Côte d'Ivoire completed and validated the National Emergency Action Plan for the Fight against Cross-Border Trafficking in Children. In 1999, the government of Nigeria funded the establishment of a 10-member police anti-trafficking task force that has since facilitated the repatriation of over 400 women and girls (US Department of State 2001a). An anti-trafficking bill, sponsored by an NGO, is currently under consideration at the National Assembly.

Local and national NGOs in almost all countries concerned provide victim assistance and shelter to trafficked persons, conduct educational and public awareness campaigns in high-risk areas, and lobby for stronger legislation.

To conclude, the often transnational component of human trafficking requires multilateral approaches between governments, and between governments and NGOs. Governments must address both the supply and demand sides of the illicit market. To do this, however, specific legislation must be in place and enforced, and financial means must be available to investigate, prosecute offenders, and implement prevention and protection projects for victims. A national legal strategy must be adopted, coupled with support for victims at local level. Destination countries must punish the exploiters and assist source countries to stem the flow of victims through educational prevention projects, employment opportunities, and the reintegration and protection of trafficked victims.

Notes

The statements and opinions contained in this chapter are those of the authors, and do not necessarily represent the position or views of the UN Interregional Crime and Justice Research Institute or the UN Centre for International Crime Prevention.

1 In June 2000, 58 Chinese nationals, trying to enter the United Kingdom illegally, suffocated in the back of a truck.

2 In April 2001 the *Etireno* disappeared, allegedly carrying 250 child slaves. When the boat finally docked, it was found to have 43 minors on board, some with their parents. While it is not known what happened to the children, or if 250 were previously on board, the incident served to draw attention to the region's trade in children.

3 West and Central Africa comprise the countries of Senegal, Gambia, Guinea-Bissau, Guinea Conakry, Sierra Leone, Liberia, Côte d'Ivoire, Ghana, Togo, Benin, Nigeria, Cameroon, Equatorial Guinea, Gabon, Burkina Faso, Mali, Mauritania, Niger, Chad, Central African Republic, Republic of Congo, and Democratic Republic of Congo.

4 In line with international concern surrounding the trafficking of human beings, the United Nations Interregional Crime and Justice Research Institute (UNICRI) is involved in two projects concerned with the trafficking of human beings in the West African nations of Benin, Nigeria and Togo. UNICRI together with the United Nations Centre for International Crime Prevention (CICP) of the Office for Drug Control and Crime Prevention in Vienna, Austria, launched the Global Programme Against Trafficking in Human Beings in March 1999. The Global Programme encompasses a number of projects in various stages of development in the Philippines, the West African nations of Benin, Nigeria and Togo, the Czech Republic and Poland, and Brazil. Also within the framework of the Global Programme, UNICRI has designed an extensive research and technical cooperation and assistance project between the governments of Italy and Nigeria.

5 In the European Union, for example, trafficking in human beings encompasses the following violations: exploitation of prostitution, forms of exploitation and sexual violence involving minors, the trade in abandoned children, the production, sale and distribution of child pornography. The definition, at present, does not include exploitation of labor.

6 As of July 2002, 141 countries had signed the Convention, 107 had signed the trafficking Protocol, and 103 the smuggling Protocol. Fourteen countries have ratified the anti-trafficking Protocol; before it may come into force, it must be signed and ratified by 40 countries. The Convention was adopted by the UN General Assembly at its Millennium meeting in November 2000 and was opened for signature at a high-level conference in Palermo, Italy, in December 2000. The new instrument spells out how countries can improve cooperation on such matters as extradition, mutual legal assistance, transfer of proceedings and joint investigations. It contains provisions for victim and witness protection and shielding legal markets from infiltration by

organized criminal groups. Parties to the treaty would also provide technical assistance to developing countries to help them take the necessary measures and upgrade their capacities for dealing with organized crime. The UN Convention and both Protocols can be downloaded from the Web at www.uncjin.org/documents/conventions/dcatoc/final_documents_2/index.htm The UN Protocols address the States that are members of the UN and signatories of the documents. The complete set of international obligations regarding trafficking is found in three documents: the UN Protocol to Prevent, Suppress, and Punish Trafficking in Persons, especially Women and Children; the UN Convention Against Transnational Organised Crime; and the Imperative Notes (Travaux Préparatoires) to the Trafficking Protocol. A valid tool to understanding these documents is A. Jordan, *The Annotated Guide to the Complete UN Trafficking Protocol* (May 2002, International Human Rights Law Group). The guide can be downloaded from the Web at www.hrlawgroup.org/resources/content/Protocol_annotated.pdf

7   The consent of a victim of trafficking in persons to the intended exploitation shall be irrelevant where any of the means set forth (in the definition) have been used. Furthermore, the recruitment, transportation, transfer, harboring or receipt of a child for the purpose of exploitation shall be considered "trafficking in persons" even if this does not involve any of the means set forth in the definition.

8   Internal trafficking occurs as well as, and possibly to an even greater extent in many countries than, transnational trafficking. It is the subsequent exploitation, and not the crossing of international borders, which defines trafficking of human beings.

9   Prostitution is not an illegal activity in all countries. In the Netherlands, for example, prostitution by adult women, if voluntary, is not an offense. It is, however, a criminal offense to force an individual into prostitution.

10 Karl Marx explained that criminal law "was used and abused by powerful classes in the processes of primitive accumulation of land and labour" (Sumner 1982: 30, citing Marx's *Capital, Vol. I*).

11 This is particularly true in Italy.

12 Police and Italian NGOs report that women incur debts ranging from US$50,000 to $60,000 to pay back to their Maman.

13 Meeting of a UNICRI officer with Nigerian Embassy officials, November 3, 2000.

14 Penal codes punish the abduction of victims. Civil codes often dictate the responsibilities of parents to their children and punish those parents who endanger the child. Administrative codes regulate travel documents and transporting minors out of the country. Labor codes regulate safety and working conditions and minimum age for employment of children.

15 Since 2001, the US Department of State has published an annual update on the situation of trafficking in persons worldwide. The latest version, published in June 2002, can be downloaded form the Web at http://www.state.gov/g/inl/rls/tiprpt/2002

References

Adamoli, S., Di Nicola, A., Savona, E., and Zoffi, P.(1998) *Organized Crime Around the World*. Helsinki: European Institute for Crime Prevention and Control (HEUNI).

Anti-Slavery International (1994) Forced begging in West Africa. *Child Workers in Asia*, October–December.

Arlacchi, P. (1998) Some observations on illegal markets. In V. Ruggiero, N. South, and I. Taylor (eds.), *The New European Criminology*. London: Routledge, 203–15.

Aronowitz, A. A. (2001) Smuggling and trafficking in human beings: The phenomenon, the markets that drive it and the organizations that promote it. *European Journal on Criminal Policy and Research*, 9, 163–95.

Aronowitz, A. A. (2003, forthcoming) *Coalitions Against Trafficking in Human Beings in the Philippines – Phase I, Research Activities*. Final Report. Turin: United Nations Interregional Crime and Justice Research Institute.

Bales, K. (1999) New slavery. The transformation of an ancient curse. *Global Dialogue*, 1, Summer, 102–13.

Bales, K., and Robbins, P. T. (2001) No one shall be held in slavery or servitude: A critical analysis of international slavery agreements and concepts of slavery. *Human Rights Review*, 2(2), January, 14–22.

Bajrektarevic, A. (2000) *Trafficking in and Smuggling of Human Beings – Linkages to Organized Crime – International Legal Measures*. Statement Digest. Vienna: International Centre for Migration Policy Development.

Bazzi-Veil, L. (2000) *The Status of Child Trafficking for Economic Exploitation in West and Central Africa*. New York: UNICEF.

Bureau for International Narcotics and Law Enforcement Affairs (2001) *The U.S. Government's International Anti-Trafficking in Persons Initiatives Fact Sheet*. US Department of State, July 12, available online at http://www.state.gov/g/inl/rls/fs/2001/index.cfm?docid=4051

Business Week (2000) Workers in bondage. November 27, 57–68.

Diop, R. (1994) The sale of child labour in Côte d'Ivoire. *Child Workers in Asia*, October–December.

ECPAT (End Child Prostitution, Child Pornography, and Trafficking of Children for Sexual Purposes) (2001) *ECPAT Newsletter*, 34, March.

Entraide Universitaire Mondiale du Canada (1999) *Projet de Lutte contre le Trafic des enfants au Bénin*. August.

ESAM (Enfants Solidaires de l'Afrique et du Monde) (1998) *Les enfants placés au Bénin*. Rapport de recherche.

ESAM (Enfants Solidaires de l'Afrique et du Monde) (1999) *Séminaire de Restitution de l'Etude sur le Trafic des enfants entre le Bénin et le Gabon*. Rapport de recherche. Lomé, August 11–13.

Europol (2000) *Europol Situation Report THB 1999*. The Hague: Europol.

Feige, E. L. (1990), Defining and estimating underground and informal economies: The new institutional economics approach. *World Development*, 18(7), 989–1002.

Fleming, M., Roman, J., and Farrell, G. (2000) The shadow economy. *Journal of International Affairs*, 53(2), 387–409.

Francis, A. (1995) The economics of the African slave trade. Available online at: http://dolphin.upenn.edu/vision/vis/mar-95/5284.html

Global March. "Benin," "Côte d'Ivoire," "Nigeria." *Worst Forms of Child Labour Data*. Available online at: http:// www.globalmarch.org, last accessed July 16, 2001.

Gunnatilleke, G. (1994) Summary of the Report of the Rapporteur, International Cooperation in Fighting Illegal Immigration Networks. IOM Seminar on International Responses to Trafficking in Migrants and the Safeguarding of Migrant Rights, Geneva, October 26–28.

Herzfeld, B. (2001) Child slave labour still a global issue. April 17, Reuters.

ILO (International Labour Organization) (2002) *A Future without Child Labour. Global Report under the Follow-up to the ILO Declaration on Fundamental Principles and Rights at Work*. ILO Conference, 90th Session, Report I (B). Geneva: ILO.

IOM (International Organization for Migration) (2000) *Migrant Trafficking and Human Smuggling in Europe: A review of the evidence with case studies from Hungary, Poland and Ukraine*. Geneva: IOM.

IOM (International Organization for Migration) (2001) *Trafficking in Migrants*; *Quarterly Bulletin*, 23; April.

Jantsch, H. (1998) Law enforcement: Germany's perspective. Report of the U.S.–EU Trafficking in Women Seminar, Lvov, Ukraine, 9–10 July, 51–4.

Kekeh, R. K. (1997) *Le Trafic des Enfants au Togo. Etude Prospective à Lomé, Vogan et Cotonou*. Rapport définitif. WAO Afrique, September.

Kelly, L., and Regan, L. (2000) *Stopping Traffic: Exploring the Extent of, and Responses to, Trafficking in Women for Sexual Exploitation in the UK*. London: Home Office Policing and Reducing Crime Unit, Research, Development and Statistics Directorate.

Kendall, R. (1999) Recent trends in international investigations of trafficking in human beings. Paper presented at the International Conference on "New Frontiers of Crime: Trafficking in Human Beings and New Forms of Slavery," Verona, October 22–23.

Kouakou K. (1998) *International Child Trafficking between Mali and Côte d'Ivoire*. New York: UNICEF.

Ojomo, A. J. (1999) Trafficking in human beings: Nigerian law enforcement perspective. Paper presented at the International Conference on "New Frontiers of Crime: Trafficking in Human Beings and New Forms of Slavery," Verona, October 22–23.

Raymond, J. (2001) *Guide to the New U.N. Trafficking Protocol*. North Amherst, MA: Coalition Against Trafficking in Women.

Richard, A. O. (1999) *International Trafficking in Women to the United States: A Contemporary Manifestation of Slavery and Organized Crime*. Washington, DC: Center for the Study of Intelligence, State Department Bureau of Intelligence, US Department of State.

Robinson, S., and Palus, N. (2001) An awful human trade. *Time*, April 30, 34–5.

Ruggiero, V. (1996) Trafficking in human beings – Slaves in contemporary Europe. Paper presented at the Law and Society Association and Research Committee on the Sociology of Law of the International Sociological Association Joint Meetings, University of Strathclyde, Glasgow, July 10–13.

Ruggiero, V. (1997) Criminals and service providers: Cross-national dirty economies. *Crime, Law and Social Change*, 28, 27–38.

Salah, R. (2001) Child trafficking in West and Central Africa: An overview. Paper presented at the first Pan-African Conference on human trafficking organized by the Women Trafficking and Child Labour Eradication Foundation (Wotclef), International Conference Centre, Abuja, February 19–23, 4. Available online at: http://www.unicef.org/media/newsnotes/africchildtraffick.pdf

Savona, E., Adamoli, S., Zoffi, P., and DeFeo, M. (1995) *Organized Crime Across the Borders*. Helsinki: European Institute of Crime Prevention and Control (HEUNI).

Sheil, M. (2001 Child slaves hawk goods for their owners in the market in Libreville, the capital of Gabon. *Black Star*, May 22.

Sumner, C. S. (1982) *Crime, Justice and Underdevelopment*. London: Heinemann.

Synopsis of the Transatlantic Slave Trade: A Timeline 1441–1888. Available online at: http://www.middlepassage.org/timeline.htm

Talens C. (1998) *Trafficking of Children in West Africa*. Paris: CCEM.

Talens, C. (2000), Smuggling and trafficking of human beings in West Africa. Unpublished desk review, Turin: UNICRI.

Taylor, I., and Jamieson, R. (1999) Sex trafficking and the mainstream of market culture: Challenges to organized crime. Paper presented at the International Conference on "New Frontiers of Crime: Trafficking in Human Beings and New Forms of Slavery", Verona, October 22–23.

UNICEF. News Notes, Background on child trafficking. Available online at: http://www.unicef.org/media/newsnotes/01nn01.htm Last accessed August 17, 2001.

UNICEF (1998a) *The Issue of Child Domestic Labour and Trafficking in West and Central Africa*. New York: UNICEF.

UNICEF (1998b) *Child Domestic Workshop*. New York: UNICEF.

UNICEF (2000) Sub-Regional Study on Child Trafficking in West and Central Africa. New York: UNICEF.

US Department of State (1999) *Human Rights* Report. Washington, DC: US Department of State.

US Department of State (2001a) The U.S. government's international anti-trafficking in persons initiatives. July 21. Available online at: http://www.usinfo.state.gov/topical/global/traffick/fsintl.htm

US Department of State (2001b) *Trafficking Victims Protection Act of 2000, Trafficking in Persons Report*. Available online at: http://www.state.gov/g/inl/rls/tiprpt

Verbeet, D. (2000) Combating the trafficking in children for labour exploitation in West and Central Africa. Draft working document based on the studies of Benin, Burkina Faso, Cameroon, Côte d'Ivoire, Gabon, Ghana, Mali, Nigeria, and Togo. Abijan, Côte d'Ivoire: International Labour Organisation.

WAO-Afrique (1999) *Child Trafficking in West and Central Africa*. Submission to the UN Working Group on Contemporary Forms of Slavery.

WOCON (Women's Consortium of Nigeria) (2000) Girls for sale: The crisis in Nigeria. *On the Record: Your Electronic Link to Civil Society in Nigeria*, 12(2), June 20.

Part VI
Globalization, Crime, and Information

22

Globality, Glocalization, and Private Policing: A Caribbean Case Study[1]

Maureen Cain

Globality is achievable in that moment when there is the possibility of instant worldwide connections across time and space. Other conditions, however, reduce actual globality to a subsection of those for whom it is potentially available. These are participation in, or being affected by, global power-bearing networks of relationships and reflexive awareness of participation in such relations, or what Shaw (2000: 12) characterizes as "a common consciousness of society on a world scale." Each of these characteristics identified by Shaw is a necessary, but none alone is a sufficient condition of globality as an achieved condition: for that, all three are necessary (this is why globality was not achieved by the Roman or later empires: time–space conflation by instant communication was not present).

Such a definition is an advance on the processual concept of globalization because it offers criteria by which the extent of that process can be assessed. However, both concepts, globality and globalization, imply that all participants in the process are making the same journey or have the same point of arrival. There is an implicit denial of the differently situated experiences and knowledges which are generated by the various globalizing processes, and which characterize global relations themselves. Waters (2000 [1995]), for example, celebrates the possibility of living in multiple social worlds in class, ethnic, and gender terms: the reduction of these erstwhile intractable distinctions to lifestyle choices. And indeed, if and where that is happening, it may be producing a reduction of conflict and social exclusion which is worthy of celebration, even though in the UK the rate of social mobility in socioeconomic terms has fallen. But it is precisely that closure of the lowest socioeconomic strata, that locking of people into lowly statuses, that is at stake in assessing globalization as a concept, for what is denied is that globalization and localization are part of the same process.

Bauman (1998: 70, following Robertson) has captured the intrinsic relationship of these processes with the concept of *glocalization*. The nature of that relationship becomes apparent only when the abstraction of globalization is taken apart and reconstructed in terms of the particular relationships allegedly moving towards globality. Relations of both productive and finance capital have certainly achieved the state of globality, and the discourses of freedom of choice for the individual-as-consumer and of human rights are in different ways quite clearly in the process of globalizing. Labor, however, is less evenly, and as Beck too has argued (2000), even less necessarily than in the past, a part of that process. Redundant labor is locked into the local, and both within the "advanced" economies and in the less developed south and east "the *connection* between the growing misery and desperation of the grounded many and the new freedoms of the mobile few" (Bauman 1998: 73, my emphasis) is rendered invisible. Watching the unattainable lifestyle of the global few on television does not mean that this global way of living is shareable. Rather, this penetration of the living room by global lifestyles serves only to deny the validity of the local, to reduce local ways of being to a problematic absence (1998: 54). Yet separate causes are adduced for the transcultural successes and the local immiserations: the *single* glocalizing process is denied. In this context, policy developments which punish or abuse the poor – most notably, in the United Kingdom, the ill-educated young and lone mothers – while extolling the virtues of globality, inevitably enhance the polarizing relations which give rise to the problems of social exclusion on a global as well as a local scale.

The argument of this essay is that such processes of societal glocalization impact upon, and are internally reproduced within, the private security industry in the Caribbean, and Trinidad and Tobago in particular. While the discussion is based upon a small case study in a small nation, the methodological and theoretical conclusions have, it is argued, an applicability in the West as well as, more obviously, in other less developed countries.

The discussion has the following form. In the next section I describe the case study; next I consider the post structural adjustment context in which it took place. There follows a discussion of the "globality" of private policing organizations which includes a challenge to the "McDonaldization" model of global influence, a consideration of the market for private security, and a discussion of the role of an international professional organization. After this the perspective shifts to that of the workforce in a glocalized economy and, finally, to the exploration of a possible symbiosis between the "big boys" and the "fly-by-night" firms. The methodological and theoretical lessons are then drawn.

THE METHODOLOGY

The case study investigated a broad range of "non-public" and "quasi-public" security measures in Trinidad and Tobago and St. Lucia. It was carried out mainly in 1997, following a pilot study in 1996, and supplemented by several return visits. In addition to interviews with chief executives or security managers from 20 security firms, and observations and conversations with private security officers in the course of 11 neighborhood/alarm response patrols – the two data sets which I rely on in this analysis – interviews were also carried out with in-house security heads, neighborhood watch committees, groups concerned with family violence, police special reservists and special constables, docks and harbor police, union officials, officials of traders' associations, municipal police, and hotel and guest house keepers.[2]

The data acquired from the full body of interviews informs the analysis in both conscious and unconscious ways. This is also the case for the statistical and other data gathered or constructed as part of my teaching responsibilities at the University of the West Indies, and for the feedback received from serving on public committees and from talks about penality and penal reform on television and to a range of organizations such as schools, women's groups, the Chamber of Commerce, and public-service graduating cohorts, among others. Colleagues in the women's movement, in the church, on the social work program's Curriculum Development Committee, and in the Alternatives to Custody pressure group also kept me on my toes, shaped my opinions, and gave me courage. The friend with whom I stayed for most of the field research also deserves a place in the text rather than the acknowledgments. It is a privilege to debate one's pet and emergent theories, and to have them challenged, within the four walls of what is, for the time being, "home." The interpretations offered here, and some taken-for-granted "facts" which may have slipped in, have been shaped by all these influences, as well as by particular friendships, the warmth of which remains with me but which cannot be categorized in a list.

Methodologically, I have tried to present an account which at least addresses Trinidadian perspectives and concerns. My knowledge of St. Lucian culture is far more limited. I lived there only for the research period and I never became a member of that society, although I received rich hospitality and a warm welcome during the fieldwork. However, insofar as there are common Caribbean concerns, I hope the work is relevant for the Lucians too.

Reverting from methodology (who is speaking?) to technique, respondents in the pilot study were identified by chain-referral sampling; in the main study a random sample of firms listed in the *Yellow Pages* was taken. Not all firms conducted routine or neighborhood patrols. I tried to vary my requests to observe by size of firm, but make no claim to representativeness here. I deem the insights achieved invaluable, however, as I argue below.

Finally, copies of the report on the pilot study were returned to the heads of security (both in-house and from the firms) whom I interviewed during the pilot. In some cases this was a matter for brief but courteous discussion, or suggested revisions of interpretation, as I had hoped. My use of recorded vernacular speech, for example, was questioned. This "light Creole" is common parlance, and I would without thinking speak it myself, but one respondent was afraid I was making fun of people by putting it in writing. I had not anticipated this, and no doubt whatever I said was inadequate. But in all reported speech derived from this study I have left the "light Creole" text for its vivacious, specific formulations and for the rich, untranslatable additions to the conventional lexicon which respondents also used. I am also embarrassed that anyone should be made ashamed of the way they choose to speak by a visitor from an alien culture: me.

Such comments may have been distressing, but getting feedback is always rather painful, and they were what I had come for. What astonished me more was the evidence that there had in the meantime been some discussion of me among ASIS members,[3] apparently as a result of the report. "Who are you really?" and "What *is* the Leverhulme Trust?" one in-house head asked me; another with whom I had, as I thought, had a helpful and enjoyable conversation first time around, said nothing either new or about the report, although we kept a good dialogue going in which I gave rather than received information, which of course I was quite willing to do, even though I was becoming increasingly puzzled. A third more openly interviewed me, throwing the drugs trade into the conversation and saying, "Aha, I thought you would be interested in that," and winding up the interview, turning round as he walked out of the door, saying, "Networks are important, aren't they?" I remember my reply: "For all of us," I said, as sweetly as I could, but feeling miffed. It wasn't much, but I was fearful for the rest of the research: these were influential men. However, either because I passed whatever test, or because they couldn't be bothered, or because their own networks weren't extensive enough, or because I had misinterpreted the situation in the first place: for whatever reason, the response in the remaining interviews was not affected.

IMMISERATION AND THE CRIME RATE

Trinidad and Tobago took its first IMF loan in 1988, the economy having suffered from 1983 onward, after the OPEC-induced boom in oil prices ended. In the same year, offenses against property increased dramatically, to be followed in subsequent years by increases in offenses against the person. As in the United Kingdom, after the Thatcherite structural adjustment program, offenses against the person continued to rise even after the overall crime rate had stabilized.

The conditions of the Trinidad and Tobago loan entailed a "freeing up" of the exchange rate (hitherto pegged at a fixed rate to the US dollar), as a result of which the value of the Trinidad and Tobago dollar (TT$) fell sharply, eventually to settle at approximately TT$10 to the pound sterling. This "freeing up" also entailed markets. It meant that capital was now free to leave the country for investment overseas, and that unlimited imported goods could enter the local market, thereby putting small local producers out of business. We all began eating apples, and again baking cakes with sultanas and currants from Florida rather than dried paw-paw and carambola ("five fingers") as had been possible in the past. Meanwhile state enterprises were being "right-sized," sold off, or both. Thus in both the public and the private sectors jobs were lost, and this in a society where unemployment payments are available only to those with dependants. The tax regime was also "reformed" (as a high earner, my income almost doubled), so the state was starved of the resources which might have enabled it to meet more gradually some of the unemployment-creating demands of the IMF. All this happened on the back of a plunge in oil revenue – then and now the main support of the island's economy. Carnival went on, with calypso demands to "ease de tension."

From 1987 to 1989, the median income in Trinidad and Tobago dropped from TT$ 1,500 per month to TT$1,300 per month, yet, tellingly, the mean was less affected, falling from TT$1,800 to TT$1,700 in the period[4] (Cain and Birju 1992; Sampson 1994). This anomaly is explained by the immediate polarization of society brought about by structural adjustment. In absolute terms, between 1987 and 1991 the numbers in the highest income bracket (TT$5,000 per month and over) rose from 5,600 to 8,000 (males) and from 700 to 1,400 (females); at the same time the numbers in the lowest income bracket (less than TT$250 per month) also increased from 6,000 to 9,200 (males) and from 4,600 to 10,900 (females).[5] Inequality rose, and the social structure was stretched – suddenly, at that. From Durkheim (1952 [1895]) to Bennet (1991) this situation has been regarded as anomic, and in Bennet's case has been demonstrated to be crimino-genic cross-nationally.

Some of the increase in crime may be guessed to be instrumental: an increase in the already common practice of praedial larceny, the stealing of fruit for resale or food; the increase in property offenses already alluded to. Some theft from the person may also have been of this kind. We don't know, because there is even less research with offenders in the Caribbean than in the West. But what also happened at this time was a change in the organization of illegalities, an expansion of the local drugs trade, made possible by the main island, Trinidad's, value as a trans-shipment center on the narcotics trade route from Latin America to the United States and the West. Unemployment ran at 9.9 percent in 1980 but was over 20 percent by 1987. Between 1987 and 1989 from 34.2 percent to 35.6 percent of young men in the 20–24 age bracket were unemployed. Many, having no income at all, were vulnerable to recruitment as petty traders in drugs, and equally readily became users and cocaine addicts (little heroin or "crack" was traded at this time). The society became more violent at a petty level: street robberies to fuel an addiction. Internecine violence between traders also developed: in another island I heard live gunfire for the first time since the 1940s as I sat on a hotel porch while, reportedly, drug dealers murdered each other in the nearby high street. Less anecdotally, over the ten years 1980–9 in Trinidad and Tobago, reported offenses against the person rose from 439 to 1,171 (absolute numbers). All serious offenses in the period rose from 12,223 to 17,983 (Cain and Birju 1992: 143).

In a discussion of immiseration and the crime rate, one important point to note is that while ad hoc instrumental criminality may be reduced when the economic situation is less severe, the structural changes are likely to persist. Once established, the drugs trade is always likely to be more lucrative than any job available in the island for a person of low to middling education. Most people, of course, earn legal livings in any event, but the criminogenic incentives are now also structurally established. And so long as "the trade" persists, there will be guns to be bought cheaply. Again, other factors affect the level of force people decide to use, but the island was built upon forced relations, and a gun does not seem an unusual way for a vulnerable person to want to "make strong."[6]

The second point, which brings the discussion back to the core topic of this essay, is that these developments affected the demand for security. The burglar-bar industry for domestic and industrial properties boomed in the 1980s, as did the demand for guards. At the same time, the ability of both residents and business people to pay for services polarized along the lines of the society as a whole. Those local businesses which already hired security now, in many cases, needed to find a cheaper service in order to maintain their profitability. The security industry was affected by the global economic chain of events which had led Trinidad and Tobago to seek a loan, by the loan conditions imposed by a global institution, and by the local responses to these twin global pressures. But, as always, some in the industry flourished in the face of these developments, while others were positioned only to be victims. Before exploring this theme further, in the next section I consider colonial global influences on private policing, international companies in Trinidad and Tobago and St. Lucia, and the direction of global influence when globalization is direct and internal to the industry, as opposed to those indirect influences via the market for security considered above.

DIRECT GLOBALIZATION OF THE SECURITY INDUSTRY AND PATTERNS OF CHANGE

Global influences have directly shaped the form of private security in Trinidad and Tobago and St. Lucia in two ways: first in the form of ordinances constituting colonial private police, and secondly in the familiar form of transnational private security firms. I will discuss the colonial situation in relation to Trinidad, which was made a Crown Colony shortly after its cession to the British in 1797. As a result the governance was more clearly from London, albeit in response on occasion to economic and settler lobbying, rather than being by settler representatives in conjunction with colonial officials, as elsewhere in the region. This was because of the undeveloped and under-settled character of the island at the time of the British takeover from Spain and of the unsatisfactory nature – even to London – of the notoriously brutal Picton regime, which attempted to impose UK-style racism on the by then multi-ethnic (French and mulatto) planters and slaveowners.

In Trinidad the state police were established in 1834 when slavery ended. In 1864 local recruitment began and the paramilitary organization was strengthened, presumably to secure loyalty from the workforce. The organization was further reinforced in 1889 when the British army left the island. The political economy of these moves in terms of maintaining colonial order seems fairly transparent. The development of the Supplemental Police, and the private police in particular, was affected by a more complex set of pressures. The Supplemental Police Ordinance of 1906 created Estate Police, state authorized "in-house" police forces employed by owners of private property, but with full police powers not only in relation to suspected offenses and offenders on the property of their employer, but also throughout the division in which the estate or other property is situated. These privately hired police forces were – and are – under the control of the Commissioner of Police in two senses. The Commissioner has the authority to confer these powers on individual privately hired officers by means of a "precept"; in addition estate police (precepted officers) may be called upon by the Commissioner in emergencies (in effect by Divisional

Superintendents), at which times they fall under the jurisdiction of contemporary policing legislation and standing orders. The Commissioner is also responsible for the issue of Firearm User's Certificates, and these days the holding of a precept is deemed a prerequisite for a private security officer to be issued with such a certificate.

The main industries in Trinidad were oil, first discovered in commercial quantities in 1902 (Anthony 1985), and sugar, and already in the early years of the twentieth century the largest of these estates were foreign-owned. Local property owners and proprietors of less land-based commercial properties, however, also avail themselves of the opportunity to hire precepted estate constables under the 1906 Act. Until 1967, however, officers of private security firms were not eligible to be precepted since they worked not on the estate of their employer but on the properties of the firm's clients, where a precept would carry no authority. Lobbying by the two international companies operating in Trinidad in the post-war years, Wells Fargo and Brinks, led to the passage of Act 29 of 1967, whereby firms may apply to the Ministry of National Security for registration as Protective Service Agencies (PSAs).[7] Officers of registered PSAs may apply to the Commissioner for a precept in the usual way, and also for Firearm Users' Certificates, if the employing firm is appropriately licensed. However, their delegated police powers apply only in relation to those properties which they are contracted to protect: they do not have police powers throughout the division in which the property is located as in-house precepted officers do.

Further executive rather than legislative changes occurred after the brief coup d'état in 1990, when it was felt that the weaknesses of both in-house and private firms in relation to assisting the state police in such crises were revealed. The training and examination necessary to qualify for a precept were improved and formalized. Examinations are now held four times a year at police headquarters.

This history – as unique in the region as the oil by which it makes its living – means that the state in Trinidad and Tobago has considerable control over the quality of the workforce in security firms, where between 25 percent and 60 percent of the officers in the sampled firms were reported to be precepted.[8]

It also indicates that there have been global influences affecting the shape of private security in Trinidad for almost a century. The invention of this unique public–private partnership in security between the state and estate owners so soon after the discovery of land-based oil in a remote southwestern forest was plausibly not a coincidence.[9] British and American firms rapidly developed the industry, so that by the 1930s "most of the investment was in the hands of foreign companies" (Craig 1988: 18), with 5 of the 22 companies accounting for 88 percent of the output, most of it again sold on to the two foreign-owned refineries. By "1936 Trinidad produced 62.8 percent of the empire's oil" (1988: 20). Oil is still the major foreign currency earner for Trinidad and Tobago. The argument proposed is that indirect economic pressures to secure so valuable a resource in a relatively poor agricultural colony and in a region that in 1902 was a day and a half by boat from the capital (Anthony 1985) encouraged creative thinking about security. A less speculative history of that creativity has still to be written. It remains plausible to suggest, however, that "global" economic pressures shaped the form and structure of the state/private security relation in Trinidad and Tobago.

It is less speculative to argue that commercial security companies follow rapid economic expansion such as occurred in Trinidad as oil became commercially exploited. Why Brinks and Wells Fargo[10] wanted their men to carry precepts is unknown, since both firms have left the island and there was no one with knowledge of the institutional history whom I could interview. My guess is that over half a century a customer culture or expectation of private policing had developed based on the known examples, the in-house Estate Constables policing the sugar and oil industries. As industrialization by invitation proceeded after independence, and soap factories, chocolate factories, soft-drinks factories, and car-assembly plants were founded, their managers looked for the same level of protection as their oil and agricultural colleagues in the Chamber of Commerce. Added to this, the two US international security firms would have been accustomed to offering armed officers to their customers, yet without precepts they were unable to do so in Trinidad. Whether demand or supply led as far as their motives are concerned, two informants explained that it was international companies that led to the revision and extension of the practice of precepting to include Protective Service Agencies. Note too that the State gained less than the companies from the 1967 legislation: these PSA police would be of less value to the Commissioner than the in-house officers because they carry no police powers beyond the limits of their clients' properties, even in an emergency.

Today, indirect global economic influences affect private security, as well as direct, company-led policies. What will become clear in the following two sections is that these direct and indirect pressures affect different levels of the private security industry in different ways.

GLOBALITY AND GLOBAL INFLUENCES

Chief executives and other senior personnel from three international companies were interviewed, two in the course of the pilot study and one in the main study. These were the only international companies operating in the two islands. I also interviewed the senior manager in a formerly international company which is now wholly owned locally.

The preoccupying question in relation to international capital in the service sector concerns the direction of influence, in particular of cultural imperialism or the "McDonaldization" hypothesis. While analysis of other data sets from this study have called this notion of a unidirectional influence into question (Cain 2000a), the hypothesis remains a useful Aunt Sally, posing questions in terms of which the current situation may be described. These concern company structure, relative size, operational practice, and workforce organization.

Company structure is linked to the history of the two US companies trading in Trinidad in the 1960s: Brinks and Wells Fargo. Brinks, so well established that "brinksman" was still occasionally a generic term for security guard, sold up in 1991 to a syndicate in which a local bank (itself with a complex ownership structure) and a local manufacturing company each owned one-third, while a British-based security firm which was already operating in the island bought the remaining third.

The second American company to arrive in the island, Wells Fargo, was incorporated in 1965 as Wells Fargo of Trinidad and Tobago. In "1975, or '76 or thereabouts" this company too was bought out and became wholly locally owned.[11] Another respondent company bore the name of an American firm, and was affiliated to a security company in Barbados, which formerly also bore the US name but now carries a UK company name. The US firm, I was told, is "probably" the largest single shareholder in a group consisting of "one or two" other corporate shareholders and some "local shareholders." The company has been operating at least since the early 1980s.[12]

Moving in the opposite direction, another company which had originally traded locally subsequently became affiliated to a US-based security firm which currently owns a 25 percent stake and has one director on the board. The Trinidadian firm is now renamed, bearing both its original and the American title. Thus the analysis of company structure gives few clues as to influence, although on balance it would seem that the proportion of the capital in the security industry which is foreign-owned has probably declined since the mid-1960s.

These three remaining companies which are at least in part internationally owned are among the largest, one employing around 440 guards, another around 600, with no information as to size having been requested from the St. Lucian company. The now wholly localized company employs 350 armed officers, with a total staff of between 400 and 500 people, including administrative personnel. However, a more recently founded local company claimed "a guard strength of almost 1400 officers." During the fieldwork period this company beat off both its multinational and local rivals to secure a high-profile state contract. Big as they are, the three multinationals are neither the largest companies operating, nor are they necessarily the dominant players in the marketplace.

All three managers of multinational companies indicated that technical advice and support was the main input from the international name-giving company, and one reported also getting irrelevant information about thefts of "jewellery and valuables" abroad "which really doesn't enter our markets." One of my respondents had been responsible for the merger of the workforces of two international companies following the buyout of one of them. While the UK buyer called the technical tune on many issues, the interchange of cultural practices was by no means one-way. UK-based "parent" companies, for example, do not arm their personnel, yet in Trinidad and Tobago officers are precepted and bear arms, following the same strict rules about the storing and distribution of weapons and the checking in of ammunition as those with US "parents" and many local firms. Where vehicles are concerned one company insisted on the use of its own secure van design, while a St. Lucian company claimed that without design adjustments heavily armored vehicles would be inappropriate for the mountains, and that most companies therefore used a lighter, locally modified, semi-armored vehicle. In the company which merged the two workforces, there was resistance from the local officers of the firm "taken over" to the new parent company's insistence on the wearing of helmets (the temperature never falls below 80 degrees Fahrenheit in Trinidad and Tobago). In order to prioritize putting vital new cash-collection and delivery procedures in place, the local management of the new "parent" decided to leave the helmet question until later, only to find that their original staff had also joined the "helmet rebellion." Arguments such as that the workforce would only be covered by insurance if they did wear helmets were heard politely, but to no avail. "We failed to gain our point and we withdrew," said the manager.

The three points to emerge are: that local customs are likely to prevail over "foreign" practices when the local customs enhance the powers of the company either directly, as in the case of firearms, or indirectly by enabling it to respond to market demand; that "foreign" practices will be ignored if irrelevant, and abandoned if the cost in worker resistance is too high; and that a unionized workforce will adopt the practice, whether local or foreign, which is to the greatest advantage of its members.

This last point is well illustrated in the case of discipline. A local respondent company is held by the union to the official rate of fines, by now outdated and trivial: "not exceeding TT$5-00," less than the rate for an hour's work for a precepted officer. Other punishments allowed under the Supplemental Police Regulations include confinement to barracks and punishment drill. Both are expensive to the employer, who in the one case has to supply maintenance and in the other has to take an officer away from an "earning" task to direct the drill. "If you fine a man TT$5-00 from his TT$56 or TT$84 a day, he laughs at you." Foreign companies, also with a high proportion of precepted officers including those with individual membership of the union, use elaborate systems of warnings and proactive attempts to influence behavior, with an ultimate sanction of suspension. One manager (not the CEO) said:

> "I don't remember anyone being fined for any disciplinary action since I'm here with the company."
> MC   "So what do you do, then?"
> R   "They've always been suspended or they've been given a written...."
> [answer tails off and MC interrupts]

In another company the power to fine rests with middle management, while the power to suspend for up to 48 hours lies with supervisors, implying (though I did not ask) that this is the sanction in most frequent use. Suspension is not governed by the old regulations and conditions of service, and is therefore preferred by companies, while the elaborate system of warnings in all but extreme cases is preferred by the officers and accepted by the Estate Constables' Association (the union). In this case, therefore, the old colonial rules can be used to the workers' advantage in one case, modern (foreign) proactive management techniques in another. It is in the smaller companies which invest less in precept and other training, and have no experience of working with a union, and which may have insufficient staff to cover suspensions, where the workers lose out, as the penultimate section of this essay will argue.

The conclusion to this section is clear. Particular practices are welcomed, accepted, or rejected on an issue-by-issue basis – by both management, the workforce, and the union. *Direct* globalization provides technical and managerial resources. True, one manager a year may be sent to the UK for training. This is doubtless experienced as a privilege or a perk rather than cultural domination. Vehicles may be air-conditioned, whereas in northern climates this was not necessary, but in these direct contacts outcomes are negotiated, not unidirectional, and certainly not all sinister even from the workers' perspective. As far as direct globalization of the commercial supply of private security goes, the McDonaldization hypothesis is a dead duck.

Professional organization

In Trinidad and Tobago there is an active chapter of the American Society of Industrial Security (ASIS). ASIS has an international membership and, arguably, a global influence. It has, therefore, to be considered in this discussion of direct global influences. A few security managers in St. Lucia were members or attended meetings of the Trinidad chapter.

The first point to note about ASIS is that some of its members were passionate about security as a profession involving specialized skills relating to all aspects of personal safety and the security of the employer's property, including information. Advice as to procedures (and hardware) to prevent loss was regarded as central, so the second characteristic of note is the preventive ethos of the members. Thirdly, the members were aware of themselves as an elite group with a proselytizing mission to gain recognition for the security profession, and to raise both the status and the standards of the occupational group. Fourth, a high proportion of ASIS members were heads of in-house security departments with reasonably high levels of resources potentially at their disposal. Heads of firms who were ASIS members held similar views about standards but were perforce more market-driven in their service delivery. Finally, and valuably, from my point of view, because of the collective nature of professionalizing activities, the members were known personally to each other. They formed a close network, which most probably helped them in their work and certainly helped me to become familiar with the industry before I began cold-calling my random sample. Importantly, it brought in-house men (all my ASIS respondents were male) into contact with senior personnel of the firms.

ASIS was a globalizing influence in two ways: it facilitated networking with colleagues in the United States as well as in the Caribbean itself, and it brought global (or American) ideas about both management and security to the region. In this sense ASIS is facilitating a shift from overt and negative to covert and disciplinary power. If someone won't let you search their bag at the gate, don't attempt coercion or create a scene: all that is bad for business; the procedure is to report the person to their line manager, who will deal with it, again according to procedures (and perhaps by a closer surveillance). ASIS stands for order rather than confrontation, for predictable expenditure or procedures rather than for the lottery of dealing with trouble after it has occurred, and perhaps, in contrast with the oral traditions of Trinidad, for *agreed* measures of effectiveness rather than the excitement of permanently negotiable truth. Procedures for the movement of company property prevent losses: when an item is "removed from the location it was in to somewhere else where somebody wanted it to work . . . what we have here is a procedure then for the movement of company property that either didn't exist or was not adhered to" (in-house manager, July 1996).

A security problem has come up. It will be more effective to treat it as a matter of procedural inadequacy than as an attempted theft.

These ideas are promulgated among ASIS members by meetings and conferences with visiting speakers, and by educational programs. Several had attended an extra-mural program in security management run by the University of the West Indies, and when I was there a campaign was mounted (eventually successful) for a more permanent program. I was consulted about distance-learning degree programs out of the United Kingdom. Professionalization does involve openness to global influences. How these are being selected from or reinterpreted in the context my respondents did not say. Certainly no one said it was all foreign and irrelevant (as has been said of Western economics, sociology, and criminology). Equally certainly, ASIS offered its members a self-image, a way of understanding their very real expertise as of value, despite the low regard in which – as they told me – the security industry is held.

INDIRECT GLOBALIZATION: THE FIRMS AND THE FREE MARKET

Unemployment may have dropped back since the crisis years of structural adjustment, from the mid-twenties to the mid-teens in terms of percentages. But there is still a plentiful supply of literate but otherwise unskilled labor in Trinidad, as well as, following the privatizing of the state enterprises and the reduction of the workforce, a supply of underemployed lower-middle-class and working-class labor (see Moonilal 1997). On the other hand these same structural adjustment processes, via the creation of a criminogenic and unpredictably violent society,[13] have without a doubt generated a massive growth in the demand for private security. However, something appears to have gone wrong with this idyll of a free-market situation in which the demand for and the supply of labor grow together. Not only is the workforce unhappy, as we shall see, but so too are the security managers. The reason for this lies in the reduction of income of those involved in local productive enterprises resulting from the opening up of the market for commodities: producers under pressure want to pay less even for their existing level of security; it lies in the declining spending power, already documented, for those in the bottom half of society, the reduction in their monthly earnings coupled with the falling value of the Trinidad and Tobago dollar, that is, the reduction in what each of these fewer dollars will buy. The lower levels of the retail trade are affected by this, and they too want more security at the same or even a lower price. Middle-class homeowners, whose demand for security in the 1980s was relatively new, want to minimize the burden of this additional item on the family budget. Everyone feels the pressure after the gloriously spendthrift decade of 1973–83 when oil prices were booming and money was officially no object.

The outcome was and is competition on price. This is the point at which globalization – the global oil market, detrimental loan conditionalities set by a global agency – has an impact on the security industry. This indirect impact sharpens the polarization within the industry itself between the big companies, not all foreign, as we have seen, and the medium to very small firms.

Security is a labor-intensive industry. In all the companies I interviewed the guard force was the largest revenue-earner. Putting a guard out involves an investment: advertising for and checking the background of recruits (however cursorily), training, equipping, funding non-productive time (holidays, illness, maternity leave), and wages. Cutting back on these investments enables a firm to tender for work at a lower price. Thus training in the smaller firms might consist of one or two days familiarization with the work, whereas one large company boasted three regional sites for in-house classroom training as well as field-training officers, and others indicated regular refresher courses in centralized training schools.

All firms had two things in common. The first was a requirement that an officer attend, and pass, a six-week training program in order to be precepted by the Commissioner of Police, to be followed by an additional course in firearms training in order to be awarded a user's certificate. These central programs were well regarded but expensive. A precept empowers the officer in relation to a particular employer, and restricts his or her mobility; a projected change to a system of precepted individuals was viewed with concern, for the company bearing the cost of the training might not reap the commercial profits from a precepted officer who decided to change jobs. The second thing the interviewees had in common was a resentment of the "fly-by-night" firms, in this context those who "take people off the road and put them into uniforms" (interview, July 1996). This both gives them an "unfair" cost advantage and lowers the status of security work.

The cost of equipment varied. Some firms paid the full cost of a uniform, for example, whereas others asked the employee to meet up to 50 percent of the cost, and deducted the employee's share in arrears from wages. Some officers reported having to meet the entire cost of the uniform, while another firm felt that officers should buy their own boots. The argument for making the employee pay was usually that he or she would not take care of the uniform otherwise.

Officers working from vehicles – a small minority – could be held responsible for damage. Cutting back on the provision and maintenance of equipment is another way of cutting costs. Officers from one very large firm were found on site with bits of the uniform missing and with radios that did not function, though to be fair, the supervisor I was traveling with took immediate action to put this right (patrol, 1997).

In many cases, officers had to be employed for two years before becoming eligible for paid holidays, although one small firm gave two weeks' paid leave after one year. Although I discussed the gender of the workforce with both male and female CEOs and managers, no one raised the issue of maternity leave.

That leaves wages. Rates for unprecepted officers started at TT$3.50 per hour in 1996, but by 1997 a minimum wage of TT$5 had been introduced.[14] Some firms, however, started their rates as high as TT$5.50 or TT$6.00 per hour. Representatives of the Security Managers' Association of Trinidad and Tobago (SMATT) reported that the minimum wage was not policed and that undercutting persisted. Another CEO reported seeing a tender for a job charging TT$4 per hour for a man and a dog, suggesting a very low (and illegal) remuneration for the man. Talk of the dogs being paid more than the men was frequent among the officers. On the other hand, top rates of pay for precepted officers could go up to TT$12 per hour, and promotions also increased earning capacity.

The minimum wage did not, reportedly at least, prevent undercutting, so price competition was still a major problem at the time of my second visit. The second endemic problem was high turnover, ranging from 2.7 percent to 10 percent per month. Turnover among precepted officers was lower. By local standards they were well paid, and I saw them pointed out to young officers as "the estate constable," suggesting some prestige. Companies, having paid for their training, wanted to hold on to them. If they left it was for better pay and conditions within the security business. These officers were also entitled to join the union, the Estate Constables' Association, and while only one of the firms was unionized, there was a standard set here by the union's agreements with this firm and the in-house officers.

For the unqualified men high turnover was regarded as a part of life. "They come and go," said one CEO. "I always say no one tends to make security their career" (interview, 1997). Of 45 officers, only a third had been employed for three years. Larger companies are in a stronger position to attract and retain workers, but even there four to five years was regarded as a long-term recruitment. "This is a boring field, the guarding side of it, so you're not necessarily going to find someone to stay 20 years" (interview 1996). Larger companies, however, tended to offer better conditions of work, to locate officers at worksites near their homes, and to provide variation in the work experience itself.

In Trinidad and Tobago, there are two rival organizations of managers of private security. The dominant concern of these organizations (or at least of the one whose officials I interviewed) is to manage the marketplace for security and to create a "level playing field" for security companies in terms of running costs, pay and conditions of security staff, training requirements, and other personnel matters. This is presented as an effort to raise standards of service and to eliminate the questionable practices of "fly-by-night" firms. Such legislation – a draft bill has been in the ministerial pending tray for seven years or more – would put some of the undercapitalized companies out of business. Although neither the union nor the managers were happy with the bill as drafted, this cannot explain the lack of progress, for discussions between concerned parties have also fallen into abeyance. In my conclusion, I argue that in spite of the universal denigration of the "fly-by-night" firms, there is, in the context of glocalization, a symbiotic relationship between the small firms and the large ones, including those with multinational connections. Before I do that, however, I want to change perspective.

Glocalization and the security workforce

The indirect impact of global economic and ideational forces affects managers and employers, as we have seen, as competition becomes more intense. But the impact of global economic influences on the workforce at the bottom end of the market has been little short of disastrous. These are the men and women whose quality of life is the bargaining counter deployed by the companies. Social scientists do not have to adopt the management perspective, police perspective, or any other top-dog perspective (Becker 1970; Gouldner 1973: ch.2). I cannot claim to be able to have adopted the standpoint of the guards, as Moonilal (1997) and Trotz (1998) did, but I can ask myself why, when nurses, policemen (*sic*), coalminers, bakers, and secretaries have had their worldviews sympathetic-ally presented, security workers have so often been presented in the literature as the problem;[15] and surely in order to explore the downside of the glocal I must address the question: What does it actually mean, to be paid less per hour than a dog?

My rather lightweight data here (for me, too, the workers' perspective was an afterthought) were gleaned in casual conversations on patrol and elsewhere. I am confident about them because Moonilal's data were collected independently but in the same year, and either support mine or present an even worse situation.

If you are a person with a family who has lost a job, then you search everywhere for work. If you are unemployed without dependants then, in the context, you are not eligible for state benefit, and you too search everywhere for work. If you have no qualifications, or if your experience is deemed not to count (like housework, agricultural work), you search for a job in private security: you become a guard. This is not a career choice: this is rice and peas.

In such a situation of vulnerability, you will agree to go to work without the belt or the hat, or in a pair of pants that is not quite your size. You will agree to pay half or even the entire cost of your uniform (I talked to such men), not thinking what a hole that will leave in your pay packet. But when you do try living on the hole, you first of all look about to find ways of increasing your pay. In this way, you meet the needs of the undercapitalized firms at the bottom end of the market. You may, for example, agree to work on your leave day at very short notice, sometimes even responding to a call-in on that same day. Most men, according to their managers, prefer to work 12-hour shifts to boost their wages. By being willing to forego your leave day, you can increase your earnings to TT$420 per week – almost US$75 at current exchange rates (before deduc-tions for uniform and national insurance, that is). This is *not* a miscalculation on my part. You may be working your twenty-fifth successive hour (and I met someone who was) but the wage rate remains the same. Overtime is not paid by most firms. However, even in Trinidad US$75 does not go far towards paying the rent and running the car (essential if you work unsocial hours), let alone feeding and clothing a family and buying the school books. So if your boss asks you to "do a double" – to work two 12-hour shifts end on end, you may well agree if it is followed by 12 or even 24 hours before resuming work. I have talked to a man who was doing a double: it happens. But what the men minded most was not the hours, but the unpredictability of them. Twelve-hour shifts in themselves would not put paid to family life, but "doubles" and unpredictability both wreck the home. And the wife saying "I wouldn't mind, but all you get for it is $75."

Boring work, low pay, extremely unsocial hours, having to pay travel costs to unlikely work sites: if this were not enough, there is also the attempt at negative control of the workforce, the punitive disciplinary measures which have their strongest impact on unprecepted officers, who are not covered by the disciplin-ary regulations negotiated by the union for their members, the precepted staff. For these low-paid officers, even if they are earning the statutory minimum (and not all were), a standard fine of TT$75 for sleeping on duty takes them below survival level and into debt, probably again to the company who may agree to deduct the fine from future wages. A man working six 12-hour shifts at TT$5 per hour would earn TT$360 per week, no more than US$62 at a good rate of exchange; such a fine would reduce his income by between a quarter and a fifth, down to TT$285. Most fines are for lesser offenses, and carry lower fines. One company told me that TT$10 was their standard fine, although Moonilal's respondents reported TT$20 as the lowest fine, with TT$40.00 being the modal sum, and TT$300 being the highest reported. Some of the men I worked with told me that TT$100 was the standard fine for sleeping on the job, so my calculations above underestimate the problem. But as with the hours, it was the irrationality of the system that proved, all too often, the last straw. They felt that fining was in itself unfair; worse, you can be "fined for any little thing." Other men, arguing that their company "doesn't bother about the law," found their whole under-the-dog's-pay work experience outside of both legality and rationality.

From my point of view, too, the system, if it is that, seems irrational, since all these stopgap measures exacerbate the problems of high turnover which cost the firms so much. At some point, feeling unappreciated, underpaid, and harassed, and having still well over a year to wait for a holiday, a man (I spoke to no guard-level women) will simply stop coming to work, or be too tired to do so. Certainly the last thing these men need is for a foreign sociologist to add to the generalized denigration, to add to the chorus of those who berate them for pulling down the status of security work.

Rather, it seems to me, these officers[16] exemplify Bauman's concept of the glocalized worker. Struggling to make ends meet, to keep awake long enough to talk to the children, to maintain some self-respect in the face of life's abuse, these men have been locked into the local by global forces which have created security as the only growth industry in the island. They lack both the material and the cultural capital to move. Unless they have social capital – a relative living in Canada, say – they are doomed to drift from one dog-paid job to another, too tired and with too little time to educate themselves, and with an ever greater effort required to maintain self-esteem whether at home or at work. Locked into the local by globalization, the unprecepted security officer guards the homes of transcultural, globally free individuals and the physical capital of local global power. I admire him anyway: he trades no lethal powders, the harms he does are small; he dares sometimes to hope for something better; he makes a contribution. That is a lot.

In Conclusion

What, then, has this essay been about? First, I have argued that the structure and powers of the security industry in Trinidad and Tobago have historically been shaped by global economic and political forces. Today, however, direct global influences in the form of global companies do not necessarily have a deleterious, culture-imposing effect on those whom they employ or, indeed, on those whom they serve. Outcomes in relation to each cultural contradiction are negotiated separately, shaped by the powers of the various parties and the salience of the issue to them. When a major shareholder says he will withdraw his support and his highly marketable name otherwise, that is salient. When a workforce threatens industrial action, that is salient. Low-level "politics" goes on, and "McDonaldization" is revealed as at best a crude oversimplification of a complex and complicated situation, and at worst as a misleading and incorrect account.

Beyond these direct meetings of the global and the local, global economic and cultural forces impact upon societies in indirect ways. Not separate international industrial capitals, but abstract capital, operating through global agencies, is what reshaped Trinidad and Tobago's society in less than a decade. The message of this small case study for social scientists working in this area is that we may need to refocus our research to the abstract global rather than the transnational level of analysis, and develop the methodological tools with which to do it.

Thirdly, I have shown that abstract global capital impacts differently on, and creates different problems and opportunities for, different classes and sectors of society. Here, Bauman's concept of glocalization has captured the polarizing character of global economic processes. The polarization effected in Trinidad and Tobago was demonstrated, together with its results. The irreversibility of one of these results, the re-ordering of the social structure of criminality, was also discussed, indicating that a long-term need for a reordering of those relationships designed to secure the safety of people, possessions, and knowledges has been generated.

Only one of the many responses to this need was discussed here – the expansion of private security, not so much by expanding already existing firms as by a proliferation of "protective service agencies."

The reasons for this proliferation lie in the structural clash arising when a newly globalized market in capital and commodities meets an always localized market for unskilled labor, and in the price competition which results. Small and new firms compete from a lower cost base: the pressure on wages and conditions is downward. To the consternation of those firms which aspire either to economic globality or to professional globality, the pressures on standards of service and on social prestige are also down. Unskilled workers and employers are captured in a polarizing force which neither of them wants. Firms hold their own, restructure, find safe markets among their shareholders, and weather the storm. The unskilled workers survive, too. They take the breaks, freedoms, and clothes their employers do not give them by job hopping, by using the freedoms of their own localized marketplace for labor, which they cannot transcend.

The humanitarian problem is that it's "the poor wot takes the pain" – and the blame, too, in some accounts of private security. The political-economic problem is where and how to intervene to halt the process. The sociological/criminological problem is to go beyond analysis of the existing situation, to acknowledge that private security workers, at least in the Caribbean, are not so much villains as an exploited labor force, and to enquire how the radical insecurity of the lives of the security providers may be addressed.

This brings me to a methodological and substantive footnote. If we talk only to security managers, we will be directed to what *they* define as problems: self-evident. But their definition of security and insecurity may differ, for example, from those who define security as predictable access to adequate food, shelter, clothing, education, and healthcare. For many reasons we should not forget the problems of *class* just because we have discovered culture, race, and gender differences. It is class polarization that is going on in the world of security.

Secondly, security managers, like people of most social groupings, tend to present a fairly similar worldview based on their experiences. They blame their troubles on market forces, yes, but specifically on "fly-by-night" companies as the demons of the marketplace, coming and going, not subject to law, and constantly undercutting and undermining the honest traders.

In spite of some limited experience of disappearing security companies (the one that closed down between appointment and interview; the premises with a phone number outside that was never answered; the company I spotted by chance and then could never find again), in my judgment the predominance of "fly-by-night" companies at the bottom end of the market is a myth. My own respondents, from larger companies and ASIS members, though the smaller firms also alluded to them, assessed the "fly-by-night" numbers as from 100 to 120, or even 150 – more than twice as many as the 57 listed in the *Yellow Pages* (Moonilal (1977) had a similar experience). I would then tell them that I really wanted to talk to the managers of such firms. Only one respondent suggested a name, and that was a company listed in the *Yellow Pages*. Commercial organizations know their rivals. This inability to name names suggests to me that I was forcing them to concretize a mythology. This mythology is used to account for the difficulties of all the firms, irrespective of size. It saves then from naming each other, while supplying a demon for whom no one is responsible to explain their difficulties – a demon, indeed, far more abstract than the global forces which continually structure their marketplace, forces which they could not be against because they live by them too.

The (mythical?) "fly-by-night" firms, and, indeed, the smaller firms from whom their real competition comes, are symbiotically of value to the big firms in other ways:

1 The rhetoric against the "fly-by-nights" enhances the status of the big boys.
2 The rhetoric also provides them with a clear statement of what they are not, assisting them to understand what they are, or what they are for, in the process.
3 "Fly-by-night"/small firms provide staff – or at least sustain them through unemployment – in an ever-circulating labor pool.
4 "Fly-by-night"/small firms protect the commercial poor. If they did not do this, the polarization of safety standards in the society would be even more glaringly exposed, with unknown consequences for the larger firms.
5 "Fly-by-night"/small firms bear the scapegoat's burden of illegal practice. The eye of the seeker after injustice (?me) is turned on them, and other social harms as a result remain unexplored.

Oddly, then, although it creates their diurnal difficulties of price competition and staff retention, glocalization and its mythologies may sustain the power of larger capitals in the private security field.

Notes

1 An earlier version of this essay was presented at the British Society of Criminology Annual Conference, Keele University, July 17–20, 2002.

2 Some of the results of this study are discussed in Cain (2000a, 2002b).

3 The American Society of Industrial Security, members of which figured disproportionately in my pilot "chain."

4 *Annual Statistical Digest*, 36, 1989, Central Statistical Office, Port of Spain, Table 4, pp. 82–3.

5 *Annual Statistical Digest*, 38, 1991, reanalyzed for Sampson 1994, Table 10, p. 31. Central Statistical Office, Port of Spain.

6 Harriot (1996) has described an ever-more dramatic restructuring of crime in Jamaica.

7 Information given by a respondent. Security managers argue that the "add-on" nature of these provisions means that security firms are still governed by inappropriate legislation, designed for a different employment situation (field data).

8 Moonilal (1997), however, argues that "the bulk" of security officers are unprecepted, and working in unregistered firms. Moonilal interviewed a larger proportion of officers from small firms than I did. My *Yellow-Pages* sampling frame biased my sample in favor of the larger and relatively stable firms (although one went out of business between making the appointment and the date of the interview). My respondents gave a range of 25–60 percent of officers precepted.

9 The first oil well was drilled as early as 1867, but oil in commercial quantities was discovered in 1902. In 1938 Sir Stafford Cripps wrote in *Tribune* that the oil company directors were "the real Governors of Trinidad" (cited in Craig 1988: 18).

10 Source: interview data. It is noteworthy, and contrary to any clear-cut economistic interpretation, that this international company pulled out just two years into Trinidad's most prosperous decade, following the oil-price rise of 1973.

11 Interviewee's report.

12 At the pilot stage, I still had not realized how important accurate historical information would be.

13 See Harriot (1996) for evidence that in similar circumstances there has been not just an absolute increase in violence, but also an increase in the proportion of acts of violence which are directed against strangers.

14 Between my first and second field trips, a minimum wage of TT$5 per hour was introduced. The TT$3.50 referred to here was legal at the time it was paid.

15 Nigel South's early contribution to this field (1988) abandoned the attempt to work with the workers in favor of an historical and theoretical overview, and this has perhaps defined the field.

16 Some of the officers actively sought my help in publicizing their plight.

References

Anthony, M. (1985) *First in Trinidad*. Port of Spain: Circle Press.

Bauman, Z. (1998) *Globalization*. Cambridge: Cambridge University Press.

Beck, U. (2000) *What is Globalization?* Cambridge: Polity.

Becker, H. (1970) Whose side are we on? In H. Becker, *Sociological Work*. London: Allen Lane, 123–34.

Bennet, R. (1991) Development and crime: A cross-national time-series analysis of competing models. *Sociological Quarterly*, 32(3), 343–63.

Cain, M. (2000a) Through *other* eyes: On the limitations and value of Western criminology for teaching and practice in Trinidad and Tobago. In D. Nelken (ed.), *Contrasting Criminal Justice*. Aldershot: Dartmouth, 265–93.

Cain, M. (2000b) Orientation, occidentalism, and the sociology of crime. *British Journal of Criminology*, 40(2), 239–60.

Cain, M., and Birju, A. (1992) Crime and structural adjustment in Trinidad and Tobago. *Caribbean Affairs*, 5(2), 141–53.

Craig, S. (1988) *Smiles and Blood: The Ruling Class Response to the Workers' Rebellion in Trinidad and Tobago*. London, New Beacon Books.

Durkheim, E. (1952) [1895] *Suicide: A Study in Sociology*. London: Routledge.

Gouldner, A. (1973) *For Sociology*. London, Allen Lane.

Harriot, A. (1996) The changing social organisation of crime and criminals in Jamaica. *Caribbean Quarterly*, 42(2–3), 54–71.

Moonilal, R. (1997) Trade unions and the informal/unregulated sector: The case of the private security industry in Trinidad and Tobago. Ph.D. thesis, Cipriani Labour College, Trinidad and Tobago.

Sampson, J. (1994) *Report of the Cabinet Appointed Committee to Examine the Juvenile Delinquency and Youth Crime Situation in Trinidad and Tobago*. Port of Spain: Ministry of Social Development.

Shaw, M. (2000) *Theory of the Global State: Globality as Unfinished Revolution*. Cambridge: Cambridge University Press.

South, N. (1988) *Policing for Profit*. London: Sage.

Trotz, A. (1998) Guardians of our homes, guards of yours? Economic crisis, gender stereotyping, and the re-structuring of the private security industry in Georgetown, Guyana. In C. Barrow (ed.), *Caribbean Portraits: Essays on Gender Ideologies*. Kingston: Ian Randle, 28–54.

Waters, M. (2000) [1995] *Globalization*, London, Routledge.

23

The Rise of the Surveillant State in Times of Globalization

Thomas Mathiesen

In 1985, an important meeting was held in the small town of Schengen in Luxembourg. Germany, France, and the Benelux countries met to sign the so-called Schengen agreement. The purpose was to establish a free zone of travel between the countries and, as a control measure intended to balance this freedom, intensified common-border control against third countries. Enhanced police cooperation to balance off the internal freedom to travel was also envisaged.

In 1990 the five countries again met in Schengen, to sign an implementing convention, afterwards called the Schengen Convention.[1] The Schengen cooperation was established for European Union (EU) member states, but during the first years it formally existed outside of the EU. At that time, the principle of flexibility, allowing given member states to stay outside common arrangements, had not yet been developed, and it was clear that Britain and Ireland wished to maintain their own national border controls.

As time went on, other EU member states joined the arrangement. In 1995 it became operational in seven member states, and at the EU summit in Amsterdam in 1997 it was formally integrated into the EU structure. Norway and Iceland, though outside of the Union, became associated members, and as of 2001 the arrangement was operational in 15 European states.

The arrangement has enormous proportions. The so-called Schengen Information System, the SIS, is its heart and brain: A common database has been established in Strasbourg, with identical national databases in all of the participating states. On a single day in 1998, there were 8.8 million entries of information in the SIS.[2] On a single day in the same year, close to 800,000 persons (in addition to objects) were in the SIS, aliases not included.[3] Since then, figures have increased considerably because the SIS has become operational in more states. Police authorities frequently claim that Schengen deals with the detection and prevention of serious organized crime operating across national borders. As

I shall document later, this is rather far from the truth: Toward the end of the 1990s, close to 90 percent of those registered in the SIS were entered pursuant to Article 96, so-called "unwanted aliens."[4] This is why Schengen often is referred to as "Fortress Europe." Some of the unwanted aliens may have committed crimes, but hardly the large bulk of them, and certainly not very serious crimes.

In 1997, close to 50,000 police and border-control computers across Europe had access to the system.[5] Today, the number of computers is still higher. Information about a person, which is fairly standardized (name and forename, date and place of birth, sex and nationality, whether the person concerned is armed, whether they are viewed as violent, reason for the report, and action to be taken), is entered into the SIS according to national legislation. But any and all of the other states may take the information out according to *their* national legislation. Information about persons entered by a given state may therefore be widely diffused and scrutinized throughout Europe.

Though Britain still maintains her own border controls, the country has decided to participate in the Schengen Information System. Wide categories of persons may be registered in the system (Articles 95–99 in the Schengen Convention): Persons wanted for arrest for extradition purposes, aliens who are reported for the purposes of being refused entry ("unwanted aliens"), people who have disappeared or persons who need provisionally to be placed in what is called "a place of safety," witnesses, persons summoned to appear before judicial authorities or who are notified of a criminal judgment or of a summons to serve a custodial sentence, and persons who are to be subjected to "discreet surveillance."

If a person is subjected to discreet surveillance (Article 99), further information may be communicated about him/her to the police of another country who have entered the alert in the SIS for discreet surveillance. For example, information about passengers may be communicated. The conditions under which a person may be subjected to discreet surveillance are partly rather precise, but also partly extremely vague, opening up discreet surveillance of broad categories of people. For example, in Article 99.2 it is stated that discreet surveillance may be used "where there are real indications to suggest that the person concerned intends to commit or is committing numerous and extremely serious offences." This is a fairly precise formulation. But then the text goes on to say "*or* [my italics] where an overall evaluation of the person concerned, in particular on the basis of offences committed hitherto, gives reason to suppose that he will also commit extremely serious offences in the future." This is a vague and open stipulation ("overall evaluation," "gives reason to suppose"), in addition to being exclusively oriented toward possible – quite hypothetical – future acts.

Furthermore, Article 99.3 opens up discreet surveillance of political behavior: It states that "a report may be made in accordance with national law, at the request of the authorities responsible for State security." In plain Norwegian, "authorities responsible for State security" means the intelligence services. Such reports may be made when "it is necessary for the prevention of a serious threat by the person concerned or other serious threats to internal or external State security." The content of "other serious threats," presumably not created by "the person concerned," is unclear, to say the least. It must necessarily involve persons other than "the person concerned," that is, persons other than the person who is targeted for discreet surveillance. Most likely, it involves a circle of associates of "the person concerned." There is not one word in Article 99.3 about offenses or qualified criminal acts. Article 93, which defines the general purpose of the SIS, explicitly refers to the maintenance of "public order and security, including State security," as a main goal, conceptualizations which certainly may cover political protests of various kinds. I shall return to the issue of political surveillance later.

In short, the background for storing information in the SIS is wide and discretionary, many items of information are evaluative, and "discreet surveillance" opens up political surveillance and surveillance of a wide circle of individuals around the main person.

The various regulations clearly raise data protection issues. The Schengen Convention contains rules regulating data protection in the SIS. There are rules concerning information quality and rules concerning application security. The problem, however, is that the rules are demonstrably inefficient: The Joint Supervisory Authority (JSA) of Schengen is weak in terms of influence and sanctions, the police and legal cultures throughout Europe, which constitute the contexts of Schengen practice, vary greatly, so that common rules are practiced differently,[6] and modern technology develops by leaps and bounds, making rules obsolete even before they are enforced. As regards the Joint Supervisory Authority, it states in its official report for 1999–2000 that "[e]ver since the convention was implemented on 26 March 1995 the JSA has had an uphill struggle in getting its competence and independence recognized by the decision-making bodies of Schengen."[7] As an example of the problems involved, it may be mentioned that in late 1997, secret SIS documents with sensitive personal information were found at a train station in Belgium. The documents were accessible to everyone who passed by. Sensitive material was also seized in the apartment of a Belgian who had been arrested. Needless to say, the affair created a big stir, but in any case it showed the impotence of the various control measures.[8]

In addition, checking information quality in many cases presupposes access by the person concerned. Such access is limited. The right of a person to have access to data relating to him or her is to be exercised in accordance with national law (Article 109.1), and national law throughout Europe may vary in this respect, not necessarily providing access to police registers. Furthermore, there are broad obligatory exceptions in the convention itself (Article 109.2): Access shall be "refused if it may undermine the performance of the legal task specified in the report or in order to protect the rights and freedoms of others." The police decide whether it "may undermine the performance of the legal task." Furthermore, access shall "be refused in any event during the period of reporting for the purposes of discreet surveillance." In practice, a person does not have much of a chance when confronting a system of this kind.

In short, a gigantic police-run surveillance system is currently developing in Europe, reaching from Iceland in the north to the Mediterranean in the south, from Portugal's shores in the west to Polish border in the east.

THE SIRENE SYSTEM

And Schengen does not stand alone. First, the SIS has an auxiliary system and practice of information exchange which may be called *the Sirene system*. Each member state has a so-called Sirene office, in charge of administering the SIS, and between the Sirene offices information supplementing the standardized information in the SIS may be exchanged. The Sirene system is not even mentioned in the Schengen Convention, nor is it regulated there.

While the information contained in the SIS is fairly limited, a vast amount of information may be exchanged through the Sirene system, including very personal information and so-called "soft data." Thus, in Norway, the Ministry of Justice has officially stated that information which is in the many national databases of the police may be exchanged.[9] The Ministry views this as a consolation, because national police registers are permitted and regulated pursuant to Norwegian law.[10] The question is whether it is such a great consolation: The national databases of the police are full of sensitive information. A single example from one part of one Norwegian national database, the database concerning police data on foreigners, may be given (the information is taken from the relevant police manual in 1999[11]): The database includes registration number, registration date, police office code, identification (birth) number, citizenship, passport number, ethnogroup, country of origin, sex, name/alias, address, telephone, height, age, bodily features, date of death, hair, language/dialect, spouse (with name and identification number), occupation, position, employer, information about automobiles, information about close acquaintances, persons who are closely tied to the person, the person's history ("should provide a brief history of the person's escapades; . . . supplementary information should be entered as time passes"), as well as "soft info" ("information we don't wish others to see"). Add to this information concerning where the person comes from, "in order for us in the future to take out information about a whole nationality."

The operation of the Sirene system is detailed in a secret manual, which is continuously updated.[12]

EUROPOL

Secondly, there are the Europol Computer Systems. In contrast to Schengen, Europol does in fact deal with serious organized crime. At the same time, the data-protection problems are even greater than in Schengen. Europol became operational in 1999, and has three important computer systems:

1   A *central information system* with standardized data about sentenced people and suspects, as well as about possible future offenders within Europol's competence. We should note the diffusely future-oriented character of the system.
2   *Work files for the purposes of analysis.* These are special, temporary work files set up for the analysis of specific areas of activity. The files may contain extensive personal data, not only about persons registered in the central information system, but also about (quotes from the Europol Convention[13]):
    – possible witnesses ("persons who might be called on to testify");
    – victims or persons whom there is reason to believe could be victims ("with regard to whom certain facts give reason for believing that they could be victims");

– "contacts and associates"; and
– informants ("persons who can provide information on the criminal offences under consideration").

In short, a very wide circle of individuals loosely tied to persons who have been sentenced or are under suspicion.

3 *An index system* which enables one to find one's way around the vast amount of information.

Let us look more closely at the second of these levels, the work files. The kinds of personal information which may be stored in these are not specified in the convention, only in so-called "implementation rules," given pursuant to the convention. As an example of the kinds of personal information for which the work files are designed, mention should be made of a proposal presented in 1996 concerning supplementary information of a highly personal and intimate nature (my emphasis):

> It shall be forbidden to collect personal data *solely* on the grounds that they relate to racial origin, religious or other beliefs, sexual life, political opinions or membership of movements or organizations that are not prohibited by law. Such data may be collected, stored and processed only if they supplement other personal data stored in the analysis file and only where they are absolutely necessary, taking into account the purpose of the file in question.[14]

The important word here is "solely." It will be seen that the proposal in fact *opens up* for inclusion of data about "racial origin, religious or other beliefs, sexual life, political opinions or membership of movements or organizations that are not prohibited by law."

Later, the proposal went through various new editions, following criticism by the European Parliament. But the final formulation still opens up the inclusion of such intimate personal data. The implementation rules applicable to analysis files states:

> Europol shall also specify in this order whether data related to racial origin, religious or other beliefs, political opinions, sexual life or health may be included in the analysis work file, . . . and why such data are considered to be absolutely necessary for the purpose of the analysis work file concerned.[15]

With regard to contacts and associates, victims, possible victims, possible witnesses, and informants, such data can only be included after special grounds are given and upon the explicit request from two or more member states. In practice, these limitations are not particularly strict. For other categories of persons, no such limitations are given.

The implementation rules applicable to work files allow the processing of around 70 (at least 68) types of "personal data, including associated administrative data," about persons registered in the central information system. The personal data are grouped into 12 categories, and they are:

"Personal details" (14 types of data);

"Physical description" (2 types of data);

"Identification means" (5 types of data; including forensic information such as fingerprints and DNA evaluation results, though "without information characterizing personality");

"Occupation and skills" (5 types of data);

"Economic and financial information" (eight types of data);

"Behavioral data" (8 types of data; including "Life style [such as living above one's means] and routine," "Danger rating," "Criminal-related traits and profiles," and "Drug abuse");

"Contacts and associates" (subtypes not specified);

"Means of communication used" (a wide range of means given as illustrations);

"Means of transport used" (a wide range of means given as illustrations);

"Information relating to criminal activities" under Europol's competence (8 types of data);

"References to other data bases in which information on the person is stored" (6 types specified, including "Public bodies" and "Private bodies");

"Information on legal persons associated with the data referred to" under economic and financial information and information relating to criminal activities (10 types of data).[16]

To reiterate, the above-mentioned types of data may not only be included about persons registered in the central information system, but also about possible witnesses, victims, or persons whom there is reason to believe could be victims, contacts, and associates, and informants.

People working in Europol have immunity within the EU, and though it is denied by Europol authorities, the Europol police force is said to be rapidly approaching the status of a European FBI.

EURODAC AND ENFOPOL

Thirdly, there is the Eurodac system,[17] a European "central register" where fingerprints and other information about all asylum seekers in Europe over 14 years of age is entered and stored for a period of 10 years. There are only two exceptions: Information about persons who have attained citizenship is to be deleted, and information about persons with formal refugee status pursuant to the UN Convention relating to the status of refugees is to be kept for a shorter period, and is only to be used for statistical purposes. Fingerprints are also to be entered for all so-called "illegal immigrants." The Eurodac register is supposed to facilitate the enforcement of the so-called Dublin Convention determining the state responsible for examining applications for asylum within the EU.[18] In fact, the register contains possibilities for the surveillance of large population groups in Europe.

In the fourth place, there are the Enfopol papers, documents produced from inside the EU structure containing far-reaching plans for interception and storage of telecommunication data – telephone, fax, e-mail, and the Internet. The contents of the Enfopol papers were first revealed by the internet journal *Telepolis*.[19] The planning of interception and storage of telecommunications data started in the early 1990s, as a collaborative effort between the EU and the American FBI. Accordingly, the British civil liberties bulletin (and organization) *Statewatch* refers to it as "the EU–FBI complex,"[20] and as focusing on criminal justice issues. In this respect, it is different from the Echelon system, which is a regular spy system, also engaged in industrial espionage and involving the United States, Britain, Canada, New Zealand, and Australia as the main participating states. Echelon appears to be able to take down vast amounts of telecommunications data from satellites, finding relevant information by means of a system of codewords. It is uncertain how far the technology has come; what is certain is that Echelon exists and that the technology is developing rapidly. A report to the European Parliament by the journalist and researcher Steve Wright may be quoted to indicate the activities of Echelon:

> A wide range of bugging and tapping devices have been evolved to record conversations and to intercept telecommunications traffic.... However, planting illegal bugs...is yesterday's technology.... [T]hese bugs and taps pale into insignificance next to the national and international state run interception networks.... Modern technology is virtually transparent to the advanced interceptions equipment which can be used to listen in.... Within Europe, all email, telephone and fax communications are routinely intercepted by the United States National Security Agency, transferring all target information from the European mainland via the strategic hub of London then by Satellite to Fort Meade in Maryland via the crucial hub in Menwith Hill in the North York Moors of the UK.... The ECHELON system works by indiscriminately intercepting very large quantities of communications and then siphoning out what is valuable using artificial intelligence aids like Memox to find key words. Five nations share the results.... Each of the five centers supply "dictionaries" to the other four of key words. Phrases, people and places to "tag" and the tagged intercept is forwarded straight to the requesting country.[21]

Three features characterizing these and other systems should be emphasized: First, the systems are becoming increasingly integrated, showing the contours of a vast, interlinked surveillance system. Secondly, insofar as crime detection and prevention are the goals of the systems, their success is mediocre. So-called organized crime across national borders easily escapes the kinds of control which the systems contain. Thirdly, in addition to picking up petty offenders and certainly masses of foreigners defined as "unwanted aliens," the systems may be used in a broader political effort to stall political protest and enhance what the establishment would call public order.

A few further comments on these three features are called for.

INTEGRATION WITH THE SIS

The various systems are established as well as operated by the same or professionally very similar organizations and agencies. When Schengen was formally outside the EU, planning was organized so that essentially the same people could discuss Schengen issues in one meeting and other issues in the next. It is also possible to be more specific. I select Europol as an example.

The Europol system was clearly planned with a view toward far-reaching integration, inter alia, with the SIS. For one thing, Article 10.4 No. 1–3 in the Europol Convention established a whole range of authorities and bodies within the EU from which Europol could request information: The European Communities and bodies within them governed by public law, other bodies governed by public law established in the framework of the EU, and bodies based on an agreement between two or more member states within the EU (also, Article 10.4. No. 5–7 established that information could be requested from international organizations and subordinate bodies governed by public law, other bodies governed by public law based on an agreement between two or more states, and Interpol). Clearly, this opened up integration with the SIS. As a matter of fact, on April 9, 1997, before Europol was operational, the High Level Group on Organized Crime explicitly recommended that Europol should be given access to the information stored in the SIS.[22] This and other recommendations were on the agenda of the Justice and Home Affairs' council meeting on December 3–4, 1998 in connection with the action plan on establishing a so-called area of freedom, security, and justice, and were also discussed in a report of February 26, 1999.[23] The report, inter alia, discussed the issue of whether Europol's authority should be extended to actual searches in the SIS (pursuant to the Europol Convention Article 3 (1) point 2, Europol has the task to obtain, collate, and analyze information and intelligence, but no authority to search).

Furthermore, concrete work directed toward facilitating and easing compatibility between Europol, Schengen, and other systems has been going on for a long time. The then Norwegian liaison officer at Interpol, Iver Frigaard, outlined a number of the issues, problems, and possible solutions in a lengthy paper as early as 1996.[24] Frigaard saw Europol, Schengen, and Interpol as three "mutually interlocking" and "overlapping" policing initiatives. He discussed their relationship on a systems level and on the level of exchange of information in concrete cases. On the systems level he pointed to the fact that by 1996 "only" 10 of the 45 states linked to Interpol's information system were also linked to Schengen and Europol. The number of states linking up to all three systems should and could, he argued, be increased. In connection with the exchange of information in concrete cases, he pointed to a lack of harmonization of the various data systems, and discussed what he viewed as the great need for compatibility between them, as well as how compatibility might be attained technologically. The vigorous tenor of the paper clearly suggested that this was a matter of high priority.

It may be added that at its meeting on March 19, 1998, the JHA (Justice and Home Affairs Ministers of the Member States) Council agreed, without debate and as an "A" point, on rules allowing Europol to request and accept information from non-EU sources (pursuant to Article 10.4. No. 4 of the Europol Convention). The report covered the receipt of data from "third States and third bodies" (a relevant country was Turkey), and included only the most minimal safeguards on data protection. The plans were to be supplemented by a series of "memorandums of understanding" between Europol and the central services of each of the non-EU states with whom data were to be exchanged.

CRIME DETECTION AND PREVENTION

When it really gets going, Europol may have some success in the detection and prevention of serious organized crime. This success will, however, probably be very moderate: As alluded to already, so-called organized crime across national borders easily escapes the kinds of control which Europol and other systems contain. Insofar as they exist, "organized criminals" are professional people who are able to circumvent many of Europol's and other systems' policing efforts.

As also alluded to earlier, as far as Schengen goes we have concrete data. Statistical information from Germany, as well as statistical information and reports from Schengen itself, show that the Schengen system of cooperation to a very large extent is focused on identity papers and unwanted aliens, such as asylum seekers who have been refused entry and have gone underground.

For one thing, this comes out in a 1995 report from the German Ministry of the Interior.[25] The report showed that close to 70 percent of the 2.3 million information records (*Datenzätze*) which up to that time were entered in the SIS by Germany alone, concerned unwanted aliens and identity papers. Close to 90 percent of the persons who were registered were entered pursuant to Article 96 in the Schengen Convention, concerning aliens who are reported for the purposes of being refused entry. Some of these may have committed serious, traditional crimes, but surely not the majority. The same report reviewed the Sirene system, which goes into greater detail, and which indicated that the aliens to a large extent were asylum seekers who had been refused entry in Germany, and who had gone underground.

Similarly, a look at a report from the German Ministry of the Interior about the Schengen Cooperation in 1996[26] shows that of the 4.2 million requests for information during 1996, 62 percent concerned unwanted aliens or identity papers. The second largest category were requests concerning motor vehicles, which amounted to 20 percent. The third largest category concerned forged bills, which amounted to 13 percent, while 4 percent were requests concerning weapons. Of the 4.2 million requests that year, over 476,000 concerned persons. Of these, 413,000, or 88 percent, were requests pursuant to Article 96 concerning unwanted aliens. The Annual Report of the Central Group in Schengen, dated March 26, 1996, is somewhat less clear because of ambiguities in data collection, but it gives the same overall picture.

The Annual Report on the State of Affairs along the External Schengen Border during 1996, published on March 20, 1997, tells the same story, only more clearly so. The report points to several technical problems relating to the border control, especially in seaports (less so at airports), and details some of the problems for the individual countries. By way of introduction, it emphasizes the struggle against cross-border crime and illegal immigration as two functions of the external border control. When going into detail, however, the report says nothing about serious control of cross-border crime. Rather, the returning of third-country citizens to third countries, the control of visas, forged documents, and so on, are reported. Crimes in a traditional sense may be hidden in this material, but they are hardly conspicuous. A total of 563,423 control actions are reported at the external borders: 41 percent concerned refusal of entry from third countries, 28.5 percent concerned third-country citizens apprehended without a residence permit near the border, 24.5 percent concerned the returning of third-country citizens to third countries, 3 percent concerned third-country citizens in possession of forged documents, and 0.5 percent concerned "apprehended people smugglers" (*festgenommenen Schleuser*). In addition, 4.8 percent were unclassifiable due to unreadable reports. It appears abundantly clear that the crux of the matter is a policy of shutting out aliens. It also appears that insofar as the apprehension of organized people-smugglers is a Schengen goal, Schengen border control is close to a failure. The fact that the crux of the matter is a policy of shutting out aliens has remained systematically uncommunicated by the media and the authorities. That the crux of the matter is such a policy, is also abundantly clear from an important and honest report from the Belgian Sirene office, entitled *The Schengen Information System and its Implementation in Belgium* (1994). But the Belgian Sirene report also shows, most importantly, that the policy of shutting out aliens is intimately related to the maintenance of public order and state security. The two aspects of Schengen are two sides of the same coin: In line with Schengen thinking, aliens currently constitute what is believed to be a primary threat to public order and state security.

The Belgian report explicitly states that the SIS is not a "criminal police service", but a service responsible for the control of all aliens who have been or will be refused entry into the Schengen territory. In more detail, we are told that the SIS "is not meant to replace or imitate Interpol," and that the two are "totally different." While the purpose of Interpol, the report says, is to coordinate "the combating of crime," the purpose of the SIS is "to guarantee the security within the Schengen countries; thus, all aliens to whom the entry is to be refused are introduced into the S.I.S" (p. 39). The connection between control of aliens and maintenance of public order and security is abundantly clear.

In addition the SIS is, according to the Belgian report, responsible for storing information about persons in general who are supposed to threaten state security: The last quote given above continues as follows: "as well as persons reported by the State security." Such persons may also be aliens, including aliens who reside in the Schengen countries, but they may of course also be other kinds of "troublemakers."

POLITICAL PURPOSES

This brings us to the third and final feature of the systems in question: The use of them *for political purposes*. The danger is imminent that such a use will develop. In the recent past we have seen how Schengen in fact has been used politically:

- In September 1998 it was reported that a Greenpeace activist who had protested against the French nuclear armament tests in 1995 was declared unwanted in France. For that reason she was barred entry into Schengen territory at Schiphol Airport in Amsterdam. The decision was made pursuant to Article 96 in the Schengen Convention, concerning unwanted aliens.[27]

- Several Norwegian demonstrators who were arrested and deported during or after the EU summit in Gothenburg, Sweden, in June 2001 (and who had done nothing wrong except be there), were addressed by Swedish police officers with a gleeful "Welcome to Schengen!" Whether they were actually entered in the system is uncertain; at least, Schengen was used as a serious threat.[28]
- In early December 2001 a Swedish citizen and member of a legal Swedish left-wing party was helping his Belgian friends paste up anti-EU posters in Brussels, advertising an anti-capitalist meeting previous to the EU summit in Laeken. Pasting up posters without a permit is illegal in Belgium, and for this he was arrested and expelled from the country, as well as subjected to a general Schengen ban in all Schengen countries except Sweden. In other words, he was not allowed to travel through any of the other 14 Schengen states (including the neighboring Nordic countries). The Belgian police gave two reasons for the expulsion and the general Schengen ban: First, that the Swede did not carry a passport (passports are not required for travel within Schengen territory, but useful for the obligatory registration in hotels); secondly, and with reference to Article 96 in the Schengen Convention concerning unwanted aliens, he had caused "serious problems for public order." The Swede had done nothing except paste up posters. Swedish police authorities responsible for Swedish cooperation in Schengen were "astonished" at the fact that the imposition of the Schengen ban had no time limit.[29]

These are, to repeat, some examples from the recent past, and they are only the beginning. The September 11, 2001 onslaught on the World Trade Center and the Pentagon in the United States spurred a feverish activity the world over in designing new systems, rules, and regulations for the prevention of terrorism, and in investing existing systems, such as the ones I have described, with new powers.

- After September 11, 2001 the US Patriot Act, the British Terrorist Act, and similar German, French, and other national legislation within the EU were rapidly put into place. The legislation in question implies serious infringements on the civil rights of citizens.
- The core of the problem is the wide and diffuse definition of "terrorism" which now is being developed. The EU as such has on short notice provided us with a proposed definition of this kind, covering a highly diffuse and wide range of political protests. A process of compromise involving the EU Commission, the EU Parliament, and the JHA Council had taken place in advance, resulting in a long list of acts and offenses. The problem, however, is the definition of a "terroristic purpose," which makes a given act or offence terroristic – with all its legal and social consequences. The JHA Council of ministers agreed politically on a definition of a terroristic purpose on December 6–7, 2001,[30] and a large majority in the EU Parliament supported it on February 6, 2002. It reads as follows:

i) serious intimidation of a population, *or* ii) unduly compelling governments or international organizations to execute or to abstain from executing any act, *or* iii) seriously destabilizing *or* destroying the fundamental political, constitutional, economic or social structures of a country or an international organization. (my emphasis, my translation)

What does "serious intimidation of a population" mean? Were the demonstrators who probably intimidated people at the EU summit in Gothenburg, or for that matter Council members present there, terrorists? What does "unduly compelling governments...to execute or to abstain from executing *any acts whatsoever*" (my emphasis) refer to? Certainly, the environmentalist movements such as the activist movement Greenpeace, or the anti-nuclear power movements, try to compel relevant governments to abstain from executing something, and they do so in a manner which often is defined by the authorities as "undue." What does "destabilizing" a structure mean? Certainly, and whether we like it or not, some demonstrators in Gothenburg and Genoa had "destabilization" in mind. Were they for that reason terrorists? I can think of many legitimate groups and people who wish to "destabilize" given economic or social structures, for example, structures where some people on top run the whole game and the rest of society is characterized by destitution and poverty. Today, structures of this kind often develop and thrive on the basis of global capitalism, a major target of attention of demonstrators at the summits. The definition of purpose is very open indeed. Some reservations in No. 10 of the Preamble and in a Council Statement do not sharpen the definition substantially or satisfactorily.

- On December 27, 2001 the Council adopted (under Article 15 of the Treaty on European Union) a so-called "common position on combating terrorism,"[31] which says (Article 4) that measures "shall be taken to suppress any form of support, *active or passive*, to entities or persons involved in terrorist acts" (my emphasis). The implication is that no line is drawn between those who actively engage in terrorist support, and those who may agree with their political aims but take no measures to help them. Suppression may be wide-scale indeed. People far outside of any reasonably narrow definition of terrorism may now be stigmatized and treated as "terrorists." Europol, which had terrorism as part of its mandate before September 11, 2001, will be engaged in the investigation of "terrorism" in this broad and diffuse sense.
- In the EU there is also agreement on a European arrest warrant, involving the arrest and surrender of EU citizens between the member states. Planning started long ago, but was greatly speeded up after September 11, 2001. Political agreement on the European Arrest Warrant was reached at the JHA Council meeting on December 6–7, 2001, supported by a large majority in the EU Parliament on February 6, 2002. Demands for arrest and surrender are to be entered as alerts in the SIS.
- There are plans to extend the SIS to cover "potentially dangerous persons" who are to be prevented from entering countries for "sports, cultural, political or social events." Suspects will be tagged with an alert on the SIS. *Statewatch* reports that a new database on the SIS is in the pipeline.[32] If the Norwegian demonstrators in Gothenburg in June 2001 referred to above were not entered into the SIS at that time, they will at least be entered when and if this extension of the SIS is adopted and they appear at a different summit site.

- There are also plans to extend the SIS to cover all "foreigners" who have not left Schengen territory within the "prescribed time frame," that is, when their visas expire. Again, *Statewatch* reports that a new database on the SIS is in the planning.[33] These plans interlock with fingerprint registration in the Eurodac system, tightening up the total surveillance system.
- Both of the latter extensions are noted in the post-September 11 EU "Anti-terrorism Roadmap," version November 15, 2001, to "Improve input of alerts into the SIS."[34]
- In the name of terroristic threats, Article 2 (2) in the Schengen Convention, which makes the reclosing of national borders possible on short notice, is now being invoked to bar demonstrators from crossing the borders to countries hosting EU summits and other top-level meetings.[35] To be sure, there may be "troublemakers," prone to throw bricks and bottles, among those who want to get in, but are they for that reason "terrorists"? Anyway, most demonstrators are ordinary people who want to express their opinion. Also, many of them will easily be barred from entry. During the World Bank Summit in Oslo in June 2002, a number of foreign demonstrators were stopped at the border and checked as to whether they were registered in the SIS.[36] No such registrations were found, but the checking shows that the SIS was used for political purposes. Several of the demonstrators were refused entry.
- An initiative of the Spanish Presidency of the EU Council introducing "a standard form of exchanging information on terrorists" was adopted as "A Point" (withtout discussion) by the Competitive Council of Ministers on November 14, 2000. The proposal had six drafts; the first two referred to "violent radical groups with terrorist links," the third changed this to "exchanging information on terrorists." But the content and intent did not change. The first two drafts, in clear reference to the demonstrations in Gothenburg and Genoa in 2001, state that information should be exchanged on "incidents caused by radical groups with terrorist links...and where appropriate, prosecuting violent urban youthful radicalism increasingly used by terrorist organizations to achieve their criminal aims, at summits and other events...."[37] But there have been no terrorist attacks at EU summits or other international meetings held in the EU, only political protests.
- The SIS is going to be technologically modernized and streamlined into a SIS II, with, inter alia, a far greater information capacity. This has long been in the pipeline, but has recently been greatly speeded up.[38]
- These are only a few of a number of new Schengen plans, or plans speeded up, in the wake of September 11, 2001. A number of further reforms of the SIS are proposed, such as opening the SIS for use by a number of public and private authorities (whatever is the meaning of the latter), thus integrating the overall system further. Specifically, an opening of the SIS to intelligence services is being proposed (since such services already do have access, the meaning here is probably a more efficient and easier access).[39]
- As early as September 20, 2001, nine days after the World Trade Center and Pentagon events, the JHA Council met and, inter alia, requested the European Commission "to submit proposals for ensuring that law enforcement authorities are able to investigate criminal acts involving the use of electronic communications systems and to take legal measures against their perpetrators."[40]

To be sure, the JHA Council also said that it would make "a particular effort to strike a balance between the protection of personal data and the law enforcement authorities' need to gain access to data." In effect, however, such powers to law-enforcement authorities would require, inter alia, all communication providers to retain data from telephone calls, e-mails, faxes, and so on. This relates directly to the Enfopol plans mentioned earlier.

- In 2002, a secret proposal (not yet adopted) to make the retention of telecommunications traffic data mandatory for a period of 12 to 24 months in all member states was revealed by *Statewatch*.

So we could go on. It is very important to note the following.

On the one hand, measures of this kind will not stop actual terrorists like those who were responsible for the World Trade Center and Pentagon events. Such persons are far too professional, and certainly able to maneuver to avoid the measures and to be ahead of them. In late December 2001 a man was caught on board an American Airlines plane with explosives in his shoe. Notably, he was caught by resourceful flight personnel and passengers *after boarding and when the plane was in the air*, not in advance by any of the great number of refined information or registration systems.

But the measures which I have outlined in this essay will, on the other hand, easily prevent and silence legitimate political protests. Ordinary protesters defined as "terrorists" will be vulnerable and easily subject to extensive surveillance. They will easily be scared to silence. We are seeing the contours of a new McCarthy era, only with global dimensions. This way, the measures strike at the core of our democratic rights and civil liberties.

Notes

Many thanks go to Nicholas Busch, the editor of *Fortress Europe?* and Tony Bunyan, the editor of *Statewatch*, for generously providing me with extensive information and many comments useful for this essay. Information on the development of surveillance after September 11, 2001, which is discussed in the later part of this essay and which may be of particular interest, is extensively covered on *Statewatch*'s website at http://www.statewatch.org and in *Statewatch Bulletin*. This essay was finalized in May 2003.

1 Convention of June 19, 1990 applying the Schengen agreement of June 14, 1985.
2 *Statewatch Bulletin*, May–August 1999, 22.
3 Ibid.
4 Ibid.
5 *Statewatch European Monitor*, 1(1), 1998, 30, with full text reference to Report dated September 1997 from the SIS Steering Committee.
6 Examples may be found in *The Schengen Information System. A Human Rights Audit*, issued by the human rights organisation JUSTICE, London, 2000.
7 Schengen–Joint Supervisory Authority: *Fourth Annual Report on the Activities of the Joint Supervisory Authority, March 1999–February 2000*. SCHAC 2533/1/00 REV 1, pp. 6.
8 Ibid. In addition, Press Release of the Joint Supervisory Authority, December 1997, and Danish *Information*, December 3, 1997.
9 Bill No. 56 (1998–9), pp. 66–8.

10 Ibid., pp. 123–4.

11 Further details may be found in Thomas Mathiesen: *Siste ord er ikke sagt. Schengen og globaliseringen av kontroll* ("Last Word is Not Yet Said. On Schengen and the Globalization of Control"), Oslo: Pax Forlag, 2000, 48–50.

12 For further details, see ibid., pp. 44–5.

13 Convention of July 26, 1995.

14 Proposal for rules applicable to analysis files, January 4, 1996 4038/96 Europol 2.

15 Official Journal of the European Communities: Council Act of November 3, 1998 adopting rules applicable to Europol Analysis files (1999/C 26/01) Article 5.2.

16 Ibid., Article 6.2.

17 Council Regulation No 2725/2000 of December 11, 2000 concerning the establishment of Eurodac for the comparison of fingerprints for the effective application of the Dublin Convention.

18 "Convention of June 15, 1990 Determining the State Responsible for Examining Applications for Asylum Lodged in one of the Member States of the European Communities," in force September 1, 1997.

19 See http://www.telepolis.de/tp/deutsch/special/enfo6329/1.html.

20 In various issues of *Statewatch Bulletin*.

21 S. Wright, *An Appraisal of Technologies of Political Control*, PE 166.499, January 6, 1998, pp. 18–19, revised ed. September 1998.

22 See doc. 7421/97 JAI 14.

23 6245/99 Europol 7.

24 I. Frigaard, Police Cooperation: Current Problems and Suggestions for Solutions in Interstate Police Co-operation in Europe. Paper delivered *at the Fourth Schengen Colloquium: Schengen and the Third Pillar of Maastricht*, European Institute of Public Administration, Maastricht, February 1–2, 1996.

25 Report from the German Ministry of the Interior, Fall 1995.

26 Delivered to the Federal States in June 1997.

27 See *Statewatch Bulletin*, September–October 1998.

28 Statements by several demonstrators, reported in Öyvind Brungot Dahl et al. (eds.), *Göteborg 14. til 17. juni 2001–15 norske beretninger fra EU toppmøtet* (Gothenburg 14 til 17 June 2001–15 Norwegian Accounts from the EU Summit). Oslo: published by the authors, 2001.

29 The reliable Swedish daily *Dagens Nyheter*, December 11, 2001; news release from fredpax@online.no and vlerner@interpac.net

30 Brussels, December 7, 2001, 14845/1/01 DROIPEN 103 CATS 49.

31 *EC Official Journal* L 344 28, December 2001.

32 *Statewatch Bulletin*, November–December 2001.

33 Ibid.

34 Ibid.

35 E.g., during the Nobel Peace Prize ceremony in Oslo, Norway, fall 2001, and during the World Bank meeting in Oslo in June 2002.

36 Statement in the Norwegian Parliament, July 5, 2002, by the Minister of Justice, Odd Einar Dørum.

37 Statewatch.org/news/2003/apr/16spainterr.htm

38 Memorandum to the Swedish Parliament, November 22, 2001, communicating 22 proposals from the EU Chairmanship to the EU Council on the upgrading of the operations of the SIS.

39 Ibid.

40 Conclusions adopted by the Council (Justice and Home Affairs), Brussels, September 20, 2001, Point 4.

24

The Politics of Crime Statistics

WILLIAM J. CHAMBLISS

Statistics on crime are indispensable for the criminologist. Variations in crime rates between countries cry out for explanation, as do changes in crime rates within a country. But all too often criminologists uncritically accept as fact data provided by government agencies with a vested interest in showing crime rates as high or low in light of political considerations. In the United States this problem is particularly acute since the nation's major law-enforcement agency, the Department of Justice, controls the gathering and reporting of virtually all data on crime and criminal justice. These data, although widely used by criminologists, are often driven more by political and administrative considerations than by concern for accuracy.

There are two major sources of crime data in the United States, both of which are controlled by divisions of the Department of Justice: the Uniform Crime Reports (UCR) published by the Federal Bureau of Investigation (FBI), and the National Criminal Victim Survey (NCVS), a nationwide survey conducted by the Census Bureau, the results of which are reported by the Bureau of Justice Statistics.

The overall trends in crime reported by the UCR and the NCVS often contradict one another. For example, in October 2000 the FBI issued a press release stating that the downward trend in violent crime had "leveled off" between 1999 and 2000 (US Department of Justice 2000: 1). The media picked up the story and it was dutifully reported by newspapers and on television across the country. In June 2001 the NCVS reported that between 1999 and 2000 the crime rate had continued its 27-year decline: "The number of criminal victimizations estimated for 2000 is the lowest ever recorded since 1973 when the NCVS (National Criminal Victimization Survey) began" (Bureau of Justice Statistics 2001: 4). Contrary to the FBI report, the victim survey found that violent crimes dropped by 15 percent and property crimes decreased by 10 percent between 1999 and 2000. How can we explain this discrepancy between the FBI news release and the findings of the NCVS? To answer this we must examine how the FBI obtains its data and the systematic biases built into their reports.

The Uniform Crime Reports

The oldest established source of national data on crime rates and trends in the United States is the annual publication of the FBI's *Uniform Crime Reports* (UCR). These reports are based on data supplied to the FBI by local police departments, and include information on crime trends, the seriousness of crime, expenditures on criminal justice, arrest data, and data on the number of people employed in police work.

The FBI is masterful in disseminating its information. News releases are carefully prepared to highlight the most alarming statistics that can be culled from the Reports. These releases are sent to every newspaper in every city and hamlet of every state and to news outlets in other countries. The report itself is widely distributed and is constructed so as to give the media ready access to crime clocks, graphs, and tables designed to spread the FBI's propaganda. The media, for its part, uncritically accepts the data provided by the FBI as uncontestable fact. In reality the FBI reports are neither uncontestable nor fact.

In its reports and news releases the FBI resorts to gimmicks and tricks to make the problem of crime appear as threatening as possible. The first few pages of the annual UCR contain a "crime clock" that purports to show how frequently claims occur. This is done through a picture of a 24-hour clock. How often a crime occurs is shown in seconds and minutes. In 1999, for example, the UCR clock showed a murder occurring every 27 minutes, a forcible rape every 6 minutes, a robbery every 59 seconds, a burglary every 13 seconds, etc. (FBI 1998: 4). Rendering the data in this manner is designed to exaggerate the seriousness and frequency of crime. To make these alarming statements the FBI combines virtually every imaginable type of offense, including minor offenses and attempted, but not completed, crimes. A report that sought to convey honestly the real state of crime in the country would not combine attempts and minor offenses with the most serious offenses. Furthermore, the number of crimes per second or minute obviously depends on the size of the population. Imagine what a similar chart in China, India, or Indonesia would look like.

The FBI does not distinguish between attempted and completed crimes: "Generally, attempts to commit a crime are classified as though the crimes were actually completed. The only exception to this rule applies to attempted murder wherein the victim does not die" (FBI 1984b: 12). In most years the FBI and local police departments are under pressure to increase the reported number of crimes in order to buttress their budgetary requests for more personnel and more funding. Occasionally, however, political pressure mounts to show a decrease in crime in order to show that the police are effectively controlling crime.

The UCR is consistent in only one thing: the tendency to distort and mislead. In 1992 the front cover of the UCR showed a graph. Under it, the words "Crime in the United States" appeared. The line of the graph went up from the bottom left-hand corner to the top right-hand corner. Clearly, the cover was designed to depict the crime rate as accelerating rapidly. The data provided to the FBI, however, told a very different story. The crime rate for most major crimes had *declined* by 4 per 100,000 inhabitants for all offenses and by 5.1 per 100,000 in the homicide rate. To discover that the crime rate declined, however, required looking past the cover, past the introductory statements, and past the crime clocks. Something few politicians, journalists, and even many academics bother to do.

COUNTING CRIMES

Homicide

The FBI selects for its crime reports data that will show the highest crime rate possible. For example, they do not distinguish between murder and non-negligent manslaughter but group the two very different types of crime under the single category "homicide." Most states and the federal government define murder as "the intentional killing of a human being." The FBI, however, chooses not to report the murder rate but to combine murder and "non-negligent manslaughter." Non-negligent manslaughter is "death due to injuries received in a fight, argument, quarrel, assault, or commission of a crime" (FBI 1984c: 6). The category "homicide" then includes both intentional and unintentional deaths. In the reports the FBI frequently refers to the homicide rate as the "murder rate," which it is not. In 1999 the UCR reported 13,194 murders in the United States for 1998. Without the inclusion of unintentional deaths, the murder rate would be substantially lower, although we cannot know how much lower, because the FBI does not release these data.

Furthermore, the instructions from the FBI to local police departments state that if a police officer finds a dead body and believes the cause to be murder or non-negligent manslaughter, the event is to be recorded as homicide. It matters not if the next day the coroner says it was suicide or the prosecutor determines that it was justifiable homicide or accidental death. It was and remains a murder for the purposes of the UCR: "Do not count a killing as justifiable or excusable solely on the basis of self-defense or the action of a coroner, prosecutor, grand jury, or court.... For UCR purposes, crime counts are based on law enforcement investigation" (FBI 1984b: 6). That the FBI's combining non-negligent manslaughter with murder to come up with a "homicide" rate confounds the real murder rate is suggested by the fact that the number of convictions for murder every year is considerably less than the reported homicide rate. In 1999, for example, the FBI reported 15,530 homicides in the United States but there were only 11,430 convictions for murder in state and federal courts (Maguire and Pastore 2000: 418, 453). For the purposes of criminological research, convictions would be a better, though far from perfect, estimate of the murder rate than the rate reported in the UCR.

In their ceaseless effort to justify expending more and more money on crime control, US politicians and law-enforcement agencies like to compare the US murder rate with that of other countries. It is accepted as "truth" by most criminologists as well as politicians that the United States has a murder rate many times greater than the murder rate in other industrialized countries. In a speech at the National Press Club, former Chief Justice of the Supreme Court, Warren Burger, fanned the flames of fear and called for tougher laws against criminals by claiming that Sweden and Denmark, with a population of 12,000,000 people, have fewer homicides than Washington, DC with a population of 650,000 (Burger 1981).

Because of differences in how murder rates are calculated, comparing the murder rate in Scandinavian countries with that in the United States is little more than political rhetoric. In addition to the problems with the way homicide rates are counted in the United States, there is a difference in how homicide and murder rates are recorded. Sweden and Denmark, like most European countries, report murder and homicide rates based on health statistics as determined by an autopsy, making comparison with US data reported by the FBI meaningless.

Crimes in general

The Uniform Crime Reporting Handbook instructs police departments to count each person who commits a crime and each victim as a separate incident. If five men are fighting with five others, the police report ten aggravated assaults. If three men are involved in one carjacking, it is counted as three carjackings: "If a number of persons are involved in a dispute or disturbance and police investigation cannot establish the aggressors from the victims, count the number of persons assaulted as the number of offenses" (FBI 1984c).

The instructions do not require that the legal definition of assault be met in order to be reported as an "assault." A simple "dispute or disturbance" is sufficient to be counted as an "assault." Remember, in this context, that no charges need ever be brought: police officers do not arrest someone for assault simply because they are involved in a "dispute or disturbance." Failure to make an arrest, however, does not keep the incident from being reported as a crime (in this case a violent crime) known to the police.

FBI data are misleading also because the categories used in the UCR are not uniform from one jurisdiction to another and changes in reporting policy by the police and the FBI confound the meaning to be attached to the data. Burglary, for example, is legally defined in many states as the use of force for breaking and entering, but the FBI instructs local police departments in all states to report the crime of burglary simply if there is unlawful entry. Merging unlawful entry with breaking and entering makes statistics on "burglary" ambiguous and, of course, *increases* the number of burglary offenses reported.

Structured distortions

J. Edgar Hoover was a master at manipulating public opinion. He held the media in the palm of his hand and fed them whatever served his interests. For years Hoover even went so far as to claim that the FBI did not cost the taxpayer anything since it recovered more in stolen property than its annual budget. To accomplish this astonishing result Hoover relied on the FBI's enforcement of the Dyer Act. The Dyer Act (1919) made the interstate transportation of stolen cars a federal crime: "sponsors of the law were primarily concerned with full-time commercial car thieves, [but the FBI] soon turned its attention to the far easier task of prosecuting and imprisoning young men who were stealing cars on a casual, spur-of-the-moment basis" (Subin 1965: 2). Over 90 percent of automobile thefts are "joyrides." The car is stolen, driven around for usually less than 24 hours, and abandoned. These cases are "solved," not by remarkable police work, but by locating the abandoned car. The FBI, however, counted the recovery of all stolen vehicles as part of the cases they "solved."

According to Harry Subin, a professor of law at New York University: "the whole federal auto-theft program was part of a fraudulent effort by Hoover's FBI to polish its image. It's clear that Dyer Act investigations are of primary importance in the Bureau's evaluation of its overall accomplishments" (1991: 4). In addition to demonstrating the diligence of the FBI in solving serious property crimes, the huge number of automobile theft cases handled by them enabled Hoover to claim that the FBI was *profitable*. By counting the estimated cost of stolen automobiles returned to their owners as money "returned to the government" the FBI could claim that it returned more money to the government than its appropriation. Unless you assume that all the vehicles returned by the FBI were government-owned, it is nothing but sleight-of-hand accounting to claim the cost of automobiles returned to their owners as money "returned to the government." A scam of this nature perpetrated by the CEO of a bank would be considered outright fraud.

J. Edgar Hoover established a tradition that has been followed by every Director of the FBI since. When Louis J. Freeh was appointed Director, he addressed the nation over C-Span, National Public Radio, and the Internet. In his address he pursued the same distorted, misleading, alarmist approach to the crime problem that served so well his many predecessors: "The rate of violent crimes has increased 371 percent since 1960 – that's nine times faster than our population has grown. In the past 30 years, homicides have nearly tripled, robberies and rapes each are up over 500 percent, aggravated assaults have increased more than 600 percent." Freeh came up with these alarming statistics by carefully choosing a year that had one of the lowest homicide rates in 60 years and comparing it with a year that had the highest reported homicide rate in that same period. Even using the FBI data on homicide, which is, as we shall see, highly suspect, a more honest depiction of changing homicide rates would show that it ebbs and flows from year to year. Equally, one could select 1992 to compare with 1978 to demonstrate that the homicide rate actually went down in the 14-year period preceding Freeh's appointment as Director. But this comparison would not serve his interests, nor the interests of the ever-hungry-for-expansion bureaucracy he heads.

Police and prosecutors' charges

In the United States over 90 percent of the criminal cases brought to court are settled by a guilty plea. The is obtained through a bargaining process in which the prosecuting attorney confronts the accused with the charges brought against him or her and warns of the possible dire consequences if the person is found guilty of these charges. In order to expedite the case, the prosecuting attorney offers to accept a guilty plea to a lesser charge that carries with it a less severe punishment than the charges brought by the police. Knowing that plea-bargaining will take place, police officers and prosecutors exaggerate the charges in order to ensure that the defendant will be disadvantaged in the bargaining process. The official statistics, however, report the *most serious crime* charged against the defendant, not the crime for which the defendant pleaded or was found guilty. The crime initially charged is most often fabricated to increase the bargaining power of the prosecutor and increase the likelihood that the defendant will plead guilty to a lesser charge. The charge brought does not reflect the reality of what transpired. A case in point is that of Willie Butts (a pseudonym) who was arrested late at night walking down an alley in Jacksonville, Florida. Butts was charged with "possession of controlled substance (crack), resisting arrest with violence and battery of law enforcement officer." The report written by the officer making the arrest states:

> The investigation revealed that on 06-06-87 at about 0020 I saw a vehicle drive to the 800 block of X street from Y. Its lights off, stopped and talked to someone. The person drove off in less than one minute. I then drove to that area without lights. When I saw someone walk up to my vehicle, I turned on my lights to confront the suspect. As I began to exit my vehicle, the suspect reached into his front left pocket, pulled out a crack pipe and cigarette pack and threw it behind him to the ground. As I attempted to place the suspect against my car, he threw another object across the top of my car. When I attempted to search the suspect, he tried to reach in his pants pocket again. When I blocked him, he fought with me in an attempt to run. After the suspect was secured, I found a penknife in his left pocket. I then found a piece of crack cocaine in the cigarette pack which the suspect threw earlier. (Chambliss and Holman 1994: 3).

The defendant pled guilty to possession of crack cocaine: the charges of battery on a law enforcement officer and resisting arrest with violence were dropped. The official report to the FBI, however, contained the more serious charges, "Arrest with violence and battery of a law enforcement agent." The fact that, in all likelihood, the prosecutor would not have been able to obtain a conviction given the police officer's report of what actually happened, is irrelevant to the crime statistic. The reality of what actually transpired, as revealed in the words of the police officer, does not correspond with the official statistic reported, nor does it reflect the real nature of the crime. Multiply this case by hundreds of thousands of others reported by local police to the FBI and "dutifully reported" in the UCR and you have some idea of how grossly distorted are the crime statistics which form the basis for the media and public image of crime.

Property crime

The FBI report includes theft of any object as a Type I or very serious crime. The crime rate is drastically skewed by including these offenses since they are by far the most common crime committed. Here again, the FBI uses every trick available to exaggerate the extent and seriousness of the crime. In most jurisdictions a distinction is made between felony theft and misdemeanor theft. Felony theft in most jurisdictions requires the theft of something valued at over $159. Not so for the FBI. They report as felonious theft "the unlawful taking, carrying, leading, or riding away of property from the possession or constructive possession of another." Since (a) theft accounts for more criminal events than any other crime and (b) petty thefts are much more common than felony thefts, the FBI statistics grossly distort the reality.

Local police are not above manipulating the data to suit their own purposes. In Washington, DC when Nixon wanted to demonstrate that his "get-tough-on-crime" policies would lower the crime rate. The Chief of Police rallied his officers to lower the crime rate: "Either I have a man who will get the crime rate down in his district or I'll find a new man" (quoted in Seidman and Couzens 1974: 482). At the time, theft of anything over $50 was categorized as a felony. In the year following Nixon's use of Washington as a demonstration city, police officers began reporting most thefts as property valued at $49 and did not report these to the FBI, even though the instructions from the FBI said they should. In this way Washington's official crime rate declined dramatically after the "get-tough" policies. The Chief "found the man" who would get the crime rate down, if not the incidence of it.

In New York in the 1990s, after Rudy Giuliani was elected Mayor he made a concerted effort to "clean up the City." He instructed the Police Commissioner to rid the streets of panhandlers, homeless people, and people at stop lights with squeegees who offered to wash car windows. That done, he instructed the Commissioner to lower the crime rate and, voilà, the crime rate was lowered. Public opinion polls showed that people felt safer, and the Mayor was given credit for reducing crime. Victim surveys, which give a much more reliable measure of changes in crime rates than police statistics, showed no difference in the crime-rate trends before and after Guiliani's campaign. It was politics that changed the official crime rate reported by the police, not any real difference in the amount of crime. Seeing the wonderful (political) results in New York, other cities quickly followed suit and crime rates declined in Los Angeles, Houston, Chicago, and Detroit in the following years. That the crime rate declined across the nation in an orderly fashion from one large city to the next is so unlikely that it defies logic.

A 1982 study of how the police in Indianapolis constructed crime rates found that the rates were made to fluctuate according to whether those in political power wanted the rates to go up or down (Pepinsky and Selke 1982). The Indianapolis study echoes the Seidman and Couzens findings from Washington, DC when the police chief "got the crime rate down" in response to Richard Nixon's decision to use Washington, DC as a "demonstration city" to show how his "war on crime" was effective (Seidman and Couzens 1974).

Just as the police and prosecutor can escalate charges brought against suspects, they can also downgrade the charges. Burglary can become trespass, aggravated assault can become simple assault, and even murder can be classified as "accidental death." Roland Chilton has shown that in New York deaths classified by the police as caused by an accident went up by 40 percent when deaths reported by the police as homicides declined (Chambliss and Chilton 1998).

Murder by strangers

Faced with police departments in some of the nation's largest cities (New York, Chicago, Houston, and Los Angeles) reporting lower violent crime rates for the first time in decades, the FBI reacted quickly to attribute the lower crime rates to increased numbers of police officers and longer prison sentences. But these claims are belied by the facts. Victim surveys show that violent crime has been declining in the United States since 1973: long before the increase in the number of police officers, mandatory sentences, and longer prison sentences (see table 24.1).

To further fan the flames of fear, the FBI attempts to counterbalance the good news of lower violent crime rates with data designed to sustain the fear of crime: namely that (1) people are in more danger than ever of being victimized by strangers and (2) demographic changes in the most criminogenic population foretell a crime wave in the near future.

The FBI sent a news release to media outlets across the United States in 1994 claiming that for the first time murders were more often committed by strangers than acquaintances and that the percentage of murders committed by non-family members had increased:

> Historical statistics on relationships of victims to offenders showed that the major-
> ity of murder victims knew their killers. However, in the last few years (1991
> through 1994) the relationship percentages have changed. In 1994, less than half of
> murder victims were related to (12 percent) or acquainted with (35 percent) their
> assailants. Thirteen percent of the victims were murdered by strangers, while the
> relationships among victims and offenders were unknown for 40 percent of the
> murders. (FBI 1995)

The *Washington Post*, along with newspapers across the country, reported in a front-page article headed "The New Face of Murder in America: Family Slayings Decline; Fewer Cases Solved; Killers Are Younger," that the "number of people killed ... by unknown persons has grown in the 1990s" (Thomas 1995: A04).

Table 24.1 Violent crime rates in the United States, 1973–2000 (per 1,000 persons aged 12 or over)

Year	Violent crime rate	Year	Violent crime rate
1973	47.6	1987	43.9
1974	47.9	1988	44.0
1975	48.3	1989	43.2
1976	47.9	1990	44.0
1977	50.3	1991	48.7
1978	50.5	1992	47.8
1979	51.6	1993	49.0
1980	49.3	1994	51.1
1981	52.2	1995	46.0
1982	50.6	1996	41.5
1983	46.4	1997	38.7
1984	46.3	1998	35.9
1985	45.1	1999	32.8
1986	41.9	2000	27.9

Source: Bureau of Justice Statistics 2001.

The FBI news release and the media's knee-jerk reproduction of the findings is a classic case of law-enforcement propaganda masquerading as fact. The increase in "murders by strangers" is a statistical artifact accounted for in part by an increase in unsolved murders. Between 1991 and 1994 the number of murders where the police made an arrest dropped by more than 5 percent compared to the preceding 10-year period.

A second reason why there appears to be more "murder by strangers" is due to an increase in murders resulting from "drive-by shootings." The police categorize these as "murder by strangers." But the fact is that drive-by shootings often are brought about by turf battles between competing gangs selling drugs; the chances are very good that the assailant was well known to the victim, well known enough to be killed for competing or "snitching" on those who shot him.

The FBI news release, which was also reported by newspapers including the *Washington Post*, goes on to state that "In 1965, nearly a third of the murders in this country were family related . . . [but by] 1992, a little more than one out of 10 of the nation's homicides were family related" (1995). The *Post* quotes Gilford S. Gee, a contributor to the UCR, who noted: "Criminologists and sociologists used to point to the fact that most murders were committed by family members or acquaintances . . . . That was indeed the case, but no longer" (1995).

The *Post* accurately reported the data it received from the Justice Department. But the Justice Department fails to point out that the number of *unmarried* couples living together has increased dramatically in recent years: from 1980 to 1997 the figure increased over 260 percent to over 4 million such couples (Bureau of the Census 1998). If a live-in boyfriend kills his partner the FBI does not report it as murder by a family member. The decline in murders by family members is explained by the fact that more people living together are not married. Furthermore, the proportion of unmarried couples living together is highest in the poorest social classes, precisely where the greatest likelihood of murder among family members takes place.

Thus the FBI claim that family and acquaintance murders no longer constitute the majority of homicides is erroneous. FBI data show that in 1994, 47 percent of all murders were of family members or acquaintances. Assuming that the unsolved murders contain the same proportions, then the observation by criminologists and sociologists that most murders are between "family members or acquaintances" is as true today as it ever was.

Selective reporting

Comparing selected years with dramatic increases in crime is another "dirty trick" used by law-enforcement agencies and politicians in order to manipulate public opinion. In the 1994 UCR, for example, the FBI presented a comparison of homicide rates between 1991 and 1994 which showed an increase in "stranger" homicides for those years. In fact, a comparison of 1991 and 1994 was about the only comparison that would have shown the increase in stranger homicides the FBI sought.

In 1980 the FBI reported that in 36 percent of homicides the assailant was unidentified. The rate drops to 27 percent in 1985 and rises again in 1988 to 33 percent. In fact, the 1996 rate remains lower than the 1980 rate (see FBI 1981, 1986, 1989, 1995).

In the FBI news releases there is no mention of the fact that the category of *substantiated* stranger homicides, that is, the number of homicides where it was determined that the assailant was a stranger, has remained fairly constant. With little fluctuation through the years, the figure now stands at 15 percent, the same as 1980 (FBI 1997: 17). Since these data will not serve to fan public paranoia about crime, the FBI prefers to draw faulty conclusions about the nature of unknown murder assailants.

Teenage "superpredators"

In addition to raising a false alarm about a dramatic increase in "stranger murders," the FBI and local law-enforcement agencies periodically point to allegedly dramatic increases in the number of crimes committed by juveniles. Citing FBI sources, the *US News and World Report* published a warning in 1970 that the nation was experiencing an "explosion in Teen-age crimes":

> Deep worry is developing among the nation's leaders over juvenile delinquency that seems to be getting out of hand across the United States. More youngsters are getting arrested every year – at lower ages and for more serious offenses. Many will be graduating into the ranks of a criminal army that is costing America billions of dollars a year. (1970a: 74)

In 1970, the *US News and World Report* also published a story claiming that "In Long Beach, Calif., Police Sgt. James D. Reed says that young thugs who 'stalk older people, like animals stalking their prey,' robbing and brutally beating their victims, want 'excitement and money in their pockets'" (1970b: 19). *Look* magazine disclosed in 1966 that "More and more youngsters are involved in burglary, auto theft, shoplifting, and a variety of lesser crimes" (Maskin 1966: 24).

The data for these years make a lie of these alarmist reports. In 1966, 21 percent of the arrestees for violent crimes and 23 percent of the arrestees for all offenses were under 18. In 1969 the percentages were 22 percent and 26 percent, respectively. Juveniles accounted for 23 percent of the violent crime arrests and 26 percent of all arrests in 1971 and 1973. On average, juveniles accounted for around 22 percent of violent crime arrests and one-quarter of the arrests for all offenses from 1966 to 1973 (see FBI 1967, 1970, 1974, 1989). These data do not support the police and FBI claims reported in the press that there was a dramatic acceleration in juvenile crime in recent years.

Panics over youth crime are as persistent in Western society as are panics over the stock market but they, like so many other alarm bells, are based on political law enforcement propaganda, not facts. Arrest rates are the best index we have of the extent of juvenile crime and these data show that juvenile crime keeps pace with the number of juveniles in the population.

Today we are witnessing another spate of law enforcement-driven propaganda about the "time bomb" of juvenile crime, a campaign closely linked to the creation of anxiety over the state of the family in the United States where children are growing up "fatherless, jobless, and godless" and dependent on "welfare Moms" (Zoglin 1996: 52).

In fact, there has been a slight decline in the percentage of arrests accounted for by the arrest of juveniles since the 1960s and 1970s. In 1994, individuals under 18 contributed to 19 percent of violent crime arrests and 19 percent of arrests for all offenses compared to 22 and 25 percent, respectively, in the period 1966–73. Figures from the past few years also show a reduction in the percentage of arrests accounted for by juveniles compared to the 1960s and 1970s. Juvenile arrests accounted for under 20 percent of total arrests for both violent crimes and all offenses from the mid-1980s to the present (see FBI 1984a, 1986, 1988, 1990, 1992, 1998).

That the percentage of arrests accounted for by juveniles is less today than in the 1960s and 1970s is explained by demographics. In the 1960s and 1970s people under 18 made up a larger percent of the population than they did in the 1990s. In 1960, 35.7 percent of the population was younger than 18, and this proportion remained relatively stable over the next 10 years, rising to 36.1 percent in 1966 and falling to 34.2 percent in 1970 (Bureau of the Census 1998). From 1980 to the present, the proportion of the population under 18 has held steady at about 26 percent of the population, substantially lower than two or three decades ago (ibid.).

Following these demographic changes, the distribution of arrests by age change as well. Between 1971 and 1994 the percentage of adults arrested increased from 74.2 to 81.4, reflecting the increase in the proportion of the population over 18.

Current panics over juvenile crime

While the arrests of juveniles remained relatively stable between 1990 and 2000, there has been an unending public diatribe about the increasing danger posed by juvenile crime. This time the panic is directed at the "near future" when demographic changes will supposedly once again create a massive increase in juvenile crime. The panic is fueled not just by law-enforcement agencies but publicity-seeking criminologists as well.

Newsweek announced in 1995 that "Criminologists are already warning that the United States can expect another wave of violent crime in the coming decade, and some say it will be much worse than the one that is now subsiding" (Morgenthau 1995: 42). *Time* magazine warns that individuals between 14 and 17, "the age group that in the early '90s supplanted 18- to-24-year-olds as the most crime prone . . . is precisely the age group that will be booming in the next decade" (Zoglin 1996: 52). These media cite not only the FBI and local police but right-wing criminologists like John DiIulio of Princeton University who warns that in the near future the nation will face a generation of "superpredator" teenagers. James Alan Fox, head of the Department of Criminology at Northeastern University, joins this chorus: "So long as we fool ourselves in thinking that we're winning the war against crime, we may be blindsided by this bloodbath of teenage violence that is lurking in the future" (quoted in Zoglin 1996: 52).

According to the Bureau of the Census the percentage of the population under 18 will not increase in the future, it will in fact decline from 26.2 percent in 1996 to 25.9 percent in 2000 and to 23.6 percent by 2025. In 1996, 14–17-year-olds represented 5.5 percent of the population and will decline to 5.3 percent by the year 2025. If the alarmists like Fox and DiIulio are correct that shifts in the size of the juvenile population affects violent crime rates, we should see a decline in violent crime over the next 25 years, not an increase.

Other criminologists point to the future of a "bloodbath of teen-age violence" by claiming that there will be a dramatic increase in teenagers among minorities. Fox and Pierce maintain that "the amount of 15–19-year-olds will rise 28 percent among blacks and 47 percent among Hispanics" (1994: 26). The conclusion that an increase in the number of teenagers among the black and Hispanic populations translates directly into an increase in violent crime is not supported by the facts. From 1980 to 1997 the black population between the ages of 15 and 34 increased by 27 percent, but the overall violent crime rate for the age group 15–34 did not experience an equivalent increase. For example, juvenile urban violent crime, often one of the most violent criminal sectors, has decreased by 6.8 percent since 1995 (see FBI 1997).

Fox and Pierce fail, also, to point out that the increase in the black and Hispanic population as a percentage of the total population will be only minimal: the percentage of African American youths between 14 and 24 will increase from 2.3 percent of the population in 1995 to 2.4 percent in 2005. The percentage of Hispanics will increase slightly, from 1.9 to 2.3 (Bureau of the Census 1998).

The Department of Justice also employs percentage increase statements in ways that exaggerate and spread fear among the population. In *Juvenile Offenders and Victims: A National Report*, prepared by the Office of Juvenile Justice and Delinquency Prevention (OJJDP), a headline warns that "If trends continue as they have over the past 10 years, juvenile arrests for violent crime will double by the year 2010" (Snyder and Sickmund 1997: 1). The report estimates 261,000 juvenile arrests for violent crimes in 2010, a 101 percent increase from the 129,600 arrests for the same offenses in 1992. Once again, such a statistic has little utility since it is not placed in the context of all arrests. Both the number of juvenile and adult arrests will increase in the future because the total population continues to grow, expanding the pool of potential arrestees.

Furthermore, the OJJDP's dire prediction is based on the premise that arrests of juveniles for violent crimes over the next 15 years will mirror the annual increases in arrests for violent crimes that occurred between 1983 and 1992. However, recall that while the juvenile population has remained relatively stable at 26 percent of the population since 1980, it will decrease to 24.6 percent by 2010. Clearly, the Justice Department's assumption that juvenile arrests will keep pace with the past when the percentage of the population under 18 is declining reveals a desire to fuel the public's anxiety about a teenage "bloodbath" rather than a prediction based in fact.

Even more misleading are the OJJDP's statistics about arrest rates for juveniles. The report claims that "The increase in violent crime arrest rates is disproportionate for juveniles and young adults" and presents six graphs, all showing juvenile arrests for violent offenses outdistancing adult arrests for the same categories (ibid.: 112). These "facts" were then presented by the conservative Council on Crime in America (1996), whose membership includes the right-wing criminologist John DiIulio, and published under the title *The State of Violent Crime in America*.

To arrive at the conclusion that the juvenile violent crime rate is accelerating faster than the adult violent crime rate, the authors compared juvenile arrests per 100,000 people aged 10–17, not, as the title of the figure claims, per 100,000 population. People under 10, the report tells us, were eliminated because they are rarely arrested. The arrest rate for adults, however, is based on a population of everyone over 18. By the same logic that led to isolating the 10–17 age group and comparing it with the youth population most likely to be arrested, it would be necessary to limit the adult arrest rate to adults in the age groups most likely to be arrested: at the very least, to eliminate persons over 65 because they, like children under 10, are very unlikely to be arrested. Even more interesting would be to compare the 10–17 age group with people aged 18–35, since these are the adult years in which most arrests occur. Once again we see a US Department of Justice report that conducts so-called research in a fashion designed to spread fear and panic. We also see the media and generously funded right-wing think tanks spreading the news and insisting that:

> Americans must search for better, more cost-effective ways of *preventing* violent crimes and *protecting* themselves and their loved ones from violent and repeat criminals, adult and juvenile. But our first order of business must be *restraining* known convicted, violent and repeat criminals. *Restraining violent criminals* is a necessary but insufficient condition for meeting America's crime challenges, reforming the justice system, and *restoring public trust* in the system and in representative democracy itself. (DiIulio 1995: 57)

Questionable math also underlies the statements of John J. DiIulio, Jr. who has stated on numerous occasions that the number of juvenile male "superpredators" will increase significantly in coming years. In an article dubiously entitled "Crime in America – It's Going to Get Worse," DiIulio asserts that:

> The current trend in birth rates makes it certain that a new violent crime wave is just around the corner. Today there are some 7.5 million males ages 14 through 17. By the year 2000 we will have an additional 500,000. About six percent of young males are responsible for half the serious crimes committed by their age group, studies reveal. Thus, in a few years we can expect at least 30,000 more murderers, rapists, robbers and muggers on the streets than we have today. (1995)

DiIulio bases his conclusions on studies "that have shown about 6 percent of all boys are responsible for about half of all the police contacts with minors" (Zimring 1996: 12). However, studies of the 6 percent cohort in several cities indicate that "almost no life-threatening violence showed up in the youth sample that were responsible for the majority of all police contacts . . . [and that] no study of any youth population supports [a] projection of predatory violence" (ibid.).

DiIulio also argues that 270,000 "superpredators" will be added to the US population by the year 2010. However, as Zimring points out: "If 6 percent of all males under 18 are superpredators, that means we currently have more than 1.9 million juvenile superpredators on our streets. We would hardly notice another 270,000 by 2010" (1996: 12). Moreover, in estimating the number of "superpredators," DiIulio counts *all* males under 18. But very few violent crimes are committed by youths under the age of 13: "Since 93 percent of all juvenile arrests for violence occur after age 13" (Zimring 1996: 12). DiIulio has included toddlers and children in diapers to project an increase of 270,000 potentially violent youths.

Currently there are 7,961,000 14–17-year-olds in the population and there will be 718,000 added to this cohort by the year 2010 (Bureau of the Census 1998). This is a substantial increase, but nowhere close to DiIulio's estimated figure. Furthermore, to assume that the proportion of "dangerous" young males is constant is ludicrous since the social forces that create violence cannot be reduced simply to a person's age. Even the FBI acknowledges that age is only one of the variables associated with an increased likelihood of violence.

CRIME VICTIM SURVEYS

The distortion and manipulation of statistics by the Department of Justice is not limited to the FBI and local police departments. Even when data on crime are gathered objectively by the US Census Bureau, the reports based on these data emanating from the Department of Justice's Bureau of Justice Statistics (BJS) are constructed so as to maximize fear and minimize public understanding. The BJS is responsible for constructing the questionnaires and interpreting and reporting the findings. Once the data arrive in the BJS offices they are under the control of a bureaucracy with a vested interest in presenting the data in a particular light.

Characteristics of the NCVS

After pilot studies were conducted between 1967 and 1972, the first official National Criminal Victimization Survey (NCVS) appeared in 1973. Each year the survey asks a random sample of approximately 135,000 US residents in 65,000 households if they have been the victim of a crime during the past year.

Unlike the Uniform Crime Reports, the NCVS can register crimes not reported to or observed by the police. It also tallies all the crimes that occur in a particular incident, not just the most violent or "most serious."

Like any survey instrument, the NCVS findings must be read cautiously. Residents of the highest crime areas may be the least likely to be surveyed and the most reticent to accurately report their experiences. People may be reluctant to disclose their victimization. On the other hand, faced with an interviewer probing to find victims of crime, respondents may well conjure responses to fill the interviewer's questionnaire, or may inadvertently recount crimes that transpired more than a year before.

The main problem with the NCVS reports, however, are not its methodological weaknesses but the use of the reports to buttress the political and bureaucratic interests of the Department of Justice. Unlike the UCR, this is not accomplished by creative statistical gathering techniques, but by creatively summarizing the results of the annual surveys.

The 1994 BJS *Bulletin*, reporting the latest results of the Criminal Victimization Surveys, begins with the following statement: "In 1994 residents age 12 or older experienced approximately... 10.9 million crimes of violence.... In terms of crime rates, for every 1,000 persons age 12 or older, there were 51 victims of violence" (Perkins et al. 1996: 1). This statement is grossly misleading. Of the

10.9 million "crimes of violence" reported, 7.7 million (71 percent) were *attempts or threats of violence*, not completed acts of violence. A less politicized statement of the violent crime rate revealed by the victim survey would state that: "Overall during 1994 there were 3.2 million crimes of violence and 7.7 million attempts or threats of violence. In terms of crime rates, for every 1,000 persons age 12 or older there were 15 victims of violence and 36 victims of attempts or threats of violence." Even this modified statement is probably an overstatement of the frequency with which US residents are the victims of serious, violent crimes. Over 58 percent of the victims of completed, attempted, or threatened violent crimes *did not report the crime to the police* for a variety of reasons. According to the NCVS report, "many indicated that they felt the matter was private or personal in nature"; others did not report it because either it was "not important enough" or "nothing could be done about it."

In almost every category of crime reported, it is *the least serious crime that accounts for the majority of the instances*. Rape, robbery, and assaults make up the violent crimes reported in the NCVS (murder is not reported since victims are not able to respond). Assaults are the least serious of the acts categorized as violent crimes and they account for the vast majority (84 percent) of all violent crimes. Assaults can be divided into aggravated and simple. Of the 9,128,000 assaults reported in 1994, 6,650,000 (73 percent) were simple (with and without minor injury), 2,478,000 (27 percent) were aggravated. Simple assault without injury which is "an attempted assault without a weapon not resulting in injury" *accounts for nearly half (48 percent) of all violent crimes*. Even victims of aggravated assaults rarely experience injuries: among aggravated assaults less than one third resulted in injury.

The systematic attempt to make the problem of crime seem as bad as the data will allow affects the reporting of property crimes as well. The report states: "In 1994 the NCVS measured 31 million household burglaries, motor vehicle thefts, and thefts of other property.... Expressed as rates per 1,000 households, there were 54 burglaries, 18 motor vehicle thefts, and 236 property thefts" (Perkins et al. 1996: 2–3). As with violent crimes, these statements are not false, but they are clearly designed to give maximum weight to the seriousness of crime and the danger crime poses for individuals. The fact is that the least serious of the property crimes, property theft, accounts for 77 percent of all property crimes. Property thefts are most likely to be under $50 and thefts under $50 account for 22 percent of all victimizations. Only 14 percent of all property crimes reported by victims in 1994 were of property valued in excess of $250. Over 50 percent of property crime victims claimed they did not notify the police because (1) it was not serious enough, (2) nothing could be done about it, (3) the item was recovered, or (4) they could not prove it was stolen (ibid.).

The maxim that the least serious offense makes up the bulk of all offenses holds true for most of the crimes within specific categories. Thus in 1992, petty larceny (theft under $100) without contact characterized 62.3 percent of the crimes of theft and 35 percent of all crimes. Petty larceny with contact accounted for 2.6 percent of all thefts and a minuscule 1.4 percent of the total. Among household crimes, household larceny was responsible for 54.7 percent of the victimizations within the category, and burglary represented 32.1 percent of household crimes and only 14.1 percent of total crimes. Once again, the most serious crime, forced-entry burglary is the least common type, representing only 10.8 percent of all household crimes and 4.8 percent of all victimizations.

What this analysis of the facts behind the NCVS report reveals is a systematic bias in summarizing the findings to make the frequency and seriousness of crime appear much worse than it is in fact. The most consistent finding of the NCVS is that most crimes are not reported by the victim, that in almost every crime category surveyed the majority of the criminal victimizations are for the least serious offense in the category, and that there is in fact no infliction of actual violence in the majority of so-called "crimes of violence." Such data should lead the authors of the NCVS report to highly qualified, cautious statements about the extent to which there is a serious crime problem in the United States. But political and bureaucratic interests take priority over accuracy in the hands of the crime-control industry. Indeed, the opening statement of the NCVS report could say: "Last year 85–90 percent of all residents in the US were not the victims of any crime. Furthermore, the majority of those who were victimized were the victims of petty theft. Less than 1 percent of the population was the victim of any type of violent crime, and the vast majority of these victims were victims of attempted or threatened violence but suffered no actual violence" (FBI 1997: 11).

THE CONSEQUENCES

Were the politicization of crime statistics merely a matter of one bureaucracy fiddling with data to support their interests it would perhaps be possible to ignore it as "good enough for government work." Unfortunately, when the subject is crime, the consequences of misreporting data reverberate in the lives of people throughout the country. Crime in the public image in the United States is not racially neutral. Crimes in the media and the view of the general public are acts committed by young black men. Never mind that more serious crimes daily occur at corporate headquarters, banks, and on Wall Street. The public image is of violent, psychopathic, young black males. Thus for the Department of Justice to distort the frequency and seriousness of crime is to accuse the African American community of being a dangerous class in need of massive efforts to control them (Chambliss 1994).

As a consequence of generating fear, the gap between the white and black communities grows. People cross streets when they see black men walking on their side of the street. Mothers hurry to put their children in the car and lock the doors.

The quality of life *for everyone* is negatively affected as parents put fear into their children from an early age. Middle-class and upper-class children are shuttled to and from the mall rather than being allowed to ride the bus or walk home after dark, even in neighborhoods that rarely experience any type of crime. The independence of women is severely curtailed, as they are afraid to walk alone and therefore become dependent on having a man, or at least other women, to escort them.

One of the more important consequences of perpetuating the myth of "crime out of control" is that it leads inevitably to the arrest and incarceration of the poor. Since African Americans are disproportionately poor in the United States the result is closely akin to "ethnic cleansing." In Washington DC and Baltimore, Maryland, between 40 and 50 percent of the black male population between the ages of 15 and 18 is at any given moment either in prison, on probation, on parole, or has a warrant out for their arrest (see Maurer 1994; Miller 1992). The consequences for the African American community are devastating. Young men cannot marry because they cannot find employment owing to their prison record. Children grow up knowing their father through weekly visits to prison. Women with husbands in prison must work or go on welfare. If they find employment they are forced to leave their children in the care of relatives or friends because they cannot afford day care.

The perpetuation of the image of crime out of control also justifies the elimination of support systems such as welfare and job-creation programs as the residents increasingly come to be defined as "the inherently criminal danger-ous classes" and therefore "undeserving" (Gans 1985).

Another consequence is the transformation of urban police departments into militarized, heavily armed tactical units whose mission is preemptive strikes and overt actions that make a mockery of constitutional guarantees. Meanwhile the Supreme Court, itself a victim of the propaganda of the law-enforcement industrial complex, eats away at the protection of civilians from the police misuse of power as they allow more and more incursions into private spaces, such as automobiles and homes, with fewer and fewer controls over police behavior.

Finally, there is the fact that increasingly criminal justice budgets grow at the expense of all other public expenditure. For the first time in history state and municipal governments are spending more on criminal justice than education (Chambliss 1992: 18). Scarcely a politician can be found in the United States who will stand up and say, as did Lyndon Johnson, John Kennedy, and Hubert Humphrey, that the crime problem has to be solved by spending more money on education, opportunities, and job creation rather than on police, prosecutors, judges, and prisons. The distortion of priorities emanating from the successful propaganda campaign of the crime-control industry, the politicians, and the media culminated in the changing of priorities in public expenditures. Nowhere is this more dramatically illustrated than in the shift of tax revenues from education to criminal justice.

Yet homicide rates dropped by 22 percent during the 27-year period from 1973 to 2000 (FBI 2000, and see Table 24.1 above), and the overall property crime rate declined by nearly 60 percent between 1973 and 2000 (US Depart-ment of Justice 2000).

CONCLUSION

In 1931 a Federal Commission was appointed to study the need for a national system of crime reporting. Known as the Wickensham Commission, its final report warned of the dangers inherent in having law-enforcement agencies with a vested interest in the outcome of crime data responsible for gathering data about crime. Referring to the fact that the data for the UCR are gathered and disseminated by the FBI the Commission concluded:

Nothing can be more misleading than statistics not scientifically gathered and compiled. The Uniform Crime Reports...[the FBI's annual summary of crime in the US] make no suggestion as to any limitations or doubts with respect to the utility or authority of the figures presented. On the contrary they contain a graphic chart of "monthly crime trends", and along with them the bureau has released to the press statements quoting and interpreting them without qualification. It requires no great study of these reports to perceive a number of weaknesses which should impose a more cautious promulgation of them. (Wickensham Commission 1931: 64)

Unfortunately, the warnings of the Wickensham commission were ignored and the Department of Justice and the FBI are the only source of data on crime. The latter institutions are not disinterested observers of crime trends. They are instead bureaucracies with a vested interest in misleading the public.

The FBI's Uniform Crime Reports and the Department of Justice's National Criminal Victimization Surveys have lived up to the Wickensham Commission's worst fears, with consequences for the lives of American citizens that could scarcely have been imagined 60 years ago. One consequence is the emergence of a crime-control industry siphoning resources from other social services. Even more important, however, is the creation of law-enforcement bureaucracies whose survival depends on making arrests and putting people in prison. This leads in turn to the arrest and conviction of the poor for minor offenses. It also institutionalizes the division of America into two nations hostile to one another, "separate and unequal."

References

Bureau of the Census (1998) *Statistical Abstract of the United States*. Washington, DC: Department of Commerce.

Bureau of Justice Statistics (2001). *Criminal Victimization 2000*. Washington, DC: US Department of Justice.

Burger, W. (1981) Speech before the National Press Club, Washington, DC, March.

Chambliss, W. J. (1992) *Trading Textbooks for Prison Cells*. Alexandria, VA: National Center on Institutions and Alternatives.

Chambliss, W. J. (1994) Policing the ghetto underclass: The politics of law and law enforcement. *Social Problems*, 41(2), 177–94.

Chambliss W. J., and Chilton, R. (1998) Fluctuations in crime rates: Artifact or substance? Paper delivered at the American Society of Criminology, Washington, DC, August.

Chambliss W. J., and Holman, B. (1994) Creating crime. Paper delivered at the American Society of Criminology Meetings, November.

Council on Crime in America (1996) *The State of Violent Crime in America*, Washington, DC: The New Citizen Project, January.

Dilulio, J. J. Jr. (1995) Crime in America – It's going to get worse. *Reader's Digest*, August, 57.

Federal Bureau of Investigation (1967, 1970, 1974, 1981, 1984a, 1984b, 1986, 1988, 1989, 1990, 1992, 1995, 1997, 1998, 2000) *Crime in the United States: Uniform Crime Reports*. Washington, DC: US Department of Justice.

Federal Bureau of Investigation (1984c) *Uniform Crime Reporting Handbook*. Washington, DC: Federal Bureau of Investigation.

Fox, J. A., and Pierce, G. (1994) American killers are getting younger. *USA Today Magazine*, January, 26.

Gans, H. J. (1995) *The War Against the Poor: The Underclass and Antipoverty Policy*, New York: Basic Books.

Maguire, K., and Pastore, A. L. (2000) *Sourcebook of Criminal Justice Statistics – 2000*. Washington, DC: Bureau of Justice Statistics 2000.

Maskin, J. R. (1966) The suburbs: Made to order for crime. *Look*, May 31, 24.

Maurer, M. (1994) *Americans Behind Bars: The International Use of Incarceration, 1992–1993*. Washington, D.C., The Sentencing Project.

Miller, J. G. (1992) *Hobbling A Generation: Young African American Males in Washington D.C.'s Criminal Justice System*. Alexandria, VA: National Center on Institutions and Alternatives (April).

Morgenthau, P. (1995) The lull before the storm? *Newsweek*, December 14, 42.

Pepinsky, H., and Selke, W. (1982) The politics of police reporting in Indianapolis, 1948–78. *Law and Human Behavior*, 6 (3/4).

Perkins, C., Klaus, P. A., Bastian, L. D., and Cohen R. L. (1996) *Criminal Victimization in the United States, 1993*. Washington, DC: US Department of Justice.

Seidman, D., and Couzens, M. (1974) Getting the crime rate down: Political pressure and crime reporting. *Law and Society Review*, 8, 457–93.

Snyder, H. N., and Sickmund, M. (1997) *Juvenile Offenders and Victims: A National Report*. Washington, DC: US Department of Justice.

Subin, H. (1965) Review of Department Policy on the Dyer Act (18 U.S.C. 2312), January 27. Washington, DC: Internal Report for the Director of the Office of Criminal Justice, Office of the Deputy Attorney General.

Subin, H. (1991) The Impact of the Dyer Act. Unpublished paper.

Thomas, P. (1995) The new face of murder in America: Family slaying decline; fewer cases are solved; killers are younger. *Washington Post*, October 23, P. A04.

US Department of Justice (2000) *Crime in the United States, 1999*. Washington, DC: FBI national press release.

US News and World Report (1970a) Why streets are not safe. *US News and World Report*, March 16, 74.

US News and World Report (1970b) Youths stalk the elderly. March 23, 19.

Wickensham Commission (1931) *Report on Criminal Statistics*. Washington, DC: US Government Printing Office.

Zimring, F. E. (1996) Crying wolf over teen demons. *Los Angeles Times*, August 19, 12.

Zoglin, R. (1996) Now for the bad news: A teenage timebomb. *Time*. January 15, 52.

25

Two Realities of Police Communication

AARON DOYLE AND RICHARD ERICSON

INTRODUCTION

In this essay, we contrast two realities of police communication. We analyze police communication with the news media, and contrast this to communication with other institutions in everyday police work. Police occupy a central place in public dramas of crime and punishment, as the official source of news and a key icon of order and authority. Police have been termed "primary definers" (Hall et al. 1978) who fundamentally shape the news-media image of criminal justice. While that oversimplifies, police are indeed often the dominant institution in media discourse about crime. However, in their everyday operations, police communication offers a stark contrast. In this less public context, police are hardly "primary definers." Instead, police are "knowledge workers" increasingly driven by, and secondary to, the knowledge needs of other institutions (Ericson and Haggerty 1997). In concluding, we discuss how this contrast reproduces a split in criminal justice more broadly.

POLICE, CRIME, AND THE MEDIA

Deviance is a defining property of news (Ericson et al. 1987). A great deal of news focuses on when the behavior of a person or thing strays from the norm. Crime and punishment have always been staples of fiction and news. Content analyses show that contemporary news remains saturated with crime and deviance (Sherizen 1978; Graber 1980; Garofalo 1981; Ericson et al. 1991; Chermak 1995).

Police–news media relations

Journalists depend mostly on official accounts (Gans 1979; Ericson et al. 1991). Reporters seldom have the time or resources to establish facts independently.

Instead, they rely on culturally credible sources to make statements that can be quoted as fact without further investigation. Reporters rely heavily on police as the accepted authoritative source concerning crime (Chibnall 1977; Hall et al. 1978; Fishman 1980; Ericson et al. 1989; Reiner 2000; Schlesinger and Tumber 1994; Sacco 1995). The media focus their reporting on other major institutions: police have become more and more a key institution as they have expanded, centralized, and become more overtly political. The police are a central yet complex symbol in public culture. While they have multiple functions and sometimes struggle to reconcile ambiguities in an uncertain mandate, in public the police often emphasize their crime-control role for purposes of legitimation.

News workers recognize a steady public appetite for tales of crime and punishment. The constant flow from police of accounts of individual crimes provides cheap news content. Police often proactively seek media attention, while other possible sources of crime news, for example, victims, the accused, criminologists, or citizens' groups, do not have the same authority, routine availability, and/or motivation in speaking with journalists. The result is a symbiosis between police and media. News outlets participate in various forms of police work and are crucial to police legitimation. Yet relations between police and news organizations are complex, differentiated, and sometimes highly conflicted. In their well-known book *Policing the Crisis*, Hall et al. (1978) argued that routine, unquestioned reliance on official sources like police reproduces the dominance of elites:

> the media...do not simply create the news; nor do they simply transmit the ideology of the "ruling class" in a conspiratorial fashion. Indeed we have suggested that in a critical sense, the media are frequently not the "primary definers" of news events at all – in the moment of news production, the media stand in a position of structured subordination to the primary definers. (Hall et al. 1978: 59).

The authors argued that police were primary definers in the heavy coverage given to "mugging" by immigrant youths in early 1970s Britain. Hall et al. saw the media-driven "crisis" over mugging as a decisive moment in the rise of a more authoritarian state.

Policing the Crisis was very influential at a broader level, but its account of police–media relations lacked nuance. The authors did not directly observe police–media relations; they simply made inferences from looking at selected news items. Later ethnographic research revealed police–media relations are more complex and diverse. Ericson et al. (1989) observed how news content is negotiated between Canadian journalists and police sources on the downtown police news beat in Toronto, Ontario. Police and media sometimes help each other and sometimes work at cross-purposes. Media outlets vary dramatically in their police coverage. "Inner-circle" reporters tend to be from populist outlets, including tabloid newspapers and AM radio stations. Based in the extensive newsroom complex at police headquarters, such reporters are very friendly with police, and largely reflect their ideology. These reporters access more information, but self-censor to maintain close ties with police sources, and thus focus on official accounts. The "outer circle" of crime journalists, from "quality" outlets such as a government television station and an elite-market broadsheet newspaper, are much less cozy with police, and place more emphasis on police deviance. Outer-circle reporters conduct extensive investigations into police brutality and wrongful convictions. The outer circle looks down on the inner circle for not maintaining respectable distance. Outer circle reporters face much more difficulty getting information; their relationship with police is more a running battle.

Schlesinger and Tumber (1994) describe a recent "broadening out" of traditional crime reporting in Britain, with less emphasis on the day-to-day traffic of crime and more on wider policy issues. Younger reporters are now more detached from police; overall, though, crime journalists remain heavily reliant on police, who make up 70 to 90 percent of their contacts.

Police in Western nations became more proactive with the media in recent decades, increasingly seeing media as a resource, not a threat. Taking the media initiative helps police achieve political ends and closes off areas of vulnerability – the police version of a story is much more effective in heading off media enquiries than no version at all. Police in major urban centers now employ civilian public relations specialists and media officers who take the initiative in contacting journalists to promote stories and arrange media events. Scotland Yard developed a massive public relations apparatus with 145 staff and a budget of £12.5 million (Schlesinger and Tumber 1994). A large, centralized public affairs unit grew at Toronto police headquarters (Ericson et al.1989). Journalists and police sources often operate several bureaucratic steps removed from actual incidents. This choice by police limits media knowledge of events, enabling a favorable official account.

Outside official channels, reporters encounter a police culture of secrecy, but still sometimes penetrate an occasionally "leaky" police bureaucracy. There are other areas of vulnerability. The lofty public view of police crime-fighting capability leaves them open to media criticism when their limited ability to control crime actually becomes apparent (Schlesinger and Tumber 1994; Manning 2001). Police are more vulnerable when policing occurs directly in front of news cameras – for example, during riots (Doyle 2003). Unpredictable events, like the massive broadcasting of an amateur recording of Rodney King's beating by Los Angeles police, create openings when alternative sources are more likely to be quoted (Lawrence 2000).

Patterns in crime news

Crime coverage varies significantly, for example, between tabloid and quality newspapers, and print and television news (Ericson et al. 1991). In general, media focus heavily on individual crimes, rather than on broader situations in criminal justice. Journalists normally report day-to-day events occurring since the last deadline, rather than examining underlying issues, a tendency known as "event orientation" (Hall et al. 1978). Many media workers hold an implicit "middle–of–the–road" ideology, positing a fundamental consensus about central institutions like the police (Gans 1979).

Media most often report violent crime, especially homicides and sexual assaults, part of a more general media orientation to violence. The news also focuses on high-status offenders and victims (Reiner 2002). Crime stories are normally hooked on institutional events, including arrests and charges, so the news features a high proportion of solved crime, emphasizing the capability of police as crime fighters (Reiner 2002; Sacco 1995).

The news also features periodic "crime waves" (Davis 1951; Hall et al. 1978), bursts of heavy publicity for items drawn from the flow of reported crime because they fit a current news theme, for example, muggings of the elderly (Fishman 1978), or attacks on women by strangers (Voumvakis and Ericson 1984), even though the reported crimes may be unrelated to another and there may have been no rise in their statistical frequency.

News sources mostly attribute crime to individual pathology or evil, rarely suggesting it is a product of structural forces, according to a content analysis of six major news outlets (Ericson et al. 1991). Lawrence (2000) analyzed news coverage of more than 500 incidents of police use of force. She found similarly that police brutality is mostly portrayed as stemming from individual deviance, rather than systemic problems.

Media influences on audiences

Social scientists have long tried to evaluate the consequences of these patterns in crime news. Media likely have a range of diverse influences on varying audiences, and have many other impacts on the various players in the justice system. Critics charge that media-induced fear of crime detracts from personal well-being, and promotes punitiveness and "law-and-order" politics. However, extensive quantitative research to test this produces inconclusive or equivocal results (Gunter 1987; Cumberbatch and Howitt 1989: 32; Sparks 1992: ch. 4; Sacco 1995: 151; Surette 1997). More generally, social scientists have failed to isolate and quantify media effects on audiences outside of experimental situations. This likely reflects the limits of social science, not the lack of any impact.

Systems of meaning about criminal justice develop in complex interplay between media, other key players like police and politicians, and in interactions among diverse audiences. People do not make a detached assessment of criminal justice based solely on information from the news, but draw on other sources, such as experiential knowledge and popular wisdom (Sasson 1995). Crime news and TV fiction are often consumed in juxtaposition, and help shape each other's meanings for audiences. In general, being seen alongside news may add immediacy to crime fiction; being juxtaposed with fiction may add drama to crime news (Doyle 1998). Tendencies in crime news interact with broader systems of meaning about youth, class, gender, and "race." These relationships are dynamic and circular; news stories about crime do not simply cause public beliefs and attitudes.

Even so, general patterns of police news – for example, a focus on individual crimes without broader context, on violent crime, on high-status victims, on the successes of police as crime fighters, and on the attribution of criminality to individual evil or pathology – reinforce one system of meaning about crime which is prominent in public culture. In this way of thinking, society is in decline because of rising crime, specifically violent street crime of the underclasses. The answer is tougher control. Police are not too soft; instead, others hold them back. The capacity of police to control crime is exaggerated. Crime is a problem of evil or pathological individuals who are a Them less human than Us. This is often connected with categories such as "race," class, and youth. An overt profession that crime control is efficient and utilitarian is bound up with less conscious, more affectively charged undercurrents of fear and anger, identification with powerful authority, and punitiveness and retribution. Various analysts argue this punitiveness involves displacement of anxieties and angers from other sources (Garland 1990; Sparks 1992; Scheingold 1995).

Loader suggests:

> the degree and sheer intensity of much public interest in the policing phenomenon suggest that something else is at stake here other than a reasoned calculation of what police can accomplish.... Popular sentiment...is attracted to the idea of an omnipotent source of order and authority that is able to face up to the criminal Other.... In this respect popular attachment to policing is principally affective in character, something which people evince a deep emotional commitment to and which is closely integrated with their sense of self. (1997: 3)

Audiences are also often fascinated by violence, especially when authorities with which audiences can identify, such as the police, employ it.

Thus, while multifaceted, the cultural place of police often reinforces their structural position dominating the production of crime news. Surveys consistently show police are the component of the justice system most highly regarded by the public (for example, Environics 1998). However, this varies widely by audience, for example, white Americans versus African Americans, and there are alternative cultural currents, for example, narratives of police brutality.

Media influences on police and other players

Much mainstream and critical research on media focuses too narrowly on influence on audience views, often in the form of an abstracted "public opinion." An alternative that captures media influence more holistically is to focus on the media's impact in particular political and institutional contexts (Altheide and Snow 1979; Ericson 1991). Focusing at the institutional level offers a way past some key stumbling blocks in researching media influences (Doyle 2003). Surette advocates an "ecological approach" to understanding the impact of crime in the media. As he notes, "the media can directly affect what actors in the criminal justice system do without having to first change the public's attitudes or agendas" (1997: 216). For example, Fishman (1978) analyzed a media "crime wave" of reported attacks against the elderly. This "crime wave" resulted in the allocation of more resources to police and the passing of tougher laws. Thus Fishman demonstrated important effects of the media without needing to measure "fear of crime" in audiences.

The media also impact crime victims: insensitive coverage may result in a kind of revictimization or "second wound" (Levin 1992). Police interviewees see the media as having diverse organizational influences (Ericson et al. 1989: 156–69): interfering with investigations, impacting accused criminals prior to trial, promoting or hurting the image of the force, creating workload pressures, influencing individual police careers, distributing emergency information, deterring potential criminals, for example by publicizing crackdowns on drunk driving, and pressuring the police administration for various political reasons. Television cameras at demonstrations and riots have helped prompt less coercive public-order policing (Marx 1998: 257). Perlmutter (2000) spent two years riding with Minneapolis patrol officers, examining how media images of policing affected them. The officers were agonizingly conscious of the gap between media-driven public expectations and the mundane responsibilities and capabilities character-izing day-to-day police work.

The media help police by soliciting information on unsolved crimes, but also make trouble by calling attention to failure to solve such crimes. The increasing pervasiveness of surveillance cameras gives police a new investigative and pro-motional media tool. Police proactively give surveillance footage of crimes to television news. While this aids the search for suspects, these "video wanted posters" (Doyle 2003) also provide stark visuals which sensationalize particular crimes. A key example was Britain's Bulger case. Sixteen cameras captured a two-year-old being led away from a shopping mall by two 10-year-old boys who later killed him (Young 1996: ch. 5). Police sometimes release surveillance footage to the media without any investigative purpose, apparently solely for promotional reasons. The broadcast of surveillance footage in turn fuels support for further spread of the cameras (Doyle 2003).

Cops and reality-TV

Police are also the focus of many "reality-TV" programs (Fishman and Cavender 1998), pioneered and exemplified by the American show *Cops*, which first aired in 1989 and remains very popular (Doyle 2003). To make *Cops*, a video and sound team accompany police in action, a television version of the "ride-along" in which a curious civilian tags along in a police cruiser for a shift. *Cops* has been recorded in dozens of American cities, as well as in Britain, Hong Kong, Russia, and Bolivia. Numerous other shows have adapted *Cops'* approach, including the Canadian *To Serve and Protect*, *American Detective*, *LAPD: Life on the Beat*, Britain's *Blues and Twos*, and programs in Scandinavia and the Netherlands. Television executives sought innovative and inexpensive programming to fill the expanding range of channels, and police forces offered massive cooperation, part of the trend toward increasing police self-promotion in the media.

Its producers call *Cops* "unfiltered" television and "raw reality" (Katz 1993: 25). However, *Cops* offers a very particular and selective vision of policing. The program records 50 or 60 hours of videotape for each hour that airs. *Cops* is edited to offer narrative qualities such as heroes for audiences to identify with, unambiguous storylines concluding with resolution or closure, and, often, a moral or theme (Doyle 1998). While there is no formal narration, the material is edited so that the officers serve as informal narrators; their narration is edited over various visual sequences. Accounts of other officers, dialogue between officers, recordings from briefings and from police radio are also stitched together in the soundtrack to structure these storylines. To comprehend often-confusing footage, viewers must rely heavily on oral interpretation of events by police. The police definition of the situation becomes the "reality" of reality-TV (Doyle 2003).

Reality crime shows, including *Cops*, overrepresent both violent crime and the amount of crime that is solved by police. Oliver (1994) found that 69 percent of the suspects on *Cops* and four other reality shows were portrayed as arrested, a dramatic increase from the arrest rate in official and other statistics. *Cops* does not air material that will cast police in a bad light. The producers are dependent on ongoing cooperation of police; *Cops* producers themselves internalize pro-police attitudes; the producers also aim to give the audience what they apparently want. The producers are like inner circle reporters who have close ties with police, yet their dependence on police is even greater (Doyle 1998).

A Kansas City police officer who let a *Cops* crew accompany him on his midnight shift for two weeks told *Time* magazine it was an enjoyable experience. "They said that they wouldn't do anything to undermine us, and that we'd have final discretion about what ran" (Zoglin 1992). *Time* reported that "each episode of *Cops* is reviewed by the police before airing, in part to make sure no investigations are compromised."

Oliver (1994) found that five reality crime programs, including *Cops*, under-represent African Americans and Hispanics and overrepresent whites as police officers, while overrepresenting minorities and underrepresenting whites as criminals. *Cops* omits any portrayals of overtly racist behavior by police. *Cops* is also selective in focusing on crime in poorer neighborhoods. Things that happen in places like Beverly Hills, a co-producer told the *Los Angeles Times*, "aren't the kind of things that are stories for us on the show" (Doyle 1998).

Clearly not all audiences will simply accept that *Cops* is reality. Yet audience research suggests that many viewers largely do see it this way. A survey of 358 television viewers in Wisconsin and Virginia by Oliver and Armstrong (1995) showed that audiences perceive *Cops* and four similar programs as significantly more realistic than crime fiction. Industry research suggests that many viewers see *Cops* as very similar to local news (Doyle 1998). If it is like news, the storytelling of *Cops* also resonates extremely well with fictional crime programming, featuring the same simple, unambiguous, narrative structure, pumped-up action, heroic police protagonists, and high arrest rate.

Of course, some audience members subvert the police definitions of the televised situations and make their own meanings from them (Fiske 1987). Yet many viewers are already inclined toward "law and order," and these are the people to whom *Cops* will most likely appeal. Oliver and Armstrong (1995: 565) found that reality programs like *Cops* "were most enjoyed by viewers who evidenced higher levels of authoritarianism, reported greater punitiveness about crime and reported higher levels of racial prejudice." As with fictional crime shows, *Cops* does not simply cause "law-and-order" tendencies in audiences; instead, audiences who already have them may be drawn to *Cops*. The relationship is most likely one of mutual reinforcement. Like many media products, *Cops* may be not exactly "preaching to the converted," but more preaching to those who lean that way – reinforcing fear of crime and law-and-order views among people already predisposed to them. Mainstream and critical communications literature converge on one point – the strongest socializing influence of media may be to reinforce existing views (Curran 1996).

The "realities" of policing in the news and on reality-TV exemplify one kind of police communication. We now look at a very different kind of police communication and how it fits with a contrasting vision within Western justice systems.

EVERYDAY POLICING: POLICE AS RISK COMMUNICATORS TO OTHER INSTITUTIONS

Hall et al.'s *Policing the Crisis* analyzes how the police and mass media combine to shape dramatic moments of political crisis into the legitimation of a more authoritarian state. In sharp contrast, Ericson and Haggerty's *Policing the Risk Society* (1997) demonstrates how the police use computers, CCTV and other information technologies to gather and disseminate knowledge of risk. Far from addressing crises in political culture, police communication is primarily characterized by routine data gathering and distribution for purposes of surveillance, regulation, and administration. Moreover, since the police themselves have very limited capacity to respond directly to crime, accidents or other problems, most of this risk-communication work is on behalf of other institutions concerned with security, such as insurance, healthcare, business enterprise, welfare, education and regulatory agencies. The police are reactive to the knowledge demands of other institutions and think and act in their terms.

The media image of policing contrasts starkly with data revealing that police are limited in how much they can control crime, and actually spend most of their time on other responsibilities. In an analysis of British Crime Survey data, Skogan (1990: 9) found most police time with citizens was used for the exchange of information, either citizens giving police non-crime-related information (16 percent of contacts) or asking police for information (23 percent of contacts). Reporting of crime accounted for only 18 percent of contacts.

It is extremely rare for a patrol officer to encounter a serious crime in progress (Clarke and Hough 1984). While patrol officers are proactive, it is mainly to obtain knowledge about possible suspects who appear out of place and time, or for regulatory matters such as traffic and liquor violations (Ericson 1982). Reactive calls for police services are also mainly about noncriminal matters. Up to 75 percent of calls for service are screened out without being forwarded to patrol officers for further action (Jorgensen 1981; Manning 1988). Even when there is a crime call, what operators define as serious crime is changed by officers to a minor incident or no crime in one-third to one-half of all instances (Comrie and Kings 1975; Ericson 1982; Manning 1988). What officers often find at the scene is not serious crime but a kaleidoscope of trouble that requires them to provide some combination of counsel, assistance, expertise, coercion, referral, and persuasion, and to make a report (Cumming et al. 1965; Ericson 1982). For patrol officers, at least, direct involvement in crime work takes up as little as 3 percent of their working time (Comrie and Kings 1975; Ericson 1982).

There are, of course, criminal investigation specialists in police organizations – detectives – who devote all their time to crime work. However, detectives also spend relatively little time on direct criminal investigation. Draper (1978: 31) estimated that only about 10 percent of the investigator's time was spent this way. Ericson (1993: 45) found that detectives spent almost half their time in the office and that much more time was devoted to recording investigative activities than to actual investigation work.

On average, a patrol officer in Canada records one indictable crime occurrence a week, makes one indictable crime arrest every three weeks, and secures one indictable crime conviction every nine months (McMahon 1992). Even in New York City, which has an extraordinary high rate of serious crime, officers spend an extraordinarily small amount of time dealing with crime and capturing criminals. Walsh (1986) found that among 156 patrol officers assigned to a high-crime area in New York City, 40 percent did not make a single felony arrest in a year and 69 percent made no more than three felony arrests in a year.

The police simply are incapable of doing much about crime directly. This incapacity is related to the institution of privacy, which limits them in developing evidence to detect and solve cases (Stinchcombe 1963; Reiss 1987). They are also limited by their own resources, and by a criminal justice system that is designed more to divert cases than to prosecute fully or heavily. Attrition within the criminal justice system is captured by criminal justice statistics for England and Wales (Barclay et al. 1995). For a range of crimes against individuals and their property, less than half (47 percent) are reported to the police and only 27 percent are actually recorded by the police. Police clear up only 4.9 percent after investigation. A mere 2.7 percent are cleared by either a police caution of the suspect or conviction of an offender, and 2 percent result in the conviction of an offender. For domestic burglary, 69 percent are reported to the police but only 41 percent are actually recorded by them. Moreover, police only clear up 8.4 percent after investigation, with 2.3 percent resulting in either a police caution of the suspect or conviction of an offender, and 2 percent resulting in the conviction of an offender.

One might think that while the police face major limitations in detecting crime, they can be efficient in taking cases to prosecution when they do manage to apprehend a suspect. However, even when suspects are apprehended and can be prosecuted, very often they are not (Royal Commission on Criminal Justice 1993: 82; McConville 1993: 86; Meehan 1993). Rather, there is an effort to "define deviance down" (Moynihan 1993) by diverting cases to other institutions such as families, schools, restorative justice facilities, and so on.

While there has been an almost 250 percent increase in indictable offenses recorded by the police in England and Wales between 1976 and 1996, the police clearance by arrest rate decreased considerably from 43 percent in 1976 to 32 percent in 1986 to 26 percent in 1996. During the same period the absolute number of indictable convictions decreased from 415,503 in 1976 to 384,000 in 1986 and 300,600 in 1996. On the other hand the rate of police cautions rose considerably, from 97,681 in 1976 to 137,000 in 1986 and 190,800 in 1996 (Ashworth 2001).

Other data from Ashworth indicate that in 1996, 60 percent of all male juvenile offenders and 80 percent of all female juvenile offenders were cautioned by the police rather than prosecuted. Among males aged 18–20, 35 percent were cautioned, and for females in the same age range the cautionary rate was 50 percent. Male offenders aged 21 and over were subject to cautions rather than prosecution 26 percent of the time, while females over 21 were cautioned 44 percent of the time. As Ashworth (2001) also observes, "these are only the options available to the police; it would be wrong to overlook the various forms of diversion employed by the tax authorities, Her Majesty's Customs, local councils, and the many inspectorates (health and safety, pollution, etc.) which have the power to prosecute" (Ashworth 2001:7).

Despite the public image of police as crime fighters, ethnographic observation of the day-to-day world of contemporary policing reveals a very different pre-occupation. In this more private world, police are first and foremost knowledge workers who think and act within the risk-communication systems of other institutions (Ericson and Haggerty 1997). Contemporary institutions are increasingly organized around risk, and risk communication is central to all aspects of day-to-day police work. The police are not only involved in law enforcement, the maintenance of order, and social service, but in all of these roles they are also knowledge workers engaged in surveillance for the production and distribution of knowledge of risk. Whether dealing with crime, vehicle collisions, regulatory matters, social service, or public order, the police operate as a center of calculation (Latour 1987) for the risk-communication systems of myriad institutions. As such, police mobilization is not only a matter of inter-vention in the lives of individual citizens, but also reactive to institutional demands for knowledge of risk. They are required to intersect with, and broker knowledge to and from, a full range of institutions in the risk-communication network. In contrast to their dominant role in negotiating media communica-tion, in this other realm of communication, police are often secondary and subsidiary to other institutions (Ericson and Haggerty 1997).

Police reports on motor-vehicle collisions exemplify the police role as knowledge brokers. Myriad institutions require knowledge of motor-vehicle collisions as part of their risk-management systems, and they each influence the risk-communication format of police collision reports. For example, the government motor vehicles registry requires risk knowledge regarding driver records, traffic engineering prob-lems, collision prevention, and automobile industry compliance with safety stand-ards. The automobile industry requires risk knowledge regarding the safety of its vehicles for compliance and product improvement. Insurance companies require risk knowledge to allocate liability in the particular case; develop risk ratings for drivers and vehicles in general; establish premium, and deductible levels; establish levels of compensation; and undertake collision-prevention initiatives. The crim-inal courts require risk knowledge if the collision results from a driving-related offense. Last and least, the police administration requires risk knowledge to meas-ure the productivity records of its officers and to allocate resources.

An appreciation of the changing role of police within risk-communication systems can be gleaned from an examination of historical changes to their official forms for reporting occurrences. Changes to the occurrence report forms of a large urban police organization illustrate this shift (Ericson and Haggerty 1997). Before 1939 the occurrence report was simply a narrative written on a blank sheet of paper. This form remained in place until the 1960s. By 1964, there were 28 items on the form in addition to the narrative. The narrative space was reduced to half a page. By the early 1990s this police organization moved into a "paperless," computerized occurrence report system. Officers were no longer required to fill out occurrence reports by hand, but rather to do so electronically, using highly specific categories and codes. Fully printed out, the present occurrence report runs to 12 pages of fixed-choice classifications.

A veteran member of one police organization discussed the changes in report formatting over time. He attributed the changes to the combined effects of computerization and the demand for knowledge from external institutions:

When I joined, the [general occurrence] report was one 8.5 by 11 [page] that was folded into three, and the boxed information would then be on that much...and now we're up to twelve pages....Computers are driving it. The fact that we *can* now collect vast amounts of data.... The more information you have, the more information people want, so you gather more, so they want more, and you just keep going and going and going.

Given the low clearance rate for property crimes, the main task of the police in dealing with them is to provide good risk-management data for insurance purposes. Occurrence reports are designed to suit the risk-knowledge requirements of insurance companies, and in many jurisdictions the insurance companies pay for the police reports they obtain. A police official engaged in negotiation with insurers over the change of occurrence reports said in an interview: "Insurance companies now pay to get their form and so the form should look more like something they are buying rather than just a photocopy of something we are providing them – how to put it so that it could be more logical for insurance companies because they're actually the external customer."

The lengthening of a given police form and the proliferation of classifications within it have been accompanied by an enormous expansion in the number and nature of forms. For example, by 1992 the Royal Canadian Mounted Police had, because of the many federal, provincial, and municipal government jurisdictions and private-sector institutions it served, approximately 2,100 operational forms and a staff of 600 full-time "informatics" employees.

One officer observed:

> Your supervisor reads your work, the sergeant checks his work, staff sergeant looks after him, the commanding officer inspects all of it. Now it goes to another group of people and they inspect it. If they find anything they send it back. You have so many people checking up on what I do on the street it makes it kind of repetitive all of the time.

Of course, there are still murmurings in police occupational culture that information work as the means has become an end in itself, interfering with "crime fighting" as the "real" end of police work. But in the vast majority of cases information work is all there is to it. It is both the means and the end of police work, and the reason why there is such an obsession with the production of clean data. The police think and act in relation to the communication formats of external institutions that demand knowledge of risk. As a result, they are mobilized not in terms of consensual order, as criminal law theory would suggest, but rather in terms of the different risk logics of the institutions they communicate with. In this respect, something only becomes actionable as police work if it fits within the risk-knowledge requirements of external institutions.

CONCLUSIONS

These contrasting realities of police communication reflect a broader split in criminal justice. In part, this is a split between public understandings and those of criminal justice professionals. The birth of the modern justice system transformed criminal justice from a spectacle of punishment into a more private disciplinary operation (Foucault 1977), but much of public sentiment seems to have remained in important ways the same. Even if the system changed its methods, in the public and media culture, criminal justice is still often understood as a spectacular, highly emotionally charged, drama of retribution.

This gap between public and professional views became more pronounced as a set of approaches took hold in criminal justice which ran ever more counter to conventional public thinking (Simon and Feeley 1995). There is a recent orientation across post-welfare-state Western justice systems toward a range of instrumental, dispassionate managerial techniques and strategies (Feeley and Simon 1994; Ericson and Haggerty 1997; Garland 2001) more at odds than ever before with the highly emotional, retributive model that is often prominent in public discourse.

However, this is more than simply a gap between rhetoric and reality, between a public face and the private. This contrast also reproduces conflicting tendencies within Western criminal justice systems themselves. In the internal, everyday operations of criminal justice, the trend is toward treating crime as a routine, day-to-day risk to be managed calmly and rationally. Crime is increasingly dealt with by police and a web of other interconnected institutions through the production of risk knowledge and its deployment in dispassionate, technicist, utilitarian approaches aimed at prevention and minimizing cost (Feeley and Simon 1994; Ericson and Haggerty 1997). Yet this general trend is disrupted by occasional contrasting tendencies within Western justice systems toward more expressive, spectacular, emotionally and morally charged, publicity-oriented, vengeance-seeking approaches to crime, such as "three strikes" laws and the return of chain gangs and capital punishment (Garland 2001; Doyle 2003).

The two realities of police communication reproduce this split. Patterns of police–media relations – emphasizing the sensational individual crime ostensibly driven by evil or pathology, and the police role as "crime fighter" – legitimate police. They also reinforce the punitive current in public, media, and political discourse. This current feeds back into the system itself, fueling alternative tendencies toward more expressive and punitive forms of criminal justice. It also justifies the elaboration of the surveillance-oriented risk-communication systems that characterize the everyday world of police work.

References

Altheide, D., and Snow, R. (1979) *Media Logic*. Beverly Hills: Sage.

Ashworth, A. (2001) The decline of English sentencing, and other stories. Draft manuscript, All Souls College, Oxford.

Barclay, G., Tavaras, C., and Prout, A. (1995) *Information on the Criminal Justice System in England and Wales*. London: Home Office Research and Statistics Department.

Chermak, S. (1995) *Victims in the News*. Bloomington, IND: University of Indiana Press.

Chibnall, S. (1977) *Law and Order News: An Analysis of Crime Reporting in the British Press*. London: Tavistock.

Clarke, R., and Hough, M. (1984) *The Effectiveness of the Police*. Home Office Research Unit. London: HMSO.

Comrie, M., and Kings, E. (1975) *Study of Urban Workloads: Final Report*. London: Home Office Police Research Services Unit.

Cumberbatch, G., and Howitt, D. (1989) *A Measure of Uncertainty: The Effects of the Mass Media*. London: John Libbey.

Cumming, E., Cumming, I., and Edell, L. (1965) Policeman as philosopher, guide and friend. *Social Problems*, 12, 276–86.

Curran, J. (1996) Rethinking mass communications. In J. Curran, D. Morley, and V. Walkerdine (eds.), *Cultural Studies and Communications*. London: Arnold, 119–65.

Davis, J. (1951) Crime news in Colorado newspapers. *American Journal of Sociology*, 57 (1), 325–30.

Doyle, A. (1998) "Cops": Television policing as policing reality. In M. Fishman and G. Cavender (eds.), *Entertaining Crime: Television Reality Programs*. New York: Aldine de Gruyter, 95–116.

Doyle, A. (2003) *Arresting Images. Crime and Policing in Front of the Television Camera*. Toronto: University of Toronto Press.

Draper, H. (1978) *Private Police*. Harmondsworth: Penguin.

Environics (1998) *Focus on Crime and Justice*. Toronto: Environics Canada Ltd.

Ericson, R. (1982) *Reproducing Order: A Study of Police Patrol Work*. Toronto: University of Toronto Press.

Ericson, R. (1991) Mass media, crime, law and justice: An institutional approach. *British Journal of Criminology*, 31(3), 219–49.

Ericson, R. (1993) *Making Crime: A Study of Detective Work*, 2nd ed. Toronto: University of Toronto Press.

Ericson, R., Baranek, P., and Chan, J. (1987) *Visualizing Deviance: A Study of News Organization*. Toronto and Milton Keynes: University of Toronto Press and Open University Press.

Ericson, R., Baranek, P., and Chan, J. (1989) *Negotiating Control: A Study of News Sources*. Toronto and Milton Keynes: University of Toronto Press and Open University Press.

Ericson, R., Baranek, P., and Chan, J. (1991) *Representing Order: Crime, Law and Justice in the News Media*. Buckingham and Toronto: Open University Press and University of Toronto Press.

Ericson, R., and Haggerty K. (1997) *Policing the Risk Society*. Toronto and Oxford: University of Toronto Press and Oxford University Press.

Feeley, M., and Simon, J. (1994) Actuarial justice: The emerging new criminal law. In D. Nelken (ed.), *The Futures of Criminology*. London: Sage, 173–201.

Fishman, M. (1978) Crime waves as ideology. *Social Problems*, 25, 531–43.

Fishman, M. (1980) *Manufacturing the News*. Austin: University of Texas Press.

Fishman, M., and Cavender, G. (eds.) (1998) *Entertaining Crime: Television Reality Programs*. New York: Aldine de Gruyter.

Fiske, J. (1987) *Television Culture*. London: Methuen.

Foucault, M. (1977) *Discipline and Punish*. New York: Vintage.

Gans, H. (1979) *Deciding What's News: A Study of CBS Evening News, NBC Nightly News, Newsweek and Time*. New York: Pantheon.

Garland, D. (1990) *Punishment and Modern Society: A Study in Social Theory*. Oxford and Chicago: Oxford University Press and Chicago University Press.

Garland, D. (2001) *The Culture of Control: Crime and Social Order in Contemporary Society*. Chicago: University of Chicago Press.

Garofalo, J. (1981) Crime and the mass media: A selective review of research. *Journal of Research in Crime and Delinquency*, 18, 319–50.

Graber, D. (1980) *Crime News and the Public*. New York: Praeger.

Gunter, B. (1987) *Television and the Fear of Crime*. London, England: John Libbey.

Hall, S., Critcher, C., Jefferson, T., Clarke, J. and Roberts, B. (1978) *Policing The Crisis: Mugging, the State and Law and Order*. London: Macmillan.

Jorgensen, B. (1981) Transferring trouble: The initiation of reactive policing. *Canadian Journal of Criminology*, 23, 257–78.

Katz, J. (1993) Covering the cops: A TV show moves in where journalists fear to tread. *Columbia Journalism Review*, January/February, 25–30.

Latour, B. (1987) *Science in Action*. Cambridge, MA: Harvard University Press.

Lawrence, R. (2000) *The Politics of Force: Media and the Construction of Police Brutality*. Berkeley: University of California Press.

Levin, E. (1992) The victim: Twice wounded. *Media Studies Journal*, 6(1), 45–51.

Loader, I. (1997) Policing and the social: Questions of symbolic power. *British Journal of Sociology*, 48(1), 1–18.

Manning, P. (1988) *Symbolic Communication: Signifying Calls and the Police Response*. Cambridge, MA: MIT Press.

Manning, P. (2001) Theorizing policing: The drama and myth of crime control in the NYPD. *Theoretical Criminology*, 5(3), 315–44.

Marx, G. (1998) Afterword: Some reflections on the democratic policing of demonstrations. In D. Della Porta and H. Reiter (eds.), *Policing Protest: The Control of Mass Demonstrations in Western Democracies*. Minneapolis and London: University of Minnesota Press, 253–69.

McConville, M. (1993) An error of judgment. *Legal Action*, September.

McMahon, M. (1992) *The Persistent Prison? Rethinking Decarceration and Penal Reform*. Toronto: University of Toronto Press

Meehan, A. (1993) Internal police records and the control of juveniles: Politics and policing in a suburban town. *British Journal of Criminology*, 33, 504–24.

Moynihan, D. (1993) Defining deviance down. *The American Scholar*, 62, 17–30.

Oliver, M. (1994) Portrayals of crime, race and aggression in "reality-based" police shows: A content analysis. *Journal of Broadcasting and Electronic Media*, 38(2), 179–92.

Oliver, M., and Armstrong, G. (1995) Predictors of viewing and enjoyment of reality-based and fictional crime shows. *Journalism and Mass Communication Quarterly*, 72 (3), 559–70.

Perlmutter, D. (2000) *Policing the Media: Street Cops and Public Perceptions of Law Enforcement*. Thousand Oaks, CA: Sage.

Reiner, R. (2000) *The Politics of the Police* (3rd ed.) Toronto: University of Toronto Press.

Reiss, A. (1987) The legitimacy of intrusion into private spaces. In C. Shearing and P. Stenning (eds.), *Private Policing*. Beverly Hills: Sage, 19–44.

Royal Commission on Criminal Justice (1993) *Report*, Cmnd. 2263. London: HMSO.

Sacco, V. (1995) Media constructions of crime. *Annals, AAPS*, 539, May, 141–54.

Sasson, T. (1995) *Crime Talk: How Citizens Construct a Social Problem*. New York: Aldine de Gruyter.

Scheingold, S. (1995) Politics, public policy and street crime. *Annals, AAPSS*, 539, 155–68.

Schlesinger, P., and Tumber, H 1994) *Reporting Crime: The Media Politics of Criminal Justice*. Oxford: Clarendon Press.

Sherizen, S. (1978) Social creation of crime news: All the news fitted to print. In C. Winick (ed.), *Deviance and Mass Media*. Beverly Hills: Sage.

Simon, J., and Feeley, M. (1995) True crime: The new penology and public discourse on crime. In T. Blomberg and S. Cohen (eds.), *Punishment and Social Control*. Hawthorne, NY : Aldine de Gruyter, 147–80.

Skogan, W. (1990) *The Police and the Public in England and Wales: A British Crime Survey Report.* Home Office Research Study No. 117, London: HMSO.

Sparks, R. (1992) *Television and the Drama of Crime: Moral Tales and the Place of Crime in Public Life.* Buckingham and Philadelphia, PA: Open University Press.

Stinchcombe, A. (1963) Institutions of privacy in the determination of police administrative practice. *American Journal of Sociology,* 69, 150–60.

Surette, R. (1997) *Media, Crime and Criminal Justice: Images and Realities* (2nd ed.). Pacific Grove, CA: Brooks/Cole.

Voumvakis, S., and Ericson, R. (1984) *News Accounts of Attacks on Women: A Comparison of Three Toronto Newspapers.* Toronto: Centre of Criminology, University of Toronto.

Walsh, W. (1986) Patrol officer arrest rates: A study of the social organization of police work. *Justice Quarterly,* 2, 271–90.

Young, A. (1996) *Imagining Crime: Textual Outlaws and Criminal Conversations.* London, Thousand Oaks, CA, and New Delhi: Sage.

Zoglin, R. (1992) The cops and the cameras. *Time,* 139(14), 62–3.

26

Hacktivism – Resistance is Fertile?

Paul A. Taylor

Introduction

> Virtual politics...should be founded on defying the neoliberal discourse of tech-
> nology currently being fashioned by the virtual class. It is crucial to ensure that the
> political genealogy of technology, of virtual reality, of the reality of virtuality, is
> uncovered by numerous individuals, groups, classes, and new social movements.
> Indeed, without such excavations, the increasingly institutionalized neoliberal dis-
> course of technology currently being promoted by the virtual class will rapidly
> become a source of immense social power. This is why concrete, corporeal, and
> ideological struggles over the nature and meaning of technology are so important in
> the realm of virtual politics. (Armitage 2000: 1, 4)

In recent years, the rapid growth and increasing sophistication of information
technologies and their convergence with a pseudo-evangelistic e-business ideology has produced a spate of cyber-eulogies of the "New Economy" like *Living on
Thin Air* (Leadbetter 2000).[1] Such pro-globalization tracts, however, have been
matched by a growing body of both physical and online forms of anti-globalization activities and literature ranging from the physical protests of the Stockholm
and Genoa clashes to various acts of electronic civil disobedience. In *Hackers:
Crime in the Digital Sublime* (Taylor 1999), I explored in detail the culture of
computer hacking and found relatively little political focus to the activity. This
essay traces the evolution of hacking into *hacktivism* (see Taylor 2001), an
activity that began in the mid-1990s and which refers to the combination of
computer-hacking techniques with the real-world, political-activist ethos of new
social movements, DIY culture,[2] and anti-globalization protests.

The analytical aftermath of the September 11 World Trade Center tragedy has
shone the spotlight even more brightly upon the issue of global commodity
culture and its discontents. In his book *Jihad vs. McWorld* (2001), for example,
Benjamin Barber characterizes the most significant element of globalization as

the growing conflict between two diametrically opposed, yet nevertheless inimically related, fundamentalisms: extreme laissez-faire economics and religious zealotry. *McWorld* is the phrase he uses to describe the "sterile cultural monism" (Barber 2001: xiii) that results from the unbridled market's insensitivity to the particularities of the local environments into which its commodities are disseminated, while *jihad* is used to describe the "raging cultural fundamentalism" (2001: xiii) that subsequently results from keenly felt dissatisfaction with the perceived negative cultural effects of the ubiquitous spread of commodity values.

Despite being superficially antagonistic ideologies, Barber points out that both McWorld and *jihad* rely upon the qualitatively new level of international interdependence communication technologies have created and which, arguably, distinguishes debates about globalization from the previous subject area of international relations.[3] Osama Bin Laden's heinous acts, for example, made use of the same media channels responsible for the spread of the US commodity values to which he objects so vehemently and destructively. In this respect, Bin Laden provides a particularly egregious example of the general technique of reverse engineering against itself, a system to which one is opposed. We shall see in the course of this chapter that the general strategy of seeking to reverse-engineer global capital is a technique of the new hacktivist anti-corporate movement, heavily influenced by its reappropriation of pre-existing hacking techniques. However, while some conservative commentators may be quick to seize upon this remote similarity of approach to the recent World Trade Center terrorist attack by labeling hacktivists as information-terrorists, I will argue that hacktivism is an imaginative and defensible attempt to reappropriate new information technologies for society's benefit.

In our introductory quotation, Armitage argues for a "virtual politics" to compensate for the way in which capitalist values have become inextricably insinuated within new information technologies: *hacktivism* is a response to this call. The key significance of the phenomenon rests upon the way it confronts head-on Armitage's call for the paradoxical need to affirm the status of the corporeal within virtual politics. It takes politics infused with concerns about real-world conditions into the abstract heart of contemporary capitalism. Hacktivism is thus an attempted solution to the problem of carrying out effective political protest against a system that is expanding its global reach, yet in increasingly immaterial forms.

FROM HACKING TO HACKTIVISM

Levy (1984) identified the following three main hacker generations:

1 *"True" hackers*: these were the pioneering computer aficionados of the earliest days of computing, who experimented with the capabilities of the large, mainframe computers at such US universities as MIT during the 1950s and 1960s.
2 *Hardware hackers*: these were the computer innovators who, beginning in the 1970s, played a key role in the personal computing revolution which served to disseminate widely and dramatically decentralize computing hardware.

3 *Game hackers*: in the 1980s these were the creators of popular gaming software applications for the hardware developed by the previous generation.

A common key quality of all three generations was their imaginative and ingeni-
ous approach to technology. The *hack* presupposed a difficult-to-define element
of élan that tended to stem from either its concise but effective elegance or an
ability to reengineer a technological artifact for purposes that ran directly
counter to the intentions of its original designers. Additional research into the
hacking phenomenon (Jordan and Taylor 1998; Taylor 1998, 1999, 2000;
Jordan 2001) has produced the following new categories to add to these initial
generations:

4 *Hacker/cracker*: from the mid-1980s to the present day both these terms are
   used to describe a person who illicitly breaks into other people's computer
   systems. The choice of the particular phrase to be used by a commentator
   depends upon his or her moral perspective. *Hacker* tends to be used by those
   within the computer underground or largely sympathetic to its values, while
   cracker tends to be used by those who oppose it.
5 *Microserfs*: in Douglas Coupland's novel (1995) of the same name, *microserfs* is the phrase used to describe those programmers who, while exhibiting
   various aspects of the hacker subculture nevertheless became coopted into
   the corporate structure of Microsoft, the commercial driving force of the
   computer industry.
6 *Hacktivists*: the mid-1990s marked the merging of hacking activity with an
   overt political stance. In 1995 a group called *Strano Network* attacked
   various French government sites in protest over its nuclear policies and in
   1998 the *Electronic Disturbance Theater* (EDT) initiated a high-profile
   campaign in support of the Zapatista movement in Mexico.

The earliest hackers exhibited some anticorporatist values and were also present
in the second generation, as indicated by the names of some of the early start-up
companies such as the Itty-Bitty Machine Company (a parody of IBM) and
Kentucky Fried Computers (Ross 1991: 142). This spirit was not to last, however, and the initial socially liberating potential of such computers as the Apple II
eventually succumbed to their status as mere commodities: "all the bright
possibilities seem so disturbingly compatible with corporate control and commercial exploitation" (Ross 1991: 155). The commodification of information
proceeded apace with the third generation's contribution to the huge growth in
the computer gaming industry. The counter-cultural hopes pinned upon the
computer as vehicle for anti-establishment values remained unfulfilled as the
spirit of Thomas Paine evolved into the electronic appetite of PacMan. The
fourth generation exhibited ambivalent political credentials, the early hacker
desire to promote free access to computers and information, as a means of
improving a perceived democratic deficit within society at large, gave way in
time to more selfish concerns about access to computing for its own sake.

Anti-authoritarian attitudes within hacking became associated less with a
form of youthful rebellion and more with a sign of a frustrated desire to consume
computing resources (see Taylor 1999: 53–6) to the extent that: "teenage hackers

resemble an alienated shopping culture deprived of purchasing opportunities more than a terrorist network" (Ross 1991: 90). Such a pessimistic assessment culminated in Douglas Coupland's vivid "factional" account of the hacker-type lifestyles of the young programmers working at Microsoft's headquarters in Seattle. Coupland depicts the extent to which Microsoft's cooptation of hacker culture has been so successful that through such corporate-friendly characteristics as "high productivity, maverick forms of creative work energy, and an obsessive identification with online endurance (and endorphin highs)" (Ross 1991: 90), it now merely serves to valorize "the entrepreneurial codes of silicon futurism" (Ross 1991: 90). The advent of microserfs as the fifth generation of hackers marks the nadir of the original hacker ethic and represented "the first full-scale integration of the corporate realm into the private" (Coupland 1995: 211). The key significance of hacktivism is the way in which it marks a retreat from such a pervasive intrusion of commodified values into social life and a proactive reassertion of more countercultural values.

The erosion of the original hacker ethic arguably occurred because the early generations of hackers were more interested[4] in the intellectual thrills that access to computer systems could afford, rather than the potential such access contained for oppositional political purposes. Whatever the contestable differences between hacking and hacktivism may be, the two activities exhibit the same quality of technological ingenuity. There are two key aspects to this ingenuity. First, a major element of the hacker aesthetic is the deliberate reappropriation of the original purposes of any technology. Secondly, the ubiquitous nature of this urge to reappropriate encourages a tendency to look beyond the specific qualities of individual technologies and instead to treat all technology as part of a general system to be manipulated and played with.

It is only relatively recently that hacking has tended to be exclusively associated with computers, but this association has served to distract attention away from its well-documented, wider affinity with technology's systemic properties. Levy (1984), for example, identifies evidence of early hacking techniques among members of MIT's model-railway club and its complexly wired models of train networks, and there has been a long and close association of hackers with the "phone phreaks" whose enjoyment, derived from exploring complex telephone networks, closely prefigured the later thrills to be enjoyed by accessing the global networks of the Internet. It is the combination of a commitment to reappropriating and subverting the original purposes of a technology with a recognition of the crucial importance of systems and their abstract qualities that hacktivism has borrowed from hacking and developed into a political strategy aimed at confronting capitalism's pervasive yet immaterial nature.

HACKTIVISM – ELECTRONIC CIVIL DISOBEDIENCE

As hackers become politicized and as activists become computerized, we are going to see an increase in the number of cyber-activists who engage in what will become more widely known as Electronic Civil Disobedience. The same principles of traditional civil disobedience, like trespass and blockage, will still be applied, but

more and more these acts will take place in electronic or digital form. The primary
site for Electronic Civil Disobedience will be in cyberspace. (Wray 1998: 3)

We have seen how the early generations of hackers espoused a hacker ethic
which asserted that "all information should be free" (Levy 1984: 40). In this
context "ethic" is perhaps something of a misnomer because, apart from a few
politically motivated hackers,[5] the rest were much more interested in access to
information as an end in itself rather than as a means to a particular social or
political end. It is this lack of political perspective that led to the cooptation of
early hacking ethics manifested by the advent of the Microserf. In stark contrast,
hacktivism is a movement which has an a priori political intent. Hacktivism
shares hacking's ability to redefine the purposes of technology and like hacking
uses such reappropriation at the level of individual artifacts such as computers
and their functions, but also seeks to re-engineer or "hack" wider sociotechnical
systems such as the media and the messages it transmits. It thus works at both
the artifactual and semiotic levels. It arose in the context of an intellectual
climate increasingly sensitive to the effects of globalization and occurred as a
result of the convergence of two different trends: (a) hackers have become more
politically aware and (b) activists have become more technologically knowledge-
able. These two trends are reflected in the following two main types of hacktivist
protest.

Web hacks and computer break-ins

Conventional hacking techniques are increasingly being applied to political
targets while maintaining the sense of humorous mischief frequently associated
with the computer underground. Thus in 1996 the website pre-election manifesto of the British Labour Party was altered from "The Road to the Manifesto"
to "The Road to Nowhere," while in the United States the Central Intelligence Agency's website was changed to read "Central Stupidity Agency."[6] The
hacker group Cult of the Dead Cow (CDC) have sought to combine a humorous attitude with a hardened attitude to corporate power on the Net. Their
various versions of the software package entitled "Back Orifice" targets computers attached to Microsoft Windows network systems and allows the software's user to access the private files and e-mails of the Microsoft user. Back
Orifice has been downloaded 128,776 times since late February 2000(Jordan
2001), and the CDC argue that it draws attention to the surveillance capabilities
written into Microsoft software which allows system administrators access to
users' private information.

Electronic civil disobedience

A virtual sit-in is little more than a collective, simultaneous requesting of a Web
site. If one requests a Web site faster than it can be transferred and built up on the
end user's screen, the server receives, on the one hand, a message telling it that the
first request is no longer valid, and on the other hand, the new request. Scripts
running on one's own computer or on go-between servers automate this process,

and after a certain number of requests, the server under attack begins to suffer under the strain. One has to differentiate very specifically between knocking out a server for private motives and a political action openly disrupting a Web site for clearly formulated reasons and for a limited time. That's when it becomes comparable to a warning strike during wage negotiations, a means of civil disobedience signaling that one side has the willingness and courage to fight. (Grether 2000: 5)

Traditional forms of civil disobedience such as peaceful sit-ins have been replicated in cyberspace to create new forms of electronic civil disobedience. In 1998, for example, the hacktivist group the Electronic Disturbance Theater (EDT) coordinated a series of web sit-ins in support of the Mexican antigovernment group, the Zapatistas. This incident was perhaps most noticeable for its use of an automated piece of software revealingly called "Flood Net." Once downloaded on to an individual's computer, this piece of software automatically connects the surfer to a preselected website, and every seven seconds the selected site's reload button is automatically activated. If thousands of people use Flood Net on the same day, the combined effect of such a large number of activists will disrupt the operations of a particular site. Similar techniques were also used in the Etoy campaign of 1999. This was a hacktivist response to a commercial company's attempt to use the courts to remove an art collective's website domain name because they felt it was too similar to their own (for a full account, see Grether 2000). In what was described as the "Brent Spar of e-commerce,"[7] a combination of Internet and media public relations stunts were used to force an eventual volte-face by the company, greatly aided by the 70 percent decline in its NAS-DAQ stock value coinciding with these actions.

The Internet-based nature of hacktivism means that, compared to traditional social protest movements, it is well placed to deal with the increasingly immaterial nature of contemporary capitalism – to which we now turn.

GLOBAL IMMATERIALITY AND CULTURAL COMMODIFICATION

All fixed, fast-frozen relations, with their train of ancient and venerable prejudices and opinions, are swept away, all new-formed ones become antiquated before they can ossify. *All that is solid melts into air*, all that is holy is profaned, and men at last are forced to face . . . the real conditions of their lives and their relations with their fellow men. (Marx, cited in Berman 1982: 21, my emphasis)

The above quotation from Marx describes capitalism's tendency to abstract from material conditions. This immaterial aspect of capitalism first gathered pace with the Industrial Revolution, and the spate of information-based technological innovations in recent years are part of the same essential process as indicated by the term "the information revolution." What has led to claims that this new revolution is qualitatively different and merits specific attention, however, is the way new information technologies have become crucially and inextricably aligned with social trends. Capitalist values have penetrated into the social environment in unprecedented breadth and depth to produce fundamentally new social questions, such as the threat to national cultures from the global spread of commodity values (the McWorld effect: see Barber 2001; Ritzer 1996), and narrowly defeated attempts to exert commercial property rights over such basic material as human DNA (see Sulston and Ferry 2002). Marx's metaphorical description of capitalism's growing ephemerality is thus increasingly manifested in the immaterial commodity forms created by the conjunction of information technologies and capitalist markets.

Marx identified the origins of capitalism's particularly incorporeal form of value in his analysis of the way in which the commodity form moves society's focus from use-value to exchange-value. An object's social worth is no longer its practical physical usefulness, but rather its abstract monetary value in the marketplace, its exchange-value. The significance of the new global information order is that while the initial process of abstraction analyzed by Marx still tends to be embodied in physical, albeit commodified objects, new forms of informational commodity value have taken the abstract, nonphysical element of value to qualitatively new heights. The contrast between the traditional corporeally based form of capitalism and its new cyber-variant is vividly illustrated in the personal account of a computer programmer, Ellen Ullman, and her thoughts about what she could do with some New York business real estate she and her sister had inherited on her father's death:

> I imagined I really could turn this collection of mortar & bricks into a kind of bond, not a thing but an asset, that I might undo its very realness, convert it into something that will come to me in . . . dustless encrypted, anonymous, secure transactions. . . . It would be money freed of ancient violations and struggling tenants, distilled into a pure stream of bits traversing the continent at network speed, just a click away – hardly money at all, but some new measure of value: logical, dematerialized, clean. (Ullman 1997: 61)

In her highly influential anti-globalization tract *No Logo* Klein develops this argument, claiming that "Companies [are] competing in a race towards weightlessness. . . . Their apparent bigness is simply the most effective route toward their real goal: divestment of the world of things" (Klein 2001: 4). Klein's point was prefigured in *Neuromancer* (1984), the Zeitgeist-capturing fictional work of William Gibson that popularized the now hugely influential concept of cyberspace. Gibson defined cyberspace as an informational *matrix* within which the disembodied consciousnesses of computer hackers known as "console cowboys" created a *consensual hallucination*. At the end of this seminal novel, the reader finds that a corporation has transcended the material world to the extent that its identity becomes inseparable from the controlling influence of an artificial intelligence. The real-world relevance of this exaggerated fictional appreciation of contemporary social trends is evident from Klein's reliance upon similar language to describe the conjunction of corporate transcendence and the ever-more abstract commodity forms of brands:

> a select group of corporations has been attempting to free itself from the corporeal world of commodities, manufacturing and products to exist on another plane. . . . It is on-line that the purest brands are being built: liberated from the real-world burdens of stores and product manufacturing, these brands are free to soar, less

as the disseminators of goods or services than as *collective hallucinations*. (Klein 2001: 22, my emphasis)

The predominance of exchange-value leads to the subordination of physical particularities to generic abstraction. This is what Ullman is commenting upon when describing her desire to translate her father's building into a "pure stream of bits." The key significance of this trend toward the promotion of the generic, however, is the way in which the commodification process that began with a physical object's exchange-value supplanting its use-value has now extended into the cultural consciousness as implied by the phrase *collective hallucinations*.

Culture Jamming and Resistance to the New Informational Order

You reach down to pull your golf ball out of the hole and there, at the bottom of the cup is an ad for a brokerage firm. You fill your car with gas, there's an ad on the nozzle. You wait for your bank machine to spit out money and an ad pushing GICs scrolls by in the little window. You drive through the heartland and the view of the wheatfields is broken at intervals by enormous billboards. Your kids watch Pepsi and Snickers ads in the classroom. (Lasn 2000: 19)

One two-dollar can of spray can reverse a hundred-thousand-dollar media campaign. (Rushkoff 1994:281)

In his book *Culture Jam* (2000), Kalle Lasn describes the saturation of the cultural realm with corporate images as a form of ubiquitous mental pollution. What sets hacktivism apart as a new, more political extension of the previous hacking generations is its much more fully developed political strategy. It seeks to resist such pollution by hacking the communicational structures of global capitalism. The Situationists were an avant-garde group of Parisian artists and activists in the 1960s. One of their concepts was the *détournement* (turning around) which involved the rerouting and subverting of meaning. Hacktivism can be viewed in this light. Rather than being confused by capitalism's mix of the abstract and the concrete, hacktivism's oppositional strategy adapts and reenergizes the mentality of the original hackers' *hack* and uses it at both material and immaterial levels.

A good example of this dual strategy is provided by the practice of *culture jamming* which combines the manipulation of semiotic codes[8] with actual physical changes to capitalist products. Thus, the Barbie Liberation Organization switched the voiceboxes of G.I. Joe and Barbie dolls and groups such as Adbusters use techniques such as "billboard banditry" to make small but crucial changes to corporate adverts that creates a process of "subvertising." After the *Exxon Valdez* disaster, for example, the San Francisco-based Billboard Liberation Front subverted a radio promotion poster so that instead of "Hits Happen. New X-100" it read "Shit Happens – New Exxon." Broadly defined, the concept of culture jamming parallels the broad original interpretation of hacking as being a mindset applicable to a heterogeneous range of artifacts. Culture jamming turns the original purpose of a cultural artifact or piece of communication back on itself to create the opposite outcome: a semiotic version of ju-jitsu.

It has been suggested that Marx himself provided an early precedent for such a strategy when he and Engels: "planned to penetrate the international wire agencies in Brussels, through a leftist press agency, in order to distribute their messages more widely" (Dyer-Witheford 1999: 42). Information technologies may be instrumental in extending the deconceptualized abstract global reach of capitalism, but they also bring a degree of autonomy and empowerment to those who would seek to resist such a process. Computers facilitate the permeation of society by commodity values through the way in which they insert the managerial values they embody into more and more areas of everyday life, helping to create a "factory-without-walls." The same networks that are used for commercial communications and surveillance, however, can also be reappropriated to reinforce grassroots opposition: networks circulate struggle as well as commodities.

From Networks to Webs

> The terminals of the network society are static. The bonding, on the other hand, of web weavers with machines is nomadic. They form communities with machines, navigate in cultural worlds attached to machines. These spiders weave not networks, but webs, perhaps electronic webs, undermining and undercutting the networks. Networks need walls. Webs go around the walls, up the walls, hide in the nooks and crannies and corners of where the walls meet.... Networks are shiny, new, flawless. Spiders' webs in contrast, attach to abandoned rooms, to disused objects, to the ruins, the disused and discarded objects of capitalist production. Networks are cast more or less in stone, webs are weak, easily destroyed. Networks connect by a utilitarian logic, a logic of instrumental rationality. Webs are tactile, experiential rather than calculating, their reach *more* ontological than utilitarian. (Lash 2002: 127)

In his *The Practice of Everyday Life*, Michel de Certeau (1984) criticizes the expansionary nature of various systems of production that produce a society dominated by commodity value. He argues that resistance to such disciplining forces can be found in the various day-to-day subversions people make with the ways in which they consume the products of such a dominant order. He uses the example of the indigenous Indians of South America and the way in which, although they superficially accepted the framework of the Catholic Church imposed upon them by the Spanish colonizers, they developed various ways to keep their traditional values alive beneath the veneer of such acceptance and assimilation. In a similar fashion, he advocates the development of various strategies to resist the uniform, disciplinary effects of capitalism upon social life, including the reappropriation of otherwise ordered urban environments in preference for more dynamic, liberated expressions of local particularities and interactions. De Certeau seeks escape routes from the circumscribing effects of productive and organizational matrices:

> We witness the advent of number. It comes with democracy, the large city, administrations, cybernetics. It is a flexible and continuous mass, woven tight like a fabric

with neither rips nor darned patches, a multitude of quantified heroes who lose names and faces as they become the ciphered river of the streets, a mobile language of computations and rationalities that belong to no one. (De Certeau 1984: v)

De Certeau's identification of the tightly woven nature of fabric that accompanies "the advent of number" provides an early analysis of the subsequent focus upon capitalist networks such as that provided in the above quotation from Lash. Where De Certeau describes a cybernetic "fabric with neither rips nor darned patches," Lash similarly talks of the "flawless" nature of a utilitarian network. He contrasts the inherently disciplinary nature of such networks with the more organically liberatory potential image of webs. He adopts Lefebvre's (1991) association of spiders' web-making with the creation of autonomous spaces to make parallels with the potentially empowering web-forming activities of the new informational order's technoculture workers. In a very similar vein, Klein sees anti-corporate opposition making use of such webs like spiders:

the image strikes me as a fitting one for this Web-age global activism. Logos, by the force of ubiquity, have become the closest thing we have to an international language, recognized and understood in many more places than English. Activists are now free to swing off this web of logos like spy/spiders – trading information about labor practices, chemical spills, animal cruelty and unethical marketing around the world. (Klein 2001: xx)

Klein's conceptualization of activists as spiders on a global web provides the beginnings of a practical strategy with which to approach the confusing immateriality of modern capitalism. It is in keeping with Dyer-Witheford's call for oppositional groups to match the nomadic flows enjoyed by corporations due to their own "global-webs" of capital (Dyer-Witheford 1999: 143). The need for a counter-colonization of the global web is now an increasingly common call amongst radical thinkers. To those previously cited can be added Hardt and Negri (2000), whose basic premise of the need for opposition to a new global corporate empire relies heavily upon the belief that its web of capital flows and commodity circulation needs counter-populating with flows of struggle.

REFRACTORY REALITY – THE STREETS AS TERRITORY AND TROPE

The street is . . . the alternative and subversive form of the mass media, since it isn't, like the latter, an objectified support for answerless messages, a transmission system at a distance. It is the frayed space of the symbolic exchange of speech – ephemeral, mortal: a speech that is not reflected on the Platonic screen of the media. Institutionalized by reproduction, reduced to spectacle, this speech is expiring. (Baudrillard 1981: 176–7)

Graffiti is transgressive, not because it substitutes another content, another discourse, but simply because it responds, there, on the spot, and breaches the fundamental role of non-response enunciated by all the media. Does it oppose one code to another? I don't think so: it simply smashes the code. It doesn't lend itself to deciphering as a text rivaling commercial discourse; it presents itself as a transgression. (Baudrillard 1981: 183–4)

Our discussion of flows and networks risks ignoring the radical power of the street and its transgressive acts such as graffiti, both of which are celebrated above by Baudrillard. It is at this point that the Actor-Network Theory (ANT) of Bruno Latour can provide some useful insights into the relationship between the physical and the immaterial in the new global informational order. Latour argues that power in society is exercised through a complex mix of not only traditional power-brokers, but also enlisted allies of humans, non-human artifacts, and semiotic structures. He uses the notion of a *gradient of delegation* to illustrate this point in relation to traffic flows (Latour, in Bijker and Law 1992: 243). The police use various options to control traffic, ranging from actual policemen to traffic lights, signs, and speed bumps (or rather more ironically, "sleeping policemen"). For Latour, the crucial aspect of the exercise of power in this instance is not that one method is better than another but that the most effective exercise of power relies upon a pragmatic and flexible utilization of whichever method is needed at a particular time.

Hacktivists are potentially good practitioners of Latour's Machiavellian power scheme (see Latour, in Eliot 1988). Thus, despite the predominantly Internet-based nature of their activities, the webs they create move freely along the gradient of delegation between physical and immaterial strategies. They offer a fresh perspective upon Baudrillard's nostalgia for graffiti by committing such acts of semiotic vandalism as website defacements, but they also remain acutely aware of the real-world, grounded effects of the global order they criticize):

> The free market, designed and constructed and refined to exploit all situations for the sake of profit, has in the U.S. self-organized to achieve the destruction of public transportation, the ethnic cleansing of politically volatile inner cities, the mass fattening of the poorest class, the reduction of useless leisure time for all classes, and on and on and on – all the while using the language of freedom and choice and Constitution with an abstraction and distance that might be poetic if it weren't so cynical. (RTMark 2000)

Capitalism's ability to operate simultaneously at both the material and immaterial levels has been well documented. With quasi-poetic vividness Marx described how commodity value transforms physical objects into social hieroglyphics so that "A commodity appears, at first sight, a very trivial thing, and easily understood. Its analysis shows that it is, in reality, a very queer thing, abounding in metaphysical subtleties and theological niceties" (Marx 1983 [1887]: 76). These metaphysical and theological properties produce a fetishization of commodities which distracts people from critical engagement with the underlying values of the market order. The application of hacking techniques to information technologies by new social movements and alternative political groups can thus be seen as a matching response to the immaterial forms of capitalism originally highlighted in Marx's analysis of the Industrial Revolution, and now manifested in more sophisticated guises within the information revolution.

In his short story *Burning Chrome*, William Gibson uses the neo-Chandler-esque phrase "the street finds its own uses for things" (Gibson 1986: 215) to describe the way in which counter-cultural uses are frequently found for establishment technologies. The hacktivist strategy of maintaining the crucial link between online and offline worlds is informed by this notion of *the street* as a useful counter-cultural trope. Hacktivism thus fulfills Armitage's call at the very beginning of this chapter for a virtual politics that combines "concrete, corporeal, and ideological struggles over the nature and meaning of technology." It offers a web of both material and immaterial forms from which to confront global capital and hence avoids the confusion historically caused by the "metaphysical subtleties and theological niceties" of the commodity form it opposes.

CONCLUSION

New and unrecognizable modes of community are in the process of formation and it is difficult to discern exactly how these will contribute to or detract from postmodern politics. The image of the people in the streets, from the Bastille in 1789, to the Sorbonne in 1968 and Tiananmen Square, Beijing in 1989 may be the images that will not be repeated in the forms of upheaval of the twenty-first century and beyond. (Poster 1990: 154)
   radical change must focus on the code, and develop a practice to dismantle it and a strategy to create a new order of symbolic exchange with a new system of signs. (Poster 1995: 105)

The erosion of the original hacker ethic arguably occurred because the early generations of hackers were more interested in the intellectual thrills that access to computer systems could afford, rather than the potential such access contained for oppositional political purposes. The apparently complete dependence of contemporary national governments and global capitalism upon such complex communication networks, however, has created room for a more deliberately focused political agenda to be added to the anti-authoritarian, but pro-system, attitudes that have always existed within hacking. The key significance of hacktivism is the way in which it has produced a political strategy that is faithful to the combination of hacking's previously identified love of abstract systems as well as its commitment to the reappropriation and subversion of the original purposes of specific technological artifacts.

Traditional social movements rightly recognize some of capitalism's profoundly negative effects, but are inherently hindered by their relatively limited access to its immaterial field of operation and thus the odds of success are stacked against them from the very start. The global market is premised upon a matrix of abstractly homogeneous economic zones designed to communicate as smoothly as possible in order to facilitate the circulation of commodities around the world. Opposition to local manifestations of this matrix such as the *maquiladora* or "swallow factories" (so-called because, like the bird, they stop so fleetingly in one place) will inevitably have limited success due to the basic mismatch in strategies based upon the values of place-based groundedness versus the cost-driven global reach of decontextualized homogeneity.

Within hacktivism, in contrast, the imaginative re-engineering of the techno-logical code contained within the Internet actually enables them to engage more successfully than many other movements with the even more abstract capitalist code that nevertheless has very real-world effects. Whilst hacktivism does use Internet-based technologies, a significant proportion, if not a majority, of hacktivist projects are deliberately linked to events and protest movements in the real world. The EDT, for example, consistently seek to draw attention to the physical oppression of the indigenous people in the Chiapas region of Mexico, whilst the groups such as RTMark regularly seek to fund activities based upon semiotic forms of protest such as the reappropriation of corporate images and more physical hacks such as the Barbie Liberation Organization's voicebox-switching activity.

From a radical hacktivist perspective, the Internet's underlying abstract architecture of computer code is but a technological instantiation of the equally abstract but more insidiously pervasive and culturally infectious capitalist code of commodity sign-values that applies itself globally, irrespective of local cultural sensitivities. It is because global marketeers think in abstract terms rather than socially meaningful grounded spaces, that their commodities spread with such ease and become such a powerful force of cultural monism. At the same time, however, insensitivity to local context makes the globalization process potentially vulnerable to the inevitable crises caused by this unresolved tension of the grounded and the abstract. Hacktivism's willingness to use both immaterial and grounded political techniques offers a potentially innovative political strategy that remains true to hacking's original penchant for understanding and manipulating systems, whether they are the telecommunication systems of the early "phone phreaks" or the uber-system of global capitalism. Thanks to hacktivists, the McWorld ideal of virtual, friction-free capitalism may yet be met by the troublesome contingencies of refractory reality....

Notes

1 Thomas Frank (2001) describes such writing as the "corporate salivating" of "business porn."
2 For further analysis of the antecedents to online activism see Jordan (1999).
3 Although, in his leadingly entitled *The Follies of Globalisation Theory*, Justin Rosenberg (2000) engagingly questions the novelty of globalization issues.
4 This is a simplifying generalization. It should be noted that political activity has been associated with hacking activity since its earliest origins in "phone phreaking." Political values were thus evident in groups such as Abby Hoffman's Yuppies and Technological American Party (TAP) of the 1970s and the Chaos Computer Club's rise to prominence in the 1980s. However, the point remains that, taken as a whole, the computer underground primary characteristics have not been political.
5 For an account of early hacker politics see Taylor (2001), esp. pp. 61–3.
6 These instances are cited in Jordan (2001), and a more detailed list of hacked websites can be found at: http://www.hackernews.com/defaced
7 See RTMark press release, available online at: http://www.rtmark.com/etoyprtriumph.html
8 These can be seen as a working-out of Umberto Eco's (1987) call for the development of semiotic guerrilla tactics to deal with the increasing power of the media.

References

Armitage, J. (2000) Resisting the neoliberal discourse of technology: The politics of cyberculture in the age of the virtual class. Available online in *Ctheory*, an electronic journal, at http://www.ctheory.com/a68.html

Barber, B. (2001) *Jihad vs. McWorld*. New York: Ballantine.

Baudrillard, J. (1981) *For a Critique of the Economy of the Sign*. St. Louis: Telos.

Berman, M. (1982) *All that is Solid Melts into Air: The Experience of Modernity*. London: Verso.

Bijker, W. E., and Law, J. (eds.) (1992) *Shaping Technology/Building Society: Studies in Sociotechnical Change*. Cambridge MA: MIT Press.

Coupland, D. (1995) *Microserfs*. London: Flamingo.

de Certeau, M. (1984) *The Practice of Everyday Life*. Berkeley: University of California Press.

Dyer-Witheford, N. (1999) *Cyber-Marx: Cycles and Circuits of Struggle in High-Technology Capitalism*. Chicago: University of Illinois Press.

Eco, U. (1987) *Travels in Hyperreality*. London: Picador.

Eliot, B. (ed.) (1998) *Technology and Social Process*. Edinburgh: Edinburgh University Press.

Frank, T. (2001) *One Market Under God: Extreme Capitalism, Market Populism and the End of Economic Democracy*. London: Secker & Warburg.

Gibson, W. (1984) *Neuromancer*. London: HarperCollins.

Gibson, W. (1986) *Burning Chrome*, London: Grafton.

Grether, R. (2000) How the Etoy campaign was won. *Telepolis*, January. Available online at http://www.heise.de/tp/english/inhalt/te/5843/1.html

Hardt, M., and Negri, A. (2000) *Empire*. Cambridge MA: Harvard University Press.

Jordan, T. (1999) *Cyberpower: The Culture and Politics of Cyberspace and the Internet*. London: Routledge.

Jordan, T. (2001) Hacktivism: Direct action on the electronic flows of information societies. In K. Dowding, J. Hughes, and H. Margetts (eds.), *Challenges to Democracy: Ideas, Involvement and Institutions: The PSA Yearbook 2000*. London: Palgrave, 118–30.

Jordan, T., and Taylor, P. (1998) A sociology of hackers. *Sociological Review*, 46(4), 757–80.

Klein, N. (2001) *No Logo*. London: Flamingo.

Lash, S. (2002) *Critique of Information*. London: Sage.

Lasn, K. (2000) *Culture Jam: How To Reverse America's Suicidal Consumer Binge – And Why We Must*. New York: HarperCollins.

Leadbetter, C. (2000) *Living on Thin Air: The New Economy*. London: Penguin.

Lefebvre, H. (1991) *The Production of Space*. Oxford: Blackwell.

Levy, S. (1984) *Hackers: Heroes of the Computer Revolution*. New York: Bantam Doubleday Dell.

Marx, K. (1983) [1887] *Capital: A Critique of Political Economy*, Vol. 1. London: Lawrence & Wishart.

Poster, M. (1990) *The Mode of Information*. Cambridge: Polity.

Poster, M. (1995) *The Second Media Age*. Cambridge: Polity.

Ritzer, G. (1996) *The McDonaldization of Society*. London: Sage.

Rosenberg, J. (2000) *The Follies of Globalisation Theory*. London: Verso.

Ross, A. (1991) *Strange Weather*. London: Verso.

RTMark (2000) Globalization and global resistance. Available online at http://www.rtmark.com/globalization.html

Rushkoff, D. (1994) *Cyberia: Life in the Trenches of Hyperspace*. San Francisco: HarperCollins.

Sulston, J., and Ferry, G. (2002) *The Common Thread: The Story of Science, Politics, & the Human Genome*. London: Bantam.

Taylor, P. A. (1998) Hackers: Cyberpunks or microserfs? *Information, Communication & Society*, 1(4), 401–19. Also in D. Thomas and B. Loader (eds.), *Cybercrime: Law Enforcement, Security and Surveillance in the Information Age*. London: Routledge.

Taylor, P. A. (1999) *Hackers: Crime in the Digital Sublime*. London: Routledge.

Taylor, P. A. (2000) Digital deviants. In T. C. Calhoun and A. Thio (eds.), *Readings in Deviant Behavior* (2nd ed.). Boston: Allyn & Bacon.

Taylor, P. A. (2001) Hacktivism: In search of lost ethics? In D. S. Wall (ed.), *Crime and the Internet*. London: Routledge, 59–73.

Ullman, E. (1997) *Close to the Machine: Technophilia and its Discontents*. San Francisco: City Lights.

Wray, S. (1998) Transforming Luddite resistance into virtual Luddite resistance: Weaving a world wide web of electronic civil disobedience. Available online at http://www.nyu.edu/projects/wray/luddite.html

Index